Braddock's Defeat

Pivotal Moments in American History

SERIES EDITORS

David Hackett Fischer

James M. McPherson

David Greenberg

Braddock's Defeat

THE BATTLE OF THE MONONGAHELA
AND THE ROAD TO REVOLUTION

David L. Preston

OXFORD
UNIVERSITY PRESS

OXFORD

UNIVERSITY PRESS

Oxford University Press is a department of the University of Oxford. It furthers
the University's objective of excellence in research, scholarship, and education
by publishing worldwide. Oxford is a registered trade mark of Oxford University
Press in the UK and certain other countries.

Published in the United States of America by Oxford University Press
198 Madison Avenue, New York, NY 10016, United States of America.

Library of Congress Cataloging-in-Publication Data
Preston, David L. (David Lee), 1972–
Braddock's Defeat : the Battle of the Monongahela and the
road to revolution / David L. Preston.
pages   cm
Includes bibliographical references and index.
ISBN 978-0-19-984532-3 (hardcover); 978-0-19-065851-9 (paperback)
1. Monongahela, Battle of the, Pa., 1755.   2. Braddock's Campaign, 1755.
3. United States—History—Revolution, 1775–1783—Causes.   I. Title.
E199.P94 2015   973.3'31—dc23
2014038584

Printed in the United States of America
on acid-free paper

CONTENTS

MAPS

ILLUSTRATIONS

COLOR PHOTO INSERT

Washington at the Battle of the Monongahela, painting by Emanuel Leutze

The Crossing, painting by Robert Griffing

Braddock's Defeat, painting by Edwin Willard Deming

The Wounding of General Braddock, painting by Robert Griffing

The Arrival of the French, painting by Nat Youngblood

George Washington as the Colonel of the Virginia Regiment, portrait by
    Charles Willson Peale

William Augustus, Duke of Cumberland, portrait by David Morier

Sir John St. Clair, miniature by John Singleton Copley

General Braddock's Sash

Grenadiers, 43rd, 44th, and 45th Regiments of Foot, painting by David Morier

Sir Peter Halkett, portrait by Hans Hysing

Commodore the Honourable Augustus Keppel, portrait by Joshua Reynolds

Captain Robert Orme, portrait by Joshua Reynolds

Daniel-Hyacinthe-Marie Liénard de Beaujeu, miniature, ca. 1737

Eighteenth-century Iroquois war club

Braddock's Field, painting by Paul Weber, 1854

Patrick Mackellar, *A Sketch of the Field of Battle of the 9th of July, No. 1*

EDITOR'S NOTE

I N 1818, JOHN ADAMS FRAMED a central problem of American history when he asked, "What do we mean by the American Revolution? Do we mean the American war? The Revolution was effected before the war commenced. The Revolution was in the minds and hearts of the people."[1]

Those enduring questions inspired a project of quantitative research by Richard L. Merritt, who wanted to know when British colonists began to think of themselves as American. He counted symbols of American identity in the colonial press and was surprised to find that their frequency increased in a series of surges, twenty years before 1775. Merritt wrote, "The curve remained low until the outbreak of the French and Indian War in 1754. The highest point of the ensuing cycle occurred in the year of Braddock's Defeat."[2]

Why Braddock's Defeat? David Preston takes up that question in this book. We have had many studies of this epic disaster—some of high quality. The author acknowledges his debt to the work of Paul Kopperman in particular. But Preston's book reaches beyond its predecessors in its range and depth of primary research and its abundance of new materials. His previous work was on Indian communities in the eighteenth century, and he knows well the complex sources for Native American history.[3] Preston has used this material to identify more than twenty Indian nations that sent between 600 and 700 warriors against Braddock's army. Throughout the book we meet Indians as individuals, with their own diversity of experiences and goals. We also learn about complex processes of Indian diplomacy, from which Europeans were sometimes excluded. Historians have written about American Indians as "auxiliaries" of Europeans in these conflicts. This inquiry finds that it was often the other way around.

David Preston also has done manuscript research in national archives and other libraries of France and Canada, with important results. An example is a new account of the battle that turned up in Caen's Archives du Calvados. It has transformed our understanding of detailed tactical planning in 1755 by French, Canadian, and

Indian leaders. We also learn about the profound impact of Braddock's defeat on Indian victors.

Another major contribution of the book is its close attention to the people of New France—*habitants* and *seigneurs* who had been trained to war from an early age and worked closely with American Indians for many generations. They were held in high respect by allies and enemies alike, and their acts and choices were fundamental to these events. Preston proves that the battle of the Monongahela might be more accurately understood as the victory of "a veteran French Canadian officer and combat leader, than Braddock's defeat."

David Preston found his greatest abundance of new primary materials for this book in Britain and the United States. He builds on recent work by scholars who have turned up astonishing troves of manuscript sources, even for major figures who have been studied exhaustively. An example is a recent discovery by Alan Houston, who used new digital search engines and old-fashioned *sitzfleisch* to find a large and entirely unknown set of letters on Benjamin Franklin's vital role in Braddock's campaign. They were first published in 2009 and are extensively used in this book. Even for George Washington's role in these events, new primary materials have been put to work here. Some of them come from the testimony of American Indians.

With this expanding abundance of new sources, Preston offers a new understanding of his historical subject and a new way of thinking about history itself, which is developing very rapidly in many fields. The common call-name of this subject, "Braddock's Defeat," offers a quick and easy explanation of the event as driven by the acts and choices of the general himself. While Preston gives full attention to Edward Braddock (and has found new sources here as well), he also greatly multiplies the number of actors, expands their many roles, and enlarges their agency. The result is a new history in which events do not flow from a single leader or small group but from a broad web of acts and choices. Contingencies become more important in this approach, but the idea of a web implies structure, and structures entail determinants. Together they create a mediating idea of history that operates as a variable in the interplay of those elements. The frame and substance of historical inquiry is itself historicized and becomes a problem to be resolved by empirical research for each inquiry. All that is happening in this book, and it represents an ongoing revolution in scholarship.

This expanding abundance of primary sources, combined with new ways of thinking about history, also creates new opportunities for writing it. Here again, this book is a leading example in its structure and style. David Preston has used his depth of research, new materials, and comprehensive approach to create a deeply immersive work. The reader is drawn into the book by its braided narrative, with many actors and multiple plot lines.

David Preston has also found many ways to make his history vivid, and that is a vital part of this new work. He walked the Braddock Road, paddled a canoe down La Belle Riviere, and slogged through woods and swamps and steep terrain. He presents his history not merely in words on a page but also in maps and images and artifacts. David Preston and his Oxford team have worked hard at sharing these materials with readers, in many pages of illustrations and much use of color.

The result of all these elements is a classic work by one of the most gifted young historians working today. It is a book that succeeds in its own terms and also as a harbinger of things to come. The digital revolution of our time is revolutionizing the practice of history. The abundance and accessibility of historical sources—so evident in David Preston's work—is growing in every field at an exponential rate. Also expanding (despite complaints to the contrary) is an informed, educated, and intelligent public, who are deeply interested in history with a broad reach.

Preston writes that "the memory of Braddock's defeat cast a long shadow." Many people who lived through this event agreed. Many years later, Benjamin Franklin thought of Braddock's Defeat as a pivotal event. He wrote, "This whole transaction gave us Americans the first suspicion that our exalted ideas of the prowess of British regulars had not been well founded." Washington shared similar ideas about Braddock's Defeat. John Adams thought it changed hearts and minds. David Preston's book rises to this level. We have much to learn from his work.

David Hackett Fischer

Braddock's Defeat

Introduction

Remembering Braddock's Defeat

J ESSIE CALLAN WAS A YOUNG schoolgirl in Braddock, Pennsylvania, in the early 1900s, a time when soot and the smells of steelmaking permeated the town, and roaring blast furnaces were symbols of economic prosperity. It was the heyday of the United States Steel Corporation, the world's largest steel producer, and of Andrew Carnegie, the world's richest man. In 1873, the great industrialist had built the most modern steelworks in the world on what was known as Braddock's Field, where a century earlier, during the French and Indian War (also known as the Seven Years' War), General Edward Braddock's British army had been defeated by a smaller army composed mainly of Native Americans with their French Canadian allies. Carnegie named the works after J. Edgar Thomson, a business associate and president of the Pennsylvania Railroad Company. ET, as the mill came to be known, brought good times to the town of Braddock, a vibrant community of nearly 20,000 souls by the 1950s, when Jessie Callan wrote a reminiscence of how her schooling there had inspired her career as a librarian. Civic leaders and townsfolk were rightly proud of the town's past and hopeful about its future prospects. They celebrated and commemorated the "Battle of Braddock," and it formed part of the historical consciousness of the community (especially of the Borough of North Braddock, where the battle occurred).[1]

Nothing better captures the event's significance to that community than the painting *Washington at the Battle of Monongahela* by German-American artist Emanuel Leutze, who completed it in 1858 just a few

years after his best-known work, *Washington Crossing the Delaware*. When
the painting came up for sale in 1911, civic and educational leaders in
Braddock wanted to purchase and display it in the Carnegie Library of
Braddock—the first of thousands of such libraries that Andrew
Carnegie funded throughout the United States.[2] Thanks in large
measure to donations of pennies from Braddock's schoolchildren, including five cents from Jessie Callan, they succeeded. Callan and her
schoolmates had raised more than one-third of the painting's total cost
of $2,000. She recalled visits to her history classes from the superin-
tendent of schools, Grant Norris, and chief librarian and historian,
George H. Lamb, who were among those who had spearheaded the
effort to obtain the painting. "In class and out, we fought the Battle of
the Monongahela," she remembered. When Leutze's canvas was finally
displayed, each class marched to the Carnegie, "to see if it fulfilled our
young, authenticated expectations. It did." They pored over every
detail of the painting and parsed its accuracies and inaccuracies, its
combination of history and mythology.[3]

   Washington at the Battle of Monongahela (Plate 1, color photo
insert) was part of Leutze's project to narrate pictorially the rise of the
American nation through the person of George Washington: from
his youthful experiences as a surveyor, to rescuing (as the story went)
the British Army at Braddock's Defeat, to his Revolutionary War
clashes with the British at Dorchester Heights, the Delaware, and
Monmouth Court House. All of Leutze's paintings capture the contours of the nineteenth-century mythology of those historical events,
including, in this canvas, the French and Indian War. Essentially it
expresses in oil what historian Francis Parkman had written in ink
about the Monongahela—that it was a battle seemingly against nature
itself, with the beleaguered-looking British regulars being overwhelmed
by the forbidding ridge. The contrast between the dark woods and the
brightness bathing the British ranks suggests the dueling forces of savagery and civilization, of French absolutism against nascent American
republicanism, as personified in Washington. To Parkman and
Leutze, Braddock's Defeat was a battle as much moral as military in
dimension: Washington's virtue and the colonists' fighting abilities
had saved the British Army, despite Braddock's arrogant adherence
to the conventional tactics of the Old World. The preserving light of
Providence shines down upon Washington and illuminates his brave
and desperate stand against all odds.[4]

   Mythology aside, Leutze's painting accurately captures many
details of the critical moment in the battle when the British army is
beginning to disintegrate and flee in panic and disorder. While some

Redcoats rallying near the British flag continue to fire volleys, most are turning toward the rear as a few remaining officers attempt to halt them. Fear and desperation are etched on soldiers' faces. A British grenadier below the cannon fires blindly into the woods, as if trying to stem the encroaching darkness. Leutze powerfully conveys what many British officers and soldiers said of the action: that they did not see a single enemy combatant, only flashes of light and puffs of smoke from muzzles. Even the grenadiers' anachronistic bearskin hats (not in use until after 1768) evoke Washington's comparison of the retreating Redcoats to "the wild Bears of the Mountains" that could not be stopped.[5]

Given that Leutze painted the canvas a century after the battle was fought and relied on fanciful accounts, there are inevitable inaccuracies in his work. The battle occurred within an old-growth forest and not in a clearing, as the painting depicts. Leutze portrays the British column as advancing straight up the face of the ridge rather than ascending parallel to it, although his depiction of the forbidding nature of the ridge is quite similar to the battlefield's actual topography (certainly that ridge was not the tiny hillock that many historians have believed it to be). Although there is no evidence that he did so, Washington is shown directing artillery fire to cover a company of Virginia rangers, presumably those of Captain Adam Stephen, charging up the hill on the right to engage the Indians in the woods.

General Braddock is strangely indistinguishable among the British participants. He may be the wounded officer lying below the British flag, the epauletted officer on a white horse, or the officer whose head is bowed in defeat, faintly visible through the white smoke. Washington, the general's sole unwounded aide, has not only inherited the command, but, as it were, history. He is the rallying point, holding together the American units as they conduct a staunch rearguard action. The painting undoubtedly reminded audiences of a popular fable involving the battle (one for which there is no compelling evidence): that an Indian warrior took fifteen aimed shots at Washington but missed them all, foiled by the Great Spirit, who protected the future commander of the Continental Army and father of his country.[6]

Leutze's painting reminds us of another basic truth, that the story of this 1755 battle has been told largely from a British or American perspective. The name "Braddock's Defeat" captured the contemporary sense that Braddock alone bore the weight and responsibility of his crushing defeat. Even by the end of 1755, both the French and British were interchangeably using the terms "Braddock's

Defeat" ("la defaite de Bradok") and the "action" or battle of the Monongahela (Malangueulée), as did later historians.[7] The Anglo-centric conceit embedded in the battle's name and in prominent historical interpretations suggest that the campaign and battle were Braddock's to lose. Defeat was snatched from the jaws of victory. Had Braddock only allowed the Americans to engage the Indians using their tactics; had British regulars not panicked; had Braddock not alienated potential Indian allies; had he or Thomas Gage, the lieutenant colonel of the 44th Regiment, only seized a tiny hillock on the army's right flank; had Braddock only followed conventional European protocols more consistently, then the army would have been saved and the battle won.[8]

The battle of Braddock's Defeat, though crucial in itself, was but one moment in Braddock's Expedition, the military force sent from the British Isles to America in 1754 to conquer a French fort in the Ohio Valley. That expedition, in turn, was part of a larger campaign in 1755 involving British, French, and Indian forces across North America. The 1755 campaign reflected the political and strategic decisions of Indian nations and those of the British and French empires locked in a global struggle for mastery. How the Monongahela fit into that larger context, and how its important legacies shaped American history, remain a largely untold story. Students of the battle will know of the unfathomable debt owed to Paul Kopperman's 1977 *Braddock at the Monongahela*, an indispensable analysis of the primary sources pertaining to the day of the battle. This book builds on Kopperman's foundation by investigating Braddock's entire expedition, from its origins to its consequences. It gathers new or untapped sources, such as manuscript collections, maps, paintings, and portraits drawn from British, French, Canadian, and US archives and libraries in an attempt to illuminate virtually every aspect of the 1755 campaign.

For example, no study has yet fully explored French and Indian perspectives on the 1755 campaign. The French and the Indians remain nearly as invisible in modern studies as they appear in Leutze's rendering. A small, shadowy line of French marines is visible through the woods on the left, with the white royal flag of France waving above them. Not a single Indian warrior is visible. Leutze depicts a single French Canadian figure standing on a rock—perhaps meant to be the French Ottawa officer Charles-Michel Mouet de Langlade, who later claimed to have orchestrated the entire battle, at which he was probably not even present. In heroic and nationalistic accounts of *la bataille de la Malangueulée* written by Canadian historians in the early 1900s, the French captains Daniel-Hyacinthe-Marie

Liénard de Beaujeu and Jean-Daniel Dumas bravely lead their out-numbered forces against the British. They were hailed as the heroes of the Monongahela, personifying the French Canadian nobility's consummate military skill vis-à-vis later European commanders who failed to heed the lessons of Canadian warfare.[9]

Historical emphasis on individual French officers, however warranted, has obscured basic questions about the victorious forces at the Monongahela. We know little about how the French marshaled their forces to the Ohio Valley in the spring and summer of 1755; the operational and logistical difficulties they faced in the region; their diplomatic and military challenges of organizing a broad coalition of Indian allies, one drawn from twenty different nations and communities; and the identity and background of the French officers and cadets who fought at the Monongahela. French sources contain a remarkable and still largely untapped record of the officers, forces, preparations, and diplomacy with Natives in the Ohio Valley of the 1750s. For example, there is Captain Beaujeu's voyage of more than 700 miles from Montréal to Fort Duquesne in 1755—an odyssey nearly the match of Braddock's march across the Appalachians. The French perspective on the battle itself has been difficult to discern, given that accounts are few and largely secondhand, though many reflect testimony drawn from eyewitnesses (Captain Dumas's report is the only lengthy account written by an actual veteran). This study presents two new French narratives on the 1755 campaign and the Battle of the Monongahela. The account of French commissary officer Jean-Marie Landriève des Bordes, first published in 1927, but never included in previous studies of the Monongahela, offers valuable testimony on Captain Beaujeu's voyage as well as French preparations at Fort Duquesne on the morning of the battle. The second French account, from the Archives du Calvados (located in Caen, France), transforms our understanding of the Monongahela, offering the fullest and most detailed account of Beaujeu's tactical decisions from the moment he sallied out of Fort Duquesne to his attack on the British column. The Battle of the Monongahela was more Beaujeu's Victory than Braddock's Defeat, for in the end, the British general was outfought by a veteran French Canadian officer and combat leader. It was not a classic meeting engagement. Beaujeu exhibited greater tactical skill, had better reconnaissance of the battlefield and the British column, and improvised a battle plan that he had coordinated with his Indian allies, who brilliantly executed it.

The Battle of the Monongahela was above all a testament to the military power of Indian nations, which comprised more than two-thirds of the force that attacked Braddock's column. The Indians' numbers, tactical initiatives, disciplined firepower, and superior marksmanship were largely responsible for the outcome. Yet we do not know how the Indians referred to this victory accomplished by their prowess. Like Leutze's painting, Indian warriors remain invisible and anonymous in historical accounts, though the artist realized that the woods were full of them during the battle, as he remarked in a letter to a friend.[10] There is no eyewitness testimony from any Native combatants, and it is nearly impossible to identify any of them by name. Nineteenth-century chroniclers, presuming that only an extraordinary Indian leader could have orchestrated so great a victory over the British, placed virtually the entire cast of celebrated eighteenth-century Indian leaders at Braddock's Defeat, such as Pontiac (Ottawa), Guyasuta (Seneca), Black Hoof (Shawnee), and Tecumseh's father, Puckshinwa, a Shawnee warrior who presumably related the lesson to his son. But French records from the 1750s do not confirm the presence of any of those legendary individuals.[11] Both British and French sources, however, shed light on the intensive diplomacy that preceded the battle as well as the choices that Native peoples made in 1755 to participate. British and French firsthand accounts also comment on the actions and tactics of Native warriors during the battle. English captive James Smith, who witnessed the French and Indian forces returning to Fort Duquesne in triumph on the evening of July 9, concluded that Indian warriors were "the best disciplined troops." "Could it be supposed," he asked in retrospect, "that undisciplined troops could defeat Generals Braddock, Grant, &c.?"[12] The Indians' victory escalated their involvement in the war and emboldened them in future clashes with conventional armies in the Seven Years' War, Pontiac's War, and the American Revolution. How the Battle of the Monongahela shaped the arc of Native history in the late eighteenth century is as yet an untold story.

The British side of the 1755 campaign is in need of a complete retelling, for factual errors, untested arguments, myths, and outright fictions have become too encrusted in many modern renderings.[13] New sources and perspectives have been uncovered since the publication of Kopperman's foundational study nearly forty years ago: the letter book of Sir John St. Clair, one of the most significant officers in Braddock's army, became known to scholars; Sheldon Cohen discovered Major William Sparke's superb account of his experiences in the 48th Regiment during the campaign; Elaine Breslaw proved that an anonymous account long believed to have been written by a British officer was in fact written by a disgruntled civilian; and, most recently, Alan Houston discovered a trove of new documents pertaining to Benjamin Franklin's crucial role in the expedition, particularly in rescuing it from logistical failure.[14] This book will also make use of two manuscript discoveries: a new account of an Ohio Iroquois warrior who fought alongside George Washington in the disputed "Jumonville Affair" that precipitated Braddock's Expedition; and a description of the British garrison at Gibraltar, apparently written by Braddock himself, that illuminates his military career and his qualifications to command in America. Finally, abundant new scholarship on the eighteenth-century British Army and Empire permits a more contextualized and accurate portrait of both the general and the two regiments that he led to America.

This book also relies on extensive personal fieldwork on the campaign's geography and terrain. Braddock's Expedition into the western frontier offers a study in mountain warfare. The surviving traces of the route he took—Braddock's Road—are primary sources unto themselves, testifying to the daunting challenges of the Appalachian terrain that the army surmounted. With few exceptions, histories of the expedition either ignore geography or misrepresent it, as in the common argument that the British lost the battle when they bypassed and failed to occupy some little "knoll" or "hillock" on their right flank.[15] Walking the modern vestiges of Braddock's Road, studying the battlefield in North Braddock, exploring the old French portage road between forts Presque Isle and Le Boeuf, and canoeing down the French line of communications along French Creek and the Allegheny River have all exponentially increased my own understanding of written sources. I place considerable emphasis on the crucial contingency of logistics, defined as "the practical art of moving armies and keeping them supplied," for both the French and British had very tenuous supply lines during the campaign.[16] As we shall see, horses and bateaux—the flat-bottomed boats that brought Beaujeu's men and supplies to the Ohio Valley—are among the most important yet underappreciated aspects of the campaign.

The conventional notion that Braddock's arrogance or blunders were chiefly responsible for his defeat has depreciated the victory that Indian and French forces won by their superior discipline, tactical decisions, and leadership. It has also robbed the story of Braddock's Expedition of its many contingent moments: the British government's decision to send two understrength Irish regiments to Virginia; the Alexandria Congress, held in April 1755, that established the tempo of the campaign; the difficult voyages of French convoys and the seemingly miraculous timing of their arrival at Fort Duquesne;

the decisions of Indian warriors from many nations to fight in alliance with the French; the killings of six Mohawk emissaries by Chickasaws and Cherokees in early 1755 that weakened Braddock's considerable efforts to gain Indian allies; the military intelligence that Braddock received of French forces in the Ohio Valley, and how that shaped his decision—crucial, as it turned out—to split his army at the Little Meadows and proceed with a lighter and faster detachment toward his objective; and finally, the evidence showing how Braddock managed to construct a durable military road and bring his powerful army to the gates of Fort Duquesne in one of the most rapid and successful marches in early American military history.

Braddock was not defeated due to any one of these contingencies, but to all of them. The battle was not lost by one man's arrogance or bluster. Braddock's Defeat was ultimately the sum of its imperial parts, a powerful reflection of how weak the British Empire in America really was in 1755. In that respect, the British general was simply unfortunate—a term that contemporaries routinely employed to describe his fate. He was unfortunate in having been ordered to begin his expedition in a colony that was unprepared for war and often unwilling to cooperate. The colonists were largely responsible for the horrendous state of British-Indian relations, which made it so difficult for the general to gain Indian allies. He was unfortunate in that his force was deployed in a column, one of the most difficult tactical formations from which to fight a battle, when he made contact with a highly mobile enemy force. He was unfortunate in that Indian warriors quickly collapsed his flank protection, which should have been fully adequate. He was unfortunate in that the battle occurred after a river crossing and while his army was ascending a steep ridgeline, making his column all the more vulnerable. British historian J. F. C. Fuller was entirely correct when he quipped, "If Frederick the Great himself had been in command of this British column, he could not have done more than Braddock did, and he would have suffered a similar fate."[17]

Yet the defeat shaped future success. As historian Sir John Fortescue observed, "It was over the bones of Braddock that the British advanced yet again to the conquest of Canada."[18] The British avenged the slaughter at the Monongahela when General John Forbes captured Fort Duquesne in 1758. Both Braddock's and Forbes's expeditions shifted the center of gravity of American warfare to the continent's interior. Prior to 1755, the British had proven incapable of projecting large military forces west of the Appalachians. Their efforts were largely oriented to the navigable Atlantic coastline or the St. Lawrence River in amphibious expeditions against Acadia, St. Augustine, Louisbourg, or Quebec. Braddock's and Forbes's expeditions symbolized a new and decisive continental reach for British and American forces. Braddock's victory became the military road that he had constructed across the mountains, which was instrumental in securing future British control over the region. Following the capture of Fort Duquesne, thousands of colonial hunters, squatters, traders, and veterans followed British military roads into the Ohio Valley, where they displaced its Indian residents and sparked renewed conflict for the region's lands and resources.

The Ohio Valley represented the confluence not only of three rivers but of three peoples—Indian, French Canadian, and British—who struggled at the Monongahela for their respective futures in America.[19] Braddock's Defeat is thus a profoundly human story, involving a unique set of individuals who cast particularly long shadows over the history of the eighteenth century: George Washington, the ambitious Virginian who volunteered as General Braddock's aide and earned the praise of his contemporaries for his conduct during the battle; Benjamin Franklin, the aspiring Pennsylvania politician who had so monumental a role in sustaining the campaign with horses and wagons; Thomas Gage, who bravely led the advance party of Braddock's army and presided over the 1775 battles at Lexington and Concord; Captain Horatio Gates, the future victor of the Battle of Saratoga who commanded a New York Independent Company in 1755; Lieutenant Charles Lee of the 44th Foot, an ambitious British officer who later became a major-general in the Continental Army; and an unheralded frontier drifter, brawler, and teamster named Daniel Morgan who achieved one of the greatest victories of the Revolutionary War at Cowpens. The French and Indian perspectives will be supplied through the lives of French Canadian officers like Claude-Pierre Pécaudy de Contrecoeur and Captain Beaujeu, and Atiatoharongwen, a Mohawk Iroquois warrior from the town of Kahnawake. Lesser-known but important characters include the irascible Sir John St. Clair, the British Deputy Quarter Master General in America; William La Péronie, a French Huguenot officer from Virginia who served with Washington; and Silver Heels and Quintin Kennedy, the first an Ohio Iroquois warrior and the second a British officer who became close friends and together had among the most illustrious military careers of the entire war. The Battle of the Monongahela was the defining generational experience for many of these officers, who carried their veteran experiences from the Seven Years' War forward into the American Revolution.

Ever since Andrew Carnegie built the Edgar Thomson Works on Braddock's Field, the story of the American steel industry has become melded with that of Braddock's Defeat. "Who would have thought it?" Braddock asked in his dying despair, as a proud and powerful army suffered an ignominious defeat. Two centuries later, a number of steelworkers expressed the exact unbelieving words as steel mills closed their gates in the Monongahela Valley in the 1980s.[20] Few would have thought that the very mills so crucial to America's military might in the twentieth century (a small manifestation of which was the World War II destroyer, USS *Leutze*, named for the artist's son, who had become a US Navy admiral) would ever be shuttered. The odyssey of Leutze's painting in the late twentieth century has been an example of art imitating life, pace Oscar Wilde. The painting shared in the flagging fortunes of Braddock and other towns when the steel industry in the Mon Valley declined at the end of the twentieth century. Even before the blast furnaces began to idle, the US Steel Corporation had divested itself of the Braddock Carnegie Library in 1961. The derelict institution temporarily closed to the public in 1974, until concerned citizens bought it for the sum of $1.00 and gradually began to preserve and reopen it. Leutze's painting was shuffled into various banks and vaults for safekeeping, largely forgotten for more than two decades.[21]

The Edgar Thomson Works now represents the last integrated steelmaking plant left in the entire Mon Valley. But ET's roaring blast furnaces and continuous steel caster stand in stark contrast to downtown Braddock. The town has suffered from declining population, deteriorating buildings, chronic depression, and abandonment, even from presidential candidates who come to ET every few years for a photo op with the region's last basic steelworkers. Its namesake general refused to go down without a fight, however, and the town of Braddock may be recovering elements of its old civic identity and prosperity through tourism related to its military and industrial pasts. Two promising initiatives were the successful preservation of the historic Carrie blast furnaces at nearby Rankin in 2010 and the opening of the Braddock's Battlefield History Center by Pittsburgh lawyer and preservationist Robert Messner and other sponsors in 2012. Leutze's painting now appropriately resides at the Braddock Carnegie Library, next to the very ground where French, British, and Indian combatants clashed on a hot July day in 1755.[22]

CHAPTER 1

Paths to the Monongahela

I T WAS THE MOST powerful European military force yet seen on the Allegheny River. In April 1754, a French armada of bateaux and birchbark canoes carrying 600 men, supplies, and artillery was sweeping southward down la Belle Rivière—the Beautiful River as the French called the Allegheny and the Ohio. Its veteran commander, Captain Claude-Pierre Pécaudy de Contrecoeur, was bringing massive numbers and firepower to overwhelm his English foes, who were hastily constructing a fortification at the Forks of the Ohio River. Late on the morning of April 17, the French beached their craft at Shannopin's Town, a Delaware settlement about three miles east of the Forks. French *troupes de la marine* quickly formed and advanced on the British post in order of battle. At least four cannon (the British reported as many as eighteen) were quickly unloaded from the bateaux, remounted on gun carriages, and drawn toward what was called Fort Prince George, or Trent's Fort, named after Pennsylvania trader and Ohio Company agent William Trent. The Virginia commander, Ensign Edward Ward, surrendered the fort and its small garrison of forty-one men without firing a shot. But the confrontation at Trent's Fort in April 1754 bloodlessly inaugurated a decade of war that would engulf not only the Ohio Valley but the rest of the world.[1]

Like the swift current of la Belle Rivière that had carried Contrecoeur's forces to Trent's Fort, powerful imperial and demographic forces swept the French, the Indians, and the British toward violent confrontation in the Ohio Valley. The Forks of the Ohio

River, formed by the confluence of the Monongahela and Allegheny Rivers, had emerged as the most vital and strategic location in North America by the mid-eighteenth century. Claimants to the region saw their respective futures, even their very existence, as inexorably turning on the question of who controlled the region. The first settlers in the Ohio Country were Delawares, Shawnees, Senecas, and other Iroquois, who began entering the valley in the 1720s. Many came as refugees, displaced from their eastern lands by British colonial expansion and by the dominance of the Iroquois Confederacy, which saw many of its smaller neighbors as clients settled figuratively under the Tree of Peace of the Six Nations.

The Ohio Valley was above all a place of independence—"a Republic composed of all sorts of Nations," as a Cayuga Iroquois described it. Individuals and communities, not powerful headmen, determined their own courses of action. Hunters prized the valley's abundant game, and young warriors sought military distinction by following the "Warriors' Road" leading from the Ohio to their traditional Cherokee and Catawba enemies in the southeast. Memories of past wrongs fueled the Ohio Indians' determination to preserve their independence from the French, British, and the Six Nations. The Delawares (or Lenapes), for example, had formed an alliance with William Penn and the people of Pennsylvania in the 1680s. In the early eighteenth century, the Susquehanna Valley was inhabited by Delawares, Shawnees, Nanticokes, Conestogas, and other Iroquois, who coexisted with the British colonists. But by the 1750s, Pennsylvania had attracted thousands of immigrants who encroached on the Natives' lands. Later, Pennsylvania officials orchestrated a number of fraudulent land purchases, such as the 1737 Walking Purchase, in which Delawares were dispossessed of their lands. Worse yet, the land agents for the Pennsylvania government were Six Nations diplomats who asserted Iroquois land claims in treaties that signed away the lands occupied by the Natives whose interests they claimed to represent. The shade of the Tree of Peace proved to be no place of repose for either the Delawares or Shawnees.[2]

Displaced Indians sought independence in Ohio, "a Country between" the French and British rivals, as an Iroquois leader named Tanaghrisson characterized it. The Ohio Indians hoped that the Appalachian Mountains would serve as a barrier between themselves and the expansive British. But Tanaghrisson personified the ways that British imperialism and Iroquois pretensions followed the Delawares and Shawnees into the region. He was one of the Ohio Iroquois (largely Senecas), and reputed to be the child of a Catawba

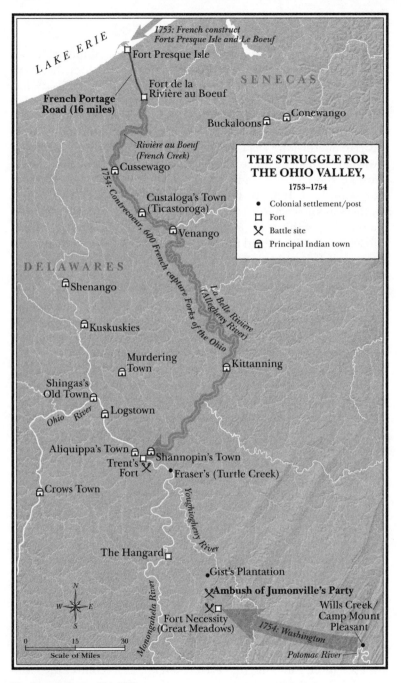

The Struggle for the Ohio Valley, 1753–1754

Glen Pawelski, Mapping Specialists, Ltd.

mother and a Seneca father. One Frenchman judged him as "more English than the English." British officials dubbed him the "Half King," a title that referred to his role as the Six Nations' emissary and his dubious ability to speak for all Ohio Indians. Traders from Pennsylvania and Virginia also followed their former Indian customers to the Ohio. They especially made inroads during the War of Austrian Succession (1744–1748), a dynastic and territorial struggle involving Britain, France, and other major European powers. Wartime shortages of trade goods in New France allowed British traders to fulfill Indians' needs during King George's War, as the conflict was known in the thirteen colonies. British officials regarded the opening of this trade as a crucial breach of New France's imperial defenses, as it enabled them to draw Indian nations into alliance with Great Britain and opened the possibilities of the far west to trade and settlement.[3]

The French laid claim to the region on the basis of Sieur de la Salle's alleged exploration of the Ohio circa 1670 but had not yet established any durable presence there. As early as the 1720s and 1730s, French governors were increasingly aware of the Ohio Valley's importance as a strategic communication route to Louisiana and of the need to maintain alliances with the Indian peoples coming into the region. In 1724, the French governor-general Philippe de Rigaud, Marquis de Vaudreuil, encouraged Shawnee bands to settle along the Rivière au Boeuf, and Baron de Longueuil's expedition against the Chickasaws floated down "the Belle Rivière route" to the Mississippi in 1739. By the late 1740s, the influx of British traders such as George Croghan had reached such a crisis point that the French responded with an expedition led by Pierre-Joseph Céloron de Blainville in 1749 to drive them away. The French discovered that their influence in the Ohio region was merely symbolic, much like the lead plates that Céloron buried along his route to assert French possession of the Ohio watershed. Onontio (as Indians referred to the French governor and metaphorical French father) was having to pursue his prodigal Native children who had run away to English traders. Sometimes Onontio did this by generous diplomacy and sometimes by brute force, as in the example made of Pickawillany, a Miami Indian town destroyed by French and Indian forces in 1752 after it had drifted too far into the English orbit.[4]

Both France and Great Britain blithely played a game of reckless escalation, gambling that each could militarily control the Ohio Valley without alienating its Indian owners or provoking a general war in America or in Europe. France had more to lose in this dangerous game. Neither King Louis XV nor his ministers wanted an open war with Great Britain, one for which they were wholly unprepared. The French hoped that negotiations with the British through the Boundary Commission created at the end of the previous war in 1748 could adjudicate territorial disputes in America. However, alarming reports from Canadian officials such as the Marquis de la Galissonière and François Bigot prompted the French government to move forcefully against the British. In his influential 1750 memoir, Galissonière argued that New France's primary value was not economic but strategic, as a barrier to British expansion (in 1754, the thirteen colonies were burgeoning toward a total population of 1,500,000 while New France's was only around 55,000). The logic of containment necessitated an aggressive response to repair the Ohio breach, which officials feared would compromise New France's existence and enable the British ultimately to gain access to the trans-Mississippi West and riches of New Spain. In 1752, the French naval minister Antoine-Louis Rouillé drafted instructions for the new governor-general of New France, the Marquis Duquesne, a brash and resolute naval officer who had been recommended by Galissonière. Duquesne was to expel British traders and reassert French control over the Ohio Valley by force of arms.[5]

In 1753, the Marquis Duquesne sent in a force of 2,600 men—as large as General Braddock's entire army in 1755—led by Captain Paul Marin de la Malgue, who was to build and garrison a chain of fortifications to anchor French control of the region. Duquesne acknowledged the "extreme boldness" of his plan but believed that the French must "seize and establish [ourselves] on the Belle Riviere, which we are on the verge of losing if I do not make this hasty but indispensable effort." Natives in the region bristled at the display of French military power, but the British had given them ample reason to acquiesce to the French presence; and they knew that French forts did not attract swarms of settlers as British ones did. By the end of 1753, the French had established two forts to secure the Presque Isle portage from Lake Erie to Rivière au Boeuf (today known as French Creek). Nevertheless, they had not yet established any fortifications on the Belle Rivière proper, only a crude encampment at Venango, where Rivière au Boeuf empties into the Belle Rivière. It had been all they could do to establish two forts in 1753 given the severe toll that toil and disease had exacted on the men, including Marin, who died that October. The French all knew that when the spring came, they would continue southward to seize the strategic prize of the Forks of the Ohio, the task that had fallen to Captain Contrecoeur.[6]

Contrecoeur's distinguished ancestry delineated much of the history of New France, established in 1608. His grandfather, Antoine Pécaudy de Contrecoeur, had come to New France in 1665 as an officer in the famed Carignan-Salières Regiment sent by Louis XIV to garrison and protect the colony from Iroquois threats. Captain Pécaudy was among the cadre of regimental veterans who remained as settlers in Canada, where he gained a seigneury on the south shore of the St. Lawrence near Montréal. The career of Pécaudy's son, François-Antoine, typified the growing military prowess of Canadian officers who spent many years in service to their king. François-Antoine campaigned against the Onondagas in Iroquoia and the English in Acadia, Newfoundland, and New England. His commands at posts such as Fort Chambly and Fort Saint-Frédéric reflected the expanding network of trade, fortifications, and alliances that had brought imperial influence in North America. François-Antoine's career culminated in becoming a Chevalier de Saint-Louis, the noble military order to which Canadian officers most aspired. Claude-Pierre, born in 1706, continued his exemplary lineage when he began his military career as a cadet in the *troupes de la marine* at the age of sixteen. By 1742, Contrecoeur was commanding troops at his father's post at Saint-Frédéric in the Champlain Valley. He was second-in-command of the 1749 expedition of Céloron de Blainville, navigating the waters of the Belle Rivière that he would one day seize for France. Contrecoeur's star had risen so brightly by 1752 that he was entrusted with command of Fort Niagara and recommended by the Governor-General Marquis Duquesne for the Croix de Saint-Louis.[7]

Captain Contrecoeur was wintering at Fort Niagara with his wife, Marie-Madeleine Boucher de La Perrière, when an urgent message arrived from the Marquis Duquesne, dated January 27, 1754. Contrecoeur read his new orders to "enter the Belle Rivière area with the detachment he commands, to march toward Chinengué [Logstown] where he will have a fort built" at the Forks of the Ohio. It was a measure of the remarkable willpower and hubris of this governor-general that he was already referring to the projected outpost as Fort Duquesne before one timber had been laid. But he had matchless confidence in Contrecoeur to execute "the most important mission that has ever been assigned in this colony." Madame Contrecoeur, on the other hand, knew the price those orders would exact on the family and was none too pleased. She and their two little girls would not see him again for nearly two years. Duquesne sent Contrecoeur a strong reinforcement of nearly 400 men, described as "the elite of the Canadians and Troupes [de la Marine]," including

Joseph-Charles Bonin, or "Jolicoeur," as he was known, a gunner in the *Compagnie des cannoniers-bombardiers* who chronicled the campaign. The troops had the unenviable and unusual task of traveling up the St. Lawrence River and over Lake Ontario during the punishing Canadian winter.[8] Contrecoeur and his detachment reached Fort Presque Isle in early March, and soon after they began their descent from Fort de la Rivière au Boeuf to the Forks of the Ohio, where Contrecoeur knew that an English force had been building a fortress since February. He had been ordered to strip all but thirty men from forts Presque Isle and Le Boeuf. With 600 men, he was to strike the English and "make a more vivid impression on the Indians," whom Duquesne believed would "die of fear when they see the king's troops marching toward their village."[9]

When Contrecoeur disembarked his artillery and troops near Trent's Fort on April 17, 1754, he sent forward an officer designed to strike fear into English hearts—Capitaine François-Marc Antoine Le Mercier. With flags, drums, guards, and an Ohio Iroquois interpreter, Le Mercier came forward to demand an immediate English surrender. The commander of Trent's Fort, Ensign Edward Ward of the Virginia provincials, could see by then the massive size of the French force assembling against him. He received Contrecoeur's summons—from the "Commander of the Artillery of Canada, Captain of the Bombardiers"—with some trepidation. He knew that this artillery officer could pulverize his little fort with his cannons. The summons read in part: "Nothing can surprize me more than to see you attempt a Settlement upon the Lands of the King my master." Ward had one hour to decide the fate of his garrison.[10] At the same moment, Le Mercier presented a belt of wampum to Tanaghrisson, which warned the Ohio Iroquois that while Onontio was coming "with enough force to crush" the English, their French father did not want them to "share the same fate," and encouraged them to withdraw. The French had laid bare the hollow nature of the Half King's authority and that of his English backers. Tanaghrisson was so enraged that he pushed Le Mercier with his hand, warning him that "the French had no Business there on their Hunting Grounds," and that "he would not allow his Brothers the English to be routed" from a fort that he had authorized. A tense "scuffle" ensued, in which Tanaghrisson and other Iroquois came close to killing the French "on the spot." But for the moment the Half King restrained his hatchet.[11]

In an hour's time, it was all over. Ensign Ward ventured to the French camp along with the Half King and an interpreter. In a forlorn bid for time, Ward told Captain Contrecoeur that he was but a junior officer and had no authority to answer his summons. But the veteran French captain expected such a reply, and insisted that he make up his mind that instant, or he would "immediately take Possession of the Fort by Force." Ward, whose command consisted of thirty-three soldiers and eight carpenters living in a ramshackle and only partly constructed fortification, had no alternative. As the English garrison evacuated the fort, the Half King "stormed greatly at the French," for his prestige and authority were bound up in that fort whose foundations he had helped to lay. The French "paid no regard" to the Half King's rants. That evening, Contrecoeur invited Ensign Ward to supper, for the two crowns of Britain and France were, after all, still at peace. Contrecoeur would long relish his "good fortune in chasing out the English" in April 1754.[12] The Marquis Duquesne greatly praised his "good and wise conduct" and remarked that "without firing a shot, the English have withdrawn, looking foolish, and in less than an hour's time you have become master of the battlefield." The ease of Contrecoeur's bloodless conquest had been deceptive. As the French set about dismantling Trent's Fort and building Fort Duquesne, the centerpiece of their Ohio Valley fortifications, the imperial situation was becoming far more volatile than simply expelling traders and cowing local Indians.[13]

Newspapers carried alarming reports of French military aggression throughout the British colonies, exaggerating the strength of Contrecoeur's force to 1,000 regular troops and eighteen artillery pieces, "which they planted against the fort," as though it were a formal siege. The reports only pointed out what was already painfully obvious to British readers: that from their chain of forts, the French and their numerous Indian allies were planning to "kill and scalp the Inhabitants, and ruin the Frontier Counties" of Pennsylvania and Virginia. The *Pennsylvania Gazette* contrasted "the Confidence of the French in this Undertaking" with the "present disunited State of the British Colonies." Unless those fractious thirteen colonies could ever agree to fight the French, "the Destruction of the British Interest, Trade and Plantations in America" would inevitably result. Contrecoeur's conquest of Trent's Fort was a galling display of French military prowess to a British world already conditioned by fear of encirclement and impotence to do anything about it.[14]

News of the French attack reached Lieutenant Colonel George Washington on April 19, 1754, on the south branch of the Potomac River, while he was riding toward Wills Creek, the forward base of Virginia's campaign to control the Ohio Valley. Washington and his

Virginia troops were now the tip of the spear, having received news the following day that Ensign Ward had surrendered the post. Royal Governor Robert Dinwiddie's instructions had authorized him to restrain any French who obstructed British forts and to "kill & destroy" them if they resisted. Contrecoeur's capture of Trent's Fort was a brazen act of war, in Washington's view, particularly after he had learned that the French had "planted eighteen Pieces of Cannon against the Fort." Governor Dinwiddie concurred, writing to the Board of Trade that "the Breach was begun by the French in taking our Fort." After news reached London, a British cabinet meeting was convened on June 26, 1754, to discuss reports that 1,000 French *regulars* had "invaded His Majesty's Dominions" and "destroyed" a fort "built by the King's order on the Ohio." French actions were later cited by both the king and the Parliament as the point "when actual War broke out" to justify military reprisals.[15] The British government responded by sending two thousand stands of arms and £10,000 in specie to Virginia, and by issuing orders for Maryland governor Horatio Sharpe, a regular officer, to act as commander in chief of colonial forces.[16] The conflict for the Ohio Valley had entered a new and more volatile phase as the British prepared to repel the French intruders.

Over the previous three decades, British officials in Virginia and other colonies had begun to conceive of their inchoate western land claims as imperial frontiers that would extend British dominion into the interior of the continent at New France's expense. Governor Alexander Spotswood was among the first to alert Virginians to the imperial and economic possibilities of the lands west of the Blue Ridge, particularly the Shenandoah (or Great) Valley. In 1716, he led an expedition across the Blue Ridge composed of gentlemen adventurers who became known as the "Knights of the Golden Horseshoe." Their keepsake golden horseshoe was inscribed with the motto *Sic juvat transcendere montes*—"thus it is delightful to cross mountains"—a telling prophecy for the subsequent history of Virginia. German and Scots-Irish settlers from Pennsylvania and Maryland also began moving southward into Virginia in a massive migration that unnerved Tidewater patricians like William Byrd II, who thought that the newcomers "swarm like the Goths and Vandals of old." The Great Valley continued to function as a thoroughfare for Native warriors from northern and southern nations engaged in perpetual wars. Occasional skirmishes between Indian warriors and backcountry farmers paled in comparison to what Virginians most feared—that these unruly borderlands might become a haven for runaway slaves. For all of those reasons, officials had awarded land grants west of the Blue Ridge and increasingly tried to settle industrious Swiss and German Protestants along the frontiers as buffers. At the Treaty of Lancaster in 1744, Virginia officials negotiated with the Six Nations for land rights in the valley. The Iroquois delegates had ceded only their claims to the Shenandoah Valley, but Virginia officials deceptively inserted language in the treaty that encompassed all of Virginia's future western land claims, including the Ohio Valley. It was on that legal fiction that British claims to the Ohio Country were mainly premised.[17]

Even before 1748, when King George's War between Britain and France had ended, powerful and wealthy Virginia leaders were already thinking of the western lands supposedly opened by the Treaty of Lancaster. Organized in 1748, the Ohio Company of Virginia petitioned the crown for a grant of land in the Ohio Valley amounting to 200,000 acres, a territory that included the Forks of the Ohio River. The Ohio Company was no ordinary joint-stock enterprise of land speculators but a powerful engine of empire. Its membership was a distinguished cast of wealthy planters, politicians, and frontier agents, including Thomas Lee (the principal Virginia negotiator at the Lancaster Treaty), John Carlyle, Thomas Cresap, Robert Dinwiddie, Arthur Dobbs, George William Fairfax, Thomas Nelson, Lawrence Washington, and Augustine Washington. With the able representation of John Hanbury, an influential London merchant and Ohio Company member, the Board of Trade and then the king approved an initial grant of 200,000 acres in 1749, with 300,000 to follow if certain terms were met.[18]

The Ohio Company's conditional grant was not merely an investment in land but also speculation in the future of the British Empire in North America. According to the terms of the grant, the company had to expand trade in the Ohio Valley and with it, the "British interest" among the Indian nations; 200 families were required to settle there; and most significantly, the crown made the construction of a fort in the Ohio Valley a condition. The Ohio Company's investors wasted no time in getting down to business. By 1749, there was a company store at the junction of Wills Creek and the Potomac River (on the Virginia shore, opposite what is now Cumberland, Maryland). Along with a second storehouse constructed at the confluence of Redstone Creek and the Monongahela River in 1752, these two posts functioned as the vanguard for British traders and even a few settlers. To reach the "Hangard" post at Redstone, the Ohio Company had commissioned frontiersman Christopher Gist in 1752 to blaze a packhorse trail from Wills Creek across the Appalachian Mountains, a route that became part of Braddock's Road in 1755. Gist had not only explored the Ohio Valley between 1750 and 1752 but also acted as a diplomatic representative of the Ohio Company. At the Treaty of Logstown in 1752, commissioners from Virginia (including Joshua Fry, Gist, and Andrew Montour, along with Pennsylvania trader George Croghan) secured from the Ohio Iroquois confirmation—if a little ambiguous—of British purchase of the Ohio Valley, and permission to build a fort and trading post at the Forks. Gist also led the vanguard of the 200 families who were supposed to settle the region. In 1753, while the French were constructing forts at Presque Isle and Le Boeuf, Gist and his family were establishing a plantation of more than 1,000 acres in a lush valley near the Youghiogheny River and the base of Chestnut Ridge. Ohio Company officials were already plotting the street layouts of a 200-acre town next to their projected fort near the Forks. All of these activities led to Ohio Indians' acquiescence to the French presence as a counterweight and to heightened suspicion of both imperial powers.[19]

If the French mission for 1753 and 1754 had simply been throwing renegade British traders out of the Ohio Country, their network of fortifications went beyond that and might very well have established control. However, the French failed to understand how and why the imperial backdrop of the struggle had shifted since Céloron de Blainville's expedition in 1749. In his summons to Ensign Ward, Contrecoeur stated that British efforts were "concerted by none but a company [the Ohio Company] who have more in View the Advantage of a trade" than of preserving peace between the two crowns. But the Ohio Company had been created and fueled by networks of power and influence reaching to London. Tales of the Ohio Valley's lush, promising lands also fueled and energized colonial traders, settlers, and soldiers who saw its agricultural and industrial possibilities, including one Virginia officer who wrote rapturously, "Nature seems to have furnished this Country in the most lavish Manner with all the conveniences and Comforts of Life. I have seen a deal of Limestone, Coal, and rich Iron Ore, all convenient for Water Carriage." Were Britain to lose it, he argued, it "would be a greater acquisition to France than the Conquest of all Flanders."[20]

Virginia's Governor Dinwiddie was as determined as his Canadian counterpart the Marquis Duquesne to fortify and possess the Ohio Valley, and his actions greatly escalated tensions with New France and deepened the British government's commitment to Virginia during the crisis. Born in 1692 to the son of a Glasgow merchant, Dinwiddie entered the British Atlantic world as a trader and colonial administrator, settling in both Bermuda and Virginia. He established himself as an expert on colonial affairs, writing reports and observations to the Board of Trade as early as 1731. That reputation, and his personal connections with influential officials such as the Earl of Halifax, Earl Granville, and Henry Pelham, gave Dinwiddie's opinions credibility. He particularly sensed a kindred spirit in the Earl of Halifax, his powerful patron on the Board of Trade, and wrote to him in a "free and open manner" on the need to reform the British colonies in America. While Dinwiddie served as Virginia's lieutenant governor from 1751 to 1758, he was a staunch defender of royal prerogative against the local House of Burgesses and its constituents, whom he found "too much on a republican Spirit." Dinwiddie believed that the "supine and unaccountable Obstinacy" of the colonial legislatures was the principal reason for British weakness in America.[21]

As Governor Dinwiddie pursued a vision of British imperial dominance over the westward lands, he privately had "the Success and Prosperity of the Ohio Company much at heart," seeing no distinction or conflict of interest between the two. His letters to the Board of Trade sounded a tocsin of British imperial defeat in

Robert Dinwiddie (1693–1770) was lieutenant governor of Virginia from 1751 to 1758. The strains of imperial crisis and warfare during his governorship are evident in this portrait by an unknown artist, ca. 1760–1765. © National Portrait Gallery, London.

America, a warning that reverberated in London, where ministers shared his concerns about French encroachments and connected them to similarly alarming reports from other colonial governors. In mid-June 1753, Dinwiddie had written to the Board with news of the French "invading His Majesty's Lands on the River Ohio." Lord Halifax read the letter in August to the Board of Trade, which considered the Ohio Valley "a point of such great national importance." He forwarded it to the Duke of Newcastle, who convened a cabinet meeting, at which a circular letter to North American governors was composed and sent, alerting them to French encroachments and authorizing them to "repell force by force" in His Majesty's dominions. Most significantly, Dinwiddie received additional instructions that escalated the conflict in the Ohio Valley and made Virginia the epicenter of that effort. Signed by King George II, the instructions urged him to "use your utmost endeavours" to establish forts in the Ohio Country and to mobilize the militia in case of French resistance. The British government took an expensive and significant step toward direct intervention in Virginia when the king ordered approximately thirty pieces of artillery (iron 4-pounders) for Virginia's use in its Ohio fortifications. Dinwiddie first had to forewarn any French trespassers to depart peaceably, then was authorized to "drive them out by force of arms" if they did not.[22]

George Washington's decision to volunteer for that diplomatic mission in late 1753 altered the trajectory of his life. He was born in 1732 to a distinguished Virginia gentry family, whose coat of arms could be traced back to fourteenth-century England. But as a youth, Washington seemed unlikely to achieve great prominence. George's aspirations were considerably shaped by the example and influence of his older brother Lawrence, who had briefly held a captaincy in the British Army. Lawrence married into the powerful family of Lord Fairfax, the proprietor of the vast Northern Neck land grant in Virginia. His marriage to Anne Fairfax brought George patronage, such as his appointment as Culpeper County surveyor. When George was commissioned as a major in the Virginia militia on Lawrence's death in 1752, he would have been the first to admit of his inexperience in diplomacy and warfare. But Washington's inclinations, as he famously said, were "strongly bent to arms," and his career as a surveyor had given him a formidable reservoir of frontier experience. Five years before Braddock's army struggled through terrain that its British officers considered alien, Washington was intimately familiar with frontier lands and topography. In 1750, Washington surveyed well over fifty tracts in the rugged Cacapon and Little Cacapon valleys of western Virginia, including two future encampment sites of Braddock's army in 1755.[23]

Washington had apparently met Governor Dinwiddie in early 1752 in Williamsburg upon returning from a trip to Barbados on behalf of his ailing brother. Having recently been commissioned by Dinwiddie, he was confident enough to volunteer for a hazardous winter mission to deliver the official summons to the French to depart their forts near Lake Erie. Along with Christopher Gist, he negotiated with key Iroquois leaders such as Tanaghrisson, Monacatootha, Kaghswaghtaniunt, and Guyasuta, and the Delaware Shingas. On December 12, 1753, at a snowbound Fort de la Rivière au Boeuf, Washington delivered the summons requiring the "peaceable Departure" to Captain Jacques Legardeur de Saint-Pierre, whom Washington thought had "much the Air of a Soldier." Legardeur was a Chevalier de Saint-Louis, expert on Indian languages, and veteran of many campaigns and explorations in the *pays d'en haut* and the far west. Few if any British colonial officers could have matched his or other Canadians' authoritative experience. Though his summons was rebuffed, Washington's rough journey had increased his confidence in his physical prowess, "a Constitution hardy enough to encounter and undergo the most severe tryals." He had also demonstrated strategic and situational awareness, alerting Dinwiddie that the triangular point at the Forks of the Ohio was "extremely well situated for a Fort." And he had given the British the best intelligence yet of the strength and resources of Fort Le Boeuf. The former surveyor cannily paced out the dimensions of the fort while the French officers held a council. Washington's thousand-mile trek from coastal Virginia through snowy mountains and icy rivers was well documented in a meticulous journal that he kept and which was later published in Williamsburg and London.[24]

Washington's arrival back in Williamsburg in January of 1754 heralded ominous events in the Ohio Valley. Not only had the French refused to depart, but Washington's intelligence of 50 canoes and 170 pirogues at Fort Le Boeuf confirmed that the French intended to "convoy their Forces down in the Spring," and that it was "their absolute Design to take Possession of the Ohio Country." They had boasted to Washington that the British were "too slow and dilatory to prevent any Undertaking of theirs." Having received Legardeur de St.-Pierre's rebuff of his summons, Dinwiddie was now authorized by his orders to use force, and he decided to employ it without delay. At that very moment in London, the British government was tacitly facilitating a colonial military campaign against the French. On

January 18, 1754, the Earl of Holdernesse wrote to Dinwiddie that additional reinforcements were coming: "You will likewise see, that the King has ordered Two Independent Companies from New York, & one from [South] Carolina, to march into Virginia, & there to put themselves under your Command, which, in conjunction with the Forces, I suppose are already raised within your Government...for erecting, & defending the Forts, you were thereby commanded to build, in some convenient Spot, on, or near the River Ohio." By the time Dinwiddie received that message, he had commissioned William Trent to raise a company of frontiersmen to proceed to the Forks of the Ohio, where he began construction of the eponymous fortification on February 17. Officer commissions to Trent, trader John Fraser, and Edward Ward meant that their work was empowered and sanctioned by the Virginia government. Dinwiddie had even received cooperation from his reluctant assembly in the form of £10,000, which enabled him to raise a Virginia Regiment, commanded by Colonel Joshua Fry and composed of 300 provincial volunteers enticed by the promise of bounties for Ohio lands. Washington, as the regiment's lieutenant colonel, was charged with leading some of the Virginia provincials ahead to support Trent's men, a march that began in Alexandria on April 2. What had been a land dispute involving the Ohio Company had escalated into an ad hoc imperial military venture composed of Virginia provincials, New York and South Carolina regulars, and artillery and money authorized by the British government.[25]

Those were the imperial, colonial, and personal paths that had led Washington to the frontier when he received news of Ensign Ward's surrender at the Forks of the Ohio in April of 1754. Washington convened a council with his officers who concluded that any advance on Fort Duquesne ran against all odds of success. Washington nonetheless believed that some advance was necessary for the sake of supporting the Half King and their Indian allies, so he charged ahead, hoping to fortify the Redstone fort until reinforcements arrived. Washington also sent an encouraging message to the Half King and the Ohio Indians, promising them "a great Number of our Warriours." He signed it with his Iroquoian moniker, "Connotaucarious" ("town taker" or "devourer of villages"), which dated back to his great-grandfather John Washington, who had been involved in the brutal murders of five Susquehannock Indian emissaries in a 1675 war. The events of May 1754 would eerily echo those of Washington's ancestor in 1675.[26]

By late May 1754, Washington and his force of 159 Virginians reached the Great Meadows, one of the few clearings in the wilderness west of Wills Creek. On May 24, the Half King warned that a French "armey" was coming to attack the English, a warning that seemed eminently plausible to Washington in view of Contrecoeur's conquest of the Forks with 600 men. Reports of multiple French parties on the advance—one report had it that the French had detached half of their force from Fort Duquesne—seemed confirmed by multiple intelligence sources that had sighted French parties at Stewart's Crossings and at Gist's plantation in the Youghiogheny Valley. Washington stoked the Indians' anger by telling them that the French had inquired about the Half King's whereabouts, suggesting that they were coming to kill him. Washington's orders now authorized him to "restrain" the French and "kill & destroy them" in case of resistance. Without hesitation, he sent out a detachment of seventy-five men under Captain Peter Hogg to reconnoiter. Washington may have lacked military experience during this campaign, but he was a decisive leader and driven by "the heroick spirit of every free-born Englishman to assert the rights and privileges of our king," as he wrote to Dinwiddie.[27]

On the night of May 27, an Iroquois warrior named Silver Heels brought word to Washington that the Half King had located the French camp, hidden in a "gloomy hollow" on Chestnut Ridge only six miles away. With Hogg's detachment departed, Washington and the Half King "planned to go hand in hand and strike the French," as Dinwiddie's recent letter to the Half King implicitly encouraged. Marching through heavy rain on a night "as black as pitch," forty Virginians and twelve Ohio Iroquois moved toward the camp and at dawn surrounded a party of thirty-five Frenchmen commanded by Ensign Joseph Coulon de Villiers de Jumonville. During a skirmish that lasted merely fifteen minutes, most of the French party was either killed or captured. The Half King, using ritual language, allegedly told the wounded Ensign Jumonville "Tu n'es pas encore mort, mon père!"—You are not yet dead, my father—and then planted a tomahawk in his skull.[28]

The so-called Jumonville Affair on the morning of May 28, 1754, remains shrouded in mystery, and conflicting historical accounts make it virtually impossible to be definitive about what had happened or to divine the motives of its actors.[29] The French maintained that Jumonville had been ordered to deliver a summons to the British to depart from lands claimed by the French and spoke of the officer's death as assassination. Washington regarded Jumonville's party as spies in a context of open hostilities begun in April, and his suspicion that the summons was a "mere pretence" that could be produced if discovered or surrounded was not unfounded. Jumonville's mission was implicitly one of reconnaissance of British dispositions, just as Washington had marked off the dimensions of Fort Le Boeuf while delivering his summons.[30] Washington's contemporaries largely hailed his victory and approved his conduct.[31]

A newly discovered document from the UK National Archives adds more context and nuance from a Native American perspective (see Appendix E). It is an account recorded in a 1754 Indian conference at Fort Cumberland (Maryland) of "the Chief Warrior" of the Ohio Iroquois—perhaps Silver Heels—who was present at the ambush of Jumonville's party. He began his speech by telling the assembled British officers that "There will now pass some sharp Words amongst us; as we are all Warriors, we shall talk like Men that are drunk, that speaks their Minds." The warrior's account provides vivid details on the tactics and sequence of the skirmish. The British and Indian force had advanced to the crest of Chestnut Ridge before turning back east toward the French encampment. The warrior's testimony reveals just how much Washington relied on the expertise of his allies. Significantly, the Iroquois "directed Col. Washington with his Men to go up to the Hill" (a rocky ledge overlooking the camp); the Half King and other warriors went to the left to block a French exit, while the Iroquois leader Monacatootha and another warrior named Cherokee Jack led others to the right. The warrior's account corroborates what Washington himself claimed, that he was the first to appear above the French camp, but adds a remarkable revelation: "When they came to the Top of the Hill, Col Washington begun himself and fired and then his people, which the French returned, two or three Fires of as many Peices as would go off, being rainy Weather, and then run off." The account thus suggests the intriguing possibility that Washington, as a signal to his men, literally fired the first shots of the skirmish that began the Seven Years' War in America. While the warrior states that the French returned two or three volleys, he is silent as to whether the French immediately scrambled for their arms (as Washington claimed) or if they attempted to read a summons (as the French claimed). The remaining French fled northward, only to meet "their Destiny by the Indian Tomayhawks," and the survivors were all captured, save one Canadian militiaman. The warrior states that Monacatootha brought French commissary officer Michel Pépin *dit* La Force to Washington, but relates nothing whatsoever regarding Ensign Jumonville. The warrior's testimony also suggests that the Half King was not an embittered leader trying to reestablish his authority in the Ohio Country by a provocative killing of Jumonville. Instead, more primal motives of self-defense and revenge are suggested. The Iroquois warriors, who were leading their wives and children from Ohio to a council in Virginia, believed that La Force was tracking them "to bring us back or to put us to Death." The Chief Warrior recalled the Half King's concern for his family as he spoke to La Force: "Immediately the Half King came up, and told the French, now I will let you see that the Six Nations can kill as well as the French, which you said we knew nothing of, and as you came after me to take my Life and my Children, I will now let you see how I used to do with some of your People before in time of old, and that I am not afraid." As the Half King raised his tomahawk to kill La Force, Washington "interposed" and prevented it. The warrior's account suggests why the Ohio Iroquois abandoned Washington a little more than a month later. After the Jumonville incident, "Col Washington never consulted with us nor yet to take our Advice" and the warriors believed that little had been done to protect their wives and children during the confrontation that they knew was coming at the Great Meadows.[32]

At Fort Duquesne, meanwhile, Captain Contrecoeur received the news of Washington's attack from one of Jumonville's men, a Canadian militiaman named Monceau, who had escaped capture during the skirmish. Contrecoeur dispatched a force of about 600 French under the command of Captain Louis Coulon de Villiers, who sought vengeance for the death of his younger brother, Ensign Jumonville. One hundred Indians, largely Abenakis, Lorette Hurons, and Canadian Iroquois from Kanesetake, Kahnawake, and Oswegatchie drawn from the St. Lawrence Valley, also agreed to fight. Following his skirmish with Jumonville, Washington regrouped his Virginia forces at the Great Meadows and constructed a small stockade there named Fort Necessity in early June. As he prepared against a French counterattack, Washington received news that Colonel Fry had died on May 31 after falling from his horse, and that Dinwiddie had appointed Washington as commander of the Virginia Regiment. Additional reinforcements had arrived at the Great Meadows, in the form of "100 fine Men" of the South Carolina Independent Company detachment commanded by Captain James Mackay. On July 3, 1754, Washington had roughly 400 men at his fortress of necessity when Coulon de Villiers's forces arrived. He gamely tried to lure the French into a conventional engagement on the "charming field for an Encounter" that he had prepared. But the French and Indian irregulars, along with torrential rain, quickly rendered the field and the fort a bloody quagmire. From the cover of the woods and with superior marksmanship, French and Native warriors inflicted appalling casualties, approximately one quarter of Washington's and Mackay's command, in a single day's action.[33] The exhausted and demoralized British accepted Coulon de Villiers's terms for surrender on July 4, 1754, though Washington and Mackay did not realize that by signing they were acknowledging that the French were merely avenging the assassination of Ensign Jumonville. Some thought the capitulation disgraceful and damned "that Rascal Vanbraam," Washington's Dutch interpreter, "who was himself the only unpardonable blunder that Washington made by making a Confidant of him," as Virginia planter Landon Carter wrote. Washington's contemporaries, including those in the Virginia House of Burgesses, hailed Washington's bravery "and the rest of the Officers and Soldiers under your command in the gallant Defence of your Country."[34] As if to underscore British America's strategic collapse, however, news of "Washington's defeat" came in the aftermath of the Albany Congress, a meeting of seven colonial delegations that drafted a "Plan of Union" for the thirteen colonies. Designed to strengthen intercolonial defense, the Albany Plan was either ignored or rejected altogether by the colonial governments. A concurrent conference at Albany with the Six Nations had been only marginally successful in restoring the faltering Anglo-Iroquois alliance. In 1754, "the whole System of our Indian Affairs was on wretched footing throughout all America," as one dispirited official reported to the Board of Trade.[35] The only stalwart British allies left, the Ohio Iroquois led by Tanaghrisson, had taken refuge at Aughwick (George Croghan's trading post) on the frontier of Pennsylvania. But even Tanaghrisson's band began to fragment when some Iroquois returned to Ohio Valley and sought French clemency. Tanaghrisson, the Half King, died at Aughwick in October 1754, the viceroy over an Ohio kingdom that had never existed.[36]

News of Washington's defeat fell upon British ministers in London with an incredibly shocking weight. A ship carrying a copy of the *Virginia Gazette* arrived ahead of any official notification from Governor Dinwiddie, and London papers printed an account of the battle on September 3, 1754. For years, leading British ministers of state, such as the Duke of Newcastle and the Earl of Halifax, had watched with alarm the growth of French fortifications and encroachments upon British claims in Nova Scotia, New York, the West Indies, and the Ohio Valley.[37] To Newcastle, news of the French victory over Washington presaged the worst: "All North America will be lost, If these Practices are tolerated," he wrote on September 5, adding that "no War can be worse to This Country, than The Suffering such Insults, as These." The Captain-General of the British Army, the Duke of Cumberland, called it "a lamentable affair," and "could not comprehend how 300 Virginians under Washington could suffer themselves to be so harrassed in their retreat by 100 Indians." Newcastle resolved that something must be done, and soon. Political pressure to act was mounting on his ministry, as the parliamentary opposition began to assail it on the charge of "doing nothing" while French power expanded in America.[38]

Over the next three weeks, King George II and the British ministry had defined the basic parameters of the 1755 expeditions, and their choices had monumental consequences for the British world and the very character of the war now under way. Indeed, their decisions and debates over the campaign exposed deep-seated attitudes about British America and its colonists. To Newcastle, French success during the 1754 campaign was a measure of the colonists' disunity and military incompetence: "Tho' We may have Ten Times the Number of People in Our Colonies," he wrote to Lord Albemarle, "They don't seem to be able to defend Themselves, even with the Assistance of Our Money." Albemarle, the British ambassador to France, responded to Newcastle that "Washington & many Such, may have courage & resolution, but they have no Knowledge or Experience in our Profession; consequently there can be no dependence on them! Officers, & good ones must be sent to Discipline the Militia, & to Lead them on." London merchant Dennys De Berdt echoed Albemarle's sentiments, writing to a high-ranking British official that if the colonists were not directly supported by British troops, their "own Efferts will be too Weak to withstand the French." The government's decision to commit regulars was partly a response to Dinwiddie's reports on the decrepit condition of the Virginia militia and his earnest pleas for British troops, and partly a reflection of imperial officials' disdain for the ability of American forces and the Independent Companies to protect the crown's interests. The 1754 campaign's principal policy lesson was the ineffectiveness of sending money, artillery, and a few Independent Companies to bolster Virginia's defenses.[39]

The Duke of Newcastle favored an initial campaign against the French in the Ohio Valley, where they had commenced hostilities. He wanted to proceed "as cheap and as inoffensive as we can," lest a general war spread to Europe. Newcastle found that the king was "in haste to have something done" in America, but that he had an "utter aversion" to parting with any of his regular regiments. Newcastle explored various alternatives and proposals, such as sending a Highland Regiment or combining the seven Independent Companies in America into a regiment. Earl Granville, Lord President of the Council, proposed "raising a Strong American Army to Consist of 5, or 6000 Men." In planning the expedition, it was almost inevitable that Newcastle would have to deal with the Duke of Cumberland, the Captain-General of the British Army. The favorite son of George II, Cumberland had earned laurels of victory and the sobriquet "Butcher" for suppressing a rebellion in Scotland in 1746. He favored not only a broad set of offensives to roll back French encroachments, but also appointing a viceroy "after the manner of the Spaniards" to execute the mission. At a meeting with the king on September 22, Cumberland nominated Major-General Edward Braddock, an officer of long service in the British Army, as the most proper candidate for commander in chief in America. Cumberland also proposed sending two under-strength regiments from Ireland that could be quickly brought to full force in America. Cumberland's proposals also intersected with the ongoing efforts of governors William Shirley and Charles Lawrence for a campaign against the French in Nova Scotia. Newcastle had qualms over the risk of a general war that Cumberland's four expeditions with 10,000 men almost guaranteed, but he accepted those risks, believing that it was politically expedient to do something. Inflaming matters more, Secretary at War Henry Fox leaked news—whether inadvertently or intentionally is not clear—of the two regiments' mobilization for America, alarming the French government, which eventually decided to send French Army regulars to America in 1755.[40]

By September 26, 1754, plans for the "Expedition to Virginia" were in place, and as one contemporary definition put it, the "very name of an expedition implies risk, hazard, precarious warfare, and a critical operation" as well as "quick resolves and rapid execution."[41] General Braddock would be commander in chief of His Majesty's forces in America (his commission was dated the 26th) and orders were sent to draw the 44th and 48th regiments from their Irish garrisons. Cumberland also ordered a powerful detachment of Royal Artillery to besiege French forts with six 6-pounders, four 12-pounders, four howitzers, and fifteen coehorns (portable mortars developed by a Dutch engineer). Although he had not seen America, Cumberland's selection of lighter brass field pieces and mortars with a few heavy howitzers was well suited to American conditions.[42] Even Braddock's axis of advance had already been determined in London. His royal instructions required him to land in Virginia, where he would bring his two regiments up to full strength. He was ordered to march to Wills Creek along the Potomac River before advancing against Fort Duquesne. Braddock did not have discretionary power to do otherwise. Later, some writers argued that Braddock should have landed not in Virginia but in Pennsylvania, where supplies and wagons were more plentiful. Such a contingency was not seriously discussed at all during the planning of the campaign in 1754, however, and it was assumed that any expedition to the Ohio would begin in Virginia, which had long been the epicenter of conflict.[43]

The British government's decision to send regular Army regiments overseas was not unprecedented. It is often overlooked in studies of Braddock's Expedition that the British government simultaneously sent a parallel expedition to India, organized along the same principles as the American venture: Colonel John Adlercron, with a detachment of Royal Artillery and the 39th Regiment (again drawn from Ireland), was appointed as commander in chief of regular and East India Company forces in India in 1754. Previous commitments to the Americas include the 6,000 British regulars sent to attack Quebec in 1711; and the 42nd Regiment of Colonel James Oglethorpe, sent to defend his colony of Georgia in 1738 and to operate against St. Augustine in Spanish Florida. During a conflict with Spain known as the War of Jenkins' Ear (1739–1742), the British organized a massive transoceanic expedition to capture the Spanish port of Cartagena in 1741. The expedition ended in military and epidemical disaster, due to both Spanish defenders and mosquito-borne yellow fever that killed more than 10,000 Britons. But British authorities had been enormously successful in recruiting more than 4,000 colonial Americans into an imperial expedition for the first time. The 43rd, or American Regiment, led by Colonel William Gooch, the governor of Virginia, featured colonials serving under American company-grade officers bearing royal commissions, such as Captain Lawrence Washington.[44] Cartagena had offered British officials a model of how to tap the patriotic energies of British Americans by offering them equal standing as a royal regiment with royal commissions. But friction between colonists and regulars had been painfully evident in the 1711 and 1741 expeditions, and that was one reason the Cartagena model would remain a road not taken in the planning for Braddock's Expedition.[45]

Imperial warfare in America was never far removed from British officials' pejorative attitudes toward the American colonists and their anxieties over the possible independence of the thirteen colonies. That was especially true in 1754, for the decision to send regular troops occurred in the context of debate over plans for the political unification for the American colonies. During the summer and early fall of 1754, British ministers had analyzed such a plan proposed by the Board of Trade and raised the possibility of proposing a bill calling for it before Parliament. But Newcastle was unwilling to risk the future of his ministry on such a union, which he felt would promote "An independency upon this Country." In early September, Newcastle discussed the merits of a "General Officer" overseeing American affairs with Arthur Onslow, Speaker of the House of Commons, and mentioned the "ill Consequences to be apprehended from uniting too closely the Northern Colonies with each other."[46]

The decision to send regular regiments from Ireland also reflected a fundamental distrust of colonial Americans' military abilities and worth. The ministry rejected those voices that preferred regimenting the Americans under their own officers in order to encourage recruitment and stoke the loyalties of ambitious colonials; and it disapproved Dinwiddie's request for blank royal commissions—"as was done in the Expedition to Carthagena"—that would have produced a "greater Equallity" between American and British officers. Instead, the "Great Persons who undervalued the American Soldiers, & Fancied wonders of their own" decided that regulars must be sent, according to Lady Anson, wife of Admiral Anson (First Lord of the Admiralty). British officer John Simcoe was representative of those who thought that Braddock's contingent of regulars should have been even larger. Like many high-ranking British officers, he condemned the "american english" as militarily unfit, recalling their "painfull campaigns" at Cartagena; and he dismissed the Americans' conquest of Louisbourg in 1745 as due entirely to the foibles of the French defenders. Members of Parliament also debated whether a "mixture of Europeans and Americans" was militarily expedient while they discussed the "defects of the constitution of our colonies."[47]

The possibility of mobilizing patriotic American volunteers into their own royal regiment was not the only lesson of the past ignored by British policymakers and officers. The 1754 expedition had been like a dress rehearsal of Braddock's Expedition, and it foretold all of the difficulties and challenges that Braddock and his regulars would soon inherit. Aside from artillery and funds from Britain, the 1754 expedition had been a largely colonial venture. It had failed miserably and weakened the colonial frontiers of Virginia, Maryland, and Pennsylvania. Comparisons of the 1754 and 1755 expeditions—one colonial, one imperial—reveal that they both failed more from structural reasons than from poor leadership or colonial incompetence. Both had as their objective the destruction of the French at the Forks of the Ohio. Both began at Alexandria and used the same route westward. The 1754 expedition failed to produce large numbers of recruits for an unpopular war that many Virginians believed was only for the benefit of the Ohio Company. The difficulty of procuring wagons, horses, and fodder was exceeded by the backbreaking work to improve trails and roads through raw mountains.[48]

Political conflict with colonial assemblies and intercolonial rivalry hindered effective cooperation. Governor Dinwiddie was unable to secure the full cooperation of the Virginia House of Burgesses due in part to their rancorous dispute over a constitutional question known as the Pistole Fee Controversy. The colonies of Pennsylvania and South Carolina also criticized Virginia for its aggressive and precipitate course of action. Governor James Glen of South Carolina cautioned that "a small spark may kindle a great Fire, and [we] are afraid that if the Flame bursts out, all the Water in the Ohio will not be able to extinguish it, but that it may soon spread and light up a general Conflagration." But Glen was concerned more with South Carolina's security than British America's, and he resisted directives to cooperate with Virginia, even to the point of receiving scolding rebukes from the government in London, which had largely dismissed him as incompetent. Colonial disunity also compromised attempts to garner any meaningful military assistance from Indian nations. Governor Glen, for example, jealously resisted what he viewed as Virginia's intrusions on diplomacy and trade with the powerful Cherokee Indians on South Carolina's frontier. Indeed, the British "interest" among Indian nations was nearing a nadir in 1754, and the actions of Washington and others had caused the Ohio Iroquois to abandon him at Fort Necessity.[49]

Washington's disputes over military rank and command with Captain James Mackay at Fort Necessity were also a bad omen. Washington warned that unequal British policies preferring royal commissions over colonial ones "Will be a canker" upon future British-colonial cooperation. But the royal government had made it clear that any colonial officer would be subordinate to a regular officer. A provincial colonel like Washington would be commanded by a British captain. A colonial captain would not have command even if his date of commission was earlier (and length of service was greater) than a regular captain's. In October 1754, Governor Dinwiddie broke the Virginia Regiment into independent companies commanded by captains, precisely to "quell the great Feud" between provincial and regular officers. Washington had lost his regiment and resigned his colonel's commission upon hearing of Dinwiddie's decision. He would not be dishonored and demoted by the discriminatory policies against colonial officers, which raised fundamental questions about British Americans' equality and worth.[50]

Failure in 1754 nonetheless had provided a foundation upon which General Braddock's Expedition would later build. Even Washington's surrender at Fort Necessity yielded an ironic benefit: Virginia officer Captain Robert Stobo had been one of the hostages detained by the French to vouchsafe the return of French prisoners held by the Virginians. While a prisoner at Fort Duquesne, Stobo drew up and later smuggled out a detailed scale plan of the fort along with other military intelligence with the help of two Indians, Delaware George and a man known simply as Moses. Stobo's map would eventually end up in General Braddock's papers. In addition, key participants in the 1754 campaign such as Governor Dinwiddie, George Croghan, John Carlyle, and Washington carried their hard-earned experience forward into Braddock's Expedition. The officer corps of the Virginia companies was more experienced in American campaigning than were any of Braddock's regular officers, save Horatio Gates. The diverse Virginia officers included men from more established Virginia families such as George Mercer and Thomas and Edward Waggoner. Most were recent immigrants to the colony: Adam Stephen, Robert Stewart, Peter Hogg, and William Polson had emigrated from Scotland; Andrew Lewis, an Augusta County frontier settler, had been born in County Donegal in Ireland; William La Péronie was a French Huguenot immigrant, and Carolus Gustavus Spiltdorf was a Swedish gentleman. While many of the rank and file in the Virginia companies were not from the frontier, a core of veterans with at least a year of campaigning or combat experience still remained in 1755.[51]

William La Péronie was among the most honorable and valiant of the Virginia officers. As a French Protestant, he was one of many such who treasured the religious and civil liberties of the British world, having witnessed the persecutions of Catholic France, and his willingness to fight reflected his gratitude for his new life in Virginia. Despite having only arrived in the colony in 1750, he was fully accepted by his Protestant brethren. His loyalty was never questioned, and his career in Virginia was one of consistent promotion. La Péronie was classically educated and urbane, and his French accent can still be heard in a letter that he wrote to Washington describing his expectation that the "wirginian Regiment" would have "more esplendour than ever: for (as I hope) notwitstanding we will Be on the British stabichment, we shall be augmanted to Six houndred." By 1755, La Péronie was a seasoned veteran of American warfare, having led scouting parties as an ensign in 1754 and fought at Fort Necessity, where he was severely wounded. Washington thought La Péronie an officer of "consummate prudence," and tellingly, a man ready "to serve his Country. (which I really believe he looks upon Virginia to be')."[52]

By the fall of 1754, colonial forces had also begun to consolidate and fortify their advanced position at Wills Creek. Following the death of Joshua Fry, Colonel James Innes of North Carolina had been appointed commander in chief of all British forces by his friend Governor Dinwiddie. An aging veteran of the Cartegena Expedition, Innes was predicted to "gather few laurels on these mountains" by Wilmington merchant James Murray. Innes did his best, under trying circumstances, to organize the forces gathered at Camp Mount Pleasant and to conduct diplomacy with nearby Indians, but his efforts were often criticized. He was eventually replaced as commander in chief by Governor Sharpe in October 1754 but remained on as the post's commandant. The three Independent Companies at Wills Creek were responsible for the most important accomplishment of Innes's command, for in November 1754 they began constructing what was later named Fort Cumberland, along with a set of barracks for the coming winter. Their heavy labor and toil had "tore their cloths to pieces" just in time for an inspection by a fiery British officer.[53]

That British officer was Sir John St. Clair, the first of many British officers in 1755 to be awakened to the political, military, logistical, and geographical issues that threatened campaigns in America. In October of 1754, St. Clair had been promoted to major and commissioned as Deputy Quarter Master General of British forces in North America, with orders to lay the logistical foundation for Braddock's march through Virginia. The origins of St. Clair's baronetcy and his early career have been unclear to biographers. But new evidence reveals that St. Clair was one of the most experienced and distinguished officers of his day, having appeared before "most Courts in Europe," most recently that of Frederick the Great of Prussia. St. Clair was commissioned in the British Army in 1735 as an ensign of the 22nd Regiment and rose in its ranks as a lieutenant in 1741 and a captain in 1748.[54] St. Clair wrote that from 1735 until 1746, he was part of the British garrison at Minorca in the Mediterranean. Yearning for release from the monotony of garrison duty, he received permission from Minorca's governor to serve as a volunteer in the Imperial Army of Austria (then Great Britain's principal European ally). From 1746 to 1748, St. Clair campaigned in southeastern Europe (primarily northern Italy) during the War of Austrian Succession, serving as aide-de-camp under the great Austrian field marshal Ulysses Maximilian von Browne. St. Clair wrote that he had "travelled above Six hundred Posts" during his service, and had "directed the disembarkation and reimbarkation of all the Austrian Artillery" during operations around Genoa. The Empress Maria Theresa of Austria and Count von Browne had both testified to his meritorious service, and the Austrian troops held him in "great esteem," according to a British diplomat.[55] St. Clair's Italian campaigns gave him immense experience in logistics, mountain warfare, and irregular tactics. Von Browne's army included Croatian light infantry and Hussars, the feared cavalrymen of eighteenth-century Europe. During Von Browne's incursion into southern France in 1747, St. Clair personally commanded a reconnaissance party composed of Croatians and Hussars (he had in fact obtained a uniform from the Hussars and brought it with him to America).[56] St. Clair's activities and reports came to the attention of the Duke of Cumberland, Newcastle, and Sir Thomas Robinson, the British Ambassador at Vienna, and their patronage resulted in his eventual appointment as Deputy Quarter Master General in 1754.[57]

Shortly after St. Clair arrived in Virginia in January 1755 aboard HMS *Gibraltar*, he pledged to Robinson to "follow the schemes I saw Count Brown lay down when he was in the Appenenes, which is much the same Country we are to march thro." He was a volatile bundle of frenetic energy, and no other figure could have set the stage so well for Braddock's Expedition. Indeed, the campaign never would have gotten under way without the efforts of this irrepressible British officer. Sir John took on his formidable duties as Deputy Quarter Master-General with an indomitable will and was often praised as "indefatigable" in his efforts. Painter John Singleton Copley captured St. Clair's determined stare, ruddy complexion, and pursed lips, all suggestive of his combative nature. Such was the force of this officer's personality that roads he constructed on the Virginia frontier were already being named after him by 1758, a distinction that remains on present-day roads in Virginia and West Virginia.[58]

Within two months of his arrival, with no staff or assistants, St. Clair had ridden or paddled nearly a thousand miles and had shaped the entire campaign. He established a general hospital at Hampton, Virginia; solicited accurate maps of the frontier and intelligence of French activities from royal governors; ordered 600,000 pounds of flour from Pennsylvania and prompted its government to build a supply road for the army; constructed bateaux for river crossings during the march; contracted for horses and forage; ordered the establishment of storehouses for provisions and supplies; supervised the construction and improvement of roads through Virginia to Wills Creek; reviewed Virginia provincial troops and regulars of the Independent Companies, weeding out soldiers who were unfit for service; established a plan for quartering troops in the Virginia tidewater; and took stock of the political lay of the land with colonial governments and Indian nations. St. Clair had even written a plan for peopling the Ohio Valley with Croatian irregulars whom he had served with in his Italian campaigns. The British had initially believed that the Potomac and Youghiogheny Rivers were navigable for canoes or small craft hundreds of miles inland. But when St. Clair took a 200-mile canoe trip in the middle of winter, accompanied by Governor Sharpe, he found that the Potomac River was so full of "shoals & falls" that it was impractical to transport provisions by boat between Alexandria and Conococheague Creek in western Maryland. Upon reaching the Great Falls of the Potomac upriver from Alexandria, St. Clair and Sharpe "were in Hopes of blowing them up," according to a contemporary report that captures the character of this British officer, determined to conquer any natural barrier that stood in his way.[59]

St. Clair's concentrated activities left him with a dismal view of the campaign's prospects, for he wrote in retrospect that "had this Country been known as well as it is now I think it wou'd not have been made use of to Carry on an Expedition." He was stunned by the colonists' geographical ignorance of their own frontiers, though he eventually obtained maps by Thomas Jeffreys, Washington, and Lewis Evans. New York governor James DeLancey admitted, "As to maps of this Country, we have none, there is one preparing by Mr. Evans I am told, which will soon be published. I use those in Charlevoise." The history of British America could rightly be summarized by a British governor's confession that he had to use maps taken from a French Jesuit priest's book for geographical information on territory that Britain claimed.[60] St. Clair realized how unimproved the road networks of Virginia really were, exclaiming that the one road west of Winchester was the "worst Road I ever travelled" and marveling that it literally went "in the Channels of the Rivers." He found the colonists largely uncooperative and "totally Ignorant of Military Affairs," and hoped that he would not have to inform his "Royal Master" that it would have been "much easier to Carry on War from an Enemy's Country" than in His Majesty's "Old Dominion."[61]

St. Clair's journey to Wills Creek offered him an especially revealing look at the weakness of America's frontier defenses. He
thought that Fort Cumberland was militarily useless and could not
fathom "what cou'd induce people ever to think of making a Fort or
a Deposit of provisions at Wills's Creek." St. Clair had come to inspect
the fortifications, review troops, and oversee the construction of barracks for Braddock's men. He also inspected the three Independent
Companies and the Virginia provincial units, and was so exasperated
by the ordeal that he exclaimed to Braddock, "no officer ever had such
a review." Two of the Independent Companies, he scoffed, had "neither Legs to get upon the Heights nor to run away thro' the Valleys."[62]

The Independent Companies were the military manifestation
of Britain's "salutary neglect" of its North American colonies in the
early eighteenth century. There were only seven such independent,
unregimented companies of the regular British Army serving in
America: four were stationed in New York and three in South
Carolina. They were poorly supplied and equipped, often filled with
older men, and their effectiveness had been deteriorated by their
monotonous garrison duties on the frontiers.[63] The Independent
Companies might have served as the basis of a more effective defense and a means of binding the loyalties of ambitious colonial
elites to their monarch, as many contemporaries realized. Instead, as
Governor Dinwiddie complained, because Virginia "never had any
Regular troops or Independent Companies established here," there
was no pool of experienced officers. New France, by contrast, was
garrisoned by numerous Independent Marine Companies (*compagnies franches de la marine*), led by veteran Canadian officers who were
skilled in wilderness warfare and often operated jointly with Indian
war parties. Archibald Kennedy, a New York customs official and re-
former, believed that the "French seldom fail of this Method" and
urged the British to follow their example. The officer corps of the
compagnies franches was dominated by Canadian officers who sought
social distinction and military glory, while the recruits were mainly
from France. There were no similar inducements for colonial
Americans in the Independent Companies, for the rank and file
were largely colonial recruits and the officers were usually native
Britons bearing royal commissions. As a result, a significant institutional divide between British regular officers and American officers
persisted throughout the Seven Years' War.[64]

The Independent Companies that the British government had
ordered to Virginia in 1754—two from New York and one from South
Carolina—probably represented those that were most fit for service.

The South Carolina Independent Company detachment was commanded by a French Huguenot officer from Georgia named Captain
Paul Demeré. The company was in "much better order and Discipline,"
lending credibility to Governor James Glen's boast that "the King has
not a finer Independent Company in any part of his Dominions." But
St. Clair was aghast when he reviewed the 3rd and 4th New York
Independent Companies, commanded by Captain John Rutherford
and Captain Thomas Clarke, a veteran of the Cartagena disaster in
1741. St. Clair thought that the New York Independents "seem to be
draughted out of Chelsea," referring to the London hospital for veterans unfit for service but deemed worthy of royal pensions. "Several
men from sixty to seventy years of age, lame and every way disabled"
appeared on a muster roll that St. Clair submitted to Braddock.
Another British officer concluded that the Independent Companies
were mostly "without discipline and very ill-appointed." In short, he
said, "they were Invalids with the ignorance of militia." The Independent Companies presented a shabby front, though they had a certain
esprit de corps, "a notion of being Independents" as one officer put it.
The uniforms of the Independent Companies were quite colorful—
red regimental coats with popinjay green cuffs and facings, as striking
as parrots' feathers. Clothing, arms, and equipment were anything but
uniform, however. The South Carolina Independents were carrying
muskets originally issued to Oglethorpe's Regiment in 1738, and the
New York troops had not been issued any new arms or accoutrements
since 1743, and many of their muskets were "unserviceable." Consequently, on March 18, 1755, St. Clair dismissed Captain Clarke's
company—"found unfit for service on account of a deficiency in
their numbers and a great number of old men"—back to Frederick,
Maryland. There, the officers were to enlist a sufficient number of
recruits to bring it to full strength by late April 1755.[65]

Of all the diverse career paths to the Monongahela Valley, that
of Captain Horatio Gates, the future victor of the Battle of Saratoga,
was perhaps the most remarkable and unlikely. Born circa 1727 in
England, Horatio Gates had entered military service in the 1740s, as
the Gates family (for reasons that remain unclear) enjoyed the patronage of a number of British aristocrats and officers. One notable
patron was Lieutenant Colonel Edward Cornwallis, uncle of the
future Lord Cornwallis whom Gates would one day face at the Battle
of Camden in 1780. When Cornwallis became governor of Nova
Scotia in 1749, he brought Lieutenant Gates into his military family
or staff as a volunteer aide-de-camp, and later helped secure Gates a
captain's commission in the 45th Regiment.[66] In 1750, Gates kept a

Horatio Gates (1727–1806). By Charles Willson Peale, from life, 1782. Gates's lengthy military career stretched from Nova Scotia to the Monongahela, Fort Pitt, Martinique, Boston, Saratoga, and Camden. Courtesy, Independence National Historical Park.

journal that vividly detailed his military experiences in a broiling insurgency in the volatile Nova Scotia borderland that came to be known as Father Le Loutre's War. Gates's Nova Scotia campaign was quite similar to Braddock's campaign: both were transoceanic expeditions of British regulars, supported by colonial troops and rangers; both advanced deep into disputed territory with the goal of establishing or capturing a fortress, and both campaigns involved *la petite guerre* (the eighteenth-century term for irregular warfare, which both the French and Indians practiced in America). Gates was thus a highly experienced junior officer, having known of ambushes, skirmishes, and the "most unheard of brutal Cruelty" during his introduction to American warfare in the woods of Nova Scotia.[67]

By 1754, Gates ventured back to London, where he secured the captaincy of the 4th New York Independent Company recently vacated by an ailing Thomas Clarke, following St. Clair's dismissal. Gates may have sensed that the Ohio Valley would become the vortex of combat in the future and undoubtedly knew that two of the New York Independent Companies had already sailed to Virginia. Returning to Halifax, he married his fiancée, Elizabeth Phillips, before proceeding to New York. In early April 1755, Captain Gates of His Majesty's 4th Independent Company of New York departed for Virginia. Before leaving, Gates drew up his last will and testament, which began: "thanks be to almighty God for the Same Yet Reflecting on the Uncertain State of this frail and Transitory Life and Knowing that it is appointed for all Mankind to Die"—a reminder of the perils that hung over Gates and his new bride as his ship set sail toward Virginia, where General Edward Braddock was already on the march.[68]

CHAPTER 2

Braddock Americanus

The General and His Army in Ireland and America

General Braddock has not yet sent over to claim the surname of Americanus.

~Horace Walpole, Member of Parliament, August 1755~

O
N NOVEMBER 26, 1754, General Edward Braddock left his house on Arlington Street in London for Portsmouth, where he boarded a British warship bound for Cork, Ireland. Dressed in a resplendent scarlet and gold general's uniform, Braddock was the plenipotentiary of British imperial might—symbolized by his uniform, his broad powers as commander in chief, and the large artillery train that he was conducting to America. At Portsmouth, Braddock boarded HMS *Centurion*, a vessel that gave effulgence to the Royal Navy's growing global mastery and transoceanic reach. By 1755, *Centurion* had already demonstrated "what one British man of war is capable of performing," as one newspaper boasted. The sixty-gun vessel with a crew of more than 400 sailors and marines was one of the most formidable vessels in the Royal Navy. During the War of Jenkins' Ear (1739–1742), a conflict with Spain that presaged Britain's global conquests in the Seven Years' War, HMS *Centurion* was the flagship of Commodore George Anson's fleet during his dauntless circumnavigation of the globe that began in 1740. When *Centurion* arrived back at Spithead in 1744, she was the sole survivor of the original expedition composed of six warships, having raided Spanish shipping and settlements off the coast of South America before sailing across the Pacific, where she captured a Spanish treasure galleon, *Nuestra Señora de la Covadonga*, in an epic duel near the Philippines. In the War of Austrian Succession, *Centurion* composed part of a British fleet that inflicted a stunning blow on the French Navy at the First Battle of Cape Finisterre in May 1747. *Centurion's*

sixteen-foot tall figurehead of a rampant lion seemed an appropriate symbol of her accomplishments.[1]

When Braddock arrived at Cork on Ireland's southeast coast in early December, his Irish expeditionary force had already been assembling. The 44th Regiment of Foot, commanded by Colonel Sir Peter Halkett, and the 48th Regiment of Foot, led by Colonel Thomas Dunbar, had been drawn from Ireland's garrisons by the Duke of Cumberland for American service. In October 1754, the officers and men of the two regiments prepared to march from their cantons to Cork. Halkett's regiment arrived at Dublin on October 31, 1754; twelve carriages arrived with 600 arms from Dublin Castle for the men drafted from other regiments. On November 6, the men of Halkett's and Dunbar's commands marched out of Dublin toward Cork, where they would embark for America. The king's viceroy or Lord Lieutenant of Ireland, the Duke of Dorset, ordered the officers of Halkett's and Dunbar's regiments to return to their posts, and by early November, a number of them had departed from London for Ireland. Newspapers openly discussed these warlike preparations, even wishing that "we shall not only dispossess the French from the Ohio, but compel them to keep such Limits as were prescribed to them by the Treaty of Utrecht."[2]

Both the general commanding the expedition and the two regiments that departed Cork in January of 1755 have been misrepresented over the centuries. Historians have often described Braddock as an arrogant, brash, and inexperienced commander, whose complacent trust in disciplined troops and slavish adherence to European tactics led him to certain defeat by skilled Indian opponents "against whom the jolly general of the London tables and St. James's clubs was wholly unfitted to cope," as one nineteenth-century account goes.[3] To understand who Edward Braddock was, and to see what his life and career can tell us about the British Army and the empire that it advanced in the eighteenth century we need to get beyond the typecasting.

Edward Braddock III and his family had long been at the center of royal power. His grandfather had come from, as one biographer has put it, a "highly respectable but undistinguished Staffordshire family." The first Edward Braddock was distinguished by a fine voice and musical abilities that earned him the impressive sum of £70 as a Gentleman of the Chapel Royal, one of twenty such choristers who sang in the king's chapel in his Whitehall Palace, and later at Westminster Abbey. Music sustained the family's fortunes and deepened its connection to the monarchy. Edward's marriage to Elizabeth

Gen.l Braddock, engraving by William Sartain, 1899, Library of Congress. No contemporary portrait of Edward Braddock is known to exist, but this engraving may have been based on an earlier and now lost original.

Cooke produced a daughter, Elizabeth, who later married John Blow, who along with Henry Purcell, was one of England's most distinguished baroque composers. As personal musician to King James II, John was also organ master at Westminster Abbey and later at St. Paul's Cathedral, where he composed majestic anthems to God's favor resting upon England.[4]

At Windsor Castle in 1682, King Charles II gave Edward Braddock's namesake son (born in 1664) a lieutenant's commission in the Coldstream Guards. The father knew that a lieutenancy in the foot guards was no ordinary commission. Posted near the seats of power in London and Windsor, and with the responsibility of protecting the monarch, the Coldstream Guards promised a sure path to wealth. The fortunes of Edward Braddock II did indeed begin to flourish, marked by his marriage to Mary, who around 1694 gave birth to Edward Braddock III, the future general. One of eight-year-old Edward's earliest memories may have been of his father, Captain

Braddock, decked out in his finest uniform, for the coronation festivities of Queen Anne in 1704. Young Edward undoubtedly absorbed the visceral sense of regal power that accompanied such dramatic scenes. Braddock's youthful military career was profoundly shaped by the Age of Marlborough. The victorious campaigns of the great Captain-General, John Churchill, first Duke of Marlborough, brought English arms "a degree of martial success and international recognition that they had not known since the Middle Ages," as historian David Chandler writes: "Few commanders born in the British Isles have achieved as much as Marlborough. None has achieved more." Indeed, Marlborough was the standard and the template for all subsequent British generals. The duke's epic 350-mile march from the Netherlands to the Danube, culminating in his most celebrated victory over the French at the Battle of Blenheim in 1704, was the best parallel in recent British history for what Braddock would eventually attempt in 1755 in the New World. The duke's march was an unparalleled logistical feat that kept his army of more than 20,000 men well supplied even through the mountainous terrain of the Black Forest and the Swabian Jura. Following his victory at Blenheim, Marlborough exultantly returned to London in scenes that were reminiscent of Roman triumphs. With the Coldstream Guards lining the route, Queen Anne attended a thanksgiving service at St. Paul's Cathedral for the duke's victory. Although Captain Braddock had not shared in Marlborough's battlefield honors, he had been promoted to lieutenant colonel in the Coldstream Guards, and eventually to the rank of major-general.[5]

This burgeoning British Empire was increasingly converging with North American affairs. In 1710, sixteen-year-old Edward Braddock gained an ensign's commission in the Coldstream Guards from Queen Anne, the same year that four "Indian kings" arrived in London from Iroquoia. Young Braddock presumably shared in the sensational reception that Londoners gave the four indigenous celebrities and other Native leaders who came to St. James's Palace in the following decades.[6] As a new ensign stationed at London and Windsor, and through his father's own experiences, Braddock learned of the politics of military command. A general officer had to be "something of a courtier as well as a soldier," as Addison and Steele wrote in *The Spectator*. In the case of General John Hill, however, the courtier won out over the soldier. In 1711, the Queen had appointed General Hill, the brother of one her court favorites, to command the land forces in an expedition to take Quebec. The Duke of Marlborough strenuously objected, decrying Hill's military capabilities and protesting that so junior an officer would bypass more meritorious ones. Under the overall command of Admiral Sir Hovenden Walker, the force of some 7,000 soldiers and a naval fleet of nine warships and dozens of transports represented the largest transatlantic military expedition that had ever been sent to North America. The expedition reflected Britain's growing ability to project power overseas, even as it underscored the limitations of that ability. More than 800 members of the expedition drowned during a hellish night on the St. Lawrence River when the winds, fog, and currents ran the expedition aground. More British soldiers died in the Quebec Expedition than would die at the Monongahela in 1755. The Walker-Hill expedition was one of several British military disasters that colonials would have been well familiar with before 1755. Benjamin Franklin had exaggerated the "exalted notions" that British colonists had of British regulars' prowess.[7]

The Hanoverian succession in 1714 marked a new era for Ensign Edward Braddock, for the vicissitudes of life rapidly and tragically deprived him of his extended family. Only a few years after he had purchased a lieutenancy in the grenadier company in 1716, Edward lost both his mother, Mary, who died in 1724, and his father in 1725. The elder Braddock's will left most of his fortune to his two daughters, Henrietta and Frances (Fanny). One item that Lieutenant Braddock inherited was his father's long, red silk sash embroidered with 1709—a memento of Marlborough's age that Braddock would one day wear into battle. The sash commemorated the year that Braddock's father had been promoted to the rank of major-general.[8]

What remained of Braddock's family became embroiled in notoriety and scandal. Edward's younger sister, Fanny, became a parable for young women of the perils of the age. Having inherited half of her father's estate, Fanny did not prudently guard either her heart or her fortune. She fell desperately in love with a suitor, known only as "the celebrated S—," a rakish man who brought her down to his dissolute depths. Fanny not only paid his many outstanding debts to free him from prison but gambled away the remaining estate, including that of her sister Henrietta, who had died in 1729. In her despair and isolation, Fanny Braddock hanged herself at Bath in 1731. Though a suicide, she was buried at the Abbey church alongside her father, "who might be said to be thus far happy, that he lived not to see or hear of so tragical a catastrophe of his beloved daughter," as the *Gentleman's Magazine* lamented.[9]

Fanny's fate undoubtedly followed her brother Edward, as it most surely remained a subject of conversation—even of literature and plays—of that era. Edward Braddock did little to unseat the public's image of the family, though poor conduct had come to be expected throughout the British Army's ranks. Braddock gained a reputation for rakish and boorish behavior, such as when he fought a duel with a fellow officer in Hyde Park. He apparently took such deep drafts of the profligate culture of the 1730s that he might have been a perfect emblem of William Hogarth's London, immortalized in his engravings and prints. Like a scene from Hogarth's series "A Rake's Progress," one of Braddock's friends, Lord Tyrawley, began an affair with a fourteen-year-old girl, who bore a daughter, George Anne Bellamy, later one of London's most famous actresses. Because of George Anne's increasing estrangement from her father, Braddock became a "second father" to the young girl, in what was the most significant relationship of his adult life. George Anne reciprocated Braddock's parental affection. She remembered him as "my much-beloved friend" and rebuked anyone who misrepresented him as a brutal and coarse man.[10]

As his career matured over the next two decades, so did Braddock. He demonstrated competence, gained experience, and strengthened his connections to the political and military sources of British power. In 1740, the Duke of Cumberland became colonel of the Coldstream Guards, bringing Braddock under the eye of the king's favorite son, and as we have seen, the future Captain-General of the British Army who would one day appoint Braddock to command the expedition to Virginia. Braddock found that his duties in the Coldstream Guards prevented him from fighting in the great battles of the War of Austrian Succession at Dettingen and Fontenoy. Some guards officers had to remain in London, and the lot had often fallen to Braddock, just as it had to his father before him. However, Braddock gained valuable campaigning and logistical experience in the wars of the 1740s. In 1745, a rebellion broke out in Scotland, in which Jacobite forces rose up in support of Charles Edward Stuart's claim to the British throne. Braddock not only witnessed the panic that ensued when the rebel army of the "Young Pretender" advanced into northern England, but he also participated in a long, frigid winter march from London to Litchfield to confront the Jacobites. A few days before he left on the march, Braddock was commissioned lieutenant-colonel of the Coldstream Guards. George II personally appeared before the officers of the foot guards, who affirmed their fundamental loyalty to their monarch. The Duke of Cumberland's crushing victory over the Jacobites at the Battle of Culloden in 1746 brought an end to the rebellion known as the "Forty-Five." But

Braddock did not share in the duke's triumph, as he was sent with a detachment of foot guards back to guard London's palaces.[11]

Braddock gained even more significant campaigning experience in Flanders in 1747, but he never tasted battle during the war. A battalion of his Coldstream Guards deployed to Flushing (Vlissingen), a Dutch seaport on the Scheldt Estuary, and Braddock reported to Cumberland that he was ready to execute his commands "with all expedition and punctuality." While Braddock and his men remained in a supporting role, however, great battles and sieges were taking place at Lauffeld and Bergen-op-Zoom, depriving him yet again of any chance at battlefield distinction. The Peace of Aix-la-Chapelle was confirmed the following year, ending both the war between Britain and France and Braddock's short-lived European campaign. The Coldstream Guards returned to their numbing routine of securing public order in London and sending detachments to the king's residences at Windsor, Kensington, and Hampton Court. London's 1749 fireworks and celebrations of the peace, accompanied by George Frederick Handel's majestic *Music for the Royal Fireworks*, were probably all of the explosions that Braddock ever beheld during the late war.[12]

In the early 1750s, however, Braddock became a regimental commander and general officer and was entrusted with a major command at Gibraltar. He had grown increasingly closer to powerful figures within and without the British government. William Anne Keppel, Duke of Albemarle, had received the colonelcy of the Coldstream Guards in 1744 and had been the titular governor of Virginia since 1737. He would eventually become the British ambassador to the Court of France and undoubtedly knew his lieutenant colonel quite well. Unlike his father, who never enjoyed regimental command, Braddock was approved by the royal government for command of the 14th Foot, recently vacated by Colonel William Herbert in 1753. Braddock was fortunate to command a regiment that was distinguished on the battlefields of the late war and was on station at Gibraltar when he took charge of the unit. In a peculiar way, Braddock's relationship with George Anne Bellamy connected him to key members of the British government. By the early 1750s, George Anne Bellamy was a prominent actress and living with John Calcraft, one of the most important army administrators of the era. Braddock naturally made Calcraft his regimental agent or supplier, knowing that it would redound to George Anne's benefit. Calcraft's principal patron was Henry Fox, the secretary at war, who was in turn an ally and friend of the Duke of Cumberland.

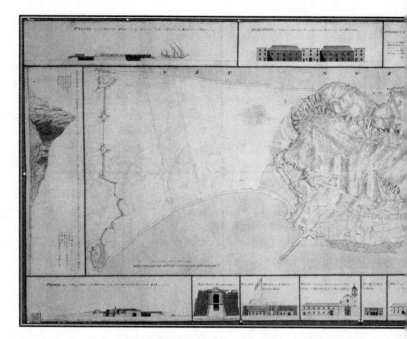

James Gabriel Montresor (1702–1776), *Plan of the Isthmus, City and Fortifications & ca: of Gibraltar*, 1751. Montresor was the chief engineer at Gibraltar in the years before General Braddock took command there in 1753. His map testifies to the knowledge of siegecraft that Braddock gained at Gibraltar. Montresor was selected as chief engineer of Braddock's Expedition but was too ill to participate. His son, John, was a lieutenant in the 48th Regiment and wounded at the Monongahela. © British Library Board, British Cartographic Items Maps K.Top.72.36.2.TAB.

Braddock even made Calcraft a joint executor of his will. It is not difficult to imagine that such relationships laid the foundation for Braddock's future military career.[13]

Most have glossed over Braddock's command at Gibraltar from 1753 to 1754, but it contains insights into the reasons for Braddock's eventual selection as commander of the expedition to America and his leadership on Britain's imperial frontiers. Major General Thomas Fowke had been appointed the "Governor of the Town and Garrison of Gibraltar" in 1753, but did not arrive at the post until the spring of 1754.[14] In the interim Braddock acted as lieutenant governor and commander in chief of the entire Gibraltar garrison, which consisted of three regiments (the 14th, 21st, and 36th) and Royal Artillerymen.[15] Despite the hellish reputation of "The Rock," Braddock earned many accolades for his conduct. "Colonel Braddock makes us all

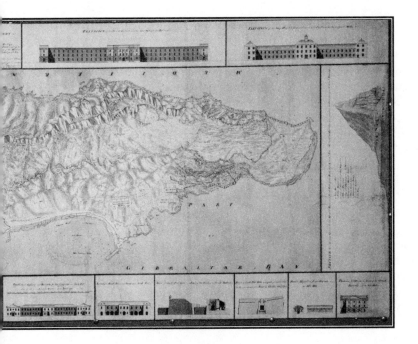

happy," a Gibraltar merchant reported in praise to a British newspaper, citing Braddock's ability to obtain for soldiers and civilians alike "an open and free Market for Butchers Meat" during the harsh winter months. Thomas Birch, a British historian, reported from London that "his Behaviour in command at Gibraltar, as the Superior officer there, gave more Satisfactions in the whole Garrison, than was expected from him." Even the habitually caustic Horace Walpole admitted that Braddock had "made himself adored, and where scarce any governor had endured before."[16]

Braddock's service on the frontiers of empire at Gibraltar prepared him for service in America. He dealt with daily logistical challenges in keeping his garrison well supplied. His governorship involved frequent engagements with civilian authorities, merchants, and contractors, and intercultural negotiations with Gibraltar's multiethnic population of British Protestants, Jews, Moors, and Catholic Spaniards, Portuguese, Genoese, Minorcans, and others. Gibraltar's very survival depended upon maintaining good relations with foreigners, such as merchants, seamen, and laborers who lived in the garrison community as well as the rulers of Morocco and Algeria in North Africa.[17] Braddock also gained experience in sifting and evaluating military intelligence, as the Gibraltar garrison lived under the constant threat of attack from Spanish forces hemming in the British. Braddock's written orders to the garrison in 1753 and 1754 reflect his vigilance as commandant on matters relating to military discipline, readiness, and security.[18] Indeed, Braddock's command was a veritable school in the art of siege warfare, for he was responsible for maintaining Gibraltar's elaborate fortifications bristling with 225 artillery pieces ranging from 6 to 32 pounders, and 45 mortars of various calibers. A newly discovered work at the Royal Library at Windsor Castle, which Edward Braddock apparently wrote and presented to Adjutant General Robert Napier in 1754, was titled "A Particular Description of the Peninsula of Gibraltar with its Several Works." One representative section described a fortification called Princess Anne's battery, "mounted with 5 twelve [pounders] Iron which Commands the Strand and flanks The Enemy in their approaches."[19] Braddock's commentary demonstrates a thorough mastery of siegecraft and knowledge of Gibraltar's history and its inhabitants. His experiences at Gibraltar, if anything, equipped him for precisely the kinds of situations that he faced in America, ranging from logistical challenges, to negotiations with potential Indian allies and colonial officials, to besieging French outposts.

A turning point in Braddock's career was his promotion to the rank of major-general in the spring of 1754—a promotion that placed him at the forefront of unfolding events in America. The Duke of Cumberland selected Braddock to command the expedition to America for many interrelated reasons: he had personally known Braddock during the 1740s when, as we have seen, they were the colonels of the Coldstream Guards and had campaigned together in 1745 and 1747. Second, the effectiveness and popularity of Braddock's command at Gibraltar demonstrated qualities that the duke, at least, believed had been evident throughout Braddock's army career. Braddock was a trustworthy and competent commander, a firm but not draconian disciplinarian, and an able negotiator and administrator. Unlike modern conceptions that equate military effectiveness with combat experience, in the eighteenth century experience was demonstrated by competent and lengthy service. Cumberland told Sir Thomas Robinson that he unequivocally "thought of Major General Bradock as the properest person to command the troops in North America." King George II also saw the merits of his selection, having "a good opinion of Mr Braddock's Sense and Bravery, and has heared is become very stayed." The expedition was, in the king's view, "as the highest national Service" and not to be entrusted to an unworthy officer. The Duke of Cumberland's patronage was a considerable expression of his trust, which he never let Braddock forget: "His Royal Highness takes a particular Interest in [the expedition], as it concerns you, whom he recommended to His Majesty, to be nominated to the chief Command."[20]

Braddock received news of his nomination in October 1754. He quickly made his way to Britain via Italy, then, paradoxically, through France. He arrived in London at his Arlington Street house on Sunday morning, November 10, 1754. Preparations for his expedition were already well under way. That same day, he went before King George II and the Duke of Cumberland, the first of Braddock's "several audiences" with the duke, in which he gave "particular explanation of every part of the service." He also met with Thomas Penn, the son of William Penn and proprietor of Pennsylvania, who prejudiced the general against the colony's Quaker-dominated assembly, with which Penn was locked in rancorous conflict. Before departing London, Braddock told George Anne Bellamy of his mission to conquer the French and "cut their way through unknown woods." Showing her a map of America, he remarked "Dear Pop, we are sent like sacrifices to the altar."[21]

The general may have been, as his royal instructions declared, "our trusty and well-beloved Edward Braddock" but his private reputation as a "rough & haughty" man continued to precede him. Walpole maligned Braddock at every opportunity, and acerbically referred to him as "a very Iroquois in disposition," invoking the contemporary British stereotype of the Iroquois as the most warlike and aggressive of all Indians. A more objective and insightful look at Braddock's personality comes from the correspondence of Colonel Charles Russell, with whom Braddock served in Flanders from 1746 to 1747. Russell had already been well aware of Braddock's reputation before serving with him. He was surprised by Braddock in person, and they appear to have socialized together quite frequently. He reported to his wife that nobody was "so immensely civil to me as Colonel Braddock." Russell hinted that "by having been now and then taken down"—perhaps frank talk from his friends or patrons—that Braddock was now "greatly reformed, behaves well, and, to me, continues to be the most polite, civil creature imaginable." Throughout their time together, Russell wrote, Braddock continued "to behave with great politeness" and acted the part of "a refined Frenchman," which hinted at Braddock's epicurean interests. Another assessment of Braddock's public character came from Thomas Birch, who wrote to a correspondent that Braddock "was known here to be rough & haughty; tho,' as I am inform'd of a Gentleman who has been very conversant with him, of better sense than most of his profession."[22]

George Washington wrote perhaps the most perceptive assessment of Braddock's character. Washington remembered his former commander as a man "whose good & bad qualities were intimately blended. He was brave even to fault and in regular Service would have done honor to his profession—His attachments were warm—his enmities strong—and having no disguise about him, both appeared in full force. He was generous & disinterested—but plain and blunt in his manner even to rudeness."[23] Washington captured the complexities of Braddock's character in ways that later chronicles and historians have flattened. General Braddock may have possessed a greater share of roughness and haughtiness, but he differed little from his contemporary general officers except that he did not disguise them. Had other British generals such as the Earl of Loudoun or Jeffery Amherst been the commander at the Monongahela, there probably would have been little difference in how colonial Americans and later historians would have remembered them. All of them might be typecast as blunt, arrogant, uncompromising conventional officers who disdained colonials and Indians.

Uncharitable judgments of General Braddock's character may also reflect views of rank-and-file Redcoats of the British Army. Contemporary attitudes toward the Redcoats were not kind. They were traditionally viewed with deep suspicion as a potential threat to English liberty. Their unpopular peacetime duties included suppressing civil disobedience, riots, and smuggling; that police role diminished whatever popularity they may have earned in wartime. The common stereotypes of the British rank and file as dregs of society drawn from the sewers and taverns of London also underlay those negative views. Most agreed with one British governor, who described them as "the scum of every country, the refuse of mankind." Lieutenant Colonel James Wolfe, the future victor at Quebec, referred to his men as "dirty, drunken, insolent rascals" and "terrible Dogs to look at." The army's officer corps clearly imbibed these views, which became part of their mindset and were reflected in their treatment of their soldiers. Some officers spoke of their men as peasants whose "stubborn disposition" and "awkward clownish ways" needed to be conquered. Officers such as Bennett Cuthbertson seemed even to embrace a Calvinistic view of Redcoats' "general depravity," as if it were somehow explained by original sin. In general, the British public feared and despised the Redcoats in peacetime, reviled them as rascals and cowards in defeat, and attributed any battlefield successes more to the skill of officers than the valor of ordinary soldiers. As historian Stephen Brumwell put it, "enthusiasm for British victories should not be confused with enthusiasm for Britain's Army."[24]

Although Braddock had spent most of his career in the Coldstream Guards, the two regular regiments under his command were far from elite units. Halkett's 44th and Dunbar's 48th were, as noted earlier, under-strength regiments plucked from garrison duty in Ireland. The precise reasons the Duke of Cumberland selected them for the American expedition are unclear. As we shall see, favoritism of the regimental commanders does not appear to have been an important consideration in his decision, and there was little in the two units' service histories to merit their selection. There was a greater number of regiments of foot in Ireland in the early 1750s (twenty-five infantry regiments compared with only ten cavalry or dragoon units), making it more probable that any expeditionary force would be culled from there.[25]

Approximately 12,000 soldiers on average, or about one-third of the British Army, were maintained on the Irish Establishment and garrisoned in Ireland. The Irish Establishment was a separate administrative entity, funded by the Irish Parliament, with a separate commander in chief, and under the authority of the Lord Lieutenant.[26] Maintaining regiments in Ireland was an important contribution to the British Empire, but from the standpoint of the officers and men, service in Ireland was not to be envied. Officers viewed an assignment to Ireland as a mark of disfavor that would relegate them to professional stagnation and estrangement from family and friends in England. The Irish Establishment of the British Army was chiefly a garrison force, but it was also regarded as a strategic reserve upon which the British government could draw as and when necessary.[27] The under-strength Irish regiments functioned as cadres, around which completed units could be formed in wartime, but it is difficult to assess how effective and experienced these cadres truly were. In the early 1750s, the 44th and 48th foot consisted of nine foot companies and one grenadier company per regiment. Each company consisted of a captain, lieutenant, two sergeants, two corporals, a drummer, and twenty-nine privates. The two regiments numbered 374 officers and men each, for a total of 748.[28]

To all appearances, the 44th and 48th were professional and fearsome infantry regiments whose massed volleys and fixed bayonets were more than capable of striking terror into their foes. David Morier's vivid period paintings of British grenadiers portray the parade-field look of the British infantry: regimental coats with elegant lace, white gaiters buttoned tightly, revealing the calves' contours; a cartridge pouch with a large buff leather shoulder strap; a waist belt with a leather appendage on the left side holding the bayonet and hanger (a short sword). The color of the Redcoats' storied regimental coats came from the madder plant (hence "madder red") of the *Rubiaceae* family, used as a cheap dye for centuries. Madder-red wool was the cheap and durable cloth of the rank-and-file soldier. Halkett's men of the 44th were distinguished by their bright yellow facings, cuffs, and turnbacks. A white lace with a yellow stripe flanked by blue and black zigzag lines bordered the regimental coat and waistcoat. Dunbar's 48th Regiment had buff facings, with lace accented by an elegant green scroll bordered by straight green and yellow stripes. These regimental insignia not only established an esprit de corps but distinguished the units from each other amid the smoke and confusion of battle.[29] Black shoes and cartridge pouches were black-balled, literally, with small orbs made of beeswax and blacking. Cracks, scratches, dents in the musket stocks were covered with beeswax; metal and brass parts were cleaned and brightly polished with a combination of oil, brick dust, emery cloth, and rock abrasives such as whiting or rottenstone. The yellowish-brown hue on buff leather belts was maintained by applications of ochre balls; and white pipe clay made an excellent medium for whitening gaiters.[30]

But the parade-ground appearances of the British Redcoats, though visually impressive and magnificently captured in Morier's paintings, were deceiving. An accurate assessment of the previous combat experiences, peacetime training, and military effectiveness of the 44th and 48th regiments has been lost in mythic portrayals of Braddock and his Redcoats as exemplars of "Hyde Park discipline." The Irish background of the 44th and 48th regiments, for example, is crucial for understanding what later happened to them. Thanks in large measure to work by recent historians, a more balanced picture has begun to emerge of the fighting capabilities of the two Irish regiments that found themselves in the American wilderness in 1755. The 44th and 48th regiments perfectly symbolized the British Army's deficiencies and weaknesses that accrued from what historian J. A. Houlding called "the friction of peace." The British Army's peacetime role as "guardian of civil order" took precedence over "efficient performance of its wartime battlefield role." As a result, peacetime duties often corroded military readiness so severely that many regiments were inadequately trained for the next war and barely maintained any proficiencies gained in the previous war.[31]

British units were so dispersed and subdivided for peacetime garrison duty in the British Isles and overseas posts that few of them had drill experience among formations larger than a regiment. With units so widely dispersed, most companies and regiments stressed the most basic aspects of drill and scarcely had either the time or the opportunity for complex maneuvering or tactical scenarios involving multiple regiments. The Irish regiments, on the other hand, had more occasions for such large-scale drills, as they tended to be concentrated into garrison towns such as Dublin, Kinsale, Limerick, and Cork; but the drills and formations were more suited to Flanders' fields than to America's woods. The 44th and 48th regiments had been on dispersed garrison duty in Ireland since 1749, shifting locations every year. Their fighting capability inevitably began to slacken under the monotony of dispersed garrison duty. Lax discipline and training, according to one British officer in 1750, was "something of the rule in Ireland." The Irish Establishment also had a degree of independence from London's War Office by virtue of its own funding, distinct command structure, and separate commander in chief. Uniformity in drill and training had a tendency to drift from English standards set by the Duke of Cumberland.[32]

Before embarking for America, the military effectiveness of the 44th and 48th regiments was also deeply affected by drafts of men from many other units. Drawing men out of other units was another common practice of the peacetime British Army, a short-term fix to bring an existing unit up to its full establishment numbers, but the practice compounded the problems of dispersed garrisons in Ireland. The greatest potential risk was that a regiment would only receive the "refuse of other Regiments," as one British officer characterized them.[33] Both Halkett's and Dunbar's regiments were augmented by 256 draftees from multiple units: 112 officers and men from Bockland's 11th Regiment went to Halkett's 44th, while the same number went from Bury's 20th Foot to Dunbar's Regiment. The 11th and the 20th regiments appear to have been selected for no other reason than their proximity to Portsmouth, from whence their drafts could be more easily sent to Ireland. An additional seventy-eight men each were drawn from four other Irish regiments: the 2nd battalion of the 1st Royal Regiment, the 10th (Pole's), 26th (Anstruther's), and 28th (Bragg's) regiments.[34] The overall quality of these drafts is hard to determine. Secretary at War Henry Fox censured the 11th Regiment

(Bockland's) as "extreamly faulty" in its discipline. James Wolfe of the 20th Foot, on the other hand, thought quite highly of his soldiers drafted for Braddock's Expedition: "it appears that the soldiers did behave themselves upon that occasion with all the steadiness, chearfulness, and obedience that may be expected from brave men and good subjects, and not a man declined the service, and all marched off with a resolution never to dishonour the corps they served in, and to do their utmost for his Majesty's service and the good of their country."[35] From their initial strengths of 374 men each, Braddock's two regiments received more than 270 draftees apiece. To bring the units up to full strength, about 350 provincials would have to be recruited in America.

A total of 1,332 officers and men of the 44th and 48th regiments embarked at Cork, Ireland, in 1755.[36] They were not the "mindless military marionettes" of legend, nor were they the dregs of society whipped into shape and kept in the ranks by a regimen of draconian discipline.[37] In 1752, the Lord Lieutenant of Ireland, Lord Dorset, issued "Rules and Orders for the better discipline of his Majesty's Army," which illustrates what British Army drill and discipline routinely emphasized. Lord Dorset's orders concerned the proper method of detailing returns; various regulations for performing guard, outpost, or picket duties; the proper "method of parading Guards"; the duties of a field officer; and wearing white spatterdashes on parade. It was thought "highly Improper" should officers "go to the Coffee Houses the play or any place of public Entertainment while on Duty." A unit that was deemed "well disciplined and fit for Service" reflected the discipline of regulations like Lord Dorset's "Rules and Orders," not the inner discipline and initiative emphasized today. Soldiers were to be "well made men" with bright arms and proper clothing. A well-disciplined unit demonstrated great proficiency in the manual of arms and the basic movements, and it was expected to perform basic tactical maneuvers, such as wheeling and platoon firing. Emphasis was also placed on the commissioned officers' and sergeants' ability to maintain discipline and duty. An orderly book kept by an officer of the 44th Regiment in Ireland between 1748 and 1755 records such expectations for Halkett's men. In 1752, for example, a sergeant and a corporal were ordered to report to Dublin for new instructions on the manual of arms, "as the Regiments of Foot in Ireland differ greatly in their time in Exercising the Manual." The men of the 44th were merely relearning the most basic rudiments of drill, such as the "proper time" of the manual of arms (i.e., sequence and positions for holding and firing a musket). The discipline of the mid-eighteenth-century regulars was thus, as Houlding puts it, an "endless practice of the 'mechanical' phase of basic training."[38]

The Long Land Pattern musket carried by Braddock's troops and described in that manual of arms was a formidable weapon, and arguably the best infantry musket in Europe. It was nearly sixty-two inches long, with an elegantly carved walnut stock and brass fixtures, weighing eleven pounds. The .75 caliber musket fired a roughly .69 caliber lead ball at a maximum effective range of around 100 yards. A 14-inch bayonet attached to the muzzle added even more heft and shock power to the musket. Of the 1,400 muskets provided to the 44th and 48th regiments, some were of the newer "King's Pattern without nosebands and steel rammers." Others retained the older wooden ramrods, which swelled in humid conditions and were easily broken.[39] The Brown Bess, as it came to be known, was beloved but notoriously temperamental. Damp and humid conditions affected the powder, frizzen, flint, and ramrod, and heavy rains made the weapon all but inoperable. Getting the musket to spark took a combination of good flint and a sharp edge that any soldier knew how to knap. The quality of the powder also varied (soldiers of the 44th in 1757 were still using cartridges made in Ireland in 1754). British regulars' muskets bore individual, regimental, and royal identification marks. Soldiers often scribed their regimental and company numbers on the small brass thumb piece on the top of the musket's wrist (one surviving musket shows such marks for the 44th Regiment). The lockplate featured an engraved crown with the initials "GR"—Georgius Rex—symbolic of the emerging centralization of the British state that oversaw the manufacture and regulation of the muskets.[40]

The ability of British soldiers to deliver on the formidable firepower of their muskets depended upon their training and the condition of their arms, both of which revealed symptoms of that "friction of peace." Regiments were commonly equipped with decades-old firearms, and the quality and quantity of ammunition issued to the troops was inferior. The 44th and 48th regiments had received new muskets in 1754 and 1755 and appear to have avoided this problem, but the Independent Companies in Braddock's army had much older and often unserviceable muskets.[41] An even greater problem was that British rank-and-file soldiers were afforded almost no live-fire practice in their basic training before the 1750s, due to the expense of ammunition. Most soldiers before the 1750s were therefore not trained to aim at targets or fire with individual discretion. The officers ordered volley fire in platoon, company, or battalion formations as the best way to maximize firepower. In the sequence of firing commands, officers ordered their men to "present" their arms, then "fire." Rather than aiming down the barrel, upright soldiers held their muskets chest high and pointed their muzzles in the enemy's direction, a firing position illustrated in drill books of the period. As one discerning lieutenant colonel foresaw: "the explanation of the word Present in the Manual of Exercise, is very different in my opinion from what Men shou'd do when Firing at an Ennemy, this gives them a Habit of doing it wrong, and I have room to believe that the Fire of our Men is not near so considerable as it would be, were any pains taken to make them good Marks men." The musket's gentle push upward, and a tendency to present "too high without Aim," as William Howe noted of one regiment, often resulted in soldiers overshooting their targets. Poor firearms training led to poor fire discipline during initial engagements, while the general inaccuracy of the smoothbore muskets meant that even a well-disciplined regiment might hit targets at seventy-five yards only a quarter of the time.[42]

The 44th and 48th regiments were unwieldy amalgamations as they assembled at Cork for their long journey to North America in January 1755: the original core of English, Scots, and Irish recruits were melded with drafts of Redcoats from other regiments and, later on, recruits from the American colonies. There was little time for unit cohesion to develop among components so hastily assembled. These regulars ultimately understood the mechanics of soldiering quite well, but fewer had any experience in large-scale maneuvers, let alone combat experience. Given the dispersed nature of British regiments, there was little else that companies, garrisons, and detachments could practice except the mechanics of basic drill. Recruits were taught the posture and bearing of a soldier, the correct techniques of marching, and the manual of arms. The rank and file were ultimately the products of their own deficient training, which emphasized exclusive obedience to their officers' commands.[43] Very little of their training prepared them for what they would face in America.

Both the 44th and 48th regiments had recently been tested in combat, though not always in ways that presaged success in North America. They had fought in the 1745 Jacobite Rebellion or in the War of Austrian Succession (before 1750, the 44th was numbered as the 55th Foot of Colonel John Lee, and the 48th was numbered as the 59th Foot of colonels Francis Ligonier and Henry Seymour Conway). In actions that eerily foreshadowed what was to come in the New World, British forces suffered a trio of losses against Jacobite forces at Prestonpans, Falkirk, and Moy in 1745 and 1746.[44] The stain of dishonor had never entirely disappeared from the reputation of the 44th Regiment for its involvement in what Lieutenant Colonel Sir Peter Halkett called "the Unhappy affair at Preston pans" on September 21, 1745. Lieutenant-General John Cope's British forces were evenly matched against the Jacobite army in a set-piece action that occurred in completely open fields in which both forces were drawn up in conventional lines of battle. One British captain remembered that the Highlanders "came running up with a Confused noise and Hallowing" in a shocking charge that threw the British regulars into confusion and gutted their morale.[45] The Redcoat infantry displayed little discipline, fired in an irregular way, and were deaf to officers' commands and attempts to rally them. Cope described how "Pannick seiz'd the Foot…they ran away, notwithstanding all the Endeavours used by their Officers to prevent it." Sir Peter Halkett, the senior officer commanding five companies of Lee's 55th Foot, fought with a handful of officers and men until the bitter end and then surrendered with honor to the Jacobites, who paroled them. Wagon drivers in the train were among the first to flee the action, and the general's headquarters papers and military chest were captured by the rebels. An official military board the following year concluded that the defeat was caused by the "shameful Behaviour of the Private Men, and not to any Misconduct or Misbehaviour of Sir John Cope." Despite Cope's exoneration, the Prestonpans debacle made clear that many British observers were unforgiving of their defeated generals but even more so of regulars who panicked. For British officers, the lesson of the disastrous battles of the '45 was that the disorderly and panic-prone nature of their rank-and-file men needed to be offset by discipline.[46]

Some came out of the '45 with their reputations intact. Sir Peter Halkett had especially "acted a distinguished part" in the battle according to one eyewitness. Born in 1695 at his father's estate in Scotland, Halkett was one of the regiment's most notable officers, having been a Member of Parliament from Stirling Burghs between 1734 and 1741. His earliest known military commission was a captaincy dated June 12, 1717, suggesting a lengthy dual career as an officer and politician. He did not stand for his seat again when he became lieutenant colonel of Lee's 55th Foot in February 1741. A clear measure of Halkett's character was his refusal to break his parole after the Battle of Prestonpans, though the Duke of Cumberland had insisted that Halkett and other officers were not bound by any parole given by rebels. In answer to the duke's threat that officers who did not return to their regiments would be superseded, Halkett and the officers replied "that he was master of their commissions, but not of their probity and honour."[47] Upon his father's death in 1746, he became Sir Peter Halkett of Pitfirrane and colonel of the 44th Regiment in 1751. Perhaps the Duke of Cumberland intended some opportunity of redemption for Sir Peter; or he may have assigned Halkett to a hazardous mission as a measure of revenge for refusing to break his parole.

The 48th (59th) Regiment, led by colonels Francis Ligonier and Henry Seymour Conway, had earned a more distinguished combat record than the 44th Regiment during the campaigns of the 1740s. Cumberland was also more familiar with the 48th Regiment, which had fought under his direct command on two occasions. The regiment participated in the 1746 Battle of Falkirk, yet another "scandalous affair" for the Redcoats during the '45 rebellion, as Brigadier-General James Cholmondeley recounted, for they "gave a feint fire, and then faced to the right about" and fled before the charging Highlanders' broadswords. Ligonier's 59th Foot was one of the reasons that the Jacobite victory at Falkirk was not a complete defeat. It had been one of the units that stood its ground, fired into the Highlanders' flanks, and were praised for the "spirit they shew'd." Later that year, the 59th shared in Cumberland's victory at Culloden. Under the command of Colonel Conway, the 59th was in the second line of British regiments and helped repel a Jacobite breakthrough. In 1747, Conway's 59th tasted battle in the Low Countries in an allied British-Austrian army commanded by the Duke of Cumberland, but it experienced a severe defeat at the Battle of Lauffeld at the hands of the French field marshal Maurice de Saxe. Cumberland praised the behavior of the British regiments, especially the 8th, 19th, and 59th regiments, which had "stormed the avenues" of the town at bayonet-point in fierce urban combat against the French, and suffered severe casualties during the action.[48]

Following the end of the war in 1748, the 59th was transferred to Ireland, renumbered as the 48th Foot, and received a new regimental commander. Colonel Thomas Dunbar was an officer of long service, dating back to 1722 when he became a lieutenant in the 35th Foot. He subsequently spent most of his career in the 18th or Royal Irish Regiment, entering the unit as a captain in 1734 and becoming its major in 1744 and lieutenant colonel in 1745. Based on the unit's history, Dunbar saw very little action during the wars of the 1740s. In 1746, the Duke of Cumberland ordered Dunbar to lead a detachment into an area of Scotland called Strathearn, as part of his brutal repression of the Highlands population following his triumph at Culloden. Dunbar executed his orders well, seizing approximately

450 cattle, horses, sheep, and goats from the people and capturing a suspected rebel.[49] Beyond that action, little else is known of Dunbar. The Duke of Newcastle once confessed that he was a "perfect Stranger to me," and that few thought him "a proper Person to have so great a Command."[50]

Given all this, we might wonder how much combat experience the officers of the 44th and 48th regiments carried forward to America in 1755, and whether their leadership might have compensated for the deficiencies of their peacetime units. It has often been suggested that Redcoats in the American wilderness of the 1750s brought great experience in irregular or *petite guerre* conditions from their campaigns in the Low Countries and in Scotland against the Jacobites.[51] That assumption tends not to hold up under a close examination of the officer lists of Braddock's two regiments. There was simply no basic continuity in the leadership of the two regiments between the 1740s and 1750s. Only four officers of the 44th who had been with the unit since its creation in 1741 were present during Braddock's Expedition; and only three veteran officers of the Battle of Prestonpans, for example, were present at the Monongahela in 1755.[52] The manuscript and published Army Lists reveal a high level of turnover in the officer ranks of the two regiments between 1741 and 1755. Of the thirty-six officers and staff listed on the 48th/59th Regiment's Army Lists covering the years 1736 to 1751, twenty-nine had retired, died, or obtained commissions in other units, taking their experience with them.[53]

While field officers and captains typically had more than a decade of service, the younger lieutenants and ensigns often entered service late in the war or missed combat altogether. Moreover, the men of the 44th and 48th regiments did not experience irregular warfare in Europe comparable to what they would face in America. In fact, conventional warfare, such as the massed ranks and open fields of battle at Prestonpans and Culloden, and urban combat at Lauffeld, characterized the actual combat experiences of both regiments in the 1740s. The Jacobite forces fought in a conventional manner and organized themselves into regiments so that they would be seen as the legitimate army of their king, not as a mob of irregulars. As difficult as the Highlanders' massed charges and the mountainous terrain of Scotland may have been, there was little in the British officers' experiences that prepared them for the irregular tactics of mobile Indian war parties and for the unique topography and environment of the Appalachian Mountains.[54]

By and large, the officers were strongly motivated not only by an aristocratic and gentlemanly code of conduct, but often by a deep loyalty to the monarchy developed through honorable service across generations. They tended to have many decades of service in their military careers and demonstrated merit for promotion even as they purchased their commissions. While there was a growing sense of professionalism in the mid-eighteenth-century British Army, most younger officers had formed whatever expertise they possessed through studying manuals, guidebooks, and historical works by ancient and modern authors such as Thucydides, Caesar, Vegetius, and Humphrey Bland, whose *Treatise of Military Discipline*, first published in 1727, was the unofficial guide to basic drill and maneuver for young officers. The officers' own lack of formal training, along with their mechanistic daily regimens, prevented them from achieving competency much beyond the level of basic training that they were expected to perfect in their soldiers. While some senior officers had tasted battle, the first test of combat leadership for many of the junior officers or subalterns came on the banks of the Monongahela.[55]

David Kennedy, laird of Drummellane in Ayshire, was a captain in the 44th Regiment and had fought at Prestonpans. He gained commissions for both of his sons, Quintin and Primrose, as officers in the 44th. The eldest, Quintin, had quite a unique military career, participating in almost every great campaign of the French and Indian War. Primrose became an ensign in the regiment in 1756 and rose to the rank of captain, serving in both that war and the War for American Independence twenty years later.[56] Captain Robert Cholmley of the 48th Regiment was born at Whitby in 1726. His father, Hugh, had been a surveyor-general of crown lands, sheriff of Yorks, and Member of Parliament for Hedon between 1708 and 1721. He became an ensign in 1745 at the age of nineteen and a lieutenant the following year. According to contemporary documents, Cholmley had been "very dangerously wounded" during the 1747 Battle of Lauffeld, and by 1749, he had earned a captaincy in the 48th Regiment, though he was apparently a brevet captain at Lauffeld.[57] In December 1754, before he departed Ireland, Cholmley drew up his last will and testament, notable for its somber phrasing: "As no Man is sure of seeing tomorrow, especially when going on a Voyage at a bad Season of the Year, which being my Case at present I think it highly incumbent on me to settle my little Affairs to prevent Disputes about them after I am gone." He left instructions to divide various effects among his family and fellow officers, leaving his clothes to his servant (or batman) who accompanied him during the expedition. "As to my Body," he requested, "where the Leaf falls, let it rot."[58]

Two officers boarding the transport ships at Cork in 1755 mattered historically more than most: Lieutenant Colonel Thomas Gage and Lieutenant Charles Lee of the 44th Regiment. Born in 1732 into a prominent family in Cheshire, Lee was nearly predestined for army life. His father, Colonel John Lee, was the first commanding officer of the 55th Regiment when it was raised in 1741, and it was undoubtedly his and the family's connections that gained his son Charles (then aged fourteen) an ensigncy in the unit in 1746. Gage, born in 1719 or 1720, was the second son of Viscount Thomas Gage and Benedicta Maria Theresa Hall, a family of English Catholic heritage in Sussex. Gage's military career probably began in the 1730s, for he was a captain and aide-de-camp to the Earl of Albemarle at the Battle of Fontenoy in 1745 and was among the "old Cullodeners" in the 48th Regiment who had fought against the Jacobites in 1746. Following the war, Gage became lieutenant colonel in Halkett's 44th Regiment in 1751 and formed a close friendship with Charles Lee through their many years of service together. Both Gage and Lee went on to have lengthy and important careers during the Seven Years' War and would one day become foes during the American Revolution.[59]

The warships and transports crowding Cork Harbor were a powerful reminder that Braddock's Expedition owed its launch to the Royal Navy. Braddock was fortunate that his Royal Navy counterpart was Commodore Augustus Keppel, who though aged thirty years, was an old salt by virtue of having joined the navy at age ten. One admiral declared that there was "no better seaman than Keppel, few so good, and not a better officer." Keppel commanded *Centurion* in 1755, a ship on which he had been acting lieutenant when his patron, Commodore George Anson, had circumnavigated the globe between 1740 and 1744. The wars of Jenkins' Ear and Austrian Succession demonstrated the Royal Navy's growing proficiency in amphibious operations, or what contemporary writer Thomas More Molyneux called "Conjunct Expeditions," meaning those "carried on jointly by the Fleet and Army." Molyneux calculated that between 1603 and 1758, England had conducted sixty-eight different amphibious operations. Of the twenty-seven "Great Expeditions" of more than 4,000 troops, only seven had been victorious. But "Small Expeditions," like that of Braddock, had succeeded in twenty-three cases and failed in only eleven cases. Braddock and Keppel had such an uncommonly harmonious relationship that one officer thought that there were "never, I believe, two men placed at the head of different Commands [who] co-operated with more spirit, integrity and harmony for the publick service."[60]

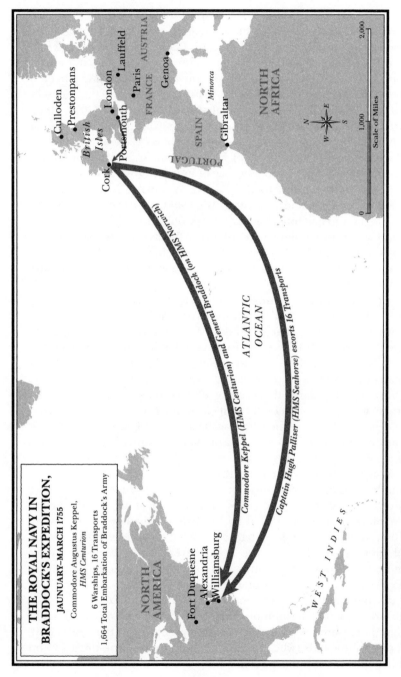

The expedition finally embarked on January 9, 1755, and the ships set sail for North America four days later, on January 13.[61] Six Royal Navy warships—*Centurion, Norwich, Syren, Garland, Sea Horse,* and *Nightingale*[62]—escorted the thirteen transports and three ordnance ships, carrying Braddock's force of approximately 1,664 personnel and the artillery train.[63] Captain Hugh Palliser, a Royal Navy officer, had full responsibility for the immense logistical undertaking of embarking all of the men and materiel for the Atlantic crossing. Each vessel carried around 100 tons of fresh water along with supplies of bread, salt beef and pork, butter, peas, oatmeal, cheese, flour, vinegar, brandy, and beer to sustain the crew and passengers for many weeks. Braddock's artillery train included four light 12-pounder and six 6-pounder brass cannons and four heavy 8-inch brass howitzers—guns that weighed from nearly half a ton to over three-quarters of a ton. The train also included fifteen portable coehorn mortars and the requisite wagons and carriages.

Braddock's complement of artillery included light brass 6-pounder and 12-pounder field pieces, portable 4.5-inch coehorn mortars, heavy 8-inch howitzers, and an array of tumbril carts, powder carts, and ammunition wagons. Fort Ligonier, Pennsylvania. Author Photograph.

The arsenal intended for use to besiege Fort Duquesne ranged
from 572 barrels of gunpowder, 6,450 cannon balls and shells, 1,606
entrenching tools, and 144,388 flints. To sustain an army the size of
a small town, 1,000 barrels of salt beef and 100 tons of Irish butter
were included for the troops' use in America. The Duke of Cumberland
also approved St. Clair's request for twelve "Rifled Barrel Carbines"
and signal rockets, and he included three sets of armor to protect the
engineers during siege operations in the woods.[64] Cumberland and
the Board of Ordnance had appointed James Montresor, the chief
engineer at Gibraltar from 1747 to 1753, as the chief engineer of the
expedition, assisted by Patrick Mackellar, Harry Gordon, and Adam
Williamson. Though Montresor later fell sick and missed the expedition entirely, the engineers brought experience in siege warfare and
in military road-building that was instrumental to Braddock's success.
Harry Gordon, for example, had engineered military roads through
the Scottish Highlands in the 1740s, and his exquisite maps still survive in the UK National Archives. Both Mackellar and Gordon later
drafted maps of Braddock's campaign that remain vital historical
sources.[65] Finally, there were tents and supplies for a general hospital,
including two regimental medicine chests for the use of the hospital's
twenty-nine personnel, one of whom was Charlotte Browne, a recently
widowed gentlewoman and hospital matron who chronicled the journey. Within the medicine chests was a goodly supply of Doctor James's
Powder, a medicine patented by Dr. Robert James in 1746 containing
antimony and calcium phosphate. This eighteenth-century cure-all
medicine was destined to bring relief to an ailing George Washington
months later.[66]

Although several of Sir Peter Halkett's officers grumbled over
the provisions and general conditions of the transports, the Atlantic
passage in January and February 1755 was not the ordeal that it
might have been. Braddock had embarked on *Norwich* with his *aide-
de-camp*, Robert Orme, a thirty-year-old lieutenant whom the general
had known in the Coldstream Guards (Orme apparently took on a
brevet rank of captain during the campaign). Orme's particularly
close relationship with Braddock elicited the envy of those who did
not enjoy such favor. The confident bearing that drove many of
Orme's enemies to accuse him of having an undue influence over
the general was well captured in Sir Joshua Reynolds's painting of
Orme.[67] Braddock's entourage also included his secretary, William
Shirley Jr. (whose father was the royal governor of Massachusetts),
his personal servant, Thomas Bishop, and his cook, Francis Delboux.
Captain Roger Morris of the 48th Regiment was later appointed

as another *aide-de-camp* in Virginia. Winter storms had damaged *Norwich's* and *Centurion's* masts, but the remainder of the fleet enjoyed comparatively easier sailing. Captain Palliser, on board *Sea Horse*, escorted the transports on the southern passage of the Atlantic. Major William Sparke, who had been in the 48th Regiment since 1742 and wounded at Culloden, wrote that "hard gales of Wind" had soon dispersed the fleet, while sailors lamented the lack of grog on board Charlotte Browne's transport, the *London*. A poem published in the *Pennsylvania Gazette* of January 1755 called for the regulars' safe arrival across the Atlantic and expressed the colonists' high expectations of what the British regulars would accomplish upon landing in America:

> The ponderous Cannon o'er the surges sleep;
> The flaming Muskets swim the raging deep;
> The murd'rous Swords, concealed in scabbards, sail,
> And pointed Bayonets partake the gale:
> Ah! Swiftly waft her to the longing shore;
> In safety land her, and we ask no more!"

Major Sparke thanked Providence for safely delivering his vessel to Hampton Roads on March 12, after being "roughly attack'd by North Westers" as they neared the American coast. One unfortunate man had been washed overboard but no rampant illnesses were reported among the passengers.[68]

It had taken *Norwich* a little more than one month to deliver General Braddock to American shores. She arrived at the Virginia Capes on February 19, 1755, and sailed on to Hampton on February 20, followed by *Centurion* a few days later. Palliser's *Sea Horse* and other transports began arriving at the Virginia Capes on March 8, 1755. General Braddock, Captain Orme, and Mr. Shirley rode into Williamsburg, Virginia, on Sunday, February 23, 1755, affording the townsfolk a view of the new commander in chief as the entourage rode up the main thoroughfare, Duke of Gloucester Street. Governor Dinwiddie received General Braddock at his house, derisively known as the governor's "palace" since the days of its completion during the opulent governorship of Alexander Spotswood. Dinwiddie thought Braddock was "a very fine Officer, and a sencible, considerate Gentleman." During his stay in Williamsburg, Braddock may have either stayed or dined at the Raleigh Tavern kept by Alexander Finnie, for the general's bay horse was lost or stolen from its nearby stable.[69]

Sir John St. Clair charged into Williamsburg on February 24 to report on his preparations for the march and to discuss the preliminaries to the campaign. He had earlier written the general with a plan for cantoning (quartering) the two regiments across different towns in tidewater Virginia and Maryland. But Braddock, Keppel, and Dinwiddie had decided by February 25 that the best course of action was to land the two regiments at Alexandria, near the head of navigation on the Potomac River in northern Virginia. Shortly after Palliser arrived with the bulk of the transports, they all set sail north for Alexandria on March 13. When the last transport, the *Severn*, arrived on March 18, General Braddock and Governor Dinwiddie finally set out for Alexandria on March 22. As the transports sailed up the broad and pleasant Potomac River, the batman or personal servant of Captain Robert Cholmley noted "many gentlemen['s] Houses on Boath Sides"—the impressive houses of Virginia's tidewater planters. Occasionally the ships saluted "with our Great Guns and answered again from the Gentlemen Houses with their great Guns and Colours flying."[70]

From Mount Vernon, overlooking the Potomac River, George Washington probably glimpsed the sight of British warships and transports sailing past his plantation toward Alexandria. A letter that arrived at Mount Vernon on March 14, 1755, from Captain Orme would change his life, for it contained an invitation to the young Virginian to join Braddock's "family," or inner circle of staff officers. Orme's letter soothed Washington's provincial insecurities by addressing him as "a person so universally esteem'd." Braddock knew that Washington's knowledge and experience would be beneficial to his expedition. He had also heard of the young Virginian's "desire to make the Campaigne"—perhaps a reflection of how Washington may have dropped hints on his availability. The general had also learned of his principled "disagreeableness" over the preference given to regular over colonial officers, and he was willing to accommodate him. By serving as a volunteer aide, Orme wrote, "all inconveniences of that kind will be obviated." Friendship between Washington and Orme blossomed in the weeks and months to come.[71]

In his reply, dated March 15, Washington fell all over himself in responding to Captain Orme and the British commander in chief: "You do me a singular favour in proposing an acquaintance, which cannot but be attended with the most flattering prospect of intimacy on my part; as you may already perceive by the familiarity and freedom which I now enter upon this correspondence; a freedom, which, even if it is disagreeable you must excuse, as I may lay the blame of it at your door for encouraging me to throw off that restraint which otherwise might have been more obvious in my deportment on such an occasion." The issue of officer rank soon surfaced. Braddock had offered Washington a brevet (temporary) captain's commission. Washington, however, would not brook an offer that was "too degrading" to his honor and sense of British equality. He had resigned his commission as a colonel on principle months before, refusing to serve in the campaign as a demoted captain: "the disparity between the present offer of a Company, and my former Rank [Colonel], too great to expect any real satisfaction or enjoyment in a Corps, where I once did, or thought I had a right to command." Washington assured a friend, however, that "My inclinations are still strongly bent to arms," and hoped that his participation would bring honor to British arms and the "approbation & esteem" of his countrymen, especially if it came in the form of a royal officer's commission. Washington lost no time in sending Orme and Braddock "a small Map of the back country," one that the former surveyor undoubtedly drew with meticulous care in order to impress the officers. He asked for the indulgence of joining the general at Wills Creek so that he could settle business at Mount Vernon, which was approved.[72]

General Braddock's brief sojourn in Williamsburg had revealed many promises and perils for his American campaign. He and Governor Dinwiddie had quickly gotten down to the business of the expedition. The general immediately raised the subject of a common colonial fund and wrote a circular letter to colonial governors, along with invitations to attend a council at Annapolis in early April. He expected the colonies to provide supplies, wagons, and recruits for the expedition. The two men settled on a plan to form two companies of carpenters, four companies of rangers, and a company of light horsemen from the old Virginia Regiment's remains. Dinwiddie was lavish with promises of colonial cooperation: he boasted that his colony had voted the impressive sum of £20,000, in contrast to the "Lethargick Supineness" of Maryland's and Pennsylvania's legislatures; that he had secured an immense supply of flour from Pennsylvania and cattle from North Carolina; that hundreds of Cherokee and Catawba warriors would be awaiting him for the expedition, especially after Virginia mediated a peace between them and the Six Nations, to be concluded at Winchester that spring.[73]

Dinwiddie's oversell would come to haunt him. St. Clair's letters to Braddock contained the list of his disappointing discoveries: the distance over the mountains was not a mere fifteen miles, as initially believed, but sixty to seventy miles; the Potomac was unnavigable above the Great Falls; and the only route to Wills Creek was the "worst Road I ever travelled." Worse yet, the colonials were "totally

ignorant of Military Affairs," St. Clair warned. "Their Sloth & Ignorance
is not to be discribed." Roads would have to be cut; floats, batteaux,
and magazines constructed; and colonial forces properly disciplined.
St. Clair also fully awakened Braddock to the reality of colonial dis-
union and the petty jealousies that had rendered their governments
ineffective in the current crisis. He singled out "Pennsylvania, the
richest and most populous of all these Provinces," adding that the
colony "will do nothing, and furnisheth the French with Provisions."[74]
Before Braddock could conquer the French and claim the title of
Americanus as Horace Walpole expected, he first had to confront
the colonial and imperial weaknesses that threatened to undermine
the expedition even before it had begun.[75]

CHAPTER 3

Confrontations

Braddock's Army, Colonial America, and the British Empire

The General and all the Officers were surpris'd, declar'd the Expedition was then at an End, being impossible.

~Benjamin Franklin~

ON MARCH 22, 1755, British transport ships carrying Halkett's and Dunbar's regiments anchored in the channel of the Potomac River at Alexandria. British regulars caught their first glimpse of the colonial port town, perched on a crescent-shaped shelf of land overlooking a shallow bay. One eighteenth-century traveler was enraptured by the raw potential of this "small trading place in one of the finest situations imaginable," where the Potomac was a mile wide and opened into a large bay roughly twice that diameter. The house of Scots merchant John Carlyle stood with conspicuous grandeur on a bluff at the center of the bay. Georgian-Palladian in style, the elegant house was made of Aquia sandstone, quarried nearby, and distinguished by handsome quoining on the corners and frontispiece. The building's keystone—engraved with the year 1752 and initials JSC—reflected the intertwined fortunes and hopes of Carlyle and his wife, Sarah. John vividly remembered March 24, 1755, when the transports "Landed In high Spirits about 1600 men, besides A fine Train of Artillery 100 matrosses [artillerymen] &c & Seemed to be Afraid of nothing but that the French & Indians Woud not Give them A Meeting, & try their Courage." The regulars disembarked and marched from the wharves, taking Oronoko Street up the embankment to their camp at the edge of town, while officers billeted at a refurbished tavern or other private homes in town.[1]

It was fitting that Alexandria (then also called Belhaven) became the starting point of Braddock's march toward Fort Duquesne and that Carlyle's magnificent home would play a part. The Virginia House

John Carlyle House, ca. 1752, Alexandria, Virginia. Author Photograph.

of Burgesses had authorized the town's founding in 1749 to serve as an entrepôt for the western frontier, and Carlyle became one of the trustees. Carlyle's career embodied the Virginia ruling class's broad web of interests that had turned the Ohio Valley into a coveted prize. He had become a prosperous merchant and landowner after his arrival in the colony from northern England in the 1740s; his marriage to Sarah Fairfax in 1747 connected him to that influential family. Carlyle was a member of the Ohio Company and served as major and commissary of the Virginia forces fighting for his land claims. During the 1754 campaign, he gained experience in the business of supplying armies.[2]

As news of their arrival spread throughout the region, the regulars became a spectacle during their encampment, which lasted nearly three weeks. The attention of many Virginia colonists, like Fredericksburg merchant Anthony Strother, "was so taken up with so unusuall a sight" as Redcoats. It had been more than seventy years since regulars were stationed in the colony (King Charles II dispatched 1,000 regulars in 1676 to help suppress Nathaniel Bacon's rebellion of disgruntled planters and oppressed servants against the royal government of Virginia). The Maryland planter and politician

Daniel Dulany, "having heard much of their gallant appearance," was overcome by curiosity and visited the Redcoats' camp. Scots residents in the area gravitated to officers such as fellow Scot Sir Peter Halkett of Pitfirrane and extolled his character (often in contrast to Braddock's). Curious colonials were also conspicuous bystanders at the grand review of March 31, 1755, when the 44th and 48th regiments were formally mustered and General Braddock personally inspected each company.[3]

The distinguished trio of Braddock, Governor Dinwiddie, and Commodore Keppel had arrived at Alexandria on March 26; the general and his military family lodged at Carlyle's house (presumably at his invitation) but as Sarah was expecting their fourth child things became tense. John admitted that Braddock had generally displayed a "Great deall of Freindship," paid him £50 for the use of his house, and given him a lucrative commission as a store keeper. But the Scots merchant remained petulant. Braddock had taken "every thing he wanted abused my house, & furniture, & made me little or No Satisfaction." Carlyle judged him to be a man of "Week understanding, Possitive, & Very Indolent, Slave to his Passions, Women & Wine, As Great an Epicure as could be in his Eateing." He was elated when Braddock and the army finally departed in early April, and his letter to his brother written months later, still dripped with resentment over British conduct toward provincials:

> they [despised] us & [the French] & by Sum means or another came In So prejudiced against Us, our Country, &c that they used us Like an Enemys Country & Took every thing they wanted & paid Nothing, or Very little for it, & When Complaints was made to the Comdg Officers, they Curst the Country, & the Inhabitants, Calling Us the Spawn of Convicts the Sweepings of the Gaols &c; which made their Company very disagreeable.[4]

The army's encampment in Alexandria in the spring of 1755 was symbolic of British Americans' broader confrontation with the very nature of the British Empire, personified in the Redcoat regiments and their commanding general with nearly viceregal powers. Braddock's Expedition began to expose some of the deep fault lines on which the Thirteen Colonies and the British Empire ultimately divided, bringing light to the colonists' second-rate status within that empire. Civil-military friction also sharpened a sense of difference, sometimes to the surprise of colonists who thought of themselves as loyal British subjects rather than disaffected malcontents, which is how some British officers viewed them. As he contended with colonial governors and their assemblies, General Braddock encountered the unruly political constitution of the Thirteen Colonies. The Virginia assembly was already well accustomed to military governors-general such as Alexander Spotswood and William Gooch, and had masterfully adopted Whig political rhetoric to paint such executives as agents of arbitrary military power.[5] Braddock and his regulars would also confront the military, logistical, and geographical challenges unique to campaigning in the colonies. America's weather, its provincials, and its Indian inhabitants all contributed to the regulars' sense that this nominally British world was indeed aberrant and strange.

Braddock's arrival in America represented the first time that the British crown had appointed a commander in chief with such consolidating powers over the Thirteen Colonies. A British pamphlet reported that General Braddock was "expected to advance the deep-projected reformation of our *American* colonies by a military government, subjecting them all under such salutary laws as reforming Soldiers have, in all similar circumstances, imposed."[6] Rumors circulated that Braddock's military success in America would translate into the governorship of an important colony like New York.[7] Braddock's appointment as commander in chief in America seemed to answer the yearnings of many imperial officials for a powerful Marlborough-like captain-general who would bring order to the disunited colonies and their defective constitutions. His office became a precedent for imperial efforts to centralize military and diplomatic affairs in the American colonies through a powerful executive.[8] The general carried three sets of royal instructions—marked "Secret," "Private," and "General"—that empowered him in innovative ways. Braddock received substantial authority over Indian diplomacy in America. He was personally charged to cultivate good relations with Native nations; ordered to appoint two royal superintendents of Indian affairs (whose powers diminished those of individual colonies); and given authority over the distribution of Indian presents that colonial assemblies had voted. In the conduct of military affairs, the colonies were clearly subordinate to the commander in chief. Colonial assemblies were expected to contribute money for military ventures to a common fund administered by Braddock (John St. Clair had arrived in America bearing a circular letter to all colonial governors detailing the common fund). The general was also ordered to prevent illegal trading between the British colonies and the French that had rankled many imperial officials. The instructions required colonial governors to "observe & obey all such orders" that Braddock issued regarding quartering, impressment of recruits, and collection of supplies. Last, the general was enjoined to convene a council of governors who were most concerned in the 1755 offensives.[9]

The Alexandria Congress of April 14–15, 1755, involved Braddock, Commodore Keppel, and five colonial governors, meeting to coordinate military strategy for the 1755 expeditions. Despite his unpleasant and inconvenient guests, John Carlyle took rightful pride that "there was the Grandest Congress held at my House ever known on This Continent." Even Benjamin Franklin, fresh from the Albany Congress, perceived the magnitude of this "grand Congress."[10] Braddock convened the governors in an ornate Palladian room in Carlyle's house on April 14, although additional meetings were still being concluded the following day. The five governors were Robert Dinwiddie, Horatio Sharpe of Maryland, Robert Hunter Morris of Pennsylvania, James De Lancey of New York, and William Shirley of Massachusetts. The latter's son Captain William Shirley Jr. served as Braddock's official secretary during the campaign and recorded the minutes of the meeting.[11]

The April 14 meeting was in many respects a continuation of themes that had been unresolved since the Albany Congress of 1754, when colonial leaders met to address problems of intercolonial defense and Indian diplomacy. It began with a formal reading of Braddock's commission and his royal instructions, one of which was to establish precisely such a council of war—since that is effectively what the Alexandria Congress was—with colonial governors.[12] Braddock discussed with them the common fund to which colonial assemblies would contribute money. The fund raised a vital issue of imperial governance, the colonies' financial responsibilities for their own defense, upon which the British Empire in America would ultimately run aground.[13]

Braddock also discussed his task of appointing a "proper person" to negotiate a new treaty with the Six Nations and to have "sole Management & direction of the Affairs of the Six Nations of Indians & their Allies." The man destined to become Superintendent of Indian Affairs in the northern colonies had in fact traveled from New York to Alexandria in the company of governors DeLancey and Shirley. William Johnson was born into a prominent Anglo-Irish family in 1715. Within ten years of his arrival in New York in 1737, Johnson had become arguably the colony's most important liaison to the Six Nations. He settled in Mohawk territory west of Albany and was soon "joined in brothership" to his Mohawk neighbors at Tiononderoge, who adopted him and named him "Warrighiyagey." His Iroquoian name—"in the midst of affairs"—was apt, for by 1746 Johnson had become a prosperous fur trader and landowner, formed

Sir William Johnson (1715–1774) ca. 1750–1752 by John Wollaston (1736–1767). General Braddock defined the trajectory of William Johnson's influential career by appointing him royal Superintendent of Indian Affairs and commander of the Crown Point Expedition in 1755. Oil on canvas, ht.30 1/16" × w.25", Albany Institute of History & Art, gift of Laura Munsell Tremaine in memory of her father, Joel Munsell, 1922.2.

political alliances with key Iroquois leaders, fathered a number of children with a Mohawk woman named Elizabeth, and been appointed as "Colonel of the Six Nations" by the New York government. By the early 1750s, William Johnson was acknowledged in imperial circles as "the best judge in America of [the Indians'] disposition," as William Shirley wrote. Although Johnson was not present at the April 14 council, and apparently met with Braddock privately, the Congress profoundly shaped his future career and significance in the British world.[14]

The third and fourth proposals were drawn from Braddock's "Secret Instructions" detailing exact military expeditions projected against French forts in America. Braddock's own expedition to the Ohio was the priority, as his instructions required him to "take the Field much Sooner" than the other expeditions. After Fort Duquesne was captured, he made it clear that the Pennsylvania, Maryland, and Virginia governments would be jointly responsible for garrisoning the new fort at the Forks of the Ohio, and for providing its supplies, artillery, and ammunition. His instructions enjoined him not only to eject the French from the Ohio but also to proceed northward to Lake Ontario and seize Fort Niagara—an ambitious odyssey of more than 500 miles.[15] Braddock's strategic grasp of North America was keen, as he referred to Fort Niagara—not Fort Duquesne—as the most important enterprise of all, knowing that control of Lake Ontario would "cutt off the French communication with the western countries." But Braddock could not alter his orders and take personal command of the Niagara expedition. So he offered the job to Shirley, a man whose integrity and devotion to the king he had come to respect. Shirley's willingness to take the assignment, along with his political abilities and expertise in the northern colonies, made him "the most capable"—as Braddock wrote to Sir Thomas Robinson—of finessing the New England governments and securing their cooperation.[16] The previous day, the Massachusetts governor also briefed Braddock on the projected campaign, already under way, against French encroachments on Nova Scotia such as Fort Beauséjour. Braddock approved and appointed Lieutenant Colonel Robert Monckton commander of the expedition on April 14.[17] Braddock then proposed that a provincial army of more than 4,000 New Englanders, New Yorkers, and Iroquois allies, commanded by William Johnson, would proceed against the French fort at Crown Point. Braddock viewed Oswego as an important staging point for the Niagara expedition, and proposed reinforcing it with two of the New York Independent Companies and two companies of Pepperell's 51st regiment, and constructing one or two vessels to ply the waters of Lake Ontario and keep watch.[18]

The governors unanimously asserted that a common fund could "never be established in the Colonies without the aid of Parliament," a shocking admission to Braddock that "the King's Pleasure" could not be gratified in his American colonies simply upon his word. Chronic disunity among the colonies and contention between their respective assemblies and governors had virtually incapacitated them from effective military responses. Even worse, the governors unanimously warned that the expeditions would completely break down from want of money unless Braddock secured funding from home. Braddock appeared "somewhat dissatisfied" over colonial intransigence, as Governor Sharpe put it mildly, as he realized that he would have to rely heavily on his own contingency fund—an outcome that the British government had in fact anticipated in its instructions to the general. The governors promised to approach their assemblies yet again on the issue of funding, but by now Braddock had been rudely awakened to the dysfunctions of colonial politics.[19]

The April 14 discussion of parliamentary taxation of the colonies did not make the Carlyle House "the place where the Revolution was born," as some have suggested.[20] Nor was the Alexandria Congress the first time that colonial governors had suggested direct taxation by Parliament. The Revolutionaries of the 1770s did not look back on the meeting as establishing some kind of precedent. The Congress was a significant enough moment in the history of the British Empire in America: its participants approved four major campaigns in the broader struggle against New France, and they came face-to-face with Britain's imperial weaknesses as they tried to advance that empire. Braddock's reports from Alexandria and his subsequent conflicts with the colonial governments shaped a negative perception of Americans in the minds of British officials, many of whom were already disturbed by the republican drift of the American colonial governments.[21] The general and the governors certainly anticipated the need for parliamentary taxation of America for purposes of imperial defense. Shirley, for example, observed to Robinson that "nothing would be a firmer cement of His Majesty's Colonies" than a common fund and a plan of union, but he also believed that neither would happen without an act of Parliament. Braddock in turn warned Robinson of how expensive the American campaigns would become and of "the Necessity of laying a Tax upon all of His Majesty's Dominions in America, agreeable to the Result of Council, for re-imbursing the great Sums that must be advanced for the Service and Interest of the Colonies, in this important Crisis."[22] Braddock's other less-problematic proposals were unanimously affirmed by the harmonious council. Although some governors claimed after the fact that they urged Braddock to proceed against Niagara, the general had his orders to advance through Virginia to Fort Duquesne. And in the end, the governors had unanimously approved four military offensives and William Johnson's diplomatic effort to gain the assistance of the Six Nations and other Indian nations.[23]

William Johnson felt a strong rapport with General Braddock when they met on April 14 or 15. The general as we've seen very quickly entrusted him with both the Indian superintendency and command of a provincial army with the rank of major-general. Johnson would oversee a new treaty with the Six Nations and deliver speeches in Braddock's name to the Iroquois. Johnson was at first wary of acting as "Plenipotentiary" to the Six Nations, though he accepted the office as he discerned Braddock's engagement in Indian affairs, his familiarity with the ways in which the Albany Commissioners of Indian Affairs had aggravated relations with the Iroquois, and of the illegal fur trade that Albany merchants conducted with the

French in Montreal. Johnson was, further, undoubtedly swayed by Braddock's uncommon generosity toward the Indians. The general went far beyond the governors' recommendation of £800, advancing Johnson an astonishing £2,000 for Indian gifts—"whatever it may cost," to use Braddock's exact words—for diplomacy with the Six Nations. Braddock moreover insisted that officers in Johnson's Indian department up to the rank of captain would receive equal pay as any British regular officer—a reflection of how significantly he viewed their roles. No subsequent British commander in chief would prove so supportive of Johnson's superintendency of Indian affairs. Braddock offered only high praise for Johnson's character and conduct in letters to the British government, which launched his already significant career toward loftier heights. Before leaving Alexandria, Johnson personally drafted the speeches that Braddock would himself deliver to Ohio Indians at Fort Cumberland the following month.[24]

During his stay in Alexandria, Braddock had a number of meetings with other gentlemen who were in the governors' entourages. One was with Thomas Pownall, a self-taught student of American colonial affairs with broad connections to the British government. The meeting undermines one of the key myths surrounding the campaign—that Braddock arrogantly rejected Indian rights to the land. Pownall and Johnson had provided a rhetorical strategy for Braddock's diplomatic messages to the Six Nations and other Native peoples. Indeed, Pownall advised Braddock to frame his and other British expeditions as an effort to *protect* Indians' land rights, not as an effort to "possess their Lands & take ye Dominion of them." The British would only drive the French off their lands and build forts to protect Indians' lands "for their own Use according to ye True Spirit & Tenor of our Alliance & Covenant Chain." Braddock enthusiastically announced, "This by God is giving some reason for what we are going to do!" and Pownall added "not only a *Reason,* Sir but a *Right.*" On April 16, 1755, Braddock empowered Pownall to draft a set of additional instructions to Johnson. Braddock now ordered Johnson to communicate a new diplomatic message to the Six Nations, one that recalled earlier deeds and treaties concluded between the Iroquois and the New York government:

> You are in my Name to Assure the Saied Nations that I am come by his Majesty's Order to destroy all ye saied Forts & to build such others as shall protect & Secure the saied Lands to them their Heirs & Successors for ever according to ye Intent & Spirit of the Saied Treaty & therefore call upon them to take up the Hatchet & Come & take Possession of their own Lands.

Rather than denying any Indian right to inherit the land, Braddock had authorized diplomatic messages saying, "I am come here upon no other Design, than to retake these Lands from the French, and preserve them for [the Indians'] use."[25]

One of the other gentlemen who came to visit the governors before their departure from Alexandria was George Washington, who as we've seen had recently accepted Braddock's invitation to serve as a volunteer aide. He wrote to William Fairfax that he had "the Honour to be introduced to the several Governours; and of being well receiv'd by them all; especially Mr Shirley, whose Character and appearance has perfectly charmd me." He thought the council had been a "favorable presage I hope, not only of the success of the Expedition, but of the future greatness of this Town."[26]

As the governors departed Alexandria on April 17, 1755, they had set in motion a plan that was sound in theory, for it applied potentially overwhelming weight on New France's strained forces. Governor Shirley best captured the raw potential that many, including his son, sensed in the council's decisions: "According to this plan," the governor wrote, "the French will be attack'd almost at the same time in all their incroachments in North America; and if it should be successfully executed in every part, it seems highly probable that all points in dispute there with them may be adjusted this year, and in case of a sudden rupture between the two Crowns the way pav'd for the reduction of Canada."[27] Nonetheless the strategy devised at the Alexandria Congress was not without flaws. Its very composition reflected colonial disunity, for Governor James Glen of South Carolina was strangely never invited even though he had called for precisely such an intercolonial congress of governors. Though there is no conclusive evidence for this, it is likely that his rival Governor Dinwiddie excluded him from the proceedings. Had Glen been present, Braddock would surely have pressed him to recruit Cherokee or Catawba warriors for Braddock's army. The governors had unanimously agreed to an ambitious plan, when they knew better than anyone the particular difficulties of American campaigning. They had also underestimated the inherent challenges of securing intercolonial support and supplies for the expeditions against Niagara and Crown Point. Because Shirley's and Johnson's forces had Albany as their base of operations, the rival commanders competed over political support, finances, supplies of ammunition and food, and Iroquois allies for their respective expeditions.[28]

The council had made important and far-reaching choices concerning the campaign's tempo. Braddock did not see the four campaigns that were being planned as in isolation from one another. Indeed, he argued that victory "would very much depend upon their being carried into execution at or near the same time." According to Captain Orme's journal, the general agreed with Shirley and Johnson that their trio of expeditions would reach their targets at "the end of June, nearly in July, and the General assured them he would use his utmost endeavours to be at Fort Du Quesne by that time." As we shall see, that choice constrained Braddock in two ways: first, he believed that French reinforcements to Fort Duquesne would be delayed because of Shirley's threat to Fort Niagara and second, it meant that he could not relent in his rapid advance on Fort Duquesne, having agreed to reach there by the end of June. "I perceive so strict a Connection between each of these Projects, that the Success of one, will procure us that of the other," Braddock reported to Sir Thomas Robinson shortly after the council. Indeed, he was so anxious to get the campaign under way that his regulars were already on the march into Maryland and Virginia while the Alexandria Congress was taking place.[29]

The general's determination to make the campaign a success extended down to the most minute details of the army's operations. Braddock's ambition was to be a soldier's general, like the great Duke of Marlborough, who had displayed uncommon concern for his men's welfare and needs. "I must say that a Soldier here should have every Advantage," he wrote to Robert Napier shortly after the troops had begun their marches, "as their Fatigue is very great and their pay not near sufficient in this dear and desolate Country." He encouraged his men in small but significant ways, such as allowing them a limitless daily ration—"in as great proportions as it will be possible to provide them"—depending upon supplies. Private Duncan Cameron of the 44th Regiment recalled the general as a "brave old experienced Officer, in whom we had a great deal of Confidence." Braddock reciprocated that confidence and praised the two regiments under his command, which "behave well and shew great Spirit and Zeal for the Service." He was not proving the draconian disciplinarian of legend, for he pardoned a deserter condemned to die. One of his first orders at the Alexandria encampment called for a fair and humane way of dealing with the dangerous combination of alcohol and encamped armies. His orders took it for granted that soldiers would get drunk; and that "whilst they are in Liquor often make use of Insolent Expressions which bring upon them heavy Punishments" and "indanger their Lives by Words tending to Mutiny." Officers were forbidden from reprimanding or conversing with drunken soldiers, to avoid provoking them into insolent or mutinous talk. Rather, the inebriated soldiers were to be immediately confined and dealt with after they had sobered up.[30]

Braddock also adapted his regulars for American conditions long before the creation of light infantry and ranger units that would occur later in the French and Indian War. His conviction that "a Soldier here should have every Advantage" was expressed in the modifications he made for his soldiers' comfort in the field. When the 44th and 48th regiments had formally mustered in the grand review at Alexandria on March 31, the regulars' appearance was not that of slavishly conventional infantry fresh from a parade at Hyde Park. Laced regimental coats and cocked hats remained *de rigueur,* but the soldiers were issued new waistcoats and breeches made of cooler osnaburg linen, "as the excessive heat would have made the others [made of wool] insupportable," Robert Orme recalled. Brown spatterdashes or gaiters were issued to protect the men's legs during road building and marches through the woods. Perhaps the only questionable addition was a "Bladder or thin Leather to put between the Lining and crown of their hats to guard against the Heat of the Sun."[31]

Braddock also lightened the marching load of the typical infantryman. With uniforms, accoutrements, and musket, the total weight carried by a Redcoat of the 44th or 48th in full marching order in 1755 was probably no more than sixty pounds, based on a return done later in the war.[32] Soldiers were permitted to leave behind their heavy buff leather shoulder belts, waist belts, and hangers in Alexandria. The twelve-inch bayonet at least had some practical combat and camp uses. But the ornamental hangers, or short swords, were viewed as irritating "incumbrances" that hindered movement. British officer Henry Bouquet later referred to such weapons as a "joke": "They could not kill a chicken with this tiny knife." Shedding those accoutrements considerably lightened the soldiers' load. In their place, they now wore a simple twelve-hole cartridge box affixed around their waist by a small buff strap with a bayonet holder. All that remained was an osnaburg haversack for rations, a tin canteen, and a knapsack containing personal belongings, extra gear, and a blanket.[33] Commissioned and noncommissioned officers were also permitted to dispense with traditional instruments of their rank. Sergeants were allowed to stow their halberds—a symbol of their office and a useful tool for keeping men in line. Braddock permitted the commissioned officers to purchase fusils (lighter and shorter muskets) and leave behind their espontoons (a half-pike that officers used to signal movements and carried in formal duties such as mounting guard or parading). He probably acted on St. Clair's recommendation that fusils were "of more use than Spontoons and Halberts in this Woody Country."[34]

Braddock reminded his Irish regulars that they had served under the Duke of Cumberland and were "very well acquainted with military discipline," and "to set the most soldier like example to the new Levies of this country." Completing the ranks of the 44th and 48th regiments was one of the main priorities during the army's encampment at Alexandria, and parties scoured local Virginia and Maryland communities for recruits. Over the ensuing weeks, recruiters successfully swelled the ranks of the two regiments by almost 400 men, but they were still below full strength of 1,050 each. Braddock was disappointed in the "very indifferent Men" recruited in the provinces, for it "cost infinite pains and labour to bring them to any sort of Regularity and Discipline." In the long term, the recruitment of colonials into the regular ranks made the regiments even more unwieldy amalgams and prone to rampant desertion.[35]

The colonists were also discontented. What particularly galled them was the recruitment of irreplaceable laborers into the ranks of the British and provincial forces, and army recruiters' disruptive infiltration of their neighborhoods. Robert Blackburn, a Maryland servant from Antietam, was one such recruit into the 48th Regiment. Described as a twenty-four-year-old man, five feet and eight inches high, and pockmarked from smallpox, Blackburn apparently found the army so intolerable that he deserted at the first opportune moment. "Numbers of Mulattoes and free Negroes" became batmen in the army or served in the ranks, such as "William Holmes, a Mullatoe," a Virginia recruit who later deserted, and a Guinea slave who had been a servant during the campaign.[36] Indentured servants were especially susceptible to impressment, and many "flocked in to enlist" to escape their hardships. A litany of complaints, bad blood, and desertion followed in the army's wake. Maryland planter Daniel Dulany believed that the 48th Regiment's officers were guilty of "great injury and oppression of many poor people, whose livelihood depended in great measure upon their property in servants." Lieutenant Percival Brereton of the 48th Regiment, for example, had an unlucky career as a recruiter. On one occasion, he enlisted four convict servants—James Tobin, Cornelius Newhouse, Nicholas Stone, and William Beadle—whose masters were unwilling to part with them. He had also aggravated Maryland merchant Christopher Lowndes when he enlisted four servants who were outfitting his ship at Rock Creek.[37] One of the exceptions in this recruiting drive of 1755 was Chestertown, Maryland, where, according to one newspaper account, men were so eager that they were volunteering even "before the Drum was beat" for recruits—"such is the commendable Spirit of that Place!"[38]

Such moments of imperial unity were fleeting, however, as many colonists neither forgave nor forgot the British military oppression they experienced in 1755. Leading figures such as Carlyle, Dulany, and the Scottish-born doctor Alexander Hamilton (no relation to the future statesman) all condemned the rapaciousness of the British Army. Carlyle, as we've seen, went so far as to say that the British had "used us Like an Enemys Country." In the context of a slave society, many provincials such as Dulany bristled that "our people were treated as slaves" by a "licentious soldiery." Benjamin Franklin's son, William, had personally witnessed much of the "arbitrary and unwarrantable insults" of the "petty tyrants" whose abuse was "scarce to be paralleled." Ordinary colonists' lasting grievances were best expressed by John Baldwin, a tavern keeper in Chester County, Pennsylvania. In 1757, he termed the British army as "a burden upon the Country." Baldwin and his tavern toughs assaulted a recruiting party, complaining that the army only "deprived the people of their hands, and that if the Country served them right they would kick them all out, like a parcel of Scoundrells as they are, for they would never do the Country any good." Memories of British oppression contributed to a growing American consciousness and formed a strong foundation of future resistance.[39]

If the regulars treated the provinces as "an Enemys Country," it was in large measure a reflection of how many saw them that way. The two regiments that had been so involved in fighting Jacobites in the 1745 rebellion seemed to bristle at the Scots character of tidewater Virginia and its inhabitants. Rumors swirled that Captain William Polson, a Scot commanding a Virginia provincial company, had been a Jacobite "in arms in the late Rebellion in Scotland"—accusations that Polson denied and that Braddock declared to be groundless. As they marched through Maryland and Virginia in April 1755, the regulars regarded the other provincials they came upon as strange, even foreign. The account published by an anonymous British officer mercilessly lacerates the American colonists and the alien landscape. "I reckon the Day I bought my Commission the most unhappy in my Life," he wrote, "excepting that in which I landed in this Country." One letter seems to denigrate everything about the provinces as incomparably deficient to England. "America is a very disagreeable Place," he believes, for "the least Shire-Town in England has more Pleasures than the best Town in North America." The Virginians he describes as "a half-starved, ragged, dirty Set," and asks his correspondent, "you see, Sir, what a wild set of Creatures our English Men grow into when they lose Society?" He also believes that American slavery is "excessively disagreeable" and that corrupted masters are the "most troublesome Company upon Earth." The language of this British officer, and many of his fellows, expresses a sense of the American colonists' inalterable differentness. Responding to these prevailing British sentiments, Marylander Daniel Dulany quipped that "Perhaps in less than a century, the ministers may know that we inhabit a part of a vast continent, and the rural gentry hear that we are not all black, that we live in houses, speak English, wear clothes, and have some faint notions of Christianity." Such impressions of colonial Americans—abundantly communicated by many British generals and officers to London—had a powerful shaping influence on the attitudes of British ministers that subsequent successes never fully erased.[40]

BRADDOCK'S 300-MILE-LONG MARCH TO FORT DUQUESNE—the heart of his campaign—finally began on April 10, 1755, when six companies of Sir Peter Halkett's regiment stepped off from Alexandria. They marched through the Virginia backcountry toward Fort Cumberland, a distance of 173 miles from Alexandria. Colonel Dunbar's 48th Regiment had to march through Maryland soon after, on April 12. From the very beginning, the British advance was plagued by logistical troubles and uncooperative wagoners, prompting Braddock to divide his forces on either side of the Potomac River. The general reported to London that he was obliged to send Dunbar's regiment through Maryland to access horses and wagons, for the Maryland colonists refused to take their teams across the Potomac into Virginia. St. Clair had also planned to float supplies by boat from the mouth of Conococheague Creek to Wills Creek and claimed to have been building a road through western Maryland that Dunbar's troops could access. The march thus began on an improvised note: there were not enough wagons and supplies to sustain a march to the Ohio.[41]

Leaving Alexandria's modest prosperity, Halkett and his men tracked westward into a rugged area known mainly to wagoners and local farmers, along a road leading to the Blue Ridge Mountains that had only been improved at St. Clair's insistence. As late as 1774, a traveler named Nicholas Cresswell still found the area "very thinly peopled along the road, almost all Woods." It was not countryside of rural towns and villages but of isolated farms and taverns known as

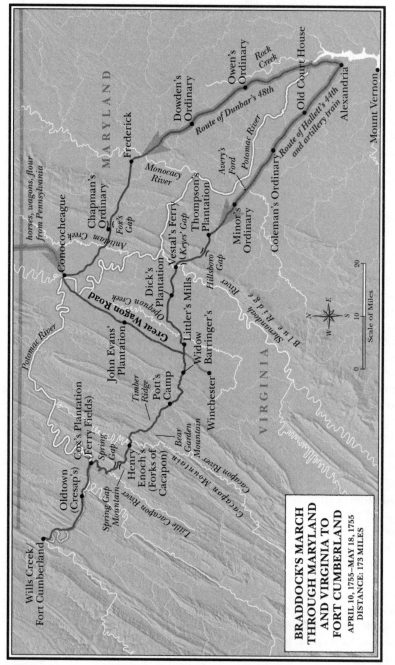

Braddock's March through Maryland and Virginia to Fort Cumberland
Glen Pawelski, Mapping Specialists, Ltd.

ordinaries. The army's route of march revealed the dispersed nature of Virginia society, with destinations like Fairfax court house, Coleman's Ordinary, Avery's Ford at Goose Creek, Minor's Ordinary, and Edward Thompson's Plantation, owned by a Quaker farmer. After passing through the conspicuous Hillsboro Gap, the troops began the steep and steady climb up their first major mountain ridge, passing through Keyes's Gap over the Blue Ridge, a "high barren mountain, producing nothing but Pines," as Cresswell recorded. From its crest, soldiers glimpsed a grand and beautiful valley below them—the Shenandoah Valley—and could see on the western horizon the endless line of ridges that they would soon cross. They encamped at the nearby plantation of Gersham Keyes, along a broad and fertile plain next to the Shenandoah River. Horses, wagons, and supplies were floated across at John Vestal's ferry, while the infantry plunged across the Shenandoah at a ford located just a few hundred yards upriver. Halkett's column marched southwestward over gentle swales and then steeply descended to the ford of Opequon Creek before encamping north of Winchester around April 16. The Shenandoah Valley had "some of the finest land I ever saw either for plough or pasture," as one British soldier admiringly wrote. The verdant landscape was dotted with new peach and apple blossoms in the spring of 1755.[42]

Colonel Dunbar's march through Maryland was dogged by transportation difficulties and by violent weather. After departing Alexandria on Saturday, April 12, Dunbar's column marched twelve miles northward to cross the Potomac River. Although the British had pressed all of the available boats into service, they still had too few craft. Braddock appealed to Commodore Keppel, who sent a party of sailors in the boats of HMS *Seahorse* and HMS *Nightingale* to ferry supplies over to the Rock Creek camp and reload them into wagons.[43] Braddock hailed Keppel as "an Officer of infinite Merit" for his manifold contributions to the expedition: four additional naval 12-pounders with 1,000 rounds from HMS *Norwich*, 50 barrels of powder, and extra salted rations. Keppel's most important contribution to the expedition, however, was a detachment of thirty-five sailors under the command of Lieutenant Charles Spendelowe, who materially aided Braddock's march. Knowing that his army counterparts were not as skilled in using block and tackle as his sailors, Keppel ordered "Thirty good Men—with a midshipman from each ship to attend the Army as far as General Braddock shall have use for them." Spendelow's sailors were to help transport the artillery over the mountains with block and tackle; to construct floats for river crossings; and to build and crew one or two vessels on lakes Erie or

Ontario when the general advanced on Niagara. The sailors were equipped for combat, as the enlisted men carried "Bright Barrel" Sea Service muskets, along with cartridge boxes, bayonets, and slings. Braddock and Keppel had managed to form an uncommonly harmonious relationship between army and navy during the disembarkation. Privately, however, Keppel entertained "strong doubts" about Braddock's ability to get his heavy artillery over the mountains.[44] Midshipman Thomas Gill of HMS *Norwich* recorded the proceedings of the Royal Navy detachment in his journal, which became one of the most vital sources on the campaign.[45]

Dunbar's march through Maryland offered only a few variations on Halkett's march through Virginia. With Spendelow's Royal Navy detachment leading the way, the men endured a fifteen-mile march on April 14. The dusty roads choked the men and sullied uniforms by the time they encamped at Owen's Ordinary. The next day brought a sweltering sixteen-mile march to another ordinary—very modest in proportions—that settler Michael Dowden had opened in 1754. America's volatile weather was fully displayed to Dunbar's men on the night of April 15 at Dowden's Ordinary. That oppressively hot day had given way to powerful thunderstorms and falling temperatures throughout the night; the next morning the soldiers awoke to blizzard-like conditions and more than a foot of snow. Cholmley's servant remembered that the snow was "so Vialent" that they had to clean it off the tents sagging under the heavy weight. The local weather added to the sense of strangeness with which British regulars perceived the land. One British officer noted that the thunder and lightning storms were so severe that "all the Elements seems on Fire." The storm halted the advance for an entire day, as the men struggled to find shelter and fodder for the horses. When Dunbar's column resumed its march to the Monocacy River on April 17, the men found it flooded from the recent rains and were forced to cross over on a float. That evening, the British made camp at Frederick, a small town founded only ten years earlier, whose largely German inhabitants were described as industrious people by Midshipman Gill.[46]

When Braddock himself finally departed Alexandria for Frederick on April 20, he was under no delusions about the expedition. He grimly assessed the "Circumstances peculiar to the Nature of the Service in America," and the delays incurred by colonists' shortcomings. "I have been greatly disappointed by the neglect and supineness of the Assemblies of these provinces," he reported to London. The colonists' promises rang hollow, and he openly charged that they "obstructed the Service" of His Majesty. In subsequent weeks,

Braddock became ever more convinced that the colonists' maxim was "never to speak Truth upon any account."[47] When the general and his staff arrived at Frederick on April 21, the campaign was on the brink of collapse. The supply situation was in utter disarray. No cattle had been delivered to the army as promised. With a paltry twenty-five wagons, the expedition could not proceed. It would be "impossible to convey the whole to Fort Cumberland in proper time," as Orme realized. Braddock appealed for assistance from Governor Sharpe when he came into Frederick on April 21. Much of the blame for wagon shortage fell on Sharpe, who had promised ample wagons, though he knew from his 1754 experience that the scarcity and high cost (£70) of a wagon and team would make it impossible for him to honor his word. It had apparently taken Dunbar's march to make Sharpe understand how difficult it actually was to procure wagons in his own province. British parties had no choice but to impress wagons and teams of horses from local farmers, sowing bitter seeds of hostility against the army. Braddock suddenly faced the mortifying and humiliating prospect that his campaign would be stillborn, as had so many previous British expeditions against the French.[48]

St. Clair charged into Frederick on the evening of April 21, heralding even more disastrous news for Braddock. He had ridden in from Fort Cumberland, where he had met a few days earlier with the Pennsylvania commissioners overseeing the construction of a supply road across the Pennsylvania frontier. Progress was minimal, and there was hell to pay for the road commissioners John Armstrong, James Burd, and George Croghan. St. Clair "stormed like a Lyon Rampant," Croghan recalled, as Sir John's accumulated anger and frustration at Pennsylvania erupted. By God, he raged, the road should have been finished by now; and as the troops were preparing to march, that "doing it now is doing nothing." St. Clair damned the Pennsylvanians for delaying the entire expedition and warned them that it "may cost them their Lives because of the fresh Numbers of French" that were pouring into the Ohio Valley. The beleaguered commissioners were mortified. The "rampant lion" threatened to "march his Army into Cumberland County to cut the Roads, press Horses, Wagons, &ca."; with "Fire and Sword," he would "treat the Inhabitants as a Parcel of Traitors to his Master," Croghan reported. St. Clair was deadly serious. Before setting out for Frederick, he had written a letter to Colonel Halkett, announcing his intention to ask Braddock for such a party of men to teach the disaffected Pennsylvanians a lesson. Otherwise, he warned, "our expedition must be at a stop."[49] St. Clair boasted to Braddock that he would "talk to the Germans in the language they have been brought up under in Germany" as he pressed wagons and supplies. He was wearing the uniform of a Hussar cavalryman that he had obtained during his service in southeastern Europe during the previous war, and which he had brought to America "for that purpose."[50] His Hussar uniform struck terror into the hearts of numerous settlers along the nearly sixty-mile route from Winchester to Frederick.[51]

Rather than St. Clair's intimidating uniform, however, it was none other than Benjamin Franklin who saved Braddock's campaign and changed the entire course of the war in America. The one-time runaway apprentice from Boston had risen to astonishing heights of fame and status by 1755. He had become a cosmopolitan figure who had been to London and gained great recognition for his scientific pursuits, including the Royal Society's Copley Medal in 1752 for his studies of electricity. Franklin had recently embarked on a political career, having been elected to the Pennsylvania Assembly in 1751 and selected as deputy Postmaster General for North America in 1753. It

Benjamin Wilson's *Portrait of Benjamin Franklin* was painted in 1759 in London. Franklin's contributions to Braddock's Expedition helped to launch his transatlantic political career, as he served as Pennsylvania's colonial agent to the British government between 1757 and 1775. Courtesy of White House Historical Association (White House Collection): 981.

was in his capacity as Postmaster General that Franklin came to Frederick, ostensibly to coordinate the regular delivery of Braddock's dispatches to the colonial governments. But Franklin was also on a political mission, for the Pennsylvania Assembly had charged him with correcting the general's "violent Prejudices" against their colony.[52]

Franklin was dining with Braddock on the evening of April 22 when the general received a report that only twenty-five wagons were available. Braddock and his officers "declared the expedition was then at an end." St. Clair exploded against the "damned people of Pennsylvania" who were all "Traiterous Frenchmen in their hearts." Franklin must have squirmed apprehensively as he heard St. Clair ask Braddock for a body of troops to seize wagons and horses, and "chastise the Resistors with Fire and Sword." When the officers railed against the British ministers for "ignorantly landing them in a Country destitute of the Means of conveying their Stores," Franklin casually observed that "it was pity they had not landed rather in Pennsylvania, as in that Country almost every Farmer had his Waggon." Braddock instantly seized upon Franklin's suggestion: "you, Sir, who are a Man of Interest there, can probably procure them for us; and I beg you will undertake it." He instantly gave him a commission—dated April 22— and the next day entrusted him with nearly £800 in gold and silver specie to procure wagons. Franklin's mission was essentially to organize an entire wagon corps for Braddock's army. He would contract for 1,500 horses and 150 wagons, which were to proceed to Fort Cumberland with full loads of corn or fodder.[53]

Braddock and Franklin had formed an instant connection, despite the brevity of their meetings. The general "was on all occasions very obliging to me," Franklin confided to his wife, Deborah. As they discussed the campaign plan recently concluded at the Alexandria Congress, Franklin delivered his prophecy to Braddock that the real danger to his march was "Ambuscades of Indians, who by constant Practice are dextrous in laying and executing them." Braddock allegedly replied to Franklin's comment, saying "These Savages may indeed be a formidable Enemy to your raw American Militia; but upon the King's regular and disciplin'd Troops, Sir, it is impossible they should make any Impression." As he prepared to depart Frederick, Franklin remained convinced that Braddock "had too high an Opinion of the Validity of Regular Troops, and too mean a One of both Americans and Indians." Although they appear in his *Autobiography*, written thirty years later, those words seem to reflect what he believed in 1755. Franklin wrote in August of that year to Peter Collinson, an English botanist, that "the General presum'd too much, and was too secure. This the Event proves; but it was my Opinion from the time I saw him and convers'd with him."[54]

In a matter of three days, Franklin had revived Braddock's flagging hopes and decisively shifted the general's political relationships with the colonies. Franklin departed Frederick on April 23, 1755, making his way toward the town of Lancaster. On April 26, he published an advertisement in both English and German that was a masterpiece of his wit and diplomacy. Addressed to "Friends and Countrymen" in Lancaster, York, and Cumberland counties, it read like a personal letter relating his recent journey to Frederick. Braddock and his officers were so "extremely exasperated" that they proposed sending "an armed Force immediately into these Counties, to seize as many of the best Carriages and Horses that should be wanted, and compel as many Persons into the Service as would be necessary to drive and take care of them." In a neighborly tone, he encouraged all "good and loyal Subjects to His Majesty" to contract their wagons out to the army. The path of least resistance would be paved with £30,000 pounds in gold and silver in compensation. The service would be "light and easy," teamsters would go no more than twelve miles a day, and they would be in the safest part of the column. Teamsters were assured—and this was no small guarantee— that they would not be "called up to do the Duty of Soldiers."[55]

Having dangled those carrots, Franklin then revealed the stick. "If you do not this Service to your King and Country voluntarily," he warned, "your Loyalty will be strongly suspected." Braddock's expedition could not be stopped, and the "many brave Troops, come so far for your Defence" would naturally reward their ingratitude with "violent Measures." He closed with an even more dire warning if Pennsylvanians failed to do their duty. In fourteen days, he was obligated to report back to General Braddock, and "I suppose Sir *John St. Clair* the Hussar, with a Body of Soldiers, will immediately enter the Province, for the Purpose aforesaid, of which I shall be sorry to hear." Pennsylvanians truly had no better "Friend and Wellwisher" than Franklin.[56]

He did not of course invent the persona of "Sir *John St. Clair* the Hussar," as is commonly believed. During his time in Frederick, Franklin had witnessed Sir John's ranting against Pennsylvania, describing him as a "most violent Creature." But it was St. Clair's Hussar uniform that had given Franklin "a hint which he immediately improved."[57] Franklin's advertisement struck immediate fear in it is intended targets. John Smith, an emigrant from County Tyrone in Ireland and a Lancaster County magistrate, wrote that "Our Country

Sir John St. Clair had obtained a uniform from the Hussars he had served with
in Italy in the 1740s. He brought the uniform to America and purposefully wore it to keep
German frontiersmen in subjection as the British Army obtained supplies and wagons. David
Morier, *Private, Regiment of Hussars "Kalnoky,"* ca. 1748. Supplied by Royal Collection Trust /
© HM Queen Elizabeth II 2014.

is seized with a very great panic lest Sir John St. Clair should be as
good as his Word." Quaker leader Israel Pemberton thought the
"Madman" St. Clair and the British Army "seemed more intent on an
Expedition against us [Pennsylvania] than against the French."[58]

When British officers received a copy of Franklin's advertisement weeks later, they thought it uproariously funny, especially the
reference to "Sir *John St. Clair* the Hussar." "I cannot but honour
Franklin for the last clause of his advertisement," Secretary William
Shirley commented. Braddock laughed "an hour together at it,"
Captain Orme related. Even St. Clair "looked on it as a kind of com-
pliment," that is, until he heard how much laughter it had provoked
among his fellow officers. Franklin's closing was, of course, a caricature of St. Clair's personality, "a very proper ridicule and resentment
of the ill Manners shown by the person described," Shirley thought.
Franklin had humorously and slyly played with the tensions between
the army and the obstinate German inhabitants, who knew a thing or

two about marauding European armies. "It answered its End tolerably among the people," he confessed, for "the Germans understood mighty well the word *Hussar*."[59]

The officers had a far greater appreciation for Franklin's contribution of 150 wagons and 262 horses that he had procured in a mere two weeks. His efforts had given the army the means to proceed over the Allegheny Mountains, instead of being stranded at Fort Cumberland, unable to advance any farther west. Like his character of Poor Richard, Franklin's industriousness had accomplished more in two weeks than the Pennsylvania government had in the previous year—a damning indictment of the government's incompetence. Franklin openly admitted, however, that even he had "fallen short of the Number of Horses," and that was perhaps his greatest failure, given the fact that horses were more important to the expedition than wagons. By the end of May, as the army prepared to march upon Fort Duquesne, Braddock had roughly 200 wagons at his disposal.[60]

The fate of Braddock's campaign now turned indispensably on the wheels of wagons contracted from ordinary settlers from the Pennsylvania, Maryland, and Virginia frontiers. The Scots-Irish settlers at Paxton, for example, contributed five wagons and twenty horses.[61] Samuel Jenkins, a young black slave of Virginia planter Charles Broadwater, drove a team during the expedition.[62] Urbanus Aschenbrenner was one of the many German immigrants to Pennsylvania, having arrived in the colony from Rotterdam in 1740 at the age of thirty-seven. He settled in Paradise Township west of the town of York and there contracted with Franklin for his wagon, team of four horses, and a driver on May 2, 1755. The terms of the contract stipulated that Aschenbrenner would carry a load of oats, corn, or forage to Wills Creek by May 20 and then "attend the Orders of General Braddock."[63]

But not even Benjamin Franklin could prevent heated quarrels breaking out between the army and the populace over the terms of the wagon contracts. He had been empowered by Braddock to appoint two wagon masters, and he lost no time in appointing his brother-in-law, John Read, and son William Franklin to appraise the value of individual wagons. William Franklin was aghast at the "Scene of Confusion" he encountered in early May (probably at York) when settlers had their wagons appraised. No one was satisfied with the estimates, and the younger Franklin heard "nothing but cursing and swearing at the appraisers, nay even threatening their lives." When he arrived at Conococheague Creek in western Maryland a few days later, William reported that "hardly a farmer in Frederic County has either Horse, Waggon or Servant to do the business of his plantation." Many settlers were "intirely ruined" as Dunbar's Regiment pressed wagons and horses into service, detained any farmers who protested, and refused to pay tavern keepers for their bills. British officers hotly swore that "they are the Law during their stay in this Country," William reported, "and that their Will and pleasure shall be the rule, by which the people shall square their Conduct."[64]

The mainstay of the expedition was the Conestoga wagon, a fusion of German and English styles that had developed in Pennsylvania in the first half of the eighteenth century.[65] It was much smaller and lighter than the sixteen heavy "King's waggons" that Braddock's army had brought from Ireland, and which could weigh as much as 2,500 pounds.[66] The Conestoga was used by farmers and traders throughout the Great Valley, with slight regional variations in Pennsylvania and Virginia styles (including the "Opekan Waggons"). The typical Conestoga had a boat-shaped box with a graceful curve rising to steeply angled end gates. The box was roughly eleven to twelve feet long and nearly four feet wide with iron hardware that was both functional and decorative. Smaller front wheels gave it maneuverability. It could carry loads of up to fifty bushels of grain (about one ton) and had a linen cloth canopy supported by eight metal bows to protect its cargoes. Franklin's contracts stipulated that each wagon was to have such a cover, as well as a sickle to cut grass. The wagoners undoubtedly brought other necessary tools and supplies, such as sets of horse shoes, nails, kegs of pitch for greasing the axles, and extra harnesses and linchpins.[67] The quality of horses, however, was far inferior to the classic wagons that they pulled. Orme dismissed most of the horses as the "offcasts of Indian traders, and scarce able to stand under one hundred weight." Orme was not exaggerating; traders along the Susquehanna River had furnished many underpowered horses to the army.[68]

The influx of so many civilians into the army created inevitable conflicts over discipline. "Those Waggoners are the most irregular set of People that I ever had to do with," wrote one British officer during the war, a judgment shared by Braddock and others.[69] The wagoners' often unruly character was captured in the journal of Matron Charlotte Browne. She had remained in Alexandria with the hospital's sick until June 1, when she journeyed by wagon with a party of British soldiers to Fort Cumberland. Her coachman, "Mr. Gore," was protective and caring of his distinguished passenger and his horses, but intimidating to anyone else who got in their way. The gruff old driver defiantly threatened that the regulars would "feel the soft end

This early nineteenth-century Conestoga wagon captures the graceful lines of its eighteenth-century ancestors used in Braddock's Expedition. Courtesy of Division of Work & Industry, National Museum of American History, Smithsonian Institution.

of his Whip" if they didn't allow Matron Browne's wagon to proceed ahead of them. The troops protested when her wagon set off first the next day, choking them with dust. But Mr. Gore stood down the British troops, saying that "he had but one Officer to Obey and she was in his Waggon, and it was not right that she should be blinded with Dust."[70]

The journey and "Extreme bad roads" had "almost disjointed" Browne, she wrote, and that was even before she had crossed the Blue Ridge. When she observed that Gore's two horses, named Black and Brown, were scarcely able to stay on their feet because of the treacherous roads, he replied that "they were right tough and good, and that everyone was not to be taken by their Looks." He insisted that Black and Brown "were as good as ever stretched a Chain." But in an ominous foreshadowing of the fate of horses during Braddock's march, Browne noted, "the poor horses no longer regard the smack of the Whip or beat of the Drum." Black never stretched his chain to Fort Cumberland, having given out during the strenuous climb up the Spring Gap Mountain northwest of Winchester.[71]

Despite Franklin's assurance that they would not be "called up to do the Duty of Soldiers," teamsters and their horses and wagons were subjected to British military discipline and order when they joined with the army. As Colonel Gage led his column across Virginia in early May, he issued orders at Thompson's plantation calling for wagoners to be "Punished" if their horses were not ready when the troops assembled. When Braddock's march across the Appalachians began in June, he organized and subordinated the wagons under a "Wagon Master General" and deputies who would oversee "forty wagons, and horse masters over 100 horses, and drovers over 7 horses." They were charged with maintenance of the army's wheeled vehicles and their drivers, who would be "punished according to their Deserts" if delinquent. Wagon masters even had to "muster their horses every night and morning" and submit a daily return, as though the horses were infantrymen during roll call. Horses, like the soldiers, had a careful order of march each day.[72]

A frontier drifter, brawler, and teamster in the expedition named Daniel Morgan personified the frontiersman's rough-hewn independence and resistance to such discipline. Morgan had been in the colony of Virginia for scarcely two years, the result of a self-imposed exile from his Welsh parents' Delaware Valley household following a dispute with his father. A migrant laborer, Morgan had worked a succession of odd jobs in the Shenandoah Valley, from farmhand to sawmill superintendent, and finally to wagon driver. To someone as youthful and headstrong as Morgan, driving a wagon was a route to independence and improvement, and wagoners like him were valued for their experience in plying the largely unimproved mountain roads between the valley and tidewater ports such as Alexandria, Dumfries, Falmouth, and Fredericksburg. Many wore long protective frocks reminiscent of the fringed hunting shirts that Morgan would one day make symbolic of the frontier rifleman.[73]

Morgan was already notorious for his coarse jesting, brawling, gaming, and drinking. He likely volunteered his wagon and team for Braddock's campaign, as it is so difficult to imagine him allowing anyone to press him into service. Subjugation to army discipline did not come easy to Morgan, and this was to have stinging consequences. During his service as a wagoner, "he was sentenced to receive five hundred lashes for insubordination to an officer, (perhaps he struck him)," according to a friend's account. Morgan afterward "in a jocular way" would tell people that "King George was indebted to him one lash yet, for the drummer miscounted one & he knew well when he did it, so that he only received 499 when he had promised him

Daniel Morgan (1736–1802). By Charles Willson Peale, from life, ca. 1794. Peale's portrait captures Morgan's dauntless character as well as the scar on his cheek from a wound he received during a skirmish with Indians in 1756. Morgan was the quintessential product of the American frontier who absorbed its independence and emulated the tactics and dress of Indian warriors. Rising to the rank of brigadier general in the Continental Army, he laid a "devil of a whipping" on the British at the Battle of Cowpens in 1781, in return for the 499 lashes he received for his altercation with a British officer in Braddock's army in 1755. Courtesy, Independence National Historical Park.

500." Multiple sources confirm the general truth of Morgan's story, though the exact circumstances of the altercation with the British officer remain sketchy (one account has none other than St. Clair himself sentencing Morgan to 500 lashes—a tribute to enduring memories of "St. Clair the Hussar"). Morgan repeated the story to his close friends, and also to a captured British officer, Captain Samuel Graham. The story first appeared in print shortly after the Americans' glorious 1781 victory at Cowpens, where the old wagoner cracked his whip over the British.[74]

In any case, and despite these setbacks, grateful tributes to Franklin's indispensable role flowed in from all points. The Pennsylvania Assembly voted its distinguished member their thanks and praised him for his prudent conduct. Franklin was the only exception to the rule of colonial intransigence and incompetence, Braddock wrote to a British minister, and "almost the first Instance of Integrity, Address and Ability, that I have seen in all these Provinces." Even St. Clair had to "draw in his Horns" and acknowledge that the army could not have sustained itself at Fort Cumberland or during the march across the Alleghenies were it not for the wagons provided by the people of Pennsylvania. The 48th Regiment's chaplain, John Hamilton, wrote to Franklin that he had saved the officers from "a worse Death than being shot": the campaign never proceeding at all.[75] Franklin also arranged for a committee of the Pennsylvania Assembly to send what amounted to luxurious care packages for the less-affluent subalterns of the two regiments. We can only imagine the officers' delight when twenty packhorses came into Fort Cumberland on May 20, 1755, bearing packages of sugar, Hyson and Bohea teas, coffee, chocolate, biscuits, pepper, vinegar, Gloucester cheese, butter, Madeira wine, rum, ham, rice, and raisins.[76]

Franklin had in the process decisively shifted the campaign's political and logistical center of gravity toward Pennsylvania, and that would have immense importance in future years. Braddock was becoming utterly disillusioned with the governments of Virginia and Maryland, and he infrequently communicated with their governors for the remainder of the campaign. Pennsylvania, however, had become Braddock's new ally, and he acknowledged that his "Chief Dependance" was on Governor Morris's province. Franklin had also set out to change the political discourse that had cast the colonists in so negative a light. He knew the weight that the army officers' representations would carry with the home government and was keenly aware of the grand imperial stage on which the campaign was being acted out. Franklin sent copies of the officers' grateful letters to a colonial agent in London, asking him to show the British ministry that "notwithstanding the Publick Reproaches thrown on this Province, as unwilling to assist the King's Forces, we had really been more serviceable to them, and had more of their Good Will than any of the neighbouring Provinces."[77]

But Franklin's contributions to the campaign were not as straightforward as he portrayed and remembered them. Despite his insistence to Colonel Dunbar that "the more you know us, the better you will like us," familiarity between Americans and regulars was breeding contempt. The experience of civilian teamsters such as Daniel Morgan and the aggrieved farmers who had horses, wagons, and servants pressed into service were sources of resentment between the army and the colonial population. Moreover, Franklin's contributions had allowed the campaign to continue, but they did not end the chronic shortages of horses and wagons that plagued it. Nor could they compensate for lost time: colonial shortcomings had stalled the entire march for many weeks. The flour ordered from Pennsylvania still had not arrived by late April and was not delivered until late June, months after it had been requested. Braddock had to send Mathew Leslie, one of St. Clair's assistants, to obtain oats and forage from Pennsylvania.[78] Colonel Dunbar's column was stalled at Frederick for nearly two weeks and did not finally march out until April 29, 1755. The entire month of May 1755 was lost, consumed in delays and transporting the enormous backlog of supplies from Alexandria, Frederick, and Conococheague to Fort Cumberland. British participants such as Thomas Gage, William Sparke, and Harry

Gordon later concluded that these cumulative delays had been disastrous to the campaign, and with good reason.[79]

As spring arrived in April and May 1755, the vast British and provincial columns streamed across Virginia and Maryland toward Fort Cumberland like tributaries flowing into a mighty river. British troops marching northwest from Winchester to Fort Cumberland began to truly experience the unique challenges of a mountain campaign in America. Sir Peter Halkett's six companies, which had been encamped near Winchester while Braddock and Dunbar were delayed at Frederick, finally arrived at Fort Cumberland on May 2, nearly a month after leaving Alexandria.[80] Colonel Dunbar's column had departed Frederick on April 29, marching eighteen miles due west on a well-established road over Catoctin Mountain, and then over South Mountain. The men camped that evening in the thinly settled area west of Fox's Gap, near an ordinary owned by Moses Chapline.[81] The following day, the red-coated column marched off South Mountain and crossed a bridge over Antietam Creek, with far greater ease than would a blue-coated army more than a hundred years later. At Governor Sharpe's request, local inhabitants had constructed the bridge, "supported on Triangular Piers made with Logs & filled with stones."[82]

Dunbar's destination was the Conococheague, a point of immense logistical importance to Braddock's expedition. Conococheague Creek, flowing southward from Pennsylvania, joined the Potomac River near the Great Wagon Road to Philadelphia and two river ferries. Both Conococheague and Shippensburg to the north were crucial supply bases on which the expedition ultimately depended. The wheat that Braddock had contracted for from Pennsylvania, for example, was slated to be shipped to Conococheague. When Dunbar had reached Frederick, he had sent the 48th Regiment's grenadier company to Conococheague to cover the movement of supplies and troops. Officers were ordered to impress any boats or canoes in the vicinity for ferrying supplies across the Potomac or floating them upriver all the way to Fort Cumberland, as St. Clair had anticipated.[83] By mid-April, Captain Horatio Gates had arrived at Frederick and taken command of his reconstituted New York Independent Company, which numbered approximately five officers and ninety-nine men. Braddock immediately ordered Gates and his company to remain at Conococheague to guard the stores while wagons hauled ammunition and supplies up from Rock Creek. Gates and his New York Independents would be among the last units to arrive at Fort Cumberland in late May.[84]

The departure of Braddock and his entourage from Frederick on May 1 suggested the changing political relationships of the campaign. George Washington had rendezvoused with the general near Frederick and then proceeded southward to Winchester. Governor Sharpe, who had fallen into such disfavor after the colony's failure to supply wagons, ceased to be a central figure in the campaign. It was symbolic that Sharpe left the company of Braddock, Orme, Roger Morris, Washington, and Shirley at Swearingen's Ferry on the Potomac River, as they continued into Virginia. Suspicious of Marylanders' intentions, Washington hoped that the three-day ride to Winchester would give Braddock "a good oppertunity to see the absurdity of the [Maryland] Rout, and of Damning it very heartily." But Braddock damned the route from Winchester to Wills Creek even more heartily, as an area "almost uninhabited, but by a parcel of Banditti who call themselves Indian Traders, and no Road passable but what we were oblig'd to make ourselves with infinite Labour."[85] The general's entourage rode into Winchester on May 3, a town of "about sixty houses rather badly built" (Washington had himself once described it as a "vile hole"). Braddock's arrival accented yet another contemptible failure of colonial undertakings, for he had come there "hoping to meet the Indians." But a conference that Governor Dinwiddie had planned with Cherokees and Catawbas was a complete bust. Braddock would remain at Winchester until May 7, awaiting the arrival of the invaluable artillery train from Alexandria. Braddock ordered that the four heavy iron 12-pounders given him by Commodore Keppel, each weighing more than a half-ton, be left behind at Winchester. Perhaps Gage's experience getting them across the Blue Ridge had convinced Braddock that it would be impossible to transport them any farther.[86]

Meanwhile, Colonel Dunbar's troops crossed the Potomac at Williams Ferry into Virginia on May 1. There was as yet no wagon road cut on the north bank of the Potomac, and Dunbar had no choice but to proceed southward up the Great Wagon Road toward Winchester. By May 3, the troops reached the neighborhood of Hopewell, a few miles north of Winchester, where British columns flowed from the north and east onto a single westward road leading to Fort Cumberland.[87] Colonel Gage, leading the artillery train, was the last Regular unit to march west from Alexandria and the most in need of horses and wagons. The artillery train, divided into two divisions, departed Alexandria on April 27, marching over the same route that Halkett had taken over the Blue Ridge at Keyes's Gap. Colonel Gage had to send out press gangs "for many miles round, and he was obliged to continue this method the whole march, having neither pasture nor forage on the road, not even at those places where it had been said to have been provided," as Orme recalled. Adjutant Daniel Disney's orderly book recorded that by May 3, Gage's train had passed over the Shenandoah River and encamped at a plantation owned by Charles Dick. In the preceding weeks, Lieutenant John Hamilton and men from Polson's Company had been busily constructing a bridge over Opequon Creek for the artillery's passage. With the heavy guns and wagons successfully across the Opequon by May 7, Braddock and his staff departed for Fort Cumberland the following day.[88]

Halkett's, Dunbar's, and Gage's columns had each marched at different intervals, taken different routes through Virginia and Maryland, and would arrive on different days at Fort Cumberland. But they all experienced the same rugged road from Winchester over the mountains toward Fort Cumberland. Their marches took them from Shenandoah's settlements into wooded mountains and steep ridges—a foretaste for the regulars of even greater tramontane hardships. After the soldiers had crossed over the Opequon Creek bridge, they marched due west across gentle swales into the Hopewell neighborhood, settled by the Society of Friends in the 1730s. Some troops encamped at Quaker homesteads such as "Widdow Littlers Mills" (an industrious complex of sawmill, gristmill, and tavern founded by Mary Littler and her husband John, who had died before 1748); they marched past the Hopewell Friends' meeting house, a log structure on a small rise south of the road; and were refreshed at a spring at "Widow Barringer's," a farmstead begun by Josiah and Mary Ballenger in 1735. Charlotte Browne recorded that Mrs. Ballenger "bid me wellcome" and that they dined on veal, greens, wine and milk punch, some of the last tastes of civilization for Matron Browne.[89]

The army columns ascended three formidable ridges northwest of Winchester: Hunting Ridge, Timber Ridge (on which the road is especially visible, like a scar), and Bear Garden Mountain. St. Clair's road then threaded the daunting Cacapon Mountain through the Bloomery Run water gap. Midshipman Gill described that strenuous route through "prodigious mountains, and between the same we crossed over a run of water 20 times in 3 miles distance." Troops, wagons, and horses enjoyed a fairly level march along the bottomlands of Bloomery Run as they descended down to the Forks of Cacapon, which one Virginia officer described as "a beautiful prospect and the best land that I ever saw." The Forks of Cacapon was one of the few open spaces in the valleys northwest of Winchester, having been cleared and cultivated by Henry and Enoch Enoch, who were among the first European settlers there. George Washington had surveyed several of the Enoch family's land claims in the 1750s and humorously referred to their current accommodations as "the Palace of Enoch Enoch's" in a letter to Robert Orme. St. Clair thought the Cacapon River was significantly large enough to order Captain Polson's company of carpenters to build a float for the passage of wagons and supplies.[90]

From the Forks of Cacapon, the soldiers had a panoramic view of the mountains that now engulfed them like cresting waves. When the troops departed Enoch's Camp, they gained a gently rising spur that brought them toward the massive Sideling Hill. They followed the rounded contours of Sideling Hill down into a gap created by Crooked Run, a small mountain stream clogged with massive rocks and boulders. Turning sharply northward, the troops climbed out of the Crooked Run valley and slowly ascended Spring Gap Mountain, where some units encamped. Named for a refreshing spring that emanated from the gap at an elevation of 1,600 feet, Spring Gap Mountain was the last and highest mountain that the troops had to surmount east of Fort Cumberland. From here it would be mostly downhill. The mountain's steep western descent tested the stamina of horses and wagoners, who strained to keep from sliding out of control. The troops then came down to the Little Cacapon River, a serpentine stream carving its way through the flat bottomlands and at times through sheer rocky cliffs and outcroppings. Indeed the stream is so serpentine that British troops had to ford the Little Cacapon as many as fourteen times before reaching its junction with the Potomac River. Nonetheless, for the rank and file of Dunbar's Regiment, the cool waters were quite refreshing on a "prodigiously hot" afternoon.[91] They finally halted at another pocket of settlement along the level plain where the Little Cacapon emptied into the Potomac River. In 1750, a thirty-year-old settler named Friend Cox and his brothers Isaac and Gabriel had carved out small plantations in the area. Washington had surveyed Friend's tract at the mouth of the Little Cacapon in that year. Cox's plantation offered a tranquil encampment site with "plenty of corn, oats, and stock of all kinds."[92]

The Potomac River crossing was a laborious task, as men, supplies, artillery, wagons, and horses were loaded onto floats constructed earlier by Captain Polson's Virginians. The army enjoyed relatively easy marches along the Potomac's northern bank all the way to Fort Cumberland. Eight miles east of the fort, many detachments

According to Sir John St. Clair, Braddock's Road occasionally went "in the Channels of the Rivers," such as the Little Cacapon River, shown here. Braddock's forces had to ford the Little Cacapon as many as fourteen times before coming to an encampment site along the Potomac River known as Cox's plantation. Author photograph.

halted at the plantation of Colonel Thomas Cresap, a trader and Ohio Company member who acted as a commissary during the campaign. His settlement was called Oldtown, an earlier Shawnee community named Opessa's Town, after its principal leader. One Virginia officer thought Cresap's plantation "delightfully situated," on a "piece of low ground entirely surrounded by the mountains, the prospect very romantic, high rocks on the sides of the mountains some hundreds of feet perpendicular to the Potomac River." Cresap had strategically situated his trading post directly on the Great Warriors' Path, the principal north-south path for Indian warriors in the eighteenth century, and near a convenient ford of the Potomac River. Washington's first encounter with Indian peoples happened at Cresap's back in 1748, when he witnessed an Indian war party composed of thirty men dancing and drinking there. Old habits of revelry died hard in Cresap's Oldtown: the British war party passing through on May 8 and 9 held a horse race to entertain Braddock.[93]

On May 10, 1755, Colonel Dunbar's column departed Oldtown for Wills Creek, a march that Midshipman Gill thought "very pleasant by the water side." At high noon, the 48th Regiment's fifers and drummers sounded the "Grenadiers' March," a robust musical accompaniment for General Braddock and his staff, escorted by Captain Stewart's light-horsemen, as the scarlet-clad entourage dashed along the elongated column. While the British troops continued on their way, they heard the seventeen thunderous booms from Fort Cumberland, saluting General Braddock as he made his grand entrance. At 1:00 P.M., the troops were halted and formed in a circle to hear the special instructions of Colonel Dunbar. He informed the army that "as there were a number of Indians at Will's Creek, our Friends, it was the General's positive orders that they do not molest them, or have anything to say to them, directly or indirectly, for fear of affronting them."

The column of British regulars and sailors arrived at the fort at 2:00 P.M., where they found (in the words of Midshipman Gill) "Indian men, women and children, to the number of about 100, who were greatly surprised at the regular way of our soldiers marching, and the numbers." Braddock's march across Maryland and Virginia had underscored his confrontations with British Americans. At Fort Cumberland, Braddock and his regulars prepared to encounter the original Americans.[94]

AS FORT CUMBERLAND CAME INTO their view, British troops beheld a grand panorama framed by the Potomac River and the Allegheny Mountains beyond. Like a ship run aground on the eastern front of the Alleghenies, Fort Cumberland symbolized the geographical limits of Britain's imperial expansion in mid-eighteenth-century America. It sat atop a bluff overlooking the junction of Wills Creek and the Potomac River, with Wills Mountain towering above it just a short distance west. As Dunbar's regulars splashed across Wills Creek and up the steep embankment into the fort on May 10, they must have thought it an odd frontier post. Fort Cumberland was "so irregular," one visitor later quipped, "that I believe Trigonometry cannot give it a Name." The large rectangular fort had four quadrilateral bastions equipped with ten artillery pieces, but it also featured a longer arrowhead-shaped appendage containing five log officers' quarters, and three parallel rows of twenty-seven barracks, making the fort more than 400 feet long and 100 feet wide. Two flanking buildings outside the palisades housed a commissary and a hospital.

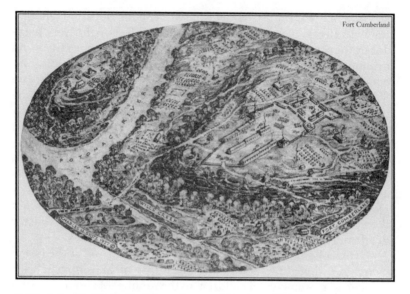

Fort Cumberland, by Charles Morse Stotz. Courtesy of Thomas and Katherine Detre Library and Archives, Senator John Heinz History Center, Pittsburgh, Pennsylvania.

Matron Browne called it "the most desolate Place I ever saw," and British engineers thought the fort militarily indefensible.[95] Yet it was instrumental in sustaining Braddock's campaign and the hopes of its namesake, the Duke of Cumberland. Though it is often claimed that Braddock christened the outpost after his patron, the name "Fort Cumberland" was definitively in use long before he arrived there.[96]

By the middle of May 1755, the vicinity of Fort Cumberland was bulging with more than 2,000 regulars, sailors, provincials, camp followers, wagoners, and Indians. Colonel James Innes commanded the fort's small garrison and acted as virtual quartermaster, paymaster, and postmaster along Braddock's communication line back to Virginia.[97] White canvas tents were spread across the bottomlands and plateaus nearest the fort, while the Ohio Iroquois encamped in the woods a quarter of a mile away. Fort Cumberland became a bustling scene of enterprise and industry as Braddock's men prepared for the next phase of the campaign. Regulars of the 44th and 48th regiments and the Independent Companies practiced platoon firing during field days; Ensign James Allen of Halkett's regiment drilled the "Americans," who still appeared "languid, spiritless and unsoldierlike" to Robert Orme. A carpenter from HMS *Seahorse* oversaw the building of a bridge over Wills Creek. Blacksmiths beat out tools for pioneers and workers. Bakers baked biscuits in large ovens for the march ahead. Saws squared timbers, hammers clanked, officers shouted commands, muskets snapped, British drums beat by day, and Indian drums by night.[98]

British regulars and Native Americans encountered each other for the first time at Fort Cumberland, offering both groups opportunities for wonder, astonishment, diversion, and aversion. "In the day [the Indians] were in our Camp," Midshipman Gill recorded, "and in the night they go into their own, where they dance and make a most horrible noise." Curiosity drew British officers and soldiers to the Indians' camp and dance circles, "round which we the Spectators stood, as at a Cricket-match in England." They commented, usually unfavorably, on the Natives' exotic appearance, clothing, bodily painting and decorations, weapons, lodges, musical instruments, and religion. One British officer wrote that the Indians' war dance, like everything in America, was "in the Stile of the Horrible." The Indians' "Ball" or "Masquerade" invoked "Terror, Fear, and all dreadful Passions," he thought, but "no pleasing ones." At one point, Native warriors sang "the most horrid Song or Cry" that this officer had ever heard, which would "strike Terror into the stoutest Heart." Determined to prevent any indiscipline or harmful incidents, Braddock forbade the troops from selling liquor to the Indians and entering their camp, on pain of court-martial or corporal punishment. Notwithstanding his stringent orders, both officers and soldiers continued to trade and interact. When Pennsylvania's provincial secretary, Reverend Richard Peters, visited Fort Cumberland in late May, he reported that British officers had created "high Quarrels" among the Natives, as Indian women brought "money in Plenty which they got from the Officers, who were scandalously fond of them." Peters righteously condemned the "Consequences of this Licentiousness" to General Braddock. Charles Lee of the 44th later claimed that he had married Bright Lightning, the daughter of Kaghswaghtaniunt (one of Braddock's scouts), was adopted by the Iroquois, and given the name "Boiling Water." While the name was entirely befitting Lee's volatile disposition—his English friends called him "Boiling Water" long after the war—it is possible that Lee first interacted with Bright Lightning at Fort Cumberland, as she was indeed present there in 1755.[99]

Diplomacy with Native Americans was one of Braddock's major endeavors during the four weeks that the army remained at Fort Cumberland—and restoration of Indian lands continued to be the grand theme of his diplomacy, as it had been in his messages to the Six Nations through William Johnson. There were many conferences, private meetings, and public ceremonies involving Braddock, his officers, Ohio Iroquois (Mingoes), and Delawares from the Ohio Country. The Iroquois families at Wills Creek that spring had been refugees from their own country for nearly a year at Aughwick, George Croghan's frontier homestead on the Pennsylvania frontier. Croghan had escorted the warriors, numbering about forty men, and their families to Fort Cumberland in early May. The paltry number of Indians surprised Braddock, who asked Croghan privately where the rest of them were. He had been expecting around 400 Cherokees and Catawbas to be awaiting him, as Governor Dinwiddie had promised. Braddock took the initiative to request that Croghan communicate invitations to both the Delawares and Shawnees in the Ohio Country, which the trader immediately did.[100]

May 12 marked the first of at least three major public conferences with the Indians—"an Asembaly with our Indiens," as Captain Cholmley's batman recorded. All officers were ordered to report to Braddock's tent at 11:00 A.M., in what must have been a resplendent scene of scarlet red coats, glimmering gorgets, and gold lace. When Scaroyady and the Ohio Iroquois came into the area, an officer in the general's guard barked the command, "Rest your-Firelocks!" at which the men crisply shifted their muskets to the right, leaning back on their right foot in a respectful salute.[101] A copy of the actual speeches that Braddock delivered to the Ohio Iroquois at the first major meeting on May 12 is preserved in the UK National Archives. Its significance never fully appreciated, this crucial document discredits recent stereotypes of Braddock's diplomacy with Indians. "Brothers," the speech begins, "With this String of Wampum I wipe open and clean your Eyes that you may see the Sun plainly, & to hear what we have to say to you; as we have always spoken with our Hearts & Minds freely to you, I hope you will open your Hearts & Minds freely to us." The speech rehearses the paths that had brought them to that point: the fight against the "treacherous & perfidious French" that had begun the previous year, and how the King of Great Britain had sent "one of his great War Captains to conduct his Army against this treacherous Invader of Your Peace." Braddock's speech expresses friendship for the Six Nations, Delawares, Twightwees, and other allies, and promises that any previous wrongs would be forgotten and buried under "this great mountain." The General notably promises the Indians the "happy repossession of you & ourselves" on their Ohio lands, which he calls on them to fight for. We know beyond any dispute that these words were actually spoken at Fort Cumberland, because Royal Navy Midshipman Thomas Gill was an eyewitness to the proceedings and accurately paraphrased the main points in his journal. Braddock "shewed them the greatest Marks of attention and esteem," Captain Orme recorded, "and conferred with them agreeably to their forms and customs."[102]

Agreeable to Native expectations that conferences should be unhurried and considered a meeting of hearts and minds, the British called for the next public congress with the Indians to be held on May 18. The occasion was a somber one, as the British had earlier that morning laid to rest Captain Henry Bromley of the 44th Regiment, a veteran of fourteen years' service who had recently died of a fever. The coffin passed between two ranks of guards at the position of resting upon their arms with muskets inverted. Braddock then offered condolence for the death of "our deceased Brother" Tanaghrisson, the Half King who had died the previous fall: "in hopes that you would willingly join with me, to revenge him, I cover his Death with this BELT." He again appealed to the Ohio Iroquois warriors to take up the hatchet and encouraged them to send their families back to Aughwick, where he pledged "in the King's Name" that the Pennsylvania government would maintain them. He then offered gifts to the Ohio Iroquois warriors and their families: guns, powder, and ammunition to the warriors, and typical trade goods such as woolen strouds, linen, knives, beads, rings, and vermilion.[103]

Most significantly, Braddock once again assured the assembled Natives that he intended to restore them to their rightful possession of their lands:

> I declare unto you, in the Presence of your Chiefs and Warriors here assembled, and according to the Instructions I have received from the great King your Father, that if you will unanimously grant me your Assistance, I will put you again in Possession of your Lands, of which you have been dispossessed by French Deceit, and cheating Tricks, and secure unto you a free open Trade in America, from the Rising unto the Setting of the Sun. It is very well known, that I have no particular Views, nor Design, but that of serving mutually the Interests of the King of England, your Father, and of the Six Nations, and their Allies; and I promise you, to be your Friend and Brother, as long as the Sun and Moon shall last.

Braddock, the Indians' "Friend and Brother" who pledges to restore their land rights again challenges conventional stereotypes of the general's diplomacy. His speeches of May 18 were also recorded in a register book, and Midshipman Gill's journal again verifies that those words were spoken. Gill noted, for example, that three wampum belts and one wampum string were presented, which corresponds *precisely* to those mentioned in the register.[104]

On the evening of May 19, the Ohio Iroquois leaders Scaroyady, Kaghswaghtaniunt, and Silver Heels came to Braddock's tent to deliver their responses and thoughts, which Gill faithfully recorded in his journal:

> that they were greatly obliged to the Great King their Father, who had been so good as to send us all here to fight for them, and that they would all give their attendance, and do what was in their power of reconnoitring the country and bringing intelligence. That they were obliged to the General for expressing concern for the loss of the Half-King our Brother, and for the presents he had given them.

Braddock again pledged to them that "he was their Friend, and never would deceive them." The British and the Indians celebrated their alliance that evening, as Ohio Iroquois warriors symbolically declared war by taking up Braddock's hatchet and singing the war song. That morning, Braddock had intentionally ordered all regimental drummers and fifers to report to the head of the artillery train after beating retreat (the ceremonial end to daily duties). He had planned a formal demonstration for the Indians of the destruction that the British artillery would rain down on the French. Drums and fifes played the standard army tune, "Point of War," as Royal Artillerymen rammed live rounds into a few heavy howitzers, light 12-pounders, and small Coehorn mortars. The musical and martial firepower "astonished and pleased the Indians greatly." Native warriors concluded the evening's festivities with the war dance, expressing "the exploits of their ancestors, and warlike actions of themselves," a spectacle that equally astonished and pleased their British allies.[105]

A total of twenty-four Ohio Iroquois warriors eventually joined Braddock's Expedition; only eight warriors remained with the army for its entirety; the other sixteen joined the army by July 10, too late to see any action. Though few in number, those who joined Braddock's expedition were stalwart fighters who had been with Washington at Fort Necessity in 1754, and all but one of them can be correctly identified.[106] Scaroyady (or Monacatootha) was described by Reverend Richard Peters, who visited the fort that May, as "a Warrior, a brave and stout Man, and has an Aversion to the French, and wants without any good Reason, to strike them." He was the Indian "who attends the

General," suggesting an advisory role.[107] Scaroyady's son, name unknown, joined his father and he proved to be an intrepid warrior and scout. The Seneca warrior Kanuksusy was the son of Queen Aliquippa, and received the English name "Newcastle" following the Monongahela. Washington had met this "great Warrior" in 1753 during his journey to the French Fort Le Boeuf.[108] Kaghswaghtaniunt (also known as "'Belt of Wampum' or 'White Thunder' who always keeps the Wampum") was described as one of the "Chiefs now entrusted with the Conduct of Publick affairs among the Six Nations" on the Ohio and "amongst the greatest Warriors."[109] His stepson, Aroas, or Silver Heels, fought at the Monongahela and had perhaps the most distinguished combat record of any eighteenth-century Indian warrior. He later spoke of his "Love for the English in general" and was deeply concerned that the war he saw brewing would bring harm upon his English brothers.[110] Gahickdodon (or Kahuktodon), the son of the deceased Tanaghrisson, also participated in the campaign. He was also known by the English name "Johnny" and was among the surviving warriors who came to Philadelphia in August 1755.[111] Finally, there was Skowonidous, also known as "Jerry," who was possibly Delaware in ethnicity but had lived in the Ohio Country and eventually made his home among the Tuscaroras.[112] Another veteran negotiator in Braddock's expedition was Andrew Montour, a *métis* of French Canadian and Iroquois parents, praised by Washington for his "hearty attachment to our glorious Cause," though it is unclear whether Montour acted as an interpreter, scout, or warrior.[113]

The allegedly controversial meeting between the general and the Indians took place on May 27, 1755, when Delaware leaders arrived at Fort Cumberland in response to Croghan's invitation. The Delawares came to Braddock's tent and "told him that they were come to know his intentions, that they might assist the Army," as Midshipman Gill recorded in his journal: "the General thanked them, and said he should march in a few days towards Fort Duquesne." George Croghan wrote that the Delawares "promised in Council to meet the General on the Road, as he marched out, with a number of their Warriors." The other British account of the meeting, Robert Orme's journal, also reported that the Delawares promised to meet Braddock during the march, "which they never performed." A freak storm may have brought the meeting to an early end, as it "blowed and rained hard" at noon that day.[114]

None of those three eyewitness accounts remotely indicates that Braddock purposefully spurned the Delawares, as was suggested in a later narrative written by Pennsylvania settler Charles Stuart, whom the Delawares had taken captive in 1755. Stuart wrote a speech supposedly given by the Delaware leader Shingas regarding his meeting with Braddock at Fort Cumberland. The Delawares had asked the general "what he intended to do with the Land if he Cou^d drive the French and their Indians away." Braddock supposedly answered, "that the English Shoud Inhabit & Inherit the Land." When an astonished Shingas queried whether Indian allies to the English would be able to live, trade, and hunt in the Ohio Valley, Braddock bluntly replied that "No Savage Shou^d Inherit the Land." The following day, Braddock was even more demeaning and dismissive, saying that "he did not need their Help and had No doubt of driveing the French and their Indians away."[115]

Such words would have been wanton violations of the king's explicit orders that Braddock cultivate good relations with Indian chiefs. Braddock's surviving speeches and correspondence and other British accounts provide a more accurate sense of how Braddock loyally attempted to fulfill those royal instructions with the Delawares. Braddock had promised the Natives that he would forget any past transgressions and receive them as brothers if they joined with him. The general's personal sentiments toward the Delawares were clearly revealed in a letter he wrote to Governor Morris that spring. He asked Morris to send them messages that he was coming to "restore that Country to our Allies, the Indians, & to protect them in ye Enjoyment of it." He believed that they would "be very usefull to me in the Course of the Expedition." Finally, Braddock brought along a wagon load of Indian presents in the march to Fort Duquesne, an indication of how he planned to engage in diplomacy with the Ohio Indians after driving out the French.[116]

Modern historians have uncritically taken Stuart's narrative at face value, for Shingas's potent words appear to provide a Native perspective and sustain a popular portrait of Braddock as an arrogant European officer. But Shingas's account is not an authentic Native voice and amounts to hearsay taken from a narrative written years later by a Pennsylvania settler. Eyewitness accounts from Fort Cumberland do not corroborate Stuart's version of events and often contradict key details (there were no Shawnee leaders present, for example, as Stuart claims). To whatever degree Stuart's account reflected Shingas's views, it occurred in the highly charged context of a warrior speaking to captives whose families he had just killed and whose settlements he had destroyed in November 1755. Shingas wanted to justify the Delawares' attacks on their former Pennsylvania allies and prove that "the English and not the Indians were Cause of the Present War." Shingas's Braddock may have been a metaphorical personification of the Delawares' long-standing suspicion that the English intended to permanently dispossess them.[117]

Two other captivity accounts seem to corroborate Stuart's version of Shingas's encounter with Braddock, but both of them point directly to French propaganda as a source of the Delawares' caricature of an imperious British general. The first is a deposition by twenty-two-year-old John Craig who was taken captive in Pennsylvania in February 1756 and adopted by Shingas as a son. When Craig challenged his Indian father about murdering the Pennsylvanians, a heated argument ensued. Shingas "replied that what he said was all a Lie for that *the Indians had found out by Letters taken from the English* after the Defeat of General Braddock that the two Crowns of England and France had struck up a Bargain to divide between them the Lands belonging to the Indians." Another colonial captive, Elizabeth Fleming, related a claim of Tewea, also known as Captain Jacobs, that Braddock "threatened to destroy all the Indians on the Continent, after they had conquered the French." But Fleming's narrative continues that the Delawares "were informed by the French" of such plots against their lands. In language nearly identical to the captives' accounts, the French in 1754 were already warning the Indians that the British were coming to "cut you entirely off from the face of the earth and then divide the lands between us." The three captives' accounts may indeed reflect the Delawares' perceptions, but they clearly point to a French influence on their caricature of Braddock, based on those "Letters taken from the English."[118]

In any case, the myth of Braddock as an ethnocentric, racist general who contemptuously spurned potential Indian allies, refuted their claims to the land, and scorned their military abilities, simply cannot be sustained by eyewitness evidence. The belief that Braddock or the British somehow must have alienated the Indians developed only after the 1755 battle, as people began to cast blame upon Braddock for having only eight Indian warriors with the army. It was *assumed*, as one British officer thought, that there "must have been wrong proceedings some where" with the Indians. Benjamin Franklin's *Autobiography* falsely accused Braddock of having "slighted and neglected" the Indians and dismissed their abilities. It had also become painfully clear that if the British "had fifty Indians instead of Eight," as Croghan put it, "that we might in a great measure have prevented the Surprise that Day of our unhappy Defeat."[119]

What had gone wrong? Braddock had been openhanded in his gifts to the Natives during the conferences and could not be accused of tightfistedness. One of William Johnson's officers, Lieutenant John Butler, visited Fort Cumberland and reported back that the general had "received [the Indians] very kindly" and given a "handsome present." Veteran Indian negotiator George Croghan also affirmed that Braddock kindly and generously ordered him to "let them want for nothing." Nor did the general violate some unchanging set of Native diplomatic protocols, which the experienced colonists themselves almost always failed to honor. Braddock never forbade his Indian allies from scalping, as one account proposed. To the contrary, Braddock emulated standard colonial procedure by offering cash bounties of £5 for every enemy scalp brought to him.[120] Perhaps the costliest and least generous result of these meetings was Braddock's insistence that the Ohio Iroquois remove their families to Aughwick. Along with Colonel Innes, Braddock believed that the presence of Indian women and children would be "very troublesome in the Camp," despite William Johnson's warning that provisions for warriors' families "must be promised & fulfilled to them." But the Indians themselves had also insisted upon returning to their Aughwick settlements, as Richard Peters observed.[121] Nor were Native families alone in their removal from the camp. On the very day that Braddock urged the Iroquois families to return to Aughwick, he limited the numbers of civilian women who could accompany the army and also sent the remaining women to Pennsylvania. Supply shortages at Fort Cumberland, not ethnocentrism, were likely the preeminent considerations in Braddock's mind concerning both Iroquois and British families. Whatever the reasons, Braddock's request redounded to his detriment. Around forty Iroquois warriors promised to rejoin the general during the march but did not, fearful as they were of "the French coming to their Cabbins to destroy their Families." The sixteen warriors who kept their promise when they came to Dunbar's Camp on July 10 arrived far too late to have any impact.[122]

It was Braddock's singular misfortune to campaign in America when the Virginia, Maryland, Pennsylvania, and South Carolina colonies had already diminished if not destroyed British hopes of obtaining Indian allies. The general correctly assigned the failure of British diplomacy with the Indians in 1755 to "the conduct of our Governments to these Nation's for some Years." Decades of relentless settlement expansion, intrusions on Indian hunting grounds, ineffective colonial diplomacy, and outright land frauds such as Pennsylvania's "Walking Purchase" had effectively alienated many potential Native allies. The Shawnees were already at war with the English in 1754, as a result of South Carolina's imprisonment of six warriors. William Johnson explained that "our Indian Interest had many years ago been wounded; it had been long on the decay, had been recently under a very lax injudicious management—Our Power by the Indians, was little respected—Our intentions greatly suspected—they were exasperated by the avarice and dishonesty of our Indian Traders. The claims on their Lands and the unrighteous methods (in many instances) made use of to obtain them, enraged and allarmed them in the highest degree." Johnson suspected that the Iroquois viewed "Mr Braddocks enterprize, as one encroachment making War upon another." Neither French nor British claims to the Ohio Valley were valid or worth fighting for.[123]

Braddock also received little help from his vaunted supporting cast of skilled frontier negotiators, including Croghan and Andrew Montour, whose influence among the Indians in 1755 proved to be nonexistent. Colonel Innes also undercut Braddock's diplomatic initiatives with the Indians. Braddock's secretary, William Shirley, wrote that when they arrived at Fort Cumberland they "found Indian Affairs so ignorantly conducted by Col. Innes" that novices could have done better. William Johnson's agent, Lieutenant Walter Butler, similarly reported that the Iroquois messengers with him were "greatly disgusted at Col. Innes' behaviour & displeased with the whole of his treatment of them," and that was not the first account that Johnson had received of Innes's meager "Arts of Manageing" the Indians. Croghan also believed that Braddock had been misled by Innes, who advised the general to send away all but ten of the Iroquois who would be "very troublesome on the march" (given Braddock's strenuous efforts to recruit Natives, and Innes's lack of experience, it is unlikely that Braddock acted on his advice). Innes later tried to deflect criticisms of his conduct onto Braddock, writing to Dinwiddie in 1756 that the general "could not endure to see [the Indians], and ordered him to let no more come to his Tent."[124]

However, there is a crucial and overlooked reason for the failure of Braddock's diplomatic initiatives—an event that took place in Indian country far to the south. The killing of six Mohawk emissaries and renewed warfare between the Iroquois and their southern enemies in 1754 and 1755 foreclosed the possibility of Indian allies joining Braddock's campaign. In late 1754, Monacatootha had sent a speech to the Catawbas from the "Warriors of the Six Nations, Dalaways, and Shainnas," delivered by Captain James Mackay when he returned to South Carolina following the Fort Necessity capitulation. Monacatootha had invited Catawba warriors to come northward to Winchester in the spring of 1755—"when the Turkeys gobble"—to confirm the peace between them. The Catawbas received the message in early January 1755 along with a delegation of six Mohawk envoys who had been sent by the eminent Mohawk leader Hendrick Theyanoguin to the Catawbas, Chickasaws, and Cherokees. The envoys were "treated like Brothers" by the Catawbas. But a few days after their departure, Chickasaws ambushed and killed five of the six Mohawk emissaries, and Cherokees later waylaid and killed the sole survivor. This incident renewed warfare between the northern and southern Indians in early 1755. As the Cherokees became fearful of attacks on their communities, they became less inclined to support the British in Virginia, and the Six Nations were reluctant to join Braddock's forces, because southern Indians were rumored to be present and they would all "spill one anothers blood in his camp," as William Johnson explained.[125]

A large party of Cherokee warriors had, in fact, started northward to join Braddock's army in the spring of 1755. Nathaniel Gist, a Virginia trader and son of Christopher Gist, had journeyed southward to persuade his Cherokee trading partners to join the British campaign to Fort Duquesne, and he was initially successful. But a dispute between Gist and another rival trader named Richard Pearis doomed his efforts. During their travels northward, Pearis challenged Gist's credentials, telling the Cherokees that he had not been authorized by the Virginia government. That was apparently all that the Cherokees needed to hear to dissuade them from going any farther. Finally, Governor Glen did nothing to encourage Cherokee participation in the expedition against Fort Duquesne and instead held a major conference with them at Saluda in mid-June 1755. The deaths of six Mohawks, a petty rivalry between two frontier traders, and the actions of a narrow-minded royal governor had destroyed the slender hope that General Braddock could recruit larger numbers of Indian allies.[126]

Moreover, the lack of substantial commitments from Iroquois, Delaware, Shawnee, Cherokee, or Catawba warriors was a reflection of British imperial weakness in early 1755. Larger contingents of Native scouts would undoubtedly have formed a bulwark of protection for Braddock's column, provided advance warning of enemy threats, and gained timely and detailed intelligence of French activities at Fort Duquesne. Of all the contributions that Native warriors might have made to the expedition, intelligence gathering was perhaps the most critical, for Braddock's knowledge of actual French and Native strengths at Fort Duquesne was poor (estimates ranged from 200 to 1,200, with more than 3,000 French and Indian forces in theater).

For that reason, the general's eight Indian scouts were immediately sent out to gain intelligence of the French when the conferences ended. Monacatootha and his young son ventured all the way to Fort Duquesne in late May and early June, bringing back accurate reports on French activities: 170 French and Indians were preparing to depart to harass the British column; low water on Rivière au Boeuf had delayed an additional 200 men; and the French had recently emplaced six cannons in the fort.[127]

Gaining accurate intelligence of the enemy was one of the most problematic aspects of campaigning in the woods of eighteenth-century America, in which rumors and distortions abounded. Braddock had appointed Christopher Gist as his "head Guide," along with other seasoned frontiersmen and Indian traders such as George Croghan, John Fraser, Thomas Burney, and John Walker, who certainly knew the Forks of the Ohio very well (such guides were defined as "country people in the neighborhood where the army encamps...to give you intelligence"). Walker was praised by St. Clair as "the best Woods man I ever knew."[128] But as the general and his army prepared during those May days at Fort Cumberland, obtaining good intelligence remained a paramount challenge. "We have no certain accounts of the French on the Ohio," Washington lamented. Rumors of French reinforcements coming down from Canada made him fear that "we shall not take possession of Fort Duquesne so quietly as was imagined." Braddock had earlier gained a very accurate map of Fort Duquesne and its defenses courtesy of Robert Stobo's espionage, and the British used Stobo's information to plan possible avenues of besieging the fort. But the French had sent Stobo to Quebec in September 1754, depriving Braddock of a potentially valuable spy in their midst. Another principal conduit of military intelligence was deserters and prisoners whom the French once called "live letters," because of the detailed information they freely revealed to their captors. Braddock lacked any such human intelligence, for not a single French deserter or prisoner was taken by the British during the march to Fort Duquesne, while the French gained valuable intelligence from multiple English deserters and captives. Braddock and other senior British officers instinctively distrusted the Indians' information, though he admitted that it was the "only Intelligence I have been able to obtain of the Number of French in the Fort." Without a large contingent of Indian scouts, Braddock lacked much in the way of actionable intelligence on the numbers and locations of French and Indian forces during his march. He knew generally that the French garrison was "at present inconsiderable, and that the

French expect large Reinforcements," as Braddock wrote to Newcastle, which he hoped would be diverted toward the other British threats to Niagara and Crown Point.[129]

Along with poor intelligence, the campaign was being doomed by troubling deficiencies in supplies and shortages of wagons and horses that were increasing as the army prepared for the over-mountain march from Fort Cumberland to Fort Duquesne. Braddock seemed amply justified in his charge that "the Disposition of the People, not only puts back the Designs of his Majesty, but also doubles the expences."[130] Dinwiddie could not deliver 600 cattle that he had contracted in North Carolina in April, and an unscrupulous middleman subsequently demanded a higher advanced price. When the cattle finally arrived in Virginia in October, Braddock's campaign had come to its fatal conclusion and the cattle were generally "unfit for use."[131] Even salted meat could be hard to come by. Thomas Cresap earned a reputation as a "Rattle Snake Colonel and a D—d Rascal" because of his incompetent contracting. Colonel Cresap had provided twenty barrels of salt beef to the army shortly after its arrival at Fort Cumberland. But Royal Navy officers Lieutenant Spendelow and Midshipman Gill inspected the casks and instantly called for the nauseating meat to be buried. There was no pickle in the meat, because porous "dry casks" had been foolishly used, instead of "wet casks" actually capable of holding brine. Better news came on May 20, in form of ninety-one wagons from Pennsylvania, along with twenty packhorses bearing Franklin's gifts for the younger officers. Mathew Leslie's efforts in Pennsylvania also yielded sixty wagons full of forage and oats bound for Fort Cumberland. But the army's supplies at Conococheague were greatly mismanaged by Daniel Cresap (Thomas's son), as he failed to send enough of the Pennsylvania flour supply and then spoiled the remaining flour by storing it in barrels made of green, unseasoned wood. If Cresap had been a "French commissary he could not have acted more to their interest," Braddock angrily reported. The expedition was delayed yet again, as Braddock had to detach more wagons and horses back east to bring up supplies.[132]

Lack of horses continued to be the greatest threat to the campaign. As Robert Orme recalled, "we lost our horses almost as fast as we could collect them," so that the army was "every day less able to undertake the extraordinary march we were to perform." These shortcomings again underscore the crucial role of logistics, highlighting how difficult it might have been for the British to sustain a permanent presence in the Ohio Valley. The delays also compounded the ravaging toll that diseases were exacting on the encamped army.

By early June, there were sixty-six men in the hospital and more than a hundred listed as sick but present.[133]

With the march set to begin shortly, General Braddock called two councils of war in late May to discuss with his officers the order and disposition of his march to Fort Duquesne. The general emphasized the critical necessity of adequate flanking protection during the march, amounting to one-third of his effectives, and outlined careful procedures for defensible campsites, which the council uniformly approved. Braddock called a second council two days later, probably on May 27 or 28, when the Delawares were also in camp. He had just received intelligence of French movements past Fort Oswego and was anxious to begin the march. If the army waited for wagons and horses to return from the Conococheague, he lamented, the march would again be delayed. The council unanimously approved Braddock's plan to expedite the march by detaching 600 men under Major Russell Chapman and a working party under St. Clair to begin building the military road from Fort Cumberland to the Great Crossing of the Youghiogheny, where they were to construct a supply magazine. Finally, the council approved Braddock's recommendation to march out of Fort Cumberland in three separate divisions led by Colonel Halkett, Lieutenant Colonel Ralph Burton, and Colonel Dunbar.[134]

"The troops were now joined," Robert Orme wrote in his journal toward the end of May. This was true, with the exception of Captain Edward Brice Dobbs's North Carolina ranger company, which was the last unit to arrive at Fort Cumberland on May 30. Dobbs was a lieutenant in the 7th Royal Fusiliers, though his captaincy was a provincial commission from his father, Governor Arthur Dobbs, a staunch advocate of British westward expansion and Ohio Company shareholder. Dobbs's company, composed of "Stout fellows" in blue regimental coats and red facings, were "not a Despicable reinforcement" in the eyes of one Virginian. One of the teamsters in Dobbs's company was twenty-year-old Daniel Boone, who personified the expansive and restless energies of colonial America and its frontier settlers who had absorbed Indian ways in hunting, dress, and tactics. Born in Pennsylvania in 1734, Boone and his family had migrated southward to the Yadkin Valley of North Carolina by 1750. He had already engaged in the first of his many "long hunts" by 1755 and would hear of a promised land called "Kanta-ke" while serving in Braddock's Expedition.[135]

The full strength of Braddock's 2,500-man army was finally apparent unto itself for the first time, imparting a sense of incredible potency to those who witnessed it. As the army prepared to move out of Fort Cumberland in late May and early June, Britons in the home country and in America were taking stock of Braddock's Expedition. Many were presumptuous of victory. Governor Dinwiddie expressed complete confidence to Braddock that "the French will surrender on Sight of your Forces." Others' sentiments ranged from cautious optimism to outright despair over the difficulties that the army still faced. Sir John St. Clair applauded Braddock, who "pursues his Schemes with a great deal of vigour and Vivacity," though St. Clair feared the possibility that they would be "obliged to abandon our Conquests for want of Sustenance." Richard Peters came away from the camp with a foreboding sense similar to that of Benjamin Franklin. The Anglican minister, interestingly, was the only person who warned Braddock of the real threat he might face: "if there should be an Army of Indians conducted by French Officers, he would not, with all his Strength and Military skill, be able to reach Fort Duquesne without a Body of Indians and Several Companies of Rangers." William Shirley Jr., the general's own secretary, based on his several months' experience, wrote even more damningly of his chief: "We have a [general] most judiciously chosen for being disqualified for the Service he is employed in, in almost every respect," though he thought Braddock "may be brave for ought I know, and he is honest in pecuniary Matters." Shirley also believed the whole enterprise to be rotten, from the British ministry's "ill concerted" plans down to the inept colonial governments. Such clashes of personality and opinion are ineluctably part of the politics of command in any army, but these unrefined initial judgments of the general's or the campaign's inherent weaknesses would only grow more hardened.[136]

The erratic relationship between George Washington and Edward Braddock was a summary reflection of the larger confrontations between British colonists and the British Empire during the 1755 expedition. Washington certainly relished the opportunity to demonstrate his loyalty and to "push my Fortune in the Military line." As a member of the general's military family, he knew that victory at Fort Duquesne might bring the royal commission that he yearned for. The affable and respectable Washington formed fast friendships with officers like Colonel Gage and Captain Orme, who wrote of their affection and esteem for him. Washington's harmonious participation in the campaign, however, had come—as we've seen—at the "degrading" cost of resigning his colonelcy. Even as he loyally served the king, Washington was becoming Americanized: "We can not conceive that because we are Americans, we shou'd *therefore* be deprived of the

Benefits common to British Subjects," he complained to Dinwiddie. His service as a volunteer aide-de-camp had only temporarily masked the essential inequality that he perceived in the British government's privileging of royal officers, and the seeming inability of meritorious provincial officers to gain royal commissions. As Braddock's aide-de-camp, Washington was "freed from all commands but his, and give his Order's to all, which must be implicitly obey'd." The young Virginian returned the "Affection" that his military father bore for him, and wrote that Braddock treated him with "freedom" and "respect" during the thirty-odd days that he was with the general. In contrast to those who thought Braddock imperious, Washington characterized him as informal and open, as he "uses, and requires less ceremony than you can easily conceive."[137]

As the sole colonial American on the staff, however, Washington was inevitably drawn into political disputes in which he had to defend the honor and patriotism of His Majesty's provincial subjects. In a letter to William Fairfax of June 7, Washington recalled that during his time at Fort Cumberland, he had heated disputes with Braddock, who "charges all his Disappointments to a publick Supineness, and looks upon the Country, I believe, as void of Honour and Honesty." These disputes were "maintaind with warmth on both sides especially on his." Washington found the general, at least in his opinion of colonial governments, obdurate.[138] Washington also accurately predicted the toil, sweat, and tears that would accompany the expedition. On the very day that he left Mount Vernon, he wrote that the march would be "very tedious indeed" and "regulated by the slow movements of the Train." It would present "difficulties to which they had never been accustomed in regular Service, in Champaign Countries"—by which Washington meant the open and level fields of the Netherlands. Whenever a "proper occasion" presented itself, Washington tried to impress upon his chief and his principal officers of "the mode of attack which, more than probably, he would experience from the *Canadian* French, and their Indians on his March through the Mountains & covered Country." But "so prepossed were they in favor of *regularity* & *discipline* and in such absolute contemp[t] were *these people held*, that the admonition was suggested in vain," as he recalled years later. Yet the young Washington bore a greater resemblance to Braddock than the elder cared to remember. The young aide was just as impatient as the general to begin the campaign, dismissive of "trifling" French and Indian threats to the army, and willing to divide the army for a rapid advance on Fort Duquesne.[139]

What did Edward Braddock think of his campaign during quiet moments of reflection in his headquarters tent? Countless historians' impressions of Braddock as an ignorant and complacent officer are simply not borne out in his personal correspondence. In his own words: He knew well the "Difficulty I fear in the Service I am entrusted with." He knew that his column would require constant flank security, "to prevent any Surprize from the Indian Parties, which is always very much to be feared, notwithstanding all the Precautions that can be taken." He foresaw that the campaign might end in logistical failure, given the chronic want of forage, horses, and wagons, in which case, "the Men must Starve and his Majesty's Arms be dishonoured (should they prove successful)." He realized the enormous challenge of a long march "thro' an uninhabited Wilderness over steep rocky Mountains and almost impassable Morasses."[140] Two months of campaigning had left Braddock an increasingly disillusioned but realistic officer of the Crown who tried his level best to execute his orders.

Still, Washington's point about the general's obdurateness toward the colonies holds true. Braddock's letters and their bitter invective against America played out on a larger political and imperial stage. The general's grasp of American realities had awakened him to the fault lines of empire, and his letters to the ministry (some of which were also read in Parliament) reinforced prevailing attitudes that there was something amiss in the constitution of British America. "The Conduct of these Governments seems to be without a Parrallel," he wrote to Robinson, adding that he would never finish his letter if he were to list the "innumerable Instances" of colonists' dishonesty. His bitterness had sprung from repeated confrontations with the independent-minded American assemblies. There was something wrong in British America as a whole, and Braddock would not be the first imperial official to denounce the "false dealing of all in this Country" which he looked upon "as void of Honour and Honesty," according to Washington. He bitterly condemned "the folly of Mr. Dinwiddie & the roguery of his assembly" as he increasingly cast his "Chief Dependence" upon Pennsylvania. Braddock further denigrated the governments of Virginia and Maryland that had "promised everything and had performed nothing," while Pennsylvania had "promised nothing and had performed everything," as he related to Franklin.[141] Colonial circumstances had shaped virtually every aspect of his campaign: from the commencement of the march (far later than he had hoped); the composition of the army (fewer Indian allies than he had expected); the disposition of the march (fewer horses and wagons than he needed); and the supplies for his troops (deficient and delayed). "I hope however in spite of this that we shall pass a merry Christmas together," he wrote to Governor Morris. Notwithstanding so many disappointments and broken promises, Braddock was determined to press forward and overcome them. Surprisingly, his counterpart at Fort Duquesne, Captain Contrecoeur, had an equally grim and despondent assessment of French fortunes as he prepared to defend la Belle Rivière.

CHAPTER 4

Beaujeu's Voyage

French and Indian Forces Converge at Fort Duquesne,
April–July 1755

C APTAIN CLAUDE-PIERRE PÉCAUDY DE Contrecoeur, the forty-nine-year-old commandant of Fort Duquesne, yearned for release from this troublesome outpost of French dominion. Much had changed for Contrecoeur since having, as he put it, "the good fortune of chasing out the English on the 16th of April, 1754." By June 1755, the burden of responsibility that now rested on his shoulders far outweighed those fleeting laurels. The veteran officer felt in his bones that this would be his final campaign, and he was happy to receive the Marquis Duquesne's confirmation that another officer would soon assume command in his stead. Devout in his Catholic faith, Contrecoeur prayed that God would somehow make his departure from the Ohio Valley as blessed as his entrance when he seized the Forks of the Ohio for his king.[1]

Fort Duquesne was the centerpiece of New France's strategic grip on the upper Ohio Valley. A few weeks earlier, on May 23, 1755, Contrecoeur was preparing to report to the Marquis Duquesne that the works of the governor's eponymous fortress were nearing completion.[2] From the commandant's quarters across from the guardhouse, Contrecoeur viewed the nearly completed fort, projecting strength over the strategic Forks of the Ohio. Fort Duquesne was also the largest of all French posts in the Ohio Valley, and imposing enough in its military engineering to require any attacking enemy to besiege it. On a contemporary French engineer's map, it appears as an imposing square fort with four bastions, covering an area of 24,000 square feet. The fort appeared self-sufficient, with a bake house, a powder magazine, a blacksmith's forge, officers' quarters, and cadets' quarters. Outside the ramparts, cornfields were being prepared for planting. Surmounting the view were six 6-pounder iron cannons that Contrecoeur had recently emplaced in May 1755 and that Scaroyady's son had seen during his reconnaissance. It now contained a sufficient number of cannons to threaten any British assault.[3]

However, Contrecoeur understood better than anyone that he commanded but a mere façade of French power. A veteran officer like Contrecoeur could not blind himself to the significant weaknesses of the post he commanded, located on a peninsula and within potential range of artillery from the north. Flooding was a perennial problem, and in February of 1755, spring waters had flooded and caused damage to the fort. He knew that the English were assembling a force of 3,000 with a powerful train of artillery to attack him. Even the fort's designer, Captain François-Marc-Antoine Le Mercier, acknowledged that it was "too small to be able to sustain a siege." Robert Stobo, the British prisoner and spy, significantly noted that "the Guard consists of Forty Men only and Officers. None lodge in the Fort but the Guard except Contre Coeur; the Rest in Bark Cabins around the Fort." Contrecoeur, his officers, and a few dozen men might comfortably reside within the fort, but as the French engineer Gaspard-Joseph Chaussegros de Léry reported in 1755, the fort could, "during a siege, with much inconvenience to them, hold two hundred men," and a third of those men would be exposed on the ramparts. The fort's quite limited ability to sustain a sizable permanent garrison was revealed each winter, when the garrisons were reduced to skeleton crews. Unless reinforcements arrived in the spring and summer, Contrecoeur would face the British with only 258 officers and men who had remained during the winter of 1754–1755, along with 100 Native allies. The total French force among all of the Belle Rivière outposts at the beginning of 1755 consisted of 9 officers, 19 cadets, and 437 Marines and militia.[4] At best, Le Mercier concluded, the fort will "oblige the enemy to make some preparations and to open trenches" for a siege. But in Léry's judgment in April 1755, everything depended on reinforcements coming from Montréal. "It is hoped," he advised, "that they will be numerous enough to engage the enemy before the formation of a siege." He placed his faith not on defending the fort from within but from outside its walls.[5]

Rumors had circulated that Contrecoeur was "inadequate for a difficult command," as one French officer reported. A mysterious

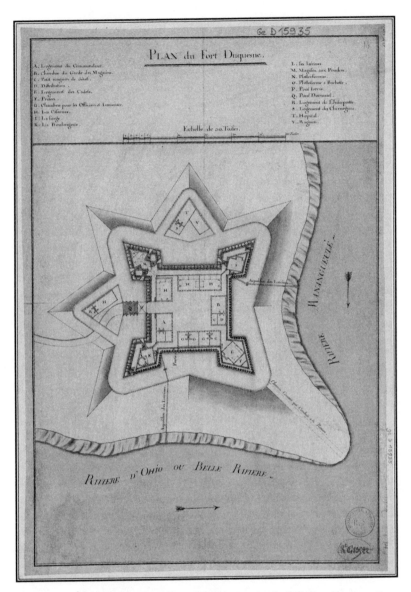

Plan du Fort Duquesne, 1755. Courtesy of Bibliothèque nationale de France, département
Cartes et plans, GE D-15935.

physical accident in February 1754 had apparently begun to take its toll on his health. Like an old soldier who had been away far too long, he was more determined than ever to devote himself to his wife, his two little girls, his two younger sons (an officer and cadet in the *troupes de la marine*), and the affairs of his seigneury. Through five years of expeditions and constant deployments to various outposts in New France, "I have lost everything I had been able to put in my household during the 26 years since I had one, which means that today my family is scattered," as Contrecoeur explained to Governor Vaudreuil. Besides, as he and his men knew well, service on la Belle Rivière was extremely taxing, and he was not sanguine as he contemplated the impending clash of arms.[6]

Contrecoeur's deeply apprehensive state of mind in mid-June 1755 was captured by a letter that he received from one of his subordinate officers, Lieutenant Antoine-Gabriel François Benoist, the commandant at Presque Isle. Contrecoeur's previous letter must have been heavy with anxiety, which Benoist summarized sympathetically, beginning with the fact that "no food had been delivered to the little fort. You do not know how to account for such a thing; you cannot sleep for worrying about it; you are terribly fearful; and you look upon the necessity of abandoning Fort Duquesne, for lack of food, as if it were an actual misfortune which already threatened you." At that moment Contrecoeur believed that the greatest threat to Fort Duquesne's existence was not Braddock's approaching hosts but more basic lack of sustenance.[7]

Contrecoeur's anxiety was eased somewhat by his standing orders from the Marquis Duquesne to remain in a defensive posture: Louis XV's desire was to "most carefully to avoid giving them [the English] any just cause of complaint" and to "stand on the most exact defensive" unless directly threatened by British forces.[8] While senior French officials such as Duquesne took great precautions, they were also contemptuous of English military abilities. Duquesne jested to Contrecoeur in April, "I shall not believe Fort Duquesne will be besieged until you have sent word to me that the English have opened the trench [i.e., parallel]. . . . I advise you to relax also, for the English on this continent are not inured enough to war to lay any sieges." He thought that the French had the advantage of time: "To raise an English troop more time and threats are necessary than for levying Canadians." Also, both Duquesne and Contrecoeur were highly skeptical that the English could get heavy artillery across the Appalachian Mountains. To succeed in breaching the fort's defenses, he believed, "they would need cannon of a caliber which it is impossible to think of transporting." According to another French officer, Duquesne had dismissed intelligence of enemy preparations as "an empty boast, and said that it was only a flash in the pan." Such complacency, filtering down through the ranks, was perhaps as great a threat as lack of food.[9]

But Duquesne was more than bluster; he was also the aggressive governor-general who had initiated the French fortifications at Presque Isle and Rivière au Boeuf in 1753 and the seizure of the Forks of the Ohio in 1754. For all of his contempt for British abilities, both he and Contrecoeur deserve much credit for their efforts to reinforce the Ohio posts and to seek the aid of Native warriors. Duquesne knew that in February 1755 the French court had sent a substantial reinforcement to New France, in the form of six battalions of *troupes de la terre* (French Army regulars). Their commander, Maréchal de Camp Jean-Armand, Baron de Dieskau, was in many respects the French counterpoint to Braddock: an experienced regular army officer leading a substantial commitment of regulars from Europe.[10] Duquesne had also strengthened the Belle Rivière posts in the early spring of 1755 by encouraging Canadian Iroquois from the St. Lawrence Valley and Ottawa and Sauteux (Ojibwa) Indians from Michilimackinac to come to their French Father's aid. Finally, he sent convoys of cannon, men, and supplies to reinforce Fort Duquesne that spring, led by one of the most remarkable officers in the history of early America.

Captain Daniel-Hyacinthe-Marie Liénard de Beaujeu was an experienced officer who led the largest detachment to the Ohio Valley. Contrecoeur counted Beaujeu as "my dear friend," and the two would form a command partnership that betrayed no hint of petty jealousy or rivalry. Duquesne had appointed Beaujeu to assume command of Fort Duquesne, relieving Contrecoeur, a testament to his faith in the officer's merit and trustworthiness. Beaujeu's odyssey to the Ohio Valley is a story that parallels and rivals that of General Braddock's march in its significance. Yet in most historical accounts, he remains only a bit player or caricature: the Canadian in Indian dress who leads the reluctant warriors against Braddock at the Monongahela. Some nineteenth-century descendants and hagiographers attempted to lionize Beaujeu, referring to him as the "Hero of the Monongahela" and the "conqueror of Braddock," the very embodiment of French Canadian military glory and nationalism. These early writers portrayed Beaujeu as the primary architect of French victory, even arguing that "the savage nations venerated and adored him as the equal of the Manitou."[11] Myths aside, there is much evidence in his surviving journals and correspondence that he was uncommonly effective, fearless in combat, and adept in the art of persuasion in councils with Natives. His career prepared him for his impending confrontation at the Monongahela.

Beaujeu's expedition to la Belle Rivière between April and July 1755 illustrates the contingencies involved in the near-miraculous assembly of French and Indian forces at Fort Duquesne by early summer. The logistical challenges that French commanders faced in their military campaigns on northern waters have not been fully appreciated. The story of Beaujeu's convoy in particular also illustrates the central question of whether French forces would even arrive at Fort Duquesne in time and in sufficient number to defend it from Braddock's advance. French reinforcements would ironically be delayed and nearly done in by the water routes that were supposed to guarantee them such strategic freedom of movement. Beaujeu's convoy was part of the most powerful coalition yet assembled for battle against British forces—but the French and Indians first had to assemble and unify that coalition. By early July 1755, hundreds of Native warriors from twenty different nations and communities converged on the Forks of the Ohio, changing the course of the 1755 campaign and of the French and Indian War. Their story became inseparable from Beaujeu's when together they sallied out of Fort Duquesne against the British.[12]

Beaujeu's military career personified that of the sons of many French Canadian elite families. He was born at Montréal in 1711 to Thérèse-Denise Migeon de Branssat and Louis Liénard de Beaujeu, a family with noble status and strong royal patronage, which facilitated the father's efforts to achieve wealth in New France. Beaujeu's father had been the commandant at the distant post of Michilimackinac, at the strait connecting lakes Michigan and Huron. He dabbled in the fur trade and fought in the Fox Wars, a fierce conflict that the French and allied Indians waged against the Fox Indians over control of that trade. According to a contemporary French account, he was "loved and feared by the french, respected by the Indians, and applauded by the Missionaries" for aggressively attacking the illicit brandy trade at Michilimackinac. Daniel-Hyacinthe-Marie continued in his father's footsteps, most likely entering the ranks of the marines at an early age. We can only imagine the part the distinguished experiences of his father played in his own understanding of military service, Indian relations, and New France's strategic situation. Although his earliest officer commissions and dates of service are obscure, Beaujeu was a lieutenant by the age of thirty-five in 1746, and a captain two years

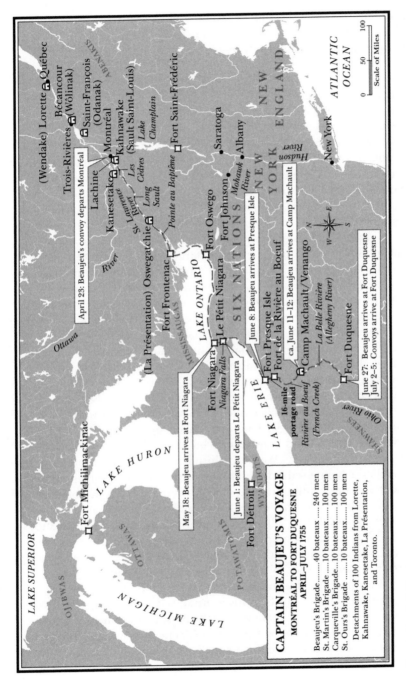

CAPTAIN BEAUJEU'S VOYAGE

MONTRÉAL TO FORT DUQUESNE
APRIL–JULY 1755

Beaujeu's Brigade.........40 bateaux ..... 240 men
St. Martin's Brigade.......10 bateaux......100 men
Carqueville's Brigade.....10 bateaux......100 men
St. Ours's Brigade.........10 bateaux......100 men

Detachments of 100 Indians from Lorette, Kahnawake, Kanesetake, La Présentation, and Toronto.

April 23: Beaujeu's convoy departs Montréal

May 18: Beaujeu arrives at Fort Niagara

June 1: Beaujeu departs Le Pétit Niagara

June 8: Beaujeu arrives at Presque Isle

ca. June 11–12: Beaujeu arrives at Camp Machault

June 27: Beaujeu arrives at Fort Duquesne
July 2–5: Convoys arrive at Fort Duquesne

Captain Beaujeu's Voyage
Glen Pawelski, Mapping Specialists, Ltd.

later. His signature was one of several affixed to a 1748 conference in which Iroquois delegates asserted their sovereignty and independence before the governor-general and other leading French officials in Québec. By 1755, the young Beaujeu had received an education in the lessons of empire through his military and diplomatic service as a marine officer.[13]

One overlooked episode in Beaujeu's life provides insight on his later actions at the Monongahela. In a lengthy journal, he detailed his combat experiences in a brutally cold winter campaign in Acadia in 1746 and 1747. The fighting between British and French forces in Acadia often involved conventional operations, such as the New England and Royal Navy forces that besieged the fortress at Louisbourg in 1745; but *petit guerre* actions—irregular warfare—were also common, and Beaujeu gained experience in both operations during the campaign. A French expedition led by Captain Nicholas-Antoine Coulon de Villiers targeted an outpost of roughly 500 New Englanders ensconced in a fortified winter encampment at Grand Pré on Acadia's western coast.[14] Beaujeu recorded that "our force was composed of around 300 men, including Indians." As acting major of the party, Beaujeu had responsibility for dividing the assault force into 10 different detachments, each composed of anywhere from 25 to 50 Canadian militia and Indians. The expedition departed from Beaubassin and marched for twenty days through blizzard-like conditions to the vicinity of Grand Pré. The attack occurred in the snowy, pre-morning darkness of February 11, 1747. Beaujeu himself killed one of the British sentinels who spotted the French columns—striking down his enemy filled him with "la joye," he wrote—and combat ensued as the British garrison desperately fought back. "We heard heavy musket fire all around us," Beaujeu remembered in his journal, and "we saw everything in movement around us without being able to distinguish if it was our men or the enemy." The chaos of battle engulfed the Canadian force, especially after Captain Villiers fell, gravely wounded by a musket shot above his forearm. Command fell to Beaujeu, who rallied his men and continued the assault. The New England forces suffered heavy losses in comparison to the Canadians and surrendered the next day. Beaujeu had proven himself to be the kind of natural combat leader who, in the words of his journal, "aller aux coups de fusils que nous entendions" (goes toward the musket shots that we heard). The attack also presaged the kind of tactical formations of small French and Indian detachments that Beaujeu would employ at the Monongahela.[15]

On April 23, 1755, Beaujeu's large convoy set out from Montréal in icy and snowy conditions. It consisted of 40 laden bateaux carrying 240 men, one of whom was Jean-Marie Landriève des Bordes, a commissary officer who had been ordered to inspect the fortifications and supplies at the Belle Rivière posts along with Beaujeu.[16] The convoy had to be utterly self-sufficient: it carried provisions for four months, along with all the equipment and supplies necessary to sustain the posts' needs. Beaujeu's men could not forage for supplies among a civilian population along the route, and they were not to drain the posts they were sent to reinforce. The convoy also carried 26 horses, which were soon to be a necessity during one of the most difficult portages these men had ever encountered. Beaujeu's convoy was followed by three others that departed Montréal in May 1755, each composed of roughly 10 bateaux and 100 men: the brigades of Lieutenant Jean-Jacques Gorge de St. Martin, Lieutenant Claude-Antoine Drouet de Carqueville, and Ensign Pierre-Philippe de Saint-Ours.[17]

New France's Native allies in the St. Lawrence Valley were also mobilizing against the British. Atiatoharongwen, a Mohawk warrior from the town of Kahnawake near Montréal, was one of many Indian allies who opposed Britain's imperial ambitions in 1755. Born on the New York frontier to an Abenaki Indian woman and an African slave around 1740, he was captured by a Kahnawake war party in 1745 during an attack on the settlement of Saratoga and adopted into the Mohawk community. The illustrious military career of this Catholic, French-speaking Mohawk likely began at the Monongahela.[18] He may have been among the twenty-two Kahnawake Iroquois, twenty-two Lorette Hurons, eighteen Kanesetakes, and twelve Nipissings who departed for la Belle Rivière in May 1755. Six Iroquois from the mission of La Présentation and twelve Mississaugas from Toronto joined the Kanesetake party en route. Significantly, each of these Native contingents was escorted by an officer and often included parties of Canadians with personal ties to those particular Native communities. One such Canadian officer was sixteen-year-old Ensign Joseph-Dominique-Emmanuel Le Moyne De Longueuil, who had led contingents of Lorette Hurons to the Ohio Valley in 1754 and 1755 and had fought at Fort Necessity.[19] These convoys and Indian contingents represented significant reinforcing of the Belle Rivière posts, totaling 617 Canadian troops and another 100 Indian warriors drawn from the St. Lawrence Valley. The hard part was getting them to Fort Duquesne.[20]

While many have viewed dominance of interior waterways as one of New France's greatest advantages, few have appreciated the

Kahnawake, also known as Sault Saint Louis, was one of many Canadian Iroquois towns in the St. Lawrence Valley whose warriors fought at the Monongahela. By the early 1750s, some Kahnawake Mohawks were permanently residing in the Ohio Valley. *Veue de la Mission du Sault Saint Louis*, eighteenth-century sketch. Courtesy of the Bibliothèque nationale de France.

sizable labor and logistical challenges involved in the passage of Beaujeu's men to the Belle Rivière in time to confront Braddock's troops. French officers like Contrecoeur were under no illusions about the challenge. They also knew that their posts were at risk of abandonment if supplies did not come through. Men, supplies, and communications had to cover more than 700 miles to get from Montréal to Fort Duquesne; moreover, by 1755 the supply line from Presque Isle to Duquesne had existed for only one year, making it more of an experiment than a reliable lifeline.[21]

Supply issues were every bit as precarious for French troops in the Ohio Valley as they were for the British. Navigation of the St. Lawrence, Great Lakes, and the upper Ohio River was perilous, exhausting, and cumbersome for men, boats, and cargoes alike, involving numerous portages, back-breaking labor, and strenuous paddling. After the "great freeze-up" ended in mid-April, the St. Lawrence River was ice-free and again open to French forces and supplies heading west to reinforce la Belle Rivière. Montréal remained the jumping-off point for the convoys, as it had been since its beginnings as a fur

John Trumbull, *Captain Joseph Lewis or Louis, of the Oneida Indians*, ca. 1785–1786, pencil sketch, Yale University Art Gallery. The military career of Atiatoharongwen (c. 1740–1814) spanned the French and Indian War, the Revolutionary War, and the War of 1812. According to oral history from his daughter, Mary Kawennitake, he fought against the British at the Monongahela in 1755.

trade entrepôt. The town's storehouses were ultimately the most important supply base for the western posts. Decades of experience plying the turbulent waters of the region had yielded the bateau, a craft of exceptional utility and durability. French bateaux were large, flat-bottomed, shallow-draft boats eminently suitable for hauling large cargoes and heavier loads such as cannons. Constructed of red oak and white fir, these vessels were sturdy and durable in rapids and rough waters. A contemporary measurement shows that a typical bateau was 36 feet long, with a beam of more than 6 feet, and was 2½ feet in depth. Native contingents going toward Fort Duquesne used either elm or birch-bark canoes, though smaller French detachments used bark canoes as well.[22]

The various detachments, including Beaujeu's, departed Montréal in the late spring of 1755, putting in at Lachine, opposite Kahnawake, so that they could bypass Sault St. Louis (the rapids of St. Louis). The French bateaux-men paddled west over Lac St. Louis, past Île Perrot, toward the next series of rapids west of Montréal. At Les Cèdres, Beaujeu's men towed and poled their bateaux through the dangerous, churning rapids and rocks that seemed as though they were "boiling into what look like abysses," as Captain Pierre Pouchot of the French Army described them. "The bateau has to be controlled by a rope held by several men," he observed, while "other men go into the water up to their shoulders in order to move it forward & haul it round the headland." Boatmen knew that one false move would throw them into Le Trou—as one particularly infamous rapid was known by name—a watery hole and grave. In addition, the prevailing southwest winds could be "furiously violent," as were the "violent squalls with lightning" that arose. Reefs, shoals, and rocky obstacles made "progress downriver dangerous & difficult": they could break a canoe's keel, split its seams, and fill the vessel with water. French flotillas became divided because of rapids, winds, storms, and fog. Men were at constant risk of drowning, as in the case of the unfortunate "nine men coming from Belle Rivière [who] had fallen into the Rapide du Buisson" in the year 1754. The word "violence" recurs with uncommon frequency in French travelers' accounts of the St. Lawrence, a telling indication of how greatly they felt themselves at the weather's mercy.[23] For those who went down to the waters on ships, there were rituals that invoked higher powers than nature. At a narrow channel of the Thousand Islands called Le Petit Détroit, veteran voyageurs symbolically baptized "those who have never traveled up the river" at Pointe au Baptême. It was a reminder to army officer Louis-Antoine de Bougainville of how deeply "naval customs [were] established in this colony," similar to the ritual crossing of the equator. The point was indeed auspicious for the French flotillas, for after threading their way through the archipelago of the Thousand Islands, with "channels between them [that] are all deathtraps," they had passed the worst nautical obstacles in their westward journey.[24]

When Beaujeu's convoy came to Fort Frontenac and Lake Ontario in early May, he knew that there was yet another Scylla and Charybdis to thread. French officers were ordered—especially if they were leading Indian warriors—to "pass by the north of Lake Ontario to remove all their desire of stopping at Choueguen." Independent-minded Indian allies might seek out opportunities for trade among the British at Fort Oswego, which the French called Chouaguen, on Lake Ontario. Beaujeu's convoy and the others were ordered to put part of their cargoes on larger barks when they reached Fort Frontenac so that they could quickly bypass Chouaguen and avoid contact with the British. On the other hand, venturing far out onto Lake Ontario had dangers of its own—violent and sudden storms and squalls "so rough that the canoes ran a risk of being broken," as Chaussegros de Léry recalled. "I had no idea of the whereabouts of the canoes. It is true the lake was so rough that there were times when the mainland was not visible."[25]

Passing near Oswego proved too great a temptation for one dis-affected Frenchman, Jean Silvestre, who refused to go to the Ohio Country for the fur trade; "he did not care to risque it in a Country then in dispute between the two Crowns," according to his deposi-tion. Silvestre provided detailed intelligence of French movements and numbers to the British. His estimate of the total strength of Beaujeu's convoy (950 men) was uncannily accurate. Oswego itself functioned as a listening post astride French communication lines. And British officers Hitchen Holland and John Bradstreet were lis-tening. Both men noted when Beaujeu's convoy passed Oswego in mid-to-late May. Taken together, Silvestre's and Bradstreet's intelli-gence would decisively affect the 1755 campaign when it came into General Braddock's hands.[26]

By May 18, 1755, Beaujeu had arrived at Fort Niagara, at the junction of the Niagara River and Lake Ontario. Niagara was the key to the western parts of New France: it was "the most frequented [passage] of the American continent," according to Pierre Pouchot, the fort commandant. In particular, the eight-mile portage around the Niagara Falls and Gorge was one of the most vital points in North America, controlling trade and military movements into the interior of the continent.[27] Beaujeu's memories of the years 1749 to 1751, when he was the commandant at Niagara, undoubtedly influenced his thinking.[28] Beaujeu's garrison had been a constant source of frus-tration and grief. He railed against the "garrison composed of old drunkards from Montréal" that he commanded and how difficult it was to "repress the insolence" of his soldiers.[29] The condition of his garrison was also a problem, ranging from his arsenal of unreliable trade muskets, to bedbugs infesting the soldiers' barracks.[30] Beaujeu described how La Maison—the trading house constructed in 1726—"will never be sturdy and [is] always in danger of falling into the Lake (Ontario)." It was still that way in 1755.[31]

Beaujeu's two years at Niagara provided him a strategic educa-tion in North American affairs. His tenure there involved frequent diplomacy with the Seneca Iroquois and a vast array of Native peo-ples trading at the fort, imparting to him a wealth of experience in negotiating with New France's Indian allies and a healthy apprecia-tion for the limits of French power. The Senecas never allowed the French to forget that they had allowed them to build the outpost on their territory, and many of Beaujeu's letters describe the indepen-dence of New France's Indian allies. On one occasion, Indians came to express their goodwill to Beaujeu, before—gallingly—heading on to trade with the British at Oswego, something he admitted "I have

Fort Niagara, Youngstown, New York. The French constructed this stone trading post in 1726–27 in Seneca Iroquois country at the strategic junction of Lake Ontario and the Niagara River. Captain Beaujeu was commandant at Niagara from 1749 to 1751, and it was there that Captain Contrecoeur received Governor Duquesne's orders in early 1754 to seize the Forks of the Ohio. Author photograph.

worked in vain" to stop.[32] But through all these problems, Beaujeu's letters also displayed a dauntless and resolute spirit. Damning the consequences, Beaujeu once slapped a Seneca named Théon8ayné in irons for stealing from French traders' canoes along the portage, then had the audacity to tell assembled Seneca leaders who were upset over the "imprisonment of one of their brothers" that he was "surprised that you addressed me in this manner." Beaujeu maintained a hard line and kept Théon8ayné in the prison until he made restitution for the stolen goods. Both sides were able to salvage their pride and defuse the situation when Théon8ayné broke out of the French jail and sent Beaujeu a horse as restitution.[33]

Beaujeu's time at Niagara had not only taught him the limitations of French power but also the logistical difficulties of the Niagara portage—the exhausting labor of transporting boats and cargoes.[34] To avoid the perilous Niagara gorge and the falls, French boats and supplies had to be unloaded at a point a few miles south of Fort Niagara (today, Lewiston, New York) and hauled eight miles overland to Le Pétit Niagara, or the Little Portage (a small post on the Niagara River upriver from the falls). It would take Beaujeu's convoy the better part of two weeks to clear the eight-mile Niagara portage, in comparison to the mere three weeks it had taken to travel nearly 400 miles from Montréal. Beaujeu was at the Little Portage on June 1, 1755, still awaiting the other brigades and detachments led by St. Martin, Courtemanche, Longueuil, and Montigny, which did not arrive at Niagara until June 11–12. The older bateaux in the convoy had taken a beating, as Beaujeu learned upon close inspection. Canoe repairmen were typically on hand at portages to repair damaged canoes with gum or pitch and prepare them for refloating. But Beaujeu remained leery of using them and only partially loaded them with cargoes for the next stage of the journey.[35]

On June 8, 1755, skirting the south shore of Lake Erie, Beaujeu and his convoy finally saw Fort de la Presque Isle coming into view on a high bluff as they entered Presque Isle bay. It was a substantial square fortress with four bastions, with squared horizontal timbers making up the fort walls and palisade.[36] It had taken the various French detachments, including Beaujeu's, six weeks to cover roughly 500 miles to Presque Isle. But once there, the French advance slowed to a crawl, as it would take them nearly a full month to advance the mere 200 miles to Fort Duquesne. Lieutenant Antoine-Gabriel François Benoist, the garrison commander of Fort Presque Isle, had earned accolades from the French army officer Louis-Antoine de Bougainville as "a very truthful man if there is one in Canada." But the Presque Isle command was draining him, he complained, and he soon found himself "terribly disgusted" with the exhausting monotony: "continual making of lists to prevent dual consumptions, wide awake at 3 A.M., in bed at 10 P.M., eating nothing but salt pork," and worse yet, "about to run out of wine. That is my situation."[37]

To British observers, the French invasion of the Ohio seemed a quintessential example of New France's strategic advantages. But among French officers, the Belle Rivière quickly earned a reputation as "indisputably the weakest part of the colony and the most difficult to sustain," as the Chevalier de Lévis wrote.[38] A seasoned commander like Beaujeu immediately spotted glaring weaknesses in the provisional French occupation of the upper Ohio. New France's entire strategic position at Fort Duquesne rested on a deceptively short sixteen-mile portage road between Forts Presque Isle and Le Boeuf and the equally difficult passage from Rivière au Boeuf to Belle Rivière.[39] For those who had never seen its actual terrain, moving goods across the portage might seem like a simple task, involving travel along flat coastal ground "as easily as one goes from Montréal to La Prairie," as the Marquis Duquesne assumed in 1754. But Beaujeu's men disembarked their cargoes and began a steady uphill ascent from the lake. As the portage road reached the Lake Erie escarpment, watersheds divided: waters to the north flowed into Lake Erie and the St. Lawrence, while streams like Rivière au Boeuf flowed southward, ultimately toward the Mississippi. The Old French Road, as it is still known today, goes over exceptionally uneven ground scoured by glaciers. At times the portage road went up incredibly steep grades then down into deep ravines cut by rivulets such as Rivière au Gravois.[40] The most serious challenge that French road builders confronted, however, were swamps and bogs, the watery vestiges of glacial times. French and Native porteurs slogged their way through swampy ground that was "killing the horses," according to Ensign Duverger de St. Blin, the commandant at Fort de la Rivière au Boeuf. Most of the portage road, in fact, had to be corduroyed with timbers, but even in 1755 these bridges were in "bad condition" and required constant maintenance.[41] A small detachment might take eight to twelve days to portage their supplies and canoes over; but the glut of detachments that came in the spring of 1755 bogged down everything. It would take weeks for all of the detachments to get over the portage and to Venango. Like General Braddock's army, French forces also suffered crippling supply problems from poor road conditions, exhausted horses, and wagon shortages—a testament to the logistical difficulties of the American wilderness.[42]

Beaujeu had been instantly struck by the miserable condition of the portage road and wrote back to the commandant at Niagara on the poor quality of horses and lack of wagons and Indian porteurs. He knew that his men would be stalled there for quite some time.[43] The portage was ironically consuming the very reinforcements and supplies intended for Fort Duquesne and hindering Contrecoeur's ability to strike Braddock's army with any significant forces. The labor of clearing forests, constructing two forts and numerous boats, building a sixteen-mile portage road, and clearing the Rivière au Boeuf had virtually destroyed Marin's command in 1753 and 1754. The Marquis Duquesne, who initially disbelieved reports of such horrendous conditions, was later astonished that anyone "could enter the Belle Rivière with such cadavers." In 1755, French soldiers—not horses—were again shouldering the burdens of this portage, suffering as greatly as the British men and horses on Appalachian ridges. There was no relief: the horses available to the French were pitifully small in number (averaging 10 to 12) and always dwindling. The portage work attracted only a handful of nearby Senecas and Mississaugas, and they were reluctant to part with their horses.[44]

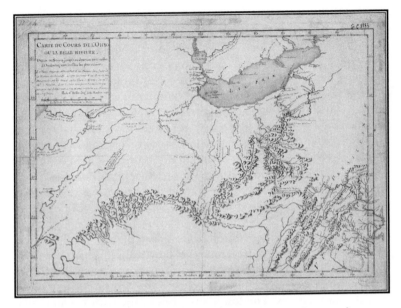

Jacques-Nicolas Bellin, *Carte du cours de l'Ohyo ou la belle rivière*, 1755, Courtesy of
Bibliothèque nationale de France. Bellin's map expresses French claims to the entire Ohio
Valley watershed. It depicts the difficult French portage road between forts Presque Isle
and Le Boeuf and the principal French posts, Indian towns, and paths in the region.

Ensign St. Blin reported that they only had ten carts, and that even
they were "beginning to wear out and even break down in the portage," along with his "lame and broken down" horses. The ten "cha-
reste" that St. Blin referred to were only two-wheeled carts called
charrettes with limited capacity. French laborers were the true beasts
of burden, hauling massive supply packs over the portage on their
backs. And the volume of supplies and provisions they moved was
astounding: Lieutenant Benoist recorded that between May 10 and
July 4, 1755, laborers had moved 2,378 barrels of food sixteen miles
from Presque Isle to Rivière au Boeuf. The abundant quantities of *les
vins* and *l'eaux de vie* that Beaujeu's men carried were perhaps the
most important sustenance of their morale and forward progress. If
the Presque Isle portage made it notoriously difficult to supply the
Ohio River posts, the next part of Beaujeu's route—la Rivière au
Boeuf—was an even more problematic passage.[45]

On his arrival at Fort de la Rivière au Boeuf, Beaujeu would
have noted activity that made the post seem more like a naval base
than a frontier fortress. It was the crucial forward French base from
which ammunition and provisions were sent to Fort Duquesne. He

might have been astonished to learn that Rivière au Boeuf, which was overlooked from the small rise on which Fort Le Boeuf sat, was no *rivière* at all, but a narrow, winding, and languid trickle. In the broad flats below the fort, carpenters constructed new pirogues (dugouts hewn from large beech tree trunks and fashioned into sturdy if wobbly vessels) and repaired other craft in a makeshift boatyard. Thirty-six-foot bateaux were nearly useless on the Rivière au Boeuf. The French could convoy supplies down its shallow and winding seventy-mile course only in canoes or pirogues. Hundreds of such pirogues and canoes lay along the shore, just as Washington had observed in 1753. Coming down the Rivière au Boeuf in 1755, Pierre-Philippe de Saint-Ours recorded the impressive carrying capacity of his forty-two pirogues "loaded with 584 sacks of flour, 305 barrels of salt pork, 7 sacks of Indian corn, 10 barrels of powder, 754 of vermillion, 6 bales, one hundred thirty-two men."[46]

Trees frequently fell across the labyrinthine channels of la Rivière au Boeuf (French Creek) and obstructed navigation; constant maintenance was required to clear timbers from the waters lest they damage canoes. The lower stretches of the river became mercifully broad and faster, for the French even encountered riffles and small rapids as they neared the junction of Rivière au Boeuf and la Belle Rivière, where the old Indian town of Venango had been

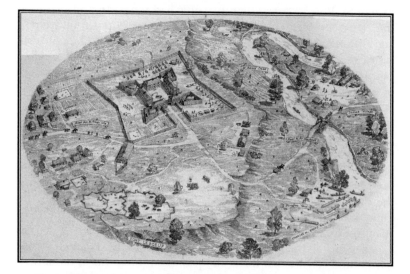

Fort de la Rivière au Boeuf, by Charles Morse Stotz. Courtesy of Thomas and Katherine Detre Library and Archives, Senator John Heinz History Center, Pittsburgh, Pennsylvania.

situated. But the greatest challenge of this waterway to the Ohio River was insufficient water. The river became exceptionally shallow, especially in dry weather. Canoes scraped along its rocky bottom or could not proceed at all unless towed from the shoreline. The drought of 1755 that enabled Braddock's army to cross the Youghiogheny and the Monongahela rivers with ease made la Rivière au Boeuf increasingly impassable. The French were not only racing against Braddock's advance but also against the brief window of time in which they could float supplies on la Rivière au Boeuf. By early July 1755, the waters would be "so extremely low that it is almost impossible for any detachments to travel by water," as a French officer warned Contrecoeur and Beaujeu.[47]

Beaujeu himself spent only a few days along the Presque Isle portage, overseeing the movement of the various detachments and their supplies. He had a special mission to accomplish, in view of his previous command at Niagara and knowledge of logistics. The Marquis Duquesne had not only given him the command of Fort Duquesne but had also charged him with building a new fort at Venango, at the junction of Rivière au Boeuf and la Belle Rivière. The latter order reflected the French higher command's sense that Fort Duquesne was not immediately threatened and that Beaujeu need not proceed with all possible haste to reinforce it. The governor-general wrote to Paris that summer that Beaujeu was to "build a little stockaded fort at the mouth of the Rivière au Boeuf, merely to surround the storehouses which we are using as a supply post." Beaujeu probably arrived at Camp Machault (as the French renamed Venango) in company with its new commander, Lieutenant Michel Maray de La Chauvignerie, sometime between June 10 and 13, 1755. La Chauvignerie was well-chosen for this task, given that he was a veteran Indian diplomat and interpreter. Governor Vaudreuil later reported that "he thoroughly understands the dispositions of the Delawares and Chaouanons" and their relations with the Iroquois.[48]

Camp Machault, named after the French naval minister, Jean-Baptiste de Machault d'Arnouville, had evolved very little from its beginnings as Fraser's trading post, named for the erstwhile English trader John Fraser, who had established trade there as early as 1741. When the French occupied the region in 1753, Fraser abandoned his post and blacksmith shop. Like many traders, he was a slippery character who sensed contrary winds and tacked accordingly. He even maintained a friendship of sorts with his French rival, Captain Philippe-Thomas Chabert de Joncaire, who ended up seizing Fraser's settlement for himself, though some of the Englishman's Delaware customers had claimed that Fraser had given it to them. The Delaware towns of Venango and Ticastoroga along Rivière au Boeuf were inhabited largely by French-allied Delawares such as Custaloga, a leader whom Washington had encountered in his 1753 journey. La Chauvignerie reported that Indians were "here everyday," and it was necessary to supply them with food, which further drained French supplies.[49]

Histories often mistakenly posit that the French built Fort Machault in 1753 and 1754, but when Beaujeu and La Chauvignerie came there in June 1755 there was no fort to speak of, only an armed camp that was the advanced staging point for the final float down the Belle Rivière to Fort Duquesne. A motley scattering of barracks, huts, and storehouses now stood around Fraser's old buildings. Beaujeu invested enough time at Venango to select the site for a future fort, draft a formal "plan" for it, and estimate the amount of timber necessary to build it, as La Chauvignerie later reported. The basic problems remained manpower and horsepower. The Presque Isle portage drained away most horses from the Machault garrison, so it was difficult to haul large oak timbers from the nearby forest to construct a fortress. The small garrison of roughly thirty men was insufficient to construct a fort, and most of the surplus manpower was at work on the portage road or shuttling pirogues and canoes between forts. Fort Machault would not be completed until 1757, and even toward the ends of its career it remained a fort in name only: "a supply post" that was "too weak to sustain a siege," and might only "resist musketry-fire," as the Marquis de Vaudreuil admitted. Like many posts throughout New France, Machault asserted control over the principal waterways in its purview, though it was completely dominated by hills that towered above it just a few hundred yards to the west. Nevertheless, it soon became one of the most important posts along the French communication between Duquesne and Presque Isle, providing a staging point and storage facilities for the 125-mile trip down la Belle Rivière to Fort Duquesne. If Fort Le Boeuf was principally important for its boatyard, Machault increasingly functioned as "the last supply depot for Fort Duquesne," as one officer termed it. The French had found that their initial practice of running goods all the way from Le Boeuf to Duquesne had resulted in the spoilage and loss of provisions due to bad weather. Beaujeu dutifully began to improve Camp Machault, and along with Landrième, was already organizing carpenters to prepare timbers for cutting. The final version of Fort Machault reflected the deep imprint Beaujeu would leave on the region.[50]

Sometime around June 14, an urgent letter came to Camp Machault from Captain Contrecoeur at Fort Duquesne, dated a week earlier and addressed to "my dear friend," Beaujeu. The letter related that "an English deserter arrived here yesterday who tells us that the English are on the march." Contrecoeur warned that the English force was 3,000 strong, bearing "fourteen or fifteen eighteen-pound brass pieces of cannons, with mortars and bombs and many grenades." Fearing it would demoralize them, he cautioned Beaujeu to "not mention this artillery to your detachment." "Since the English are coming on fast, I beg you, my dear friend, to come with as many men as possible, as soon as you receive my letter, and bring all the food you can." Beaujeu departed shortly after receiving it, though he was apparently still at Camp Machault on June 17, when he sent ahead four pirogues loaded with the essentials: cannonballs, gunpowder, flour, and bullets.[51]

Beaujeu finally arrived at Fort Duquesne on June 27, 1755,[52] though his entire detachment was still strung out along the Rivière au Boeuf. Most of the brigades (those of Beaujeu, St. Martin, Carqueville, and Courtemanche) that had departed Montréal in April and May of 1755 had remained at Presque Isle for most of June 1755. Not until June 23—a little more than two weeks before the Monongahela—did the detachments begin to depart Presque Isle. Carqueville's was the last of these four convoys bound for Fort Duquesne; one additional brigade, that of Saint-Ours, left Presque Isle on July 6, too late to participate in any combat but bearing much-needed supplies. The delays were so significant that it took part of Saint-Ours's men two full weeks to travel from Fort Le Boeuf to Camp Machault "because the river was so low."[53]

When Beaujeu's convoy descended the Rivière au Boeuf in the last days of June, a majestic vista opened at the river's mouth at Venango. Truly, la Belle Rivière was the beautiful river: tall hills towered above the broad river on both sides, and tranquil waters cast stunning reflections of the mountains and bluffs above. La Belle Rivière's fast current promised some relief to the stiff and sore limbs of French paddlers. With "a fine deep water and a stream in our favour," as one Frenchman recalled, the voyage from Venango to Duquesne could be covered in as little as four or five days. Nine miles downriver from Venango, the French travelers saw a massive, twenty-foot high boulder with one flat, angled face upon which Native peoples had inscribed petroglyphs, "rudely enough carved" in French eyes. During the 1749 expedition of Céloron de Blainville, the French convoy had stopped at the rock, embedded a lead plate, and placed the king's arms on a nearby tree. Some officers insisted that the symbols were the work of Europeans, while a Jesuit priest said that they reflected "the unskillfulness of savages." The priest described the entire route southward as surrounded by a "double chain of mountains" that obscured the sun in the early morning and late afternoon. This section of the river gave French troops probably one of the few chances to reflect on their natural surroundings. Later in life, the French gunner named Joseph-Charles "Jolicoeur" Bonin could still evoke the "very beautiful" variety of trees and wildlife he had seen in the Ohio Country. Beaujeu's convoy finally reached Fort Duquesne on July 2, 1755, seventy days after setting out from Montréal. Other detachments arrived in the following days.[54]

Three components of French and Native forces that would fight the Battle of the Monongahela had converged at Fort Duquesne, including the 600 to 700 Native allies drawn from as many as twenty different nations and communities, the *troupes de la marine,* and the Canadian militia. The concentration of French and Native warriors at Fort Duquesne by early July was nearly miraculous, as their diverse journeys had converged despite difficulties of travel and an

La Belle Rivière (Allegheny River), a few miles downriver from Venango (Franklin, Pennsylvania). Photographed from the author's canoe.

unpredictable line of communication and supply. By early July, La Chauvignerie was reporting from Camp Machault that the water on Rivière au Boeuf was so low that it was nearly impossible for detachments to get through.[55] Timing is everything in warfare, and the arrival of the French reinforcements and Native war parties, while serendipitous, could not have been more fortunate. Had the French reinforcements been delayed any longer, or had Braddock arrived only one week earlier, Fort Duquesne would have been dangerously undermanned. Alternatively, if Braddock's army had been delayed until August or September, the French would have found it impossible to provision so large a concentration of manpower.

The forces assembling at Fort Duquesne in July 1755 represented the entire spectrum of New France and its Indian alliances drawn from half a continent.[56] Contrecoeur's allied army was typical of such joint French-Indian military ventures in the eighteenth century. Certainly, there was nothing uncommon about the 600 to 700 Native warriors who were present at Fort Duquesne. In retrospect, what makes this force of warriors unique is that they constituted the largest Indian army ever engaged in any previous Anglo/French conflict to that point. They were larger than, for example, the Native contingents in Longueuil's Expedition (1739), Céloron's Expedition (1749), and the large-scale attacks on Schenectady (1690), Deerfield (1704), Saratoga (1745), Fort Massachusetts (1746), and German Flatts (1757).[57] When this Indian army met Braddock's army in the forest, there was no precedent for a confrontation of this nature, one in which the French acted more as auxiliaries. The raw military power that the Native allies added to the defense of Fort Duquesne can scarcely be exaggerated. With the Indians present, that defense was militarily possible; without them, Contrecoeur would most likely have been compelled to abandon the Forks of the Ohio to the English. Fort Duquesne was a perfect symbol of French America: an indefensible outpost of empire, save for the Native peoples who came there for rendezvous, diplomacy, and war.[58]

The Natives' incredible journeys began at disparate points of the compass such as Michilimackinac, Détroit, Scioto, Kahnawake, and Lorette. Approximately one-third of the Indian warriors were *domiciliés* or residents of the Seven Nations—Iroquois and Nipissings from Kahnawake and Kanesetake, Hurons from Lorette (Wendake), and Abenakis from St. Francis (Odanak) and Bécancour (Wôlinak) in the St. Lawrence Valley.[59] Perhaps one-half or more were Anishinaabeg—Odawas, Ojibwas, and Potawatomis who were stalwart French allies from the *pays d'en haut* (the upper country of the Great Lakes region).

Though present in much smaller numbers, fighters from the far west who journeyed eastward to Fort Duquesne in the summer of 1755 included Sac, Fox, and even Osage Indians from west of the Mississippi River.[60] Another sizable contingent was Ohio Valley and Great Lakes Indians such as Delawares, Shawnees, Miamis, Wyandots (Hurons), Mississaugas, Senecas, and other Ohio Iroquois who had cast their lot with the French.[61] The Shawnees had already engaged in hostilities against the British and were present at Fort Duquesne. The Delawares—the peoples who had the greatest justification to seek vengeance upon the British—were ironically the most divided. Although some Delaware leaders later claimed to have been neutral, other warriors were firmly committed to the French side in 1755. Beginning in 1753 and 1754, a number of Ohio Indian communities and bands had resettled closer to the French forts, such as the pro-French Delawares led by Custaloga, the "domiciliated Mississagués of Presqu'isle," and the "Iroquois of the vicinity of Fort Duquesne."[62]

Contemporary sources shed little light on the paths, literal and figurative, that brought so many Indian nations to the Ohio Valley in the summer of 1755, though one Native route that can be reconstructed concerns the Wyandots, Ottawas, and Potawatomis who settled around Détroit. In the winter of 1754–1755, Contrecoeur had been authorized to call on the commandant at Détroit, Captain Jacques-Pierre Daneau de Muy, for militia and to solicit the help of Indians settled there. Contrecoeur had sent letters to De Muy in late January, warning of impending English plans to attack Fort Duquesne and advising him to have Native contingents ready to come to his aid. He pressed Chaussegros de Léry to leave Détroit and oversee improvements to Fort Duquesne: "According to information which reaches us daily by the Indians, the English mean to attack Fort Duquesne this spring," Contrecoeur wrote, adding, "you will be most useful to us here as we have the greatest need of an officer capable of planning and carrying out works necessary to put this place in a state of defense. Messrs. Dumas and De Lignery wish you to come as soon as possible." In March of 1755, some warriors from the vicinity of Fort Détroit began to depart for the Forks of the Ohio to aid their French father. It was yet another example of Contrecoeur's diligence and foresight as a commander: his appeals to Native allies for help were rooted in his desperation, but they nonetheless brought Wyandot, Ottawa, and Potawatomi warriors to his beleaguered post.[63]

The Native allies who came to the Ohio Valley in 1755 were well armed with weapons that prepared them for both long-range and face-to-face combat. Indian warriors were generally armed with trade muskets originally derived from either the French or the British. Indians who were long-standing allies of New France undoubtedly carried hunting or trade muskets (*fusils de chasse* or *fusils de traite*) typical of that period. Most if not all Indian warriors at the Monongahela were armed with smoothbore muskets, not rifles. Captain Le Mercier, the officer who had designed Fort Duquesne, wrote to the ministry that "there is no other country, My Lord, where there is such a high rate of gun consumption than in this colony with regards to the Natives, since we are in the habit of arming them each time we have them go to war." Native warriors, in addition, were fastidious when it came to their firearms, preferring the *fusil de chasse* made at the Tulle manufactory in France, for its "lightweight and robust construction." According to one governor-general, "the Natives know them [the Tulle *fusils*] and will not accept any others."[64] Native warriors also carried weapons that enabled them to demonstrate raw courage against their enemies. Tomahawks, scalping knives, and war clubs were used to gain the scalps of enemies killed in face-to-face encounters (warriors often etched their clubs with tallies of scalps, captives, or combat actions). Warriors carried decorative burdenstraps and cords for securing captives, perhaps the ultimate symbol of military victory, who were ritually adopted into Native communities.[65]

The Independent Companies of the Marine (*Compagnies franches de la marine*) were French regulars who formed the second component of Contrecoeur's forces in 1755. Also known as the *troupes de la marine* and the *troupes du Canada*, these independent marine companies were the garrison troops of New France. The French Naval Ministry had historically administered overseas colonies and had sent marine companies to New France beginning in 1683. They were under the overall command of the governor-general and numbered between 700 to 900 men in total for the first half of the eighteenth century. Despite their naval affiliation, however, the *troupes de la marine* functioned as line infantry and had little, if any, maritime service. Though few in number and not without weaknesses, the *Compagnies franches de la marine* rendered excellent service to New France in its various wars. The best independent marine companies outclassed their English counterparts, and constituted a strong cadre of regulars around which the Canadian militia and Native allies could operate.[66]

The garrison uniform coat of the *Compagnies franches* was a gray-white *justacorps*, a knee-length coat with blue cuffs and lining, complemented by a blue woolen *veste* (waistcoat) and *culotte* (breeches), and capped with a black tri-folded *chapeau*. Given the rough nature of service in the western posts, to say nothing of the trials of the long passage from Montréal, this uniform was considerably modified. The *Compagnies franches* at la Belle Rivière in 1755 wore most likely a motley-looking admixture of Marine uniforms and Indian clothing and equipment. Moccasins, *mitasses* (leggings), breechclouts, tomahawks, powder horns, and beaded pouches were most likely used among the rank and file, as well as by the officers who, stripped to their waist and wearing only gorgets, led Indian allies against the British. The fact that Beaujeu's Niagara garrison was partly armed with *fusils de traite* (trade guns) cautions against any generalizations about the standard firearms in French service. The French marines were sometimes armed with grenadier muskets (*fusils grenadiers*) from French manufactories in Tulle and Saint-Étienne; on average, these lengthy weapons (60 inches or more) weighed around seven pounds and fired a .62-caliber round ball. A 1755 document shows that *fuzils fin de Traitte et Tulle* (fine trade guns and Tulle guns) were among the firearms sent to Fort Duquesne.[67]

The *Companies franches de la Marine* were therefore the French mirror-images of the British Independent Companies: poorly funded, fragmented, sporadically supplied, lacking regularity in discipline in training, and not always militarily effective. Native warriors openly laughed at French marines drilling at Détroit in 1754, performing what they thought were utterly useless wheelings and maneuvers. Contemporaries generally believed that the Canadian militia were superior guerilla fighters and tended to see the independent marine companies as ineffective and sometimes dissolute garrison troops. Reinforcing that image was the fact that the rank-and-file men were largely unemployed tradesmen from French cities and towns, recruited for a grim period of service in Canada, ranging from six years to an *engagement perpetuel* (i.e., until discharged by the king due to old age or infirmity). Given their backgrounds, many of Contrecoeur's *troupes de la marine* were most likely inexperienced as well, though it is reasonable to conclude that most of the fittest and hardiest men were sent to the Ohio Valley posts. In 1750, the French government had doubled the numbers of *troupes de la marine*, resulting in a major infusion of roughly 900 new recruits from France. In other words, at least half of these recruits differed very little from Braddock's forces, which are routinely characterized as inexperienced in New World combat. For some of the newer marine recruits who were undoubtedly in the mix at Fort Duquesne, any combat experience would have been derived from their actions in the 1754 campaign.[68]

French Naval Infantry, c. 1754. Painting by Don Troiani, http://www.historicalimagebank.com.

The third component of Contrecoeur's army at the Monongahela was the Canadian militia volunteers. Beginning in 1669, when King Louis XIV had ordered the formation of militia companies, male Canadian *habitants* ranging in age from fifteen to fifty had provided much of New France's defensive manpower in the eighteenth century.

With so few units of *Compangnies franches*, it was absolutely essential for the Canadian militia and Indians to supplement their numbers. In 1750, there were 11,687 militia out of a total population of 51,908. The Canadian militia, like the British militias, were often reputed by European officers to possess some innate skill for fighting, like the Indians, and to be properly hardened to the American climate. Not all Canadian militia, of course, were battle-hardened, veteran guerilla fighters of legend.[69] The caliber of Canadian militia who served in the Ohio Valley against the British is difficult to gauge. Most likely, as noted, the militiamen were similar to their British provincial counterparts, with many youthful rank-and-file men like Pierre Simard of Petite-Rivière, aged twenty-three, who were novices at war, serving along with veteran officers who were bulwarks of leadership and experience. Captain Contrecoeur asserted that his "best militia had remained at the Rivière au Boeuf to portage provisions" and that the militia at Fort Duquesne "were unfortunately only children." What can be said with certainty is that vast majority of Canadian militia present were not drawn from the western posts, such as a Détroit, but from the St. Lawrence Valley. Surviving rolls for Beaujeu's detachment and others bound for la Belle Rivière in 1755 show that the militia hailed from places and seigneuries in the St. Lawrence such as Montréal, La Prairie, Boucherville, Île Perrot, Pointe-aux-Trembles, Saint-Ours, and La Corne.[70] The Canadian volunteers would have been equipped in the most rudimentary summer garb, "wearing shirts and their backsides bare in the Canadian style," as Pierre Pouchot observed.[71]

The most significant distinction between the independent companies of New France and those of British America involved the Canadian officer corps who led the *troupes du Canada* and militia, and often accompanied Indian war parties.[72] While the rank-and-file men of the *Compagnies franches* were predominantly French recruits, the officer corps was dominated by Canadians, many of noble rank (British Independent Companies, by contrast, were officered by native Britons and filled with American recruits). For elite Canadians, military service fulfilled their longing to honor the king, to gain military glory for themselves and their family name, and to garner posts of profit through their military successes. Canadian officers were the principal landholders, seigneurs, and slaveholders of New France; they tended to have quite lengthy terms of service, and the officer corps often functioned as a kind of patrimony that a father tried to pass along to his son. Sons of the Canadian elites typically began their military training at an early age. Two cadets were assigned to

each marine company: a *cadet-soldat* and a *cadet à l'aiguillette*, referring to the blue and white silk cord worn on the right shoulder to
distinguish the most senior officer candidate (one of Contrecoeur's
sons, René-Marie, was one such *cadet à l'aiguillette* in the Ohio Valley
in 1755). Promotion did not come about through purchase, as in
the British Army, but through seniority, merit, and a healthy dose of
family connections or business interests.[73]

The incomparably superior Canadian officer corps that assembled at the Forks of the Ohio in 1755 was one of the principal
advantages the French held over British forces during the campaign.
Based on a French account that lists officers by surname,[74] and with
the help of excellent official records and Québécois genealogies,
Appendix C identifies the thirty-six officers and cadets who were reported as present during the combat of July 9. Their service histories
reveal that every one of the captains, lieutenants, and ensigns, and
even some cadets, had previous campaign or battle experience in
petit guerre conditions. They had great familiarity with their Indian
allies, by virtue of joint military actions, diplomatic experience, or
garrison duty in the distant outposts of New France. Some had fought
against the Fox or Chickasaw Indians in the 1730s. Others brought
combat experience gained on the frontiers of Acadia, New England,
and New York in the 1740s. Some had participated in Céloron de
Blainville's Expedition in 1749, helped to establish French fortifications in the Ohio Valley in 1753, and fought at Fort Necessity in
1754. For all those reasons, the Ohio Valley became a proving ground
for numerous French Canadian officers who had distinguished
careers as partisan fighters during the Seven Years' War. In 1754,
Contrecoeur had been permitted by the Marquis Duquesne to personally select many of the officers who would serve under his command in the Ohio Valley: "You will have in your fort the best cadets
of the colony and officers of your choice."[75]

The collective biographies of the officers at the Monongahela
in 1755 make clear that Contrecoeur's ranks had an unusual concentration of the most experienced Canadian officers and cadets.
Beaujeu, as we have witnessed, had engaged in Indian diplomacy,
seen the logistical challenges of service in western posts, and participated in campaigns with Indian allies. Along with Beaujeu, two
additional captains with conspicuous records were present at Fort
Duquesne. François-Marie Le Marchand de Lignery was one of the
most battle-tested French officers—a veteran of the Fox and Chickasaw
wars in the 1730s who had also fought alongside Beaujeu at the
Grand Pré battle in Acadia. François-Marie's father, Constant Le

Marchand de Lignery, was a veteran officer of the Fox Wars, who had led a multiethnic coalition of French, Mission Indians, Ottawas, Potawatomis, Chippewas, and Hurons in 1728 (Beaujeu's father was second in command of that expedition). How this family history may have shaped François-Marie's knowledge of Indian peoples can't be known, but it is certain that the younger officer displayed a certain skill in Indian diplomacy: Duquesne affirmed that "besides being an excellent subject, he understands and directs the savages perfectly." Lignery would act as Contrecoeur's second-in-command until Beaujeu's arrival.[76]

The second distinguished captain was Jean-Daniel Dumas, one of the rare native-born French officers who had gained a commission in the *troupes de la marine* in Canada. Dumas began his military career in the Régiment d'Agenois of the French Army and gained the rank of captain during his service in the War of Austrian Succession.[77] For reasons that remain unknown, Dumas became a captain in the *troupes de la marine*, emigrated to Canada in 1750, and was briefly stationed on the frontiers of Acadia. He had been at the Belle Rivière outposts from their beginnings in 1753. During a brief time as commander of Fort de la Rivière au Boeuf that year, Dumas revealed a brash personality and an ability to outlast his rivals. When his commanding officer, Sieur de Marin, feuded with him over problems at the camp, Dumas challenged him to relieve him: "I cannot see that there will be much glory for me in this campaign, and I shall thus avoid the unpleasantness of which I am already getting a foretaste." Although temporarily relieved of duty, Dumas was considered too valuable and talented an officer to lose and was promptly sent back. Dumas and Lignery appear to have enjoyed a cordial relationship, and with Beaujeu, would help to lead the detachment that confronted Braddock's army on July 9.[78]

The three captains were assisted by four veteran lieutenants at the Battle of the Monongahela: Claude-Antoine Drouet de Carqueville, Paul Le Borgne, Jacques-François Legardeur de Croisille de Courtemanche, and Jean-Baptiste-Philippe Testard de Montigny. Both Le Borgne and Courtemanche, for example, had participated in Céloron de Blainville's expedition in 1749, and both had served briefly as commanders at Rivière au Boeuf and Presque Isle in 1754, respectively. Among the six ensigns, a few are especially noteworthy: the Sieur de Corbière, later praised by the French general the Marquis de Montcalm as an officer of "zeal and intelligence," famous for his later attack on British forces at Sabbath-Day Point in 1757. Some of the ensigns were well known to Beaujeu, such as François de Bailleul, who

Jean-Daniel Dumas (1721–1794). Drawing by Marie-Claudine-Ursule Boze, ca. 1788. Dumas's career as a formidable partisan fighter began at the Monongahela. As commandant of Fort Duquesne, he orchestrated the collapse of the Pennsylvania and Virginia frontiers. During the Quebec campaign in 1759, he tracked down and destroyed parts of Robert Rogers's famed rangers and fought valiantly at the Plains of Abraham. Library and Archives Canada, Archival Reference Number R12615, e008300002.

began his military service in 1729. The Marquis Duquesne described Bailleul as a "very zealous and competent officer." As a young cadet in 1745, he had participated in the attack on Saratoga, New York, that netted the young captive Louis Cook. Two years later, Bailleul had served in combat with Beaujeu in Acadia, leading a party of twenty-five Micmac and Maliseet Indians. He came to the Ohio Valley in 1753 and fought against the British at Fort Necessity in 1754. Contrecoeur would entrust him with scouting expeditions against Braddock's army in 1755. While some of the youthful cadets had never tasted battle, all having been born in the mid-to-late 1730s, many had gained some campaign experience in 1754 and some degree of familiarity with Indian peoples and diplomacy. Contrecoeur also attached cadets to the Indian scouting parties that he sent out in June and July of 1755 in order to give them experience.[79]

One French officer most likely *absent* at the Monongahela was Ensign Charles Mouet de Langlade, who is often and mistakenly given credit for orchestrating the battle against Braddock. Edward

Deming's iconic painting of Braddock's Defeat in the Wisconsin Historical Society has helped to perpetuate the myth that Langlade coordinated the ambush of Braddock's column.[80] None of the contemporary French records on the Ohio Valley—even the copiously detailed *Papiers Contrecoeur* and numerous rolls of French officers down to the names of ensigns, cadets, and rank and file men—contain any reference to Langlade, who was a commissioned officer in 1755 (an ensign) and would have been quite well known to senior French officers because of his involvement in the action against Pickawillany in 1752.[81] Langlade not only boasted to British officers in the Revolutionary War that he had been at Braddock's Defeat but also that he had managed the whole affair. Nineteenth-century historian Francis Parkman's wholesale acceptance of these claims, also embedded in nineteenth-century oral tradition, have been the foundation of Langlade's supposed presence and significance in the 1755 campaign. There is no evidence that Beaujeu needed any prodding from a considerably younger ensign, and it further defies belief that an ensign would be selected over the senior lieutenants and captains who were far more experienced to orchestrate a battle plan.[82] If Langlade had indeed been present, he fought not as a Canadian ensign but as an Ottawa warrior. But his absence in the French records of 1755 for the Ohio Valley speaks with greater authority than boasts and legends.

The myth of Langlade obscures a more basic fact: there were other French officers present at Fort Duquesne who matched if not excelled Langlade's skills in forest warfare and diplomacy. Lieutenant Jean-Baptiste-Philippe Testard de Montigny (b. 1724) had been leading Canadian and Indian war parties since the 1740s, when he had participated in or personally led more than thirty destructive French-Indian attacks on the frontiers of New York and New England. By the time he led a contingent of Canadian Iroquois from Montréal to the Belle Rivière in May 1755, Montigny was already a seasoned veteran of nineteen years' service on New France's frontiers, having served at posts ranging from Michilimackinac to Fort Saint Frédéric.[83] Officers like Montigny had prior experience with specific Native nations and usually accompanied them in travel and in battle. In 1754, for example, when Lieutenant Chaussegros de Léry was at the Chautauqua portage, he wrote in his journal that "M. de Villiers, captain, at the head of the Nepissingues and Algonkins, M. de Longueuil, commander, at the head of the Iroquois, M. de Montesson, lieutenant, at the head of the Abenakis, and M. de Longueuil, second ensign, with the Hurons of Lorette, arrived here." Among the officers active in the 1755 campaign were La Chauvignerie, an officer and interpreter to the Indians; Lieutenant Joseph Godefroy de Normanville had "been with the Miamis" in 1754. Lieutenant Courtemanche had led "his savages," the Lorette Hurons, to Fort Duquesne in 1755, along with Ensign Longueuil. Some of those men were among the "officers in command of the Indians" at the Monongahela. Embedding French officers among Indian war parties was the standard French practice that Beaujeu, as we shall see, continued in July 1755.[84]

The component parts of a Franco-Indian army had assembled at Fort Duquesne, but it took effective French leadership and diplomacy to forge them into a powerful coalition. Contrecoeur's diplomacy with Native allies in May and June 1755 mirrored Braddock's parallel negotiations at Fort Cumberland. Contrecoeur played the role of Onontio (as Indians referred to the French governor and metaphorical French father), creating consensus on how the Natives would resist British intrusions, resolving tensions among Onontio's children, generously supplying his allies, and arranging joint expeditions of French officers and Indian warriors to scout Braddock's

Jean-Baptiste-Philippe Testard de Montigny (1724–1786). Entering marine service in 1736 at the age of twelve, Montigny personified the deep reservoirs of experience with Indian relations and *petite guerre* that French Canadian officers brought to the Monongahela. Montigny's knightly portrait features his Croix de Saint-Louis, which King Louis XV awarded him in 1762 for his distinguished military career in New France. © Château Ramezay—Historic Site and Museum of Montréal.

army.[85] Contrecoeur walked a delicate balance in what historian Peter MacLeod termed "parallel warfare," in which Natives fought for their own objectives even as they acted as French allies against the British. Not only were there differences in military goals and tactics, but significant tensions also remained among Contrecoeur's Native allies. There was a great deal of suspicion and mistrust, for example, between some Ottawas and Potawatomis over the killing of a Potawatomi from St. Joseph by an Ottawa war party from Arbre Croche in the fall of 1754.[86]

Effective and persuasive French diplomacy was necessary to assemble and unify a multiethnic coalition of Indian warriors on which the French so greatly depended. French efforts were facilitated by a network of able interpreters and traders in the region, such as Jacques and Antoine Baby dit Dupéront (among the Shawnees), Philippe-Thomas Chabert de Joncaire (among the Senecas), and Lieutenant La Chauvignerie (among the Delawares near Venango). A Shawnee leader named Ackowanothio later recalled what a French officer, perhaps Contrecoeur or Beaujeu, had told the Indians upon the approach of Braddock's army: "Children, now the Time is come of which I often told. Such an Army is coming against you, to take your Lands from you and make Slaves of you—You know the Virginians;—they all come with him.—If you will stand your Ground I will fight with you for your Land, and I don't doubt we will conquer them." The text of only one of Contrecoeur's speeches to assembled Indians survives. On June 16, he addressed Senecas (Sonontouans), Cayugas (Goyoguins), Shawnees (Shawenons), and Delawares (Loups), though Ottawas, Potawatomis, and St. Lawrence Iroquois seem to have been present too. He appealed to them as Onontio's representative, reminding them that "your Father has only been seeking the means by which to bring peace to this land, and that he wants to put you under his wing." He presented the English as the aggressors and "our common enemy." He asked the assembled warriors to take up Onontio's hatchet, adding that they had once promised to do so "if they passed beyond the height of the land." "They have scorned your words," he told them. "Now it is up to you to show them your resentment." That day and the next, parties composed of Shawnees, Delawares, Senecas, and Cayugas went out to scout the British army.[87]

The absence of the Natives' reply to Contrecoeur's speech in the official record means that we have no real understanding of why so many Native warriors were ultimately willing to respond to such French entreaties and journey to the Ohio Valley in 1755. The standard interpretation of Indian motivation—defense of their lands—is not entirely convincing in the case of the 1755 campaign. Some Delawares, for example, whose lands were most directly threatened by British encroachments, were the most neutral and noncommittal. Natives who were farthest removed from territorial threats were among the most willing to fight alongside their French allies.[88]

Bonds of Indian alliances with the French were manifold and often intertwined. Native warriors who came to the Ohio Valley sought captives, scalps, and war materiel, all of which were all prized as symbols of military victory. Personal ties to French Canadian officials and traders, a shared Catholic faith, prior service in French expeditions, and common geopolitical goals—all might further explain Native eagerness to participate in the 1755 campaign. The *domiciliés*, such as the Canadian Iroquois and Abenakis, proved to be the most resolute French allies. Composing one-third of the Indian forces at the Monongahela, there was little exaggeration to Governor Vaudreuil's boast that they were "as a rampart to their Father." Canadian Iroquois had previously fought in the Ohio Valley in 1754, and at least 100 had remained at Fort Duquesne that winter. As one Kahnawake warrior explained, "the French & we are one Blood & where they are to dye we must dye also. We are linked together in each others Arms & where the French go we must go also." Some Canadian Iroquois—especially Kahnawake Mohawks—had maintained a seasonal occupation of Ohio Valley hunting grounds for decades and wanted to preserve those lands. Everyday life in the multiethnic towns of the Ohio Valley also cemented new ties among families and communities. When Céloron de Blainville came to Chiningué (Logstown) in 1749, he noted that the town was composed of Iroquois, Shawnees, Delawares, Kahnawake and Kanesetake Mohawks, Nipissings, and Abenakis. The French also gained strong diplomatic leverage by defining their claim to the Ohio Valley watershed up to the "height of land"—the crest of the Appalachians—as "the natural boundary between France and England as far as the Ohio." They defended the Appalachian Mountain border that the Ohio Indians themselves wanted to preserve with the British colonists to the east. And of course, there was the trump card: reminding Onontio's children of their past experiences with the British, who would become "as numerous as Muskeeto's and Nitts in the Woods" if the Indians did not drive them away, as Ackowanothio recalled.[89]

Yet there remains an element of mystery surrounding the Natives' exact motives. For all of the apparent bonds of Franco-Indian alliance, much that happened among the Natives' own counsels will forever remain invisible, and for this there are only fleeting glimpses in French records. The French had remained suspicious of their Native

allies in the early 1750s—especially the Ohio Indians who had gravitated toward British trade and alliance in the late 1740s. They were
never quite sure of their intentions, hearing rumors of intrigue with
the English ("the Hurons and Cha8anons [Shawnees] were plotting
evil deeds," wrote Chaussegros de Léry in his journal) and of mysterious intertribal councils and wampum belts ("the savages have been
talking in riddles"—which, of course, the French did not get).[90]

The French, in truth, were only peripheral witnesses to the
speeches, belts, and messages that Native leaders and diplomats
exchanged in the winter of 1754 and spring of 1755. An intertribal
council in the fall of 1754 is perhaps one of the best indications of
what Natives were saying about the impending clash of arms. In early
1755, Chaussegros de Léry recorded one of the faint glimpses of what
was actually said at a meeting of Shawnees and Miamis during the previous fall (though he learned it from his informant, a Wea Indian who
witnessed the proceedings, making it a third-hand account). Shawnee
leaders had appealed for unity with Miamis, Weas, Piankashaws,
Kickapoos, Mascoutins, and other northward Indians. The Shawnee
speaker encouraged a Miami sachem named Latortue. "If all of you
come to see us, my brothers," he said, "come when the grass is half
way to your knees, so we may all assemble together. This is when the
French and the English are to fight each other, and we shall see who
is stronger." It was in these ways that diplomacy among the natives in
1754 and early 1755 often redounded to the benefit of the French.[91]

Some Natives at Fort Duquesne were fighting for each other,
drawn to action precisely because of their alliances and relations
with neighboring Indians. The Delawares' testimony of their dispos-
session by the English presumably alarmed their Native neighbors
who had less experience or contact with them. And as the case cited
suggests, the Shawnees effectively appealed to other nations as they
explained their reasons for making war against the English. In late
1754, for example, Shawnee leaders had presented a tomahawk and
war belt to the Wyandots, with a declaration of "eternal war on the
English" who had seized and imprisoned several Shawnee warriors in
South Carolina after an attack on the Catawbas had gone awry. They
also presented English scalps (taken in a revenge attack on colonists living on Buffalo Creek in Carolina that fall) to the Wyandots,
to Captain Contrecoeur at Fort Duquesne, and to various Native
communities along la Belle Rivière. The reply of Wyandot leader
Sastaretsy testifies to the ultimate effect of such appeals. "We are
in mourning because of the misfortune which has befallen you, my
little brothers," he told the Shawnees. "As you consider us your elders,

we are ready to help you in your affliction," he added, and ritually consoled them with gifts of wampum. Sastaretsy then received "with joy, the slave, the scalp, the belt and the hatchet you gave me," but cautioned that "the hatchet will remain lowered until Father Onontio has told you and us where it shall fall." By the spring of 1755, Onontio knew where the hatchet would fall, and Wyandot warriors came to aid their little brothers at Fort Duquesne.[92]

By late June 1755, Fort Duquesne was New France in microcosm, with all of its inherent strengths and weaknesses, its bonds and frictions of alliance. While historical accounts tend to treat a French-Indian victory at the Monongahela as virtually inevitable, there was very little confidence among the French officers at the Belle Rivière. That July, the Marquis de Vaudreuil wrote of his "dread" of receiving news from Fort Duquesne, which he had essentially written off as an inevitable English conquest.[93] Fort Duquesne's chronic weaknesses still remained. It was the terminus of supply lines that were overextended to an unsustainable degree. The sheer numbers of men present at the Forks of the Ohio could be sustained for only a few weeks. Within a year following Braddock's Defeat, Fort Duquesne was becoming increasingly untenable, and Governor Vaudreuil admitted to the "impossibility of victualing that post from this colony [Canada]." The fort would owe its continued existence in future years only to food and supplies coming upriver from the Illinois Country, which could provide them "sooner and more easily than from the heart of this Colony [Canada]."[94]

Upon Beaujeu's arrival at Fort Duquesne on June 27, his thoughts undoubtedly turned to the conundrum of defending an indefensible post. Despite his abundance of Indian allies, Contrecoeur and Beaujeu would encounter many difficulties in gaining intelligence of Braddock's advance. Whether the Native warriors would commit to battle or acquiesce in a British conquest of the Forks of the Ohio remained unclear. The records unfortunately shed little light on Beaujeu's exact activities once he reached Fort Duquesne. The only precise indication of French plans in the event of a British attack is a letter from Contrecoeur dated June 21 to the Marquis de Vaudreuil, whom he informs, "if we are attacked, I plan to put all our savages outside. They will have the woods to themselves, with the French to guide them, in order to strike behind the army day and night."[95] Contrecoeur's health was poor enough that he could not lead men into battle. As the senior officer who would become commandant upon Contrecoeur's departure, Beaujeu knew that he would likely lead that attack on the British, once more into the supreme chaos of battle.

CHAPTER 5

Braddock's March

Conquering the Allegheny Mountains, May 29–July 8, 1755

> We began our March, but surely such a one was never undertaken before....I apprehend [it] will be look'd upon as Romantick by those who did not see, and therefore cannot comprehend the difficulties of that March.
>
> ~Major William Sparke, 48th Regiment, 1755~

DRUMMERS BEATING ASSEMBLY ON the morning of May 29, 1755, announced the beginning of the march across the Allegheny Mountains. The noise roused 650 men who had been drawn from the 44th and 48th regiments, the New York Independent Company of Captain John Rutherford, the South Carolina Independents of Captain Paul Demeré, the Virginia ranger companies of captains William La Péronie and Thomas Waggoner, and William Polson's company of Virginia artificers. They all fell in fully accoutered, with two days' provisions, fresh ammunition, and ten flints apiece. Braddock had signed these men into motion the previous day, with orders to Sir John St. Clair to "open & prepare a Road over the Allegany Mountains, towards the great meadows." They were soldiers, road-builders, engineers, sailors, and Indians, and were under the overall command of Major Russell Chapman, who had responsibility for defending both the working party and the convoy of fifty wagons and two field pieces that accompanied them. St. Clair was the ideal officer to spearhead the conquest of the formidable natural barriers that lay ahead of them. The detachment departed Fort Cumberland at first light, but the sheer difficulties of marching through the Allegheny Mountains became apparent even as the sun began to set on May 29: the detachment had barely proceeded three miles, the convoy of fifty wagons was still getting over the immense mountain overlooking Fort Cumberland,

and multiple wagons had been utterly destroyed or damaged in the descent.[1]

Braddock's Campaign was unprecedented for its mountainous character—"surely such a one was never undertaken before," as Major Sparke believed. The first challenge that the army faced was conquering the Appalachian Mountains and the nearly 125 miles that lay between Fort Cumberland and Fort Duquesne.[2] Men and horses would face exhaustion and defeat at the hands of geographical forces, even before they might challenge French and Indian foes. It is difficult to exaggerate the sheer brute power required to overcome these obstacles, for the weapons of this warfare were axes, shovels, whip-saws, wagoners' whips, block and tackle, and barrels of blasting powder. The mountains, rocks, boulders, forests, ascents, descents, rivers, streams, and swamps that these men and animals confronted must have seemed insurmountable.[3] The surviving traces of Braddock's road are primary sources unto themselves, testifying to the laborers' toil and engineers' logic. In addition, the British had to be entirely self-sufficient during the march, while taking enough supplies to sustain them once in the Ohio Valley. An eighteenth-century Royal Navy admiral employed a striking nautical metaphor to describe the advance of a British field army into the interior of America: it was like "the passage of a ship through the sea whose track is soon lost." The land, like the sea, threatened to swallow up the army immediately after its departure from Fort Cumberland.[4]

British officers said as much to their unbelieving audiences in Britain. The vast American continent, the rugged character of its mountains, and the strength it afforded defenders were noted by a number of British officers from the 1750s to the 1780s. Charles Lee wrote to his sister Sidney in England in 1756, "there is a magnificence and greatness through the immense extent (which we have seen of this Continent) not equal'd in any part of Europe; our Rivers and Lakes (even the greatest) are to these little rivulets and brooks; indeed Nature in every Article seems to be in great here what on your side the Waters, she is small." St. Clair, among the few who had any campaigning experience in mountainous countries in Europe, wrote, "What was looked on at home as easy is our most difficult point to surmount, I mean the passage of this vast tract of Mountains; Had we a Country we coud subsist in after we get over them, the thing wou'd be easy." The baronet believed that the English had no idea of how to carry on a war in such a "Mountaneous Country." "I cannot conceive," another British officer baldly stated, "how war can be made in such a country." And after a year on the continent,

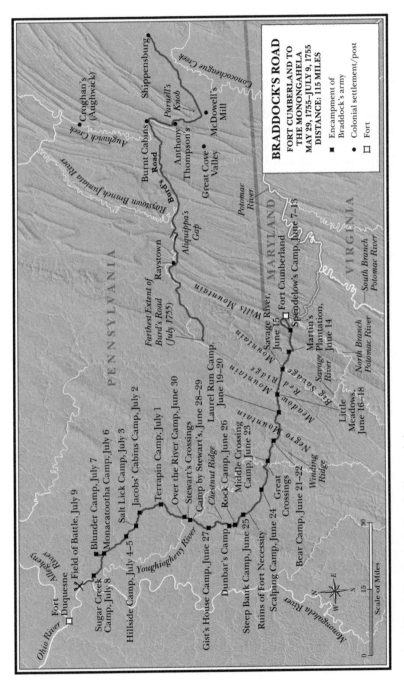

Braddock's Road: Fort Cumberland to the Monongahela

Glen Pawelski, Mapping Specialists, Ltd.

St. Clair reminded a correspondent, with considerable understatement, that "the War in North America differs widely from that in Europe."[5]

The campaign was nearly undone from the start when St. Clair and Chapman experienced difficulty in getting over the first ridge southwest of Cumberland, known as Wills or Haystack Mountain. After departing the fort, the detachment began its precipitous climb of the 1,400-foot-high mountain, building a new military road along an old trail that had been blazed by previous explorers and soldiers such as Christopher Gist and George Washington (the army was not following an Indian path called "Nemacolin's Trail," which was a later historian's invention).[6] Robert Orme wrote in his journal that "the ascent and descent were almost a perpendicular rock." The road was so rocky and descended so abruptly (200 feet) into Sandy Gap at the southern end of Haystack Mountain that three wagons crashed down the precipice and were "entirely destroyed," while "many more were extremely shattered." Washington recalled that the climb had been equally "destructive to our Waggon Horses." If the army continued to suffer similar casualties while surmounting the Alleghenies, the expedition would be in grave danger. Haystack Mountain was absorbing so much labor and time that General Braddock personally inspected the route, and sent 300 men to make the road passable to his artillery.[7]

On June 2, Lieutenant Spendelow of HMS *Centurion*, commanding the detachment of thirty-five Royal Navy sailors, went out to inspect the road, along with Colonel Ralph Burton, Robert Orme, and Midshipman Gill. Spendelow, whom Orme praised as a "young man of great discernment and abilities," was dissatisfied with the current route and with earlier scouting done by St. Clair. So he departed his companions on June 2 and scouted the countryside for an alternative to the grueling Haystack Mountain road. In a few hours, he had discovered a passage that even seasoned students of the land, including Gist and Washington, had failed to observe in their previous journeys. Spendelow discovered that the army could march northwest through the Narrows, the enormous water gap that Wills Creek had scooped out of Wills Mountain a short distance west of Fort Cumberland. With Haystack Mountain now looming harmlessly on his left, Spendelow found a gentler southwest ascent along a rivulet known today as Braddock's Run (or Four Mile Run) that the army could follow to a point just west of Sandy Gap, and continue following it westward through the water gap it created between Dans Mountain on the south and Piney Mountain on the north. Braddock was so convinced of the route's superiority that he immediately sent

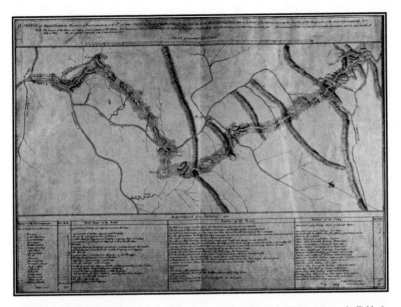

A Sketch of General Braddock's March from Fort Cumberland on the 10.th of June 1755 to the Field of Battle of the 9.th of July near the River Monongahela. Attributed to Engineer Harry Gordon, who had significant experience building military roads in Scotland in the years before Braddock's Expedition. Supplied by Royal Collection Trust / © HM Queen Elizabeth II 2014.

crews to construct the new road through the Narrows. Spendelow had single-handedly spared Braddock's army from the debilitating climb and destructive descent of Haystack Mountain.[8]

The road-builders in St. Clair's party, however, were not spared the physical toll that the mountains exacted. Provincials constituted the bulk of the party, though Braddock authorized, incentivized, and sometimes ordered British Redcoats to work on the roads or push wagons. In any serious ascent of steep mountain ridges, soldiers were expected to help muscle the wagons over. The general issued orders at Fort Cumberland that "every subaltern superintending work upon the road should receive three shillings per day; each serjeant one shilling; each corporal nine pence; and every drum and private man six pence." But with few sutlers or settlers to buy provisions from, Braddock held on to the troops' supplemental wages until their winter quarters. The composition of Chapman's 650-man detachment suggests who was doing the guarding and the working. Nearly half of his command (279 men) were regulars of the 44th and 48th regiments. The other half were Americans of the Independent Companies and the Virginia companies.[9]

Building a twelve-foot-wide wagon road over the consecutive mountain ridges tapped an extraordinary range of skills and occupations. Sawyers, or "hatchet men," wearing leather aprons cut swaths through old growth timber. Blacksmiths were constantly sharpening axes, saws, and tools. Miners used gunpowder to blast their way through boulders and rocks larger than themselves. Diggers graded and leveled the roads. Teamsters and wheelwrights repaired the wagons' axles and wheels; and British military engineers had to make quick topographical choices as they laid out the road ahead. Each day was an exhausting ordeal of "cutting, digging, and Bridging" and various degrees of blowing rock, as engineer Harry Gordon described the roadwork in his *Sketch of General Braddock's March.*[10] Already a seasoned hand at colonial road-building in 1755, St. Clair knew the importance of tools and the need for lots of them. In April, when St. Clair was working on the roads around Cacapon, he had had the foresight to write Robert Orme to employ blacksmiths in Frederick, Maryland, to produce more basic tools and equipment that he knew would be necessary: 100 "felling axes," 12 whipsaws, and 3 sets of miners' tools for "breaking and blowing rock." After a year's service in America, St. Clair was even more convinced that "the proportion of Entrenching Tools made out for Service in Europe will by no means answer in America." Referring to the paltry number of such tools sent with Braddock's troops from Ireland, he reminded his superiors that "one hundred felling Axes were sent out Last, when one Thousand wou'd have been too small a number for the work we had to do: digging is the great Work in Europe as cutting is here."[11]

Those uninitiated to the American wilderness felt an increasing sense of isolation and distance as the army entered what seemed an utterly foreign landscape. A pall seemed to hang over their undertaking, one British officer sensed, as if "the very Face of the Country is enough to Strike a Damp in the most resolute Mind." Charles Lee was struck by the "darkness and thickness of the woods" in America. The workmen cut an incalculable number of old growth trees whose diameters were best measured in feet. As the army plunged deep into the woods, felling the old growth timber and battling laurel thickets, the road must have appeared as an unnatural swath of light through the woods. The long, grayish trunks and branches stretching upward of 100 feet or more were now contrasted against the dark interior of the woods, still shielded by dense canopies. The road itself was strewn with small rocks and tree stumps sawn low enough to clear the wagons' axles. Much digging was required, as crews dug and leveled sidehill-cut roads, as the British engineers typically avoided directly uphill climbs, preferring instead to follow the contours of mountains for gentler, gradual ascents.[12]

St. Clair's working party had departed Fort Cumberland on May 29, but by June 1 it had covered only eleven miles, reaching a camp near George's Creek. Captain Cholmley's batman remembered the monotonous halts "Every hundred yards" as they waited on crews to mend the "very Bad Roads." St. Clair had foreseen the necessity of having miners' tools and was likely the force behind Braddock's orders in early May for a "return to be sent in of the numbers of men who understand the springing of rocks, & those men that are fitt are to be told that they will receive proper encouragement." One of the volunteers was likely Robert Hilton of Bristol, a twenty-year-old enlisted man in the 48th Regiment, who was a lead miner by trade. Braddock formed a special company composed of experienced miners, who accompanied St. Clair's work party for the entirety of the march. As the crews built along the route from Martin's Plantation to Little Meadows from June 2 through June 5, there was a "great deal of blowing" of immovable boulders on Big Savage Mountain, a ridge that was (and remains) awash in a sea of stones and boulders that the forces of nature and geology had strewn as far as the eye could see. Some boulders were so large, Cholmley's servant reported, "that we were obliged to Blast them several times before we Came to our ground" near the Savage River. Chapman and St. Clair's detachment finally arrived at the Little Meadows on June 5 after a miserable march over two more craggy ridges followed by swamps that required corduroying the road. Violent thunder storms created terrible conditions for the men and horses that day, as they slipped to their knees, struggling in the mud. Sir John aptly summarized that "the Roads are either Rocky or full of Boggs, we are obliged to blow the Rocks and lay Bridges every Day; What an happiness it is to have wood at hand for the latter!" On June 6, after unloading supplies, St. Clair's working party began clearing the encampment site at the Little Meadows. Major Chapman and the regulars returned eastward to escort the wagons, arriving back with the main body of the army on June 10.[13]

One of the most incalculable aspects of Braddock's march is the physical toll it exacted on the soldiers. The forty-one days of this march may have left the army in so exhausted a condition that it was a spent force by the time it reached the Monongahela. Soldiers may not have received enough calories in their provisions to offset the heavy, unrelenting labor and were perhaps as gaunt and emaciated as their horses. Road-building surely exacted a debilitating toll, etching into the men's bodies the physical price of the campaign. Men suffered from hernias, herniated discs, strained and torn muscles, and daily soreness. As one British officer observed in 1760, "soldiers are wrought like horses" while serving in America. Redcoats were ordered to "Assist the Waggons When Any pinch of a hill or Difficulty That may Append." The parade-ground appearance of Braddock's regulars was a casualty of the toil, so that "misshapen tricornes, and ragged, motley clothing" and torn gaiters were the norm. After one year of American service, Lord Loudoun reported, the 44th regiment was "in Rags but look like Soldiers."[14]

The story of a slave provides one indication of the physical toll on the road-builders. He was the slave of George William Fairfax, who had written to Washington in May 1755, seeking his help in returning three horses and his slave, whose name was Simpson, who had been impressed by the British Army. Washington was never able to locate Simpson (his only name), but was told later in the march that he "was taken ill upon the Road while he was with Sir Jno. St. Clairs Detachmt," perhaps through incapacitation or illness during his strenuous road work. Simpson's story establishes the presence of blacks in Braddock's army, though their invisibility in the sources is a measure of how expendable these laborers were.[15]

Soldiers' complaints of poor provisions during the campaign were nearly chronic. The common men, according to a later investigation, "were greatly Harrass'd by Duty's unequal to their Numbers Disperited by want of sufficient Provisions and not being Allowed time to dress the Little they had, with nothing to Drink but water and that often Scarce and Bad."[16] Though Braddock had tried to avoid it, the army had already begun to rely on salted provisions while it was at Fort Cumberland in May. These provisions, high in fat and protein, had enough caloric value for heavy work but the constant diet, as Braddock predicted, could "disable the men from undergoing the fatigues and hardships they were to meet with on their March to the Ohio." An unnamed British officer wrote that on the march they "can get nothing but *Indian* corn, or mouldy Bisket; the fresh Bread we must bake in Holes in the Ground having no Ovens, so besides the Mustiness of the Flour, it is half Sand and Dirt. We are happy if we can get some rusty salt Pork, or Beef, which hath been carried without Pickle" on pack horses. The army drove herds of sheep and cattle as a moving food supply, but the officer complained that "they are so lean that they are Carion and unwholesome," a judgment borne out at the end of the campaign, when Colonel Dunbar recommended killing emaciated cattle that were unfit to be given to the troops. At the Little Meadows, Braddock's Iroquois allies lifted the men's morale by bringing in deer, turkey, and other wild game. Cholmley's batman is equivocal on the subject of food, expressing the opinion that men needed more provisions, but also mentioning meals of mutton, bear, and rattlesnake.[17]

Far worse dangers to man and beast presented themselves in the woods: bad water, snakes, poisonous plants, mosquitoes, and ticks. A British officer complained especially of "a Kind of Tick, or Forest Bug, that gets into the Legs, and occasions Inflammations and Ulcers, so that the Wound itches and makes one ready to tear off the Flesh; this hath greatly distressed both Men and Officers, and there is no Help nor Cure for it but Patience." Toxic mountain laurel (*Kalmia latifolia*) and rhododendron that grew plentifully in the mountains tempted horses that lacked steady sources of forage. Braddock ordered that "horse drivers must take perticuler care to prevent their horses eating of Lawrell As it is Certain Death to them." Captain Edward Brice Dobbs, commanding the North Carolina ranger company, was temporarily blinded "by some stinking Weeds in the Woods" (most likely Jimson weed—*Datura stramonium*—which blossoms in the summer months, or smoke from poison ivy vines burning in a campfire). Strangely enough, it was Jimson weed or Jamestown weed that had brought a few English regulars to grief, when a few of them ingested a hallucinogenic and toxic salad of *Datura* greens while stationed in Virginia in the late 1600s, following Bacon's Rebellion.[18]

On a rainy June 7, with crescendos of thunder and cracks of lightning, Sir Peter Halkett's 44th regiment marched from Fort Cumberland, leading the advance of Braddock's main body under ominous gray skies. They marched along Spendelow's new route, a wet and muddy slog given the rainy weather. The troops and 100 wagons carrying supplies and ammunition had to cross Wills Creek four times, even before their route intersected with Four Mile Run. The army camped about five miles from Fort Cumberland and west of Sandy Gap, at what was called Grove Camp or Spendelow's Camp, which thankfully had good forage. "The first days March," wrote Harry Gordon, "Convinc'd us that it was impossible to Get on with so many Carriages so heavily Loaded," and most of the heavy wagons and artillery had yet to move. Indeed, Halkett's regiment would remain at Grove Camp for another five days awaiting the rest of the army.[19]

The second division—largely the American units—marched on June 8, under Lieutenant Colonel Burton, who led the New York and

Robert Orme, *A Plan of the Line of March with the whole Baggage* (Thomas Jefferys, 1758). Orme shows the disposition of the British column as it departed Fort Cumberland on June 7 until its arrival at the Little Meadows camp on June 17. Map reproduction from the Richard H. Brown Revolutionary War Era Maps Collection of the Norman B. Leventhal Map Center, Boston Public Library.

South Carolina Independents, as well as all of the Virginia, Maryland, and North Carolina provincial companies. This division escorted the artillery train with most of its ammunition and other supply wagons. Given the massive labor involved in hauling the heavy artillery over such rugged ground, the third and final division of Braddock's army did not march until June 10. General Braddock and Colonel Dunbar, whom the general relegated to the rear of the army for the entire campaign, led the 48th Regiment out of Fort Cumberland with the remainder of the supply wagons. The last thing that remained to do was to transfer custody of Fort Cumberland to the governor of the fort, Colonel Innes, and his garrison of about fifty men, mostly invalids. Braddock gave Innes his final instructions, for the moment when he "shall receive Advice from me of my being in Possession of the Fort of Duquesne." The march on June 10 was described by an officer in the 48th Regiment as "attended with many difficulties owing to ye road & cariages being bad, & though ye line of March was intended to be only two Mile & an half in Extent, Yet they were frequently twice that distance." An aerial view of Braddock's divisions would have revealed a long, red line, stretching out for five miles from Fort Cumberland.[20]

General Braddock called another council of war at Spendelow's Camp on June 11 to discuss the slow pace of the march. The impetus for this meeting was Colonel Burton's observation that while Spendelow's route was "a better road than we were to expect afterwards," even this gradual ascent of five miles along a stream had resulted in "extreme faintness and deficiency of the horses." What would happen to them when the army had to scale massive ridgelines? Braddock immediately took action, recognizing that "it would be impossible to continue the March without some alterations." He recommended that officers sacrifice any and all excess baggage and tents, asking them to volunteer any extra horses for wagon service. According to Orme, Braddock "excited them to it by his example; he and his family contributed twenty horses." The officers provided a total of nearly 100 horses, with "great chearfulness and zeal," according to Washington.[21]

The June 11 council substantially altered the dispositions of Braddock's immense train. The officers present—Halkett, Dunbar, Gage, Burton, Chapman, and Sparke—unanimously agreed to send two 6-pounders and four coehorn mortars back to Fort Cumberland, immediately freeing up twenty wagons. The "King's Wagons"—the heaviest ones used to haul gunpowder and requiring the largest draft horses—were simply too cumbersome for the wilderness roads and were also sent back. The council further agreed to reduce the wagon weight, which had been from 18–20 hundredweight (approximately 2,016 to 2,240 pounds, or more than a ton) to 14 hundredweight (approximately 1,600 pounds or three-quarters of a ton). Abler horses would pull the heavy howitzers in teams of seven, the 12-pounders in teams of five, and the traditional four to each wagon. The weaker horses, deemed "the offcasts of Indian traders," were converted into pack horses, carrying hundred-pound sacks of flour and bacon. It took two days at Spendelow's Camp to institute these changes and reload wagons.[22]

Halkett's brigade began its march to the next encampment site along George's Creek at 4:00 A.M. on June 13. A British officer described the long day as "tedious with some accidents." Even with the retrenched baggage, the army was becoming impossibly distended. Captain Orme recorded that Halkett's brigade reached the next encampment on the evening of the same day, but that Dunbar's brigade did not get there until 11:00 A.M. the following day—which meant that the army had been strung out for five miles, and that Dunbar's column most likely camped along the road on the night of June 13.[23]

The army's encampment site on June 13 and 14 was a forward outpost of colonial settlement called Martin's Plantation, located along a branch of George's Creek near present-day Frostburg. The plantation had "very good feeding [forage], fine water," and may have been the one spoken of in Braddock's orderly book as "Mr. Martin's where the troop of Light Horse graze."[24] Though no land records with the name of "Martin" can be found, it is possible that the settler family were kin of the family of John Marshall, later chief justice of the United States. A letter dated June 15, 1755, from Elizabeth Marshall Martin to her brother Thomas, mentions that Braddock and his staff "camped here last night" at their plantation named after her husband, Abram Martin. Frontier settlements like the Martins' would soon be in mortal danger from Indian attacks, which was presumably the reason the family never persisted long enough to obtain any formal right to the land. It was perhaps with such families in mind that Braddock had warned the governors of Virginia, Maryland, and Pennsylvania of the threat of Indian attacks along the frontiers the army was leaving behind.[25]

From the clearings at Martin's Plantation, Braddock and his men could begin to perceive their greatest challenge on the western skyline. Big Savage Mountain was unquestionably the most difficult geographical obstacle that the army encountered during the march.

Halkett's brigade stepped off at 5:00 A.M. on June 15, but after seven hours, the army's trailing wagons had only climbed out of the George's Creek valley and gotten up to the steep spur leading to the crest of Big Savage. The climb in elevation from Martin's Plantation to the crest of Big Savage was nearly 1,000 feet covering a distance of about two miles along a steep and rocky road (a 9 percent grade). Even a short ascent with a fully loaded wagon rapidly exhausted a team of horses, and this one tested the limits of human and animal endurance. Braddock had earlier canvassed Dunbar's regiment, Gates's New York Independent Company, and the American units for any men "fitt for Waggoners or Horse Drivers," indicating how troops were to be used in the march. One officer recalled that throughout, "we were all Work'd and sweated both man and beast to get the Waggons up the hills *which the horses never Could have done without the men.*" The hot weather made the march up Big Savage all the more draining. Half of the troops, Robert Orme recalled, were ordered to "ground their arms and assist the carriages" up and down the mountain. As the wagoners came to the gentle saddle on the summit of Big

Trace of Braddock's Road, one-quarter mile from the crest of Big Savage Mountain, Savage River State Forest, Maryland. Author photograph. A company of miners had to blast huge boulders and rocks with gunpowder from this and other sections of Braddock's Road.

Savage Mountain, they must have cringed as they saw what lay ahead—the road simply dropped off the mountain's "very rugged and almost perpendicular" western face, in Orme's description.[26]

The descent of Big Savage Mountain and other such ridges tested the wagoners' skills and their teams' endurance, even as it showcased the unique contributions of Lieutenant Spendelow's sailors. A common method of slowing wagons going downhill was to fasten a large tree to the back of the wagon and lock the wheels, while travelers tugged with all their might on ropes fixed to the axles or wheels. Royal Navy sailors used their block-and-tackle skills throughout the march to lift wagons stuck in mud or to aid them as they descended steep hills. Despite these efforts, the British lost control of a number of wagons, which careered down the western slope, crashing and overturning their supplies, so that "we intirely demolished three waggons and shattered several." Yet in the face of incredible hardships, Halkett's brigade almost miraculously made a march of five miles before camping near the Savage River. The end of that exceptionally wearisome day was reflected in the terse entry in Colonel Halkett's orderly book:

Camp at Savage River June 15th: 1755

The Parole is Marlborough

Field Officer for to Morrow is Lieut Col: Gage

The Troops to March to Morrow. The Genl to beat at 4 oClock.[27]

No sooner had the army conquered Big Savage than it confronted diverse but equally difficult terrain. Nowhere were Europeans' fears of the wilderness more pronounced than under the "Shades of Death," a tract of tall white pines and hemlock that seemed to enclose the soldiers in a gloomy and dark embrace. Adam Stephen described them as "a dismal Place," that only needed Cerberus, the three-headed dog that according to Greek mythology guards the gates of hell, to appropriately complete the scene. Pine trees soared as high as 180 feet, "many of them without a limb for 100 feet," creating an impenetrable canopy. Watered by a rivulet called Two Mile Run, dampness permeated everything in these dark woods, from the moss on fallen trees and lichens on rocks, to the diffused gray light that occasionally penetrated the darkness under the forest canopies. It was "one of the most dismal places I ever saw," reported one later traveler, "the lofty Pines obscure the Sun, and the thick Laurels are like a Hedge on each side, the Road is very narrow and full of large stones and bogs." Low areas where mountain runs, springs, or runoff flowed over the road created morasses of mud that had to be filled and maintained.[28] Coming off of Red Ridge, the army now had to cross a "bogg" whose watery descendant is still visible today. St. Clair and the road-builders had "with infinite labour" created a corduroy road over this swampy ground; they were "obliged to blow the rocks and lay Bridges every day." Before arriving at the pleasant-sounding prospect of the Little Meadows, the army had to march from soggy ground up the face of Meadow Mountain. This proved another horrible ordeal for the horses, who struggled up the concentrated and steep ascent of nearly 250 feet in a half of a mile along a switchback. Cholmley's batman described the route as "very Bad Roads Over Rocks and Mountains," and it is still covered with mammoth boulders and rocks to this day.[29]

Halkett's brigade finally arrived at the Little Meadows on a stiflingly hot June 16, but the two hills had prevented Dunbar's brigade from reaching it until the next morning. In the space of a few days, the army had gone from Big Savage Mountain's immense heights down its nearly vertical western slopes, through the Shades of Death,

The engraving *Braddock's March* depicts how the British column of 2,500 soldiers and civilians often extended for miles along the twelve-foot-wide military road. In William Cullen Bryant and Sydney Howard Gay, *A Popular History of the United States*, Volume 3 (New York, 1881), 260.

across bogs and swamps, and finally over the boulder-covered slopes of Meadow Mountain. The army had also crossed the Continental Divide (near modern Walnut Hill), leaving behind "the last water that empties itself into the Potomac." With its flat, broad, and well-watered clearings, the Little Meadows offered respite to horses hungry for fodder and a spacious setting more befitting regulars from Ireland, one of whom commented that of all the places they camped, the Little Meadows was "the only one where regular Troops could make Use of their Discipline and Arms." The Little Meadows, significantly, would be the only fortified outpost along Braddock's Road. St. Clair and the working party had prepared an abattis around the entire encampment, following Braddock's orders to "establish a small Post and to lay a Deposit of Provisions."[30]

It was at the Little Meadows encampment that Braddock made a crucial decision about the speed and tempo of the campaign. A march of only twenty-one miles—from Fort Cumberland to the Little Meadows—had brought Braddock's army to a physical and logistical breaking point. The bloody flux and fevers that incapacitated many at Fort Cumberland were still afflicting soldiers, who complained of bad water during the march.[31] The campaign was beginning to come apart at its logistical seams, as Robert Orme summarized: "By these [past] four days' marches it was found impossible to proceed with such a number of carriages. The horses grew every day fainter, and many died: and the men would not have been able to have undergone the constant and necessary fatigue, by remaining so many hours under arms; and by the great extent of the baggage the line was extremely weak'ned." The column was so dangerously extended, Washington observed, and "the Soldrs Guarding them so dispersed that if we had been attackd either in Front, Center or Rear the part so attackd, must have been cut [off] or totally routed before they coud be sustain by any other Corps."[32]

When Braddock approached his aide-de-camp on June 16 or 17, Washington was himself growing more ill by the hour, wracked with "violent Fevers & Pains" that incapacitated him for weeks. Washington later maintained that "at the little Meadows there was a 2d Council called" to discuss the urgent need for horses. Braddock had asked his "private Opinion concerning the Expedition" before the officers had met in council. For days, Washington had been thinking of the "insurmountable obstacle" that the army faced if it continued with so large a train. He urged Braddock to further lighten the load and to push forward with a "small but chosen Band," bringing only the guns necessary to besiege the French, while leaving the heavier wagons and baggage behind with the army's rear division, "to follow while we were advanced in Front." He believed that a rapid advance could catch the French in a weakened condition at Fort Duquesne and arrive there ahead of the French reinforcements that were coming. Both Washington and Braddock became more certain that the French had no "sufficient force to make a serious assault."[33]

We have only Washington's letter to verify that a formal council of war took place at the Little Meadows. It is possible that he had raised his plan previously, for a letter by William Shirley Jr. related that a proposal to detach a column had already been discussed at the June 11 council at Spendelow's Camp. Perhaps Braddock merely informed his senior officers at Little Meadows that they would now proceed along that previously discussed plan. Colonel Dunbar later wrote that Braddock had simply issued orders at the Little Meadows for "a Detachment of About twelve hundred of the best Troops" to march onward, and that "was the first Sr Peter Halkett or I knew of this design." St. Clair's account also corresponds to Dunbar's, that "about the 17th of June General Braddock sent for me and told me, he laid down a Scheme of his own for marching on, which before that time, had been given to the Brigade Major [Francis Halkett] in orders."[34]

Crucial intelligence also came into Braddock's hands that decisively shaped his thinking on the campaign. Sometime before June 9,[35] while the army was preparing to depart Fort Cumberland, the general had received a visit from Lieutenant John Butler, one of Indian Superintendent William Johnson's agents and interpreters. Butler accompanied a delegation of four Tiononderoge Mohawks down from New York, and he was carrying recent intelligence on French strength and movements.[36] It was a copy of Johnson's examination of Jean Silvestre, the erstwhile French trader who had refused to go on to the Ohio Country and went to British Oswego instead. According to Silvestre's estimates, there were only 300 men on the Belle Rivière, but 950 reinforcements under Captain Beaujeu were on their way.[37] Butler brought a specific report from Johnson that 500 or 600 French troops were stalled at Rivière au Boeuf, "lying at the River Ohio not able to proceed, the Waters being so very shallow." Johnson had charged Butler to urge Braddock "to advance with the utmost Dispatch to Fort Du Quesne."[38] Around the time that the army was at the Little Meadows, Braddock received a second strand of intelligence from Captain John Bradstreet at Fort Oswego, with more detailed information on French troops then passing the British outpost on Lake Ontario.[39] This precise fix on French reinforcements confirmed Silvestre's account and, perhaps, Braddock's resolution to march quickly to beat them to Fort Duquesne.[40]

In any event, Braddock decided to split the army in half in his pursuit of a quick and speedy victory. He pared down the army to create a leaner "flying camp" or "flying column"[41] of about 1,200 men. He selected about 900 officers and men of the "Old Standers"—the original Irish veterans of the 44th and 48th regiments, including Private Duncan Cameron, who perceived that the general's "Dependance was chiefly upon us Regulars that he brought from Ireland." Braddock also included his finest New York Independent Company, that of Horatio Gates, and the most experienced Virginia companies of Polson, La Péronie, and Waggoner, as well as Robert Stewart's lighthorsemen. By sifting out all of the American recruits from his regular regiments and leaving them with Dunbar, Braddock betrayed a fundamental distrust of their discipline and martial qualities.[42] The general also took only the minimum amounts of artillery and ammunition to level Fort Duquesne: four 12-pounders, four 8-inch howitzers, two 6-pounders, and three Coehorn mortars. The four heavy howitzers would have a total of 200 rounds (50 each), suggesting that Braddock did not anticipate any lengthy siege. St. Clair would have three wagons of requisite tools for building roads and siege works. The total number of carriages in the pared-down train was approximately thirty-four, including artillery, supply, and ammunition wagons. Pack horses would now carry thirty-five days' worth of provisions, suggesting that Braddock expected Fort Duquesne to be captured, Dunbar's column to come forward, and Burd's Road to Pennsylvania to be opened within that time.[43] Finally, and perhaps most significantly, Braddock included one wagon filled with Indian presents, presumably for his Indian allies as well as future negotiations with Ohio Indians after the presumed fall of Fort Duquesne, proving again that he did not intend to scorn the Ohio Indians, as he has so often been accused of doing.[44]

Braddock had divided his army not only physically but also politically. Every officer eager for laurels and preferment knew that glory

---

Opposite: Robert Orme, *A Plan of the Line of March of the Detachment from the Little Meadows* (Thomas Jefferys, 1758). From the Little Meadows to the Monongahela, Braddock pressed forward with a flying column that was divided into an advanced party (or vanguard), the main body guarding the artillery and wagons, and a rearguard. Approximately one-third of Braddock's forces were deployed as flanking parties protecting and screening the column's advance.

Map reproduction from the Richard H. Brown Revolutionary War Era Maps Collection of the Norman B. Leventhal Map Center, Boston Public Library.

was in the advance column, while those in Dunbar's column would languish. Two young officers carrying dispatches to Braddock desperately sought to accompany Braddock's column as volunteers. Captain Mathew Floyer of Hopson's 40th Regiment and Captain William Stone of Lascelles's 47th Regiment had arrived at the Little Meadows and "earnestly solicited the General to be permitted to accompany the Troops up to Fort du Quesne." The general granted permission to Floyer and Stone but to none of the officers in Dunbar's column, including Charles Lee, who would thus lose an opportunity for professional advancement were the campaign to succeed.[45] In retrospect, it meant that Braddock's most bitter and vitriolic critics would survive the campaign. Captain John Rutherford, commanding the 3rd New York Independent Company left behind, was one of them. He mockingly wrote of how the army "marched out the Knight [St. Clair] swearing in the Van, The Genl Curseing & bullying in the Center & their Whores bringing up the Rear" (historians enjoy citing this because it reinforces conventional if distorted stereotypes of Braddock and provides some comic relief).[46]

Braddock's decision stoked a fiery debate among his senior officers about the proper approach to Fort Duquesne. Political divisions are common to all armies in every age, but Braddock's army seemed to have an abundance of "many unhappy Divisions," as Governor Sharpe reported. There was, however, little criticism of Braddock's plan to proceed with a smaller and faster corps. Even the skeptical St. Clair knew that dividing the army "was the only way we Could have brought up our Convoy." But a fierce dispute arose over the question of whether to reunite Braddock's and Dunbar's columns as they approached Fort Duquesne. Halkett and St. Clair were especially adamant that the army establish a forward outpost or base as they neared the French stronghold. "Had the General used less Dispatch in marching to Fort Duquesne," Governor Sharpe later wrote, "making places of Defence at proper Distances as they marched...the Enemy would have been kept in Suspence on the Ohio while things were carried on" northward. They essentially favored the slower methodical advance that General John Forbes adopted during his advance on Fort Duquesne a few years later. Had Braddock proceeded down that road not taken, it is possible that the army might have developed a secure supply lifeline to Pennsylvania via Burd's Road and arrived at Fort Duquesne in the early fall—after French Indian allies had departed for their homes.[47]

Braddock's final advance on Fort Duquesne was perhaps the fastest by a conventional army through mountainous wilderness ever accomplished in early American warfare, but in the end the general lost the race with French reinforcements under Beaujeu. He had predicated his strategy for the remainder of his expedition on advancing to Fort Duquesne "as fast as possible" before the French reinforcements arrived, and of gaining accurate intelligence of French and Native strengths at the Forks of the Ohio. Neither Braddock nor Washington was wrong in his understanding that low waters on Rivière au Boeuf would significantly delay enemy reinforcements. But the expedition's accumulated delays ultimately proved fatal to the premise of Braddock's flying column. Had the British Army arrived at Fort Duquesne only a few weeks earlier, as he had once hoped, French forces would have been much smaller. And finally, Braddock did not gain significant intelligence of French strength at Fort Duquesne even as he drew near it in early July.[48]

Braddock's plan to supply British forces in the Ohio Valley was coming to fruition, thanks in part to Pennsylvania, the province that had once invoked Braddock's wrath and was now earning his affectionate praise. The general thanked Governor Morris and "your little Government" for their efforts to construct a supply road across Pennsylvania's frontier and for sending along additional provisions. The Pennsylvania road came to be known for its principal commissioner and overseer, James Burd, a Scottish immigrant.[49] The ninety-odd completed miles of Burd's Road began near Shippensburg and roughly followed paths used by squatters and traders to access points west. It rounded Parnell's Knob, crossed the Tuscarora Mountain at Anthony Thompson's trading post, and coursed alongside the Juniata River through Aliquippa's Gap to Raystown, before turning west-southwest toward the Allegheny Front. Its end point was the Turkey Foot, so-called because it was where the Youghiogheny River forked into three branches. Burd's Road was to intersect with Braddock's Road, though it was yet to be determined where exactly that would happen.[50]

Braddock increasingly saw the Pennsylvania road as essential to the campaign. "It is a road of the utmost consequence," provincial secretary Richard Peters told Burd on May 27, as Braddock "expects his provisions by this road." Braddock indeed intended for Pennsylvania to establish a huge supply magazine at Shippensburg (paid for with the bills of credit from South Carolina). He assumed that supplies laid up there—three months' worth—would sustain his men after they took Fort Duquesne in July. Completion of the road was stymied, however, by usual colonial roadblocks: Morris's bare-knuckle fights with the Pennsylvania assembly to fund it; wagoners who would not

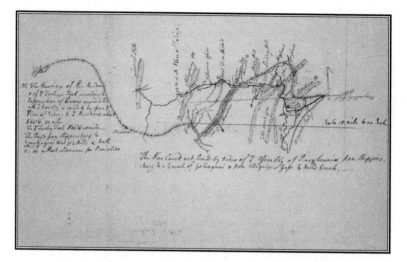

Burd's Road, shown in this unpublished 1755 map, was intended to be Braddock's principal supply line from Pennsylvania to the Ohio Valley. Parts of Burd's Road were later incorporated into Forbes's Road of 1758. Thomas Pownall, "The New laied out Roads by Order of ye Assembly of Pennsylvania from Shippensburg to a Branch of Yohiogenni & from Alliquipis Gap to Wills Creek," ca. 1755, Loudoun Papers, LO 530, Courtesy of the Huntington Library.

work for Burd unless paid the same wages as Braddock's teamsters; and terribly poor provisions for workers. Yet for all these problems, Burd's Road was in "tollerable Forwardness" by early June, and 108 workers were extending the route ever farther westward. Braddock had also detached Captain Peter Hogg's Virginia ranger company, numbering around 100 men, northward to cover the working party. By June 17, the road-builders had threaded their way through Aliquippa's Gap, and they reached Raystown on June 19, the same day that Braddock left the Little Meadows encampment for the final march on Fort Duquesne.[51]

THE ARMY HAD OVERCOME the greatest geographical challenges of the campaign, though many more ridges still stretched across the western horizon, and it would have to contend with multiple crossings of the Youghiogheny and the Monongahela rivers. Braddock's decision to detach a flying column seemed to be paying off. Nonetheless, shortly after splitting his army in half, he faced a new challenge. On June 19, the advanced guard of the army led by Colonel

Gage would confront a significant French and Indian force at the crest of an enormous mountain, an event that signaled a new phase in the westward progress of the army, testing whether it could withstand a series of concentrated French and Indian probes and attacks.

Thus far, the French had done little to contest Braddock's march. But now, the British were beginning to enter what the French called the "height of land" that they had demarcated in 1754 as their territorial claims. Governor Duquesne had directed Contrecoeur in the spring, "whenever he [Braddock] passes beyond the big mountain, you must harrass him and take up the hatchet."[52] Contrecoeur had sent out a few scouts to reconnoiter Fort Cumberland beginning in May 1755, and they had reported back that the English were "not at all on the march." Not until around June 7 did Contrecoeur sense the British were advancing, and that intelligence came not from Indian scouts but from a deserter who had made his way to Fort Duquesne (the deserter was from one of the Independent Companies in St. Clair's working party). The deserter's report had prompted Contrecoeur, as we've seen, to send his urgent letter to Beaujeu at Camp Machault, asking him to come on immediately, and warning him to keep Braddock's powerful artillery train a secret from his men. The next day, June 8, Contrecoeur sent out his first large detachment, led by cadet Joseph Godefroy de Normanville and composed of eighty-seven Indian scouts and eleven cadets, including René-Marie Pécaudy de Contrecoeur, the twenty-three-year-old son of Fort Duquesne's commandant and a *cadet d'aiguillette*.[53] Their express mission was "to attack the English on the sly, so that we can divert and hold them up while we await the arrival of our men"— meaning, Beaujeu's detachments. Sieur de Normanville's detachment would confront the British at the crest of the "immense mountain" on June 19, and they would shadow Braddock's army throughout the following week.[54]

A day earlier, on June 18, Gage had marched out of the Little Meadows with the advanced party of Braddock's smaller, lighter, and mobile column. St. Clair was tasked with carving out the military road to the Great Crossing of the Youghiogheny River. The units under Gage's command included Gates's New York Independents, the two Virginia ranger companies of Waggoner and La Péronie, and two companies of the 44th and 48th commanded by captains John Beckwith and William Morris. Royal artillerists accompanied the column as well, to service the two 6-pounders. The following day, June 19, Braddock set off with the main body, following the road that St. Clair's workmen had built. After leaving the Little Meadows,

Braddock's flying column ascended a small ridge and forded the Little Crossings of the Youghiogheny (Casselman River) before descending into the deep defile of the Shade Run Valley, formed by Shade Hill to the east and the steep slopes of an "immense mountain" to the west. Later known as Negro Mountain, after a black soldier who died in battle in 1756 along its crest, it was nearly 3,000 feet in elevation. The ascent up Negro Mountain was nearly as grueling as that of Savage Mountain—a steady climb of 700 feet over two miles of "very rough and stoney" ground. The British engineers constructed a traverse road with two sweeping arcs that curved nearly ninety degrees to the north, following the mountain's contours, before again turning ninety degrees to the west up toward the summit. As Gage's detachment neared the crest, Braddock's guides and his Indian allies, led by Scaroyady (also known as Monacatootha) were screening the advance.[55]

Braddock and the main column were just a short distance behind Gage, having just marched down into the defile of Shade Run, when panicked and frightened guides rushed into the camp, warning that a "great body of the enemy were marching to attack our advance guard." Braddock ordered forward an aide-de-camp who soon "found Lieutenant Colonel Gage in possession of the top of the mountain, and his men very advantageously posted." Braddock's faith in both Gage his "old standers" must surely have increased as he heard of this. Earlier that day, the guides and Native allies had discovered enemy tracks. French and Indian forces had achieved a great coup by capturing none other than Scaroyady himself, who had been a thorn in the French side for nearly two years. Normanville and Contrecoeur *fils* bound Scaroyady to a tree and pressed their Native allies to execute the influential Iroquois leader. But the French-allied warriors—some of whom were Iroquois—refused to kill a warrior of such stature, especially after Scaroyady appealed to them to be released. He eventually found his way back to British lines. In the meantime, Gage's advance party had secured the crest of Negro Mountain and remained there "about two hours under arms." Given that the enemy made no appearance, Gage sent out patrols to "scour the neighboring woods," and when they returned, they set up camp for the night.[56]

The sparing of Monacatootha's life reveals that Native warriors with the French had their own agenda, one that made the European combatants seem peripheral. Contrecoeur was clearly frustrated that his allies had prevented the party from returning to Fort Duquesne with Scaroyady. A British officer with the expedition also reported what had transpired during Scaroyady's brief captivity. The French-allied Indians had interrogated him for their own purposes: "They asked him many questions about our Numbers & what Artillery, & were excessively surprised at his account." Scaroyady must have told the French allies of the artillery that the British carried, for the British officer's account relates that the French cadets tried to persuade the Indians that "it was impossible to march Artillery through such a Country"—a statement that perfectly matches the sentiments of Duquesne and Contrecoeur. The French officers insisted to their allies that "what Monacatothe said was entirely false," but the Native scouts were forming their own conclusions about Braddock's approaching army.[57]

Tensions between the French and their Indian allies were common in May and June 1755, during which time Contrecoeur sent out a total of at least 550 Frenchmen and Indians from Fort Duquesne to scout and confront Braddock's column. The parties were variously composed of Abenakis, Senecas, Shawnees, Delawares, Cayugas, Potawatomis, and Ottawas, accompanied by officers such as Lieutenant Pierre-Louis Boucher de Niverville Montisambert, a veteran of the 1749 Céloron Expedition, or interpreters and traders such as Louis-Amable Pertuis and Louis, Jacques, or Antoine Baby, dit Dupéront.[58] Contrecoeur's stated goal in sending out these detachments was to slow the British march until reinforcements arrived. He was optimistic that "the English will be surprised when they see themselves attacked in the savage way almost every day and night." He even had the peculiar idea of giving the Indians spears to destroy English horses during the night, which would further delay Braddock's advance: "they will have all our savages on their back and some Frenchmen, which will hinder them a great deal in their march."[59] It remained to be seen, however, whether Contrecoeur's Indian allies would actually fulfill his mission.

Meanwhile, Braddock's army had continued on its westward course after the nonconfrontation on Negro Mountain on June 19. The army had advanced seven miles down into the Puzzely Run valley before ascending Keyser's Ridge and onto the next encampment site named Bear Camp. Gordon described the route as "1/2 mile in steep turnings [down the west face of Negro Mountain], ½ mile good [Puzzely Run], 2 miles very rough and stoney [Keyser's Ridge], 4 miles tolerable [to Bear Camp]." The monotonous work of road-building, according to Gordon, involved "a great deal of cutting and digging," as well as the creation of a few bridges over low-lying areas. The column was far from "flying," as an impatient George Washington complained, for "instead of pushing on with vigour, without re-garding a little rough Road, they were halting to Level every Mold Hill, & to erect Bridges over every brook; by which means we were 4 days getting 12 Miles." The main body of the army had indeed halted twice, at Laurel Run and at Bear Camp, awaiting St. Clair's road-builders to complete their tasks. The old surveyor's estimate of the distance they covered was spot on—the distance from the Little Meadows to Bear Camp is exactly twelve miles. But Washington's famous critique of Braddock's march did not take into account the immense challenge of hauling artillery over Negro Mountain and Winding Ridge, and it failed to note the army's first significant encounters with French and Indian forces in that section of the march. Wagoners might also have scoffed at Washington's character-ization of "a little rough Road."[60]

Washington was deliriously ill by this time, so much so that he could no longer ride a horse or bear the jarring movements of the wagons, even proceeding at their allegedly snail-like pace. Braddock left his young aide behind at Bear Camp, along with his word of honor that he would bring Washington forward as they neared Fort Duquesne. The general also ordered his physician to prescribe Doctor James's Powder, mentioned earlier, and the medicine brought Washington "immediate ease, and removed my Fevers & other Com-plaints in 4 Days time." Washington fondly remembered Braddock's care and seemed to take particular delight in extolling the virtues of Doctor James's Powder, even decades later.[61]

During the march, the army took many calculated risks while moving through the landscape of ridges and valleys that offered a multitude of perfect locations for French and Indian ambushes. By June 23, the main body of the army was advancing up one of the steepest slopes that it had yet encountered, so steep that the main body had to halt two days while the working party created multiple switchbacks ("zigzags" in Gordon's words) to ascend the 10 percent grade of Winding Ridge. There were already hints of imminent dan-gers lurking in the woods. A sentry at Bear's Camp, spooked during his nighttime watch, "Fired at two Men as he thought which Alarm'd the Camp." And as the army marched on June 23 and 24, Cholmley's batman reported that they "drove many French Indians before us." The same day that it passed over Winding Ridge, the army threaded its way into a narrow defile created by a small stream (later called Braddock's Run). The streambed was laden with rocks and boulders that had to be moved as the army crossed, which it did five times.[62]

As the army encamped that night within a mile of the Great Crossings of the Youghiogheny, three Mohawk Indians (presumably Canadian Iroquois) from Fort Duquesne came into the camp "pretending friendship," as Orme recorded, though their motives were unclear. They related entirely accurate intelligence to Braddock that Fort Duquesne had received minimal reinforcements, that more were expected, but there was "very little provision" there, and that low water on Rivière au Boeuf had stalled French movements. The intelligence appeared to confirm William Johnson's earlier reports and to vindicate Braddock's decision to push forward with the flying column before those reinforcements reached Duquesne. In Captain Orme's description, General Braddock "caressed them, and gave them presents" as they departed, again displaying his earnest diplomacy. One of Braddock's Indian scouts, however, the man named Skowonidous, or Jerry, used the occasion of the three Mohawks' visit to desert the army. The British had "very long suspected" Jerry's loyalties, and the long stares had perhaps finally gotten to him. They would meet him again. In the meantime, he presumably shared with the French and other Indians all the intimate knowledge he had gained of Braddock's force. For his part, Braddock could do very little with his intelligence of the French situation except press quickly onward.[63]

On June 24, the army marched to the mouth of the run, gazing upon the dazzling spectacle of the Youghiogheny River, which Orme gauged to be about 100 yards wide and three feet deep. Another British officer wrote that crossing the brown waters of the Youghiogheny "was extreamly beautifull & aforded us a pleasant prospect," in part because it offered relief from the "continued thickett" through which they had been marching. The crossing, and the narrows by which the army passed on the west bank, were again ideal places for ambush. A British officer reported that guides had seen "Indians frequently lurking round our line which we had reason afterwards to think true." Shortly after crossing the river, the army's guides had come upon a recently abandoned Indian camp and estimated the number of the party to be approximately 170. Ominous signs were left on stripped and painted trees, "upon which they and the French had written many threats and bravados with all kinds of scurrilous language." Such pictographs depicting the scalps and captives the warriors had taken were common among eastern woodland Indian warriors. Bent and twisted saplings warned enemies that they were united and strong.[64]

In the early morning hours of June 25, wagoners like Daniel Morgan were already stirring, knowing that drums would beat the general soon, and they undertook their daily ritual of going into the woods to retrieve their horses and hitch up their teams. One wagoner wandering far from the camp stumbled upon a party of French-allied Indians, who fired four shots into his stomach at close range. He somehow managed to flee back to the safety of the camp, but died a horrendously painful death a few days later. Around the same time, other wagoners—as many as four—were similarly shot and scalped while retrieving their horses. Hearing the firing, British Indian scouts ran to the fight, as did other patrols. One French or Indian warrior was killed, as the British later found a trail of his blood leading to a shallow grave.[65]

The British expected even greater trouble on that day's march, for their route would take them through the Great Meadows, giving the regulars a glimpse of the rotting remains of Fort Necessity, where Washington had fought the year before. The ground was still littered with bleached bones. The enemy's threatening omens along the trail and the ruins of Fort Necessity must have sparked conversations in camp about Native tactics and given rise to stories about scalping, probably told by Virginia and South Carolina troops who were veterans of the battle. "It was strongly imagined," one British officer wrote, that "if we met with any opposition, ye Meadows would be ye place; but we marched through without any Molestation or alarm." Throughout the day's march, Indians continued to hover along the flanks of the column. But the army was beginning to gain a certain level of tactical confidence. Near the Great Meadows, a party composed of Stewart's light horsemen, Indians, and volunteers went out to surround enemy fighters. For his part, Orme noticed a certain "alacrity and dispatch" in how the soldiers formed their next encampment, located on a site about one mile west of the Great Meadows. He noted that "marching through the woods, which [the soldiers] at first looked upon as unnecessary fatigue, they were now convinced to be their only security, and went through it with the greatest cheerfulness." That night, Godefroy de Normanville's detachment tried to "reconnoitre the camp," but sentinels discovered and fired on them. The next morning, Braddock deployed his men essentially as light infantry to flush out any hidden enemies. He sent two captains with fifty men each at the front and rear of his encampment. The two captains were to "divide the detachments into small parties," spread out into a half-mile-wide skirmish line, then sweep the flanks of the column, forcing into the open any enemy fighters who happened to conceal themselves overnight. None were found.[66]

The climax of the campaign's geographical obstacles and Contrecoeur's challenges came at Chestnut Ridge, which the army started to ascend on June 26. The climb of 600 feet up to Chestnut Ridge was so difficult that the army struggled to move even 3.5 miles that day. When the troops arrived near the crest that evening, they stumbled upon a large French and Indian campsite that had been abandoned only moments before, judging from the burning campfires. Soldiers found "many odd figures on ye trees expressing with red paint, ye scalps and Prisoners they had taken with them." The French, mimicking their Indian allies, also left their own "insolent expressions" that British officers translated. They were men of Normanville's party, for Normanville had either dropped his commission or left it as a calling card for the British to find. Three French names were also scrawled on the trees: Rochefort, Chauraudray, and Picaudy, the latter being the cadet René-Marie Pécaudy de Contrecoeur.[67]

Captain Contrecoeur's attempt to halt or simply delay the English advance was an unequivocal failure. Very little had been accomplished by the 500 Frenchmen and Indians who went out in May and June from Fort Duquesne. One horse had been wounded in the neck. A few British wagoners or servants had died or lost their scalps, and one French or Indian fighter was killed. No ambushes had occurred. No British horses ever died from spear-throwing Indians during the night. Contrecoeur's stream of war parties only appeared to be a great show of force, but in fact they underscored French weaknesses. The French had neither the manpower nor the supplies to indefinitely sustain any large force at a great distance. Governor Duquesne had specifically cautioned Contrecoeur to avoid "having a large corps march en masse unless it is close enough to get food, because it would be too dangerous for us not to be able to sustain such a bold measure," adding that "it would have a very bad effect on the spirit of the savages." Contrecoeur later offered praise of Braddock's vigilance and security during his march, when he admitted to Governor Vaudreuil that "these troops [Braddock's] maintained themselves so well on their guard, always marching in order of battle, that all the efforts the detachments made against them became useless."[68]

Despite Contrecoeur's express orders, French officers had not been able to mount any serious attack on the British, and it seemed as though they had been the auxiliaries of their reluctant and cautious

Native allies, whose actions revealed their independence and their own agenda. A large number of Native warriors had never before engaged (or even seen) a conventional army of the power and size of Braddock's. They had observed the army's weaponry and tested the tactical responses of the British troops. Canadian Mohawks had even approached the commander of this strong army directly—perhaps a way to diplomatically "clear the road" between the Indians and the British, in the event that Braddock's army proved an unstoppable force. The Indians' reconnaissance had given them wisdom on how, or whether, to engage this new and strange army.

If anything, French and Indian threats to the column between June 19 and 26 had conditioned the British to seize the tactical initiative at the slightest hint of an Indian threat. British troops were immediately sent forward into the woods, based on the notion that Natives would be easily brushed aside whenever disciplined regulars were deployed against them. Over the centuries, most observers have assumed that Indian threats and warnings encountered around the Great Meadows intimidated the British soldiers, who became unnerved by this shadowy foe in the woods and their fighting techniques "in regard to their scalping; and mohawking [tomahawking]." But British accounts convey increasing confidence and effectiveness in the woods, as they repeatedly faced down an enemy that apparently avoided them in any confrontation.

Not only were Contrecoeur's hopes of slowing Braddock's advance unfulfilled, but French commanders seemed infatuated with the idea that the British could not possibly get artillery across the Appalachians. They remained unclear about the army's precise location, despite the many scouting parties sent out to find it. The French were reduced to mere acts of desperate bravado: a few warnings and curses scrawled on trees as they hastily departed. A geographical and moral turning point had been reached at the Rock Camp, as it came to be known, on June 26, 1755. From the heights of Chestnut Ridge, the British troops could overlook the broad valley below, knowing that the worst of their mountainous passages were behind them. They had dealt with Indian assaults, and the French had not dared stand against them. That night, General Braddock dispatched Captain Robert Dobson of the 48th, a veteran of the Battle of Lauffeld, with two subalterns, ninety men, and guides, to pursue and fall upon Normanville's fleeing detachment: to "hunt the Indiens," as Captain Cholmley's batman bluntly wrote.[69] There was a palpable sense of rising morale as the army descended Chestnut Ridge the following day. Victory seemed near.

AT 5:00 A.M. ON JUNE 27, Braddock's column marched north out of the Rock Camp to begin their nearly eight-mile march and descent from the dominant ridgeline into the valley below. Some of the Virginia troops were already familiar with the route, which led past the site of Washington's skirmish with Ensign Jumonville a year earlier. The road then turned slightly to the north-northeast as it gained the crest of the ridge, a narrow backbone that the army followed for about a mile. The view eastward at the mountains must have reminded the men of all of the difficulties they had overcome. During the steep descent off Chestnut Ridge, the western prospect could only have cheered their hearts. A gentle and green valley appeared before them, where "ye mountains begin to diminish & a fine pleasant rich Soil is seen," as one British officer wrote. This "Pleasent Cuntry" suggested the future promise of the Ohio lands they were ultimately fighting for. The man perhaps most invested in that day's march was Christopher Gist, who had settled with his family on these rolling hills in 1753, marking out a plantation of more than 1,000 acres. All that remained of it now was a blackened shell, for it had been burned by the French in 1754. Dreary though they were, the ruins must have appeared as a harbinger of future prosperity in so pleasant a valley. The following morning, at Gist's plantation, Braddock warmed his Redcoats' hearts with "a quantity of Rum for each man which his Excellency is pleasd to give the men in Consideration of their good Behavour" in surmounting the worst of their mountainous ordeals. It was yet another indication of how much Braddock was a "soldier's general."[70]

The challenge the army now faced was overconfidence. Euphoria, like rum, could impair an army's senses, blinding it to its true situation and masking its own weaknesses. The deeper the army advanced into the heart of enemy country, the longer became their supply lines, as the distance between Braddock's and Dunbar's columns became greater. Braddock and his principal officers also needed timely intelligence of the exact situation at Fort Duquesne as they planned their final advance to crush the French. The rivers, Indian paths, and mountains along the route also needed reconnoitering. Should a fortified base camp be established as the army neared the French? That question and others became the subjects of heated debate among Braddock, his staff, and leading officers.

A false sense of security was developing in Braddock's army: everywhere that they had expected the enemy to appear, he retreated; every dangerous defile they had passed had been undefended; at every show of Redcoat strength, the enemy had evaporated. British commissary officer William Johnston noted that they "had gone through several dangerous passes, and finding the enemy had not taken any advantage from them, it was imagined they were extremely weak and would not stand a siege, much less meet him in the woods." The army departed Gist's plantation on June 28, led by St. Clair's work party consisting of Gates's New York Independent Company, Waggoner's and La Péronie's companies, and a detachment of fifty-two men from both of the regular regiments. Braddock's extra rum ration that morning had been perfectly timed, as the heavens opened during the day's march, the most "terable Rain that Ever hapnd" in the experience of Cholmley's batman. The torrential rains damaged the column's flour supply. Braddock urgently sent back to Colonel Dunbar, with orders to forward "with the utmost diligence one hundred carrying horses with flour, with some beeves, with an escort of a Captain and one hundred men."[71]

Overconfident or not, everyone expected trouble at the army's final crossing of the Youghiogheny River. The army encamped the nights of June 28–29 at Stewart's Crossings, where it faced a significant ford about 200 yards long and through waters three feet deep. A French and Indian force arrayed on the northern bank would find the army in a compromising position. On June 29, soldiers had their ammunition replenished to twenty-four rounds each. On June 30, the army was on alert as the advanced party splashed across the ford and "took post" on the north bank, defending the wagons and baggage during the crossing. To everyone's surprise, a British officer wrote, they "crossed the river without any opposition, which was not expected." The army had overcome yet another obstacle, one that their increasingly contemptible enemy could have easily defended. Near the crossings, there was an old Indian fort used by northward Indians in their wars against Catawbas.[72]

The troops encamped about a mile north of Stewart's Crossings after a march totaling only two miles that day. Engineer Gordon found the road "uneven to the ford [and] the ford rough," probably a reference to embankments that needed to be graded, lest the wagons break under the strain. The short march was undoubtedly due to morasses of mud created by heavy rains, "so slippery that the horses could not keep their feet in pulling but fell constantly to their knees." The army also did not advance any farther because of an imposing "steep bank" over which a road had to be built. The encampment site was right beneath that steep bank—an example of the calculated risks taken during the march on ground ideally suited for attack. That evening, Orme wrote to Washington, who later quoted him as saying that "they have sent out Parties to scour the Country thereabouts, and have Reason to believe that the French are greatly alarmed at their approach." If Washington's summary of Orme's letter is accurate, it again indicates the officers' burgeoning optimism as they advanced closer to Fort Duquesne, passing likely points of ambush with no opposition whatsoever.[73]

Had Orme been witness to the travails of Washington and of Colonel Dunbar's column, his confidence would have been greatly dampened. When Washington received Orme's letter on July 2, he was at the Scalping Camp, six miles east of the Great Meadows. Washington had earlier written Orme on June 30 from the Great Crossing of the Youghiogheny, warning of impending disaster for Dunbar's column. The rear column was sputtering to a halt as horses became sick and scarce. Washington warned Orme, "you may rest assurd, that Colo. Dunbar cannot move from his present Incampment [near Great Crossing] in less than two or three Days; and I believe really, *it will be as much as he possibly can do to reach the Meadows at all*; so that you will be greatly advanced before him." Washington forewarned his brother, John Augustine, that the column would soon not "be able to stir at all," a prediction that came true when it finally ground to a halt near the crest of Chestnut Ridge, at a place now known as "Dunbar's Camp."[74]

It had taken Dunbar's column thirteen days to cover only twenty-five-odd miles between the Little Meadows and the Scalping Camp, a march that Braddock's flying column had covered in six. Dunbar had been left with a nearly impossible task and was bitter about it. He had disingenuously claimed that Braddock would never be "more than a days March" ahead of him, and that they would be able to signal each other by firing a six-pounder. But if the two columns were to always remain within supporting distance, what was the purpose of separating in the first place, and proceeding with a lighter and faster column? If the two columns indeed grew apart, it was by design. Dunbar's genuine problem was not having "a sufficient number of horses for all our waggons" (commissary officer William Johnston recorded a total of 150 wagons). The poor horses were literally caught in a vicious circle. They drew as many wagons as their numbers allowed to the next encampment, then were unhitched and sent back to pull the remaining wagons forward. The strain on the horses was exponential as they pulled the same loads twice each day, and the army's rate of march was proportionally halved. The unfortunate horses were further weakened by the "want of forage" in the mountains. The shoestring supply chain evident in Dunbar's column may have eventually forced Braddock "to abandon our Conquests for want of Sustenance," as St. Clair foresaw.[75]

There were other problems brewing, well behind Dunbar's column and stretching back to Fort Cumberland. Braddock had warned the governors that Indian war parties would strike the frontiers of Pennsylvania, Maryland, and Virginia. And indeed Indian attacks on the Holston River, New River, and Patterson's Creek resulted in the deaths of dozens of settlers. Two colonial families living just two miles away from Fort Cumberland had been attacked on June 26. Warriors had clubbed and scalped a seven-year-old boy, who was found alive but in shock, sobbing and standing in a pool of water when a party sent by Colonel Innes to bury the dead came upon the scene. Hospital matron Charlotte Browne cared for this boy when he was brought to Fort Cumberland, but he survived for only four days. The boy's skull fractures had been too severe. Other panic-stricken families soon began to pour into the vicinity of Fort Cumberland or abandon the frontier altogether. Governor Dinwiddie initially dismissed such threats as so much "French Bravado." Subsequent events forced him to call out Virginia militias, whose actions showed just how unprepared and weak colonial defenses really were. Whether or not Natives intended to interdict supply and communication to Braddock's army, the effect was the same. Washington warned in late June that the communication between the Youghiogheny and Fort Cumberland would "soon be too dangerous for single persons to pass," and Braddock himself mentioned such disruptions in a letter to Governor Morris, telling Morris that his "Chief Dependence" would be upon supplies coming from Pennsylvania via Burd's Road, which he hoped would soon be finished.[76]

Even Burd's Road was becoming unsafe. An eighteen-year-old road-builder named James Smith was working west of Raystown on July 3. As he and others were preparing to ascend the Allegheny Front looming on the horizon, three warriors lying in wait—a Kanesetake Iroquois and two Delawares—opened fire on the unsuspecting workers. Smith's startled horse threw him off, and the warriors instantly took him prisoner. The Indians killed Arnold Vigoras with two shots. Smith looked helplessly on as his captors scalped his companion, leaving his body on the road. They knew enough English to ask Smith if there were any forces nearby and promptly set off for Fort Duquesne. Some Delaware warriors, at least, had in their own way fulfilled their promise to Braddock to join him during the march.[77] These attacks foreshadowed the Indians' destruction of the Virginia, Maryland, and Pennsylvania frontiers, and were a

frightening reminder of all that hung in the balance for British settler families.

Meanwhile, the man who would one day defend the Virginia
frontier remained deathly ill, lying in a wagon in Dunbar's train.
While at the Scalping Camp on July 2, Washington wrote that doctors had forbidden him even to write letters (orders he obviously
disobeyed) and revealed that he had planned to depart Dunbar's
column the following day. Braddock had apparently made good on
his promise to bring his young aide forward as they reached the vicinity of the French fort. Sometime in late June, perhaps hearing of
Washington's improvement, Braddock had sent a note to him via his
aide Captain Roger Morris that "If Mr Washington would bring up
Jervais the groom, the General would be [willing]." Still too "weak
and low" to ride a horse—but undeterred—Washington departed in
a covered wagon along with the beeves and supplies that his old comrade, Captain Adam Stephen, was taking to Braddock's column. To
his credit, Colonel Dunbar responded with "utmost diligence" to
Braddock's request for provisions. Stephen's convoy included his
own Virginia rangers, who most likely were responsible for herding
100 oxen and the pack horses loaded with flour; a detachment of
fifty-two men of the South Carolina Independent Company led by
lieutenants Probart Howarth and John Gray; and a smaller number
of officers and men from the 44th and 48th regiments who were joining the flying column. The detachment made an astonishing march
of more than forty miles in three days, departing the Scalping Camp
on July 3 and joining Braddock's column on July 5, when it was
encamped near a stream called Thicketty Run. The column must
have met with a ravenous reception in the hungry British camp.[78]

After crossing the Youghiogheny on June 30, Braddock's column
had confidently pushed ahead into the pleasant and curious country. Some commented on the sights they came across—tall grasses,
salt licks, a bear sitting in a mulberry tree, and abundant outcroppings of coal which the soldiers gleefully burned. The army's route
northward roughly paralleled the Catawba Trail, an ancient Indian
thoroughfare and one of the main campaigning corridors between
northern and southern Indians locked in chronic combat. The army
gained "a very long & high ridge" coming out of the Youghiogheny
Valley near Stewart's Crossings. Nonetheless, it halted at the Terrapin
Camp on July 1, "by reason of a great swamp which required much
work to make it passable," as Orme wrote. The pioneers' axes dulled
under the labor of creating a corduroy road through swampy ground,
enough to support the wagons and artillery. The army resumed its

march through the great swamp the next day, making only about five to six miles on July 2 before encamping at Jacobs' Cabins. Named after the Delaware leader Captain Jacobs, this abandoned hunting camp was a reminder of Native life in the Ohio Country and the colonial encroachments that had driven the Delawares westward long before Braddock's arrival. Jacobs had once lived in the Juniata Valley among traders and squatters in the 1740s. But he carried deep grievances against them as he relocated farther westward to such places as the abandoned hunting cabins that Braddock's army passed by.[79]

On July 3, Braddock convened a formal council of war. The army was now within a few days' march of Fort Duquesne, and critical decisions had to be made about the army's final advance. Earlier that day, the army had moved sharply northwest from Jacobs Cabins, managing to cover only four miles to a place called the Salt Lick Camp, "from a lick being there, where Deer, Buffaloes & Bears come to lick ye Salt out of ye Swamp," as a British officer wrote in his journal. That evening, St. Clair proposed to Braddock privately that he should "halt with the detachment, and bring up Col. Dunbar with his Convoy." He pointed to the "great Advantages of this Strong ground" as a forward base—the high ground overlooking the valley of Sewickley Creek. Sir John later disingenuously claimed that Braddock had always ignored his advice and that this proposal was "Rejected with great indignation." Braddock respected his Deputy Quartermaster's advice enough to call a council of war to address this very suggestion.[80]

The council's discussion offers insight on the mindsets of the leading British officers as they stood within a few days' march of Fort Duquesne. With Braddock presiding, it consisted of St. Clair, Halkett, Gage, Burton, and Sparke. They discussed St. Clair's proposal. Dunbar's column was strung out between the Great Crossing and Scalping Camp and could not possibly rejoin the flying column in less than two weeks. The council agreed that "no advantage seemed to accrue from this junction." Rejoining the two columns would only compound the problem of moving forward and make Dunbar's force even more vulnerable to attack. The vital factor, again, was Dunbar's horses; "through their weak situation [they] were not judged capable of performing it." Moreover, if Braddock's column was simply to wait for two weeks or more, its supplies would be quickly expended. The urgency in Braddock's original decision to split the army was also a point of discussion. If the army waited, "the French would have time to receive their reinforcements and provisions, to entrench themselves, or strengthen the fort, or to avail themselves of the strongest passes to interrupt our march." Some officers "conjectured they [the French] had not many Indians or great strength at the fort, as they had already permitted us to make passes which might have been defended by a very few men." In the end, as Orme recorded, "the council were unanimously of opinion not to halt there for Colonel Dunbar." The advance would continue in its spirit of exuberant haste, to arrive at Fort Duquesne ahead of French reinforcements.[81]

The council also discussed the need for timely intelligence of Fort Duquesne and the exact route the army would take toward it. Following the council, Braddock called for the "Indian manager," George Croghan, ordering him to "prevail with the Indians to go towards the fort for intelligence." Some kind of dysfunction and discord had beset Braddock's relations with his Indian scouts, though there is almost no clear evidence for its origins, and all British generals of that era had some degree of friction with Indian allies. Sometime later, Scaroyady allegedly stated that Braddock "looked upon us as dogs, and would never hear any thing what was said to him." The Indians, he continued, "often endeavoured to advise [Braddock] and tell him of the danger he was in with his Soldiers, but he never appeared pleased with us." But those were likely the words of Pennsylvania officials anxious to cast blame on the general and redeem their colony's reputation in London. Orme reported that Braddock had "often assayed, but could never prevail upon [the Indians] since the camp at the great Meadows" to go scouting. "They now likewise refused, notwithstanding the presents and promises which he constantly made them." The army continued its northwesterly course to the Thicketty Run or Hillside Camp, through country described as "less mountainous and rocky, and the woods rather more open, consisting chiefly of white oak." Captain Stephen and his convoy with 100 oxen and pack horses loaded with flour arrived there of course on July 5, and British officials were finally able to persuade two of the remaining seven Indian warriors to scout Fort Duquesne (one of whom was Scaroyady's son). Christopher Gist, who knew the area well from prior journeys to the Forks, also went on a separate reconnaissance, "unknown" to the Indians, which suggests that Braddock wanted Gist's independent confirmation of the Indians' intelligence. All three men departed on July 4 for the roughly twenty-four-mile journey to the Forks.[82]

For nine days, from June 27 to July 5, no encounters with French-Indian parties were recorded in the surviving accounts of Braddock's officers or men. The French, it seemed, had completely lost track of Braddock's army. Reconnaissance had undoubtedly taken place, but the French and Indian parties were maintaining so careful a distance that they were all but cloaked in secrecy. During those nine days, the British were tightening their operational security. Orderly books revealed a sense of heightened awareness. One such order, issued on June 29, concerned fire discipline: "Where as by the connivance of some of the Officers several of the men fired their peices [muskets] this morning in a very Ireguler manner It is His Excellencys Orders that for the future if Any [Officer] of whatsoever Rank shall suffer the men to fire their peices in that Ireguler manner They shall be put Under An Arrest." In fact, such irregular firing was a rarity, and whatever the exact situation was that prompted the firing, it was not soldiers spooked by Indians but "the connivance of some of the Officers." Braddock doubled the advanced pickets for greater nighttime security and forbade them from lighting fires. He also ordered officers to inspect the men's muskets on a more frequent basis and insisted on basic safety measures, such as fixing thumbstalls over their frizzens, to prevent accidental discharges.[83]

The events of July 6 tested these stringent security regulations. The general assembly beat at 6:00 A.M. that morning, the troops setting off shortly thereafter. The army's two Indian scouts had returned around 10:00 A.M., bringing new information on Fort Duquesne, followed by that offered by Christopher Gist upon his return that afternoon. The advance was uneventful, except for "cuting through four thickets" that offered excellent opportunities for cover. With the addition of so many cattle and pack horses, however, the British column now extended "a prodigious length," in Orme's words. It was perhaps no coincidence that a French and Indian party, sensing opportunity, again struck Braddock's column. The French cadet accompanying this party (possibly composed of Ottawas, Potawatomis, or Mississaugas) was Sieur de Godefroy de Roquetaillade, the son of a Détroit settler named Pierre Godefroy de Roquetaillade, and cousin of Godefroy de Normanville. Around 11:00 A.M. that morning, a woman tending cows and three soldiers, perhaps part of the flanking parties, became the unfortunate victims. The Indians killed and scalped the woman and a soldier. They had wounded another man in the shoulder, and as Cholmley's batman reported, "Began to Scalp a Nother Soldier but had not got it of[f] before our Rear guard Came." The batman's journal mirrors a French account, that Roquetaillade "had fixed on the Enemy and had kill'd some of them; but the Indians (according to their cruel Custom) had not been able to scalp them; the English always keeping in good order." Braddock had heard the firing and immediately sent back a company of grenadiers.

Robert Orme, *A Plan of the Encampment of the Detachment from the Little Meadows* (Thomas Jefferys, 1758). The well-protected encampments of Braddock's army, encircled by a line of pickets, rendered ineffective the French and Indian efforts to contest the British advance. Map reproduction from the Richard H. Brown Revolutionary War Era Maps Collection of the Norman B. Leventhal Map Center, Boston Public Library.

The French-Indian party fled, but was still lingering in the area, perhaps ensconcing itself in the deep laurel thickets that Gordon had described.[84]

In a state of heightened alarm, the army was subjected to another attack in the early afternoon. Braddock's flanking parties on the right of the column had come upon a group of Indians, perhaps of Roquetaillade's detachment. The Indians fired, and to the chagrin of one British officer, "put ye Men in a good deal of confusion." Order was soon restored, however, and the British "returned ye fire very briskly & obliged them to retire." Many details of the encounter remain murky: Orme's account relates that it was the Indian scouts who had discovered the French-allied Indians, while an anonymous British officer has "our own Indians interfereing" at the beginning of the fight, while Cholmley's batman similarly describes "Our Indiens Coming to our Asistance." White smoke from the volleys clouded the sylvan scene, and in the confused melée tragedy unfolded. The Indian scouts had decided that discretion was the better part of valor and "made the agreed countersign, which was holding up a bough and grounding their arms." A .69-caliber ball from a British volley tore through the son of Monacatootha, apparently killing him instantly. The intentions and regularity of the British musketry cannot be known definitively, but its deadly effect was the same. Cholmley's batman stated that two other Indian scouts were wounded—although no other British account mentions additional wounded. But if true, Braddock's Indian scouts were possibly dwindled down to only four effective men, depending on the severity of their wounds. The army's encampment on the night of July 6 bore the name of the tragic events of that day: Monacatootha Camp. Braddock called for Scaroyady, the other Indians, and the officers to his tent. He later presided over a funeral for Scaroyady's son and "condoled with and made them the usual presents." Braddock demonstrated respect for his Indian allies during this military funeral that concluded with soldiers firing a volley in tribute to the fallen warrior. Captain Orme remembered that Braddock's conduct was "so agreeable to the Indians, that they afterwards were more attached to us." But old Scaroyady remained inconsolable in his grief, "hardly able to support his loss," according to one British officer who probably witnessed the burial. Scaroyady may have said something to the effect that "had he been killed by the french it would have been trifling, but what he regretted most was his being killed by our own people." It remains unclear what role, if any, the grieving father played in the subsequent days.[85]

PLATE 1. Emanuel Leutze, *Washington at the Battle of Monongahela*, ca. 1858. By permission of Braddock's Battlefield History Center and Braddock Carnegie Library Association. Photograph courtesy of David Kissell.

PLATE 2. *The Crossing*, by Robert Griffing, depicts the British army's second crossing of the Monongahela on July 9, 1755, which George Washington remembered as a "beautiful spectacle." Courtesy of Paramount Press, Inc.

PLATE 3. *Braddock's Defeat*, by Edwin Willard Deming, ca. 1903. The painting elevates the role of French ensign Charles Mouet de Langlade in orchestrating the attack on the British column, despite the lack of authentic evidence for his presence at the battle. It more accurately depicts the ways that Indian warriors used the cover of trees and rocks to fire into the dense British ranks and at conspicuous officers on horseback. Courtesy of Wisconsin Historical Society, WHS-1900.

PLATE 4. *The Wounding of General Braddock*, by Robert Griffing, shows the general surrounded by his principal officers and aides (from left to right): Captain Robert Orme, Lieutenant Colonel Thomas Gage, George Washington, Captain Robert Stewart, Scaroyady, George Croghan, and Captain Roger Morris. Courtesy of Paramount Press, Inc.

PLATE 5. In *The Arrival of the French*, by Nat Youngblood, Captain Contrecoeur's forces are disembarking and advancing upon Trent's Fort on April 17, 1754. Youngblood's paintings strikingly depict key events and everyday life in western Pennsylvania history. Courtesy of Robert MacLachlan. Photograph courtesy of Peter West/World West Galleries.

PLATE 6. Charles Willson Peale, *George Washington as Colonel of the Virginia Regiment*, 1772. Courtesy of Washington and Lee University. Peale's portrait captures the colonists' growing awareness of "being Americans," as Washington wrote, even as it evokes his distinguished and loyal service to king and empire in Braddock's and Forbes's expeditions. The wooded setting and the order of march in his waistcoat pocket call to mind Washington's genius in adapting his Virginia Regiment to both regular and irregular warfare in the woods of America.

PLATE 7. *William Augustus, Duke of Cumberland*, by David Morier, ca. 1748–1749. © National Portrait Gallery, London. Cumberland's decisions in 1754 defined the basic parameters of Braddock's Expedition to Virginia.

PLATE 8. The indefatigable Sir John St. Clair was the Deputy Quarter Master General responsible for establishing the logistical foundation of Braddock's Expedition in 1754 and 1755. John Singleton Copley, miniature, ca. 1757. Image copyright © Metropolitan Museum of Art. Image source: Art Resource, NY.

PLATE 9. General Braddock's Sash, ca. 1709. George Washington preserved Braddock's sash as a memento of his service as the general's aide-de-camp and his narrow escape at the Battle of the Monongahela. Courtesy of Mount Vernon Ladies' Association.

PLATE 10. David Morier, *Grenadiers, 43rd, 44th, and 45th Regiments of Foot*, ca. 1751. The grenadiers of the 44th and 48th regiments represented the formidable elite troops of Braddock's army who spearheaded the advance on July 9, 1755. Supplied by Royal Collection Trust / © HM Queen Elizabeth II 2014.

PLATE 11. Hans Hysing, *Portrait of a Man* (said to be Sir Peter Halkett, Second Baronet of Pitfirrane, d. 1755), ca. 1735, Scottish National Gallery, NG 2159. Sir Peter Halkett (ca. 1695–1755) was the commanding officer of the 44th Regiment of Foot, a veteran of the Battle of Prestonpans in 1745, and a former Member of Parliament. Hysing's portrait captures the earnest nature of this officer who was uniformly praised for his conduct during Braddock's Expedition.

PLATE 12. *Commodore the Honourable Augustus Keppel*, by Joshua Reynolds, 1749, National Maritime Museum, Greenwich, London. Caird Fund. One admiral declared that there was "no better seaman than Keppel, few so good, and not a better officer." Keppel commanded the Royal Navy squadron that transported Braddock's forces to Virginia and contributed a detachment of sailors under Lieutenant Charles Spendelowe of HMS *Centurion*.

PLATE 13. *Captain Robert Orme*, by Sir Joshua Reynolds, ca. 1756. Image copyright © The National Gallery, London. Image source: Art Resource, NY. Orme was a lieutenant in the Coldstream Guards who was a brevet captain and Braddock's principal aide during the expedition. Reynolds fully captures the young officer's confident bearing, while the horse with bowed head and the forest battle in the background evoke Orme's fallen chief.

PLATE 14. Daniel-Hyacinthe-Marie Liénard de Beaujeu (1711–1755), miniature, ca. 1737, © Château Ramezay—Historic Site and Museum of Montréal. According to family tradition, Daniel presented this miniature to his wife, Michelle-Élisabeth Foucault, on their marriage in 1737.

PLATE 15. This eighteenth-century Iroquois war club was found at the Gilchrist farm near Braddock's Field. Denver Art Museum Collection: Permanent Collection, Gift of Mrs. Effie Parkhill, 1951.300, © Denver Art Museum.

PLATE 16. Paul Weber, *Braddock's Field*, 1854. Courtesy of Fort Ligonier, Ligonier, Pennsylvania. Weber's painting beautifully represents the steep clay embankments that gave the Monongahela its name and shows the towering ridge line of 1,200 feet that Braddock's army ascended on July 9, 1755.

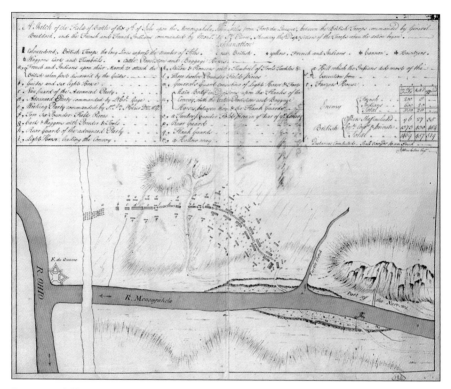

PLATE 17. *A Sketch of the Field of Battle of the 9.th of July Upon the Monongahela*, by Patrick Mackellar, Engineer, CO 5/46, f. 135, National Archives (UK). Mackellar's scale map shows the exact disposition of the British column after crossing the Monongahela on the afternoon of July 9 to avoid the Narrows (shown on the right). The final British advance on Fort Duquesne did not parallel the Monongahela River, as Mackellar indicates (the area to the left of the double vertical lines he drew is not to scale, as it covers a distance of about twelve miles).

Back at Fort Duquesne, Contrecoeur had been unable to slow the British advance, and as late as July 6 had no precise fix on its location, despite having sent out those 500 French and Indian scouts in May and June. For all of the problems that Braddock had with his own Indian scouts, the breakdown of French intelligence-gathering is somewhat astounding, given their advantage of numerous Indian allies. Contrecoeur had seemingly lost track of Braddock's army, only "hearing always that these troops were approaching." The initial report fixing Braddock's location at approximately eight leagues (three days' march) of his own post came to Contrecoeur on July 6, 1755, from four Hurons who had been out scouting. Contrecoeur and Beaujeu apparently did not believe their allies and sent out a separate party led by Ensign Jean-Baptiste Léon Tarieu de Lanaudière de La Pérade, whom Beaujeu considered "un fort bon officier," to confirm the report. Ensign La Pérade and a small party were guided by an Ohio Iroquois warrior who was not willing "to conduct him above 3 or 4 Leagues" and they were forced to turn back. An entire day was lost. The French commanders were also greatly concerned by reports that the British were "coming by different ways to invest the fort." On July 7, Contrecoeur and Beaujeu sent out two separate reconnaissance parties, led by the ensigns La Pérade and François Bailleul and composed of French and Indians. These parties presumably scouted the Monongahela River's north and south sides. La Pérade and Bailleul returned back to Fort Duquesne, as did the party of Lieutenant Rigauville, who had been out since June 28. Contrecoeur and Beaujeu fully realized the gravity of the situation they faced upon hearing their reports on the evening of July 7: the British were only eight leagues' distance, numbered 3,000 men, and had brought artillery. They had, at best, three days before the British army would entirely trap them on their triangular peninsula.[86]

Braddock, however, was even more unfortunate, receiving misleading and faulty intelligence from his scouts when it mattered the most. While having to meet two Indian attacks on his column and console Scaroyady, he had to digest the intelligence that his two Indian scouts and Christopher Gist had brought back to the army on July 6. Scaroyady's son and another enterprising Indian (perhaps Silver Heels) presented a French scalp to Braddock that they had taken within a half-mile of Fort Duquesne. The unfortunate victim of this ambush was a French Canadian militiaman named Pierre Simard, an inhabitant of the Petit Rivière parish below Québec who had probably been out hunting along the banks of the Allegheny. The two Indian scouts took his scalp and made a hasty exit, fearful of pursuit. According to Orme, the two men reported that "they saw very few men there, or tracks; nor any additional works. That no pass was possest by them between us and the fort, and that they believed very few men were out upon observation. They saw some boats under the fort, and one with a white flag coming down the Ohio." Gist, who was also pursued, told Orme that his "account corresponded with their's." How all of these parties managed to miss the presence of hundreds of French and Indian troops encamped in the vicinity of Fort Duquesne is a mystery explained only by the difficulties of gaining accurate information in wooded terrain. Not all of the Indian warriors were absent from the fort: there were significant enough numbers present on July 6 to hold a conference with Contrecoeur. The scouting of Gist and the two Iroquois allies was obviously superficial and incomplete. Quite possibly, they never climbed the heights overlooking Fort Duquesne (near what became known as Grant's Hill) to afford themselves a sweeping view of the Forks. Although there is no direct evidence as to how these intelligence reports shaped Braddock's final approach to Fort Duquesne, it is likely that they merely confirmed what he and many of his officers apparently believed: that French reinforcements had not arrived; that Fort Duquesne was in a weak state and that the French were not going to contest their advance. If these reports indeed influenced him in those ways, the supreme irony is that he was misled by the false intelligence of Iroquois allies who were allegedly the masters of scouting and warfare in the woods.[87]

The army itself became misled on July 7 as it marched off from Monacatootha Camp heading due north, for reasons that remain mysterious. The British had previously been following an Indian trail leading toward the Monongahela River (the same route that Washington had followed in his 1753 mission). But on July 7, the army "turn'd off the Indian path to avoid Long Run," according to Harry Gordon and to avoid "the dangerous pass of the narrows," in Robert Orme's journal. As they neared Fort Duquesne, British commanders especially feared two difficult narrows (passes) that were the most likely sites for ambushes: the first narrows in the Long Run valley were dominated by hills very close to the Indian path (the hills still loom sharply above Lincoln Way east of McKeesport, Pennsylvania). The second narrows, near the mouth of Turtle Creek on the east side of the Monongahela, were located along a sharp river bend where time and erosion had left only a small sliver of bottomland next a sheer cliff rising up to 1,000 feet in elevation (even today, only railroad tracks thread the thin gauntlet where Braddock's men could have built a road). The Turtle Creek narrows were an especially dangerous axis of advance: an enemy force positioned on the heights above the British right flank could easily pin the entire column against the riverbank with no means of maneuver or escape.[88]

Braddock's apparent goal on July 7 was to avoid such dangers by locating a high ridge northward of Turtle Creek that would enable his army to march on high ground all the way to Fort Duquesne. Two British military maps of the vicinity of Fort Duquesne from the 1750s reveal why Braddock had diverged from the Indian path and the precise route that he wanted to gain for the final drive on Fort Duquesne. A map by John Montresor (a lieutenant in the 48th Regiment and the son of James Gabriel Montresor) demarcates a "Ridge proposed by M.r Guest [Gist] & Indians for the army to march on but not followed." The second map, drawn during Forbes's Campaign in 1758, labels the ridge route to Fort Duquesne as "Bradock's intended Road."[89] So the army marched on July 7, "and quitting the Indian path, endeavored to pass the Turtle Creek about 12 miles from the mouth [at the Monongahela], to avoid the dangerous pass of the narrows," in Orme's telling. But when the army finally arrived at the Brush Creek branch of Turtle Creek, the officers and wagoners were stupefied. The heights above Brush Creek were shockingly steep, worse than anything the British had seen, and they knew it would be impossible to descend without significantly delaying the expedition. Braddock then ordered St. Clair, a captain, 100 men, the Indian scouts, the guides (presumably including Fraser and Gist), and some of the Virginia light horse on a mission to "reconnoitre very well the country." St. Clair returned after four hours, informing Braddock that "he had found the ridge which led the whole way to fort Du Quesne, and avoided the narrows and Frazier's [Turtle Creek]." But, he added, some labor would be required to hew a wagon road down and up the rugged valley walls, and to ease the wagons down with block and tackle. The army encamped on July 7 on the high plateau overlooking Brush Creek (modern Browntown, at Larimer). There, Braddock made a crucial decision: he would backtrack and march due west, risking an advance through the dreaded Long Run narrows instead of crossing Brush Creek to access the ridge route.[90]

Christopher Gist labeled the army's July 7 encampment site "Blunder Camp" on his map of Braddock's road. Gist was the only person to refer to the encampment by that name (other British accounts or maps simply called it the Turtle Creek Camp) and the question is why. Some British officers accused the guides of having "lost their Way" and leading them "to a precipice which it was impossible to descend"—charges that are difficult to believe given the intimate knowledge of the area that experienced woodsmen like Gist, Fraser, and Croghan possessed. Nor is it likely that Gist named the encampment after his own blunder.[91] Perhaps Gist believed that Braddock's "blunder" was in departing the Indian path and attempting to access the ridge route via Turtle Creek, where the defiles and steep descents were very forbidding. But if Montresor's map is correct, Gist may have believed that the British erred by foresaking the safer ridge route that he had advised and risking a passage through Long Run and the Monongahela. Gist and the guides may have been leading the army to the Sewickley Old Town path, which led northward to the ridge route and could be accessed just a short distance to the west of Blunder Camp (modern Trafford, Pennsylvania).

Whatever the case, the events of July 7 made an enormous difference, as they essentially delayed Braddock's army from any substantial forward progress for an entire day. Had the army crossed the Monongahela on July 8, it would have advanced on Fort Duquesne when the French and Indian forces were in a state of disarray, still organizing and debating what to do about Braddock's approach.[92]

At Fort Duquesne on July 8, the situation was chaotic but not desperate. The news of Braddock's approach sparked fresh preparations for battle, as well as diplomacy with cautious Indian allies. But French officers were undoubtedly careful, for the sake of their Indian allies, to disguise any signs of panic or desperation. Contrecoeur and the French certainly were not making preparations to abandon Fort Duquesne after a token defense, as Thomas Mante reported in his *History of the Late War in America* (1772). French commanders, au contraire, were organizing the strike force on July 7 and 8 that would assail the British column in a spoiling action outside of the fort. Contrecoeur entrusted leadership of the detachment to his most capable officer, Beaujeu, along with captains Dumas and Lignery. Dumas later claimed that "it was my remonstrance alone that urged M. de Contrecoeur to send us to fight them on the road," but this is highly doubtful, given that Contrecoeur had determined long before that the only hope for holding Fort Duquesne was to fight outside of its walls. Beaujeu was also "very anxious to prevent the siege," according to one French account, and determined to attack. A Virginia deserter from Captain Polson's company had come over to the French during that time and may have provided valuable information on Braddock's army. Undoubtedly much of that day was taken up in the arduous process of distributing bulk ammunition and powder in large barrels, equipping Native allies with muskets, tomahawks, and other implements. There must have been a palpable sense of gravity, as the French knew that their garrison's future rested on the result of Beaujeu's attack.[93]

It was on July 8—not the morning of July 9 as countless historians have written—that Indian warriors made the decisions to do battle against the British, as Captain Beaujeu rallied them and sang his war song. Consensus and unified action were crucial conditions of the Native allies' participation with the French. On July 6, an Ohio Iroquois had refused to guide La Pérade's party three to four leagues past the fort. A number of Indian nations also "detained" the Ottawas and Ojibwas from Michilimackinac who were preparing to go out that day. They all met with Contrecoeur on July 6, a conference that resulted in broad agreement that "all the Indian Nations should march together," but the scouting party was delayed until the next day. On July 8, there was a grand council to which "all the Indian Nations were called together, & invited to joyne & assist the french to repulse the English." Shawnees and Ohio Iroquois living near Fort Duquesne also came to meet with Contrecoeur, and already having heard that "he was determined to oppose the English," resolved to stand with him. During this July 8 council, Beaujeu offered his famous speech to the Natives, and drawing deeply on his experiences at Niagara, appealed to the warriors in Onontio's name: "I am determined to confront the enemy. What—would you let your father go alone? I am certain to defeat them!" "With this," the account goes, "they decided to follow him," as he sang the war song.[94] Beaujeu's actions rallied all but one of the nations—the Potawatomis of the Détroit area. The Potawatomis did not refuse to fight, simply "not to march till the next day," which gave the other Indians pause. Undeterred, French officers spared no expense and refused no requests of their Indian allies, a reflection of how deeply they relied upon them. At Fort Duquesne that evening, hundreds of Indian warriors encamped about the fort and across the river, smoke arose from hundreds of flickering campfires, and vast amounts of goods and ammunition were distributed as Indian and French fighters prepared themselves for battle.[95]

English captive James Smith had arrived at Fort Duquesne in the midst of this grand mobilization. The Delaware and Kahnawake war party that captured him along Burd's Road on July 3 had returned to Fort Duquesne on July 7, letting out war cries that announced fresh scalps and captives. Shouts and celebratory volleys from the hundreds of French and Indians near the fort greeted the returning warriors. To Smith, it seemed like "thousands" of warriors had gathered at Fort Duquesne. Smith had to run through a gauntlet of warriors who beat him unconscious, perhaps a measure of how willing they were to do battle against Braddock. He awoke within the walls of Fort Duquesne, where a French doctor was treating his wounds with brandy. As soon as he had regained his senses, Indian warriors were there interrogating him with questions about Braddock's army: How many men were present? How well armed was the force? The following day, July 8, one of Smith's English-speaking Delaware captors paid him a visit and conversed about the rituals of captivity. Smith quizzed him about news of Braddock's army, to which the Delaware warrior replied that "the Indians spied on them every day, and he showed me by making marks on the ground with a stick, that Braddock's army was approaching in very close order, and that the Indians would surround them, take trees, and (as he expressed it) shoot um down all one pigeon." Smith's account provides a glimpse of the Indians' preparations: they had cautiously studied this new enemy and gathered intelligence on his numbers, composition, and precise order of march. Having finally committed to battle, they were supremely confident of their ability to hunt down and kill him.[96]

Contrecoeur sent out one additional reconnaissance party on July 8 that yielded crucial intelligence. It was led by two cadets named Normanville (perhaps brothers): Joseph Godefroy de Normanville and Jean-Baptiste Godefroy de Normanville. The Indians had again been reluctant to depart, but the Normanvilles persuaded them to go. Joseph's father, Louis Godefroy de Normanville, had been commandant of the French outpost of Ouiatenon on the Wabash River, where he may have gained a familiarity with Indians. The Normanvilles' party located Braddock's army at a distance of six leagues from Fort Duquesne (presumably as it passed through the Long Run narrows or as it neared its next encampment). French commanders knew that there were two possible avenues of British advance: either the south bank of the Monongahela, or the northerly track through the narrows and across Turtle Creek. The Normanvilles' detachment scouted the fords of the Monongahela River where the British eventually crossed, and they were presumably responsible for suggesting the lower ford as an ambush site—"a favorable spot which had been reconnoitered the night before" (July 8).[97] The French battle plan for July 9 was to ambush Braddock's army at the river crossing.[98]

The general assembly beat among the British ranks at 5:00 A.M. on July 8, rousing men and horses to prepare for the day's march. Rumors and heightened security measures had alerted everyone to the potential dangers of the route ahead. Braddock had ordered that the rearguard be strengthened. He wanted the pack horses to march on the left of the main column and within the protective screen of flanking parties on the left. The men were to remain vigilant even when halted. Half of the advanced party was ordered to "remain Under Arms with fixt Bayonets facing outwards" while the others rested. "The General seems very anxious about marching through the Woods," one British officer observed, "and gave very particular Orders." The march through the Long Run valley was a calculated risk: two miles "through a bad Defilé," "very much commanded on Both Sides by Steep hills." Those hills on their right and left became more pronounced and steep, and at some points the ridges hemmed in the column's flanks, narrowing the defile to a width of just fifty yards. Because the hills were so close to the Indian path, Braddock ordered Colonel Burton to secure them with 350 men from the advanced party. To Harry Gordon and the troops in the column, it seemed as though "Every proper precaution was taken to secure us." British soldiers in the main column gazed upward to see Redcoats on the crests of the ridges right above them. But just ahead, the ground rose sharply again, "which shut up the valley in our front." The grenadiers of the 44th went forward to clear and claim that high ground. "No Enemy appear'd" during the army's march to its last encampment before crossing the Monongahela River, near the headspring of Sugar Creek. Because of the column's difficult and lengthy passage through the Long Run narrows, the army did not make camp until 8:00 P.M., as Captain Cholmley's batman recalled. As the army bedded down on the high plateau above the Monongahela Valley, its conduct of July 8 was a credit to the operational security of Braddock's entire march.[99]

Although still "very weak and low," George Washington had doggedly pushed along in the back of a covered wagon, determined to be present in time for the final drive on Fort Duquesne. When he finally rejoined Braddock's column on July 8,[100] he found the high command locked in tense debate. Braddock took counsel of officers and guides that evening and may have called a formal council of war.[101] Two decisions confronted Braddock and his officers on the night of July 8: should the army again risk passing a dangerous defile (the Narrows below Turtle Creek) or undertake two risky crossings of the Monongahela? And should a detachment be sent forward to invest the fort, or was it best to preserve a united force to advance upon Fort Duquesne? The impulsive St. Clair, perhaps drawing on his experiences in southeastern Europe, advised Braddock and Orme on either July 7 or 8 to "march on a Detachment, to take post

Robert Orme, *A Plan of the Disposition of the Advanced Party, consisting of 400 Men* (Thomas Jefferys, 1758). The advanced party, which included many flanking parties, gave notice of impending dangers and defended St. Clair's working party as it constructed the military road. Map reproduction from the Richard H. Brown Revolutionary War Era Maps Collection of the Norman B. Leventhal Map Center, Boston Public Library.

near the Fort in the night, and then to bring up his Convoy for that no General had ever led up his Convoy at noon day to the place he was to besiege." St. Clair specifically "begged him to send 400 men to take Post before it in the night to hinder any Sorti to be made on the Convoy. These Men I prayed he wou'd give me the Command of" (a request similar to that of James Grant in 1758, that probably would have ended the same way). Sir John was essentially asking for the kind of independent detachment he had led at the beginning of the campaign, when he advanced from Fort Cumberland to Little Meadows.[102]

It is not difficult to imagine the informal council of war developing around Braddock's tent. Orme remembered St. Clair "being asked whether the distance was not too great to reinforce that detachment in case of an attack," to say nothing of a dangerous nighttime advance that St. Clair was suggesting. Other officers suggested it would be better to send such a detachment from the next encampment, which would be only six or seven miles from the fort. Halkett allegedly cautioned Braddock on the night of July 8 to beware of ambush. Although this later claim has no basis in any eyewitness account, generations of historians have often repeated it to show that Halkett was full of premonitions of disaster.[103] The officers especially discussed the question of "whether it would be more advisable to make the pass of the Monongahela or the narrows, whichever was resolved upon, with our whole force." That night, Orme remembered, the guides were summoned and they suggested that the army cross the Monongahela's "two extreme good fords, which were very shallow, and the banks not steep." The guides described the dangers of the narrows and particularly pointed out the difficulty of making a passable road through them. While the river crossings had their own dangers—"if the Enemy should have possession of it, they would not be able to get over without great loss," said one British officer—the troops would at least have clear fields of fire. According to Orme, Sir John "immediately acquiesced" to the prudent measures that Braddock had planned for July 9.[104]

On that evening of July 8, the two fundamentally different approaches and factions underlying the entire campaign were starkly apparent since their development at the Little Meadows. St. Clair represented those who favored establishing a strong base of operations closer to Fort Duquesne by bringing up Dunbar's convoy and of marching on the fort with a strong detachment, not "clogged with a Convoy." Braddock and others favored a rapid thrust by a powerful column that could force the French to evacuate by placing a large train of artillery outside of Fort Duquesne (as Contrecoeur had done to Trent's Fort). As St. Clair put it, "the General and his Advisors were so much prepossessed that nothing was wanting at Fort Du Quesne for the Reduction of it, but his Presence, that he went on with this unlucky Supposition." In that respect, Sir John's warning to Braddock—that "a few days wou'd show who were his good and who were his bad Councillors"—was all that was left to be said.[105]

The British, French, and Indian worlds awaited the issue of Braddock's campaign. Anticipation was palpable everywhere as people followed news of Braddock's advance. Captain Contrecoeur's eldest son, writing his father from Montréal, remarked, "there's no doubt about it now: we really are at war." At Québec, Governor-General Vaudreuil believed that the next letter from Fort Duquesne would relay news of its fall, while his Virginian counterpart, Governor Dinwiddie confidently expected that "the first News I shall have from the Gen'l will be from the Ohio." Dinwiddie adjourned the House of Burgesses on July 9, 1755, full of "great Hopes." Native villagers in the *pays d'en haut* got along without the hundreds of warriors faithfully fighting with Onontio, anticipating their return with captives, scalps, and war materiel as evidence of victory. Ohio Indian leaders carefully calibrated how the advent of Braddock's army in the Ohio Valley and the possible expulsion of the French would affect their lands. In England, army officers followed the fortunes of their brothers overseas. Colonel James Wolfe, with "high hopes of his [Braddock's] success," wrote of a "favourable account of the General's proceedings" in a letter to his father.[106]

"May the Great GOD OF HOSTS Crown their Enterprize with Success." The anonymous writer who penned this blessing in the *Maryland Gazette* revealed how many Britons registered their hopes and uncertainties in heaven as they awaited the campaign's issue. John Gates, a diarist in Stow, Massachusetts, observed a day of fasting and prayer "to implore the Blessing of allmighty God on the several Expeditions against our Neighbouring Enemies," and "to humble our selves Before God for our provoking sins which hath provoked him to Bring upon us a distructive war." On June 24, the feast day of St. John the Baptist, Philadelphia's Freemasons processed from a service at Christ Church to their newly constructed lodge at Norris Alley, where they made a toast "to General BRADDOCK, and Success to his Majesty's Forces. Prosperity to Pennsylvania, and a happy Union to his Majesty's Colonies." Lodge member Benjamin Franklin was concerned by the premature celebrations that he had seen. Two acquaintances had recently come to his home with a subscription to raise money for "the Expense of a grand Firework," to celebrate the news of Fort Duquesne's capture. Franklin warned them that it would "be time enough to prepare for the Rejoicing when we knew we should have occasion to rejoice." The two doctors, their confidence stunned, replied, "Why the Devil! You surely don't suppose that the Fort will not be taken?" The subscription was dropped after Franklin admonished them, "the Events of War are subject to great Uncertainty."[107]

CHAPTER 6

The Battle of the Monongahela

I join very heartily with you in believing that when this story
comes to be related in future Annals, it will meet with unbelief
& indignation; for had I not been witness to the fact on that
fatal Day, I should scarce have given credit to it even now.
~George Washington to Robert Jackson, August 2, 1755~

THE GRENADIERS OF HALKETT'S and Dunbar's regiments
formed in the dark stillness of the morning of July 9 at 2:00
A.M. These were the best soldiers, unfrightened of adversity,
as the Latin motto "nec aspera terrent" on their caps proclaimed.
They would be the vanguard of Thomas Gage's advance party chosen
for the difficult crossings of the Monongahela River on the way to
Fort Duquesne. But the grenadiers had gotten at most only three to
four hours' sleep and were still exhausted from having arrived at the
Sugar Creek encampment at 8:00 the previous evening. After setting up the encampment, Braddock's troops had received twenty-
four rounds of ammunition and were issued two days of meat and
flour rations, which they dutifully stowed in their haversacks. The
two-day supply would enable them to subsist until July 10, by which
time Braddock's flying column of nearly 1,400 men would establish
a new encampment closer to Fort Duquesne and besiege it. The
column's order of march would remain the same: an advance guard,
the working party, the main body with wagons and artillery, a rearguard, and dozens of flanking parties surrounding the entire column.
Under Gage's command, the two grenadier companies marched
out shortly after 2:00 A.M., along with Horatio Gates's New York
Independents, two 6-pounder cannons, and the guides, led by trader
George Croghan, who knew the terrain. The men in St. Clair's working
party, which followed them, had also enjoyed precious little sleep, as
they marched at 4:00 A.M. to begin clearing a road down to the first
ford of the Monongahela. Drums beat general assembly for the

remainder of the army as the working party left, and troops were ordered to ram down fresh rounds into their muskets, given that
combat might be likely. At 5:00 A.M. Braddock and the main body of
the army marched out of camp, following closely in the wake of Gage
and St. Clair.[1]

Descending from the heights down to the ford was difficult. Gage's
men struggled to pull the 6-pounders through the uncut woods, as they
were ahead of St. Clair's road-builders. The wagoners especially "had a
great deal of trouble with the road" because of the steep grade. A warm,
still smoldering enemy campfire near the ford was an indication of the
enemy's mysterious presence. Indians had fled the army's advance,
leaving even weapons behind. Some soldiers, seeing muddied waters,
believed that they had just departed. These warriors were probably attached to the scouting party led by the Normanville cadets. Now rumors
circulated among the men that "a great many" French Indians were on
the other side of the river. Gage cautiously led his men across the knee-
deep ford, drawn up in line of battle, with two 6-pounders ready for
action. As the men waded across the 200 yards of river, the brown
waters gently tugging at their wet gaiters and shoes, the advanced guard
confronted the obstacle for which Natives had named the river
Mehmonawangehelak, or "falling in bank river": its sheer embankments of soft clay, ranging from six to twelve feet high, that often collapsed into the river. A roadway had to be dug and graded before any
wagons could get up the embankments to the bottomlands above. The
advance party then deployed on the flat plain to provide security for St.
Clair's working party and the main body of the army under Braddock,
following close behind. William Dunbar (no relation to Colonel
Dunbar), a lieutenant in the grenadier company of the 44th Regiment,
thought their mission had been smoothly accomplished—"executed
with[out] any disturbance from the Enemy."[2]

Around 8:00 A.M., when the main body arrived at the first
crossing, Braddock sent forward a small covering party of 150 men
ahead of the wagons; another party of 150 men covered the second
division of wagons, as the sounds of lowing cattle and packhorses
splashing through the ford announced the tail of the column. The
rearguard still on the heights was afforded a spectacular view of the
long red column curling its way across the ford and onto the bottomlands of the river's south side. The soldiers sensed how close they
were to Fort Duquesne, as they again were deployed in the usual line
of march toward the next ford, only about two miles distant. As the
column slowly moved onto the broad floodplain of this "extremely
fine" river, soldiers enjoyed a rare uninterrupted view "of at least 4

This unpublished map by engineer Patrick Mackellar records the army's route from the July 8 encampment at Sugar Creek to the two crossings of the Monongahela on July 9. The square formation in the lower left marks the "Camp of the British Troops the Night before the Action." Mackellar indicated that "the Engagement began where the Daggers cross," which he drew at the second ravine at the head of the British column. *Sketch of the Ground & Disposition of the Brittish Troops & Indians when the Engagement of the 9th July began, 1755*, by Patrick Mackellar, Duke of Cumberland Papers, Box 61/A3, Royal Archives, Supplied by Royal Collection Trust / © HM Queen Elizabeth II 2014.

Miles up the river." They beheld the immense bend of the Monongahela arcing northwest toward Fort Duquesne, which some soldiers strained to spot downriver. They were thankful to have entirely
avoided the dangerous pass on the opposite bank, when they saw the
imposing rocky strata of the Narrows tapering down to the river's
edge just to the east of Turtle Creek's mouth. Braddock was in the
midst of reforming his column into its line of march to head to the
second ford when a message arrived from Gage.[3]

By about 9:30 A.M., Gage was leading his advanced guard across
the Monongahela's second ford opposite the mouth of Turtle Creek.
The fatigue brought on by early rising and road-building would be
offset by the exhilaration of the river crossings, which the men did to
the triumphant refrain of the "Grenadiers' March." "Having posted
himself agreeably to his orders," Gage sent word to Braddock of his
uncontested passage to the north bank of the river. The advanced
guard deployed to provide security for St. Clair's vulnerable work
party, busily grading and sloping the steep clay embankments to
make them passable to the wagons and artillery, a job that took the
better part of two hours to complete. Many of Gage's weary men had
around two hours to prepare something to eat before they were
called to order when the main army crossed. Captain Robert Cholmley
relished a bite of Gloucestershire cheese and some milk that his
batman prepared. While some enlisted men cooked rations, others
had nothing whatsoever. But all of them were struck by the enemy's
absence, welcome though it was. If there was any time when the
French and Indians could have caught the army in a compromising
position, it would have been during the river crossing. But forward
enemy scouts, well hidden, were watching Gage's men as they ate
during their halt.[4]

High noon on July 9 was a majestic scene of the full panoply of
British armed might. As the high command had decided the previous evening, the army marched "over the river in the greatest order,
with their bayonets fixed, Colors flying, and Drums and Fifes beating
and playing, as they supposed the Enemy would take a view of them
in the crossing." The pickets on the heights above the crossing,
where Braddock had deployed them for security, had the finest view
of the varied hues of madder red and provincial blues mingled with
gleaming bayonets in the brownish waters of the Monongahela. As
an eyewitness later remembered, "a finer sight could not have been
beheld, the shining barrels of the muskets, the excellent order of the
men, the cleanliness of their appearance, the joy depicted on every
face at being so near Fort Du Quesne, the highest object of their

wishes.—the music re-echoed through the mountains. How brilliant the morning." Viewing the crossing from his saddle, Washington would forever be struck by the "beautiful spectacle." He had rejoined the army only the day before and was still so "much reduced and very weak" that he had to mount his horse "on cushions" as he resumed his duties as one of Braddock's aides.[5]

The dangerous crossings were over at last, as wagoners cracked their teams up the newly graded embankments, and the rearguard marched onto the gravelly and muddy flats. The uncontested crossings and the martial music stoked the soldiers' hearts with renewed ebullience, and as the soldiers assembled in the lowlands near the burned remains of John Fraser's plantation their morale was high. Harry Gordon recalled how the soldiers "hugg'd themselves with joy at our Good Luck in having surmounted our greatest Difficultys," but added that they "too hastily Concluded the Enemy never wou'd dare to Oppose us." There was a sense in the army, from Braddock and Washington down to the officers and men, that "the French would not attack them, as they might have done with so many advantages a little time before," in the words of one British officer. It seemed to him that Braddock was "now thinking ye dangerous passes were over." Some soldiers, however, felt that this was dangerous overconfidence. From the rearguard, it seemed to Virginia Captain Adam Stephen that British officers were expecting to "hear the Explosion of the French fort blown up and deserted, before We approached it." But another officer best expressed the many reasons for the British soldiers' stout hearts that day:

> [We] thought we had got over our greatest Difficulties, for we look'd upon our March through the Woods to be such: We were sure we should be much above a Match for the *French*, if once we got into the open Ground near the Forts, where we could use our Arms. We had a Train, and a gallant Party of Sailors for working our Guns, full sufficient to master better Works than those of the *French* Forts, according to the Intelligence we had of them.[6]

The closer that they got to Fort Duquesne, the tighter the British could draw the noose around the French, who would be trapped on a peninsula. If the French were foolish enough to remain, a hellish iron rain would soon fall upon them.

At Fort Duquesne that morning, French marines, Canadian militia, and Indian warriors were making preparations to strike Braddock's column. The forces had been organized and the Natives had committed themselves to battle on July 8, but the Potowatomis' procrastination and Natives' insistence on unity had delayed the attack for a day. Inside Fort Duquesne, captive James Smith stumbled out upon the ramparts, where he "viewed the Indians in a huddle before the gate, where there were the barrels of powder, bullets, flints &c." Commissary officer Jean-Marie Landrière des Bordes opened French storehouses of arms, powder, ammunition, and other trade goods to Native allies. Landrière wrote that "he contributed in everything that depended on him to [Braddock's] defeat, in providing all of the needs of the detachment of French and Indians who marched out against that general," and his conduct was later commended by French officers such as Captain Dumas. The French typically shipped powder in huge fifty-pound kegs, and a Native warrior might get as many as 100 shots from a pound of powder. Warriors filled their shot pouches with extra flints, wad-extractors, and round lead balls from large open barrels. Smith estimated that there were only 400 French and Indian forces busily equipping themselves.[7]

Captain Beaujeu was in the chapel of Fort Duquesne before dawn on the morning of July 9, one of many spiritual preparations that French and Native warriors made before the battle. Récollet priest Denys Baron, *aumonier* or chaplain to the garrison, recorded that Beaujeu had "been at confession and performed his devotions the same day." Beaujeu then turned to the organization and departure of his assault force.[8] He had wanted to march out at daybreak but was now despondently impatient, knowing that any possibility of an ambush depended upon a timely arrival at the ford of the Monongahela, located about twelve miles away. But his Native allies "not being quite ready retarded him." Beaujeu even started marching his French troops out of the fort down the trail to "hurry [the Indians] to advance."[9] The record is silent as to what caused the delays that were so frustrating to Beaujeu, but in any case Native warriors' reluctance on the morning of July 9 has been overstated. The allies had already agreed in council to fight the British when they "immediately joined" Beaujeu on July 8 by singing the war song following his speech. Cajoling Native warriors to fight was not Beaujeu's problem when the French and Indian forces finally departed Fort Duquesne, shortly after 8:00 A.M.[10]

A large host of French and Indian forces had assembled on the plains around Fort Duquesne early that morning. Contrecoeur had detached a significant part of his entire garrison. Beaujeu's strike force consisted of 108 officers, cadets, and men of the *troupes de la marine*, 146 Canadian militia, and 600 to 700 Indian warriors drawn from a broad mosaic of twenty different nations or communities. The principal subordinates under Beaujeu were captains Dumas and

Lignery. Beaujeu's command included four lieutenants and six ensigns such as Montigny, Courtemanche, La Pérade, and Bailleul, who, as we've seen, were veterans of many previous campaigns and battles. Twenty-three Canadian cadets were also present, each one eager to distinguish himself.[11] Beaujeu's main detachment, with French marines, Canadian militia, and Indians went along the main Indian path leading to the Monongahela ford. Some officers at the head of the force wore only gorgets and were dressed like Indians (perhaps even Beaujeu himself, though this is not conclusive).[12] While his detachment did not advance down the forest trail like some disorganized mob, from the moment the forces left the fort, Beaujeu may have commanded a divided force. In the account of Godefroy, a French officer at Fort Duquesne and most likely a particip-ant, "Three hundred of the Indians took a route different from that of their commander. They crossed the Monongahela River, so that as it approached the enemy the detachment was very weak." If Godefroy's account is accurate, it means that nearly half of Beaujeu's entire Indian force was marching off in a different direction, crossing the Monongahela River and advancing along the south side, before eventually rejoining Beaujeu's command. The reason for this divi-sion remains unclear. Contrecoeur reported that his scouts had been telling him that the British were advancing on Fort Duquesne from different directions to lay siege to the fort. Concerned by the possi-bility that the British would indeed advance along the south side of the Monongahela, Contrecoeur and Beaujeu may have ordered this division of force themselves. Nonetheless, as the detachment "pre-pared to strike," Godefroy related, the 300 Native warriors who were reconnoitering the south side of the Monongahela returned to join the main force.[13]

A separate but key issue is the route that Beaujeu's French and Indian detachment used as they sallied forth from Fort Duquesne, for it has enormous implications regarding the battle and of the route the British were following toward the fort. A 1755 French map in the Library and Archives Canada provides a definitive answer to this crucial question. It is the only French map of the battle known to exist and was most likely drawn by a French eyewitness (perhaps Captain Dumas or another high-ranking officer). It depicts the exact route the French took from Fort Duquesne, revealing that there was no direct trail along the Monongahela from Fort Duquesne to Turtle Creek, although many British maps give that mistaken impression. Instead, Beaujeu took his forces northeast on an old Indian trail leading along the Allegheny River to Shannopin's Town (modern

Lawrenceville), where they turned sharply southwestward toward
Turtle Creek and John Fraser's cabin. The map shows that the trail
terminated at the ford of the Monongahela (marked with the word
quay, to indicate where, in nautical terms, the English were fording
the river). The French and Indian forces were on a direct collision
course with Braddock's army as they marched along the path from
Shannopin's Town.[14]

A newly discovered account from the Archives du Calvados in
Caen offers the fullest understanding to date of French preparations
and dispositions after Beaujeu's force left Fort Duquesne (Appendix F).
Like nearly all French accounts of the Monongahela, it was written
not by an eyewitness but by a French lieutenant in the Louisbourg garrison named Michel-Pierre-Augustin-Thomas Le Courtois des Bourbes.
The depth and accuracy of his description, however, suggest that he
relied on eyewitness testimony. Le Courtois's account reveals new

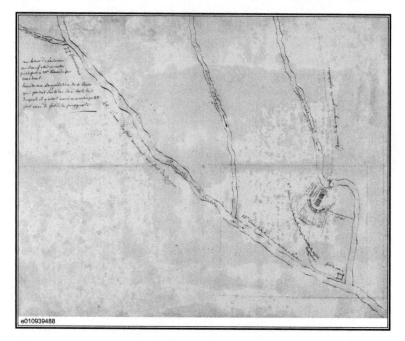

e010939488

This 1755 map, entitled *Bataille du fort Duquesne defaitte de Bradok,* depicts the route that
Beaujeu's forces took on July 9, proceeding northeast from Fort Duquesne along the
Allegheny River to the vicinity of Shannopin's Town (modern Lawrenceville, Pennsylvania)
before turning southwest on an Indian path leading to Turtle Creek and the Monongahela
ford, a distance of three leagues (about nine miles). Library and Archives Canada,
NMC 7755.

insights on the tactical skill and leadership of Captain Beaujeu. It further reveals that the Battle of the Monongahela was not a classic meeting engagement, one in which the French were just as startled as the British after the two columns collided. Beaujeu first sent out Indian scouts before him, who brought back exact intelligence as to the location of Braddock's forces. As he neared the Monongahela ford, he knew that the French had arrived too late to contest—let alone ambush—the British Army at the crossing. The scouts informed him that the British had halted in the woods (presumably this was Gage's advance party, whose men deployed on the north bank of the Monongahela and were enjoying a moment's rest) and that they were marching in a column. Another French account similarly confirms that "Our Scouts had indeed about that time discovered the English Army [had called] the Halt (who probably had receiv'd intelligence of us) & immediately acquainted Monsr. Beaujeu who was at No very great distance." Beaujeu thus had a precise understanding of the British column's disposition. Indian scouts, according to Le Courtois's account, provided him an exact description of the column, "the entire center of which, from the head to the tail, was filled with their waggons and baggage; that a few grenadier companies marched at the head of this column, around 15 men abreast supported by 2 pieces of cannon, that 2 small corps of light cavalry formed the advanced guard and the rear guard of this army, and that the rest of the artillery was located toward the center."

The new account plainly reveals that Captain Beaujeu, upon learning of Braddock's location and disposition, not only organized an immediate frontal attack but improvised an ambush along the British flanks. "Certain of the enemy's position"—a key phrase in the document—Beaujeu organized his detachment into three parallel columns, similar to the tactical organization that he had seen in his Grand Pré expedition in 1747. Such a division of forces was recalled by one veteran of the action, who remembered that "the army marched through the woods in three columns to meet the enemy, with our scouts always in advance." Beaujeu's columns arrived at the heights overlooking the Monongahela and descended the ridge that the British were beginning to ascend—putting the French and Indians into position to control that high ground. Knowing that battle was imminent, Beaujeu then deployed his Indian allies in the woods on either side of the trail, and as Le Courtois's account relates, he "placed at the head of each nation an officer or cadet who spoke the language," for purposes of command and control. Beaujeu instructed the Indians to "reveal themselves only when he had attacked the enemy." He then formed his marines and militia in the road, about fifteen ranks deep, which was the same front that the British grenadiers presented. It was sometime after 1:00 P.M. when he moved his force forward for an immediate attack, with his characteristic aggressiveness and "intrepid courage," according to Le Courtois.[15]

Two hours was all that separated the British army from its next defensible encampment. With Fort Duquesne still more than twelve miles away, Braddock probably intended to establish a base camp that evening before laying siege to the fort, as he expected to do on July 10. Around one o'clock, at the same moment that Beaujeu was planning to attack, Captain Roger Morris rode up to Gage and St. Clair, where they had posted their commands, about 200 yards northwest of Fraser's plantation. Braddock's aide had brought them new orders to ready their men and to march on for two hours. Gage and St. Clair then discussed relocating the two 6-pounders to the front of the working party. In the morning's march, Gage's men had laboriously lugged the cannon along with them through uncut woods. Gage supposedly replied—according to the account written by Cholmley's batman—"I do not think we Shall have much use for them" and reminded St. Clair of the difficulty they had moving them. As the troops marched off, Cholmley's batman thought that "There Never was an Army in the World in more Spirits then we were, thinking of Reaching Fort de Cain the day following."[16]

The only scouting party ahead of Gage's column consisted of six of Captain Robert Stewart's Virginia light horsemen and the handful of guides led by Croghan. Gage later wrote that there were "only three or four Guides for our scouts." If Gage defined "Guides" as white woodsmen, it suggests that none of Braddock's six remaining Ohio Iroquois scouts were in this party and were stationed elsewhere in the column.[17] Guides such as Croghan and Fraser were in familiar territory anyway. But they were located only about 200 yards ahead of Gage's men. They could not possibly provide much warning or timely intelligence of enemy attacks, which would therefore fall upon the British before they could form and potentially throw them into immediate confusion. A lack of any deep forward reconnaissance to apprise him of enemy movements from Fort Duquesne was perhaps General Braddock's greatest command failure that day, but his exact reasons for the composition and location of the scouting party remain unknown.[18]

Gage's leadership of the advanced guard has also been the source of historical controversy, with some arguing that he was guilty of negligence by bypassing some "small rounded hill" or tiny "hillock" or

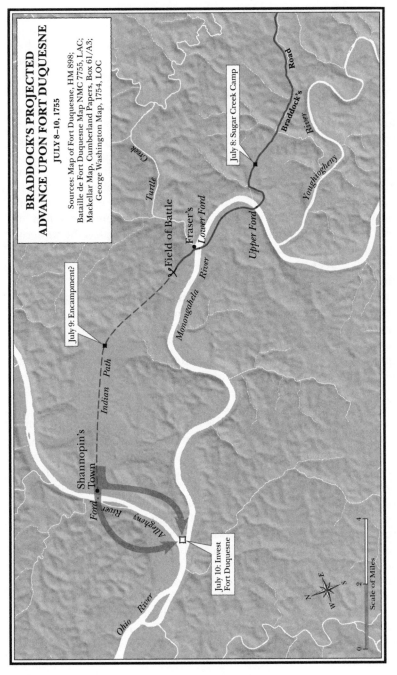

BRADDOCK'S PROJECTED
ADVANCE UPON FORT DUQUESNE
JULY 8–10, 1755

Sources: Map of Fort Duquesne, HM 898;
Bataille de Fort Duquesne Map NMC 7755, LAC;
Mackellar Map, Cumberland Papers, Box 61/A3;
George Washington Map, 1754, LOC

Braddock's Road

July 8: Sugar Creek Camp

Youghiogheny River

Turtle Creek

Field of Battle

Fraser's
Lower Ford

Upper Ford

Monongahela River

July 9: Encampment?

Indian Path

Shannopin's
Town

Ford

Allegheny River

July 10: Invest
Fort Duquesne

Ohio River

N
W   E
S

Scale of Miles

0   2   4

Braddock's Projected Advance on Fort Duquesne
Glen Pawelski, Mapping Specialists, Ltd.

"knoll"[19]—terms that inaccurately minimize the actual terrain. Gage's exact route has also been misunderstood. The British were not advancing to Fort Duquesne on some forest trail paralleling the Monongahela River, for no such trail existed. The British were not bypassing but *ascending* a massive ridge because that is where the path to Shannopin's Town led. The guides had led the column north along a well-trod Indian trail linking Fraser's settlement with Shannopin's town on the Allegheny River. Gist undoubtedly remembered the frigid winter of 1753 when he and Washington had journeyed along that very path during their return from Fort Le Boeuf. It was a steep ascent up an enormous ridgeline, the crest of which was more than 1,100 feet above the Monongahela River's elevation of about 700 feet. The Monongahela bottomlands were dominated for miles downriver by similarly high plateaus averaging between 1,100 and 1,300 feet in elevation.[20] The ridge that they were now ascending was the western geological continuation of the dreaded Narrows, visible to the east of Turtle Creek. Perhaps it was the element of familiarity, along with the conspicuous absence of any French or Indian parties at the river crossing, which led the army to confidently proceed up what was effectively a mountainous defile. From this path, Braddock apparently hoped to regain the ridge route that St. Clair had located on July 7 for his final advance on the French bastion.[21] One of the general's headquarters maps of Fort Duquesne provides unmistakable evidence that he planned to ford the Allegheny River at Shannopin's Town and besiege Fort Duquesne from the north as well.[22]

From his horse, Gage viewed the advance party's methodical march through increasingly dense woods. His men encountered the first of two ravines, a "hollow way" running down the ridge and across the army's route, and formed most likely by small streams or erosion.[23] The army did not abandon its conventional precautions, as Engineer Gordon would later argue.[24] Gage's advance party, numbering approximately 301 men, was led by the elite grenadier companies of the 44th and 48th regiments, numbering 73 and 78 men, respectively.[25] He also had 150 men from the battalion companies of the 44th and 48th. An adequate proportion of Gage's fighting strength—as many as 110 men—was deployed as flanking parties. Indeed, impressively, one-third of Gage's entire command was in the woods as flankers, detached into squads of 10 men, with a sergeant or a subaltern, to screen and protect the column. Through the woods, which were relatively free of underbrush, Gage could see them, for they were deployed at a distance of anywhere from 100 to 150 yards on either side of the column. Gage was confident as he

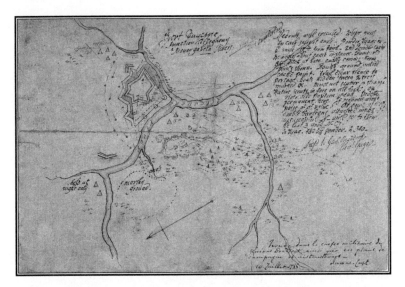

Discovered by the French among General Braddock's headquarters papers, this map of Fort Duquesne reveals British intentions of crossing the Allegheny River and besieging the French fort from the north as well as the east. "General Braddock's Military Plans, captured by the French before Fort Duquesne," 1755, HM 898, Courtesy of the Huntington Library.

looked at the steeply rising ground on his right, which he believed was "partly already possess'd by an Officer's Party that was scouring our Right Flank." In a short time, Gage would reach the crest of the ridge.[26]

By this point, the front of the British advance was about an eighth of a mile in width (between 200 and 300 yards across) and the column stretched for about a mile in length. The vanguard of Gage's party consisted of about 106 grenadiers in a column of fours, while another 45 grenadiers were deployed as the forwardmost flanking parties on the right and left.[27] Behind the grenadiers, also in column, were men of the battalion companies who were similarly not deployed as flanking parties. Immediately behind them, Gage's men could hear the sounds of shovels scraping and axes chopping from St. Clair's working party, busy clearing a road for the artillery and wagons. The working party consisted of the Virginia companies of captains La Péronie, Polson, and Waggoner. At the tail of the working party was Gates's New York Independent Company, numbering fifty-seven officers and men, which functioned as the rearguard of both St. Clair's work party and Gage's advanced guard. Altogether, St. Clair's working party of four companies numbered a little more than 200 men.[28]

Just behind the working party, at a distance of about 100 yards, were Captain Robert Stewart's lighthorsemen, who were at the head of the main body of Braddock's army, including the wagons and artillery. "The General," one British officer noted, "did not suffer ye advanced party to proceed any farther than ye distance of a few Yards from the main body"—a point that has occasioned some controversy, as it seemed to compact the column too closely.[29] Given that it extended a distance of slightly more than one mile, the column occupied a number of different terrains. In the bottomlands past the ford and Fraser's cabin, the undergrowth "Continued very thick for about one quarter of a mile," as St. Clair described it. Robert Orme recalled that the "place of action was covered with large trees, and much underwood on the left." Much of this undergrowth was probably young, for it had sprouted after the clearing that Fraser had done in the area. But Gage's men toward the front were beginning to climb up the ridgeline in front of them, following its contours for a gradual ascent. Roughly three-quarters of a mile from the ford, Gage's party entered an old growth forest with large trees and boulders, which was "free from underwood." The trees, mainly white and red oaks and walnut, formed a dense canopy. As a result, "this wood was so open the Carridges Could have been drove in any part of it," as St. Clair later described it. Another British officer noted "immense large trees fallen on each other" that offered natural breastworks. Lieutenant Dunbar remembered that the woods were "open" but still spread upon a steep incline, yet another indication that Gage and his grenadiers were not bypassing but ascending the steep heights. Those in the main column—midway between the river and Gage's men—were deceived by what they saw as "gradual riseings" on their right, for what was masked from their view was the fact that this "rising ground" continued to rise sharply for more than half a mile before reaching the top of the ridge, more than 1,200 feet in elevation. Rather than inclining gradually, the ground became abruptly, even forbiddingly steep the closer it got to the crest of the ridge. Better reconnaissance of the terrain would have revealed this, but as St. Clair remarked, "one may go twenty Miles without seeing before him ten yards" in the woods. British impressions of the field would remain just that: fleeting glimpses of terrain that they would have very little opportunity to study.[30]

"THE INDIANS ARE UPON US!" one of the forward guides frantically shouted, as Harry Gordon was riding up to their position about 200 yards ahead. Gordon had come to mark the road or to explore the terrain ahead, as the path climbed toward the crest of the ridge. Gordon and the guides caught their first sight of the enemy, coming at them in force stronger than Braddock's army had yet experienced. Gordon and guide George Croghan had a "free sight of the Enemy as they approached," and both men estimated that there were roughly 300 French and Indians ahead. They probably saw only the center column of French and Canadian fighters, and were unaware of the other Indian parties on the flanks. Croghan saw "three French officers with hats in their hands"—perhaps Beaujeu, Dumas, and Lignery—"with which they gave a signal for the firing." Unforgettably, Gordon saw a French officer "at the head of them dressed as an Indian, with his gorget on, waved his hat, and they immediately dispersed to the right and left, forming a half moon."[31]

When the guides streamed back to Gage to report the enemy's approach, it might have seemed to Gage a repetition of his encounter with the French and Indians atop Negro Mountain a few weeks earlier. The look in the eyes of the guides perhaps told him that this was to be a far different encounter. Gage would have little time to react. A warning sign emerged when the leading element of the vanguard, about twenty grenadiers under an officer, "came to the Right about," and turned back toward Gage's main column. The officer commanding these men, either through curses, threats, entreaties, or the blunt edge of his sword, stopped them from running in and "prevaild" upon them "to face again." The rank-and-file grenadiers had a disconcertingly narrow view of the field. All that they knew was the alarm of the scouts and a sense of impending confrontation. Officers such as Captain Robert Cholmley immediately called for their horses and mounted for action. Gage barked out the command, "Fix your Bayonets," as the clanking of cold steel sounded through the forest and steeled the nerves of the grenadiers. He most likely ordered that the two 6-pounders with the working party be readied for action. The British grenadiers, formed in line of battle, were now moving toward the French.[32]

Beaujeu was also pressing his attack, "with much daring," according to his second-in-command, Captain Dumas, but as he advanced toward Gage's grenadiers, the British were in a position of strength by fluke of terrain. The grenadiers came toward the eastern brow of a second "hollow way," or ravine that ran perpendicular to the path, from right to left (on one unpublished map Engineer Patrick Mackellar marked this ravine as where the engagement began). To the French, as a result, it seemed that the British possessed the high ground: "The enemy troops cried out and struck back from high ground, which was very disadvantageous to us," one French eyewitness reported. The French marines fired a hasty volley while out of range and may have overshot the British grenadiers, who displayed great resolve and responded with a "heavy fire."[33]

The battle at the ravine pitted Gage's grenadiers against the French marines and Canadian militia who were at the center of the French advance. Shattering volleys that sounded like tearing sheets ripped through the forest and into the French ranks. The grenadiers responded to the engagement with the spirit they were famous for, even shouting "God save the king" as they drove the French back. The grenadiers, with the front rank kneeling, had fired two smart volleys into the woods, which were already becoming obscured with white smoke.[34] In the battle's initial moments, Gage had immediately deployed the two brass 6-pounders located at the front of the working party, and the artillery had a devastating initial effect on the French forces. Le Courtois's account confirms that the grenadiers "opened their ranks after every discharge to the right and to the left to leave a free passage to the cannons that they concealed, charged with grapeshot." The two guns hurled at the enemy ranks as many as 100 rounds of case shot, or "Tin Cases fill'd with Iron Shot" that splintered trees and drilled fear into French and Indian hearts.[35] That iron shot severely wounded Lieutenant Paul Le Borgne and cadet Joseph-Marie Rémy de Montmédy, both of whom suffered broken arms. British musket rounds struck the mouth and leg of Ensign François de Bailleul, and seriously wounded cadet Joseph Hertel de Sainte-Thérèse. Most of these French casualties were probably incurred in the battle's opening volleys.[36]

Beaujeu's detachment slowly fell back, a few steps here, a few steps there. As the 1755 French map of the battle shows, there was an initial attack by a concave line of battle heading straight toward the British ("1.ere attaque generale ou l'on est reypoussé"—first general attack where we were repulsed). The veteran commander again sensed the disorder and chaos of battle that he had witnessed at Grand Pré years earlier, as his command began to fragment. Some Indians, terrified by what was undoubtedly their first encounter with artillery in battle, fled the field. The Canadian militia—whose quality Contrecoeur had doubted—became panicked by the British artillery fire, and around 100 of them ran off the field shouting, "Sauve qui peut!" (every man for himself!).[37] If Dumas's estimate was correct, there were now, astonishingly, only a mere 150 French and Canadians in Beaujeu's detachment to do battle against a force nearly ten times greater. Beaujeu's disorganized and uncertain command was reforming

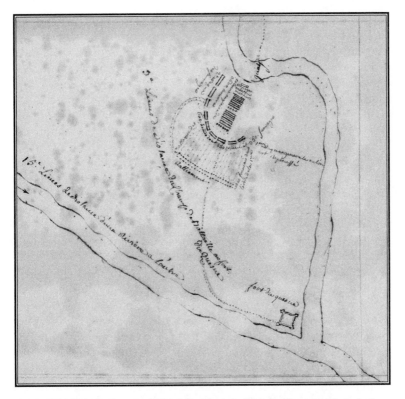

Detail of *Bataille du fort Duquesne defaitte de Bradok, 1755*, shows the "first general attack where we were repulsed," the "rallying of the French in the order of the first," and the "second attack of the Indians," forming a half-moon along the right flank of the British column. The map numbers the opposing forces as 250 French and 350 Indians against 3,600 English troops. Library and Archives Canada, NMC 7755.

and rallying ("Ralliement des français dans l'ordre de la 1ere") when the British grenadiers fired a third volley. A ball struck Beaujeu, killing him instantly, as he fell near the ravine.[38] The battle raged around his lifeless body and leaderless army as Captain Dumas found himself in command: "Our defeat appeared before my eyes as the most unpleasant viewpoint; and so as to not be charged with the bad maneuvers of others, I wished nothing more than to be killed myself."[39]

Led by the grenadiers of Gage's advance guard, Braddock's army had largely won this first phase of the Battle of the Monongahela, repulsing Beaujeu's initial attack and putting around 100 Canadian militia hors de combat. Yet in so doing, the British had transformed the very nature of the battle. It was now essentially a confrontation between Braddock's army and an army of 600 to 700 Indian warriors, a test of British heavy infantry against Indian light infantry. No sooner had Gage's vanguard thrown back the French, than Braddock's army had ironically lost the initiative. Native warriors, from the moment of first contact, had been developing the battlefield both psychologically and tactically for the second phase of the fight. The 1755 French battle map rightly depicts a "2$^{d.}$ attaque des sauvages" (second attack of the Indians), with lines advancing on the British right flank. Le Courtois's account describes how "all at once our Indians, who had advantageously posted themselves behind trees," fired a shocking and destructive volley into the British ranks and raised their massed war cries. It was the Indians' diversionary volleys that "diminished the effort that [the British] had made toward the front" and gave the French "time to reform and to fight more equally."[40]

Dumas claimed full credit for rallying both the demoralized French and Indian forces after Beaujeu's death. "It was then," he reported to the French ministry, "that by word and gesture I sought to rally the few soldiers who remained. I advanced, with an assurance born of despair." Dumas boasted that he orchestrated a "withering fire that astonished" the hapless British. Nonetheless Dumas had not acted alone as he rallied the French troops within earshot. He and Captain Lignery both "surpassed themselves in encouraging our men," and leading the remaining French *troupes de la marine* and Canadian militia as an effective blocking force on the road. Dumas maintained that the Indians had been so terrified by Braddock's artillery that they had fled along with the Canadian militia and that only when they saw his heroic stand did they return, at which point Dumas gave them orders to "seize the enemy's flanks." Both the French and Indians, having endured the pummeling volleys of musketry and cannon, realized that "the gunfire was doing little damage." The British were firing too high, and the trees protected them from the blasts of case shot. Each Frenchman and Indian behind trees "continued to do his best in the position he found himself in," as Pierre Pouchot described. Dumas deserves credit for his role in rallying the French, but it is clear that Beaujeu and individual Indian war captains had already taken the fight to the British flanks long before Dumas took command.[41]

The pivotal moment of the battle occurred when the Indians attacked along the British flanks in a half-moon formation that wrenched the initiative away from the British and rendered futile all of their subsequent responses. The Native forces at Braddock's Defeat were essentially an army of skilled light infantry and were unquestionably the most disciplined military units on the field. Each Indian warrior was "like a king and captain" and fought "as though he was to gain the battle himself," as two British observers noted. Experienced war captains led their men along the flanks of the Braddock's column with great efficacy, seeking opportune places to strike as well as cover that offered security to their men. Native squads functioned like modern fire teams as they extended the killing zone, a movement described in one British report as a "kind of running fight" as the warriors leap-frogged along the length of Braddock's column.[42]

It seems likely that Beaujeu and the leading French and Indian captains had discussed and agreed upon a battle plan in advance, for their rapid movement toward the baggage train at the very beginning of the fight suggests an overall strategy. Moreover, the tactical movements of hundreds of multiethnic Indians could hardly have been controlled by one man such as Beaujeu. French officers and cadets attached to individual war parties helped to execute their commander's intent. Lieutenant Courtemanche later recalled that he maintained an exact discipline among the Indians that he "commanded" as they pressed their attacks on the British. But both French and Native leaders had to exercise tactical leadership by personal example, persuasion, and consent. Courtemanche could not command in any meaningful sense, any more than Indian war captains could command their own warriors. "Since no operation was undertaken without Indians," another French officer openly admitted, "it was they who were in charge, whether on the march or in the attack." As the American frontiersman Robert Rogers, commander of Rogers' Rangers, later said, an Indian war captain was "a general without any real authority, and governs by advice only, not by orders."[43]

The speed with which the warriors developed the battlefield and moved along the British flanks does not suggest an ad hoc response but a calculated intention that reflected weeks of planning. For more than a month, Native scouts had been quietly studying the nature and organization of the British column and had tested its responses with small probing attacks. Those who had passed by this very spot were perhaps familiar with the tactical possibilities of the location. Although few warriors had ever encountered a European force of such potent firepower and size, the British column was vulnerable on the side of a high ridge, and Natives sensed that it would be a certain victory with minimal casualties. Native war parties conducted their

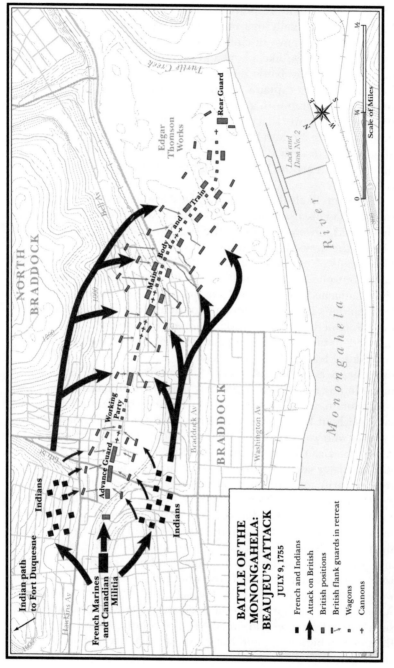

Battle of the Monongahela: Beaujeu's Attack
Glen Pawelski, Mapping Specialists, Ltd.

own battle parallel to that of their French allies, who were being quickly reduced to the status of auxiliaries. Were it not for the decisive ways in which Indian warriors shifted the momentum, the British grenadiers might have triumphed in the wooded setting.[44]

Redcoats perceived the first shots of the battle coming not from the French to their front, but to the "left of the advance Guard which Gradualy Came to the front and extended to their Right something like a half moon." Another British officer, perhaps located toward the rear of the advanced party, also thought "our first flank upon the left was fired on." Engineer Gordon, who had a bird's-eye view of the initial engagement, stated that "*as soon as the Enemy's Indians perceiv'd our Grenadiers*, they Divided themselves & Run along our right & Left flanks." A primal fear struck some soldiers as they saw through the cloudy smoke that Indian warriors were getting behind them and were gaining the steep heights on their right.[45] The euphoria of British soldiers after their unopposed crossing of the Monongahela was erased by shock at the unexpected collision and the unearthly sounds they heard. "The Indians instantly set up the War Cry as is their Custom," as one Frenchman reported. Their blood-curdling battle cries intensified under the dense forest canopy, magnifying their numbers and psychologically disarming the British rank and file.[46] Throughout history, such war cries, along with music, have accented battlefield triumphs, and the Monongahela is probably one of the greatest examples of their tactical effectiveness.[47] British soldiers described the Indian war cry as a "violent and horrid scream," "perhaps the most horrid sound that can be imagined."[48] Mathew Leslie, the commissary officer who had issued Braddock's celebratory rum to the troops on June 28, never forgot this first sound of battle: "the yell of the Indians is fresh on my ear, and the terrific sounds will haunt me until the hour of my dissolution."[49]

Musketry and artillery fire sent leaves falling and trees and limbs crashing to the ground, a forest carpet for the soldiers who themselves "dropped like Leaves in *Autumn*," as one British eyewitness remarked. Among the first to fall were those in the leading flanking parties, exposed at distances of at least 100 yards on the right and left of the column. The French were initially impressed by how well the British were "covering their forward positions & their flanks." But Native warriors began to overwhelm the flanking parties, rapidly collapsing the protection they were supposed to have provided for the main column. Much of that fighting was undoubtedly hand-to-hand, for which the Indians' weapons, the tomahawk and the war club, were well suited. The grenadiers and other men of the

Indian warriors like these extended the kill zone around Braddock's vulnerable column through their skillful tactical initiatives, terrifying war cries, and disciplined firepower. *War Party from Ticonderoga.* By Robert Griffing. Courtesy of Paramount Press, Inc.

44th and 48th regiments in Gage's main column began to hear the death throes of the small flanking parties as Indian warriors fell on them. The sounds of cracking skulls punctuated the frightening prospect that any wounded man left behind would receive no quarter and have his scalp lifted.[50]

Redcoats from the flanking parties began running in on the main column, creating disorder and dread, a contagion that spread "a visible Terror and Confusion appeared amongst the Men," as Gage himself witnessed it. Despite the actions of the officers, none of the troops would obey Gage's orders to move toward the rising ground and strengthen one of the flanking parties still holding its ground. A sense of being surrounded and cut off took hold, and soon Gage's main column was facing outward (a fact confirmed in the Le Courtois account, which notes that the British were "compelled to face on both sides of the road"). Officers yelled "Make Ready!" The soldiers' muskets were at full cock, ready to be presented and fired at the officers' commands. However, lack of sleep and emotional exhaustion—the alternating peaks and troughs of euphoria and fear—were beginning to take their toll on Gage's men. Discipline was the next casualty, as the men "threw away their Fire" without waiting for the commands of officers, more and more of whom were dead or wounded. The batman of Captain Cholmley of the 48th saw his master felled from his horse and killed in the first ten minutes of the fight. One account of the battle related the "hellish Treatment of poor Capt. Chomondeley" by two Indian warriors who were alleged to have rushed in, scalped him as he lay wounded, and rubbed his brains on their joints. Traumatized and terrified Redcoats who witnessed such acts began to fire at anything that moved amid the smoke that began to cover them like a shroud. Gage witnessed the confused British musketry kill "several of our Men on the Flanking Parties who came Running in on the Detachment." Captain Charles Tatton of the 44th was one of the officers leading a flanking party on Gage's right. Tatton was likely standing his ground, as he had done at the Battle of Prestonpans ten years earlier, when a ball from a Brown Bess made him the victim of friendly fire.[51]

Gage himself was one of the few officers miraculously still on horseback, though he probably received his wounds during the advance party's ordeal by fire. His command began disintegrating despite his attempts to arrest it. His flanking parties and even the vanguard of grenadiers had run in on his main column. He could see that the Natives had taken possession of the rising ground on his right and were pressing hard for the rear. Gage issued an order to move the advanced guard fifty or so yards back, where a makeshift line of battle "confusedly form'd again." One of the soldiers wounded early in the engagement was Duncan Cameron, the thirty-three-year-old private in the 44th Regiment, who was "for a while pretty much stunn'd." Cameron lay helpless on the field, as he saw Gage's men abandoning him and Indians overrunning their positions.[52]

Gage was praised for his bravery, but few officers could have salvaged their commands from so hopeless a tactical situation. After the Indians had collapsed his flanking parties and killed or wounded many officers, he was left with an immobile and disordered column. To press an attack forward against the French marines who were in front of him would extend the column and expose St. Clair's party and the main body of Braddock's army to attack, and perhaps allow Native warriors to isolate and destroy his command in detail. Regulars had not been trained to fight as light infantry, and therefore attacking into the ambush and sweeping along the enemy's flanks was a difficult proposition. Gage and the British were ultimately beholden to a line of battle, a problematic formation in a forest composed of huge old growth timber. With astonishingly speed, Native war parties had completely mauled Gage's advance party, rendering it combat-ineffective. Major William Sparke reported that only 11 men of 78 in the 48th Regiment's grenadier company survived unscathed, and only

13 of 70 men in Halkett's grenadier company came off the field. The killed and wounded included almost every commissioned officer in the grenadier companies, and 15 out of 18 officers in Gage's entire advanced guard. With good reason, Lieutenant Dunbar recorded that "before the Genl came to our assistance, most of our advanced Party were laid sprawling on the ground."[53]

When the working party of American companies heard the first shots and Indian war cries, St. Clair "immediately form'd" his men and readied the two 6-pounders for action, perhaps at Gage's request. Captain Polson's provincials were thirsting for battle—"much Readier to fight than to work," St. Clair remembered—and they were the first that formed for action. The snapping musketry that they heard, however, was soon followed by Redcoats from the advanced guard streaming back upon their lines. St. Clair characteristically rode forward to find out for himself what was happening, and instantly sensed the extreme peril that the column faced, for Native warriors were advancing deeper along its flanks. Just then, a musket shot tore through Sir John's right lung, breaking a collar bone and damaging his shoulder blade. He nonetheless returned to his men and deployed Captain La Péronie's and Captain Polson's companies to cover the two 6-pounders, which were at that moment booming into action. Having secured his command, St. Clair rode up to General Braddock, who was a few dozen yards behind the work party with the army's main body. Blood-soaked and gasping, St. Clair provided one of the first reports of what he had seen ahead, pleading "for God-Sake to gain the riseing ground on our Right to prevent our being Totally Surrounded." His desperate plea (perhaps spoken in Italian so that any bystanders would not perceive it as panic or overt criticism of his chief) came at a critical moment in the battle's development, as it seared Braddock's sense of the battlefield with an objective of questionable tactical worth. Suffering shock and loss of blood, St. Clair collapsed into unconsciousness, sparing him from witnessing the future horrors of this day. Battle now stormed around the "lion rampant" as he lay wounded on a sheet.[54]

St. Clair had found Braddock "at the head of his own Guns," the brass 12-pounders and giant 8-inch howitzers that were to have opened fire on Fort Duquesne. Surrounding Braddock were his aides, the Royal Navy detachment, and Captain Robert Stewart's Virginia lighthorsemen, acting as the general's guard. George Washington, riding with the staff officers in the center of the column, remembered that "*We* but a few moments before, believ'd our number's almost equal to the Canadian Force, *they* only expected to annoy us."[55] To those back in the main body, it seemed as though they had just begun to march when all hell broke loose. Upon hearing the firing a half mile ahead, Braddock had treated the encounter as he had previous alarms, immediately sending forward an aide-de-camp to investigate the attack and bring back a report. The minutes between the moment that Braddock first heard the firing to when St. Clair rode up to him wounded and distraught must have seemed interminably long. As the din of battle became louder and the aide did not return, Braddock finally went forward himself, according to his aide Robert Orme who was likely by his side as he rode on ahead. Orme wrote that his chief had become convinced that the French and Indians had "taken post," meaning they were making a stand in force.[56]

The general made two fateful decisions at this moment in the battle, perhaps only fifteen or twenty minutes after it had begun. First, he coordinated with Halkett about the security of the artillery and wagon train, stretching back a half mile or more to Fraser's burned cabin and the river crossing. In Orme's words, Braddock "dispos'd the Column in such a manner as to defend it from any attack and to disengage more men for action." The wagons, which had halted and had not advanced any farther than the first ravine, were drawn up in a tighter formation. Second, Braddock planned to send forward most of his remaining regular companies, which were then deployed in column on both sides of the train. Halkett would remain in command of the train and the rearguard, which was to be secured by the two dozen flanking parties (amounting to about 260 men) deployed to the right and left of the main body (engineer Mackellar's map shows approximately twenty-four such flanking parties). By disengaging them from the train, Braddock was freeing as many as 400 men from his battalion companies to reinforce Gage's advance party to their front. As Colonel Burton's column moved ahead, Braddock gave orders to deploy the three 12-pounders on the left flank of the advanced party: this was done apparently to secure his left flank while Burton's party assaulted the rising ground on the right that St. Clair had so desperately warned was the army's salvation.[57]

There was a bewildering futility to all subsequent efforts of the British commanders to respond in any meaningful way to the Indian army they confronted. By the time that Braddock gained any awareness of the tactical situation, Native warriors had already seized the initiative from him. As Braddock and Burton prepared to lead a column forward to what they thought was the front, Native war parties

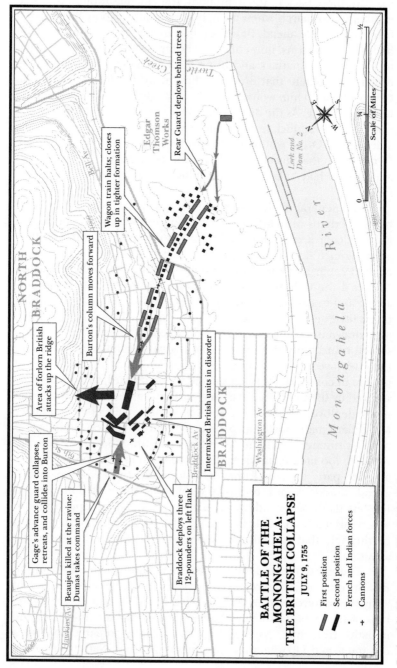

BATTLE OF THE MONONGAHELA: THE BRITISH COLLAPSE

JULY 9, 1755

Rear Guard deploys behind trees

Wagon train halts; closes up in tighter formation

Burton's column moves forward

Area of forlorn British attacks up the ridge

Gage's advance guard collapses, retreats, and collides into Burton

Beaujeu killed at the ravine; Dumas takes command

Intermixed British units in disorder

Braddock deploys three 12-pounders on left flank

NORTH BRADDOCK

BRADDOCK

Edgar Thomson Works

Turtle Creek

Monongahela River

Lock and Dam No. 2

Scale of Miles

First position

Second position

French and Indian forces

Cannons

Bell Av

Hawkins Av

9th St

Braddock Av

Washington Av

Battle of the Monongahela: The British Collapse
Glen Pawelski, Mapping Specialists, Ltd.

were at that same moment already making the rear of the British army the focus of their strikes. The speed and tactical skill with which the Indians operated had rendered the battlefield beyond the capacity of Braddock to control. There was little if anything that he could do to seriously threaten the Natives' dominance of the flanks. Caught in their column formation, the British forces lacked mobility, a defensible perimeter, and their commander's intent—how General Braddock intended his subordinates to respond to an attack by massed Indian warriors.[58] Moreover, there was no fallback point: two difficult river crossings separated them from their Sugar Creek campsite. The French and Indians could not have struck the British column at a more vulnerable psychological, tactical, and topographical moment.

Native warriors shifted the battle to the remainder of the doomed column, extending the killing zone to include the baggage train. The isolated flanking parties protecting the baggage and artillery found themselves infiltrated by Indian warriors. According to Orme's account, all but one of the flank parties "left for the security of the baggage" fled in upon the train, which was then "warmly attacked." Small parties of Redcoats began streaming down from the higher ground, wagon drivers struggled to maintain control of teams, and civilians huddled together fearing the worst. The sounds of lowing cattle and wounded horses and men were punctuated by dull thuds as soldiers, teamsters, and animals fell to Indian bullets. Within a short period, Native warriors had instilled chaos and disorder along the entire column.[59]

Riding above that fray was Colonel Halkett, uniformly praised for his conduct and character "as a good and truly heroic Gentleman," and whose bearing on horseback imparted resolve to his men. Sir Peter presumably brought forward a 12-pounder cannon that had been trailing the entire baggage train and ahead of the rearguard and emplaced it on the right flank of the baggage train. Because the four howitzers still in the column were apparently never brought into action, it was this single 12-pounder that "for some time kept the Indians off," until the warriors started to target the gun crew.[60]

One anonymous British officer later wrote that Halkett "behaved in the late action with the greatest bravery and Coolness—divided his men and fired some platoons by his own Direction." His composure and words encouraged his men in their platoon firings. The colonel's son, Lieutenant James Halkett, commanding the sixth company of his father's regiment, was likely either alongside the baggage train or in a flanking party when the battle began. One account has it that James witnessed the moment when his father, coursing about on horseback while leading the defense of the train, was toppled by Indian gunfire near a large "remarkable tree." James rushed to his wounded father's aid and was himself instantly killed and fell across his father's body. If the account is indeed accurate, it suggests that Sir Peter was killed within the first hour of the engagement. For all of his popularity, there is strangely no detailed eyewitness account of Sir Peter's last moments. In an account related by Dr. Alexander Hamilton, the Maryland civilian who was not part of the campaign, Christopher Gist looked on in horror as he was reloading his musket and caught a glimpse of an Indian taking aim at Sir Peter at close range. Gist finished loading and shot the warrior, though not in time to prevent him from killing Halkett. When British forces returned to the field years later, the skeletons of the father and son were found lying on top of one another in a macabre embrace.[61] Whatever the circumstances of his death, a senior British regimental commander had fallen near the very beginning of the battle,[62] leaving the entire baggage train and rearguard leaderless and demoralized. The Americans in the rearguard, now left to themselves, would begin to take matters into their own hands.

Yet the Natives' half-moon formation never became a full circle. The battle did not become one of annihilation, though the Natives might have easily surrounded the rearguard and cut off Braddock's army from the Monongahela.[63] It was rather a battle of opportunity, one in which Native warriors sought kills and scalps in much the same way that they hunted. The blasts of hundreds of muskets had accumulated immense clouds of dense white smoke over the entire field, which Native warriors used to their advantage. Under its concealment, the Indians accelerated their movements along the column. Once the war parties had captured the flanks, the Indians stealthily moved from tree to tree, closer to British targets. The giant oak trees on the field were remarkable bastions: their diameters were enough to provide cover for two or even three Native warriors, and the trunks provided stability for their deadly aimed shots. Sparke saw the Indians "changing their places as soon as they have fired, creeping or laying upon the Ground while they Load which they do very quick and are good marksmen." The warriors displayed disciplined firepower throughout the battle. They conserved ammunition, making every shot count. The Indians had learned to accurately fire their smoothbore trade guns through hunting, and they probably used a combination of round ball and buck shot to bring down British soldiers, as a Delaware warrior later recalled to a British emissary, Christian Frederick Post. "The *English* people are fools," he insisted, for "they hold their guns half man high and then let them snap," a quite accurate rendition of the typical British soldier's posture during the command to "present," that perhaps drew on this warrior's actual experience at Braddock's Defeat. "We take sight and have them at a shot, and so do the *French*," the Delaware continued, "they do not only shoot with a bullet, but big swan shot."[64]

The British rank and file experienced the battle enshrouded in white smoke, accented by flashes of yellowish light from the muzzles of Indian marksmen. Some testified that they never even saw their enemy in plain sight, or even a handful of warriors at any one time. But one Native enemy who was shockingly present was the Tuscarora deserter, Skowonidous, alias Jerry, who had crept forward to kill his former allies. Soldiers of the 44th Regiment recognized his face through the smoke and trees, as they saw "their comrades scalped in their sight," as one eyewitness related. There was little anyone could do about it.[65]

Using smoothbore muskets, warriors targeted British officers who were often conspicuously mounted on horseback in scarlet red coats and gleaming gorgets. Pierre Pouchot later reported that the French and Indians "fired at the officers as a priority" at the Monongahela battle. Throughout the eighteenth century, targeting of officers was an acknowledged hallmark of Indian tactics. Natives knew that by shooting down the commanders, "the soldiers will be all confused, and will not know what to do," as they told Post in 1758. Native marksmen also silenced the 12-pounder cannons by picking off the Royal Artillerymen and Royal Navy sailors servicing the guns. By killing the officers, Indians struck at the very pillars of organization, discipline, and morale in the British ranks. Redcoat officers led by personal example, often demonstrating sangfroid—the ideal of imperturbable calm—in battle. Those British officers who survived missed death by inches. Gage had clearly been targeted by Native warriors while he was on horseback, apparently for most of the whole battle: he received a slight wound in his abdomen, a ball grazed his eyebrow, shots went through his coat, and his horse was wounded twice.[66]

The disciplined firepower of the Indian warriors was quickly vanquishing the vaunted massed volleys of the British regulars. The Delaware warrior who had told captive James Smith that they would "shoot um down all one pigeon" could not have spoken a more accurate prophecy.[67] The Natives' attack on the rearguard, culminating with the early dispatching of Halkett, unfolded with tragic consequences for the remainder of the British forces, especially the reinforcements that Braddock had sent forward under Colonel Burton.

Harry Gordon was still with the alloyed remnants of the advanced and working parties, and witnessed how it all devolved. An alarm spread among the troops that the Indians were "attacking the Baggage in the Rear"—which they indeed were. This alarm intensified the soldiers' fears of being cut off from the river and massacred wholesale. Whether by instinct or by direct order, Gordon does not say, this alarm "Occasion'd a second Retreat of the Advanc'd party."[68]

The timing could not have been more unforgiving, Gordon must have thought, as the scene developed before him. The remnants of Gage's men "had not Retir'd But a few paces when they were join'd By the rest of the troops, Coming up in the greatest Confusion." Burton, leading the detachment of regulars from the main body, was marching his men in a column perhaps four abreast toward the beleaguered advanced troops. Patrick Mackellar, positioned at the rear of the working party, later depicted Burton's men in column, based on what he had witnessed during the battle. Orme best captured the multiple collisions that occurred, as Gage's men "in great confusion fell back upon the Party which Sir John St. Clair commanded, as did Sir John St. Clair's upon Col. Burton's," "whilst he was moving forward to their assistance."[69]

This series of collisions were the most catastrophic moments of the battle for the British, and controversy raged long afterward over who or what caused it. The questions were whether Burton's column moved forward in order or disorder, and whether Gage's command bore responsibility for creating the disorder when it fell back upon Burton. Orme for one believed that it was the disarray of the forward troops that caused the mayhem. For his part, Gage never denied that his men had fallen into disorder even before the arrival of Burton's troops from the main body. He admitted that the collapse of the flanking parties and vanguard, and their "Running in on the Detachment" had "completed our Disorder." But Gage also insisted that Burton's column was already disordered and panicked by the time it reached them. So, too, did Gates and Dunbar, who were in a good position to see Burton's advance. Gates saw that Burton's troops advanced in line of march (i.e., column) but were also "flank'd on both sides by the enemy which caused an immediate confusion" as they ran a gauntlet of fire. One officer (not an eyewitness) maintained that Braddock, his aides and other officers, and soldiers were moving ahead without any order, like a "parcell of school boys Coming out of s[c]hool." They were already under ferocious enemy fire, and at one point the column was facing to the right and left (two files facing right, with their backs to the other files facing left) returning fire.

However the officers might disagree on the cause of the chaos, they surely agreed that "from this time all was anarchy, no order, no discipline, no subordination," as Orme wrote.[70]

The collision crushed the integrity of the British units, so that "Blue, buff and yellow were intermix'd" into a chaotic conglomeration. Nearly 1,000 men were densely packed together in a small space. Many astonished British officers described the mob as anywhere from twelve to thirty men deep. The bunching together that many eyewitnesses noted was a common instinct for self-preservation in battle. As one British officer noted later in the eighteenth century, "men—like all animals—crowd together" in danger. British officers viewed the breakdown of military discipline among the privates as mutinous, almost like a dissolution of their social order. To sort out the mob, Braddock finally advanced the two colors carried in the flying column: the "King's colour" of the 44th Regiment rose proudly above the fray, while a soldier carried in a different direction the 48th regimental flag, a buff field with the Union in the right corner, their golden Roman regimental numerals gleaming. Some soldiers rallied to these banners. Gage saw a number of British soldiers attack up the ridge on the right of the column. But each attempt proved futile. The men began in line of battle but ended as a huddled column. Officers were killed, and the men flew back down the slope to safety. Worse still, many of these attacking British troops were killed by friendly fire as Redcoats in the densely packed mob continued to fire blindly into the woods.[71]

Braddock's efforts were directed at holding the ground through conventional tactics. After the wounded St. Clair had pleaded with Braddock "at the head of his own Guns," the general's immediate goal was to seize the rising ground on his right flank and to recapture the two abandoned 6-pounders ahead of his entangled army. Braddock sent forward the three light 12-pounder field pieces to secure his left flank. Horses and crews had to drag these guns down the first steep ravine or hollow way, then deploy them a few yards off the road. Captain Thomas Ord of the Royal Artillery had seen the slaughter of the Battle of Fontenoy ten years earlier, and under his command the 12-pounders belched out case shot and solid shot (as many as 99 total rounds may have been fired). Lieutenant Spendelow's sailors, with their tumbril filled with tools and block and tackle, had been marching ahead of the three giant guns and probably aided in their deployment. Spendelow and his crew acted as a covering force for the artillerists as their guns hurled rounds into the trees. Midshipman Haynes "behaved with great Bravery and very coming his

Station," in the words of Commodore Keppel, who praised the entire detachment to the Lords of Admiralty, who, he insisted, would find "no reason to be displeased with the Behaviour of the Sea Party at the Unfortunate Battle." Spendelow perished in the battle, along with Midshipman Matthew Talbot. Of the thirty-five men in the Royal Navy detachment, eleven were killed in action and seven were wounded (a casualty rate of 52 percent).[72]

The remainder of the battle was, for the British forces, largely a static and stationary affair. The British were gunned down in place by French and Indian muskets, and by their own comrades' Brown Bess muskets. The regulars were no match for Indian light infantry in terms of individual initiative and disciplined firepower, particularly as command and control broke down. Friendly fire occurred on a tragically greater scale after the collision of the British columns and accounted for many deaths. Washington even estimated that as many as two-thirds of their casualties were due to this indiscriminate firing, though it is impossible to measure precisely. He found it abhorrent that "our own cowardly dogs of Soldier's, who gatherd themselves into a body contrary to orders 10 or 12 deep, woud then level, Fire, & shoot down the Men before them." Some of the musketry coming from the rank and file may even have been intentionally fratricidal, directed at officers who "would have forced them to rally," as one concerned British officer wrote. Friendly fire also cut short the limited forays of small British platoons to take back the 6-pounders and attacks up the rising ground. Orme bitterly noted that the officers had "got themselves murder'd by distinguishing themselves in leading their men on."[73]

Time did nothing to diminish Washington's reaction to the chaos and panic among the British troops at the Monongahela, for he recalled years later that "by the unusual Hallooing and whooping of the enemy, whom they could not see, [the British] were so disconcerted and confused, as soon to fall into irretrievable disorder."[74] The panic that Washington witnessed was described in one contemporary account as being "like electricity," for it operated "instantaneously—like sympathy, it is irresistible where it touches." The panic mentioned in accounts of the battle was not simply fear or cowardice but resulted from a series of distorting physiological and psychological responses to combat. There was the shock of combat and the overwhelming sensations that it produced, as well as the sheer abject terror of scalping by an enemy who could appear out of everywhere and nowhere. The concentrated explosions of muskets and cannon became even more intense in some soldiers' ears. Redcoats were literally deaf to their officers' commands, for their ears excluded certain sounds and focused only on others (an effect known as auditory exclusion). Others likely experienced distortions such as tunnel vision, which rendered them unable to comprehend their surroundings, incapable of conscious action, and unable to discern friend from foe. Combat exposed the regulars' poor level of training, lack of self-discipline, and conglomerate composition, all of which reduced them to a mob that their regimental coats and uniform drill had superficially masked. The most panic-stricken soldiers, faces literally white with fear from vasoconstriction, were reduced to obeying a primal instinct for survival.[75]

The scalping had been uppermost in their minds. Over the course of the march, as we've seen, campfire chats had often turned on the subject of Indian warfare. The British rank and file had imbibed certain ideas about their Indian enemies "in regard to their scalping and Mawhawking," as one British officer wrote. They were certain they would receive no quarter if captured, suffer horrendous deaths by torture, and have their scalps hacked or sliced off their heads. Gage, Dunbar, and other British officers attributed much of their soldiers' panic to the "frequent Conversations of the Provincial Troops and Country People," who told them that "if they engaged the Indians in their European manner of fighting they would be Beat." By early July, on the other hand, many of these regulars had had experience in repelling Indian threats and displayed no fear or panic. The stories also worked advantageously for the British, for it convinced the soldiers that surrender was never an option. As a number of eyewitnesses reported, including Cholmley's batman, "If it was not for their Barbaras Usage which we knew they would treat us, we should Never have fought them as long as we did, but having only death before us made the men fight Almost longer then they was able."[76]

Panic was a cause, but not the primary cause of the catastrophe.[77] Not all British soldiers panicked, and some of them, especially the Americans, continued to fight with initiative and fortitude. Thomas Farrell, a volunteer with the expedition, rescued Lieutenant John Treby after he had been wounded and immobilized. When Farrell heard that Treby had been left behind, he "caught him up on his back, and conveyed him, at the most imminent peril of his own life, to some distance from the field of battle."[78] St. Clair was especially adamant that the rank and file not be singularly blamed for defeat: "something besides Cowardice must be attributed to a Body of men, who will suffer the one half to be diminished by Fire without being pursued in their Retreat." St. Clair had been unconscious for most of the battle, but his point seems to hold true. He had commanded four of the most combat-effective companies, all of which were composed of American recruits. He hoped "never to live to see that Argument hold good against our men," especially after he learned of the bravery that his officers and soldiers had displayed.[79]

Though they had been previously maligned by mainline British officers, the New York Independents of Captain Gates fought with great tenacity and suffered horrendous losses at the Monongahela. Ordinary soldiers such as Sergeant Francis Penford, Corporal Andrew Holmes, and privates Daniel Hart and Martin Lucorney fought with courage. Private Martin Lucorney provides one of the most revealing portraits of how a rank-and-file infantryman experienced the Monongahela. A native of Hungary and a Lutheran Protestant who could barely speak any English, Lucorney knew that "the Battle was going against the King's Troops." He came up to his comrade, Corporal Holmes, and beating his breast shouted, "The English be all killed!" encouraging him to take to the trees. Lucorney took cover with Private Hart behind a massive tree and fired away at the enemy, "watching his Opportunity to fire upon the Enemy" like a good soldier. Lucorney's heart was in the fight, and he was seen to weep over the disaster that had befallen British arms.[80]

Another demonstration of British bravery was how Lucorney's commanding officer, Gates, was saved. Gates had been seriously wounded by a ball that penetrated his left breast and immobilized his arm. Thirty years after the Monongahela, a story appeared in a newspaper about the deep gratitude that Gates felt for one of his soldiers, a man named Penfold. The writer was a British officer who had heard the story from Penfold, an "old soldier of the royal regiment of artillery who served me while the 18th regiment was at Fort Pitt and the Illinois." Penfold and Gates had both been wounded at the Monongahela, and Gates was "left among the slain." Penfold "made a shift to carry the worthy captain" off the field, and Gates always told him "that he owed his life to me." In the early 1770s, when Gates heard that Penfold had been "worn out" in such lengthy service, he invited him to Traveler's Rest, Gates's new home in Virginia: "come rest your firelock in my chimney corner, and partake with me; while I have, my savior Penfold shall not want; and it is my wish, as well as Mrs. Gates's, to see you spend the evening of your life comfortably. Mrs. Gates desires to be affectionately remembered to you."[81]

The apocryphal story is altogether true in every detail save one: the soldier's name was Penford, not Penfold. Sergeant Francis

Penford appears on returns and documents relating to Gates's New York Independent Company. He had enlisted in the company in 1754 and was a witness for Gates's last will and testament in April 1755. He remained in Gates's company until 1760, going on to serve in the Royal Artillery with the 18th Regiment, present at Fort Pitt from 1768 to 1772, when he told his story to the unnamed British officer. Penford apparently returned to England and always maintained a warm affection for the Gates family. In addition to being wounded, Gates lost all of his horses and personal baggage in the battle, but due to Penford's bravery, he came away with his life.[82] Gates and Penford were both among the few fortunate survivors of the shattered New York Independent Company. Of the fifty-seven officers and men who crossed the Monongahela, approximately twenty-seven were killed in action (nearly half) and another eighteen wounded, according to an unpublished return in Gates's papers. A staggering 78 percent of the New York Independent Company detachment was slaughtered at the Monongahela.[83]

By 3:00 P.M., the army was nearing the breaking point, under the weight of such enormous casualties and so unsustainable a position. The army's survival now hung in the balance, as did the preservation of the precious artillery and supply train, and the lives of the wounded men who might be rescued were the British to hold their ground. The question of what to do was forced upon Braddock by the independent initiatives of American units such as Gates's New York Independent Company, the Virginia companies of La Péronie and Polson, and a small number of Irish regulars who recognized that breaking ranks and taking to the trees might mean survival. The rearguard, also composed of American units—the South Carolina Independent Company and Adam Stephen's Virginia ranger company—fought on valiantly despite losing Halkett at the beginning of the action.

American units fought at the Battle of the Monongahela with the greatest unit cohesion, discipline, and effectiveness, and suffered the most for it. The four companies in St. Clair's working party (La Péronie, Polson, Waggoner, and Gates) had spontaneously begun taking to the trees and attacking the enemy around the time that Braddock and Burton were leading the regular column forward. The batman of the unfortunate Captain Cholmley may have witnessed these Virginia companies fighting in loose order when he wrote that "two hundred of the American Soldiers [had] fought behind Trees and I belive they did the most Execution of Any." Braddock's remaining Indian allies, "who all behav'd well" according to Starke, may have set the example or encouraged the men to use the cover of trees. Whatever the impetus, one British officer observed that the "American Troops though without any orders run up immediately some behind trees & others into ye ranks & put ye whole in confusion." British officers, including Braddock, instinctively believed that such indisciplined actions would contribute to confusion and desertion. "In the early part of the Action," as Washington later recalled, "some Irregulars (as they were called) *without [directions]* advanced to the right, in loose order, to attack; but this, *unhappily* from the unusual appearance of the movement being mistaken for cowardice and a running away was discountenanced."[84]

A number of combat veterans from the old Virginia Regiment seasoned the rank-and-file men of La Péronie's, Polson's, and Waggoner's companies, providing greater unit cohesion than that of the British regiments. Veterans of Fort Necessity such as John Stewart and John Harwood probably sensed the futility of staying in the open and made for the trees. In Stewart's case, he suffered a grievous wound to both thighs that rendered him "incapable of getting a Livelihood" in future years. Sergeant Thomas Longdon of La Péronie's company had also fought at Fort Necessity the year before, only to die in action at the Monongahela, leaving behind a wife and three young children whose only recompense was a sum of £10 granted by the Virginia House of Burgesses.[85]

The Virginians attacked the Indians and advanced up the steep hillside more effectively than Braddock's regulars, and they did so knowing the potential dangers of the latter's irregular firing. At some point in the melee, La Péronie and Lieutenant John Wright were killed, leaving Ensign Edmund Waggoner in command of the company.[86] As a former sergeant in the Virginia Regiment, Waggoner probably had the right touch with the men. Along with his brother, Thomas, and his company, he may have jointly led a force of at least eighty Virginians up the steep ridge, intending to hold a position on it near some large trees and fallen timbers.[87] The Virginians moved stealthily in the smoke, losing only three men, and gained the log breastwork from whence they proceeded to open fire on the Indians. The explosion of musketry on the right startled the already confused Redcoats, who apparently concentrated their fire on the Virginians at the same time, perhaps believing that Indian warriors were counterattacking. The Virginians' attack was destroyed in the cross fire. Edmund was killed, and his brother returned with only a small remnant of Virginians left behind on the hillside. A subsequent attack by Captain Polson similarly failed when he tried to prevent Redcoats located behind his Virginians to cease fire. Several Redcoats "replyed they could not help it. They must obey orders." Polson was shot through the head in one of their next volleys and his company was also destroyed.[88]

As his old Virginia Regiment officers and men steadfastly made those charges, Washington could only look on from afar at a prospect that undoubtedly stirred his affections. The battle was turning against the British, and there was one chance left to stem the tide. He made a desperate plea to Braddock: "before it was *too late*, & the confusion general an offer was made by [me] to head the Provincials, & engage the enemy in their own way; but the propriety of it was not seen until it was too late for execution."[89] What Washington may have envisioned was dispersing the Virginians behind trees and slowly clearing the flanks, a move that may have enabled the British to at least hold their ground and gain room for maneuver. Braddock initially refused,[90] for at this point in the battle he believed that everything still depended upon Burton's men and the artillery on his left. Washington was also his only unwounded aide-de-camp, and Braddock may also have refused on that basis alone. The young Virginian was not alone in his appeal to Braddock against the futile tactic of standing under withering musketry: James Burd's conversations with St. Clair, Thomas Dunbar, and other officers revealed that the soldiers had "insisted much to be allowed to take to the Trees, which the general denied and stormed much, calling them Cowards," even going so far as to strike the troops with the back of his sword to bring them to a sense of discipline.[91] Washington could only look as his former command and old comrades became distinguished in death: "The Virginian Companies behavd like Men, and died like Soldier's," as he later eulogized them. "In short the dastardly behaviour of the Regular Troops exposd all those who were inclind to do their duty, to almost certain Death."[92] Washington did not exaggerate. Of the 57 men in Captain Polson's company in June 1755, only 18 could be mustered in September 1755 at Fort Cumberland: 39 men had been killed, wounded, were missing, or had deserted: a casualty and attrition rate of 68 percent. Waggoner's company was similarly shattered, suffering 61 percent losses, while 54 percent of La Péronie's company was lost between June and September.[93]

Washington's survival had been measured by inches as he attended to Braddock. He had four bullet holes in his clothes and one through his hat, and enemy shots felled two horses under him, and he would have been killed had he simply leaned in the saddle differently.[94] Braddock and his staff were of course highly visible objects of Indian marksmen throughout the affair, as the general's military family had been "prettily pickled," as lamented Orme, who had a bullet tear through his leg above the knee, barely missing arteries. William Shirley Jr. had been shot through the head and died instantly around the time that Halkett was killed. Captain Roger Morris had a painful facial wound, having been shot through the nose according to one account. Orme and Morris were left in a wagon while the battle raged around them. Washington recalled that they "were wounded early in the Engagemt which rendered the duty harder upon me, as I was the only person then left to distribute the [General's] Orders, which I was scarcely able to do, as I was not half recoverd from a violent illness."[95] Washington's conduct at the Monongahela on July 9 is all the more remarkable given the illness that had recently incapacitated him and from which he didn't fully recover until a full month after the battle.[96] The Monongahela left Washington's mind with a profound conviction of "the all powerful dispensations of Providence," which he credited with protecting him in combat "beyond all human probability," as he wrote shortly afterward.[97]

In the end it was not up to Washington's provincial troops but to Colonel Burton's regulars to lead the forlorn hope of the British Army at the Monongahela. A "diligent Sensible Man," Burton and other officers had reasserted enough control amid the chaos to organize 150 men in a line of battle. Burton personally led a desperate attack straight up the infamous rising ground to their right. Another attack, led by officers unknown, was sent up the road, to recapture the two abandoned 6-pounders. The ridge was already covered with British and Virginian dead whose corpses marked the limits of previous attacks. The terrain itself was a formidable challenge, for in addition to the steep slope, fallen and standing trees and rocks slowed the British advance. Anyone watching the attack unfold sensed that everything hinged on whether the men could clear the slope and end the incessant firing. Native warriors responded to Burton's assault the same way they had others. They retreated up the ridge, inviting the British to attack by "always giving way," as Thomas Gage noted. But the Indians continued to hold the high ground as they absorbed and isolated the British attack. After regrouping, they then felled the officers leading at the front of their ranks. After Burton went down with a wound in the hip, the Redcoats lost heart and fled back to the comparative safety of their massed comrades.[98]

It was over. Both the rising ground and two 6-pounders had absorbed the remaining energies of the British units in fruitless and truly forlorn endeavors. There was no hilltop that if taken, would have brought security to Braddock's forces, as other British officers discovered years later. Perhaps speaking with Braddock in view, a British writer later summarized the hopelessness of attacking Indians in the woods with regular formations:

> He will not hesitate to charge those invisible enemies, but he will charge in vain. For [the Indians] are as cautious to avoid a close engagement, as indefatigable in harrassing his troops; and notwithstanding all his endeavours, he will still find himself surrounded by a circle of fire, which, like an artificial horizon, follows him every where.
>
> Unable to rid himself of an enemy who never stands his attacks, and flies when pressed, only to return upon him again with equal agility and vigour; he will see the courage of his heavy troops droop, and their strength at last fail them by repeated and ineffectual efforts.[99]

Huddled in their compact formation for security, the wagoners were among the first to sense that the battle was lost. They had been engaged by Native warriors who had attacked the wagon train from the earliest moments of the battle. Tension was palpable as teamsters and civilians could only wait and watch while the battle enveloped them. They had seen the gallant Colonel Halkett felled by enemy fire, and loaded wounded officers such as captains Orme and Morris into wagons. Indians then crushed the flanking parties that were supposed to have protected them. Gage relates that "the men that covered the wagons went off by tens and twenties, till reduced to a very small body." A Virginia wagoner named Lewin was badly wounded in the arm as Native warriors fired on the train. Wagoners struggled to control their teams, spooked by the sounds of musketry and artillery. Enemy fire was killing and wounding both men and horses, and scattering some of the pack horses and cattle. A slow trickle of soldiers and teamsters began flowing back to the ford of the Monongahela throughout the battle. Twenty-year-old Daniel Boone was one of many who chose survival over their sovereign, cutting a horse out of its harness and escaping the expedition. So many wagoners eventually fled that a British officer coming on the remnants of the wagon train realized that even had they won the battle, there would have been no horses left to pull the artillery to Fort Duquesne.[100]

By around 4:00 P.M., the desolate army was virtually leaderless, with so many officers killed outright or incapacitated by wounds. Braddock's ability to command and control the battle had fallen with them. The artillery fell silent, as crews lay dead around their 12-pounders. The pair of colors near the abandoned guns was retrieved by the 44th Regiment's chaplain, Philip Hughes. Soldiers were running low on ammunition, and muskets were becoming dysfunctional after firing twenty-four or more rounds. Misfires occurred as flints failed to spark and touchholes were caked with fouling, making many soldiers "useless spectators" in the battle as they struggled to fix their weapons.[101] Some sleep-deprived soldiers had been up for more than twelve hours and were simply exhausted. For others, lost in the abyss of combat, nothing mattered anymore. Braddock came to realize too late that he had to "engage the enemy in their own way." A Royal Navy officer recalled that very late in the battle, "when the General perceived and was convinced that the soldiers would not fight in a regular manner without Officers, he divided them into small parties and endeavoured to surround the Enemy, but by this time the major part of the Officers were either killed or wounded."[102]

Braddock had proven stouthearted throughout the battle, a symbol of perseverance and unflinching bravery in the line of fire. Wearing his elegant sash, Braddock and his mounted staff officers were visibly important targets to Native marksmen (it is unknown whether the general was wearing his full regimental coat with gold lace). Like Washington, Braddock had numerous bullet holes in his clothing. Four horses were shot from under him but he bravely remounted a new horse each time. When he was mounting a fifth, a ball struck his right arm and tore into his lungs.[103] Washington and Captain Robert Stewart attended the general, as did Gage and Croghan. The wounded Braddock lay on the ground as his attendants removed his red sash and used it for its intended purpose, as a litter. Washington, Stewart, or other officers or servants carried him to the rear, and placed him in a tumbril cart.[104] Stewart, who "had the Honour of being close by his Side," observed that more than Braddock's body had been wounded: "I believe his Misfortune wounded his very Soul." Croghan also sensed the magnitude of Braddock's despair as he lay in the tumbril insisting that he be left on the field of battle. The wounded general allegedly tried to lay hold of Croghan's pistols, wanting to "die as an old Roman,"—by his own hand—as Quinctilius Varus had when his three Roman legions were slaughtered by Germanic tribesmen in the Teutoburger Forest in AD 9.[105]

Braddock's despair stemmed from the realization that the battle had been lost and that only honor could be salvaged from the disaster. As word spread of his wounding, it further demoralized his troops. Facing the inevitable, as Gage recalled, "an order was given to beat a Retreat to bring the Men to Cover the Waggons and Carry

[off] as much as could be." Orme recalled that Braddock "endeavored to retreat them in good order; but the panick was so great that he could not succeed." All that remained was to conduct an orderly retreat, to cover the remaining wagons and artillery. At first, the troops fell back in a composed manner across the first "hollow way" to the train. The French, pressing ahead along the main road, found some British retreating "in good order," firing as they retreated. A strange, eerie silence settled over the battlefield, Gage recalled, and as troops crowded around the wagons, the firing largely ceased for a short time.[106]

But the silence was deceptive, a pause in which Native warriors prepared their weapons and their minds to deliver a final attack on the column, one that turned the retreat into a bloody rout. The account of Le Courtois related this decisive moment: "Our Indians, seeing them withdraw toward the tail of the column after having fired, took this movement for a flight, and came out of the woods, war clubs in hand, and made their horrible cries, and fell upon them with inexpressible fury." Renewed scalp cries resounded through the battlefield, and musketry again erupted from the areas where Native warriors and French officers were pressing their attacks home. Lieutenant Courtemanche recalled that he encouraged the Indians to pursue the English and prevent them from rallying. British soldiers like Gordon perceived the "Indian's shouts upon the Right Advancing," while Gage noted a "smart Fire coming from the Front and left Flank," after which "the whole took to Flight."[107]

French and Indian warriors had brought a proud army to the brink of dissolution in three hours. The British officer corps was so decimated that any effective command and control was now nearly impossible. Gage and Sparke were the only field officers remaining, the rest "rendered incapable by Death and Wounds." The rank and file recognized their leaderless condition, which only contributed to their sense of isolation as the final Indian attack came down on them. They sensed that Indians were driving toward the river crossing behind them in order to cut them off and slaughter them.[108] Like a crushing, unbearable weight, all of those circumstances finally broke the army in an instant. Aghast British officers described the army's final moments in terms of drill. "As if by beat of Drumm," one British officer observed, the remaining men collectively executed a right-about face, pivoting 180 degrees and fleeing for their lives, "every one trying who should be the first." Washington was among the few remaining officers attempting to rally the men. Both lieutenant colonels—Burton and Gage—had gotten back across the river to halt the men on the south

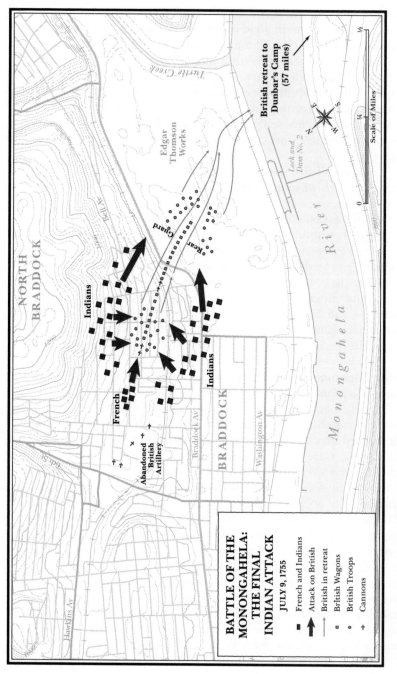

Battle of the Monongahela: The Final Indian Attack
Glen Pawelski, Mapping Specialists, Ltd.

bank, so that Washington and Sparke were the only effective leaders left. The troops were running, Washington said, like "sheep before hounds": "when we endeavourd to rally them in hopes of regaining the ground and what we had left upon it, it was with as little success as if we had attempted to have stopd the wild Bears of the Mountains or rivulets with our feet, for they [would] break by in spite of every effort that could made to prevent it."[109]

The American rearguard of Braddock's army, roughly 110 men, was all that stood between the Native contingents and the river crossing, where Captain Cholmley had earlier enjoyed his last meal of Gloucestershire cheese. To his batman, it seemed, the Indians "strove for [the crossing] with all their Force." But the rearguard, "knowing the Conciquance of it preserved the pass till we Retreated."[110] The remnants of Braddock's army were saved by two American units, one provincial and one regular, that both fought with American tactics. The South Carolina Independent Company was a regular unit led by lieutenants Probart Howarth and John Gray, but most of its fifty-four men were colonial recruits.[111] Captain Adam Stephen and Lieutenant William Bronaugh[112] led the first Virginia ranger company, numbering between fifty and sixty men.[113] Many of the officers and men in these units had fought at Fort Necessity, and they were ready to receive the Indians' attack.

At the beginning of the action, the Virginians and South Carolinians had been left to themselves following the death of their overall commander, Colonel Halkett. The units fanned out into the woods in a crescent formation a good distance from the road. It is likely that the officers ordered their men to take to the trees. Engineer Mackellar's map shows the rearguard "divided (round the rear of the Convoy now closed up) behind Trees." Another British officer credited the effectiveness of the rearguard, which he confessed "did more execution than the whole, among the Enemy, as the officer [Stephen?] had time to recolect himself Consequently made a disposition and extended his Guard in advantageous posts behind trees by which he both repuls'd and kill'd a great number."[114]

In this desperate fight for survival, Gray, Howarth, and Stephen were all wounded.[115] Stephen's company lost as much as one-third of its strength.[116] But his soldiers' steadfastness had bought time for the retreating army and enabled many wounded men to survive. One British officer was so severely wounded in the leg that he was unable to move, and his voice intermingled with those of other wounded men frantically pleading to their fleeing comrades to help them from the field. He wrote that when a Virginia soldier stopped to help, he instead leveled his gun at the officer's head, exclaiming, "I will put you out of your Misery, these Dogs shall not burn you!" The wounded officer managed to take cover behind the tree, and the smoothbore round missed its mark. The officer was saved by Lieutenant Gray and his small remnant of the South Carolina Independent Company. Adam Stephen remained greatly embittered against the "infamous Dogs," as he referred to the regulars who abandoned the field. "The few independents and Virginians that were engaged behaved better and suffered much," he later commented. The rearguard action underscored the ironic reversal of fortunes at the Monongahela: Braddock had put his confidence in disciplined Irish regulars, only to witness his army saved by the American provincials and regulars that he and others had dismissed as indifferent.[117]

Washington, Stewart, and a handful of officers brought the tumbril cart bearing the wounded Braddock down to the river. No other rank-and-file soldiers could be persuaded to help, and pulling and pushing the cart through the ford was impossible. The three wounded officers were "with great Difficulty" taken out of the tumbril, and "hurryed along across the River," either on horseback or again using Braddock's sash. The troops had "abandoned their General and their Colours," intensifying the ire that Stewart and other officers felt for the men. Major Sparke was the last field officer to leave the field. The tattered officer had somehow managed to remain on horseback for most of the battle, wounded by a grazing shot on his left leg and a spent ball that hit his stirrup and lodged in his foot. When his horse finally went down, Sparke was alone, bleeding, and hobbled, facing a considerable walk of a half-mile to the ford. As he neared the Monongahela, he found Native warriors lining the river's edge, firing at will on the hapless British.[118]

The depths of war's abyss were fathomed in the Monongahela River, as the Indians slaughtered many of the retreating soldiers and civilians, and the ground leading toward Fraser's old plantation was covered with the detritus of the defeated army.[119] Terrified soldiers threw away everything in their frenzied attempts to escape. Regimental coats, tricorn hats, drums, muskets, and accoutrements littered Braddock's Road as the British retreated over it. Soldiers of the 44th threw away approximately ninety regimental coats in the battle and retreat, and Gates's New York Independents cast aside thirty-seven muskets and greater numbers of cartridge boxes and bayonets.[120] Wounded British soldiers struggled to escape as they saw enemies closing in behind them. The wounded Harry Gordon was saved by the unstable embankments that gave the Monongahela its name. As he came to the ford, he steered his horse toward the road cut earlier that day through the steep embankment. Finding it jammed, he had no choice but to urge his horse over the edge. But the Monongahela's steep banks gave way and broke off under the weight, gently sliding horse and rider into the river. Glancing over his shoulder, he saw Natives attacking terror-stricken soldiers flailing in the water, and heard their shrieks as tomahawks cleaved their skulls and sharp knives lifted their scalps. Gordon was one of several eyewitnesses who saw Indians pursuing and killing soldiers and women alike. During the crossing, the batman wrote, "an Indien shot one of our Wimen and began to Scalp her," before her husband turned and "Shot the Indien dead." Sparke somehow evaded the Indians lining the ford and plunged into the river. The bullets, he remembered, fell "very thick" around him. He nearly drowned in a deep pool until helped out by another soldier. Sparke would forever "retain a just sense of the Almighty's protection that day." The currents carried bodies and blood downriver toward Fort Duquesne, a melancholy counterpoint to the army's triumphal crossing earlier that morning.[121]

As the terrified flotsam of a proud army washed up on the south bank of the Monongahela, Colonel Burton "made a Speech" to rally the men but to no avail. The French and the Indians were not pursuing the British across the river. But the army's backward flight was now driven by fear that they would. Washington knew that had the Native warriors passed the Narrows and driven for the upper ford, the entire army would have been cut off and destroyed. Some soldiers became lost and darted aimlessly into the woods on reaching the south side of the river. Braddock ordered Washington ahead to rally as many men as possible. After crossing the Monongahela one final time, Washington ascended the heights to their July 8 encampment site near Sugar Creek, where he found the wounded Gage attempting to restore order and rallying around 100 men. The exhausted aide turned around to report back to Braddock, who had remained with a stalwart party of men near the crossing. But the "utmost agonies" of the wounded precluded any stand by a significant number of the survivors.[122]

The setting sun brought an end to the day of slaughter. But Washington's ordeal—like that of the battle's survivors—was just beginning. Braddock ordered Washington to undertake a mission that the utterly spent aide must have thought impossible given "the weak state in which he was, and the fatiegues, and anxiety of the last 24 hours." Despite being "wholly unfit," Washington rode nearly sixty miles back to Dunbar's Camp, and conveyed orders to send reinforcements to cover the retreat and provisions for the survivors and the wounded. Washington and two guides (perhaps the redoubtable Christopher Gist) rode through the entire night, arriving like living dead at Dunbar's Camp the morning of July 10. The "gloom and horror" of that night was forever seared onto Washington's memory, a hellish descent into "impervious darkness occasioned by the close shade of thick woods." His two guides were reduced to stumbling and "groping on the ground with their hands" just to rediscover Braddock's Road. The wounded also groped through the darkness to find the marks that St. Clair's pioneers had notched on trees on each side of the road only days before. A British officer recalled, "we found [the marks] of very great Use to us in our retreat, for being obliged to keep marching ye whole night through a continued Wood, ye people frequently lost their way, & had nothing to put them right except feeling for the Marks." Many of these wounded men died lonesome deaths as darkness surrounded them, and as the solitary ordeal of walking Braddock's Road in reverse depleted what little strength they had. "The shocking Scenes which presented themselves in this Nights March are not to be described," Washington recalled thirty years later. "The dead—the dying—the groans—lamentation—and crys along the Road of the wounded for help…were enough to pierce a heart of adamant."[123]

But those in the retreat were comparatively lucky. Private Duncan Cameron, who had been wounded and abandoned when Gage's men retreated, witnessed many "Horrors" that rendered this battle the "most shocking" that he had ever experienced (and given that he had survived the hellish eighteenth-century battles of Cartagena, Dettingen, Fontenoy, and Culloden, this is an extraordinary thing to say). He was one of many British soldiers who "were left in the field of Battle and Crawl'd off afterwards." After the enemy had swept over him, Cameron hid in a hollow tree, from whence he witnessed the gruesome orgy of destruction that followed the battle.[124]

The battlefield was covered with more than 400 British dead. Hundreds of wounded soldiers, still alive and conscious, suffered the deaths by Indian tomahawks and scalping knives that they had so dreaded. Native warriors, flush with the euphoria of victory, turned to the writhing and moaning fields of battle. They could now seize the principal honors of their warfare: captives, scalps, and war materiel from among the detritus of Braddock's shattered army and baggage train. Natives stripped symbols of their conquest from the dead and the wounded, such as grenadiers' mitre caps, officers' tricorns and gorgets, 44th and 48th regimental coats, and swords and muskets. Private Cameron witnessed a French commander trying to prevent the Indians from scalping men who were still alive. The officer was perhaps Captain Dumas himself, who tersely noted, "the pillage was horrible." But the French exercised little control over the battlefield in its aftermath, becoming either participants in the looting or bystanders to the Indians' scalping. "The Bodies of a great number of men kill'd & those of eight Women or Girls entirely strip'd, lie promiscuously with dead horses for more than half a League," as one French account described the scene. The killing and scalping of hundreds of British dead and wounded cannot be explained entirely by reference to cultural practices. The aftermath reflected war's intrinsic brutality and the rage born of combat, like something out of an ancient battlefield. The Indians' piercing victory yells, the cracking of skulls by war clubs, the dying agonies of the wounded, the groaning of wounded animals— blended together in an unearthly sound that only war could compose. Indian and French warriors gathered at the supply wagons staved in two hogsheads of rum that quaffed their thirst and fueled their destructive impulses. They had discovered the wagonload of Indian trade goods that Braddock had brought in anticipation of winning over the region's Indians after they had destroyed the French. The cattle herd that might have provided a victory supper for Redcoats experienced the same fate in French and Indian hands. They found a small money chest, perhaps stored in the "Money Tumbril" among Braddock's headquarters wagons, and "plundered much gold and silver coin." The capture of Braddock's train was a blessing in disguise, Washington later observed, as it diverted the French and Indians from pursuing the defeated army.[125]

The greatest French triumph of the battle was the capture of Braddock's entire artillery train. French officers were far more concerned with securing the valuable guns and extracting their own dead and wounded than with protecting British wounded. French soldiers ransacking the wagons also came up with an astonishing find: General Braddock's headquarters papers, which were brought back to Fort Duquesne and examined that evening and the following day. French commanders may have wished to pursue Braddock's army but were fearful of a British counterattack from Dunbar's column and uncertain of its exact location. According to one French report, the Indians were "afraid that the French would wrong them of their plunder" and spread a rumor that the British had rallied and were advancing again to recover their artillery, knowing that the French would leave them alone while trying to secure it. Most of the troops, including Captain Dumas, returned to Fort Duquesne later that evening, leaving only a token force to remain with the silent guns. The battlefield and remains of Braddock's army were left largely in Indian hands. It is no surprise that Pierre Pouchot described the Monongahela as "the most vigorous & most glorious in which the Indians were involved, and a part of the glory can be attributed to the accuracy of their fire."[126]

The French had gained a monumental victory over the British at an astonishingly low cost. The total casualties (killed and wounded) for French and Indian forces were probably fewer than 50, but a precise number is difficult to arrive at. Estimates of total deaths range from 11 to 33, with the most reliable accounts ranging from 27 to 33 killed and 20 to 29 wounded. The most detailed accounting in one later report showed only 15 Indians killed, along with 2 Marines, 3 militiamen, and 3 officers, while there were 4 officers and cadets, 2 Marines, 2 militiamen, and 12 Indians wounded in action. Beaujeu's body was found in the "gully near the road" where the fighting had initially broken out and was eventually transported by canoe down the Monongahela and buried in Fort Duquesne's cemetery. Lieutenant Carqueville and Ensign La Pérade survived the battle long enough for comrades to bring them back to Fort Duquesne. Carqueville expired that evening, while La Pérade lingered on until July 10. Other wounded officers, as we've seen, included Lieutenant Le Borgne, Ensign Bailleul, and cadet Montmédy. Another cadet, twenty-two-year-old Joseph Hertel de Sainte-Thérèse, died of his wounds on July 30. Among the fallen rank-and-file soldiers were Monsieur Limoge, a Canadian militiaman from the Thousand Islands, who was buried on the field of battle; and Jean-Baptiste Talion, another militiaman from the Thousand Islands, who was brought back to Fort Duquesne wounded, but died there that evening, after receiving the sacraments of penance and extreme unction from Father Baron.[127]

At Fort Duquesne, the prisoner James Smith had spent July 9 anxiously wondering if his liberation was nigh. How could so small a force, without artillery, hope to defeat Braddock's column? He remained in "high hopes that I would soon see them fly before the British troops, and that general Braddock would take the fort and rescue me." From the walls of Fort Duquesne, Smith "heard a number of scalp halloo's and saw a company of Indians and French coming in." The Natives carried many trophies of valor and victory: scalps still wet with blood, mitre caps worn only a few hours before by proud grenadiers of the 44th and 48th regiments, along with canteens, bayonets, swords, muskets. Triumphant warriors wore British officers' coats, sashes, gorgets, and laced hats. Each successive party had more scalps than the last. One party arrived, this time with British horses, perhaps including the white charger of Braddock himself, and "a great many scalps." Natives had herded hundreds of cattle and horses off the field, all of which trampled carefully planted French cornfields at Fort Duquesne (an ironic reversal of what generally happened in the colonial period), and the Indians shot and killed French pigs for celebratory feasts. The entire evening of the battle was an orgy of celebration—incessant peals of celebratory musket fire and "most hedious shouts and yells" that to Smith's eyes and ears at least, seemed a perfect picture of hell.[128]

"About sun down," Smith continued, "I beheld a small party coming in with about a dozen prisoners, stripped naked, with their hands tied behind their back, and their bodies blacked—these prisoners they burned to death on the bank of the Alegheny River opposite to the fort." He watched until the Native warriors having tied a soldier to a stake, "kept touching him with fire-brands, red-hot irons &c. and he screeming in a most doleful manner,—the Indians in the mean time yelling like infernal spirits." While Smith only saw one of these soldiers tortured before he turned away, other sources indicate that a few captives probably suffered a similarly horrendous end.[129]

The battle was remarkable for the small number of captives taken by either the French or the Indians. The running nature of the battle had precluded Indians from taking any significant number. British accounts, drawn largely from captured settlers, seem to confirm that few members of Braddock's army were taken alive, and that the wounded were simply killed on the battlefield or left to die. Two French accounts record that Indians took only twenty captives, of which there were "Seven Women or Girls."[130] During his captivity, the Pennsylvania colonist Charles Stuart met one Agnes Hamilton, "the Wife of one James Hamilton, who belonged to the late Sir Peter Halket's Regiment": "This Woman told him, that she and thirteen others were all the Prisoners that were carried of [from] the Monongahela, the rest being butchered by the Indians; and that two of the thirteen being badly wounded, and their Wounds offensive, occasioned by the Heat of the Weather, the Savages knocked them in the Head."[131]

There is no record of any regulars of the 44th or 48th regiments taken as captives who survived.[132] Lieutenant John Hart of the 48th Regiment was reportedly taken as a captive while seriously wounded. The Indians killed and scalped him and an unknown number of wounded "who not being able to keep pace with the Victors in their Return to the Fort, were all treated in the same

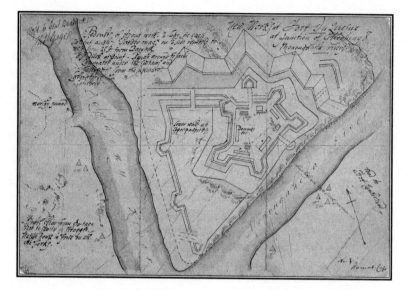

New Work at Fort Duquesne at junction of Allegheny & Monongahela rivers, 1755 Map, HM 898
"General Braddock's Military Plans, captured by the French before Fort Duquesne,"
1755. Courtesy of the Huntington Library.

Manner, only one Virginian surviving it."[133] The sole Virginian survivor was Crosby Eger, who later petitioned the Virginia government that "he was taken Prisoner by the Enemy in General Braddock's Engagement, where he received several Wounds, and was removed from Fort to Fort" until he was imprisoned at Quebec. Eger may have been the "English prisoner shot through the body" mentioned by Captain Contrecoeur in early August 1755. Eger was sent to Plymouth, then recaptured by a French privateer and taken to Bordeaux while he was voyaging back to Boston, before his long convalescence and repatriation had ended. One of the votes for his £15 for relief was cast by Burgess George Washington in 1769.[134]

Among Braddock's headquarters papers that the victorious French carried to Fort Duquesne were three maps, drawn on the back of sheet music of traditional English rounds, a musical form well suited for officers in camp. On July 10, Captain Jean-Daniel Dumas examined the maps on a table in Fort Duquesne, undoubtedly savoring the completeness of a victory that had yielded even the defeated general's own papers. The maps had been endorsed by Thomas Gage as "Ref'd to Genl. Braddock." Dumas now referred them to the governor-general of New France, writing on the captured documents, "Trouvé dans la caisse militaire du Général Braddock ainsi que ses plans de campagne et instructions 10 Juillet 1755. Dumas – Capt." The first map was a detailed plan of Fort Cumberland on the frontiers of Virginia and Maryland, upon which Dumas and his allies would soon unleash destruction. The second map, of Fort Duquesne, reflected British plans for a siege that was never laid. The third map, entitled "New Work at Fort du Quesne at junction of Allegheny & Monongahela rivers," was a detailed drawing of a massive pentagonal fort that General Braddock planned to erect at the Forks of the Ohio after he had obliterated Fort Duquesne. It was a British map of what might have been, a poignant testament to all the future contingencies that had hung in the balance on July 9, 1755. For the British world would now suffer a series of even greater disasters and miseries as a consequence of Braddock's failure to build that "New Work" at the Forks of the Ohio.[135]

CHAPTER 7

Consequences

The folly & consequence of opposing compact bodies to
the sparse manner of Indian fighting, in woods, which had
in a manner been predicted, was now so clearly verified
that from hence forward another mode obtained in all
future operations.

~George Washington~

ON THE MORNING OF JULY 10, 1755, Colonel Dunbar's
column was fixed upon the heights of Chestnut Ridge like
a ship run aground on shoals. Dunbar's forward progress
had been so slow that nearly sixty miles now separated him from
Braddock's column. Dunbar seemed incapable of devising any solu-
tion to the problem of his dwindling number of horses. The only
substantial contribution that he had made was obeying Braddock's
order to send forward a convoy of men and supplies under Captain
Stephen. Whether by lethargy or by logistical constraints, Dunbar
had not managed to move his column the eight miles to Gist's plantation, where Braddock had ordered him to encamp. Dunbar's Camp,
as it was now fittingly named, was situated in an indefensible location
dominated by a conspicuous knob along the crest of Chestnut Ridge.[1]
There the largely American recruits of the 44th and 48th regiments,
along with small units of South Carolina and New York independents, as well as the remaining Virginia and North Carolina provincials, waited for news of Braddock's victory. A party of sixteen Iroquois
allies from Aughwick, accompanied by two officers, had departed
the camp that morning, hoping to join Braddock's army for the final
action.[2]

It was around 9:30 on the morning of July 10 when terrified
and exhausted wagoners from Braddock's defeated army pulled into
Dunbar's camp, carrying with them the party of sixteen Indians that
had just set out. The wagoners spread the news of how the army had
been attacked as they were "going up a hill" in a horrific three-hour

battle. Initially, the wagoners reported that "the most part of the English were killed, that Gen:l Braddock was wounded & put into a Waggon and afterwards killed by the Indians, that S:r Peter Halket and Cap:t Orme were also killed." George Washington and his guides also arrived shortly thereafter, providing Dunbar with the first accurate reports of the battle. But the damage was done. Panic ran like electricity through Dunbar's startled men. He ordered his drummers to beat to arms, and the men were placed on high alert, not knowing what to expect. Sentries tried to stop desertion, but some determined wagoners, including Matthew Laird, Michael Hoover, and Jacob Hoover, ignored the sentries ringing the encampment and "took to flight" to Pennsylvania and home.[3]

Displaying his legendary stamina, Washington had risen from a sickbed, fought in a battle, and ridden sixty miles through the pitch darkness to Dunbar's Camp, all in the space of thirty-six hours. He delivered Braddock's orders that wagons, provisions, and medical supplies be sent to Gist's plantation under the escort of two companies of the 44th and 48th. In severe pain, the general had been carried through the long and tortuous night, arriving at Gist's around 10:00 P.M. on July 10.[4] A makeshift gurney had been made for the wounded general, using poles and fabric (perhaps again using his sash), that required six men to carry. Embers of the army's pride occasionally glowed during the retreat. Martin Lucorney of the New York Independent Company was one of the volunteers who had helped carry Braddock most of the fifty miles back to Gist's plantation. After rejoining his own decimated company, Private Lucorney found a discarded "pair of Colours, which he gave to Serjeant Anderson of the South Carolina Independ.ᵗ Companys." Some men wished to make a stand and fortify. Earlier on July 10, as the army passed its old encampments one by one, the wounded Harry Gordon proposed fortifying above the Salt Lick camp. Gordon sorely wished that Dunbar's column had been at Gist's plantation, "where a Good Camp might Easily Been had." But Dunbar's inability or unwillingness to advance eight miles farther down Chestnut Ridge to Gist's plantation foreclosed the possibility of fortifying one of those defensible locations.[5]

Private Duncan Cameron had survived the hellish night on the battlefield but was not spared the sixty-mile journey back to Dunbar's camp. Echoing Washington's painful memories, Cameron was forever haunted by the dying agonies of the wounded on Braddock's road: "I pass'd several just expiring, some so far gone as to be senseless, others making lamentable Moans and Cries, begging for God's Sake to be help'd along, and indeed the Horrors of a Battle are very great, but this seem'd to be the most piercing Scene mine Eyes had ever seen." Braddock's wounds were bringing out his qualities as a soldier's general, for he was most concerned with his wounded men like Cameron who were struggling to get to Dunbar's Camp. On July 11, having received fresh supplies from Dunbar, Braddock ordered a sergeant's party to advance beyond Stewart's Crossing at Youghiogheny and leave food and supplies for "any men who might have lost their way in the woods." At least one wounded Redcoat survived because of Braddock's regard. He had been among a group of eight wounded soldiers who had escaped the field and banded together. "They all dyed on the Roade," the sole survivor sorrowfully reported. But he found his way back to Fort Cumberland, subsisting on flour and water "which was left for them," along with "directions in wrighting to follow and the[y] should find more at such and such places" until they rejoined the army. An officer in Dunbar's Camp heard of the plight of the wounded from the accounts of stragglers, who told him that "the road was full of Dead and people dieing who with fatigue or Wounds Could move on no further; but lay down to die." The officer believed that had they stayed longer in the camp rather than moving on so quickly they would have saved "the life of many a poor fellow."[6]

On July 11, most of the stunned survivors, including Braddock, made the grueling ascent up Chestnut Ridge to Dunbar's Camp. The very appearance of the survivors struck fear into the ranks of Dunbar's men. When Duncan Cameron finally arrived at Dunbar's Camp, he found the army in the midst of a panic. It was only then that Cameron realized the full magnitude of what had happened at the Monongahela, including Braddock's wounding, which "sorrowfully affected" Cameron. Dunbar's men, such as commissary officer William Johnston, were "greatly alarmed and shocked" to see what remained of the once-mighty army. When some of Braddock's Indian scouts came in, Dunbar's men thought they were the enemy and "began to run away, but were stopp'd when they were convinced of their mistake," said one officer.[7]

Braddock's Expedition came to a deliberate end in the great conflagration at Dunbar's Camp, where on July 12, Braddock issued the order to prepare for a retreat to Fort Cumberland. There were not enough horses, however, to transport everything back. Wagons were needed above all to move the wounded, and this meant destroying virtually all of the remaining ordnance, ammunition, and supplies, lest they fall into enemy hands. The wounded were treated and loaded into the wagons throughout the day of July 12. Soldiers were employed scattering bullets, staving huge copper-hooped kegs of gunpowder in a nearby spring, breaking shells, and otherwise destroying anything of value. Huge fires of the remaining wagons and supplies glowed around the camp, the funeral pyres of a defeated army.[8]

The destruction of Dunbar's Camp only heightened the controversy surrounding the conduct of the campaign. As one unidentified British officer wrote, "Scandalous as the action [battle] was, more Scandalous was the based and hurried Retreat, with the immense destruction and expense to the Nation," which he estimated to be worth £300,000 (tens of millions of dollars today). Braddock had ordered the retreat and the destruction of the stores, but Dunbar inherited the mantle of responsibility for the decision, despite his

Musket balls and iron hardware melted by the fires at Dunbar's Camp, July 12, 1755. Courtesy of the Braddock Road Preservation Association.

attempts to avoid it. Both Dunbar and St. Clair had principled objections to destroying the "valuable Stores," but they chose to obey the orders of a man who by their own admission was "in no Condition to be spoke to or to give orders." No one, however, disputed the dishonor done to British arms, as one despondent officer wrote: "the Confusion, hurry and Conflagration attending all this, Cannot be describ'd, but I Can assure you it affected every body who had the least sense of the Honour of His Majesty or the Glory of England at heart, in the deepest manner." Washington and Charles Lee (who had remained in Dunbar's column) never forgot the chaos and disorder.[9]

The defeated army departed Dunbar's Camp on July 13, marching a short distance before a wagon containing powder and eight coehorn mortars was discovered. They halted somewhere around the old Rock Camp, from whence Captain Robert Dobson had led a detachment in pursuit of Indians on the night of June 26. Dobson called for his men to dig a hole in the ground, in which the last remnants of Braddock's siege artillery was buried—"in sight of the army." Contrary to legend, there were no 12-pounder guns ever buried at Dunbar's Camp, for those had been left behind at Winchester.[10]

Braddock's Defeat therefore became the story of Dunbar's Retreat. The general resigned the command shortly after the army's departure and his condition grew worse as the army descended Chestnut Ridge to their old camp one mile west of the Great Meadows. Around 8:00 P.M., shortly after the army had arrived at the Steep Bank camp, General Braddock died, "much lamented by the whole Army," according to a Royal Navy officer. "Who'd have thought it," he was heard to mutter, according to Robert Orme, who recounted it to Benjamin Franklin. "We shall better know how to deal with them another time" were among the last things he said. Braddock's final moments stayed in Washington's memory thirty years later:

> Genl Braddock breathed his last. He was interred with the honors of war, and as it was left to [me] to see this performed, & to mark out the spot for the reception of his remains—to guard against a savage triumph, if the place should be discovered—they were deposited in the Road over which the Army, Waggons &ca passed to hide every trace by which the entombment could be discovered.[11]

During the long retreat from Dunbar's Camp to Fort Cumberland, the demoralized army bitterly walked Braddock's Road in reverse, reflecting on the futility of all of their labor and once hopeful expectations. The soldiers now had to retrace their way along the same perilous ridges and passages—Winding Ridge, Negro

Howard Pyle, *The Burial of Braddock*, ca. 1897. Courtesy of the Boston Public Library. Pyle's imaginative work shows George Washington presiding over the interment of Braddock, flanked by the wounded officers Gage and Gates.

Mountain, Meadow Mountain, and the "nearly perpendicular" western slope of Big Savage Mountain—and ford seemingly countless rivers and streams. The plight of the wounded, jolted along the uneven roads in wagons as maggots grew in their wounds, can only be imagined. Daniel Disney, the adjutant of the 44th regiment, dutifully kept the daily orders. When the army passed the Great Meadows and crossed the Youghiogheny River on July 15, Washington was sent ahead of the retreating army with a captain's command of seventy men. His mission was to escort the lightly wounded and the officers back to Fort Cumberland, an assignment that undoubtedly conjured up memories of his retreat from Fort Necessity along this very route a year earlier. Washington's party endured a jarring ride through the rock-littered valley of Braddock Run, down Winding Ridge, and over Negro Mountain before arriving at the Little Meadows on July 16. Many of the wounded officers, such as Robert Orme, were carried on litters between horses that were exhausted by the time they reached Fort Cumberland on July 17. In the meantime, Colonel Dunbar and the remnants of the main army had continued their march and arrived at Fort Cumberland a few days later, on July 22. At Washington's request, Colonel James Innes had sent Dunbar the gifts that Governor Morris had earlier sent to Braddock and which had never been touched: the hams, cheeses, raisins, fish, biscuit, lemons, potatoes, sugar, and pickles were now the tokens of defeat rather than the fruits of victory on the Ohio.[12]

For those at Fort Cumberland, the retreating army's wagoners had again been the first heralds of disaster, bringing news to the outpost at noon on July 11. Colonel Innes passed along the news eastward in a dramatic circular letter to Dinwiddie and other governors whose effect was to raise the panic level:

> Sir: I have this Moment received the Melancholy Account of the Defeat of our Troops, the General kill'd and Numbers of our Officers, our whole Artillery taken; In short the Account I have Received is so very bad, that, as please God I intend to make a stand here, its highly necessary to raise the Militia everywhere to defend the Frontiers
>
> Your humble serv.[t]
>
> Fort Cumberland July 11th 1755   James Innes[13]

A rising tide of sorrow began to engulf Fort Cumberland as accounts of the disaster came in. Camp women and officers' wives waited anxiously for news of their loved ones. Matron Charlotte Browne noted, "It is not possible to describe the Distraction of the poor Women for their Husbands." She well understood their feelings, for her brother had been taken ill on July 1, and his health ebbed and flowed over the course of the next few weeks. On July 17, the day that the first contingent of wounded officers staggered into the fort, Browne wrote in her diary: "Oh! how shall I express my Distraction this unhappy Day at 2 in the After Noon deprived me of my dear Brother in whom I have lost my kind Guardian and Protector and am now left a friendless Exile from all that is dear to me."[14]

The widows of Braddock's Defeat had indeed become friendless exiles on the earth. Colonel Dunbar forewarned Governor Morris that the widows of John Handsard, Percival Brereton, and John Hart would arrive in Philadelphia soon and recommended that he provide assistance to them. Benjamin Franklin seconded the idea. Sarah Nartlow, the wife of Ensign William Nartlow, was one of the few spouses to receive a royal bounty, suggesting that most either failed to receive any official support or eventually remarried. The Virginia legislature routinely received petitions from survivors and their families for aid, of which some were granted. Rebecca Polson, widow of the slain captain, was granted £26 per annum for support of her and her infant child.[15] For those families left behind in the colonies and in Britain, there are only small clues to what Browne called the "torturing Suspence, Each One for their best belovd." The wife of Captain Mathew Floyer inquired to Governor Dinwiddie about her husband, unaware that he had been killed in action. Dinwiddie forwarded her letter to an acquaintance, suggesting more than a little callously, "It may prove a good Introduction as I am told she is a rich Widow." In Yorkshire, Nathaniel Cholmley inscribed in the family's Bible, "My brother Robert was killed in America under the Command of Gen[l] Braddock July 9th 1755. N.C." A portrait of his brother (now apparently lost) was the family's only means of remembrance. Robert's body was never recovered, fulfilling the pre-monition he had expressed in his will—"As to my Body, where the Leaf falls, let it rot."[16]

In late July, army officers took grim stock of the dead and wounded at the Monongahela. Captain Cholmley's batman observed "the men dying so fast daily that they digg holes and throw them in without Reading any service Over them, Altho we having two Ministers with us." Soldiers had jagged pieces of lead and flattened slugs in their wounds that hindered their recoveries.[17] In the 44th Regiment, Sergeant Richard Nichols, a fifty-year-old veteran who had served his king since 1740, was severely wounded in the left hip. Thomas King, a carpenter from Yarlington in Somerset County with fifteen years of service, lost his left arm at the Monongahela. Jonathan Lock, a tailor from North Tawton in Devonshire, would never practice his trade again, being "disabled in his right arm." In the 48th Regiment, Daniel Rann, a wagoner from Standon in Hertfordshire, had enlisted in 1753 at the age of twenty-six, only to lose his left arm. Drummer James Carmichael, aged twenty-three, was the son of a 48th regiment soldier and had been in the ranks since the age of nine. He was "Disabled by a Wound in the Foot at Monegala." Mitchell Higgins, a thirty-six-year-old gardener from St. Albans, Hertfordshire, was wounded in the face and jaw. These were among the British regulars incapacitated by wounds who received royal pensions at Chelsea Hospital for their honorable conduct at the Monongahela.[18]

The army was as collectively shattered as the men were corpo-rally. The Battle of the Monongahela is exceptional in the annals of military history for the incredibly high proportion of casualties—at least two-thirds of the entire force. Of the approximately 85 commis-sioned officers engaged there, 60 were killed or wounded, a casualty rate of 70 percent (27 killed and 33 wounded); 5 staff were also

Lieutenant Milbourne West, ca. 1774, artist unknown. Courtesy of Dr. Walter L. Powell. West was a gentleman volunteer who carried arms in Braddock's Expedition and was wounded at the Monongahela, actions that merited him an ensign's commission in the 47th Regiment in 1756. He later took part in the Siege of Louisbourg in 1758 and the Quebec Campaign in 1759.

casualties (3 engineers and a chaplain wounded and 1 doctor killed). The 44th Regiment lost not only its regimental commander but 6 additional officers killed and 9 wounded out of 24 officers engaged; the 48th Regiment lost 6 killed and 12 wounded out of 25 officers.[19] It is difficult to establish with any degree of precision the exact numbers of total killed and wounded comparing the two returns of Braddock's army done at Fort Cumberland on June 8 and July 25, respectively. The two returns for the 44th and 48th regiments, however, convey the enormous cost of combat, though they may be inflated by desertion following the battle. Halkett's regiment had numbered 858 officers and men on June 8: it was diminished by approximately 190 men, down to 668 by July 25. Dunbar's regiment fell from its initial strength of 773 officers and men to a total of 605 on July 30th, a loss of 168 men. The hospital and quarters at Fort Cumberland housed 295 wounded and 143 sick as of July 25.[20]

The most reliable and precise casualty statistics come from the reports of eyewitnesses, which reflect official returns done at Fort Cumberland. Engineer Patrick Mackellar's map records the total strength of Braddock's army on July 9 as 1,469 officers and men. Of these, 457 were killed in action, and 519 wounded (an army return published in the *Virginia Gazette* roughly mirrors Mackellar's numbers at 456 killed, 421 wounded, and 583 unwounded, for a total of 1,460 men). If 976 of 1,469 men indeed became casualties at the Monongahela, it would translate into a 66 percent loss. Robert Orme's reports have slightly fewer casualties and numbers engaged (63 officers and 714 men killed and wounded out of 1,100 engaged, or 70 percent). The anonymous British officer's journal matches Orme almost exactly, listing 60 officers and 713 rank-and-file men killed and wounded. Moreover, that journal significantly adds that 532 rank and file were not wounded, placing the total of Braddock's force, including officers, at 1,341. The numerical differences may

Major Roger Morris (1727–1794), twentieth-century copy of an original attributed to Benjamin West. New Brunswick Museum, New Brunswick, Canada. John Clarence Webster Canadiana Collection (W1182). After the Monongahela, Morris took part in the Louisbourg, Quebec, and Montreal campaigns with the 35th and 47th regiments. He married into the wealthy Philipse family of New York in 1758 and built a Georgian-Palladian mansion on northern Manhattan. A loyalist during the Revolution, his confiscated house was briefly used in 1776 as a headquarters for General George Washington, with whom Morris had once served on Braddock's staff.

p e r h a p s   be explained by whether civilian wagoners and other personnel were included in the total strengths.[21]

Not all the damage was physical. Combat stress, courts-martial, and mass desertion were also symptoms of the army's demoralization in the weeks and months following the battle. Captain Orme wrote that "the terror of the Indians" remained vividly in the men's minds. Private Duncan Cameron recorded "Court-Martial upon Court-Martial" and "most cruel Whippings," presumably of soldiers who had behaved with cowardice or disobedience. Many Virginians and Marylanders recruited into the 44th and 48th regiments deserted, especially when it became clear that the army was going on to Pennsylvania and New York. The nine Virginia, Maryland, and North Carolina companies that defended Fort Cumberland in the fall of 1755 were especially afflicted with desertion after the bloodletting inflicted on them on July 9. By September, two months after the debacle, the late Captain Polson's shattered company numbered only 1 officer and 18 men, out of its original contingent of 57 men. Death and desertion had cut the Virginia, Maryland, and North Carolina units at Fort Cumberland by approximately one-half between early June and September of 1755.[22]

In the governor's palace in Williamsburg on the morning of July 14, Governor Dinwiddie read Colonel Innes's missive. For the next ten days, Dinwiddie alternated between hope and melancholy as he tried to convince himself that Innes's initial report had been based on information from some panic-stricken deserter. Reading the letter over and over again, he concluded that a few days' time would reveal "the first News is false, or at least not so bad." Like many colonials, Dinwiddie had "never doubted of the General's Success when I considered his Forces and the Train of Artillery," as he wrote to Lord Fairfax. On the night of July 24, Dinwiddie received news from Washington, whose letter reiterated Innes's despair and substantiated its essence. "With Tears in my Eyes," Dinwiddie strained to take in that Braddock was dead. The train lost. Halkett, Shirley, and so many brave officers struck down as their men scattered. Dinwiddie's heart must have wilted when he read in Washington's letter that Dunbar was intending "to continue his March to Philadelphia for *Winter* Quarter's; so that there will be no Men left here."[23] This would be from his perspective a potentially disastrous decision for his colony. He replied to Washington, "surely You must Mistake. Colo. Dunbar will not march to Winter Quarters in the Middle of the Summer, & leave the Frontiers of his Majesty's Colonies open without proper Fortifications & exposed to the Invasions of the Enemy, no! he is a better Officer & I have a different Opinion of him." The governor's thoughts turned toward an immediate counteroffensive in light of the "very galling" prospect that the French might use their own artillery against them. He barraged Virginia's militia colonels with orders to mobilize their commands, though it had become shockingly clear to Dinwiddie that the militia was as ineffective as the political leadership that had rendered them "in so bad Order for want of Arms and Ammunition." He was even more bewildered as he began receiving reports from the Virginia frontier that sporadic attacks by tens of Indians were putting ten thousands of colonists to flight.[24]

The "Banditti of Indians" wasn't the only perceived threat to security, for British colonists in Virginia, Maryland, Pennsylvania, and Nova Scotia were becoming ever more fearful of domestic enemies. In any crisis, the Virginia militia always had to be prepared for a two-front war: "The Villany of the Negroes on any Emergency of Government is what I always feared," Dinwiddie wrote to the Earl of Halifax, for "I must leave a proper Number in each County to protect it from the Combinations of the Negro Slaves, who have been very audacious on the Defeat on the Ohio." British colonists not only feared that an "Insurrection should be occasioned by this most unhappy Event," but also expressed virulent anti-Catholicism as many heeded rumors of Catholic subversion. When news of Braddock's Defeat reached Philadelphia at 3:00 on July 18, "The Consternation of this City upon the occasion is hardly to be expressed," as one diarist wrote. "The Mob here upon this occasion were very unruly, assembling in great numbers, with an intention of demolishing the Mass House belonging to the Roman Catholics," but were dissuaded by

Quaker magistrates. Reverend Thomas Chase, rector of St. Paul's parish in Annapolis, warned his congregants that the atmosphere was like that before the Irish massacre of Protestants in 1641. The fears aroused by Braddock's Defeat were also evident in Nova Scotia, where the news dampened the recent British victory over the French at Fort Beauséjour, and strengthened British officials' resolve to expel more than 10,000 French Acadians, whose religious and political loyalties were suspect.[25]

With such anxieties and contingencies in mind, Governor Dinwiddie's pleas to the hapless Colonel Dunbar became all the more desperate. In his letter of July 26, Dinwiddie argued that a British counteroffensive might still succeed, as French strength at Fort Duquesne was likely to be weak. Believing that only 300 enemies had defeated 1,300 British, he commented that "Such advantages by so few Men is not to be met with in History, and surely must raise a just resentment in the Heart of every British Subject." "Dear Colonel," he asked plaintively but goadingly, "is there no Method left to retrieve the Dishonor done to the British Arms?"[26]

But Dunbar had already determined by July 16—even before arriving at Fort Cumberland—that the regulars would abandon the frontiers of Maryland and Virginia, and go into winter quarters in Philadelphia. He would neither wait for orders from William Shirley, the new commander in chief, nor seek counsel from other officers and royal governors. The letter that reveals his intentions was written to Pennsylvania governor Robert Morris from the Great Crossings of the Youghiogheny River on July 16, only a week after the great battle. Dunbar's decision cut off any discussion of making a stand at Fort Cumberland, or, as some advocated, renewing the offensive. Dunbar claimed that it had always been Braddock's intention to go into winter quarters in Philadelphia after conquering Fort Duquesne. He never explained why he was following a dead general's orders rather than seeking fresh orders from his replacement or counsel from royal governors. Even Dunbar's friends attested to his disordered state of mind when the command was thrust upon him. Robert Orme—who was no friend—hinted that Dunbar believed that he now had an independent command and was beholden to no one.[27]

Dunbar called a pro forma council of war on August 1 at Fort Cumberland to consider Dinwiddie's proposals—including leading a new initiative against Fort Duquesne—in his July 26 letter. Considering that Dunbar marched the army out of the fort the next morning, preparations for an evacuation were already well under way. He sent an abrupt letter to Dinwiddie. "Your Schemes & Proposals were read

& duely considered & unanimously agreed to be impracticable."
Dunbar, Gage, Sharpe, Chapman, Sparke, and St. Clair had all concluded that the offensive could not be renewed. Governor Sharpe
noted, however, that Dunbar had cast the question as whether they
"should march again immediately" to attack the French, though the
council perceived that Dinwiddie's original plan called for a more
deliberate process.[28]

From the perspective of Dunbar and his council, their unani-
mous rejection of another offensive had ample justification. Dunbar
himself was cautious, not knowing his exact authority after Braddock's
demise. The army's leadership had been decimated, and many of the
surviving officers were still recovering from wounds. The 44th and
48th regiments had been depleted of their veteran Irish contingents,
and their remnants were mostly raw American recruits. All of them
were demoralized. Sharpe cautioned that fresh orders to renew the
advance might lead one-half of the army to desert. More than anything, the army did not have the means to recommence the campaign,
having lost artillery, ammunition, horses, wagons, camp equipment,
and other stores. The only artillery left was four light 6-pounder field
pieces. However, Dunbar did not ask his council if the army should
continue to hold Fort Cumberland, where it might have offered some
protection to the frontier and become a nucleus for additional reinforcements. His decision to foresake Fort Cumberland—by marching
to Pennsylvania with all of the regular troops, including the Independent Companies, and leaving only provincials to guard it—was
his most controversial.[29]

Dunbar left entire colonies virtually defenseless when the army
marched out of Fort Cumberland on August 2, 1755, reaching their
old camp at Widow Ballenger's north of Winchester on August 6.[30]
On that very day in the Mohawk Valley to the north, General William
Shirley, the new commander in chief of His Majesty's forces in
America following Braddock's demise, was considering what to do
with Dunbar. He had initially hoped that since only half of Braddock's
army had been defeated, the remaining half might continue the
campaign. But Shirley and the New York government feared that
Braddock's captured artillery would be turned against his forces
advancing against Fort Niagara. Accordingly, on August 6, Shirley
ordered Dunbar to reinforce him in New York, without considering
the situation his departure would create on the Middle Colonies'
frontiers. Both governors Dinwiddie and Morris, however, inter-
ceded for their colonies, knowing exactly what that situation would
be. Six days later, on August 12, Shirley completely reversed himself,

ordering Dunbar to renew the offensive and besiege Fort Duquesne. But his orders were discretionary: "if thro any unforeseen Accident it shall become absolutely Impracticable" to advance, Dunbar could choose to follow the August 6 orders instead. Governor Morris, who had copies of Shirley's orders, foresaw that Dunbar could have remained to protect Pennsylvania's defenseless frontier. He urged Dunbar to obey Shirley's first command to proceed to Philadelphia, and then to deploy the army in the vicinity of McDowell's Mill, Shippensburg, and Carlisle. Morris was then locked in a battle with his Quaker-dominated legislature over the question of arming the province and the taxation of Proprietary estates.[31]

Dunbar, meanwhile, continued his march northward into Pennsylvania. At Widow Ballenger's on August 6, he held a second council of war, which approved Morris's proposal to garrison troops on Pennsylvania's western frontier. The army then marched northeast down the Shenandoah Valley, reaching Pine Ford of the Susquehanna River on August 21. There Dunbar called a third council of war to discuss Shirley's orders of August 12. The principal officers again concluded that any offensive against Fort Duquesne could not be undertaken, and that they should proceed to New York. When Dunbar explained the decision to Shirley, he also addressed reports that the new commander in chief had heard of the British burying their artillery. Dunbar lied to Shirley, averring that "there was not a Gun of any kind buried" when they abandoned their camp. Dunbar's retreat and abandonment of three colonial frontiers ended when the army arrived at Philadelphia in late August. By October 1755, when Dunbar's forces reached Albany, Shirley's expedition to Niagara had long since foundered.[32]

NEWS OF BRADDOCK'S DEFEAT FELL with great shock upon the entire British world. The first conduits of the news, as we have seen, were the teamsters who had abandoned the army, and Colonel Innes's missive to colonial governors. Upon reaching Fort Cumberland, British and provincial officers began writing the first accounts of the action, and wasted no time in defending themselves from reproach. By late July and early August, the first narratives of the battle had appeared in newspapers throughout the American colonies. On August 23, 1755, official accounts reached London when Commodore Keppel and Captain Palliser in HMS *Sea Horse* brought letters written by Orme and Washington and the long and dreary list of the killed and wounded officers.[33] Little wonder that British on both sides of the Atlantic were stunned by the "melancholly Account of the Slaughter" on the Monongahela and by early reports suggesting that a mere 300 French and Indians were responsible for one of the most lopsided defeats of the British Army. It reminded one British aristocrat, Lady Jemima Meadows, of a clash with barbarians during the age of Roman Britain. The Monongahela was the "most scandalous and disgraceful defeat that ever was heard of," Daniel Dulany of Maryland wrote, while Lieutenant Governor Spencer Phips of Massachusetts believed the defeat went "beyond what has ever befallen the English Arms in the Colonies since their first Settlement."[34] The news aroused condemnations of the Irish regiments and the "infamous Behaviour of the private Men." That behavior, one British aristocrat thought, was tinged with "a mixture of Stubbornness & Mutiny in it." Some contemporaries accused (falsely) the 44th and 48th regiments of being among the same units that had panicked at Prestonpans and Falkirk. Army officers like James Wolfe were of course apt to vilify the rank-and-file men and to exonerate Braddock, who, "though not a master of the difficult art of war, was yet a man of sense and courage.[35]

Many American colonists in the era of the Great Awakening strongly viewed the Monongahela through a religious lens. Jonathan Edwards, the great evangelical minister, observed a fast day in Stockbridge, Massachusetts, following Braddock's Defeat, as did many other congregants in the region. Edwards preached from Psalm 60: 9–12 as he rebuked the vanity of martial pride.[36] Ministers made Braddock a type of King Saul in the Old Testament as they preached from II Samuel 1:27, in which David laments the deaths of Saul and his son Jonathan in battle against the Philistines: "How are the mighty fallen, and the weapons of war perished!" William Vinal, pastor of the First Congregational Church in Rhode Island, especially denounced the "accursed thing"—"*Self-Confidence in War*"—responsible for the defeat. Presbyterian minister John Wright, in Cumberland County, Virginia, witnessed a significant spiritual movement prompted by the recent news of Braddock's Defeat. Such congregants explained the disaster as God's judgment on their sins, even as they looked for "the *beneficial consequences* aimed at by providence," as Charles Chauncy wrote.[37] New Englanders particularly mourned the death of General Braddock, and some described him as a tragic martyr for Britannia, along with other British generals killed later in the war. Martha Wadsworth Brewster, a Connecticut-born woman who was the first to publish poetry under her own name, eulogized the deceased general in her poem entitled "Braddock's Defeat, July 9th, 1755":

> And must this valiant Hero fall?
> Curs'd be the Day thro' Ages all;
> Ye Streams of proud Monongahal,
>   Be turn'd to British Tears.
> His Deeds have won Immortal Fame,
> Nor Envy can Extinct his Name,
> Old *Mars* will not allow the same,
>   But pay the long Arrears.[38]

Although colonists were more apt to mourn Braddock's death, or lament their own sinful self-reliance, some British writers expressed fears that the dishonorable defeat of royal arms would elicit thoughts of independence among the Americans, or at least breed contempt. Lady Anson, wife of Admiral Lord Anson, warned her brother Lord Royston, "your own Subjects in America must hate, & they & the Enemy despise you, & the Indians will all be lost to you." As a Member of Parliament, Royston was apprehensive that "Our American Subjects, (Allys I was going to call them), will heartily despise the Troops of their Mother Country, [which may] have in process of time, for ought I know, as bad Consequences to ourselves, as the French will reap from it now." Letters condemning the colonial governments written by Braddock and other British officers circulated after the defeat and heightened such concerns. The Earl of Halifax went so far as to say that had Governor James Glen of South Carolina been more cooperative, "Mr. Braddock's Life and the Honour of His Majesty's arms...probably would have been saved." Thomas Gage predicted that Pennsylvania and Maryland would never "act for the Publick Service, till their Constitutions are changed which sooner or later must be attempted." While Braddock's ordeal had further convinced British officials that a future remodeling of colonial governments was necessary, it had a more immediate political effect on the Duke of Newcastle, who knew better than anyone that "If Braddock or Boscawen are beat, I must answer for it." Although such observers as William Pitt questioned the decision to send "two miserable battalions of Irish" to America and the appointment of General Braddock in the first place, the Duke of Cumberland escaped the brunt of public wrath aimed at Newcastle, whose ministry collapsed under the weight of consecutive British military setbacks in 1755 and 1756.[39]

Edward Braddock became the perfect scapegoat for a disaster that contemporaries increasingly called "General Braddock's Defeat" as they discussed the "Action near the Monongahela." He had not escaped caricature in English society before his expedition, and after his death he became an even greater object of scorn and derision. In an age when the public attributed military defeats to the moral failings of the commanding officer, Braddock was condemned as violent, obstinate, haughty, impious, profane, overconfident, and rash. Outright lies and calumny were put forward as truth; words were already being stuffed into dead men's mouths as soon as the army had retreated safely back to Fort Cumberland (many of Braddock's most vociferous critics were often the officers who had remained with Dunbar's column and survived unscathed). Braddock was accused of every conceivable mistake: of landing in Virginia when he should have landed in Pennsylvania; of blindly walking into an ambuscade or ambush; of not having any flank protection; of ignoring and driving his Indian allies away; of being governed by a cabal of ambitious staff officers; of burdening the army with a heavy baggage train and more camp followers "than would have serv'd an Army of 20,000 in Flanders."[40]

Such accusations have led even the best historians awry. One commonly repeated myth is that Thomas Gage blundered when he failed to occupy a little hill along the army's line of march, which in turn allowed the Indians to seize the high ground during the battle. However, not a single officer who was present at the Monongahela accused Gage of negligently bypassing a hill, and no contemporaries faulted either Gage or Braddock for failing to follow Humphrey Bland's *Treatise* as though it were a rigid doctrinal manual. The claim is ultimately based on the observations of Governor Shirley, a presumed expert who was not present at the battle, who had simply glanced at a sketch of the battlefield and misinterpreted its terrain. He declared it "morally certain" that if Gage had occupied the hill, then the British would have defeated the Indians. But it is historically certain that Native warriors in subsequent battles overwhelmed British forces even when posted on hilltops.[41]

A more basic confusion reigned in public debate over how to describe the battle. Sir John St. Clair observed in 1755 that "Various are the Terms they give our action, some call it a Surprize others an Ambuscade, a Battle." But Braddock's army was not ambushed by the French and Indians, and the action was not a meeting engagement in the classic sense of two forces surprised by a collision with the other. St. Clair rightly argued that the most accurate description of the battle was an "Attack [on] a Convoy," adding that a column is the one of the most difficult tactical formations to defend. But most regular officers portrayed the action as a betrayal of brave officers by panic-stricken rank-and-file men, even as they were divided over who bore responsibility for the disorder that resulted from the advanced party's retreat back on the main body. One of the most intelligent, if also sympathetic, assessments of Braddock's Campaign came from James Oglethorpe, the founder of Georgia and an old soldier who had experience in American campaigning: "It was not so extraordinary that they should be defeated where they were, as it was that they got so far, and that they should not have sooner been catched on their long March and routed."[42]

The earliest reports of the battle immediately contrasted the "Indian manner" or "American way of fighting" with the "European manner," and extolled the virtues of the American provincials who had fought with great distinction. Reverend Chauncy argued that "*American irregulars*, in an *American* war, are full as necessary as *British regulars*," and that British leaders should exercise "great care to distinguish *American* merit." Within a few weeks, the Virginians' conduct during the battle had already become mythologized, due in part to laudatory accounts written by Washington, Stephen, and Stewart. Even some regular officers later praised the officers of the American companies. The Virginia Burgess and officer John Bolling thought Braddock a brave man but contrasted the "English Generals skill in bush fighting" to the Virginians' martial prowess in a letter to his son. His embellished account related that as Braddock lay wounded, he cried out "my dear Blue's (which was the Colrs the Virginians wore) give em tother Fire, you Fight like Men, & will die like Souldiers." Braddock praised the provincials and could not suffer to look upon the Redcoats during his dying moments, Bolling reported.[43] Above all, contemporaries on both sides of the Atlantic praised the "Heroick Virtue" of Washington during the battle, his "whole Behavior being extremely gallant," according to Orme. More than three months after the battle, the guide Christopher Gist reported to his old friend that "Yor Name is more talked off in Pensylvenia then any Other person of the Army," and that "all their Talk is of fighting in the Indian way." Most famously, the Presbyterian minister Samuel Davies commended Washington as a divine spark of "martial Fire," who he hoped "Providence has hitherto preserved in so signal a Manner, for some important Service to his Country." The essential contours of future American national mythology were thus already defined even in 1755.[44]

These contrasting images of colonials and regulars raised broader issues about tactics, strategy, and politics as the British Empire faced a broader war. Debate over the Monongahela also centered on traditional English concerns over the virtues of a militia versus a standing army, and the worth of American contributions.

One writer, using the pseudonym "Americanus," advised Lord Loudoun (the British commander in chief in America) that the "English Americans" would be "vastly more Serviceable" if they could fight in their own way. He offered the provincials' fighting record from 1745 and 1755 as evidence of their "natural Bravery and Intrepidity." But one British pamphleteer remained skeptical of the "*American* Militia" and argued that the colonists' woeful defense had brought them to the present crisis. He especially attacked those who linked Prestonpans, Falkirk, and the Monongahela as evidence of irregulars' superiority: "Many a brave Regiment has been surprised and dispersed by a lurking Party of Hussars; yet no one, for this Reason, ever thought of forming an Army of Hussars for their Defence." His conclusion: more regulars were necessary. Many colonists, in fact, agreed and some petitioned for even greater commitments of regiments from Britain.[45]

Contemporaries uniformly believed that Colonel Dunbar's retreat harmed the regulars' reputation as much as, if not more than, the Monongahela. Condemnations of Dunbar on both sides of the Atlantic were legion.[46] Leaving the frontier "in such haste and disorder has had a worse effect than the defeat of General Braddock," as one Virginia correspondent concluded. John Carlyle of Alexandria openly mocked the regulars who "determined to Go in to Winter Quarters in July, (O brave English Men)." Marylander Daniel Dulany was especially galled that Dunbar took the Independent Companies of New York and Carolina, leaving the middle colonies "naked, and exposed to the fury of the Indians." Dinwiddie thought it was "without Precedent" that the regulars would abandon the king's subjects to the enemy, and the king's ministers were equally astonished at Dunbar's conduct.[47] The Duke of Newcastle wrote that "Dunbar ought to be immediately recalled," and he was in November 1755. Dunbar was appointed lieutenant governor of Gibraltar, Braddock's old station, an office that he would hold until his death in 1767, achieving the rank of lieutenant-general by 1760. To some observant critics, it "appeard ridiculous to trust a person with Gibralter who could not defend Fort Cumberland."[48]

THE GREAT IRONY AS REGARDS Dunbar's retreat is that British forces abandoned the frontiers precisely when the French at Fort Duquesne were most vulnerable. The victorious French and Indian warriors had dispersed to the four winds immediately following the battle. Practically speaking, the French did not have the supplies to sustain any larger force at Duquesne. And Native warriors were eager to return home from the Ohio with scalps, horses, and other treasures taken from their defeated enemies. One of the enduring legends of the campaign—that of Braddock's gold, a cache of £25,000 (worth millions of dollars today) supposedly abandoned in the mountains[49]—has unfortunately diverted attention from the significance of what the defeated British really did leave behind. The French and their Indian allies gained three powerful strategic dividends from their victory of July 9, which ultimately brought New France to the pinnacle of its military dominance of the British colonies. The sheer abundance of battlefield treasure gleaned by Native warriors produced a massive surge in Native participation in the subsequent French campaigns in 1756 and 1757. The French had captured twenty-one British cannons and mortars that enabled their future conquests of other British posts. And finally, the French gained considerable diplomatic leverage and military advantage in both Europe and America when they captured Braddock's headquarters papers.

Captain Contrecoeur, fearing the possibility of a renewed British advance, was stunned when Native warriors from Detroit and Michilimackinac began leaving Fort Duquesne the morning after the battle, "despite my attempts to stop them." The French had focused all of their attention on July 10 to retrieving Braddock's captured artillery. Contrecoeur ordered Ensign Céloron de Blainville to take twelve canoes upriver to the battlefield, and later ordered him to send out reconnaissance parties to locate the British army. Captain Dumas led a second detachment of 100 French and a few Indians. Both officers reported seeing "nothing but dead bodies" for fourteen miles along the road. That evening, Dumas oversaw the salvaging and loading of the howitzers, 12-pounders, 6-pounders, and mortars onto canoes, presumably rigged as pontoons with platforms. By July 11, the French had successfully transported all of the captured artillery back to Fort Duquesne. The post's terrible supply problems were temporarily relieved by the capture of eighty cattle driven to the fort, "which the Indians made as great Slaughter as they had done with the English," wrote one Frenchman. Finally, Captain Beaujeu's body was solemnly placed in a coffin by Lieutenant Montigny and Ensign Corbière, and floated downriver to Fort Duquesne, where he was buried "with all the marks of Honour due to his Bravery."[50]

The scattered debris of Braddock's field—abandoned artillery, ammunition, headquarters papers, supply wagons, regimental coats, swords, and muskets—decisively shaped the course of the war in America. Contrecoeur marveled at "the amount of everything that the English had." There were, for example, 175 cannonballs for the 12-pounders, 192 howitzer shells, 17 kegs of gunpowder, 19,740 musket cartridges and hundreds of discarded Brown Bess muskets, 6,000 gunflints, wagons, carts, artillery carriages, and a multitude of tools (hatchets, shovels, picks, jacks, and sickles). By the end of July, Contrecoeur was still gleaning captured materiel, sending two officers with thirty pirogues on one occasion to haul supplies from the battlefield. Indeed, the cache of captured materiel was so extensive that Contrecoeur had to build a structure of 80-*pieds* (approximately 85 feet) in length to preserve all of it. English captive John McKinney saw this structure in 1756, describing it as "a house which contains a great quantity of tools of such broad and narrow axes, planes, chisels, hoes, mattocks, pick-axes, spades, shovels, &c. and a great quantity of wagon wheels and tire." The French marines were so exhausted from hauling captured supplies that "almost all our men had their feet crippled," according to Contrecoeur.[51]

In mid-July, French officers brought nine British deserters back to Fort Duquesne, and these "live letters" divulged even more spectacular news. They offered to guide the French to Dunbar's Camp, "where the rest of the mortars, bombshells, and bullets were located."[52] Contrecoeur immediately sent forth a number of detachments to scout British movements and to search out their "cache" of military stores lest they be used again by the British. One party under Lieutenant Louis-Charles-Jacques Renaud Du Buisson had specific orders either to seize or spike British mortars. Their route upriver along the Monongahela spared them from the sight and stench of gnawed, decomposing British bodies along Braddock's Road. The English deserters led the detachment to the site of Dunbar's abandoned camp on Chestnut Ridge. Du Buisson brought back the eight mortars that Captain Dobson of the 48th Regiment had buried in a hole during Braddock's evacuation on July 13.[53] Another parallel detachment of 130 French and Indians led by officers Joachim-Louis Robutel de La Noue and ensigns Bailleul and Jean-Clément de Sabrevois de Bleury also retrieved materiel from the camp.[54] Ensign Bleury led a detachment well beyond Fort Necessity, verifying that the English had completely evacuated and returned to Virginia. Fort Duquesne was safe for the time being, and it was well provisioned with captured English goods. The French were still gleaning materiel from Dunbar's Camp in the following year.[55]

By early August 1755, as Dunbar was taking an entire army into winter quarters, Contrecoeur reported that his skeleton force at Fort Duquesne numbered only 260 men. There were only two Abenaki Indians left at the post. It was logistically impossible to sustain a large garrison at the fort, which necessitated the dispersal of Contrecoeur's forces. Starting toward the end of July, French troops had departed Duquesne in small detachments and convoys in much the same manner that they had arrived. They left behind an undermanned fort whose supply lines remained dangerously thin as they retraced their route up the Allegheny to the parched Rivière au Boeuf. On July 22, Captain Lignery left Fort Duquesne, arriving at Fort de la Rivière au Boeuf on July 27, and at Niagara three days later, on July 30. Other detachments soon followed, including those of Courtemanche, Montigny, Longueuil, Normanville, and St. Ours. Lignery, who was accompanied by Contrecoeur's son René-Marie, had the signal honor of carrying back to Montreal all of Braddock's headquarters papers, containing secret British government correspondence, plans, and maps.[56]

The capture of Braddock's headquarters papers, as noted, was a great intelligence and propaganda coup for the French, and a decisive moment leading up to the formal outbreak of the Seven Years' War in 1756. When Lignery reached Quebec in August, the governor-general, the Marquis de Vaudreuil, immediately ordered a translation of the documents into French, which was completed by the end of September by Louis-Amable Pertuis, the skilled linguist who had also fought in the Ohio Valley that summer. Three copies were sent to Paris. Braddock's papers revealed a long-standing plan of duplicity and premeditated aggression. Royal instructions from the king and the Duke of Cumberland, along with letters from every leading British minister (Fox, Newcastle, Robinson, and Halifax), implicated the entire government in the aggression and belied all of the peaceful negotiations between the two crowns. These captured documents were later published with the admonition, "Tels sont les faits. L'Angleterre n'en peut desavouer aucun. C'est à l'Europe à prononcer" (Such are the Facts. England cannot deny any of them. Let Europe now decide).[57] While the British were crying for peace in 1754, the Duke of Cumberland and the leading ministers of state were busily planning preemptive war against Canada. Yet another treachery uncovered was the espionage of Robert Stobo, who had smuggled out a sketch of Fort Duquesne. French propagandists had much delicious material to cast the British as aggressors: the assassination of Ensign Jumonville, four premeditated attacks on forts

Beauséjour, Duquesne, Niagara, and Crown Point, and the Royal Navy's seizure of the French warships *Alcide* and *Lys* in June 1755. A formal memorandum from the court of Louis XV to that of George II in December 1755 declared, "It is scarce possible to conceive how these [peaceful] assurances can be reconciled with the orders for hostilities given in November, 1754, to General Braddock, and in April, 1755, to Admiral Boscawen." The British ministry, embracing war's inevitability, sardonically replied to Louis XV's message that a "signal proof" of George II's peaceful "moderation" and "forbearance" was the "very smallness of the succors he sent to America" in the form of two under-strength regiments. Braddock's papers also strengthened Onontio's diplomacy with the Natives, and especially put the Six Nations on the defensive for their diplomatic overtures to the British. Vaudreuil reproached Iroquois delegates for their "most criminal treason" against their French father, asking them, "Do you doubt my having in my hands the papers of General Braddock? I have the identical Messages you have sent him; I have, likewise, your solemn conference with Colonel Johnson." Braddock's captured papers had severe military as well as diplomatic repercussions: the French not only used those captured plans to deflect other British offensives but employed Braddock's captured artillery to besiege Fort Oswego the following year.[58]

The publication of Braddock's captured papers spread news of *la bataille du Malanguelée* throughout the French world. Even in faraway Louisiana, it emboldened French diplomatic offensives among the Native peoples on the southern flanks of British America.[59] French responses to the Monongahela, like their British counterparts, often reflected on the workings of Providence. Father Baron, at Fort Duquesne, wrote new lyrics to the French noël, "Or nous dites, Marie" (Now tell us, Mary), which attributed the victory to French reliance on Mary as well as "our mountains which have thwarted [Braddock's] work." Charlotte Daneau de Muy *dite* de Sainte-Hélène, an Ursuline sister in Quebec, rejoiced, "Never did God's hand appear more obviously to humble the pride of a new Holofernes, in the person of General Bradock, who expected to have breakfast at La Belle-Rivière, dinner at Niagara, and supper at Montreal. He lost his life and the greater part of his army."[60] Mother Superior Marie-Andrée Duplessis de Sainte-Hélène, of the Hôtel-Dieu in Quebec, also ascribed French victory to divine intervention. She related the story of an English prisoner captured at the Monongahela who reported that "the English saw a lady clothed in white with outstretched arms above the French camp." He related that more than 4,000 rounds were fired at the Marian figure, which explained why the British fire overshot the French troops.[61] But other observers realized that New France would need many more divine interventions to survive the basic threat to the colony in the form of the British Royal Navy. Thomas Pichon, an irreligious, dissolute French official in Acadia (and a spy who provided critical intelligence to British forces) was not optimistic: "Our victory over General Braddock, which has been sounded so high in Europe, is far from determining our fate. The maritime power of the English is a hydra, in opposition to which we ought to set up another of the same nature."[62]

Back at Fort Duquesne, the ailing Contrecoeur again turned to thoughts of his retirement from service and requested to be relieved of command. The Monongahela was the pinnacle of his service in the Ohio Valley, a victory that he also ascribed to the fact that "God came to our side." The weight of his post's many liabilities undoubtedly dragged down the veteran French commander. Despite their overwhelming victory, French forces in the Ohio Valley would be continually plagued by logistical problems. La Chauvignerie, writing from Camp Machault on August 27, warned Contrecoeur that the very existence of his fort was at stake for want of food. The waters of Rivière au Boeuf were nearly unnavigable, brought prohibitively low by drought and summer heat. Presque Isle's commander, Lieutenant Benoist, warned Contrecoeur that his fort was not tenable and that he "may expect but few supplies this fall."[63] Contrecoeur would not endure Fort Duquesne's travails for long. Vaudreuil signed orders for transfer of command from Contrecoeur to Dumas on August 8, 1755. Dumas later lamented that Fort Duquesne was "a post too long neglected," and were it not for his subsequent efforts to obtain provisions from the Illinois Country, the post probably would have been abandoned altogether. On November 15, 1755, the man who had done so much to solidify French control of the Ohio Valley departed once and for all, finally to be reunited with his dear wife and family at Montréal on November 26. Contrecoeur entered his retirement with one of the most enviable and distinguished records of any senior Canadian officer. Praise for him poured in from his superiors for his "prudence, foresight, and firmness." Contrecoeur was reasonably confident that he would soon gain the two honors that he coveted the most from his recent victory: the Croix de Saint Louis and promotion for his two sons, the youngest of whom, René-Marie, "had the hammer of his musket broken by an enemy bullet" at the Monongahela.[64]

The battle had been a distinctly Canadian victory, for it had been Canadian officers of the *troupes de la marine* who had seemingly reversed fate. The Marquis de Vaudreuil particularly awarded veterans of the Monongahela with significant promotions and important posts.[65] King Louis XV had also taken notice. As Vaudreuil remarked in 1756, "I learn of the satisfaction that the King has taken in the combat with the English at the Belle Rivière, and that His Majesty is very pleased to reward those who have distinguished themselves in that affair." Indeed, Louis XV immediately awarded all of the captains serving at the Monongahela in 1755—Contrecoeur, Lignery, and Dumas—with the Croix de Saint-Louis, which Canadians held in "greater veneration" than almost any other such honor. Contrecoeur was particularly commended for how he had conducted himself at Fort Duquesne. By their zealous service throughout the remainder of the war, a number of Monongahela veterans would be similarly decorated. All of the surviving lieutenants—Paul Le Borgne, Jacques-François Legardeur de Croisille de Courtemanche, and Jean-Baptiste-Philippe Testard de Montigny—eventually received the Croix de Saint-Louis for their distinguished careers that included the Monongahela, as did the young ensign François de Bailleul and cadet Joseph-Marie Rémy de Montmédy.[66]

The Monongahela schooled a new corps of French officers in the Canadian way of war, and many of them went on to serve with great distinction as partisan fighters in the Seven Years' War. Yet despite the strategic magnitude of the battle, there was strangely little subsequent discussion in French circles of how this "complete victory" validated the strategy that the Marquis de Vaudreuil consistently advocated: of active diplomacy with Native nations to sustain joint French-Indian expeditions that would aggressively strike the British colonial frontiers.[67] The Monongahela should have been the ultimate model for French operational success, but its example fell victim to the rivalry between the Canadian-officered *troupes de la marine* and the metropolitan *troupes de la terre*, which were sent to New France beginning in 1755. The regular army officers who came from France generally believed that the warfare practiced by Canadians and Indians was utterly savage, illegitimate, and degrading to their honor.[68]

The outcome of an engagement in September 1755 particularly dampened French Army officers' reliance on Canadian and Indian irregulars. The Marquis de Vaudreuil had received reports in the summer of 1755 (confirmed by Braddock's captured papers) that William Johnson's provincial army was threatening Fort Saint-Frédéric. He decided to shift French forces under the Baron de Dieskau to the Champlain Valley. As he set out to confront Johnson's army in August 1755, Dieskau wrote that "we are as well acquainted as themselves with all their treacheries, from General Braddock's papers." The two armies met at the Battle of Lake George on September 8, 1755, an action that might be more properly called Dieskau's Defeat, the French counterpoint to the Monongahela. Despite his long career in the French Army and considerable experience in irregular warfare in Europe, Dieskau met with disaster in the woods of America. As Braddock had done, Dieskau divided his army and took a flying column ahead to confront the enemy. Leaving behind most of the regular troops, he relied on the nimble Canadian militia and Indian warriors who composed the majority of his force. The battle began, ironically, when British-allied Mohawk warriors and Massachusetts provincials, deployed in column and with no flanking protection, blindly walked into an ambush. Luckily for the British column, there were Canadian Mohawks in Dieskau's force who warned their southern Mohawk brethren before the trap was fully sprung. Most of the American provincials ran out of the killing zone and fled back to their camp. Hearing the fighting, Johnson started to fortify his base camp to provide a rallying point for the panicked survivors. Dieskau pursued his retreating foe and launched a disastrous frontal attack on Johnson's fortified base camp with his grenadiers. Dieskau was wounded and captured after his repulse, and while he had successfully blunted the British offensive toward Crown Point, it was seen as a debacle.[69]

The lesson that French army officers in America seemed to have taken from Dieskau's unfortunate action was the failure of irregular warfare, specifically the dangers of overreliance on Indians and Canadians. Dieskau blamed his defeat directly on his Indian allies, whom he accused of duplicity and betrayal. But he was charged, like Braddock, as being overconfident and imprudent. As a result, some French army officers took a negative view of the kind of warfare and diplomacy that had brought victory at the Monongahela. Another reason the glory of the Monongahela was partly dimmed was the Marquis de Montcalm's victory over the British post of Oswego, a conventional siege that regular army officers hailed as "an expedition more successful and extraordinary than that [over] General Bradock last year."[70]

Britons, for their part, celebrated Johnson's victory that "at once repaired and contrasted Braddock's defeat," in the words of Horace Walpole, a Member of Parliament. The Lake George battle exacerbated the essential debate over European and American warfare following the Monongahela. An American army "composed wholly of *irregulars*" and commanded by a man "totally a stranger to

European discipline" had triumphed over a French aristocrat and his elite grenadiers, Canadians, and Indians. Colonists celebrated the battle as yet another vindication of American fighting capabilities. One writer boasted that the colonials had defeated the French "as reputably and unexpectedly as the French routed the unadvised Braddock," to the chagrin of British regulars. William Johnson achieved transatlantic fame for his victory. King George II conferred upon him the title of baronet in 1755, the British Parliament voted him a reward of £5,000, and he was empowered as the sole Superintendent of Indian Affairs in 1756—all of which was made possible by the path that Braddock had set him on at the Alexandria Congress.[71] As the British would find to their dismay in the next two years, however, stalemating the French at Lake George and granting a baronetcy to Johnson did nothing to reverse Britain's flight from the frontiers—which began when the French put to use Braddock's artillery captured at the Monongahela.

Between 1755 and 1757, British arms had suffered a cascading succession of strategic defeats: the Monongahela; the capture of forts Bull, Oswego, and William Henry on the New York frontier; Admiral Byng's defeat at Minorca; and a failed expedition against Louisbourg. The two surviving regiments from Braddock's campaign, the 44th and 48th, particularly symbolized the demoralized state of British arms. After Dunbar's retreat through Pennsylvania, the two regiments had been stationed on the New York frontier. They had never fully recovered either physically or psychologically from the Monongahela disaster. Although Lord Loudoun applauded Gage's leadership of the 44th Regiment—"a good Officer [who] keeps up Discipline Strictly"—he observed that "the Regt is in Rags but look like Soldiers," a judgment echoed by the two regiments' colonels, who described the men as "in a very tatter'd condition."[72] Daniel Webb, the new colonel of the 48th Foot after Thomas Dunbar, would preside over two ignominious moments that further damaged the regulars' reputation in the eyes of Britons and Indians: his timorous responses to the French sieges of Oswego and William Henry.

The psychological wounds of the Monongahela still festered in particular in the 44th Regiment, and a deep-seated desire for vengeance erupted while the men were encamped near Schenectady in the summer of 1756. On the morning of August 5, the severed head of an Indian warrior was found in the camp sticking on a pole. Soldiers had cornered one of their old adversaries, Jerry, or Skowonidous, the scout who deserted the army only to appear during the Battle of the Monongahela killing and scalping British soldiers. Skowonidous

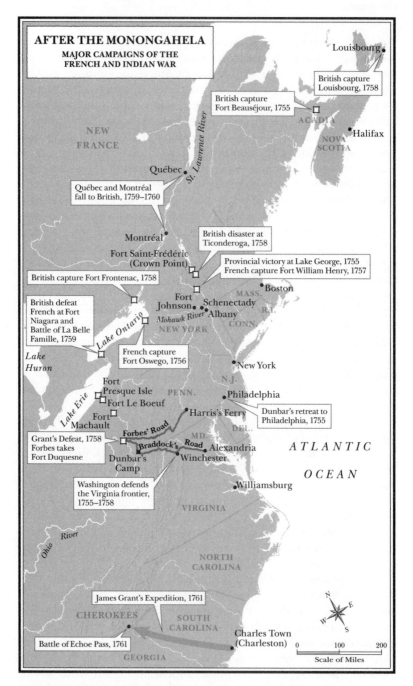

After the Monongahela: Major Campaigns of the French and Indian War

Glen Pawelski, Mapping Specialists, Ltd.

resurfaced in the summer of 1756 among the Tuscaroras of the Six Nations to whom he had "lately Join'd himself" (Jerry's ethnicity is unclear—one official believed he was a Delaware). He had audaciously visited Albany in the company of Tuscaroras, Mohawks, and Sir William Johnson, and apparently visited none other than the Earl of Loudoun. When he was at Schenectady he foolishly admitted to having killed British soldiers at the Monongahela and boasted that "no Man Dared to tutche him for it." The men of Halkett's Regiment took their revenge. No soldier was ever court-martialed for murder, and some suspected the regiment's officers of collusion. The incident further soured British efforts to gain Six Nations allies. The Tuscaroras refused to aid the British when they needed help in August 1756, and a year later, Johnson reported that the Tuscaroras were still angry over Jerry's murder.[73]

The timing of Jerry's murder was unfortunate, for the French were threatening the British fort at Oswego on Lake Ontario at that very moment. Lord Loudoun ordered Colonel Webb to march the 44th Regiment to reinforce Oswego and to improve the Mohawk Valley's defenses. When the 44th Regiment marched out of Schenectady on August 11, 1756, some of the demoralized soldiers were drunk—a fact noted in the regiment's orderly book. Webb's march up the Mohawk Valley reunited the men of the 44th with other Monongahela veterans such as Horatio Gates and his New York Independents, and Silver Heels, who led a scouting party with the British.[74] While encamped at Nicholas Herkimer's 1752 homestead at German Flatts on August 17, Webb received news that the French were besieging Oswego. He advanced to the strategic Oneida Carrying Place, where the British were constructing two fortifications to guard the upper Mohawk Valley and the communications to Oswego. Webb ordered the destruction of the two fortifications without any authorization from Lord Loudoun, then abandoned this forward outpost and retreated back to Albany, thus opening the Mohawk Valley to French attacks, which fell hard on German Flatts in 1757.[75]

The Marquis de Montcalm had captured Fort Oswego, the only British post on Lake Ontario, with artillery that included "six brass pieces, taken from Admiral Braddock." The odyssey of Braddock's artillery readily summarizes Britain's dismal fortunes from 1755 to 1757. Contemporaries instantly recognized how that captured artillery monumentally swung the war's momentum to the French. The New York Council in August 1755 feared that the French would soon "march with the Artillery they have taken from General Braddock's

Army, to reinforce the Garrison at Niagara" and to threaten Fort Oswego. According to local Iroquois, the victorious French had scornfully told them "they were very much obliged to the English for furnishing them with so many Cannon, to take their own Forts."[76] By 1757, the artillery and stores captured at the Monongahela and Oswego empowered Governor-General Vaudreuil's offensive against the frontier of New York. When Montcalm besieged Fort William Henry in 1757, his army of more than 6,000 French troops fought alongside 1,800 Native allies drawn from around thirty nations. Captured British artillery and ammunition had produced a strategic ripple effect. As Governor Vaudreuil wrote in 1758, "Were it not for the ammunition furnished successively by the Beautiful River, Chouagouin, and Fort George, I should not have had enough either for attack on defence."[77] Webb further besmirched his own and the regulars' reputation when he refused to come to the relief of Fort William Henry in 1757. Webb's decision was immortalized in James Fenimore Cooper's novel *Last of the Mohicans*, along with the infamous "massacre" of the British column by French Indian allies following the surrender.

All of these consecutive reverses had brought the British colonies in America and the British Army to the brink of defeat. Aguiota, an Oneida sachem, told William Johnson shortly after the surrender of Oswego, that the Iroquois were "quite surprised to find our selves deceived in our opinion of the English—We took them to be a more steady People, but we see that this defeat at Oswego discourages them entirely and that you seem as it were to give up all hopes." By 1757, one demoralized colonial correspondent captured the sense of many British Americans, writing that "the more we are strengthened from *Great Britain*, the more ground we lose against the *French*, whose number of regular troops is much inferior to ours." But the anonymous author of this letter in the *Gentleman's Magazine* believed that it was "want of proper management" that had rendered the regulars ineffective. Yet the British Army's leadership was already beginning to implement the lessons of Braddock's Defeat and produce the proper management—politically and militarily—that this colonial writer so desperately longed for.[78]

Indeed, if there was any glimmer of hope in the 44th Regiment's history during this dismal period, it was the regiment's tactical adaptations to the threat of Indian and French attacks. The orderly book's description of the column's tactical disposition as it marched up the Mohawk Valley in 1756 is a description of what these veterans had learned at the Monongahela:

All partys covering the Troops on a March wither in Front Flanks or Rear are on an Enemys approach & finding they are to form in Order of Battle are to Conceal themselves as much as possible behind Trees Logs in the Brush & being thus covered and protected it will be no easy matter for the Enemy to force them if they do their Duty when the Order of Battle is formed if it be found that the Flanks and Rear are sufficiently secured the partys that cover them will be Orderd in and the Officers on Receiving such Orders are to form their Men Two deep as Expeditiously as possible and proceed as they shall be Directed, Every Soldier to be told and Repeated over & over that whither he is Detached or in ye Line tho there should be Firing all round him he is not on Any occation to give his fire unless he can see any Enemys as a fair mark to fire at.[79]

One year after Braddock's Defeat, British regulars were being ordered to fight behind trees when attacked, to aim at specific targets, and to fire at the enemy with independent judgment, and to close with the enemy. The regiments so nearly destroyed in 1755 would rebuild their numbers and renew their confidence in the years to come. By 1758, the regiments were near peak strength, with significant proportions of American recruits in 1755 and 1756. The 44th Regiment numbered 22 officers and 1,020 men, while the 48th Regiment had 24 commissioned officers and 1,010 men. Both units went on to fight effectively in the final campaigns of the war.[80] In that respect, the march of the 44th up the Mohawk Valley in August 1756 symbolized the Americanization of the British Army in both its manpower and tactics.

ONE OF THE MOST IMPORTANT yet still unexplored legacies of the Monongahela is how it affected the Native warriors and nations so responsible for Braddock's defeat. Just as the Seven Years' War provided "educations in arms" to a generation of colonial Americans,[81] the Monongahela provided an education in arms to a generation of Indian warriors, one that is dimly seen in written sources but vividly demonstrated in the subsequent annals of frontier history. There was no other battle during the Seven Years' War in which Natives' cultural expectations of victorious warfare were so abundantly and powerfully realized. At the Monongahela, Indian warriors from across half a continent had triumphed over numerical and technological odds in their unprecedented destruction of an entire British army with a powerful artillery train. Native expectations were also met in the short campaigning season, for many warriors had only recently arrived at Fort Duquesne and then returned home immediately after the battle. The Natives completely routed their enemies and had little interference from the French when they took scalps and collected materiel from the battlefield: there were no conventions, paroles, or surrender agreements brokered by Europeans. And they had suffered around twenty-seven killed and wounded, an exceedingly slender cost for so grand a victory.[82] Unlike Braddock's mauled army, 99 percent of the Native warriors returned home with stories to tell and physical proof of their triumph. As Pierre Pouchot later admitted, the Monongahela was "the most vigorous & the most glorious in which the Indians were involved."[83]

The memory of Braddock's Defeat was sustained among Indian nations by the physical trophies of battle that circulated throughout Indian Country for decades. The scalps, regimentals, grenadiers' hats, swords, and other accoutrements that James Smith had beheld from Fort Duquesne were taken back to Indian towns and communities. French soldiers of the Béarn Regiment were introduced to the reality of war in America when they met Indians bearing scalps of Braddock's men at Petit Détroit on the St. Lawrence River in August 1755.[84] Iroquois visiting Fort Niagara in September 1755 "saw there many English Scalps, and much Cloaths and Furniture, in particular one very rich Saddle, all which they understood had been taken from the English at Monongahela." A Virginia officer captured in 1756 reported seeing "the English Colours, taken from Gen'l Braddock" at a Potawatomi town. And most extraordinary, a British officer in the Maumee Valley in 1764 discovered "an Indian on a handsome white horse, which had been General Braddock's, and had been taken ten years before when that General was killed on his march to Fort du Quesne."[85] In July 1776, during the American Revolution, when British general Sir Guy Carleton met in Montreal with Indian delegates from the Great Lakes region, a Hessian officer noted that one of the chiefs "wore on this occasion the coat of General Braddock whom he had killed in the previous war; and his little son of nine years the vest [waistcoat] belonging to it."[86] Even quotidian objects, such as war clubs or horses, disseminated stories of personal valor in combat throughout Indian country. War clubs were used to record an individual warrior's campaigns, and many were surely notched with scores of enemies slain and scalped at the Monongahela.[87] Warriors brought back tales of heroism, such as Atiatoharongwen's "brave and skillful conduct" in saving a French officer's life during the battle. The hundreds of horses that Natives had seized—the ones that had trampled Contrecoeur's cornfields at Duquesne—also had stories to tell even as they changed the lives of their owners. A later traveler among the Wyandots recorded that "they had no horses previous to 1755, the year of Braddock's defeat," and had captured a number of them during the battle.[88]

The Monongahela was, in sum, the standard by which many Native warriors assessed future battlefield success. In the short term, this unequivocal demonstration of Native military power drew hundreds more Indian warriors into subsequent Franco-Indian campaigns from 1755 to 1757—a surge that magnified their military power and extended the duration of the war. "The great pillage at the time of General Braddok's Defeat," one French report concluded, "has attracted some Indian tribes from very remote countries to Fort du Quesne." Undoubtedly, some Native warriors at Oswego in 1756 and Fort William Henry in 1757 were veterans of the Monongahela expecting to replicate their success, only to leave unfulfilled and betrayed by their allies. Pouchot believed that it was the Canadian and Indian quest to get plunder, "as they had at the Braddock incident," that prompted the Indians to attack the British after the surrender of William Henry.[89] The Monongahela had Indianized the war to a degree far greater than any previous Anglo-French conflict.

Braddock's Defeat, and the Natives' subsequent military successes over the British between 1755 and 1758, imbued warriors with an unqualified confidence in their warfighting. Cherokees received a deputation of Northern Indians who proudly reported that "they had entirely defeated the English Army killed the General (Braddock) and destroyed most of them & the few that were left alive." The delegates invited the Cherokees to join with them to drive the colonists into the "Salt water." Ohio Indians similarly boasted to Christian Frederick Post in 1758 that they could "over-power both the *French* and the *English* when they please." Warriors' confidence in their tactics reflected their sense that "the white people are ... nothing at all." It was "through their imagination and reason," Post concluded, that "they think themselves a thousand times stronger." The memory of the Monongahela inspired Native armies as they inflicted many such defeats on Anglo or American forces in the subsequent history of the Ohio Valley. Interpreter and trader John Long, who traveled extensively among the Indian nations of Canada and the Great Lakes, recorded a tradition apparently drawn from Kanesetake Iroquois. Braddock's conduct confirmed "them in an opinion they had before often hinted, 'that he wanted both skill and prudence in war.'"[90] Ironically, it was more the Native peoples and less the colonial Americans who took from the Monongahela the mythic lesson that vaunted British regulars could be defeated and that self-reliance and independence were desirable. Braddock's Field itself was another means by which the memory of this battle lingered in Indian minds. The battlefield carried military lessons to Indian travelers and warriors who routinely passed through it. By 1758, Braddock's Road had been "very much beat by Warriours" as they brought destruction to the Virginia, Maryland, and Pennsylvania frontiers.[91]

As Washington, Dinwiddie, and many others sensed, one of the most important short-term consequences of Braddock's Campaign was the devastation it brought upon British frontier settlements. "The service the Regulars have done," Dinwiddie concluded, "is they have opened the Road from Fort Cumberland to the Ohio, which will facilitate the Invasion of the Enemy on our Frontiers." After Dunbar went into premature hibernation in Philadelphia, the British colonial frontiers were even more exposed to what the French called *la guerre sauvage*: a total war waged against the families, settlements, and communities along the British frontiers. Many settlers went about their daily routines assuming that "Braddock's War" would somehow not affect them.[92] But Native war parties had begun striking Virginia and Maryland as early as June 1755, and attacks on Pennsylvania commenced when Delawares, Shawnees, and Mingoes destroyed the Great Cove Valley in November 1755. The French and Indian victory over the British at the Monongahela had not only shifted the weight of Indian military power to the French, but it also freed Native leaders like Shingas to pursue their own war aims against British adversaries, against whom they had many long-standing grievances concerning land and trade. Joint French and Native expeditions (often led by veterans of the Monongahela) successfully brought three British colonies to their knees by destroying farms, crops, and livestock; capturing frontier forts both small and large; killing around 1,500 inhabitants, and taking captive nearly 1,000 others. The attacks also provoked a mass exodus of refugees who sought comparative safety along the Carolina frontiers, including the ancestors of James Chesnut, the husband of famed Civil War diarist Mary Boykin Chesnut. The three-year scorched-earth campaign also caused political convulsions within the affected colonies, especially Pennsylvania, as the Quaker faction in the government bristled over the decision to fortify and arm the province. Pennsylvania's political system was in a sense revolutionized by the British retreat and the subsequent destruction of the colony's frontier settlements. A Delaware warrior named Lamullock laughed at the anemic British military responses to the campaign, telling one captive that "the English were a Parcel of old Women for that they could not travel without loaded Horses and Waggons full of Provisions and a great deal of Baggage."[93]

One of the greatest legacies of Braddock's Defeat was how profoundly it transformed the British Army and motivated its subsequent adaptations to warfare in America. Years afterward, George Washington offered one of the most famous (and cited) assessments of the Monongahela's central military legacy: "The folly & consequence of opposing compact bodies to the sparse manner of Indian fighting, in woods, which had in a manner been predicted, was now so clearly verified that from hence forward another mode obtained in all future operations." Before Braddock's Defeat, the British Army had no official doctrine or standard training on *petite guerre*.[94] However, in response to the perceived dominance of Canadians and Indians in irregular warfare, British and American officers developed and institutionalized ranger and light infantry companies that could master both the wilderness and the Indians.[95] Although British and French regular officers struggled mightily to Europeanize the conflict, the Seven Years' War in America never lost its hybrid character, a fusion of European and Indian military cultures and practices.[96]

Veterans of the Monongahela were conspicuously among the vanguard of officers who led British tactical adaptations to the challenges of American campaigning. Three officers in particular— Quintin Kennedy, Thomas Gage, and George Washington—personified British responses to the war in America. Lieutenant Quintin Kennedy was a young officer of the 44th Regiment who espoused a more radical and thorough transformation of the British Army's conduct of the war. He recognized that effective diplomacy with the Indians was necessary for equally effective combat, and he immersed himself in Iroquois culture. Both Kennedy and Charles Lee were rumored to have had relationships with Iroquois women, and both dressed and equipped themselves as Indian warriors and scouted with Iroquois allies and British rangers. Gage pioneered the first true light infantry regiment in the British Army, though his 80th Regiment of Foot ultimately reflected the inherent conservatism of senior British commanders who were unwilling to permit their light infantrymen to become true irregulars. As colonel of the Virginia Regiment, Washington combined the best qualities of disciplined regulars and adaptable irregulars, and developed a force that anticipated the Continental Army. By war's end, British and colonial American forces had achieved a formidable degree of fighting prowess by such adaptations, regardless of the exact motivations behind them. By 1760, the officers and men who had been bloodied at the Monongahela had fully avenged themselves upon the French and developed the capacity to engage Native American forces in woods they had once so greatly feared.

When Washington accepted command of the Virginia Regiment in August 1755, few commanders in military history had ever inherited a situation so grim and chaotic.[97] Defense of Virginia's 300 miles of frontier fell squarely on the shoulders of this twenty-three-year-old officer and his depleted and demoralized troops at Fort Cumberland, a paper command of more than 1,000 men. Worse yet, as Washington charged, Braddock's Road now functioned in reverse to the enemy's advantage, for Virginia was "laid *entirely* open by the *very avenue* which had been prepared." Even before accepting command, Washington foresaw the "insurmountable obstacles" he would face after Braddock's campaign had effectively depleted the countryside of recruits and supplies.[98] Virginia's defensive strategy of protecting the frontier by a cordon of fortifications was anathema to Washington, who chafed for "a vigorous offensive war" against the French or the Indians. The forts were like mere islands of safety in a sea swirling with French and Indian war parties. In 1756, the French could boast that "grass was growing in the roads communicating with Cumberland" (i.e., eastward to Virginia). Washington admitted as much to Robert Dinwiddie when he reported that the "roads over the Allegany Mountains are as much beaten [by Indians], as they were last year by General Braddock's army." At Fort Cumberland, Lieutenant Colonel Adam Stephen fumed that "the Enemy pass under our Noses without ever putting them in bodily fear." The Indians took captives literally within a stone's throw of the fort, including the consort of John Fraser, the old Venango gunsmith and veteran of Braddock's company of guides.[99]

But despite the way some historians have portrayed it, Washington's ordeal on the Virginia frontier was not his personal struggle against desperate odds. The war in Virginia between 1756 and 1758 was increasingly a joint Anglo-Indian operation, as Washington's own correspondence bears out.[100] Around 2,000 Cherokees, Catawbas, and Tuscaroras were engaged in the defense of Virginia, Maryland, and Pennsylvania at various times between 1756 and 1758. They frequently undertook joint scouting missions with Washington's Virginians and other provincial forces at forts Loudoun, Cumberland, and Frederick. Washington had an unalterable respect for Native warriors and their tactical skill, believing it to be "literally true" that 500 Indians were more capable of inflicting destruction on Virginia than 5,000 regular troops.[101]

Washington's genius as commander of the Virginia Regiment was fashioning an adaptable, hybrid American army that was capable of both regular and irregular operations, and whose strengths were fully displayed in John Forbes's campaign in 1758. It has become fashionable to portray Washington as a military conservative, who modeled himself after Braddock and only wished to transform his Virginians into disciplined Redcoats. He certainly wanted to create a body of soldiers with an inner soul of discipline and boasted that "we want nothing but Commissions from His Majesty to make us as regular a Corps as any upon the Continent."[102] However, Washington was also a military innovator who trained his men in light infantry tactics and advocated use of Indian dress and equipment. According to Adam Stephen, the Virginia Regiment knew "the parade as well as the Prussians, and the fighting in a Close Country as well as Tartars [i.e., partisans]." Washington reported to Dinwiddie that he had ordered his officers to train their men both in the "proper use of their Arms" and "the method of Indn Fighting." He discussed with senior British officers his desire to "not only cause the Men to adopt the Indian dress but Officers also, and set the example myself." He instructed Major Andrew Lewis—whose men were outfitted like Indians in 1758—to have his men "regularly practised in Shooting at Targets" while they learned the "platoon way of Exercising."[103] His Virginia provincials fought jointly with their Cherokee and Catawba allies, slowly eroding the supremacy of French and Indian war parties and creating a shared warrior culture as they fought together. In 1757, for example, a party of twenty Virginians and Cherokees advanced all the way to Fort Duquesne. Lieutenant James Baker of the Virginia Regiment followed the Cherokees' lead as they ambushed a smaller French party along Turtle Creek, not far from the site of Braddock's field. During the brief but intense skirmish, the Cherokees lost a captain, Swallow Warrior, but they and the Virginians had killed, wounded, or captured three French officers. Ensign Pierre-Philippe de Saint-Ours, a veteran Ohio Valley fighter, was killed, and François-Louis Picoté de Belêstre was captured and interrogated by Washington and Edmund Atkin, the superintendent of Indian affairs. The Virginians were sharpening their reputation as the Long Knives.[104]

On the New York frontier to the north, British officers from Braddock's shattered regiments were undergoing an education and evolution similar to Washington's. While stationed in the Mohawk Valley in 1756, they came under the influential example of Sir William Johnson and his diplomatic and military efforts with the Six Nations. At Fort Johnson in February 1756, Captain John Beckwith, lieutenants William Dunbar, James Pottinger, Charles Lee, Quintin

Kennedy, and Ensign George Pennington witnessed the Iroquois condolence ceremony and rituals involving wampum belts. Scaroyady, their old ally from Braddock's expedition, was also present and passed wampum belts to cover their dead. Johnson was not only a binding force of the shared British-Iroquois world of the Mohawk Valley but also a staunch advocate of Iroquois and British military cooperation. In King George's War a decade earlier, he had burst into Albany dressed "after the Manner of an Indian War-Captain" at the head of a Mohawk war party. He organized and equipped many joint scouting expeditions of colonists and Mohawks, and wanted to form a "Regm.ᵗ of Christians, & Indians" to jointly defend the valley that they shared. The Mohawk sachem Abraham "esteemed Colonel Johnson to be a good warriour," and some British officers took Johnson's example to heart.[105]

Quintin Kennedy experienced the most thoroughgoing transformation of any British officer of the French and Indian War. He went from Redcoat officer to Indianized warrior in a military career stretching from the Monongahela to the Mohawk and Champlain valleys, to St. Francis on the St. Lawrence, to Cherokee country in

British officers like Quintin Kennedy and Charles Lee observed Sir William Johnson's diplomacy with the Six Nations in 1756 at Fort Johnson (Sir William's first home in the Mohawk Valley; his second home is pictured here). Kennedy and Lee, who allegedly married Iroquois women, adopted Indian dress and methods of warfare.

Johnson Hall (Sir William Johnson Presenting Medals to the Indian Chiefs of the Six Nations at Johnstown, N.Y., 1772), Edward Lamson Henry (1841–1919), 1903.
Oil on canvas, ht. 21 ¼" × w. 37", Albany Institute of History & Art Purchase, 1993.44.

Carolina, and finally to the island of Martinique. The *Scots Magazine* captured Kennedy's odyssey in a colorful sketch in 1756:

> Lieut. Kennedy has married an Indian squaw, whose tribe has made him a king. Gen. Abercrombie gave him a party of highlanders joined with a party of Indians to go a-scalping, in which he had some success. He has learned the language, paints and dresses like an Indian, and it is thought will be of service by his new alliance. His wife goes with him, and carries his provisions on her back.[106]

The *Scots Magazine* referenced an August 1756 scouting party that Johnson outfitted with moccasins and green ratteen leggings made by local Iroquois women. Forty Iroquois warriors accompanied by Kennedy and his Highlanders scouted for forty days in the wilderness, advancing as far north as the St. Lawrence Valley. They burned a tavern and killed a few French *habitants* along the supply road between La Prairie and St. Jean. On their return, they destroyed lumber and naval stores near Missisquoi, where the seigneur René-Nicolas Levasseur had established a sawmill. Kennedy's wholehearted adoption of Indian warfare was reflected in his dress and in the trophy that he had lifted, "the Scalp of one Man they had kill'd at the Tavern."[107] The Ohio Iroquois warrior Silver Heels was a close friend of Kennedy, having fought with him at the Monongahela and in subsequent actions during the war. Silver Heels appears to have been instrumental in Kennedy's transformation, for Adam Stephen recalled that "He was Achates to Quintin Kennedy," evoking the matchless friendship of Achates and Aeneas in Greek mythology.[108] Kennedy's 1756 scouting expedition was one of many such missions by which the British gained experience in ranger tactics, which led to the creation of formal independent ranger companies such as Robert Rogers's celebrated command. Some British officers—for example, Lieutenant James Pottinger of the 44th—were embedded as volunteer "cadets" in Rogers's Rangers. Captain Charles Lee appears to have approved of Kennedy's methods, for during the Ticonderoga Campaign in 1758, Richard Mather of the Royal Americans wrote his brother that "Capt Lee is very well," noting that he was "in his Indian dress, which he seems very fond of."[109]

Thomas Gage was also a crucial leader of the institutional development of the British Army's first light infantry regiment. Gage had been quick to realize the military lessons of Braddock's disaster. He once told Warren Johnson, Sir William's brother, that "300 Indians [were] above a Match for 1000 Regulars," which were roughly the numbers he believed had actually been engaged at the Monongahela. He later diagnosed one of the causes of British defeat as Braddock's "own inexperience, and that of his troops, of the kind of country in which he was to engage, whose manner of fighting was new to Europeans, though adapted to their circumstances and the nature of the country, in which heavy fires from close and compact bodies would not prevail" (Gage interestingly blamed colonial governments' delays as the primary reason for the campaign's failure). The action at the Monongahela was partly the genesis of Gage's idea to form an actual unit of light infantrymen who would learn to fight effectively in America.[110]

Gage also sniffed out the possibilities for career advancement through the formation of a new regiment, especially after his hopes for command of the 44th Regiment were dashed. As the senior surviving officer of the 44th Regiment, he believed that he had a rightful claim to the colonelcy opened by Sir Peter Halkett's death. In late July of 1755, he was already lobbying for the command and explaining his actions and wounds at the Monongahela to ministers in the British government. He even petitioned King George II for command of the vacant regiment, adding "it will give him the happiness of Your Majesty's Sanction and Approbation of his Conduct, and alleviate the Mortification he suffers to have been concerned in the Disgrace of so many of his Countrymen." Lord Gage also lobbied the Duke of Newcastle on his younger brother's behalf, and though the Duke favored Thomas's promotion, army politics prevailed when the colonelcy went to James Abercromby.[111] But in 1757, Gage proposed to the Earl of Loudoun that he would personally raise a regiment of "Light armed Foot" through the sale of his commission, equipping a regiment of 20 officers and 545 men organized into five companies. Gage had the good sense to harness the talented officers and veterans of the Monongahela who were already learning the art of ranging, such as Kennedy and William Dunbar. In early January 1758, Lord Loudoun approved Gage's request, and recruitment began in earnest.[112]

Thomas Gage deserves credit for creating the first official light infantry regiment in the British Army—a movement that began in America and not in Europe. He was a competent officer, even an innovator with respect to light infantry, for his new regiment, the 80th Regiment of Light Armed Foot, symbolized the Army's adaptation to wilderness warfare. By 1759, the 80th Regiment was near full strength with 20 officers and 487 enlisted men. They were clothed in short, dark brown coats with black buttons and small black caps; equipped with shorter and lighter firelocks; and carried standard wilderness implements such as hatchets, knives, shot bags, powder horns, and moccasins.[113] But Gage's leadership and the 80th Regiment's lackluster record ultimately reflected how such adaptations could be superficial. While commanders in chief, such as Lord Loudoun and James Abercromby, certainly deserve credit for their efforts to create effective ranger companies, the British high command had reservations about the radical transformations espoused by Kennedy and Robert Rogers.[114] The Duke of Cumberland, for example, applauded the development of ranger companies while also making it clear that regular officers were ultimately to replace unreliable colonial or Indian rangers. Gage also saw his light infantry regiment as a means to an end—of obtaining the command of a regular regiment. As his brother Lord Gage explained, "The Corps which [Thomas] commands now, cannot be a very agreeable one, it gave Him Rank, and therefore He solicited it, but I believe you will not wonder, as He is a <u>Regular</u> bred Soldier, that He should wish to return to y.ᵉ <u>Regulars</u>." Gage's lukewarm commitment to light infantry was matched by his overall disdain for Indian "gentry." He viewed his Stockbridge Indian allies as a great "nuisance to the army" who "did no manner of service."[115]

The officer who brought Gage's military conservatism and reluctance into sharp relief was George Augustus Lord Howe, the commanding officer of the 55th Regiment in 1757 and 1758. Lord Howe fully embraced the ranger techniques practiced by Rogers and Kennedy, and was especially beloved by the American provincials, who knew that he respected their martial abilities. One British observer wrote to Lord Loudoun that under Howe's influence, "The Art of War is much changed and improved here. I suppose by the End of Summer it will have undergone a total Revolution." Howe's revolution was cut short by his untimely death at the head of his troops near Fort Ticonderoga on July 6, 1758.[116] At the subsequent Battle of Ticonderoga on July 8, British Redcoats seemed to revert to their old ways, demonstrating incredible bravery and sangfroid as their commander, Major General James Abercromby, ordered a series of disastrous frontal attacks against French earthworks outside of Fort Carillon. Abercromby commanded the largest British army ever assembled in North America—around 17,000 effectives—but failed to defeat Montcalm's French army of nearly 4,000. The British Army (including the hapless 44th Regiment) suffered more than 2,000 casualties in what was the bloodiest single day of the war, retreating in panic and disorder on July 9, the anniversary of Braddock's Defeat.[117] The shocking disaster further hardened colonists' impressions of the regulars' slavish adherence to conventional tactics in the wilderness. Colonial writers contrasted Abercromby's futile defeat with the victory gained by American forces in August 1758. Led by Colonel John Bradstreet, 5,000 American provincials and regulars undid much of the ignominy of Braddock's Defeat and Oswego's fall when they captured and destroyed Fort Frontenac, a key French outpost on Lake Ontario, with more than sixty cannons, including some of Braddock's pieces that were stored there.[118]

Wristplate from a Brown Bess musket belonging to the 44th Regiment (3rd Company, Musket No. 13). Found at the French settlement of Pointe-à-la-Chevelure (Crown Point, New York) around 1967, the musket had presumably been captured either at the Monongahela or at Ticonderoga. Private Collection.

The final British campaigns of the Seven Years' War in America demonstrated through glorious victory what the British Army had learned through bitter defeat. The triumphs at Louisbourg, Frontenac, Duquesne, Niagara, Quebec, and Montreal were a testament to the massive military strength that the British had committed to America and mobilized among the colonies. The spirit of *Carthago delenda est* infused British efforts to destroy once and for all the Canadian nemesis to British America. Britons celebrated the revenge they had obtained in these decisive victories for the humiliating defeats suffered earlier in the war. But glorious British victories never fully erased the memory of those defeats, nor did they eclipse the ongoing tensions of imperial identity as regulars and provincials fought together as allies.

The victorious counterpoint to Braddock's Defeat finally came in November 1758, when General John Forbes's army captured Fort Duquesne. The French abandoned and blew up the fort on the British Army's approach, just as Braddock had once anticipated. The Forbes Expedition brought together many of the principal veterans from 1755 in this successful enterprise: Washington, George Croghan, James Burd, Harry Gordon, Adam Stephen, and St. Clair. General Forbes and his executive officer, Colonel Henry Bouquet, endeavored to "learn the art of warr from enemy Indians" as they successfully overcame the challenges that Braddock had confronted three years earlier. Yet Forbes's Expedition had nearly ended in a disastrous and humiliating loss known as Grant's Defeat, an action that paralleled Braddock's Defeat and again highlighted differences between regulars and Americans. As Forbes's army came within striking distance of Fort Duquesne in early September 1758, Major James Grant received permission from Bouquet to lead a reconnaissance in force against the French outpost with a picked force of 850 men (nearly the size of Braddock's two regiments at the Monongahela). When Grant arrived near Fort Duquesne on September 13, its 1,500 provoked defenders—the overwhelming number of which were Indian allies—poured out against the British. Grant unwisely chose to fight a defensive and stationary battle from what he thought was a commanding rocky hilltop. Native warriors skillfully outflanked and surrounded Grant's position, which proved to be no advantage. The British forces were routed, and Grant himself was taken prisoner by the French; 300 of his men were either killed, wounded, or captured. In the aftermath, malicious accusations flowed between the regulars and provincials, as Grant blamed the Virginia officer Andrew Lewis. The Virginians boasted (with ample justification) that they had saved

Grant's regulars from total destruction, just as they had done in their rearguard action at the Monongahela three years earlier.[119]

On November 25, 1758, the British finally captured the abandoned and smoldering Fort Duquesne, the military and moral object for which the war had been fought. Both Braddock's and Grant's defeats had been avenged, one soldier wrote, for "upon the Spot where *Fort Duquesne* once stood... the *British* Flag flies over the Debris of its Bastions in Triumph." Washington had long relished the thought of reversing Braddock's loss, a sentiment that he knew his old friend Francis Halkett would appreciate: "Shall we revisit together, a hapless spot, that proved so fatal to so many of our (former) brave companions? Yes! And I rejoice at it; hoping it will now be in our power to testify a just abhorrence of the cruel Butcheries exercised on our friends, in the unfortunate Day of Genl Braddock's Defeat." General Forbes immediately took measures to commemorate the victory and the dead. A soldier in the army reported that Forbes ordered "a Day of publick Thanksgiving to Almighty God for our Success; the Day after we had a grand *feu de Joye,* and To-day a great Detachment goes to *Braddock's* Field of Battle to bury the Bones of our slaughtered Countrymen, many of whom were butchered in cold Blood by (those crueller than Savages) the *French,* who, to the eternal Shame and Infamy of their Country, have left them lying above Ground ever since." A burial party of nearly 100 men ventured to Braddock's Field on November 28, 1758. Francis Halkett revisited the "hapless spot" where his father and brother had fallen together. An Indian veteran of the battle guided them to a "remarkable tree" near which he had seen Halkett fall and a young soldier rushing to his assistance. As they uncovered the two skeletons lying across each other, Major Halkett exclaimed "It is my father," when he recognized his artificial tooth. One of the witnesses of this "pious expedition" was Captain Samuel West, the older brother of painter Benjamin West, who was inspired by his sibling's testimony to sketch a melancholy study, *Discovering the Bones of Sir Peter Halket,* that remained an unfinished masterpiece.[120]

The equally grim fate of French Captain Lignery symbolized the broader collapse of New France late in the war. He had been of course one of the triumvirate of French captains at the Monongahela, and then the commandant at Fort Duquesne since 1756. After destroying his post, Lignery withdrew to Fort Machault and other posts to the northward. But he intended to return to the Forks of the Ohio and strike the British again. In the summer of 1759, however, British General John Prideaux led his army through Iroquoia to besiege the

French outpost of Niagara commanded by Captain Pouchot. The only salvation for this vital French outpost rested with Lignery's French and Indian forces in the upper Ohio Valley. Hearing of the threat to Fort Niagara, Lignery rushed northward to the relief of the beleaguered garrison with a force of around 1,300 men. As he approached within a few miles of Niagara, Lignery led his columns headlong into the British ambush. The Battle of La Belle Famille, on July 24, 1759, was Braddock's Defeat in reverse and symbolized just how effective the British Army had become. The few Monongahela veterans still in the ranks of the 44th Regiment again heard the Indians' war cry, but "on this occasion it had no effect" on them. After punishing volleys from the 46th Regiment had mauled the French ranks, the 44th's light infantry company charged with "inexpressible fury," as their Iroquois allies also fell upon the retreating French. Captain Charles Lee remarked on this "happy event" in his letters, recalling how "our men received their fire with great intrepidity, and immediately rush'd in with their Bayonets." A number of French partisans and Monongahela veterans were killed, wounded, or captured at Belle Famille, such as Montigny, La Chauvignerie, Niverville, and Bailleul. Lignery was mortally wounded and died on July 29, 1759, a few days after the French surrendered Fort Niagara.[121]

Contemporaries instantly grasped the vicissitudes of Lignery's and Braddock's defeats and congratulated veterans of the Monongahela for having achieved vengeance against the very French forces that had once occupied the Ohio Valley. Thomas Boone, the future governor of New Jersey, observed to Horatio Gates that the "the 44.th [Regiment] have had thorough Revenge & have by all Accounts amply sacrificed to the memory of your Monongahela Friends" at Belle Famille. The capture of Fort Niagara further conjured memories of the Monongahela when British readers learned of a soldier of the 44th Regiment who had discovered among the French prisoners his wife, who had been captured at Braddock's Defeat. Believing that her husband was slain, she had since married a young French officer and had a child, only to discover that her first husband was yet alive. After "some Struggles of Tenderness" for the Frenchman, the account reported, she left him and her child to be reunited with her British husband.[122]

Although that story may be apocryphal, the unequivocal British victory at Niagara had severed the strategic interior waterways of New France. Lee took "great satisfaction" in being the first Englishman to cross Lake Erie when he led a small party from Niagara down the Allegheny River to link up with the British army at Fort Pitt. En route, he passed forts Presque Isle, Le Boeuf, and Machault, the abandoned remains of French power in the Ohio Valley. By 1759 and 1760, British armies (including the 44th and 48th regiments) had fully avenged the Monongahela by capturing Quebec and Montreal. A British soldier discovered one of Braddock's old mortars in the French lines at Quebec. During the Redcoats' occupation of Canada in 1760, the 44th Regiment was garrisoned near Kahnawake, the Iroquois town whose warriors had been such conspicuous French allies in 1754 and 1755. Accounts of British soldiers' robberies, assaults, and malevolence against the people of Kahnawake suggest that memories of the Monongahela still lingered in the regiment.[123]

Over the course of the war, British adaptations had resulted in an unprecedented ability to strike targets deep in the American interior and to engage Indian warriors in the woods. James Grant's expedition against the Cherokees in 1761 revealed just how profoundly the British Army and its provincial allies had developed the military and logistical capacity to destroy Native communities in long-range campaigns deep in the interior of the Appalachians. The 1761 Expedition was a sharp contrast to Braddock's Defeat and to Colonel Grant's own humiliating defeat and capture before Fort Duquesne in 1758 (he was exchanged by the French in 1759). Grant led a combined army of British regulars and South Carolina provincials with the objective of laying waste the warring Cherokees' lands. The army consisted of 1,400 regulars and a nearly equal number of South Carolina provincials, including Francis Marion (the future "Swamp Fox"), William Moultrie, Andrew Pickens, and Andrew Williamson, all of whom gained military experience that shaped their future careers as revolutionary partisans.[124] The expedition lasted a grueling sixty-six days in a march through unsettled and mountainous country more than 800 miles from Charles Town and back, a distance far greater than Braddock's march. Captain Christopher French of the 22nd Regiment wrote that the officers "agreed that no such march was ever made by Troops...even those who had been at Pitsbourg [Pittsburg]."[125]

A measure of how far the British had come since the dark days of 1755 was the presence of Quintin Kennedy's "Indian Corps" of 138 Indians and colonial rangers spearheading the army's advance. He had brought his "Old friends the Mohawks" with him from Albany down to Charleston, including his Achates, Silver Heels.[126] Kennedy's unit included seventeen Chickasaws, three Yuchis, nineteen Catawbas, six Mohawks, and fifteen Stockbridge Indians from western Massachusetts.[127] By early June 1761, more than 2,000 British and Indian forces were pressing into the mountainous Cherokee country from their forward base of Fort Prince George. At 6:00 in the morning of June 10, Grant's army began its march toward Echoe Pass, where every soldier "expected to be attacked," as Captain French recalled—quite unlike Braddock's overconfident men after crossing the Monongahela. Six hundred Cherokee warriors had masterfully prepared an ambush in the "very narrow Pass" dominated by a steep mountain parallel to the Little Tennessee River, leaving the British column in that slender gauntlet little room to maneuver. But the vanguard of Quintin Kennedy's Indian Corps, which had been "continually scouting" during the entire advance, uncovered a party of Cherokees. The sound of Indian halloos raced along both sides of the column from front to rear. The Battle of Echoe Pass (or Cowhowee) was joined.[128]

Despite the Cherokees' accurate fire and the terrifying war cries, the British responded with "great spirit and coolness," according to one eyewitness, who thought that "finding Indians round us, was no surprise." Kennedy's Indian Corps immediately attacked into the ambush, sweeping along the hillside into the Cherokees' flank and holding their positions behind trees. Colonel Grant also made a crucial movement early in the engagement, far different from his and Braddock's earlier disastrous decisions. Grant knew that "stopping and forming in disadvantageous ground against an invisible enemy could answer no good end," so he ordered the entire column to press through the killing zone. Throughout the fight, the troops maintained a "heavy fire" on the Cherokees. The battle lasted for about three hours as the lengthy column ran the gauntlet and pressed forward to its next encampment.[129]

Grant's scorched-earth campaign left in its wake eighteen Cherokee towns and 1,500 acres of crops and orchards destroyed, 5,000 homeless refugees, and numerous abandoned villages.[130] Grant extolled Kennedy and his Indian Corps, believing that the battle had reversed the British regulars' sense of inferiority in the woods and instilled "fear and dread of His Majestys Arms" among the Indians.[131]

Kennedy hoped that his battlefield distinctions and knowledge of the Indians would open a route for him similar to that of Sir William Johnson. But his hopes of becoming Superintendent of Indian Affairs for the southern department was dashed when Charleston merchant John Stuart was appointed to the office. Instead, Kennedy remained with his 17th Regiment in Colonel Robert Monckton's 1762 invasion of the French island of Martinique in the West Indies. His old Mohawk friends, including Silver Heels, also decided to join him, "being Determined to have another Touch at the Great King's Enemies," as one British newspaper proudly reported. Kennedy led a group of light infantrymen called "Kennedy's Rangers," who fought in a "good many small skirmishes" and gave the "Indian Halloo" to intimidate the French. During the conquest of Martinique, Kennedy had seized eighteen African slaves, who were escorted by Silver Heels and the Mohawks back to New York. However, Kennedy was wounded during an assault near Cape Navières on January 24, 1762, during the "warmest part" of the action, which undoubtedly contributed to his death by disease a few months later. His ambitions of becoming Indian superintendent, of gaining an independent fortune, and of spending "the remainder of my Days with my friends" in Ayrshire died with him at Martinique.[132]

Quintin Kennedy personified a road not taken in the postwar evolution of the British Army. The light infantry and ranger tactics championed by Kennedy and others had become institutionalized in the British Army with a light infantry company in every British regiment. Nonetheless the fighting prowess that had won the British Army such monumental victories in North America was a casualty of its own success. When the 44th and 48th regiments returned to the British Isles in the 1760s, they were shattered remnants. The 48th Regiment by 1763 numbered only thirty-six rank-and-file men. By 1765, the greatest theorists and practitioners of light infantry tactics were all dead—Lord Howe, John Forbes, Henry Bouquet, and of course Quintin Kennedy—and their veteran experience died with them in America. Such losses in leadership and men had rendered the British Army in America "a regular army without light troops," as Henry Clinton characterized it in 1775. British officer Charles Townshend admitted as much to the aging Lord Amherst: "for it is not a short coat or half gaiters that makes a light infantryman, but as you know, Sir, a confidence in his aim, and that stratagem in a personal conflict, which is derived from experience. This is still to learn, the Americans have it." Townshend was responding to news of the battles of Lexington and Concord in 1775, when the Massachusetts militia spectacularly defeated British light infantry in a fight that contemporaries compared to the Monongahela twenty years earlier.[133]

THE CONQUEST OF CANADA IN 1760 had rendered Braddock's Defeat a monumental victory for the future of British America and a disastrous defeat for the unconquered Native peoples who had tenaciously defended the Ohio Country. Braddock's greatest legacy became not his eponymous battle but the military road that he had built over the Appalachian Mountains. Both Braddock's and Forbes's roads channeled that great demographic force of eighteenth-century history—British settlement expansion—over the Appalachian barrier, inexorably compromising Indian settlements in the Ohio Country. The deep scars and cuts of Braddock's Road—visible even today, as I've noted—provide evidence of the many thousands of colonial settlers from Virginia and Maryland who used the road in the decades following the war. Braddock's victory was in breaching the Appalachian barrier, building a military road across the mountains, and awakening colonials to the possibilities of the west.[134]

From almost the moment that John Forbes's army took the Forks of the Ohio in 1758, Braddock's Road became a crucial supply conduit (along with Forbes's Road) to the newly christened Pittsburgh. Construction soon began on the pentagonal Fort Pitt—similar to the fortress that Braddock had once envisioned—and it became one of the largest British outposts in all of North America. Monongahela veteran Captain Robert Stewart, stationed at Pittsburgh in September 1759, wrote to his friend Washington that "this Fort, which is yet but in embryo, will when finish'd, be the grandest that has yet been in this new World, but it will require much Time great perseverance and immense Labour." His letter described an industrious and thriving British "Military Colony" on the Ohio: "this hightned by a view of three glorious Rivers, and the many Beauties Nature has been so lavish in adorning this place and it's Environs, forms a most delightfull Prospect, terminated by high romantic Mountains, which nearly encircle it: in fine the more I see of this Charming Country, the more I'm enamour'd with it."[135]

In 1759, Braddock's Road was reopened and improved upon by Alexander Finnie, an adjutant in the Virginia militia and also the former keeper of Raleigh Tavern in Williamsburg, where Braddock's bay horse had been stolen four years earlier. While visiting Fort Cumberland, Finnie became aware of how much the road had deteriorated and gained General John Stanwix's support to commence work on it, as his November 1759 petition to the Virginia House of Burgesses explained: "That the Petitioner hired at his own Expence thirty Workmen.... That he began the said Work the fourth Day of August, and finished on the twentieth when he arrived at Pittsburg with 60 Provision Waggons, 500 Sheep, and 70 Head of Cattle, and at that Time the Garison had not eight Days Provision."[136]

Following the improvement of Braddock's Road, thousands of American hunters and settlers from Virginia and Maryland began clearing land, planting corn, and hunting in the Ohio Valley in the 1760s. Some of these colonists were military veterans pursuing land grants promised to them, while others like Finnie pursued the economic opportunities afforded by the British garrisons' reliance on civilian tradesmen, contractors, and merchants. They found that the land "from the foot of the Laurel Mountain to Fort Pitt is rich beyond conception," especially the bottomlands along Redstone Creek, a tributary of the Monongahela. By 1760, there were already 146 men, women, and children living at Pittsburgh, and a year later, the population had increased to 332 inhabitants. Fort Pitt's designer, Captain Harry Gordon (the same engineer who had spotted Beaujeu's approach on July 9, 1755) marveled at the community's growth: "The Resort of numbers of People to this Place [Fort Pitt] is very Considerable—They are building good Houses fast, on the Spot Col.o Reid has very judiciously made choice of for the Town; and if this continues the thoroughfair to our Posts on the Mississipi the Number of People will soon considerably increase." Travelers equally marveled at the massive tide of emigration into the Ohio Valley during the 1760s. In 1769, a Pennsylvanian traveler recorded that he encountered 200 settlers on Forbes's Road between Carlisle and Ligonier, as "the People are going out verry fast to Settle that Country." John Parrish, a Quaker missionary traveling along Braddock's Road in 1773, "met great Numbers of People going to the new Country." One of them was Zadock Wright of Virginia, a teamster in Braddock's Expedition who escaped from the Monongahela, only to return to the promising lands he had seen years earlier.[137]

Braddock's Road sustained the memory of Braddock's Defeat and the French and Indian War among the 20,000 souls estimated to have settled the Ohio Valley by the 1770s. Settlers recalled the Hussar who threatened to storm into Pennsylvania as they traveled on "Sir John St. Clair's Road"; they viewed Fort Cumberland "going to Ruin," having been abandoned in 1765; experienced the gloomy Shades of Death; and viewed the site of Fort Necessity and Washington's action at the Great Meadows. Travelers "pass'd over Braddock's Grave" (the general location) as they contemplated the melancholy defeat of a proud British officer who had refused to listen to Washington. Even by 1773, the place where Dunbar's column had encamped was known to travelers as "Dunbar's Destruction," and "great quantities of broken Bombshells, cannon, bullets, and other military stores" were still visible in the woods.[138] During his journey through the Ohio Country in 1784, Washington was reported to have searched in vain for the site of Braddock's grave (his correspondence and diaries are silent on that score). It was not until 1804, when crews were repairing the old road as it dipped down into a ravine, that the bones of the deceased general were uncovered, along with military emblems such as metal buttons. The remains were fittingly reinterred under a broad oak on a nearby hillock.[139]

The bleached bones of Braddock's Field also spoke with great power as emblems of remembrance.[140] Braddock's Field became America's Teutoburg Forest, as Reverend William Smith had observed, where an imperial British army under Braddock was crushed in circumstances similar to those of Varus.[141] Bones were still strewn across the battlefield for decades afterward, despite General Forbes's cursory effort to bury them in 1758. Visitors to Pittsburgh in the 1760s and 1770s routinely made a pilgrimage through the "Golgotha" of the Monongahela. When the Moravian missionary John Heckewelder came upon the "dreadful sight" of scattered skulls

Grave of Edward Braddock and trace of Braddock's Road, leading down to the ravine where road crews discovered the general's remains in 1804, near Chalk Hill, Pennsylvania. Author photograph.

and bones in 1762, "the sound of our horses's hoofs continually striking against them, made dismal music." For the Reverend David McClure, the "melancholy spectacle" of the mostly unburied remains was a "disgrace to the british commanders at Fort Pitt." He noted trees scarred by grapeshot and musketry, leather harnesses lying on the ground, and scalping knife marks on the skulls. The site evoked "serious & solemn reflections on the vanity of life, & the deep depravity of our fallen nature, the dreadful source of fighting & war, & all the miseries that man delights to inflict on man." Visits to Braddock's Field further reinforced contemporary perceptions of Braddock's "obstinate adherence" to European conventions and Washington's espousal of American tactics.[142]

As early as 1761, the American settlements at Pittsburgh seemed to Henry Bouquet "a Colony sprung from Hell," and conditions only worsened in the Ohio Valley over the next decade. The establishment of Fort Pitt and other British outposts in the west had angered Natives who had fought for their territorial integrity. Pontiac's War again tore apart the frontier in 1763, and although an uneasy peace was negotiated in 1765, the British and the Indians lived constantly at the precipice of war. Euroamerican hunters and squatters provoked Natives' fears of being dispossessed, and murders fueled by lingering hatred and alcohol alienated the rival occupants of the Ohio Valley. For a time, the British Army tried, but failed, to evict squatters who violated the British ban on settlement in the region. The crisis of illegal British settlement became so acute by 1766 that George Croghan and many others warned that "if some affectual Meshers are nott Speedyly Taken to Remove those pople settled on Red Stone Creek...the Consequences may be Dreadfull and wee Involved in all the Calamitys of a Nother Gineral Warr."[143]

The man responsible for meeting this growing crisis was Thomas Gage, who by 1764 had been promoted to the rank of major general and appointed to Braddock's former position as commander in chief of His Majesty's forces in North America. Gage's tenure was plagued by what he called the "lawless Banditti upon the Frontiers" and the contemptibly weak colonial governments that could not enforce obedience to their own laws. Gage's ability to enforce British rule was waning. By 1766, he wrote to Major General Ralph Burton, who had led the final assault at the Monongahela, that regulars needed to be moved from the western posts to control His Majesty's unruly subjects in eastern port cities: "The seditious Spirit now reigning in the Provinces, and the open Declaration, that they will oppose the Execution of the Stamp Act, with their Lives & Fortunes, requires my attention to the support of the Kings service in the Inhabited

General Thomas Gage (ca. 1719–1787). By John Singleton Copley, ca. 1768, Yale Center for British Art, Paul Mellon Collection. When Copley painted this portrait, Gage was at the apex of his lengthy military career, having been appointed commander in chief of British forces in North America in 1764. Gage's tenure coincided with the growing divide between the thirteen colonies and the British Empire, a separation that was reflected in Gage's relationship with Washington. Gage had once expressed "so great an esteem" for the young Virginian when they served together under General Braddock, and they had dined together amicably at New York in 1773. But by 1775 they had become avowed enemies as they led the American and British armies at the Siege of Boston.

Country." The British Army finally abandoned Fort Pitt in 1772, effectively abdicating control of the region to the Euroamerican and Indian settlers. Seventeen years earlier, then-Colonel Gage had fought to wrest the Ohio Valley from French control, but now the commander in chief of His Majesty's army in America found it impossible to effectively govern the vast region and its increasingly rebellious peoples.[144]

One of the few officers who had the temperament for stamping out sedition and parcels of traitors was Sir John St. Clair. Following the war, in 1762, he had married Elizabeth Moland, the daughter of a prominent New Jersey family, and they had a son named John. St. Clair's health declined, however, from the lingering effects of wounds he had suffered at the Monongahela, and he died at Elizabethtown, New Jersey in 1767. Gage and other officers attended his funeral, conducted "with all military honours" for his thirteen years of service in America. During the War for American Independence, Lady St. Clair and her son, Sir John St. Clair, remained loyal to the crown—decisions that led the revolutionaries to confiscate their property in much the same manner as "St. Clair the Hussar" had once threatened in 1755.[145]

EPILOGUE

Legacies of the Monongahela

TWENTY YEARS TO THE day after Braddock's Defeat, George Washington held his first council of war as commander in chief of the Continental Army in Cambridge, Massachusetts.[1] When Washington had last visited Boston in 1756, he still yearned for the distinction of a royal commission as a British regular officer; now, he was levying war against the king and the empire that he had once so ardently defended. Meeting in the home of Reverend Samuel Langdon, the president of Harvard College, the council faced the impossible task of besieging General Thomas Gage's British Army in Boston without any proper siege artillery. Two of the officers in that council were Major-General Charles Lee and Horatio Gates, the Adjutant General of the Army. They knew the British Army well and were well known to Washington, as he had fought with them in 1755.

The Siege of Boston was a confrontation between veterans of Braddock's Defeat who again found themselves present at the opening battle of a new war. Over the previous twenty years, these men had chosen different paths of loyalty that led them to opposing sides during the Siege of Boston. Washington's thwarted career as a regular officer had been the first in a long train of grievances against British tyranny. As a member of the Virginia House of Burgesses and the first and second Continental Congresses, he had ardently defended the rights of British America. His opponent at Boston was Gage, his old comrade, the commander in chief of British forces and the royal governor of Massachusetts. Gates and Lee, both native-born Britons and regular officers, were also comrades of Gage, and they had made especially pointed acts of rebellion against George III. Gates and Lee abandoned England in the 1770s because of their republican principles, purchased plantations in the Shenandoah Valley, embraced the revolutionary cause, resigned their royal commissions, and were appointed by Congress as generals in the Continental Army. Their participation in the campaign of 1755 had stayed with them all. Lee particularly invoked the lessons of Braddock's

Defeat as he encouraged American militias, convincing them that they could defeat British regulars.[2] The invocation did not go unnoticed. One British officer at Boston averred that "there is not a Soldier or Officer in the Garrison, especially his old Regiment (44th) but woud be happy to get a Shot" at a man they considered a dangerous traitor. The triumvirate of Washington, Lee, and Gates formed an effective foundation for the Continental Army. As its chief architect, Washington designed a "respectable Army" in the mold of Great Britain's, but not as a mindless imitation. It hearkened back more to his old Virginia Regiment than to the armies of Braddock and Forbes. He created a force that was "competent to every exigency" and consistently relied on irregulars, including Indians, riflemen, and partisans.[3]

One such irregular fighter who came to Cambridge was Daniel Morgan, the former teamster in Braddock's expedition who still bore the scars of those 499 lashes he received for assaulting a British officer. Morgan personified the rifle-bearing Virginia frontier culture that had been so deeply influenced by contact with Indians and their independent spirit. He had recently fought in Lord Dunmore's War in 1774, a conflict against Shawnees on the Ohio frontier, where he and other Virginians made a formal resolution to defend American liberty in the event of a war with Britain. In 1775, he made good on that resolve, leading a company of frontier riflemen, dressed and equipped as Indian warriors, in a dramatic three-week march from Virginia to Massachusetts. Morgan became one of Washington's trusted lieutenants and went on to command a corps of riflemen. "The Old Wagoner," as he was known, earned great distinction for his roles in American victories at Saratoga and Cowpens.[4]

Perhaps the most unlikely veteran of Braddock's Defeat to arrive in Cambridge that summer was Atiatoharongwen, the Kahnawake Iroquois warrior also known as "Louis Cook" or "Colonel Louis." This Abenaki-African-Mohawk, who had perhaps fired shots in anger against Washington in 1755, ventured down from Canada in 1775 with a party of Mohawk Iroquois volunteers and appeared at Washington's headquarters in Cambridge. Washington later wrote that Atiatoharongwen had "Honoured me with a visit" and had reported that the Indians and Canadians were well disposed to the Americans. While most Indian peoples were initially neutral, indeed averse to taking any sides in the conflict, Atiatoharongwen resented British occupation of his Canadian homeland. The war presented him with an opportunity to expel them. He fought in a number of campaigns with the Continental Army, eventually securing a commission from Congress as a lieutenant colonel.[5]

Part of Atiatoharongwen's justification was the American decision to invade Quebec in 1775. Shortly before Washington's July 9 council of war, the Continental Congress had authorized an invasion of Quebec to win over the reluctant French Canadian population to the revolutionary cause as well as to prevent British and Indian forces in Canada from striking the colonies. The invasion prompted a number of Washington's old French Canadian adversaries (including a few veterans of the Monongahela) to resist the advances of his "Northern Army," commanded by General Philip Schuyler and later by General Richard Montgomery. Following the conquest of New France in 1760, British officials had closely monitored the whereabouts of the principal Canadian seigneurs, marine officers, and recipients of the Croix de Saint-Louis. They not only respected those Canadians' latent military abilities but also thought it was politically necessary to conciliate them in order to effectively govern Canada. The Quebec Act of 1774, which defined certain religious, political, and legal rights to the French Canadians, contributed to what became an unlikely alliance between conquerors and conquered. In August 1775, the British government appointed Contrecoeur, Braddock's opponent at Fort Duquesne, as a member of the Legislative Council authorized in the Quebec Act. Contrecoeur's appointment was a measure of his stature, but his health was already declining when he took office, and he died in Montréal in December 1775. Other formidable partisan fighters from the Seven Years' War took up arms against the *Bastonnais* (as the Americans were known), including Louis Liénard de Beaujeu (the brother of Daniel), François-Marie Picoté de Belestre, and the Monongahela veteran Joseph-Dominique-Emmanuel Le Moyne de Longueuil. As a young ensign, Longueuil had led contingents of Lorette Hurons to the Belle Rivière and fought against Washington and Braddock in 1754 and 1755. Twenty years later, he commanded a detachment of Canadian volunteers at Fort Saint-Jean on the Richelieu River, now a British outpost besieged by the American army. While these Canadian partisans of proven abilities did not score any victories as spectacular as the Monongahela, their political and military resistance had helped to prevent the Americans from making Canada the fourteenth colony in rebellion.[6]

More than a remarkable coincidence had brought these central figures to the great confluence of events that was the American Revolution. The lives and careers of Washington, Lee, Gage, Gates, Morgan, Contrecoeur, and Atiatoharongwen had all been forged by their involvement in the Monongahela. Colonel Adam Stephen

wrote to Lee in 1776 that "the 9ᵗʰ [of July instant], the Anniversary
of Braddock's defeat [was] a day which I will always remember."
Gage, Washington, Lee, and Gates had been in the same crucible.
A few of the letters that passed between them during the Siege of
Boston were published in colonial newspapers and pamphlets, illus-
trating the painful separation and severing of relationships in this
civil war. On July 9, 1782, late in the war, an English expatriate named
George Grieve dined with Gates at his Virginia home "Traveller's
Rest," along with Adam Stephen. Grieve recalled that their conversation turned to the anniversary of Braddock's Defeat, as Gates and
Stephen observed to him that "no less than *four* of the most distinguished of the American Generals" were present in the 1755 expedition. By 1782, however, the once-distinguished careers of three of
those generals had become tarnished by battlefield defeat (Gates),
drunkenness (Stephen), or dereliction of duty (Lee). Veterans all,
they were acutely aware of the "vicissitudes of human affairs" that
had shaped their lives. Gates and his guests marveled at the "wonderful revolution in the affairs and minds of men" that had taken
place in the years since, one that they could not possibly have foreseen or anticipated. Who would have thought that those officers,
who had once risked all for king and empire in 1755, would fight
against the British Army to secure independence? Or that their old
French adversaries—now allies fresh from victory at the Siege of
Yorktown—would encamp on the very ground in Alexandria that
Braddock's army had occupied in the spring of 1755?⁷

To Washington, as we have seen, Braddock's Defeat remained a
manifestation of the "wondrous works of Providence." It had transformed his reputation, taking him from humiliation at Fort Necessity
to virtuousness at the Monongahela. He preserved the deceased general's sash and two pistols at Mount Vernon as tokens of remembrance.
The Monongahela was an unforgettable reminder to him of "the
uncertainty of Human things," and the certainty of an all-powerful if
inscrutable Providence who ordered all things and "heretofore has
befriended & Smiled upon me." The subsequent years of the
Revolutionary War would test Washington's "perfect reliance" upon
Providence, a word that recurs with great frequency in his writings.
At New York in 1776, Washington's outnumbered Continental Army
awaited the impending confrontation with Sir William Howe's British
Army, the largest yet assembled in America. Seeking assurance for
his nation's future, his thoughts turned backward to the Monongahela
and the bloody days of 1754 and 1755, in a letter he wrote to Adam
Stephen:

> I did not let the Anniversary of the 3d or 9th of this Instant pass off without a grateful remembrance of the escape we had at the Meadows and on the Banks of Monongahela. The same Providence that protected us upon those occasions will, I hope, continue his Mercies, and make us happy Instruments in restoring Peace & liberty to this once favoured, but now distressed Country.[8]

Braddock's Defeat had altered the trajectory of the Seven Years' War in America. It escalated the war, which in turn had new and unforeseen consequences for its British, French, and Indian combatants. The battle also brought into sharp relief the fundamental nature of eighteenth-century American warfare, revealing what happened when conventional forces campaigned and fought against experienced irregular enemies in the unique environment of America's woods and mountains. Like initial battles of other wars, the Monongahela defined the military and political character of what was to come. It was an unprecedented rout of a modern and powerful British army by a predominantly Indian army. No other battle before 1775 had a more profound effect on the colonial British world. It symbolized the blend of conventional and unconventional warfare and motivated all subsequent British military adaptations to fighting in the New World. It was a defining educational experience for many British and American officers who fought both in the French and Indian War and later in the American Revolution, and also for a generation of Native American warriors.

The effects of the battle on the Indian nations allied with New France were no less far reaching. That first major clash of arms in 1755 had brought together a broad and diverse coalition of Indian warriors who collectively demonstrated the real political and military power that Indian nations of the interior still possessed. The Monongahela undoubtedly contributed to the remarkable political coalescence and unification of Indian nations in the Ohio Valley and Great Lakes region that occurred during the remainder of the Seven Years' War. Old divisions and tensions persisted, but Indian peoples in the trans-Appalachian west increasingly fought and negotiated together. During Pontiac's War, much of the same Indian coalition that had defeated Braddock also collapsed almost the entire network of British outposts in the far west, save those at Pittsburgh, Detroit, and Niagara. Although a lack of documentation makes the individual process difficult to trace, it is plausible that the Indian veterans of the Monongahela constituted the cadre of military leaders who led the resistance to British military occupation of their lands as well as the growing threat of British colonial settlement. In retrospect, the battle marked the beginning of the Indians' sixty-year struggle against French,

British, and American efforts to achieve dominion and empire in the trans-Appalachian west.

Braddock's Defeat had also been the French Canadians' greatest victory of the war, for it validated the means by which they had maintained their strategic dominance over a British colonial population roughly twenty-five times larger than that of New France. They had relied on effective diplomacy between Onontio and Indian nations; the military prowess of Native warriors; control of crucial interior waterways, however difficult; the leadership of Canadian-born marine officers and cadets with deep reservoirs of experience in American warfare; and finally, the practice of *la guerre sauvage*, which devastated entire British colonies and kept them on the strategic defensive. By the end of the Seven Years' War, however, the Monongahela also reminded them of how they might have won or stalemated the war had that strategy been maintained. The Monongahela's example, however, was eclipsed by the conflict between Canadian marine officers such as Vaudreuil and French Army officers such as Montcalm. The spectacular victory over Braddock also contained within it a seed of a still more devastating defeat: the spirit of *Carthago delenda est* that germinated in British hearts after the Monongahela, that the Canadian Carthage must be destroyed once and for all. Braddock's Defeat had rendered the subsequent war for empire explicitly one of vengeance and destruction, as French Canadians bitterly realized in *la conquête* of New France in 1759 and 1760.

Braddock's Defeat was, finally, crucially important because of the part it played in shaping a distinctly American identity and the origins of the American Revolution. It did not instantly and inevitably turn Britons into Americans. Yet there was a kernel of truth in Benjamin Franklin's assertion, written nearly thirty years afterward, that the disaster shattered colonists' "exalted Ideas of the prowess of British Regulars" and assuaged their fears of becoming independent. Braddock's Defeat stunned nineteen-year-old John Adams, who wrote to a friend in 1755 of its transcendent lesson: "All that part of Creation that lies within our observation is liable to change. Even mighty States and Kingdoms, are not exempted."[9] For many colonial Americans, the campaign had been an awakening to their provincial status within the empire, and it anticipated many of the political and social divisions that ultimately sundered the British world. Colonials were gradually discovering themselves as Americans, even as they thought of themselves as loyal British subjects (Washington and his fellow officers, as we've seen, conceived that "being Americans" was the reason they were deprived of "the benefits of British subjects").

Braddock's Expedition occurred at a moment when many British imperial authorities wanted to reform the political constitution of the American colonies, which they believed were becoming too independent of the Crown. Judging from political pamphlets, military treatises, newspapers, sermons, poems, and songs that frequently employed the word "American," no other battle before the American Revolution spawned more discussion of identity.[10] It fostered an already nascent American consciousness, defined by the colonists' prolonged relationships to the continent and its Indian peoples, and sharpened by the friction they experienced while fighting alongside British regulars. Colonists still reveled in the British Empire's triumphs by 1763, and pride of accomplishment seemed to salve many wartime irritations. But Braddock's Defeat became the cornerstone of an American counternarrative of the Seven Years' War, one that gave birth to and kept alive a number of its military and moral lessons. Colonists contrasted the regulars' embarrassing defeats not just at the Monongahela but also at Oswego, William Henry, Ticonderoga, and Grant's Defeat with their own heroic contributions to British imperial success, such as the capture of Louisbourg in 1745, the Virginians saving British regulars at Braddock's and Grant's defeats, the provincials' victory at the Battle of Lake George, and their capture of Fort Frontenac.[11] This American interpretation of the French and Indian War may initially have been in the language of loyalty to the Crown, but when colonists finally took up arms in 1775, it became one of resistance, as Franklin observed in his *Autobiography*.

Indeed, the memory of Braddock's Defeat cast a long shadow, one that stretched to include the origins of the American Revolution, and particularly the colonists' decisions to take up arms. In 1773, a Massachusetts veteran, "A Ranger," wrote that Americans must fight for their rights, and that he would readily "fight Enemies from Britain as Indians from Canada" using bush fighting tactics. "You may remember," he asked his readers, "how the French and Indians fought General Braddock's Army? That's the way we must manage our enemies." In a pamphlet published in 1774, Charles Lee encouraged the rebel militias, writing that they could defeat the British Army and recalling the "fatal experience" of Braddock's Expedition—that "men may be smartly dressed, keep their arms bright, be called regulars, be expert in all the anticks of a review and yet be unfit for real service." By contrast, Colonel James Grant haughtily predicted to the House of Commons in early 1775 that the cowardly colonial rabble would never stand before regulars and boasted that he could overrun the continent with only 5,000 men. In reply, Benjamin Franklin laid on the delicious irony that it was the Virginia provincials' "unthanked Service" that had saved Grant's regulars from destruction in 1758. Another colonial writer warned British readers that "they who remember the fatal overthrow of Braddock by a few Indians in ambush, an overthrow incurred by the very discipline in which he vainly put his trust, will be apt to doubt the facility of reducing the colonies by military force."[12]

The Massachusetts militia's victory over Gage's regulars at Concord on April 19, 1775, further reinforced the myth that American militias were more virtuous and more effective than conventional troops. Colonials compared the Redcoats' panicked flight from Concord to "that which seized the broken Remains of General Braddock's Army," while a chagrined British official compared the action to "what Braddock first suffer'd in the last war by surprize from the Indians, and his little army was sacrificed without seeing an Enemy." When Washington finally forced the British to hastily evacuate Boston in March 1776, he remarked that they made "greater havock of the King's Stores than Dunbar did upon Braddocks defeat." Such lessons were well summarized in a song by Benjamin Franklin entitled "The King's Own Regulars, and Their Triumph over the Irregulars," published in a 1776 Pennsylvania newspaper. The verses rehearsed the litany of British regulars' defeats at Falkirk, Prestonpans, Monongahela, Oswego, Ticonderoga, and Concord:

> To Monongahela with fifes and drums,
>
> We march'd in fine-order, with cannon and bombs,
>
> That great expedition cost infinite sums;
>
> But a few irregulars cut us all into crumbs
>
> O the old Soldiers of the King, and the King's own Regulars.[13]

Although one British observer believed the "shamefull Defeat at Ohio" would "scarcely find its parallel in History,"[14] Braddock's Defeat would be repeated, often with far greater loss of life, in future military catastrophes involving conventional forces and indigenous foes: the Indians' defeat of the US Army under Arthur St. Clair in 1791 along the Wabash River; George Armstrong Custer's demise at the Little Bighorn in 1876; and the Battle of Isandlwhana in the Anglo-Zulu war in 1879. Braddock's unshakable confidence in his regular troops' ability to defeat Native irregulars was witnessed again in Custer's foolhardy charge and in Lord Chelmsford's blithe contempt for Zulus.

Vulnerable columns of conventional forces, like Braddock's, have been frequently destroyed by indigenous forces in modern times, such as the US 8th Army running "The Gauntlet" of Chinese and North Korean forces near the Chongchon River in Korea in 1950, or the Viet Minh's annihilation of French *Groupement Mobile 100* in the central highlands of Indochina in 1954. American and British soldiers and marines in 2001 and 2003 entered worlds in Afghanistan and Iraq that are every bit as tribally based as the Indian country that Braddock encountered. Pashtun tribesmen still remember their monumental 1842 victory over the British Army at the Battle of Gandamak, where the descendant of Halkett's 44th Foot, the East Essex Regiment, was slaughtered.

General Braddock's story has been remembered across many generations, a parable of man's hubris and complacency. By contrast, the hundreds of ordinary British soldiers who left their bones at the Monongahela have been utterly forgotten. Buried somewhere underneath modern Braddock, Pennsylvania, their final resting places remain unknown to this very day. Therein lies a message of Braddock's Defeat for our time, and for all times.

ACKNOWLEDGMENTS

This book represents the work of ten years, but its origins are ultimately rooted in my up-bringing in western Pennsylvania, where I first learned to appreciate the French and Indian War at places such as Fort Necessity, Fort Ligonier, the Venango Trail, and the Allegheny River. The project began as a study of the veterans of Braddock's Defeat but evolved into a narrative history of Braddock's Expedition as I uncovered new sources and realized the need for a full accounting of British, French, and Indian perspectives. David Hackett Fischer's scholarship has been a source of inspiration and admiration, and I am grateful for his constant support of the project from its inception. His detailed comments on the manuscript were worth their weight in gold. I have been very fortunate to have such an outstanding team at Oxford University Press. I can imagine no finer editor than Timothy Bent, who vastly improved the manuscript and refined it with skill, grace, and humor. My wonderful production editor Joellyn Ausanka and copy editor Patterson Lamb, along with editorial assistants Alyssa O'Connell and Keely Latcham, shepherded the manuscript through the production process. Several colleagues and friends read the entire manuscript: Stephen Brumwell's scholarship has been foundational to my own, and I am deeply grateful to Stephen for his careful comments on the manuscript and our exchange of ideas; Walt Powell shared wisdom gained from a lifetime of studying the French and Indian War; Martin West also read the manuscript, and I relied heavily on conversations with him and his matchless knowledge of eighteenth-century art and material culture; and Tim Shannon has been especially supportive of the project and commented on parts of the manuscript.

Numerous colleagues at The Citadel and the College of Charleston offered encouragement and shared their expertise. Lunch conversations with Kyle Sinisi at Moe's often hinged on the fine points of Braddock's Defeat, and he was a worthy companion in our days at the gun range. Michael Barrett and Jason Coy graciously assisted with translations of German documents. Bret Lott offered valuable insight as I sketched out the book's structure over a cup of coffee, and he encouraged me in more ways than he knows. Stephen Grenier and Marcus Gillett shared observations on the Monongahela drawn from experience in Afghanistan and Iraq. Other colleagues shaped the project in ways large and small. Christophe Boucher, René Chartrand, Bob Emerson, Peter MacLeod, Michael McDonnell, Julia Osman, and Nicholas Westbrook all provided information on New France or French sources. Ian Steele graciously discussed his definitive research on Allegheny frontier captives, including those taken at the Monongahela. I relied on Erik Goldstein and Kevin Gélinas for their masterful knowledge of eighteenth-century firearms. The project was also shaped by helpful conversations with Thomas Abler, Jonathan Bell, Darren Bonaparte, Tyler Boulware, William Campbell, Simon Fowler, Michael Livingston, Kristofer Ray, John Ross, John Rowland, Matt Schumann, Peter Silver, and Patrick Speelman.

Extended research fellowships through the Gilder-Lehrman Institute of American History and the Massachusetts Society of the Cincinnati Fellowship awarded by the Massachusetts Historical Society were profoundly important in shaping the research and the manuscript. Director Conrad Wright and the wonderful MHS staff deserve credit for the fact that much of the book's outline took shape during my fellowship there. I also received invaluable feedback from participants in the conferences or seminars where I presented aspects of my research: the "1763 and All That" conference organized by Robert Olwell and James Vaughn at the University of Texas; the Filson Historical Society's "Long Struggle for the Ohio Valley" conference organized by Eric Hinderaker and François Furstenberg (John Hall provided enormously constructive feedback); and the Jumonville French and Indian War Seminar in 2011 and 2014.

Returning each fall to the Jumonville Seminar on Chestnut Ridge near the site of Dunbar's Camp has always infused the project with new energy. My friends and colleagues at the Jumonville Seminar and the Braddock Road Preservation Association hold a special place in my heart, and their dedicated study of the French and Indian War has always provided fresh perspectives: Walt Powell, Bob Nipar, Norman Baker, Bruce Egli, Doug Cubbison, Larry and Jaye Beatty, Robert Matzen, Joan Mancuso, Richard Gaetano, Armand Rousseaux, Dane Konop, David Miller, Keith Rouleau, and many others. Other colleagues in western Pennsylvania who deserve special thanks are Alan Gutchess, Director of the Fort Pitt Museum, Brian Reedy at Fort Necessity National Battlefield, and Doug MacGregor of the PHMC. I am especially grateful to Robert Messner, who inspires me with his steadfast efforts to preserve and interpret Braddock's Field. He has graciously guided me during visits to North Braddock and discussed Braddock's Defeat over many cups of coffee. His support of this book has been invaluable, and I am very thankful to him and to the Braddock Carnegie Library Association for permission to use the Emanuel Leutze painting.

This book was "studied as much from life and in the open air as at the library table," as Francis Parkman once wrote. Tracing Braddock's Road over mountain ridgelines and rivers was an epiphany that transformed my understanding of the written accounts of the expedition. My traveling companions—Norman Baker (the foremost scholar of the road), Robert Nipar, and Walt Powell—have built new roads of friendship every bit as durable. I will always cherish our times walking and bushwhacking along Braddock's Road, most of which remains on private property. Special thanks are also due to the Reverend Edward C. Chapman, Gaylord Brooks, and Justin Paulman for their Christian hospitality following a service at Emmanuel Episcopal Church in Cumberland, Maryland, as they showed me the remains of Fort Cumberland underneath their beautiful and historic church. I also wish to thank the staff at historic sites that I visited, including Carlyle House Historic Park (Helen Wirka and Sarah Coster), Cook Forest State Park, Dorchester Heights National Monument (Julia Mize), Fort Loudoun State Historic Park, the Morris-Jumel Mansion (Ken Moss), Mount Vernon, and Washington's Headquarters in Cambridge. David Burns welcomed me to "Prato Rio" (Charles Lee's Virginia home) and made possible a visit to Horatio Gates's "Traveller's Rest."

My understanding of the eighteenth-century British Army was greatly enriched by my reenacting experiences in the recreated Independent Company of South Carolina, which was historically present at Fort Necessity in 1754 and at Braddock's Defeat. I owe a great debt to many friends who shared their knowledge of the British Army and eighteenth-century material culture and life: Ashley Chapman, the extended Cherry family, Scott Douglas, Kenneth Dunne, Fielding Freed, William Jack, Carl Johnson (tailor par excellence), Sally Nuckles, Steve Smith, Steven Steele, Alan Stello, Will Tatum, Andrew Vollman (BTV 24/7), Jeff Wells, and many others.

The maps in this volume were created by Mapping Specialists, Ltd., and I am thankful to Don Larson and Glen Pawelski for taking my sketches and turning them into cartographic art. The new battle maps of Braddock's Defeat are loosely based upon those of Sydney Dillon, a US Steel engineer who superimposed Patrick Mackellar's 1755 scale drawings of the battle onto 1909 maps of Braddock, Pennsylvania.

Finally, I wish to recognize the staff members at the following institutions. During my visit to Windsor Castle, Royal Librarian Oliver Urquhart Irvine and Bibliographer Bridget Wright kindly assisted me, as did the staffs of the British Library, Dorset History Centre, National Army Museum, the UK National Archives, and the University of Nottingham. I also wish to thank the Archives du Calvados, Bibliothèque nationale de France, Carnegie Library, Daniel Library at The Citadel (ILL specialists Debbe Causey and Courtney McAllister), David Library of the American Revolution, the Filson Historical Society, Frostburg State University (Mary Jo Price), Gilder Lehrman Collection (Marisa Sharii), Harvard University Archives, Historical Society of Pennsylvania, Huntington Library, Library and Archives Canada (Isabelle Charron), Library of Congress, Mackinac State Historic Parks (Brian Jaeschke), Musée du Château Ramezay (Christine

Brisson), New-York Historical Society, New York Public Library, Pennsylvania State Archives (Jonathan Stayer); Senator John Heinz History Center (Matthew Strauss), University of Pittsburgh Archives, University of Virginia Library (Heather Riser), Virginia State Library, Virginia Historical Society, Wayne State University (thanks to Cindy Krolikowski for help with the Cumberland Papers), and the William L. Clements Library (Brian Dunnigan and Clayton Lewis).

I remain privileged to teach at The Citadel, where I am currently the Westvaco Professor of National Security Studies. The Westvaco Foundation has been instrumental in the completion of this book. I am also deeply grateful for the research funding from The Citadel Foundation that has made possible much of the research for it. Provost Samuel M. Hines Jr. also provided immense support for the project, and I am grateful beyond words that he made possible an extended research trip to the United Kingdom during my sabbatical.

I have learned immensely from my Citadel cadets and active-duty Navy and Marine Corps NCOs, some of whom are combat veterans of Iraq and Afghanistan. Special thanks are due to Dan Franzen, Matt Garnier, Kyle Hawks, Mark Morrison, Randy Stone, and Paul Whitten for their insights and friendship.

My children, Vivian, Nathanael, and Alistair, deserve much credit for helping me to complete the manuscript. When I began writing the book at my home, I made it clear to them that my office door was always open. Their boisterous intrusions were always refreshing intermissions from the eighteenth century. They never failed to leave me with a smile and provided much incentive to get back to ponies and trains instead of Braddock's horses and wagons. My extended family also gave generous support, including my father-in-law, Robert Nagy, who also read the manuscript. My wife, English, not only shared in some of my research adventures but provided judicious counsel on certain chapters. She remains my best friend and spiritual companion, and I grow more in love with her as each day passes. *Soli Deo Gloria.*

David L. Preston
Charleston, South Carolina
January 2015

Order of Battle, Braddock's Defeat, July 9, 1755

FRENCH AND INDIAN FORCES

Claude-Pierre Pécaudy de Contrecoeur, Commandant of Fort Duquesne
French and Indian Detachment
    Capt. Daniel- Hyacinthe-Marie Liénard de Beaujeu, Commanding Officer
    Capt. Jean-Daniel Dumas
    Capt. François-Marie Le Marchand de Lignery
    (See Appendix C for other French officers and cadets)

Troupes de la Marine (Compagnies franches de la Marine) (108 officers and men)

Canadian militia (146 officers and men)

Indian Nations (600–700 warriors):
    Osages
    Odawas
    Ojibwas
    Sac
    Fox
    Potawatomis
    Wyandots
    Miamis
    Delawares
    Shawnees
    Ohio Iroquois
    Senecas
    Hurons of Lorette (Wendake)
    Nipissings
    Mississaugas
    Abenakis of St. Francis (Odanak)
    Abenakis of Bécancour (Wôlinak)
    Oswegatchie Iroquois
    Kahnawake Iroquois
    Kanesetake Iroquois

BRITISH FORCES

Maj.-Gen. Edward Braddock
Maj. Sir John St. Clair, Deputy Quarter Master General
Maj. Francis Halkett, Brigade Major
Capt. Robert Orme, Aide-de-Camp
Capt. Roger Morris, Aide-de-Camp
George Washington, Aide-de-Camp
Capt. William Shirley Jr., Secretary
Guides and Scouts:
    Christopher Gist (Head Guide)
    George Croghan (Captain of Indians)
    Nathaniel Gist
    Thomas Gist
    John Fraser
    Andrew Montour
    John Walker
    Thomas Burney
Ohio Iroquois Allies:
    Monacatootha (Scaroyady)
    Monacatootha's Son
    Kashwughdaniunto (Kaghswaghtaniunt, Belt of Wampum)
    Skowonidous (Jerry)
    Cashuwayon (Kanuksusy, Newcastle)
    Attschechokatha
    Silver Heels (Aroas or Froson?)
    Kahuktodon (Gahickdodon)

GENERAL BRADDOCK'S COLUMN ON JULY 9, 1755

GUIDES/SCOUTS:
4 Guides and 6 Virginia Light Horsemen

ADVANCED PARTY (CA. 300 MEN):
Lt. Col. Thomas Gage, 44th Regiment
Grenadier Company of the 44th Regiment (73 total)
Grenadier Company of the 48th Regiment (78 total)
Battalion Companies, 44th/48th Regiments (2–3)

WORKING PARTY (CA. 200 MEN):
Maj. Sir John St. Clair, Deputy Quarter Master General
4th New York Independent Company Detachment
    Capt. Horatio Gates
    Lieut. Simon Soumain
    Lieut. Richard Miller
Second Company of Virginia Artificers:
    Capt. William Polson
    Lt. John Hamilton/Hambleton
    Ens. Hector McNeill
Third Company of Virginia Rangers
    Capt. Thomas Waggoner
    Lt. Henry Woodward
    Ens. Walter Steuart

Fifth Company of Virginia Rangers
    Capt. William Peyronnie
    Lt. John Wright
    Ens. Edmund Waggoner

MAIN BODY (CA. 600 MEN):
Virginia Light Horse Troop
    Capt. Robert Stewart
    Lt. John Fenton Mercer
    Cornet Carolus Gustavus Spiltdorft
Royal Navy Detachment
    Lt. Charles Spendelow
    Midshipman Matthew Talbot
    Midshipman Thomas Haynes
Royal Artillery
    Capt. Thomas Orde
    Capt. Lt. Robert Smith
    Lt. William McLeod
    Lt. James Buchanan
    Lt. Jonathan McCulloch
Remaining Battalion Companies (7–8)
    Lt. Col. Ralph Burton
        44th Regiment
        48th Regiment

REARGUARD (CA. 110 MEN):
Col. Sir Peter Halkett
First Company of Virginia Rangers
    Capt. Adam Stephen
    Lt. William Bronaugh
Detachment of South Carolina Independent Company
    Lt. Probart Howarth
    Lt. John Gray

2ND BRIGADE AT DUNBAR'S CAMP

Col. Thomas Dunbar
44th Regiment: Mixed companies of Irish and provincial recruits
48th Regiment: Mixed companies of Irish and provincial recruits
3rd New York Independent Company
    Capt. John Rutherford
Detachment of 4th New York Independent Company
    Lt. William Spering
Detachment of South Carolina Independent Company
    Capt. Paul Demeré
Fourth Company of Virginia Rangers
    Capt. Thomas Cocke
First Company of Virginia Artificers
    Capt. George Mercer
    Ens. Thomas Bullitt
Maryland Ranger Company
    Capt. John Dagworthy

North Carolina Ranger Company
    Capt. Edward Brice Dobbs
    Lt. Thomas McManus

DETACHED SERVICE IN PENNSYLVANIA (BURD'S ROAD)

Second Company of Virginia Rangers
    Capt. Peter Hogg

DETACHED SERVICE IN AUGUSTA COUNTY, VIRGINIA

Sixth Company of Virginia Rangers
    Capt. Andrew Lewis

OTHER CIVILIAN OR MILITARY OFFICIALS
ASSOCIATED WITH BRADDOCK'S EXPEDITION

Colonial Governors and Royal Officials

Lieutenant John Butler	Officer in the Indian Department
Robert Dinwiddie	Royal Governor of Virginia
Arthur Dobbs	Royal Governor of North Carolina
James De Lancey	Royal Governor of New York
James Glen	Royal Governor of South Carolina
Colonel James Innes	Commandant of Fort Cumberland
Colonel William Johnson	Superintendent of Indian Affairs
Robert Hunter Morris	Governor of Pennsylvania
Thomas Pownall	British advisor at Alexandria Congress
Horatio Sharpe	Royal Governor of Maryland
William Shirley	Royal Governor of Massachusetts

Logistical and Administrative Support

Robert Bristow	Apothecary (Brother of Charlotte Browne)
Charlotte Browne	Matron of General Hospital
James Burd	Pennsylvania Road Commissioner
John Carlyle	Storekeeper and Alexandria merchant
John Cherrington	Surgeon of General Hospital
Thomas Cresap	Maryland Commissary Agent
Charles Dick	Commissary and Fredericksburg merchant
Benjamin Franklin	Pennsylvania Wagon Contractor
James Furnis	Commissary of Stores and Paymaster, Royal Artillery
Colonel John Hunter	Virginia agent for London trading firm
William Johnston	Deputy Paymaster General
Robert Leake	Commissary General
Lt. Matthew Leslie	Assistant Deputy Quartermaster
John Read	Wagonmaster
Thomas Scott	Wagonmaster General
Thomas Walker	Commissary and Hampton merchant
Townshend Washington	Assistant Commissary

Medical Personnel

James Napier	General Hospital Director
John Adair	Surgeon
John Charrington	Surgeon
Charlotte Browne	Matron
Robert Bristow	Apothecary

British Officers at Braddock's Defeat

Name	Rank	Date of Commission	Casualty Status
Edward Braddock	Major General	March 29, 1754	DOW (Died of Wounds)
George Washington	Aide-de-Camp (ADC)	May 10, 1755	
Robert Orme	ADC	Lt., April 20, 1751, Coldstream Guards	WIA (Wounded in Action)
Roger Morris	ADC	Capt., Sept. 13, 1745	WIA
William Shirley, Jr.	Captain, Secretary	Appointed 1754-55	KIA (Killed in Action)
Sir John St. Clair, Deputy Quarter Master General (DQMG)	Major, DQMG	Oct. 7, 1754	WIA
Matthew Leslie, Esq.	Assistant to DQMG	Appointed 1755	WIA
Francis Halkett	Brigade Major	May 2, 1751 (capt.); March 27, 1755 (brigade major)	

44TH REGIMENT (HALKETT'S)

Name	Rank	Date of Commission	Casualty Status
Sir Peter Halkett	Colonel	February 26, 1751	KIA
Thomas Gage	Lt. Col.	March 2, 1751	WIA
Charles Tatton	Captain	January 26, 1741	KIA
Samuel Hobson	Capt.	May 25, 1747	
John Beckwith	Capt.	March 2, 1751	
Richard Gethin (Gethins, Githius)	Captain Lieutenant	December 16, 1752	KIA
Thomas Falconer (Faulkner)	Lieutenant	November 29, 1745	
William Littler (Litteler)	Lt.	March 14, 1748	WIA
Richard Bailey	Lt.	April 3, 1750	
William Dunbar	Lt.	May 1, 1751	WIA
James Pottinger	Lt.	May 2, 1752	
James Halkett	Lt.	December 16, 1752	KIA
John Treby	Lt.	March 10, 1753	WIA
James Allen	Lt.	June 25, 1755	DOW
Andrew Simpson	Lt.	June 26, 1755	WIA
Robert Lock	Lt.	June 27, 1755	WIA

Daniel Disney	Lt. and Adjutant	June 29, 1755 June 20, 1753 (adjutant)	WIA
Quintin Kennedy	Lt.	June 30, 1755	WIA
Robert Townshend	Lt.	July 2, 1755	KIA
George Clark	Lt.	July 3, 1755	
William Nartlow (Nortlow, Nartlo)	Ensign	May 18, 1748	KIA
George Pennington	Ens.	Ca. 1755: Not in Army List until 1757	WIA
William Preston	Ens.	Ca. 1755: Not in Army List until 1757	
Thomas Eyre	Ens.	Ca. 1755: Not in Army List until 1757	
Philip Hughes	Chaplain	January 4, 1752	
Henry Farrant	QM (Quarter Master)	October 7, 1754	

48TH REGIMENT (DUNBAR'S)

Ralph Burton	Lt. Col.	October 15, 1754	WIA
William Sparke	Major	June 3, 1752	WIA
Robert Chomondeley (Chomley)	Captain	April 15, 1749	KIA
Robert Dobson	Capt.	August 12, 1745	
Richard Bowyer	Capt.	August 28, 1753	WIA
Robert Ross	Capt.	September 4, 1754	WIA
William Morris	Captain Lieutenant	November 13, 1754	
Theodore Barbut (Barbat)	Lieutenant	April 7, 1747	WIA
John Walsham	Lt.	April 15, 1749	
Walter Crymble (Crimble)	Lt.	November 27, 1752	KIA
William Widman (Wideman)	Lt.	June 20, 1753	KIA
Henry Gladwin	Lt.	August 28, 1753	WIA
John Hansard	Lt.	March 12, 1754	KIA
William Edmeston (Edmonstone)	Lt.	June 26, 1755	WIA
John Hawthorne (Hotham)	Lt.	June 26, 1755	
John Cope	Lt.	June 27, 1755	
Percival Brereton	Lt.	June 28, 1755	KIA
John Hart	Lt.	June 30, 1755	KIA
Jonathan Dunbar	Lt.	July 3, 1755	
John Montresor	Lt.	July 4, 1755	WIA
Richard Croe (Crowe)	Ens.	July 3, 1755	WIA
Alexander McMullen	Ens.	July 3, 1755	WIA
Robert Stirling	Ens.	July 3, 1755	WIA
Joseph Cowart	Ens.	July 3, 1755	
Henry Harrison	Ens.	July 3, 1755	

MEDICAL PERSONNEL

James Napier	Director, General Hospital		
James Adair	Surgeon		
James Craig	Surgeon		
Robert McKinley	Surgeon, 44th Regiment	July 31, 1750	
Charles Swinton	Surgeon		KIA
James Campbell	Surgeon's Mate		
William Congleton	Surgeon's Mate, 44th Regiment		
Jonathan Lee	Surgeon's Mate, 48th Regiment		
Joseph Williams	Surgeon's Mate		

ENGINEERS

Patrick Mackellar	Engineer in Ordinary, 1751	WIA
Harry Gordon	Sub-Engineer, 1749	WIA
Adam Williamson	Practitioner Engineer, 1753	WIA

ROYAL ARTILLERY

Thomas Orde	Capt.	March 1, 1746	
Robert Smith	Capt. Lt.	March 1, 1755	DOW
William McLeod	1st Lt.	March 1, 1755	WIA
James Buchanan	2nd Lt.	March 1, 1755	WIA
Jonathan McCulloch	2nd Lt.	March 1, 1755	WIA

NEW YORK AND SOUTH CAROLINA INDEPENDENT COMPANY DETACHMENTS

Horatio Gates	Capt.	September 15, 1754	WIA
Simon Soumain	Lt.	November 10, 1750	KIA
Richard Miller	Lt.	December 17, 1751	
Probart Howarth	Lt.	March 26, 1744	WIA
John Gray	Lt.	September 13, 1754	WIA

VOLUNTEERS

William Stone	Capt. (47th Regt.)	December 23, 1746	KIA
Mathew Floyer	Capt. (40th Regt.)	October 24, 1747	DOW

VIRGINIA PROVINCIAL COMPANIES

Adam Stephen	Capt.	February 25, 1754	WIA
William Polson	Capt.	July 21, 1754	KIA
Thomas Waggoner	Capt.	July 20, 1754	
William La Péronie	Capt.	August 25, 1754	DOW
Robert Stewart	Capt.	December 1754	
Carolus Gustavus Splitdorf	Lt.	October 29, 1754	KIA

Jonathan Hamilton	Lt.	Unknown	KIA
Jonathan Wright	Lt.	October 28, 1754	KIA
John Fenton Mercer	Lt.	July 21, 1754	
William Bronaugh	Lt.	July 20, 1754	
Henry Woodward	Lt.	April 1755	
Hector McNeill	Lt.	Unknown	
Edmond Waggoner	Ens.	January 1, 1755	KIA
Walter Stewart	Ens.	July 25, 1754	WIA
James Craig	Surgeon	July 23, 1754	

ROYAL NAVY DETACHMENT

Charles Spendelowe	Lt.		KIA
Matthew Talbot	Midshipman		KIA
Thomas Haynes	Midshipman		

Sources: Sargent, *History of an Expedition*, 359–65; Journal of a British Officer, Hamilton, *Braddock's Defeat*, 54–58; Robert Orme Letter, 1755, British Library Add. Mss. 28231, ff. 359-60; War Office Annual Army Lists (WO 65/1–2), TNA; "Keppel Manuscripts Descriptive of the Defeat of Major-General Edward Braddock," *American Antiquarian Society Transactions and Collections* 11 (1909): 171–74; "Virginia officers Killed and wounded in the last Ingagement," *GWP* 1: 342; Establishment of Virginia Companies, in Braddock to St. Clair, February 28, 1755, John Forbes Papers, Box 1, Folder 10, UVA; Arthur S. Cunningham, "March to Destiny" (2001), at Thomas and Katherine Detre Library and Archives, Senator John Heinz History Center, Pittsburgh.

APPENDIX C

French Officers and Cadets at the Battle of the Monongahela

Rank	Name	Remarks: √=Chevalier de Saint Louis
Capt.	Claude-Pierre Pécaudy de Contrecoeur	√
Capt.	Daniel-Hyacinthe-Marie Liénard de Beaujeu	KIA (Killed in Action), July 9, 1755
Capt.	Jean-Daniel Dumas	√
Capt.	François-Marie Le Marchand de Lignery	√ DOW (Died of Wounds), Battle of la Belle Famille, 1759
Lieut.	Jacques-François Legardeur de Croisille de Courtemanche	√
Lieut.	Claude-Antoine Drouet de Carqueville	DOW, July 9, 1755
Lieut.	Paul Le Borgne	√ WIA (Wounded in Action)
Lieut.	Jean-Baptiste-Philippe Testard de Montigny	√
Ens.	M. de Corbière (Corebreare)	KIA, Battle of Sainte-Foy, 1760
Ens.	Pierre-Hyacinthe Céloron de Blainville	
Ens.	Joseph-Dominique Emmanuel Le Moyne de Longueuil	
Ens.	François Pierrecot de Bailleul	√ WIA, July 9, 1755
Ens.	Jean-Clément de Sabrevois de Bleury	
Ens.	Jean-Baptiste-Léon Tarieu de Lanaudière de La Pérade	DOW, July 10, 1755
Cadet	Charles-Michel d'Ailleboust	
Cadet	Joachim-Amable Benoît de Sacquespée	
Cadet	Louis-Joseph Céloron de Blainville	
Cadet	Pierre-Charles Daneau de Muy	
Cadet	Antoine-Charles Denys de Saint-Simon	
Cadet	Hyacinthe Godefroy de Linctot	"the elder"
Cadet	Daniel-Maurice Godefroy de Linctot	"the younger"
Cadet	Jean-Baptiste Godefroy de Normanville	
Cadet	Joseph Godefroy de Normanville	
Cadet	François-Claude Hertel de Beaulac	KIA, Battle of la Belle Famille, 1759
Cadet	Joseph-Hippolyte Hertel de Saint-François	
Cadet	Joseph-Hertel de Sainte-Therèze	DOW, July 30, 1755
Cadet	Joannès	Unknown

Cadet	Joseph-Melchior de Jordy de Cabanac	
Cadet	M. Le Borgne	Brother of Lt. Paul Le Borgne
Cadet	Pierre-Jacques Le Gardeur de Croisille de Courtmanche	
Cadet	Jean Le Gardeur de la Framboise	
Cadet	M. de Normanville de Roquetaillade	KIA at Battle of la Belle Famille, 1759
Cadet	René-Marie Pécaudy de Contrecoeur	Died in Shipwreck of *L'Auguste* in 1761
Cadet	Philippe-François de Rastel de Rocheblave	(possibly Pierre-Louis)
Cadet	Joseph-Marie Rémy de Montmédy	√ WIA, July 9, 1755
Cadet	François-Abel-Étienne Rocbert de la Morandière	
Cadet	Pierre-Philippe de Saint-Ours	Listed as present, but not at the Monongahela battle (*Papiers Contrecoeur*, 384). KIA, 1757 on raid near Fort Cumberland.
Cadet	François-Charles Sabrevois de Sermonville (Sonnonville)	Died in July 1755 (killed in a duel by cadet Rocheblave)

Sources: French surnames are derived from "Relation de l'affaire de la Belle-Rivière," in "Les 'mémoires' du Chevalier de la Pause," *Rapport de l'Archiviste de la Province de Québec* 13 (1932–1933): 308; and "Account of M.ʳ Roucher of Battle of Monongahela, 1755," PRO 30/8/98, ff. 1–4, TNA.

I identified the officers' full names and identities using the following archival and genealogical sources: ANOM, Archives des Colonies, Série E, Personnel colonial ancien (XVIIe–XVIIIe); Douglas Brymner, *Report on Canadian Archives, 1886,* clxxxv; Douglas Brymner, *Report on Canadian Archives, 1888,* 44–48; George Alfred Dejordy, *Les de Jordy de Cabanac, histoire d'une ancienne famille noble du Canada,* (Montréal, 1930); *Dictionary of Canadian Biography;* Yves Drolet, *Dictionnaire généalogique et héraldique de la noblesse canadienne française du XVIIe au XIXe siècle* (Montréal, 2010); Aegidius Fauteux, *Les chevaliers de Saint-Louis en Canada* (Montréal, 1940); Aegidius Fauteux, *La famille d'Aillebout: étude généalogique et historique* (Montréal, 1917); Fernand Grenier, *Papiers Contrecoeur;* Pierre-Georges Roy, *La famille Céloron de Blainville* (Lévis, 1909); Pierre-Georges Roy, *La famille Godefroy de Tonnancour* (Lévis, 1909); Pierre-Georges Roy, *La famille Rocbert de la Morandière* (Lévis, 1905).

Casualties at Braddock's Defeat

BRITISH CASUALTIES

Source	Numbers engaged	KIA	WIA	Not Wounded	Notes
Patrick Mackellar	1,469	457	519	493	CO 5/46, f. 135, TNA
Journal of a British Officer	1,245	385	328	532	Hamilton, *Braddock's Defeat*, 58: Not clear if his numbers are inclusive of officers on his list
William Dunbar	1,100	823 killed and wounded			Kopperman, *Braddock at the Monongahela*, 188
Orme Letter	1,100	777 killed and wounded (63 officers and 714 men)			Houston, "Wagon Affair," 283–84
Philip Hughes		864 killed and wounded			Kopperman, *Braddock at the Monongahela*, 203:
Seaman's Journal	1,200	896 killed and wounded			Seaman's Journal, in Sargent, *History of an Expedition*, 383, 388
Virginia Gazette, Sept. 5, 1755	1,460	456	421	583	"Return of the Troops under General Braddock, at Frazer's Plantation, near Monongahela River, July 9, 1755" (excluding servants, and teamsters, and women)

FRENCH AND INDIAN CASUALTIES

Source	Numbers engaged	KIA	WIA	Notes
Contrecoeur	250 French 650 Indians			Kopperman, *Braddock at the Monongahela*, 250
"Etat des Morts Et blessés"	n/a	3 officers 2 Marines 3 militia 15 Indians	2 Marines 2 Canadians 12 Indians	*Papiers Contrecoeur*, 390–91 (also in ANOM D2C, 48, f. 255)
Le Courtois	36 officers and cadets 72 Marines 146 Canadians 637 Indians	20 French 13 Indians		Appendix F
Landriève	250 French 600 Indians	3 officers 5 French 19 Indians		De Bonnault, "Landriève," 502
Malartic	n/a	3 officers, 40 French	100	Pouchot, *Memoirs*, 83, n. 253
Pouchot	200 French 500 Indians			Pouchot, *Memoirs*, 83
French A	33 officers and cadets 100 Marines 100 Canadians 600 Indians			Kopperman, *Braddock at the Monongahela*, 253
French B	72 Marines 146 Canadians 637 Indians	3 officers, 25 Marines, militia, and Indians	"about as many wounded"	Kopperman, *Braddock at the Monongahela*, 256
French C	250 French 650 Indians			Kopperman, *Braddock at the Monongahela*, 257
Lotbinière	250 French 641 Indians	3 officers 30 French and Indians	"a peu près même nombre de blessé"	Shea, *Relations diverses*, 42–43

La Pause/Roucher	36 officers 72 Marines 146 Canadian 637 Indians	Beaujeu, Carqueville, and La Pérade KIA	Le Borgne, Bailleul, Normanville, Hertel de Ste.-Therèse WIA	Kopperman, *Braddock at the Monongahela*, 267–68, La Pause, "Relation," *RAPQ*, 308–9
Godefroy	150 French 500 Indians	3 officers killed; 30 total KIA ("dont les trois quarts sont Sauvages")	"Peu de blessés, tant de françois que des Sauvages"	Shea, *Relations diverses*, 13
"Relation des divers mouvements"	300 French 900 Indians	3 officers 2 Marines 3 Militia 15 Indians	2 officers 2 cadets 2 Marines 2 Militia 12 Indians	Shea, *Relations diverses*, 35–36

An Ohio Iroquois Warrior's Account of the Jumonville Affair, 1754

The National Archives (UK)

 Colonial Office Papers, CO 5/15, ff.194–195

 This account of an Ohio Iroquois participant in the Jumonville Affair and Fort Necessity—identified only as the "Chief Warrior"—was recorded during a conference with Ohio
Iroquois, Delaware, and Shawnee delegates at Mount Pleasant, or Wills's Creek (future Fort
Cumberland) in October and November 1754. Colonel James Innes was the presiding officer
as commander in chief. The officers of the New York and South Carolina independent companies attended, and Andrew Montour and Captain William Trent served as interpreters. This
document has never been studied by previous scholars, and it offers new evidence on Ohio
Iroquois motives, their perspective on the Jumonville affair and Fort Necessity, and a new twist
on Washington's role in the origins of the French and Indian War.

By Colᵗ James Innes Camp Mount Pleasant Wills Creek
 Tuesday November 5.th 1754

*In the Morning we had a private Council with Monocatootha and the chief Warriors of the Six Nations,
all whom we know to have a true Heart to us; Cap.ᵗ Rutherford, Mʳ Trent, the Interpreter and myself only
present with the Chiefs above; The Chief Warrior took out three Strings of Wampum, a large French white
Belt of Wampum describing their four Forts, three of which only are completed; a black Belt of Wampum
with the Hatchet given them by the Governor of Virginia. Upon the Strings he made the following Speech.*

 *Brothers, There will now pass some sharp Words amongst us; as we are all Warriors, we shall talk
like Men that are drunk, that speaks their Minds.*

 *Brothers, We expected you would have told us more of your Minds, but as you have told us you were
done, and what was spoke in public was only to prevent some of our People from knowing what we were
about, as you suspect they will go to the French and tell what they hear; We now open our Minds to you;
and desire that you will not be fool-hardy and depend too much upon your Strength as Colᵗ Washington
did, but that you will finish your Fort, make it strong, and build another on the other Side of the River, and
if any Indians from the French pretending to come to Council, if you don't know them, don't admit more
than two into your Camp, Least the French shou'd make Use of that Stratagem to cut you off, while they
attack you without, those that you have received as your Friends may fall upon you in your Camp or
Fort.—Gave a String of black & white Wampum.*

 *Brothers—Don't delay; Send for your people that are coming; Hasten them that you may be strong:
The French are an enterprising People; they will travel Night & Day to get an Advantage over you.*

 *Brothers—We are all Soldiers and Warriors; Some sharp Words will now pass between us; we shall
talk like drunken Men. The French have told us that the King of England and the French King had made
an Agreement to cut us off, and that the French were to begin first, but if we would hearken to them, they*

would not hurt us, but might live among them; This Speech of the French is the Reason we are so much divided at this Time, and the Reason why several of our Allies keep off and don't join us. When we were coming down, the French told us the English would put us to Death; but from our long Experience of the English faith, we told them if it was so, we could only die once, we could not live for ever, and were determined to trust to the Promises of our Brothers, which they never had yet forfeited; But the other Nations who were not so well acquainted with you, could not be prevailed upon to think as we did.

Now Brothers you have given us some Reason to suspect you; For Col. Washington *whom we convoyed to the French Fort, left us there, came through the Woods, and never thought it worth his while to come to Logs Town, or near us and give us any Account of the Speeches that passed between him and the French at the Fort which he promised to do. Now Brothers, you are Strangers to us, and none of you having heard our Accounts of what have passed, you shall hear all that we know, and what we tell you is Truth. We were all with Cap.ᵗ Trent's people when the French came down the Ohio, and the Half King told the French they had no Business there on their Hunting Grounds, pushing the French Officer with his Hand, telling them he would not allow his Brothers the English to be routed from the Land, which the Half King by the Directions of the Six Nations had allowed them to build and fortify; Upon which ensued a Scuffle, and had there been any proper Person with a small Body to have encouraged the Indians, they would not have left one Frenchman alive upon the Spot. Our Brother the Governor of Virginia having taken us by the Hand at a Treaty in Winchester where Col Fairfax was Chief, told us we were to meet Our Brother the Governor of Virginia and our Brothers the Catabas on the twentieth of May next to make a firm and lasting Peace with the Catabas and their Allies. In the spring Col.ᵉ Washington being up at the large Meadows, sent a Message to the Half King and us to hasten and come to Winchester to meet our Brother Governor Dinwiddie. Accordingly in some little Time after, he set off, we and several young Men along with us, we was so narrowly watched by the French, that immediately upon our setting off with our Wives and Children being able only to travel slow, the French sent off that Party with La Force to bring us back or to put us to Death, & they travelling faster than we could, the French got before us, and when they went [off] the Road to encamp we tracked them, when we came up to that place and [torn] to tell Col.ᵉ Washington where they were: So they and our [G] traveling all Night and coming close to the place where the French were encamped, we directed Col.ᵉ Washington with his Men to go up the Hill, straight to the French where they were, not above fifty Yards off when they must come in Sight of the French Camp below them: The Half King with his Warriors went to the left to intercept them if they should go that Way, and Monacatootha with another young Warrior [f. 195] Cherokee Jack went to the Right, and left Col.ᵉ Washington: When they came near the Top of the Hill, Col.ᵉ Washington begun himself and fired and then his people, which the French returned, two or three Fires of as many Peices as would go off, being rainy Weather, and then run off, one of Col.ᵉ Washington's people being more forward than the rest and before the Company, they unluckily shot their own Man, and wounded a Frenchman in the Cheek; So the French having taken to their Heels and running, happening to run the Way the Half King was with his Warriors, eight of them met with their Destiny by the Indian Tomayhawks, upon which the others remaining Survivors turned short and ran the other Way where Monacatootha was, and upon his calling to them, they observed they were surrounded, and Monacatootha knowing La Force he came up and surrendered himself with the others to Monacatootha who carried them to Col.ᵉ Washington. Immediately the Half King came up, and told the French, now I will let you see that the Six Nations can kill as well as the French, which you said we know nothing of, and as you came after me to take my Life and my Childrens, I now will let you see how I used to do with some of your People before in time of old, and that I am not afraid, so offering with his Tomayhawk to La Force, La Force got behind Col.ᵉ Washington who interposed, otherwise we do believe they would have been all put to Death. One of the French Company having some Way got off through the Bushes went back for the French Fort, but in his Way was met with some of our Indians; They found he spoke English and therefore persuaded him to return to his Brethren the English, which he refused several Times, upon which they killed and scalped him and brought the Account thereof to the Half King and us, after which we proceeded to the Meadows, and the prisoners sent down to Williamsburgh.*

After this Col.ᵉ Washington never consulted with us nor yet to take our Advice, as we knew the French were strong, and now it was dangerous Times we wanted a place of Security or Fort for our Wives and Children that they might not be left and exposed, and have only the Woods to run to, which was no Satisfaction to us at all, and this prevented our coming to Winchester to see our Brother the Governor.

Then happened the Battle at the Meadows, before which we gave Col. Washington an Account of how strong the French were, and when they were just as hand, would not believe us; So when we saw and heard them fire at one another we thought they were in earnest, but what afterwards past in Council between him and the French we never could yet understand. Had it been us, we must have been all killed or taken Prisoners without we had run away, for we never council in Time of War. Then Col. Washington carrying all his People down to the great Towns, and leaving all this thin settled Country to be protected by a few Strangers, and never in all this Time to return back or come with other Men, as there are Men enough in all this great Province; All which gives us more Reason to suspect that what the French told us had some Foundation, and we have been easily kept from coming all this Time, from seeing our Brothers, only as we have struck the French, we cannot expect but that they will strike us when they can.

French Account of Beaujeu
at the Monongahela

Archives du Calvados, Caen, France

Fonds Surlaville, Série F-1859

Michel-Pierre-Augustin-Thomas Le Courtois des Bourbes à son cousin Surlaville, 20 octobre
1755

The account of the Battle of the Monongahela was written by Michel-Pierre-Augustin-Thomas
Le Courtois des Bourbes to his "dear cousin," Michel Le Courtois de Surlaville in October
1755. Des Bourbes was a grenadier lieutenant in the Louisbourg garrison in the 1750s. His
cousin, Surlaville, was an effective officer who brought fiscal and military reforms to the Île
Royale garrison before returning to France in 1753. Like most all French accounts of the
battle, this one was not written by an eyewitness but was undoubtedly drawn from a summary
(*précis*) written by a veteran of the action who accompanied Beaujeu. It offers the clearest evidence to date of the tactics that Beaujeu and the Indians employed from the moment they
departed Fort Duquesne to their attack on the British column on July 9, 1755.

Transcription and translation by the author.

Summary of the action that occurred in Canada three leagues from Fort Duquesne, July 9, 1755

*M. Duquesne, governor-general of Canada, informed that the English were departing from Boston
and Halifax in order to take Fort Duquesne, dispatched messieurs Beaujeu, Dumas, and Delignerie, captains, in the early spring to protect it with a detachment of regular troops of the Independent Companies of
the Marine, militia, and Indians, with orders to send several small parties to harass the enemy on his
march. Having arrived at the fort, they learned that the English were already returned to Fort Necessity,
which they had restored, that they numbered around 3000 men, and that Lord Braddock was general of
this army. M. de Contrecoeur, captain, commanded at our fort, the garrison of which numbered 200 men.*

*Our scouts reported on June 26 that the English had left their fort and that they marched with
many wagons and cannons.*

*On July 7 we learned by Huron scouts, that they were no more than 10 leagues from the fort, which
was confirmed by the return of M. Rigauville, who went out with a party of 120 Hurons and Sauteurs on
June 28.*

*July 8 was spent assembling all the Indian nations into one body. The same day the Iroquois and
Shawnees of the Five Nations who inhabit the area surrounding Fort Duquesne, and who hitherto had
remained neutral, came to join themselves to M. de Beaujeu.*

*On July 9 Captain Beaujeu departed at daybreak with a detachment of 891 men, among which
there were 2 captains, 4 lieutenants, 6 ensigns, 23 cadets, 72 men of the Regular troops, 146 militia, and
637 Indians. M. de Contrecoeur kept with him in the fort only the troops necessary to defend it.*

*M. de Beaujeu, in command, learned by the scouts whom he had sent out before him, that the English
had halted in the woods, in a road that they had built the year before, from Fort Necessity up to 3 leagues from
Fort Duquesne; that they were formed in a column, the entire center of which, from the head to the tail, was
filled with their wagons and baggage; that a few Grenadier companies marched at the head of this column,
around 15 men abreast supported by 2 pieces of cannon, that 2 small corps of light cavalry formed the advanced guard and the rearguard of this army, and that the rest of their artillery was located toward the center.*

Certain of the enemy's position, M. de Beaujeu divided the Indian nations and spread them out on both sides of the road in the woods; he placed at the head of each nation an officer or cadet who spoke the language and ordered them to reveal themselves only when he had attacked the enemy in front. Then, he formed his soldiers and militia about 15 ranks deep, which was nearly the same front that the English grenadier companies presented. In this order, he attacked them with intrepid courage. They received him on their side with a heavy fire; and opened their ranks after every discharge to the right and to the left to leave a free passage to the cannons that they concealed, charged with grapeshot; they shook our detachment a little, when all at once our Indians, who had advantageously posted themselves behind trees, fired their discharge (a discharge all the more terrible as their fire was continual, and as you know, dear cousin, no shot of theirs is ever false).

This unexpected fire surprised the English. To remedy this, they were compelled to face on both sides of the road. This movement diminished the effort that they had made toward the front, giving our detachment time to reform and to fight more equally. M. de Beaujeu, having been killed in the 3rd discharge, Dumas took command, seconded by M. de Lignerie. He ordered our soldiers to fix bayonets and charge the English. They in turn gave way and made a fire in retreat. Our Indians, seeing them withdraw toward the tail of the column after having fired, took this movement for a flight, and came out of the woods, war clubs in hand, and made their horrible cries, and fell upon them with inexpressible fury. The English, unable to withstand this shock, although they had their bayonets fixed, broke ranks and unable to rally because of the poor disposition of their order of battle, fled in disorder. Half of our detachment pursued them, almost to the banks of the Monongahela, while the other half remained to guard the battlefield.

The fighting began around 11:30 in the morning and ended around 4 or 5 in the evening. The English have lost 1,250 on the battlefield; we have captured their 4 pieces of cannon of 12-pound bore, 2 others of 6-pound bore, 4 Howitzers of 7½ inch diameter. 11 mortars all of brass. 19,740 musket cartridges. 17 barrels of gunpowder of 100 pounds, 192 howitzer shells of 43 pounds, 55 grenades of 6½ pounds and 157 shells of 7 pounds, a great number of iron shovels and tools proper for conducting a siege, many provisions, the greater of which, in truth, has been squandered by the Indians on the battlefield, several wagons, 500 horses, 100 oxen or cows, and many sheep.

The spoils taken by our soldiers and Indians amounts to more than 180,000 livres. We have taken several prisoners, among whom we found 7 women. We have also found several of these women among the dead.

The mistress of General Braddock, beautiful as love, dressed in Amazon and riding a superb horse, was killed while fighting at her lover's side, despite all our desire to protect her. Her lover himself was mortally wounded but carried off by the English. The effects and jewelry found on Braddock's mistress were estimated to be worth 10,000 livres.

We have lost on our side 20 men, among whom were messieurs Beaujeu, Quarqueville, (Lieutenant), and La Perrade (ensign), and more than 13 Indians. We have had very few wounded.

Since this action, English deserters have claimed that Braddock was dead, that all the artillery officers and engineers had been killed, and that of all the officers of this army, there were only eleven saved (of which there were five wounded), with around 300 men.

Messieurs Du Buisson, officer, and Vieux Pont Normanville, cadet, were sent out after the battle in order to observe the English retreat. They have been almost to Fort Necessity, which they found partly burned. They have found there 8 mortars for grenades, 125 half-burned supply wagons, 225 staved barrels of gunpowder in a stream, several cannonballs, 700 shells, 19 grates for heated shot, and numbers of trunks. In that of M. Braddock were found several letters of one Stobo, an English officer and prisoner at Quebec since last year, who sent word to this general of everything that had taken place in Canada. In the general's chests, the royal instructions for his campaign were found. It is said that they revealed that he must first seize Fort Duquesne, then Fort de la Riviere au Boeuf, Fort Presque Isle, and from there to establish himself at Niagara.

APPENDIX G

Midshipman Thomas Gill, Royal Navy

Author of the "Seaman's Journal"

One of the most important and revealing of all accounts of Braddock's Campaign is the "Journal of the Proceedings of the Detachment of Seamen," often called the Seaman's Journal after its heretofore unknown author, who some scholars have incorrectly identified as Lieutenant Charles Spendelow.[1] The handwriting in the original journal, currently preserved at the Library of the Royal Artillery Museum at Woolwich, reveals that one author wrote the entirety of its entries, dated from April 10 to August 1, 1755.[2] The author was unquestionably an officer, and his journal was not his personal diary but an official record of the Royal Navy detachment's proceedings. He associated with other officers such as Lieutenant Spendelow, performed the duties of an officer, and attended events for officers at Braddock's tent such as the Indian conferences, the speeches of which he accurately paraphrased. Finally, he claimed that his account of the Battle of Monongahela was "related by some of the Principal Officers that day in the field"—an unlikely association were he an enlisted sailor.

The author's identity can be definitively established by a document in the Admiralty Papers of the UK National Archives entitled "An Account of the Detachm.t of Seamen sent with his Excellency General Braddock on the Late Expedition Against Fort du Quesne, October 30, 1755."[3] The Royal Navy detachment led by Lieutenant Charles Spendelow included three midshipmen: Matthew (or Mathias) Talbot and Thomas Haynes of HMS *Centurion*, and Thomas Gill of HMS *Norwich*. All but one of those four officers were with Braddock's army at the Battle of the Monongahela on July 9, 1755. One was left behind at Fort Cumberland because of illness. The document lists Midshipman Thomas Gill as "Left Sick at Will's Creek not in the Action" [i.e., July 9, 1755].[4] Gill's own journal entry for June 10 also confirms that "The Director of the Hospital came to see me in Camp, and found me so ill of fever and flux, that he desired me to stay behind, so I went into the Hospital, & the Army marched with the Train &c."[5] Another Admiralty document confirms that Midshipman Thomas Haynes was "the only Officer that survived of the Detachment of Seamen under General Braddocks Command that were present at the Action near the Banks of the Monongahela."[6] The journal remained in Gill's possession for a time, for he expanded his original notes into a lengthier version (which was published in Sargent's 1856 *History of an Expedition*). The first and largest section of the journal (from April 10 to June 10, 1755) represents Gill's authentic observations. It is my contention that the material dating from June 15 through July 1755 (relating to Braddock's column) was largely the testimony of Midshipman Thomas Haynes, the only naval officer who survived the battle. It is noteworthy that between the original and extended versions of the journal, Gill made little if any alteration to that section pertaining to Braddock's march and the battle of July 9. This discovery establishes the authority of the author and lends greater credibility to one of the finest accounts of Braddock's Expedition.

APPENDIX H

Historic Sites Relating to Braddock's Expedition

Colonial Williamsburg, Williamsburg, Virginia
Carlyle House Historic Park, Alexandria, Virginia
George Washington's Mount Vernon, Virginia
Braddock's Road (see Norman Baker's *Braddock's Road* (2013) for the finest field guide)
Emmanuel Episcopal Church, Cumberland, Maryland
Big Savage Mountain, Savage River State Forest, Maryland
Casselman River Bridge State Park, Grantsville, Maryland
Fort Necessity National Battlefield (NPS), Farmington, Pennsylvania
Braddock Grave Unit, Fort Necessity National Battlefield
Jumonville Glen Unit, Fort Necessity National Battlefield
Jumonville Camp and Retreat Center, Jumonville, Pennsylvania (Site of Braddock Road
    Preservation Association's Annual Jumonville Seminar on French and Indian War)
Yough River Park, Connellsville Area Historical Society, Connellsville, Pennsylvania
Braddock's Battlefield History Center, Braddock, Pennsylvania
Fort Pitt Museum, Pittsburgh, Pennsylvania
Senator John Heinz History Center, Pittsburgh, Pennsylvania
Fort Ligonier, Ligonier, Pennsylvania
Bushy Run Battlefield, Jeannette, Pennsylvania
Fort LeBoeuf Museum, Waterford, Pennsylvania
Old Fort Niagara, Youngstown, New York

ABBREVIATIONS

Add. Mss.	Additional Manuscripts, British Library
ABF	Joyce E. Chaplin, ed., *Benjamin Franklin's Autobiography* (New York, 2012)
ADM	Admiralty Papers, The National Archives (UK)
ANOM	Archives Nationales d'Outre-Mer, Aix-en-Provence, France
ASQ-VV	Archives du Séminaire de Québec, Fonds Viger- Verreau
BL	British Library
BP	Sylvester K. Stevens, Donald H. Kent, and Louis M. Waddell, eds., *The Papers of Henry Bouquet*, 6 vols. (Harrisburg,1951–1994)
BOB	General Braddock's Orderly Book, in Will H. Lowdermilk, *History of Cumberland* (Washington, D.C., 1878), I–LX
BRH	*Bulletin des recherches historiques*
CLP	*Charles Lee Papers* (New-York Historical Society, 1872–1875)
CO	Colonial Office Papers, The National Archives (UK)
DCB	*Dictionary of Canadian Biography*
DP	Robert Alonzo Brock, ed., *The Official Records of Robert Dinwiddie*, 2 vols. (Richmond, 1883–1884)
DRCHNY	E. B. O'Callaghan, and Berthold Fernow, eds., *Documents Relative to the Colonial History of the State of New York*, 14 vols. (Albany, 1855)
ECCO	Eighteenth-Century Collections Online, Gale Digital Collections http://gdc.gale.com/products/eighteenth-century-collections-online/
GWP	*Papers of George Washington, Colonial Series*
GWR	Fred Anderson, ed., *George Washington Remembers: Reflections on the French and Indian War* (Oxford, 2004)
HL	Huntington Library, San Marino, California
HOB	Halkett's Orderly Book, in Charles Hamilton, *Braddock's Defeat* (Norman, 1959), 61–126
HSP	Historical Society of Pennsylvania, Philadelphia, Pennsylvania
JBO	Journal of a British Officer, in Charles Hamilton, *Braddock's Defeat* (Norman, 1959), 39–58
JSCL	Sir John St. Clair Letterbook, John Forbes Papers, University of Virginia
JSAHR	*Journal of the Society for Army Historical Research*
LAC	Library and Archives Canada, Ottawa
LO	Lord Loudoun Papers, Huntington Library
LOC	Library of Congress, Washington, D.C.
MHS	Massachusetts Historical Society
MANA	Stanley Pargellis, *Military Affairs in North America, 1748–1765* (1936)
MPCP	Samuel Hazard, ed., *Minutes of the Provincial Council of Pennsylvania*, 16 vols. (Philadelphia, 1852)
NYHS	New-York Historical Society, New York City
ODNB	H. C. G. Matthew and Brian Harrison, eds. *Oxford Dictionary of National Biography*, 60 vols., Oxford University Press, 2004

Orme	Journal of Captain Robert Orme, in Winthrop Sargent, *History of an Expedition against Fort Duquesne in 1755* (1856), 281–358.
Papiers Contrecoeur	Fernand Grenier, ed., *Papiers Contrecoeur et autres documents concernant le Contrecoeur conflit anglo-français sur l'Ohio de 1745 à 1756* (Québec, 1952)
PA	*Pennsylvania Archives*, 9 series, 138 vols. Philadelphia and Harrisburg, 1852–1949
PBF	Leonard Labaree et al., eds., *The Papers of Benjamin Franklin* (New Haven, 1959–)
PH	*Pennsylvania History*
PMHB	*Pennsylvania Magazine of History and Biography*
PSA	Pennsylvania State Archives, Harrisburg, Pennsylvania
RCB	Journal of Captain Robert Cholmley's Batman, in Charles Hamilton, *Braddock's Defeat* (Norman, 1959), 5–36
Sharpe	William Hand Browne, ed., *Archives of Maryland*, Vol. 6: *Correspondence of Horatio Sharpe, Vol. 1, 1753–1757* (Baltimore, 1888).
SWJP	James Sullivan et al., eds., *The Papers of Sir William Johnson*, 14 vols. (Albany, 1921–1963).
TNA	The National Archives, United Kingdom
VMHB	*Virginia Magazine of History and Biography*
WLCL	William L. Clements Library, University of Michigan, Ann Arbor
WO	War Office Papers, The National Archives (UK)
WMQ	*William and Mary Quarterly*, 3rd series
WPHM	*Western Pennsylvania Historical Magazine*

NOTES

EDITOR'S NOTE

1. John Adams to Hezekiah Niles, Feb. 13, 1818, in *The Works of John Adams*, ed. Charles Francis Adams, 10 vols. (Boston, 1856), 10: 282. Adams raised a similar question in another letter to Thomas Jefferson on August 24, 1815.
2. Richard L. Merritt, *Symbols of American Community, 1735–1775* (New Haven, CT: Yale University Press, 1966), 61; for the inspiration of Adams's thought see Ibid., 13.
3. David L. Preston, *The Texture of Contact: European and Indian Settler Communities on the Frontiers of Iroquoia, 1667–1783* (Lincoln: University of Nebraska Press, 2009).

INTRODUCTION

1. Jessie Callan Kennedy, "Pennies for History," *Carnegie Magazine* 33, no. 1 (February 1959): 66–69; Robert M. Grom, *Braddock, Allegheny County* (Charleston, 2008). After graduating from Braddock High School, Jessie Callan became a librarian, serving at the New York Public Library and also as head of the children's department at the Braddock Carnegie Library: *Library Journal* 39 (November 1914): 857; *Morning Oregonian* (Portland), October 2, 1919, p. 9.
2. "Planning to Buy Famous Painting for Braddock," *Pittsburgh Gazette Times*, October 4, 1911, p. 10.
3. Callan, "Pennies for History," 66–67.
4. Barbara S. Groseclose, *Emanuel Leutze, 1816–1868: Freedom Is Our Only King* (Washington, D.C., 1975), 91; Sylvia Neely, "Mason Locke Weems's 'Life of George Washington' and the Myth of Braddock's Defeat," *VMHB* 107 (Winter 1999): 45–72.
5. *GWP* 1: 339–40.
6. George Washington Parke Custis, the adopted son of George Washington, popularized this story in his 1827 play, *The Indian Prophecy*. He may have derived it from Henry Trumbull's *History of the Discovery of America* (Norwich, 1812), 114–15. The legend is superficially based on Washington's account of his 1770 meeting with the Seneca leader Guyasuta, who had met Washington during his journey to the Ohio Country in 1753, and who may have been at Braddock's Defeat. But Washington's journal entry says nothing of any conversation about the Monongahela battle.
7. Examples from 1755 include "General Braddock's Defeat" (*Sharpe* 1: 368) and Résumé de lettres de Vaudreuil, décembre 1755, ANOM COL C¹¹A, Vol. 100, f. 301 ("la defaite de Bradok"); "Action near the Monongahela July 9th 1755" (LO 696). Nineteenth-century historians continued to employ both "Braddock's Defeat" and the "Battle of the Monongahela" interchangeably—e.g., Jared Sparks, in *The Life of George Washington* (Boston, 1839), ix, 62; and in *The Writings of George Washington* (Boston, 1837), Vol. 1: xvi, 64, 77. French Canadian historians have tended to favor the name *la bataille du Malanguelée*—e.g., Albert Desbiens, "9 juillet 1755: la bataille du Malangueulé," in *Histoire du Canada: Une expérience tricentenaire* (Montréal, 1967), 51–63.
8. The interpretations described are reflected in Paul Kopperman, *Braddock at the Monongahela* (Pittsburgh, 1977), 116; Francis Jennings, *Empire of Fortune* (New York, 1988); Stanley McCrory Pargellis, "Braddock's Defeat," *AHR* 41 (January 1936): 253–69; and Robert L. Yaple, "Braddock's Defeat: The Theories and a Reconsideration," *JSAHR* 46 (Winter 1968): 194–201. Franklin Thayer Nichols's "The Braddock Expedition, 1754–1755"

(Ph.D. diss., Harvard University 1946) is the best military history to date, but it superficially dealt with French sources and dismissed the Indians as irrelevant.

9. Francis-Joseph Audet, *Jean-Daniel Dumas: Le Héros de la Monongahela* (Montréal, 1920) and Monongahela de Beaujeu, *The Hero of the Monongahela*, trans. G. E. Hawes (New York, 1913).

10. Emanuel Leutze zu Julius Erhard, 22 February 1858, Erhard Stiftung, Städtisches Museum Swäbisch-Gmünd im Prediger. Many thanks to museum director Monica Boosen for providing me with a transcription of Leutze's letter and to my colleague Michael Barrett for translation assistance.

11. See Francis Parkman, *Montcalm and Wolfe* (reprint, New York: Barnes & Noble, 2005), 112 (Pontiac); Allan Eckert, *A Sorrow in Our Hearts: The Life of Tecumseh* (New York, 1992), 127, places Tecumseh's father, Pucksinwah, at Braddock's Defeat but cites no evidence; on Guyasuta, see Series S, Draper's Notes, Vol. 4, ff. 9, 68, 94, 236, Draper Manuscripts; Thomas Abler, "Kayashota?," *DCB* 4: 408–10; Thomas S. Abler, e-mail communication with author, November 27, 2012; on Black Hoof, see Charlotte Reeve Conover, ed., *Recollections of Sixty Years by John Johnston* (n.p.: John Henry Patterson, 1915), 11, and contradictory evidence in Joseph Ficklin, "The History of Black Hoof, a Chief of the Shawnee Nation," and Joseph Ficklin to Lyman Draper, April 1, 1847, Daniel Boone Papers, Series C, Vol. 13, Draper Manuscripts.

12. John J. Barsotti, ed., *Scoouwa: James Smith's Indian Captivity Narrative* (Columbus, 1996), 163, 167.

13. E.g., Thomas E. Crocker, *Braddock's March* (Yardley, Pa., 2009).

14. John St. Clair Letterbook, in the John Forbes Papers at the University of Virginia; Sheldon S. Cohen, "Major William Sparke along the Monongahela: A New Historical Account of Braddock's Defeat," *PH* 62 (October 1995): 546–56; Elaine Breslaw, "A Dismal Tragedy: Drs. Alexander and John Hamilton Comment on Braddock's Defeat," *Maryland Historical Magazine* 75 (1980): 118–44; Alan Houston, "Benjamin Franklin and the 'Wagon Affair' of 1755," *WMQ* 66 (April 2009): 235–86.

15. Pargellis, "Braddock's Defeat," 259; Kopperman, *Braddock at the Monongahela*, 61, 64.

16. Martin Van Creveld, *Supplying War: Logistics from Wallenstein to Patton* (Cambridge, 1977), 1 (Van Creveld's paraphrase of Jomini).

17. J. F. C. Fuller, *The British Light Infantry in the Eighteenth Century* (London, 1925), 85.

18. J. W. Fortescue, *A History of the British Army*, Vol. 2 (London, 1910), 2: 286.

19. François Furstenberg, "The Significance of the Trans-Appalachian Frontier in Atlantic History," *American Historical Review*, Vol. 113, no. 3 (June 2008): 647–77.

20. William Serrin, *Homestead: The Glory and Tragedy of an American Steel Town* (New York, 1992), xxiv.

21. Marjorie Michaux, "Library Dream Moves into Action," *Pittsburgh Post-Gazette*, April 16, 1987, Section PG East, 13–14. See also Robert T. Messner, *Reflections from Braddock's Battlefield* (Braddock, Pa., 2005) for the preservation efforts of the Braddock's Field Historical Society. Messner was responsible for restoring Leutze's painting to the Braddock Carnegie Library in 2001.

22. Marylynne Pitz, "New Museum Charts Braddock's Defeat," *Pittsburgh Post-Gazette*, August 18, 2012, p. D-1; Braddock's Battlefield History Center, http://www.braddocksbattlefield .com/. The new center is located at the ravine (running along Sixth Street in North Braddock) where the British grenadiers clashed with the French and Indians at the beginning of the battle, and where Beaujeu was killed.

CHAPTER 1

1. Recent studies of the French and Indian War have usually glossed over the significance of Contrecoeur's takeover of the Forks. See the important essay by Douglas MacGregor, "The Shot Not Heard around the World: Trent's Fort and the Opening of the War for Empire," *PH* 74 (Summer 2007): 354–73.

2. *DRCHNY* 10: 206; David L. Preston, *The Texture of Contact: European and Indian Settler Communities on the Frontiers of Iroquoia, 1667–1783* (Lincoln, 2009).

3. Michael McConnell, *A Country Between: The Upper Ohio Valley and Its Peoples, 1724–1774* (Lincoln, 1992), 89; Donald H. Kent, *The French Invasion of Western Pennsylvania* (Harrisburg, 1954), 47; William A. Hunter, "Tanaghrisson," *DCB* 3: 613–14.

4. Sylvester K. Stevens and Donald H. Kent, eds., *Wilderness Chronicles of Northwestern Pennsylvania* (Harrisburg, 1941; reprint: Lewisburg, Pa., 2002), 3–5, 9–12, 14–16; Richard White, *The Middle Ground: Indians, Empires, and Republics in the Great Lakes Region, 1650–1815* (Cambridge, 1991); Hanna disputes La Salle's voyage in *The Wilderness Trail; or, The Ventures and Adventures of the Pennsylvania Traders on the Allegheny Path*, 2 vols. (New York, 1911), 2: 87–124; *DRCHNY* 10: 227 (watershed claims).

5. Paul W. Mapp, *The Elusive West and the Contest for Empires, 1713–1763* (Chapel Hill, 2010), chap. 10; Matt Schumann and Karl Schweizer, *The Seven Years' War: A Transatlantic History* (New York, 2008), 19–34; Daniel Baugh, *The Global Seven Years' War, 1754–1763* (London, 2011), 28–33, 53–59; and Frank W. Brecher, *Losing a Continent: France's North American Policy, 1753–1763* (Westport, 1998).

6. Duquesne to Rouillé, August 20, 1753, *DRCHNY* 10: 257; Duquesne to Contrecoeur, October 18, 1752, *Papiers Contrecoeur*, 17; Kent, *French Invasion*, 27–68. See Rouillé's orders to Duquesne, May 15 and July 9, 1752, in Theodore Calvin Pease, ed., *Collections of the Illinois State Historical Library*, Vol. 29, *Illinois on the Eve of the Seven Years' War, 1747–1755* (Springfield, 1940), 627–35, 648–51. For numbers in Marin's party, see Louise Dechêne, *Le Peuple, l'État et la Guerre au Canada sous le Régime français* (Montréal, 2008), 498–99.

7. Francis-Joseph Audet, *Contrecoeur: Famille, Seigneurie, Paroisse, Village* (Montréal, 1940), 30–41; André Côté, "Pécaudy De Contrecoeur, François-Antoine," *DCB* 1: 535–36; Fernand Grenier, "Pécaudy De Contrecoeur, Antoine," *DCB* 3: 547; and Fernand Grenier, "Pécaudy De Contrecoeur, Claude-Pierre," *DCB* 4: 617–18.

8. Duquesne to Contrecoeur, and Orders to Contrecoeur January 27, 1754, Pean to Contrecoeur, January 28, 1754, and Duquesne to Contrecoeur, May 11, 1754, *Papiers Contrecoeur*, 93 ("Le S.ʳ Ch.ᵉʳ Le Mercier vous mene L'elite des Canadiens et des Troupes"), 96–97, 98, 125 (mission); Contrecoeur to Minister, November 28, 1755, Stevens and Kent, *Wilderness Chronicles*, 85–86; Sylvester K. Stevens, Donald H. Kent, and Emma Edith Woods, eds., *Travels in New France by J.C.B.* (Harrisburg, 1941), 54–55 (detachment's journey); René Chartrand first identified J.C.B. as Joseph-Charles Bonin: see his *Canadian Military Heritage*, Vol. 1, 1000–1754 (Montréal, 1993), 123–24, 207.

9. Duquesne to Contrecoeur, January 27 and April 15, 1754, *Papiers Contrecoeur*, 93, 115 (Indians).

10. Lois Mulkearn, ed., *George Mercer Papers Relating to the Ohio Company of Virginia* (Pittsburgh, 1954), 86–88; Stevens et al., *Travels in New France by J.C.B.*, 55–56; Jean Pariseau, "Le Mercier, François-Marc-Antoine," *DCB* 4: 458–60.

11. "Paroles de Contrecoeur aux Sauvages," 16 avril 1754, *Papiers Contrecoeur*, 116–17 (author translation). Some translations of the *Papiers Contrecoeur* are from an unpublished translation by Donald H. Kent of the Pennsylvania Historical and Museum Commission (PHMC). I am grateful to Doug MacGregor, formerly of the PHMC, for sharing a copy of Kent's work. For the confrontation between the Half King and Le Mercier, see Appendix E.

12. "Ensign Ward's Deposition, May 7, 1754," in William M. Darlington, ed., *Christopher Gist's Journals.* (Pittsburgh, 1893), 275–78; Contrecoeur to Vaudreuil, June 21, 1755, *Papiers Contrecoeur*, 364.

13. Duquesne to Contrecoeur, May 11, 1754, *Papiers Contrecoeur*, 125 (conduct).

14. *Pennsylvania Gazette*, May 9, 1754, p. 2; *New-York Mercury*, May 13, 1754; *Boston Gazette*, May 21, 1754.

15. April 19, 1754, *GWD* 1: 174–75; *GWP* 1: 65; GW to Dinwiddie, April 25, 1754, *GWP* 1: 87; Dinwiddie to Board of Trade, June 18, 1754, *DP* 1: 206; Cabinet Minutes, June 26, 1754, in Theodore Calvin Pease, ed., *Collections of the Illinois State Historical Library*, Vol. 27, *Anglo-French Boundary Disputes in the West, 1749–1763* (Springfield: Illinois State Historical Library, 1940), 48; Robinson to Dinwiddie, July 5, 1754, in Louis Knott Koontz, *Robert*

Dinwiddie: Correspondence Illustrative of His Career in American Colonial Government and Westward Expansion (Berkeley, 1951), 573–77; "Encroachments made by the French," 1754, and King's Order for General Reprizals, 1755, Add. Mss. 33029, ff. 102–103, 318–21; and R. C. Simmons and P. D. G. Thomas, eds., *Proceedings and Debates of the British Parliaments Respecting North America, 1754–1783*, Vol. 1: 1754–1764 (Millwood, N.Y., 1982), 105, 167, 171.

16. *Sharpe* 1: 104–105; CO 5/211, ff. 39–40, 53–54.

17. Byrd to Collinson, July 18, 1736, in Marion Tinling, ed., *The Correspondence of the Three William Byrds of Westover, Virginia, 1684–1776* (Richmond, 1977), 2: 493; Warren Hofstra, "'The Extension of His Majesties Dominions': The Virginia Backcountry and the Reconfiguration of Imperial Frontiers," *Journal of American History* 84 (March 1998): 1281–312; Stephen Saunders Webb, *Marlborough's America* (New Haven, 2013), 356–58; David Hackett Fischer and James C. Kelly, *Bound Away: Virginia and the Westward Movement* (Charlottesville, 2000), 103–34; Francis Jennings, *Ambiguous Iroquois Empire* (New York, 1984), 354–62.

18. James Titus, *The Old Dominion at War: Society, Politics, and Warfare in Late Colonial Virginia* (Columbia, 1991), chap. 1; Kenneth P. Bailey, *The Ohio Company of Virginia and the Westward Movement, 1748–1792* (Glendale, Ca., 1939), 17–60, 298–303 (1748 petitions). See also Petition of John Hanbury, ca. 1754, CO 5/7, ff. 351–53 and Ohio Company Petition, 1754, CO 5/1328, ff. 69–72.

19. Bailey, *Ohio Company*, 17–60; Norman L. Baker, *Braddock's Road: Mapping the British Expedition from Alexandria to the Monongahela* (Charleston, 2013), 16–19; Francis Jennings, *Empire of Fortune: Crowns, Colonies and Tribes in the Seven Years' War in America* (New York: W. W. Norton, 1988), 37–45 (Logstown); David B. Trimble, "Christopher Gist and Settlement on the Monongahela, 1752–1754," *VMHB* 63 (January 1755): 15–27; Mulkearn, *George Mercer Papers*, 147–48 (town).

20. Mulkearn, *George Mercer Papers*, 86; Frégault, in *Canada: The War of the Conquest*, trans. Margaret M. Cameron (Toronto, 1969) argues that the French error was in "underestimating the influence of those 'few private traders'" (19); *Maryland Gazette*, January 30, 1755.

21. Dinwiddie to Abercromby, July 24, 1754, *DP* 1: 236; 1: 102 (Halifax); Dinwiddie to Halifax, October 25, 1754, *DP* 1: 366; A.W. Parker, "Robert Dinwiddie," *ODNB* 16: 251; Louis Knott Koontz, *Robert Dinwiddie: His Career in American Colonial Government and Westward Expansion* (Glendale, Ca., 1941), 51–65, 157–72; John R. Alden, *Robert Dinwiddie: Servant of the Crown* (Charlottesville, 1973), ch. 4.

22. Dinwiddie to Cresap, January 23, 1752, *DP* 1: 17–18; Dinwiddie to Board of Trade, June 16, 1753, CO 5/1327, ff. 637–42; Holdernesse to Governors in America, August 28, 1753, *DRCHNY* 6: 794–95; Instruction to Robert Dinwiddie, August 1753, LO 450; King's Order in Council, August 10, 1753, CO 5/1328, f. 1 (artillery cost of £888); King's instructions to Dinwiddie, August 28, 1753, CO 5/211, ff. 33–40; John Pownall to Dinwiddie, August 27, 1753, in Koontz, *Dinwiddie Correspondence*, 329–30; See also Steven G. Greiert, "The Board of Trade and Defense of the Ohio Valley, 1749–1753," *WPHM* 64 (January 1981): 1–32; Baugh, *Global Seven Years' War*, 59–60.

23. Stephen Brumwell, *George Washington: Gentleman Warrior* (London 2012), Chap. 1 (Lawrence); *GWP* 1: 8–37 (surveying); Washington surveyed Henry Enoch's and Friend Cox's plantations in 1750 (23, 25); 226 (bent).

24. *The Journal of Major George Washington: An Account of His First Official Mission, Made as Emissary from the Governor of Virginia to the Commandant of French Forces on the Ohio, October 1753–January 1754* (Williamsburg, 1959), 16 (Air); *GWP* 1: 51n, 60–61, 98 n. 3, 107; Joseph L. Peyser, trans. and ed., *Jacques Legardeur de Saint-Pierre: Officer, Gentleman, Entrepreneur* (East Lansing, 1996).

25. *Journal of GW*, 13, 17; Earl of Holdernesse to Dinwiddie, January 18, 1754, LO 466A; Dinwiddie to Trent, January 27, 1754, *DP* 1: 55–57; *GWP* 1: 63–69; Sewall Elias Swick, *William Trent and the West* (Harrisburg, 1947), 50–54; Titus, *Old Dominion at War*, 28–42.

26. *GWR*, 16; *GWP* 1: 88, 91 n 8 (Conotocarious); J. Frederick Fausz, "'Engaged in Enterprises Pregnant with Terror': George Washington's Formative Years among the Indians," in

Warren Hofstra, ed., *George Washington and the Virginia Backcountry* (Madison, 1998), 115–55 (John Washington).

27. GW to Fry, May 23, 1754, GW to Dinwiddie, May 27, 1754, *GWP* 1: 101, 105, 65 (orders), 86 (numbers, spirit); *DGW* 1: 191–93 (May 24–27); Donald H. Kent, ed., "Contrecoeur's Copy of George Washington's Journal for 1754," *PH* 19 (January 1952): 1–32, May 10 entry, 15–16.

28. Kent, "Contrecoeur's Copy," 21; Adam Stephen, "The Ohio Expedition of 1754," *PMHB* 18 (1894): 43–50, at 46 (Silver Heels); Dinwiddie to Half King, May 8, 1754, CO 5/14, ff. 383–84.

29. Marcel Trudel's 1952 essay in *Revue d'histoire de l'Amerique française* remains one of the finest and most objective analyses of the incident: Marcel Trudel, "The Jumonville Affair," trans. and ed. Donald H. Kent, *PH* 21 (October 1954): 351–81; see also Anderson, *Crucible of War: The Seven Years' War and the Fate of Empire in British North America, 1754–1766* (New York, 2000), 3–5, 50–65 and Brumwell, *Gentleman Warrior*, 51–53. Key primary sources include *GWP* 1: 104–25; "Affidavit of John Shaw," William L. McDowell, *Documents Relating to Indian Affairs, 1754–1765* (Columbia, 1970), 3–7; *Papiers Contrecoeur*, and Sylvester K. Stevens and Donald H. Kent, eds. and trans., *Journal of Chaussegros de Léry* (Harrisburg, 1940), 27–28 (Denis Kaninguen).

30. *GWP* 1: 110–17, 111 (pretence), 135 (suspicion).

31. See *GWP* 1: 119–22, 128, 145, 150–51.

32. Appendix E.

33. *GWP* 1: 103 (SC company), 105, 159–61; *GWP* 1: 74 n.3, 126–27 (command); D. Peter MacLeod, *The Canadian Iroquois and the Seven Years' War* (Toronto, 1996), 43–50; Anderson, *Crucible of War*, 59–65; William Harden, "James Mackay, of Strathy Hall, Comrade in Arms of George Washington," *Georgia Historical Quarterly* 1, no. 2 (June 1917): 77–98; A. S. Salley, *The Independent Company from South Carolina at the Great Meadows*, Historical Commission of South Carolina Bulletin No. 11 (Columbia, 1932).

34. John Robinson to GW, September 15, 1754, *GWP* 1: 209–10 (see also 169–70, 178, 214–16, 220 for other contemporary responses); Jack P. Greene, ed., *The Diary of Colonel Landon Carter of Sabine Hall, 1752–1778*, 2 vols. (Charlottesville, 1965), 1: 109–10. See also "Letter of Col. John Banister, of Petersburg, to Robert Bolling," *WMQ* 10 (October 1901): 102–5.

35. DeLancey to Lords of Trade, July 22, 1754, *DRCHNY* 6: 852; Wilbur R. Jacobs, ed., *Indians of the Southern Colonial Frontier: The Edmond Atkin Report and Plan of 1755* (Columbia, 1954), 3; Timothy J. Shannon, *Indians and Colonists at the Crossroads of Empire: The Albany Congress of 1754* (Ithaca, 2000).

36. *MPCP* 6: 184; Duquesne to Minister, November 3, 1754, Stevens and Kent, *Wilderness Chronicles*, 84.

37. *Whitehall Evening Post*, September 3, 1754. The British government specifically disputed French forts built upon their territorial claims, such as forts Crown Point, Chambly, Niagara, Cadaraqui, Detroit, and St. Joseph: see Halifax Memorandum, August 15, 1753, Add. Mss. 33029, ff. 96–100, and "Encroachments made by the French in America," 1754, ff. 102–103. The following narrative draws from T. R. Clayton, "The Duke of Newcastle, the Earl of Halifax, and the American Origins of the Seven Years' War," *Historical Journal* 24 (September 1981): 571–603; Schumann and Schweizer, *The Seven Years' War*; Dominick Graham, "The Planning of the Beauséjour Operation and the Approaches to War in 1755," *New England Quarterly* 41 (December 1968): 551–66; James A. Henretta, *"Salutary Neglect": Colonial Administration under the Duke of Newcastle* (Princeton, 1972), chap. 7; and Baugh, *Global Seven Years' War*, 73–91. The British government specifically disputed French forts built upon their territorial claims: see Halifax Memorandum, August 15, 1753, Add. Mss. 33029, ff. 96–100, and "Encroachments made by the French in America," 1754, ff. 102–103.

38. Newcastle to Albemarle, September 5, 1754, in Pease, *Anglo-French Boundary Disputes*, 51; Robinson to Newcastle, September 15, 1754, and Newcastle to Murray, September 28, 1754, Add. Mss. 32736, ff. 529–30, 591–94; Thomas Penn to Robert Morris, November 15, 1754, Penn Correspondence, 1754–1756, Vol. 4, f. 27 (opposition); Penn Papers, HSP; Stanley Ayling, *The Elder Pitt: Earl of Chatham* (New York, 1976), 152–58.

39. Newcastle, quoted in Henretta, *Salutary Neglect*, 338; Albemarle to Newcastle, September 11, 1754, Add. Mss. 32850, ff. 289–91; Stuart Liebiger, "To Judge of Washington's Conduct: Illuminating George Washington's Appearance on the World Stage," *VMHB* 107 (Spring 1999), 37; Dinwiddie to Board of Trade, March 12, 1754, *DP* 1: 99 (need for regulars). British leaders in 1754 realized how unfit for service most Independent Companies were and how militarily unprepared the Virginia militia was (e.g., *DRCHNY* 6: 844–45 and Robinson to Dinwiddie, July 5, 1754, CO 5/211, ff. 49–51).

40. Newcastle to Hardwicke, and Newcastle to Murray, September 28, 1754, Add. Mss. 32736, ff. 554 (haste), 591–94 (aversion); the anonymous author who wrote in 1754 "A Scheme for the Improvement & Employment of His Majesty's Forces in America, Sept. 1755 [*sic*]" was one of the advocates for a regiment formed out of the American Independent Companies: see Add. Mss. 32736, ff. 515–18; Clayton, "The Duke of Newcastle," 593–95; Robinson to Newcastle, September 15 and 22, 1754, and Add. Mss. 32736, ff. 529–30, 569–70. See also Evan Charteris, *William Augustus Duke of Cumberland and the Seven Years' War* (London, 1925), 122–33; Rex Whitworth, *William Augustus, Duke of Cumberland: A Life* (London, 1992), 156–64; Andrew C. Thompson, *George II: King and Elector* (New Haven, 2011), 233–38. Box 45 of the Duke of Cumberland's Papers in the Royal Archives contains numerous reports from America, suggesting that Cumberland had followed news of French encroachments in 1753 and 1754.

41. British documents in 1754 overwhelmingly describe Virginia as the object of the expedition: e.g., WO 47/44, f. 207 ("Expedition to Virginia"). "Expeditions," in George Smith, *An Universal Military Dictionary* (London, 1779), ECCO, n.p.

42. Fox to Duke of Dorset, October 1754, Add. Mss. 32737, ff. 139–40; Napier to Robinson, September 29, 1754, Add. Mss. 33046, f. 297, and Board of Ordnance Minutes, WO 47/44, ff. 187–88, 280. Both regiments were placed on the English Establishment: Fox to William Pitt, Paymaster-General, October 21, 1754, WO 4/50, f. 86.

43. On Braddock's orders to proceed through Virginia (and St. Clair's orders to prepare the Virginia route via Wills Creek), see Napier to Braddock, November 25, 1754, in Winthrop Sargent, *History of an Expedition against Fort Du Quesne in 1755* (Philadelphia, 1856), 398 (reiterating verbal orders from the Duke of Cumberland); *MANA*, 145; and "Secret Instructions to General Braddock," November 25, 1754, *DRCHNY* 6: 920–22: "You will, therefore, order the Troops to be carried up the Potomac River, as high as Wills's Creek"; Robinson to Dinwiddie, and Robinson to Governors, November 4, 1754, CO 5/211, ff. 219–36. None of the sources regarding plans for the expedition ever mentioned landing at Philadelphia and advancing across Pennsylvania. Lawrence Henry Gipson, in *The Great War for Empire: The Years of Defeat, 1754–1757* (New York, 1956), incorrectly states that Braddock had discretionary power to change the route (73–75), which is contradicted by his official orders, and by James DeLancey to John St. Clair, August 31, 1755, JSCL 176–77.

44. See G. M. Waller, *Samuel Vetch: Colonial Enterpriser* (Chapel Hill, 1960), chap 12; William A. Foote, "The American Independent Companies of the British Army, 1664–1764" (Ph.D. diss., UCLA, 1966), ch. 14; John Roach, "The 39th Regiment of Foot and the East India Company, 1754–1757," *Bulletin of the John Rylands Library* 41 (1958): 102–38; Webb, *Marlborough's America*, 371–413; Lee G. Offen, *America's First Marines: Gooch's American Regiment, 1740–1742* (Lexington, 2011).

45. Webb, *Marlborough's America*, chs. 9, 12, epilogue; Douglas Edward Leach, *Roots of Conflict: British Armed Forces and Colonial Americans, 1677–1763* (Chapel Hill, 1986).

46. Newcastle Conference with the Speaker, September 9, 1754, and Council Minutes, October 9, 1754, Add. Mss. 32995, ff. 309–10, 328–29. See also Alison Gilbert Olson, "The British Government and Colonial Union, 1754," *WMQ* 17 (January 1960): 22–34.

47. Lady Anson to Lord Royston, August 23, 1755, Add. Mss. 35376, ff. 127–30; Dinwiddie to Board of Trade, November 16, 1754, CO 5/1328, f. 126; John Simcoe to Lord Barrington, June 1, 1755, PRO 30/8/95, ff. 58–61. See the following in the Newcastle Papers: "A Scheme for the Improvement & Employment of His Majesty' Forces in America," Sept. 1754, Add. Mss. 32736, ff. 515–18; and "Some thoughts on the Expediency and

Manner of supporting a Regular military Force on the Continent of North America," October 1755, Add. Mss. 32737, ff. 16–21; Simmons and Thomas, *Proceedings and Debates*, 1: 135–36.

48. On 1754 difficulties, see *GWP* 1: 82, 88, 93, 141, 143 (wagons); 83–84, 186 (supplies); 83, 88–99, 124, 184–85 (Indian relations); *Maryland Gazette*, April 17, 1755 (New York Independent Company's march).

49. Glen to Sir Thomas Robinson, August 15, 1754, *Records in the British Public Record Office Relating to South Carolina, 1663–1782*, Vol. 25, ff. 84–105, Reel 8. See also Joshua Piker, *The Four Deaths of Acorn Whistler: Telling Stories in Colonial America* (Cambridge, 2013), 45; Jonathan Mercantini, *Who Shall Rule at Home? The Evolution of South Carolina Political Culture, 1748–1776* (Columbia, 2007), 122–39; Titus, *Old Dominion at War*, chaps. 2–3.

50. GW to Dinwiddie, June 10, 1754, *GWP* 1: 130 (canker); Dinwiddie to Sharpe, June 20, 1754, and Dinwiddie to Halifax, October 25, 1754, *DP* 1: 213, 369 (Virginia companies); *GWP* 1: 224–27 (rank).

51. Robert C. Alberts, *The Most Extraordinary Adventures of Major Robert Stobo* (Boston, 1965); Robert Stobo to Colonel Innes, July 28, 1754, Robert Stobo Papers, 1754, DAR.1925.05, Darlington Collection, Special Collections Department, University of Pittsburgh http:// digital.library.pitt.edu/u/ulsmanuscripts/pdf/31735060225889.pdf, accessed September 30, 2013. See biographical notes of the Virginia officers in the *Dinwiddie Papers* and *Papers of George Washington*.

52. GW to Dinwiddie, June 10, 1754, *GWP* 1: 134 and 191, n. 1; William La Péronie to GW, September 5, 1754, *GWP* 1: 203–4. La Péronie's wounds deprived Washington of the French translator he sorely needed. La Péronie was promoted to captain in August 1754.

53. *GWP* 1: 127–28, 206, n.3, 212–14, 224, n. 1; Murray, quoted in Hugh T. Lefler and William S. Powell, *Colonial North Carolina: A History* (New York, 1973), 140; John Rutherford to Dinwiddie, December 27, 1754, in Koontz, *Dinwiddie Correspondence*, 652; Sharpe to Baltimore, October 25, 1754, and Sharpe to Dinwiddie, December 10, 1754, *Sharpe* 1: 102, 136.

54. *DP* 1: 465 and *London Daily Advertiser*, February 4, 1754 (court visits); Manuscript Army List, 1736, WO 64/9, f. 54 (commissions).

55. In the Duke of Cumberland's Papers, see Sir John St. Clair (JSC) to the Duke of Cumberland, 1748, Box 35/111, Reel 55, and Lettre du General Comte de Brown, écrite de Parma à Son Altesse Royale le 20 Mai 1748, Box 35/110, Arthur Villettes (British envoy in Turin) to JSC, February 5, 1747, Box 59/293, Reel 89 (see also letters 288–317); and JSC to Sir Thomas Robinson, February 13, March 8, and July 5, 1748, Add. Mss. 23827, ff. 117, 170; Add. Mss. 23829, f. 10. For St. Clair's reputation, see Earl of Richmond to JSC, January 6, 1755, JSCL, 161–62 (esteem); JSCL 141, 174, and 208 (references to Marshal Browne), and also St. Clair to Robert Napier, July 30, 1757, Folder 20, John Forbes Headquarters Papers, UVA.

56. JSC to General James St. Clair, January 24, 1747, SP 92/52, Sardinia, 1747; JSC to Loudoun, December 22, 1757, LO 5069 (uniform). For the mountain campaigns in Italy, see Christopher Duffy, *The Wild Goose and the Eagle: A Life of Marshal von Browne, 1705–1757* (London, 1964).

57. For St. Clair's orders and promotion, see JSC to Robert Napier, August 15, 1755, and Henry Fox to JSC, November 1754, JSCL 157, 289–90. His majority was dated October 7, 1754 (WO 65/2, 1755 Army List). See also Cumberland to Count Browne, April 29, 1748, Cumberland Papers, Box 38/246, Reel 60.

58. JSC to Sir Thomas Robinson, February 12, 1755, JSCL, 25 (Apennines); *DP* 1: 453 (arrival); Charles R. Hildeburn, "Sir John St. Clair, Baronet," *PMHB* 9 (1885): 1–14; Table of Distances, 1758,"*BP* 2: 653 ("Sir John St. Clairs Road"). For other favorable views of St. Clair, see WO 1/4, f. 33 (William Shirley) and Duke of Cumberland to Loudoun, October 22, 1756, LO 2065.

59. JSCL, January–March 1755, pages 1–75; "Route to the Ohio by Water," 1754, *MANA*, 32–33; *Pennsylvania Gazette*, February 11, 1755 (Great Falls); WO 4/50, f. 355 and JSCL, 24 (Croatians).

60. St. Clair to Henry Fox, August 16, 1755, JSCL, 159; St. Clair to Napier, June 13, 1755, Little Meadows, *MANA*, 94; James DeLancey to St. Clair, February 3, 1755, JSCL, 46–47; Thomas Jefferys's 1754 *Map of the Western Parts of the Colony of Virginia* was published in the London edition of George Washington's Journal; A copy of George Washington's map of the Ohio Valley, and inscribed "J. St. Clair," is in the Cumberland Papers, Box 61 (a copy of that appearing in Freeman, *George Washington* 1: after 282); Governor Morris of Pennsylvania sent St. Clair a draft of Evans's 1755 map, which arrived by March 1755, too late to influence the basic trajectory of the campaign (*MPCP* 6: 301–302).

61. St. Clair to Braddock, February 9, 1755, and St. Clair to Lord Fairfax, February 21, 1755, JSCL, 16, 20, 35.

62. St. Clair to Braddock, February 9, 1755 and March 12, 1755, JSCL, 17, 21, 78.

63. Foote, "The American Independent Companies of the British Army"; Stanley Pargellis, "The Four Independent Companies of New York," in J. Franklin Jameson, ed., *Essays in Colonial History Presented to Charles McLean Andrews by His Students* (Freeport, N.Y., 1966), 96–123; J. A. Houlding, *Fit for Service: The Training of the British Army, 1715–1795* (Oxford, 1981), 14–19, 120.

64. Dinwiddie to Holdernesse, March 12, 1754, *DP* 1: 94; Archibald Kennedy, *Serious Considerations on the Present State of the Affairs of the Northern Colonies* (London: R. Griffiths, 1754), 13; Earl of Holdernesse, Circular Letter to Governors, January 18, 1754, LO 464A (condition of independents); see Jacobs, *Edmond Atkin Report and Plan of 1755*, 80, for a proposal to regiment the Independent Companies in America.

65. Glen to Bedford, *BPRO-SC* 26: 10; John Rutherford to Barrington, February 28, 1756, WO 1/972, f. 9; Fox to James Pilcher, October 28, 1754, WO 4/50, f. 91; St. Clair to Braddock, February 9, 1755, JSCL, 17 (Chelsea); Orme's Journal, 286 (Invalids); St. Clair to Capt. Thomas Clarke, March 18, 1755, JSCL, 80; Grant to Amherst, February 22, 1761 (arms) December 24, 1761 (notion), James Grant Papers, LOC. Peter F. Copeland and John R. Elting, "Independent Companies of New York, 1756–1760," *Military Collector & Historian* 42 (Spring 1990): 23 and plate 649; John Rutherford to Loudoun, January 21, 1756, "Memoranda on the Four Independent Companies in New York," LO 2689.

66. George Sackville to Mr. Robert Gates, September 23, 1748, and Edward Cornwallis to Robert Gates, March 18 1750, Gates Papers, Box 1, NYHS; Paul David Nelson, *General Horatio Gates: A Biography* (Baton Rouge, 1976), 6–10; Stephen Brumwell, "Gates, Horatio (1727?–1806)," *ODNB* 21: 632–34.

67. "Journal Kept on an Expedition Sent by Cornwallis, Governor of Nova Scotia, to dislarge the French and Indians from Chignecto, Sept 10 to October 8 1750," Gates Papers, Box 1, NYHS;

68. Nelson, *General Horatio Gates*, 10–12; Last Will and Testament of Horatio Gates, April 7, 1755, Gates Papers, NYHS.

CHAPTER 2

1. *London Daily Advertiser*, November 27, 1754, p. 1; *London Chronicle*, July 17, 1762, p. 6; N.A.M. Rodger, *The Command of the Ocean: A Naval History of Britain, 1649–1845* (New York, 2004), 239. HMS *Centurion* achieved even more successes in American waters after 1755, as she was among the fleets that captured Louisbourg, Quebec, Martinique, and Havana.

2. *London Gazette*, October 1, 1754, p. 2 (Dorset); *Whitehall Evening Post or London Intelligencer*, November 7–9, 1754, p. 1 (Dublin); *Whitehall Evening Post or London Intelligencer*, November 16–19, 1754, p. 1 (Gage); *London Evening Post*, October 10, 1754, p. 4 (expel).

3. Justin McCarthy, *A History of the Four Georges*, 4 vols. (London, 1890), 2: 380. Lee McCardell's biography, *Ill-Starred General: Braddock of the Coldstream Guards* (Pittsburgh, 1958), remains the only full-length biography of Braddock, and his description of the mythological Braddock is apt (p. 2); see also Paul Kopperman, "Edward Braddock," *ODNB* 7: 171–73 for an excellent brief biography. McCardell's biography, however, often uncritically accepted dubious nineteenth-century legends regarding Braddock, and completely missed important evidence about Braddock's command at Gibraltar.

4. McCardell, *Ill-Starred General*, 5–6.

5. David Chandler, "The Great Captain-General, 1702–1714," in *The Oxford Illustrated History of the British Army*, 69–91, at 69; McCardell, *Ill-Starred General*, 23–29, 41; Stephen Saunders Webb, *Marlborough's America* (New Haven, 2013); Van Creveld, *Supplying War*, 26–34 (Marlborough's march greatly differed from Braddock's in that he journeyed along established roads and settlements).

6. Eric Hinderaker, *The Two Hendricks: Unraveling a Mohawk Mystery* (Cambridge, 2010).

7. McCardell, *Ill-Starred General*, 30–31; Jonathan Spain, "Hill, John (*d.* 1735)," *ODNB* 27: 143–44; Waller, *Samuel Vetch*, ch. 12.

8. McCardell, *Ill-Starred General*, 53–54.

9. McCardell, *Ill-Starred General*, 54–58; Donna T. Andrew, *Aristocratic Vice: The Attack on Duelling, Suicide, Adultery, and Gambling in Eighteenth-Century England* (New Haven, 2013), 197–206.

10. McCardell, *Ill-Starred General*, 46, 65–66, 71; *An Apology for the Life of George Anne Bellamy*, 3d. ed. (London, J. Bell, 1785), 1: 1–14, 3: 28–29.

11. McCardell, *Ill-Starred General*, 75, 81, 93.

12. McCardell, *Ill-Starred General*, 101–7. See Edward Braddock to Duke of Cumberland, September 15, 1747, Box 27, f. 76, reel 42, and Braddock to Sir Everard Fawkener, July 19, 1745, Box 3, f. 210, reel 4, Cumberland Papers.

13. McCardell, *Ill-Starred General*, 109–15, 132; Jonathan Spain, "Keppel, William Anne (1702–1754)," *ODNB* 31: 371–73; *Albemarle Papers* 1: 199, 347; *Public Advertiser*, January 31, 1753, 1: "Colonel Braddock, of the Coldstream Regiment of Guards, to be Colonel of the Regiment of Foot now doing Duty at Gibraltar, lately commanded by Col. Herbert"; W. P. Courtney, "Calcraft, John, the elder (*bap.* 1726, *d.* 1772)," rev. Patrick Woodland, *ODNB* 9: 496–97; George Anne later stated that Braddock gave the contract to Calcraft "upon my account" (*An Apology for the Life of George Anne Bellamy*, 5: 142). The general also left Bellamy and Calcraft his expensive government plate and part of his estate.

14. *London Gazette*, May 1, 1753, p. 2 (Fowke's title); *Whitehall Evening Post*, April 30, 1754, p. 3 and July 2–4, 1754, p. 1 (Fowke's arrival at Gibraltar).

15. Warrants for Edward Braddock, November 18, 1754, for acting as "Lieutenant Governour of the Garrison of Gibraltar," and "Commander in Chief of the Garrison," AO 1/69/90, TNA; Establishment of the Forces at Minorca and Gibraltar, Anno 1754, WO 24/304.

16. Extract of a Letter from a Merchant, at Gibraltar, to his Correspondent Here, dated November 17, 1753, *London Public Advertiser*, December 24, 1753, p. 1; Thomas Birch to Lord Royston, August 9, 1755, BL Add. Mss. 35398, ff. 271–72; *LHW* 3: 334, 337; *London Magazine* 22 (May 1753): 244 (Fowke's appointment); Walpole to Mann, August 28, 1755, *Correspondence of Horace Walpole*, 20: 496; McCardell, *Ill-Starred General*, 116–19.

17. Hannah Weiss Muller, "The Garrison Revisited: Gibraltar in the Eighteenth Century," *Journal of Imperial and Commonwealth History* (2013): 1–24.

18. WO 284/3: Gibraltar Garrison Orders, Vol. 3, 1748–1756, ff. 225–314. See also Ordnance Office, Bill Books, Gibraltar, 1753, WO 53/128 for the maintenance of fortifications.

19. Edward Braddock, *A Particular Description of the Peninsula of Gibraltar with Its Several Works* (ca. 1753–1754), Royal Library, Windsor Castle (RCIN 1085523) (quote at pp. 3–4, numbers of guns and mortars at 50–55). The manuscript, bound in a green leather volume, was "Given to Col Napier by MGenl Braddock, 1753, upon Genl Braddock returning from the Command of Gibraltar." I am grateful to Royal Librarian Oliver Urquhart Irvine and Bibliographer Bridget Wright for their kind assistance during my visit to the Royal Library.

20. Robinson to Newcastle, September 22, 1754, BL Add. Mss. 32736, ff. 563–64; Robinson to Newcastle, September 23, 1754, BL Add. Mss. 32736, ff. 569–70; Napier to Braddock, November 25, 1754, in Jacob Nicholas Moreau, *A Memorial Containing a Summary View of the Facts, with their Authorities. In Answer to the Observations Sent by the English Ministry to the Courts of Europe* (New York: H. Gaine, 1757), 114; *London Gazette*, March 30–April 2, 1754, 2 (Braddock's promotion).

21. *Whitehall Evening Post,* November 9–12, 1754, p. 1; *London Evening Post,* October 31 to November 2, 1754, p. 1; McCardell, *Ill-Starred General,* 129, 133; Thomas Penn to Richard Peters, November 7, 1754, and Penn to Morris, November 15, 1754, Penn Correspondence, 1754–1756, Vol. 4, ff. 23, 27, Penn Papers, HSP; *An Apology for the Life of George Anne Bellamy,* 5: 178. The word *pop* may have been short for either *poppet, poplet,* or *popelot,* which were contemporary terms of endearment, according to the *Oxford English Dictionary.*

22. Walpole to Mann, August 21, 1755, *Correspondence of Horace Walpole,* 20: 492; Letters of Col. Charles Russell, in *Historical Manuscripts Commission, Report on the Manuscripts of Mrs. Frankland-Russell-Astley RHMC* 52 (London, 1900), 352, 354, 381, 366; ff. 271–72: Thomas Birch to Lord Royston, August 9, 1755, BL Add. Mss. 35398, ff. 271–72; see also C. T. Atkinson, "A Flanders Sideshow: Hulst, 1747," *JSAHR* 22, no. 89 (Spring 1944): 205–12.

23. *GWR,* 21.

24. Brumwell, *Redcoats: The British Soldier and War in the Americas, 1755–1763* (Cambridge, 2002), 54–56, 69–70, 101; Tony Hayter, *The Army and the Crowd in Mid-Georgian England* (Totowa, N.J., 1978).

25. See "Draught of a Map of Ireland, wherein the several Quarters of the Horse & Foot are marked," ca. 1753, Cumberland Papers, Box 45, f. 34, Reel 69; John Houlding, "Irish Army Orders, 1751–1753," *JSAHR* 72 (1994): 107–17.

26. Houlding, *Fit for Service,* 45–48.

27. Alan J. Guy, "The Irish Military Establishment, 1660–1776," in Thomas Bartlett and Keith Jeffery, eds., *A Military History of Ireland* (Cambridge, 1996), 211–30; Francis Godwin James, *Ireland in the Empire, 1688–1770* (Cambridge, 1973), 174–77.

28. Houlding, *Fit for Service,* 49, 127, 132; *Quarters of the Army in Ireland in 1752* (Dublin: George Faulkner, 1752), 20.

29. R. R. Gale, *"A Soldier-Like Way:" The Material Culture of the British Infantry, 1751–1768* (Elk River, Mn., 2007); Eric I. Manders, "Braddock's Troops, 1755: The 44th and 48th Regiments of Foot," *Military Collector & Historian* 14 (Spring 1962): 16–17.

30. Henry Trenchard, *The Private Soldier's and Militia Man's Friend* (London: G. Kearsley, 1786), 18, 20, 23, 27; John Lampton's 68th Foot, "To Clean the Brass of Your Arms," http://lambtons.wordpress.com/2011/09/06/to-clean-the-brass-of-your-arms/(accessed July 26, 2012); L. E. Babits, "Shoe Life in the 71st of Foot, 1776–1777," *Military Collector and Historian* 34 (Summer 1982): 84–85.

31. Houlding, *Fit for Service,* x, 2–3, 195.

32. Houlding, *Fit for Service,* 46–55, 276, quote at 56 ("quelque chose de règle en Irelande"); Houlding, "Irish Army Orders," 107–17; *Quarters of the Army in Ireland in 1749,* 12, 14. See "Remarks or Observations on Discipline," a report written in 1750, that describes the conventional drill practiced by the Irish regiments (Cumberland Papers, Box 44, f. 99, pages 6–10).

33. Brumwell, 67 (refuse); Houlding, *Fit for Service,* 14, 50, 120–25.

34. Fox to Wilkinson, October 11, 1754, WO 4/50, f. 79; Robinson to Newcastle, October 11, 1754, Add. Mss. 32737, f. 104–105 (Portsmouth); *Pennsylvania Gazette,* March 3, 1755.

35. Fox to Colonel Maurice Bockland, November 18, 1754, Out Letter Book of Henry Fox, 1754–1755, f. 5, D/RWR/X5, Ryder of Rempstone Archive, Dorset History Centre, Dorchester, U.K.; *General Wolfe's Instructions to Young Officers: Also His Orders for a Battalion and an Army,* 2d. ed. (London: J. Millan, 1780; reprint, Ottawa, 1967), 37–38.

36. In "State and Condition of his Maj.ˢ hired Transports on board which the Troops are Embarked for Virginia under the Care of Capt:ⁿ Hugh Palliser in Cork Harbour 10ᵗʰ Jan:ʸ 1755," Captain Palliser provides a detailed account of approximately 1,664 people in the total embarkation of troops under Braddock's command: 8 field officers, 26 captains, 75 subalterns, 84 sergeants, 13 staff officers, 48 drummers, 1,078 privates, 195 women and servants, 108 Royal Artillerymen, and 29 surgeons and hospital attendants (ADM 1/2292: Captains' Letters, 1755, Section 9).

37. Brumwell, *Redcoats*, 136.

38. Lord Dorset, Lord Lieutenant of Ireland [Lionel Crawfield Sackville, 1st Duke of Dorset], "Rules and Orders for the better discipline of his Majesty's Army," April 7, 1752, LO 341; Thomas Burges, Inspection of 11th Regiment of Foot, WO 1/972, f. 301 (see also the inspection returns in WO 27); Daniel Disney Orderly Book, Library of Congress, June 3, 1752. See also Houlding, "Irish Army Orders," 107–17. Houlding, *Fit for Service*, 269 (endless).

39. Houlding, *Fit for Service*, 139 (best), 145–56; De Witt Bailey, *Small Arms of the British Forces in America, 1664–1815* (Woonsocket, R.I., 2009), 119, 233–34; LO 6897: James Furnis, Return of Small Arms in the His Majesty's Stores at New York & Albany, January 7, 1758 (blend of iron and wood rammers).

40. Erik Goldstein and Stuart Mowbray, *The Brown Bess: An Identification Guide and Illustrated Study of Britain's Most Famous Musket* (Woonsocket, R.I., 2010), 11; Daniel Disney Orderly Book, LOC, July 15, 1757; Orders, September 19, 1755, *GWP* 2: 53. My observations of the Brown Bess here and following are based on live-fire exercises at Twin Ponds Rifle Range, Francis Marion National Forest, Awendaw, S.C., 2012 and 2013, with special thanks to my colleagues Kyle Sinisi and Steve Smith and our Citadel cadets.

41. Houlding, *Fit for Service*, 137, 146, 152; Francis Halkett, Return of Cloathing, Arms, etc. Artificers & Recruits in His Majesty's 35th 42d, 44th, 48th, 50th & 51st Regiments, August 17, 1756, LO 1962 (issues of muskets in 1754 and 1755); Capt. Hubert Marshall to Henry Fox, January 23, 1755, LO 542; Grant to Amherst, Dec. 24, 1761, James Grant Papers, LOC, Box 29 (Reel 28) (firearms).

42. Houlding, *Fit for Service*, 144–46, 262–63 (inaccuracy of muskets), 279 (plates), 280 (word Present), 350 (fire discipline); see also B. P. Hughes, *Firepower: Weapons Effectiveness on the Battlefield, 1630–1850* (New York, 1997).

43. Houlding, *Fit for Service*, 162–63, 259–60, 278, 317, 348. On the ethnic composition of the regiments, see Brumwell, *Redcoats*, 318.

44. James Wolfe to William Sotheron, January 20, 1746, in Beckles Wilson, ed., *The Life and Letters of James Wolfe* (London, 1909), 57 (Falkirk).

45. Sir Peter Halkett to Peregrine Lascelles, January 23, 1745/6, and Captain Adam Drummond to Lascelles, January 24, 1745/6, LO 10305 (Scottish), HL. Katherine Tomasson and Francis Buist, *Battles of the '45* (New York, 1962); Stuart Reid, *1745: A Military History of the Last Jacobite Rising* (New York, 1966). See also Thomas Carter, *Historical Record of the Forty-Fourth or the East Essex Regiment of Foot* (London, 1864).

46. Cope, quoted in Martin Margulies, *The Battle of Prestonpans 1745* (Stroud, UK, 2007), chap. 4 (board, 183).

47. *Autobiography of the Rev. Dr. Alexander Carlyle, Minister of Inveresk* (Edinburgh, 1860), 144; Chevalier de Johnstone, *Memoirs of the Rebellion in 1745 and 1746* (London, 1820), 125–26; The History of Parliament, http://www.historyofparliamentonline.org/volume/1715-1754/member/halkett-peter-1695-1755, accessed November 6, 2013; WO 64/9, f. 116 (Halkett's commissions).

48. Brumwell, *Paths of Glory: The Life and Death of General James Wolfe* (Montreal, 2006), 48 (Falkirk); Stuart Reid, *Culloden 1746*, 2d. ed. (Barnsley, UK, 2011), 66, 92, 104–105; Russell Gurney, *History of the Northamptonshire Regiment, 1742–1934* (Aldershot, 1935), 19–22, 352.

49. "A Report of the Detachment Commanded by L.t Col.o Dunbar ordered into the Baile of Strathern By His Royal Highness the Duke, May the 24th 1746," Cumberland Papers, Box 15/201, Reel 21; *Quarters of the Army in Ireland in 1749* (Dublin, 1749), 14; Gurney, *Northamptonshire Regiment*, 380–82; Richard Cannon, *Historical Record of the Eighteenth or The Royal Irish Regiment of Foot* (London, 1848), 44–46.

50. Newcastle to Lord Holdernesse, August 26, 1755, BL Add. Mss. 32858, ff. 289–91; see also Thomas Birch to Lord Royston, August 30, 1755, BL Add. Mss. 35398, ff. 280–82, which records one contemporary view that Dunbar's "character for Capacity & Generalship was indeed never thought very highly of by those who know him."

51. Peter E. Russell, "Redcoats in the Wilderness: British Officers and Irregular Warfare in Europe and America, 1740 to 1760," *WMQ* 35 (October 1978): 629–52.

52. Margulies, *Prestonpans 1745*, 99; Reid, *1745: A Military History*, 13, 39. Only five companies of the 55th/44th had seen action at Prestonpans, the rest being on garrison duty at Berwick. Sir Peter Halkett, Major Russell Chapman, Captain Charles Tatton, and Lieutenant William Dunbar were at Prestonpans in 1745 and in Braddock's Expedition; but only Halkett, Tatton, and Dunbar were at the Monongahela.

53. These observations are based on my study of the unpublished pre-1754 manuscript Army Lists in WO 64/9 (1736), 64/10 (1745), and 64/11 (1752) and the officers of the 55th/44th and 59th/48th regiments during the 1740s and early 1750s. The first published Army List dates to 1754 (WO 65/1).

54. Margulies, *Prestonpans 1745*, 69. See Armstrong Starkey, *European and Native American Warfare, 1675–1815* (Norman, 1998), 46–53, and John Grenier, *First Way of War: American War Making on the Frontier* (Cambridge, 2005), chap. 3, for insightful critiques of Russell's argument.

55. Houlding, *Fit for Service*, 104–5, 115 (quote), 272. Houlding significantly notes that "opportunities for advanced tactical training were infrequent at the regimental level and almost unknown at higher levels" (166); see Ira Gruber, *Books and the British Army in the Age of the American Revolution* (Chapel Hill, 2010), for the inchoate professionalism of the army at mid-century.

56. James Patterson, *History of the County of Ayr: With a Genealogical Account of the Families of Ayrshire*, Vol. 1 (Ayr, Scotland, 1847), 390; Daniel Disney Orderly Book, LOC, November 20, 1756 (Primrose Kennedy).

57. Sir Hugh Cholmley, *The Memoirs of Sir Hugh Cholmley, Knt. and Bart* (n.p.: 1870), 57–58; Newcastle to Duke of Dorset, September 20, 1754, and Lord Rockingham to Newcastle, September 25, 1754, Add. Mss. 32736, f. 548 and 577 (wounded); Army List (1739), WO 64/9, f. 101, Army List (1752), WO 64/11, f. 140; Army List (1755), WO 65/2 (Cholmley's captaincy in the 48th Foot was dated April 15, 1749).

58. I am grateful to my friend Dr. Walter L. Powell for sharing his work on Robert Cholmley, a keynote address entitled "Where the leaf falls, let it rot"—The Aftermath of Braddock's Defeat," given at the Carnegie Library in Braddock on July 9, 2005. Walt first introduced me to Cholmley's eloquent last will and testament, dated December 28, 1754, PROB 11/818/386, TNA.

59. John R. Alden, *General Gage in America* (Baton Rouge, 1948) and *General Charles Lee: Traitor or Patriot?* (Baton Rouge, 1951).

60. Boscawen, quoted in Ruddock Mackay, "Keppel, Augustus, Viscount Keppel (1725–1786)," *ODNB* 31: 361–65, at 362; Orme, 289–90. Thomas More Molyneux, *Conjunct Expeditions: or Expeditions that Have Been Carried on Jointly by the Fleet and the Army* (London: R & J Dodsley, 1759); Richard Harding, *Amphibious Warfare in the Eighteenth Century: The British Expedition to the West Indies, 1740–1742* (Suffolk, UK, 1991).

61. Palliser to Cleveland, January 10, 1755, and January 13, 1755, ADM 1/2292: Captains' Letters, 1755, Section 9, state that the embarkation was completed on January 9, 1755, and that Palliser was under sail on January 13, 1755.

62. *Centurion* (Captain William Mantell), *Norwich* (Captain Samuel Barrington), *Syren* (Captain Charles Proby), *Garland* (Captain Mariot Arbuthnot), *Sea Horse* (Captain Hugh Palliser), and *Nightingale* (Captain Dudley Digges).

63. Transports carrying the 44th and 48th regiments were *Prince Frederick, Terrible, Halifax, Anna, Osgood, Fane, Isabel & Mary, Severn, Molly, Fishbourn, Concord*, and *Industry*; the transport *London* carried the hospital personnel and three ordnance ships, *Nelly, Newall*, and *Whiting* transported the artillery and the Royal Artillery personnel. See "State and Condition of his Maj.ˢ hired Transports on board which the Troops are Embarked for Virginia under the Care of Capt:ⁿ Hugh Palliser in Cork Harbour 10ᵗʰ Jan:ʸ 1755," ADM 1/2292, Section 9.

64. "Account of Brass Ordnance Mortars Small Arms and Stores sent to North America in the Years 1754 & 1755," LO 628. See also ADM 1/480, Box 2 and ADM 1/2291 (Captain's Letters) for Keppel's and Palliser's oversight of the naval forces at Cork in 1754–1755; Board of Ordnance Minutes, November 5, 1754, WO 47/44, f. 242 and 253.

65. Montresor Family Papers, Reel 1, David Library of the American Revolution; Board of Ordnance Minutes, October 21, 1754, WO 47/44, f. 207; Harry Gordon, Maps of Scotland: Perthshire and Argyllshire, ca. 1749–1751, MR1/497, TNA. See *MANA*, 104, n.1 for Gordon's career as a Royal Engineer that began in 1742. Gordon's efforts were a continuation of British General George Wade's construction of 250 miles of roads and 40 bridges through Scotland to facilitate military suppression of highland rebellions. See William Taylor, *The Military Roads in Scotland* (London, 1976) and Carolyn Jane Anderson, "State Imperatives: Military Mapping in Scotland, 1689–1770," *Scottish Geographic Journal* 125 (March 2009): 4–24.

66. Fox to Apothecary General, October 3 and November 11, 1754, WO 4/50, ff. 51 and 125 (hospital); "Necessaries provided for the Hospital in North America in y.ᶜ year 1754," LO 526 Lulu Stine, "Dr. Robert James, 1705–1776," *Bulletin of the Medical Library Association* 29 (June 1941): 187–98.

67. Mark Hallett, "From Out of the Shadows: Sir Joshua Reynolds' *Captain Robert Orme*," *Visual Culture in Britain* 5 (2004): 41–62. I thank John Rowland for referring me to this article.

68. Palliser to Cleveland, December 26 and 27, 1754, ADM 1/2291; Keppel to Cleveland, February 25, 1755, ADM 1/480, f. 500; *MANA*, 77, 80; Charlotte Browne Diary, January 16, 1755, NYHS; HOB, 63; "A Poem occasioned by his Majesty's most gracious Benevolence to his British Colonies in America," *Pennsylvania Gazette*, January 14, 1755, p. 2; Cohen, "Major William Sparke," 549–50 (see also Gurney, *Northamptonshire Regiment* 19, 351, n.2); McCardell, *Ill-Starred General*, 137–38.

69. *Virginia Gazette*, February 28, 1755, p. 3; March 14, 1755, p. 3, March 21, 1755, pp. 3–4; Hugh Palliser to JC, May 3, 1755, ADM 1/2292, Sec. 9; Keppel to Cleveland, February 25, 1755 ADM 1/480, Box 2, f. 500; Dinwiddie to Dobbs, February 27, 1755, *DP* 1: 515.

70. *Virginia Gazette*, March 21, 1755, p. 3; Braddock to Robinson, March 18, 1755, Add. Mss. 32853, f. 346; Keppel to Cleveland, February 25, 1755, and Braddock to Keppel, Feb. 25, 1755, ADM 1/480, f. 500, 505–505b. St. Clair recommended two quartering plans to Braddock: see JSCL 16–19, 31; RCB, 9.

71. Robert Orme to GW, March 2, 1755, *GWP* 1: 241–42.

72. GW to Robert Orme, March 15, 1755, *GWP* 1: 253–45, at 245; *GWR*, 18 (degrading); GW to William Byrd, April 20, 1755, *GWP* 1: 250; GW to William Fitzhugh, November 15, 1754, *GWP* 1: 225–26. See also *GWP* 1: 224, n. 1 for rank controversy. GW to Carter Burwell, April 20, 1755, *GWP* 1: 253 (motives); GW to Robert Orme, April 2, 1755, GWP 1: 246–47 (map). GW to John Robinson, April 20, 1755, GWP 1: 256.

73. *DP* 1: 474; Orme, 284–88.

74. St. Clair to Braddock, February 9 and 10, 1755, JSCL, 16–21; Braddock to Robinson, March 18, 1755, Add. Mss. 32853, f. 346; Braddock to Napier, February 24, 1755, in Moreau, *Memorial*, 119; Braddock to Morris, February 28, 1755, *MPCP* 6: 307–308.

75. Horace Walpole to Richard Bentley, August 15, 1755, *Correspondence of Horace Walpole*, ed. W.S. Lewis, et al. (New Haven, 1973), 35: 245.

CHAPTER 3

1. Andrew Burnaby, *Travels through the Middle Settlements in North-America in the Years 1759 and 1760* (Ithaca, 1960), 36; W. W. Abbot, ed., "General Edward Braddock in Alexandria: John Carlyle to George Carlyle, 15 August 1755," *VMHB* 97, no. 2 (1989): 205–14, at 209; James D. Munson, *Col.o John Carlyle, Gent.: A True and Just Account of the Man and His House* (Alexandria, 1986), 64 (ordinary), 119–26 (house); "Major William Sparke," 550 and Laws, "R.N. and R.A. in Virginia, 1755," 196 (dates).

2. Munson, *Col.o John Carlyle*, 31–57 and James D. Munson, "New Bottles, New Wine: Changes in Colonial Alexandria's Leadership," in *Proceedings of Northern Virginia Studies Conference 1983, Alexandria: Empire to Commonwealth*, ed. James Allen Braden (Alexandria, 1983), 57–84; *DP* 1: 53–54 (Carlyle's commission).

3. Daniel Dulany, "Military and Political Affairs in the Middle Colonies in 1755," *PMHB* 3 (1879): 11–31, at 13; Anthony Strother to GW, July 9, 1755, *GWP* 1: 333; GW to Sarah Cary Fairfax, May 14, 1755, *GWP* 1: 279. On the March 31 muster, see *GWP* 1: 280, n.2. See Lee Offen, "British Regulars in Virginia, 1677–1682," History Reconsidered, http://historyreconsidered.net/British_Regulars_in_Virginia.html, accessed August 4, 2014.

4. Abbot, "Braddock in Alexandria," 209, 212; Warrant, Braddock to John Carlyle, April 10, 1755, LO 563 (commission as "Store keeper"); Munson, *Col.o John Carlyle*, 30 (children).

5. Webb, *Marlborough's America*, 352.

6. *A Modest Address to the Commons of Great Britain, and in Particular to the Free Citizens of London* (London, 1756), 9.

7. James Abercromby to Dinwiddie, May 1755, in John C. Van Horne and George Reese, eds., *The Letter Book of James Abercromby, Colonial Agent, 1751–1773* (Richmond, 1991), 149 (see 132–33 for contemporary views of Braddock's powers).

8. See Clarence Carter, "The Office of Commander in Chief: A Phase of Imperial Unity on the Eve of the Revolution," in Richard B. Morris, ed., *The Era of the American Revolution* (New York, 1939), 170–213; Jack P. Greene, "Martin Bladen's Blueprint for a Colonial Union," *WMQ* 17 (October 1960): 516–30; and Harry M. Ward, "*Unite or Die": Intercolony Relations, 1690–1763* (London, 1971), chap. 2.

9. CO 5/211, ff. 116–138 contain the three sets of instruction; see ff. 109–110 for St. Clair's distribution of the circular letter. On illegal trade, see Thomas M. Truxes, *Defying Empire: Trading with the Enemy in Colonial New York* (New Haven, 2008).

10. Abbot, "Braddock in Alexandria," 211; Benjamin Franklin to John Ridout, April 4, 1755, in Houston, "Wagon Affair," 250.

11. *Sharpe*, 1: 203; Ross D. Netherton, "The Carlyle House Conference: An Episode in the Politics of Colonial Union," in Braden, *Alexandria: Empire to Commonwealth*, 57–84. William Shirley Jr. apparently had the actual or brevet rank of captain from Braddock: see Henry Fox to Braddock, July 30, 1755, Out Letter Book of Henry Fox, ff. 19–20, Dorset History Centre.

12. "At a Council held in the Camp at Alexandria, April 14ᵗʰ, 1755," CO 5/46, ff. 17–20 (also reprinted in *MPCP* 6: 365–68 and *DHNY* 2: 648–51); cf. Commodore Keppel's account in ADM 1/480, Box 2, Part 3, ff. 548–553; Orme, 300–306, and "Proceedings of a Council of War," December 1755, Sharpe 1: 315–20.

13. *MPCP* 6: 200–202.

14. "Commission from Edward Braddock, April 15, 1755," *SWJP* 1: 465–66; *DRCHNY* 6: 945. Johnson was not listed among those present during the main council session, so he most likely met with Braddock and the governors in a separate meeting afterward. See Preston, *Texture of Contact*, 92–96, for Johnson's biography.

15. CO 5/211, f. 116; *Sharpe*, 1: 203, 210; Orme, 302; *MPCP* 6: 400.

16. Braddock to Robinson, April 19, 1755, CO 5/46, f. 11–16, at ff. 11–12; Shirley to Robinson, March 24, 1755, *DRCHNY* 6: 941–45.

17. Edward Braddock to Robert Monckton, April 14, 1755, Monckton-Arundell Family Papers, GaM2, University of Nottingham, Manuscripts and Special Collections.

18. Braddock to Napier, April 19, 1755, *MANA*, 81–82; Orme, 306.

19. *DHNY* 2: 649–50; Sharpe to Lord Baltimore, April 19, 1755, *Sharpe*, 1: 195.

20. Richard Henry Spencer, "The Carlyle House and its Associations—Braddock's Headquarters—Here the Colonial Governors met in Council, April, 1755," *WMQ* 18 (July 1909): 1–17, at 17.

21. P. J. Marshall, "The Thirteen Colonies in the Seven Years' War: The View from London," in *Britain and America Go to War: The Impact of War and Warfare in Anglo-America, 1754–1815*, ed. Julie Flavell and Stephen Conway (Gainesville, Fla., 2004), 69–92.

22. Shirley to Robinson, June 20, 1755, *DRCHNY* 6: 958; Braddock to Robinson, April 19, 1755, Moreau, *Memorial*, 129.

23. James DeLancey to John St. Clair, August 31, 1755, *JSCL*, 176–77; Braddock to Napier, April 19, 1755, *MANA*, 81–82; Orme, 301–307; *DRCHNY* 6: 943–45, 947 (Niagara).

24. Orme, 303–305; *DHNY* 2: 651–54; Braddock to Robinson, April 19, 1755, Moreau, *Memorial*, 127 (money for gifts), 143 (speeches drafted by Johnson); Braddock to William Johnson, June 9, 1755, Gratz Manuscripts, HSP, Case 4, Box 6 (Indian officers); *SWJP* 9: 171–79 (speeches). Johnson accepted the appointment as superintendent on April 15 (*SWJP* 1: 467). Johnson's drafting of Braddock's speeches is a key detail overlooked in previous studies.

25. Pownall to Johnson, August 16, 1755, *SWJP* 1: 854–55 (the "Additional Instruction" from Braddock to which Pownall refers can be found in Pownall's handwriting in "Instructions to Col. Johnson, April 16, 1755," PRO 30/8/95, ff. 56–57 and *SWJP* 13: 40–41). See also Braddock to Halifax, April 1755, in Moreau, *Memorial*, 134–35 (use). Pownall's only biographer did not realize that he had indeed met with Braddock at Alexandria: John A. Schutz, *Thomas Pownall: British Defender of American Liberty* (Glendale, Ca., 1951), 61.

26. GW to William Fairfax, April 23, 1755, *GWP* 1: 258.

27. Shirley to Robinson, June 20, 1755, in Charles Henry Lincoln, ed., *Correspondence of William Shirley, Governor of Massachusetts and Military Commander in America, 1731–1760*, 2 vols. (New York, 1912), 2: 197, 203; *MPCP* 6: 405–6.

28. Gipson, *Great War for Empire*, 70; Netherton, "Carlyle House Congress," 80.

29. Orme, 306, and Braddock to Robinson, April 19, 1755, in Moreau, *Memorial*, 130–31.

30. *MANA*, 82; *The Life, Adventures, and Surprizing Deliverances of Duncan Cameron, A Private Soldier in the Regiment of Foot, late Sir Peter Halket's* (Philadelphia: James Chattin, 1756), 10; BOB, 5 (rations); HOB, 75 (drunkenness); Brumwell, *Redcoats*, 101, 105.

31. Orme, 298; BOB, April 9, xxi; "Spatterdashes," Smith, *Universal Military Dictionary*.

32. See Lieutenant Alexander Baillie's return of August 28, 1762, in Alfred Proctor James and Charles Morse Stotz, *Drums in the Forest* (Pittsburgh, 1958), 105.

33. Houlding, *Fit for Service*, 151, n. 120; Bouquet to Forbes, July 11, 1758, *BP* 2: 182; BOB, April 8, xix and April 11, xxi; *MANA*, 486, lists "Cartouch Boxes with Straps" of "12 Holes" that were issued to the two regiments. See also Franklin T. Nichols, "The Organization of Braddock's Army," *WMQ* 4 (April 1947): 125–36 and Gale, *A Soldier-Like Way.*

34. Orme, 296; HOB, 68; St. Clair to Napier, February 15, 1755, *JSCL*, 30. See Smith, *Universal Military Dictionary*, "Halbard/Halbert," and "Spontoon."

35. HOB, 64; Braddock to Napier, April 19 and June 8, 1755, *MANA*, 83–84 (700 men each).

36. Braddock to Napier, March 17, 1755, *MANA*, 78; *Virginia Gazette*, February 28, 1755, p. 4 (Holmes); *Carlisle Gazette* 3, no. 150 (June 18, 1788) (Guinea slave). Alexander V. Campbell's essay, "'To Stand in the Face of Danger for Us': The British Army and Maryland's Indentured Servants, 1755–1760," *Maryland Historical Magazine* 94 (Winter 1999): 419–39, is a useful corrective, but ignores the related issues of impressment, delayed compensation, and the colonists' lingering memories of British military oppression in 1755.

37. Dulany, "Military and Political Affairs," 14; on servants, see JCB, 12; Sharpe to Braddock, May 7, 1755, and Sharpe to John Sharpe, May 24, 1755, *Sharpe* 1: 204–205, 211; *ABF*, 134–35; *Virginia Gazette*, May 9, 1755, p. 2 (Blackburn).

38. *Virginia Gazette*, March 21, 1755, p. 3.

39. Abbot, "Braddock in Alexandria," 209; Dulany, "Military and Political Affairs," 14; William Franklin to Benjamin Franklin, May 15, 1755, in Houston, "Wagon Affair," 271–72; "Information of James Jobb," December 14, 1757, LO 5012; Breslaw, "A Dismal Tragedy," 131.

40. BOB, xxxii (Polson); *Expedition of Major General Braddock to Virginia; with the Two Regiments of Hacket and Dunbar* (London, 1755), 5–6, 9–10, 13, 23, 34; Dulany, "Military and Political Affairs," 12.

41. Braddock to Napier, April 20, 1755, *MANA*, 82, and Orme, 296, and St. Clair to Braddock, April 10, 1755, JSCL, 94 (St. Clair's projected road); Ross Netherton, "Braddock's Campaign and the Potomac Route to the West," *Winchester-Frederick County Historical Society Journal* 1 (December 1986): 1–22; "Campaign," in Smith, *Universal Military Dictionary*, is defined as "the time every year that an army continues in the field."

42. *The Journal of Nicholas Cresswell, 1774–1777* (New York, 1924), 47–49; HOB, 78; Jefferson-Fry Map of 1751, LOC (Avery's Ford); Walter S. Hough, "Braddock's Road through the Virginia Colony," *Winchester Frederick County Historical Society Journal* 7 (1970): 1–79; Baker, *Braddock's Road*, 30–35; "Account with the Colony of Virginia" [October 1754], *GWP* 1: 221, notes "ferriages" at John Vestal's on the Shenandoah. The camp locations for Halkett's six companies are probable, based on the route that the remainder of the 44th under Colonel Gage took when it marched from April 27–May 2, 1755 (HOB, 85–86); JCB, 36 (fruit trees); Netherton, "Potomac Route," 9.

43. Orme, 299; RCB, 10; Cohen, "Major William Sparke," 550; Seaman's Journal, in Sargent, *History of an Expedition*, 367 (hereinafter cited as "Seaman's Journal").

44. Braddock to Napier, Williamsburg, March 17, 1755, *MANA*, 77; Keppel to Cleveland, Hampton, March 14, 1755, ADM 1/480, Box 2, Part 3, f. 523; "An Account of Ordnance Stores supplied his Excellency General Braddock, 1755," ADM 1/480, f. 596; and Copy of an Order to Lt. Spendelowe, March 14, 1755, ADM 1/480, ff. 610–15. The sailors were drawn from HMS *Centurion*, HMS *Norwich*, HMS *Syren*, HMS *Seahorse*, HMS *Guarland*, and HMS *Nightingale*: see Charles Spendelow, "A Return of the Detachment of Seamen," May 28, 1755, ADM 1/480, Box 2, Part 3, f. 578, and "Account of Ordnance Stores deliver'd in March 1755," f. 590. See also Bailey, *Small Arms of the British Forces*, chap. 11.

45. See Appendix G for Midshipman Gill's authorship of the "Seaman's Journal."

46. JCB, 10; Seaman's Journal, 367–68; *Expedition of Major General Braddock*, 15; "Dowden's Ordinary Archaeological Site, MN-CPPC of Montgomery County, Maryland," http://www.montgomerycollege.edu/nearchaeology/dowdens/history.pdf, (accessed July 19, 2012).

47. Braddock to Newcastle, April 19, 1755, Add. Mss. 32854, ff. 188–91, and Braddock to Napier, April 19, 1755, in *MANA*, 81–84; Orme, 288.

48. Orme, 307; Sharpe to John Sharpe, May 24, 1755, *Sharpe* 1: 211; JCB, 11; Seaman's Journal, 369. Sharpe to Dinwiddie, December 10, 1754, *Sharpe* 1: 140 (wagon costs).

49. Croghan, et al., to Morris, April 16, 1755, *MPCP* 6: 368–69; St. Clair to Halkett, April 17, 1755, JSCL 105; Seaman's Journal, 369 (St. Clair's arrival). George Croghan, John Armstrong, William Buchanan, Adam Hoops, and James Burd were appointed as commissioners by Governor Morris on March 12, 1755 (*MPCP* 6: 318).

50. St. Clair was still raging against the Germans in 1757 when he advised Lord Loudoun on the need for lighthorsemen and again volunteered his Hussar uniform: "I believe it will appear necessary for your [Lordship] to raise some of such Troops; they will serve in collecting carriages and keeping the Dutch Waggoners in Subjection, & if your [Lordship] shoud choose to dress them as Houzars there is a pattern Suit of Mine at New York which I brought to this Country for that Purpose." St. Clair to Loudoun, Dec 22, 1757, LO 5069.

51. St. Clair to Braddock, February 9, 1755, JSCL 20.

52. *ABF*, 127; Whitfield J. Bell, Jr. and Leonard W. Labaree, "Franklin and the 'Wagon Affair,' 1755," *American Philosophical Society Proceedings* 101, no. 6 (December 1957): 551–58.

53. Bell and Labaree, "Franklin and the 'Wagon Affair'"; "Memorandum of Wagon Accounts," 1755, *PBF* 6: 13–17; Commission to Franklin, April 22, 1755, and Franklin to Deborah Franklin, April 26, 1755, in Houston, "Wagon Affair," 251–52, 258–59.

54. BF to Deborah Franklin, April 26, 1755, in Houston, "Wagon Affair," 260; *ABF*, 132; BF to Peter Collinson, August 27, 1755, *PBF* 6: 170.

55. "Advertisement for Wagons," April 26, 1755, and BF to Susannah Wright, April 28, 1755, *PBF* 6: 19–22 (ad), 23–24 (German version).

56. "Advertisement for Wagons," April 26, 1755.

57. BF to Deborah Franklin, April 26, 1755, in Houston, "Wagon Affair," 258–59; *Gentleman's Magazine* 25 (August 1755): 378.

58. John Smith to BF, in Houston, "Wagon Affair," 258; Israel Pemberton to John Fothergill, May 19, 1755, *PBF* 6: 54.

59. William Shirley, Jr. to Morris, May 14, 1755, William Franklin to BF, May 19, 1755, and BF to William Shirley Jr., May 20, 1755, in Houston, "Wagon Affair," 271, 274.

60. Franklin to William Shirley Jr., May 8, 1755, and Franklin to Braddock, May 8, 1755, in Houston, "Wagon Affair," 268–69; Lewis Burd Walker, ed. *The Burd Papers: The Settlement of the Waggoners' Accounts Relating to General Braddock's Expedition towards Fort Du Quesne* (Pottsville, Pa., 1899) records reimbursements for 146 wagons and 510 pack horses; Orme, 321, and Shirley to Morris, June 7, 1755, *PA* 1st ser., 2: 347 (ca. 200 wagons at Fort Cumberland by May 1755).

61. John Harris to BF, May 2, 1755, in Houston, "Wagon Affair," 265.

62. *New England Historical and Genealogical Register* 3 (1849): 292. Jenkins had been either pressed into service by the British army or sent into the service by his master. He survived the campaign and died in 1849, at the unlikely age of 115 years, retaining "his faculties to the last."

63. *PA* 2nd ser., 17: 204–6 (Aschenbrenner's 1740 immigration); "Harbanus Ashebriner: Contract for a Wagon and Horses," May 2, 1755, *PBF* 6: 25–27. The fifty-two-year-old Aschenbrenner eventually received £81 / 17s. for his wagon and team and expenses, and likely drove the wagon himself during the campaign, as no driver was listed: Lewis Burd Walker, ed., *The Settlement of the Waggoners' Accounts Relating to Braddock's Expedition towards Fort Duquesne* (Pottsville, Pa., 1899), 54.

64. Houston, "Wagon Affair," 269, 251, 270–72.

65. Donald H. Berkebile, "Conestoga Wagons in Braddock's Campaign, 1755," in *Contributions from the Museum of History and Technology, Paper 9, United States National Museum Bulletin 218* (Washington, D.C., 1959), 142–53; Ron Vineyard, "Virginia Freight Wagons, 1750–1850," Colonial Williamsburg Foundation Library Research Report Series #345 (Colonial Williamsburg Foundation, 1994).

66. Orme, 331; *MANA*, 479.

67. Vineyard, "Virginia Freight Wagons," 27, 40–46, 137–40; Berkebile, "Conestoga Wagons," 145–46 (loads); *PBF* 6: 27; "A List of Necessarys to be provided by each Waggoner," May 2, 1758, Box 3, Folder 169, John Forbes Papers, UVA.

68. Orme, 332; William Franklin to BF, April 29, 1755, in Houston, "Wagon Affair," 263.

69. Grant to Amherst, April 25, 1761, James Grant Papers, LOC, Box 33, Reel 32.

70. Fairfax Harrison, ed., "With Braddock's Army: Mrs. Browne's Diary in Virginia and Maryland," *VMHB* 32 (October 1924): 305–20, at 310–12.

71. Harrison, "With Braddock's Army," 315–16.

72. HOB, 86; "Instructions for Waggon Master to the train of Artillery ordered to attend his Majesty's Forces in North America," [1755], Society Misc. Coll., 1676–1937, Folder 2A, Colonial Wars, No. 425, HSP; Orme, 314, 318–19, 351 (disposition); HOB, 99–100 (Gage and wagoners).

73. See note 74, and Don Higginbotham, *Daniel Morgan: Revolutionary Rifleman* (Chapel Hill, 1961), 1–4, and Joseph S. Folsom, "General Daniel Morgan's Birthplace and Life," *New Jersey Historical Society Proceedings* 14 (1929): 277–92; B. Floyd Flickinger, "Riding with Wagoner Morgan," *Winchester-Frederick County Historical Society Journal* 14 (2002): 30–41; Neal Thomas Hurst, "Fringe on American Hunting Shirts ca. 1775–1815," *Military Collector and Historian* 62 (Fall 2010): 213–15.

74. William Hill Manuscript on General Morgan, William Hill Papers, 1769–1852, reel VW2, Union Theological Seminary, Richmond, Va.; William Hill Sermon, 1802, and Notes from Benjamin Berry, Mss 7:1 M8214:1 and 2, VHS; "Account of Brigadier General Morgan," *Political Magazine and Parliamentary, Naval, Military and Literary Journal*, March 2, 1781, 173–75; James Graham, ed., *Memoir of General Graham, With Notes of the Campaigns in Which He was Engaged from 1779 to 1801* (Edinburgh, 1862), p. 71; cf. [Samuel Graham

(1756–1831)], "A Recollection of the American Revolutionary War," *Virginia Historical Register* 6 (1853): 204–11.

75. Israel Pemberton to John Fothergill, May 19, 1755, *PBF* 6: 54–55; Braddock to Robinson, June 5, 1755, Moreau, *Memorial*, 136; St. Clair, in *MANA*, 93–94; John Hamilton to BF, June 9, 1755, William Shirley Jr. to BF, May 10 and 14, 1755, in Houston, "Wagon Affair," 270–71, 275; *PA* 1st ser., 2: 322 (horns).

76. Meeting of Pennsylvania Assembly Committee, April 29, 1755, in Houston, "Wagon Affair," 261–62; Seaman's Journal, 379–80; *ABF*, 131; *MPCP* 6: 635–36.

77. *MPCP* 6: 475; BF to Richard Partridge, July 2, 1755, and BF to William Shirley Jr., May 5, 1755, in Houston, "Wagon Affair," 277, 265–66.

78. *MPCP* 6: 374; *PBF* 6: 90–91; *GWP* 1: 275 n. 3 (Leslie); J. Alan Rogers, "Impressment in Western Pennsylvania, 1755–1759," *WPHM* 52 (July 1969): 255–62.

79. "Major William Sparke," 550; *MANA*, 470; and "Queries of George Chalmers with the Answers of General Gage," *Massachusetts Historical Society Collections* 4th ser., 4:367–72, at 368.

80. St. Clair to Napier, June 13, 1755, *MANA*, 93; Seaman's Journal, 378.

81. Seaman's Journal, 370; RCB, 12; Curtis L. Older, *The Braddock Expedition and Fox's Gap in Maryland* (Westminster, Md., 1995), 172–75; Baker, *Braddock's Road*, 27–30.

82. Sharpe to St. Clair, June 25, 1758, *Sharpe* 2: 211.

83. Dinwiddie to Morris, March 10, 1755, *DP* 1: 522 (flour). For road, ferry, and river networks, see the Fry-Jefferson Map of 1751, LOC. On Conococheague, see Orme, 299, 308; JCB, 11; BOB, xxv–xxvi (boats); Older, *Braddock Expedition and Fox's Gap*, 50–52; and St. Clair to Shirley, November 10, 1755, JSCL, 185, regarding compensation for "The water Carriage up the Patomack to fort Cumberland" from Conococheague.

84. Edward Braddock to Gates, April 28, 1755, and "Return of His Majesty's Independant Company of Foot Commanded by Captain Horatio Gates," January 29, 1756, Horatio Gates Papers, NYHS; Seaman's Journal, 378 (arrival).

85. Sharpe to Dinwiddie, May 9, 1755, *Sharpe*, 1: 205; GW to John Carlyle, May 14, 1755, *GWP* 1: 274 and GW to William Fairfax, May 5, 1755, *GWP* 1: 262–63, n.2; Braddock to Napier, June 8, 1755, *MANA*, 84.

86. Orme, 309; On Winchester, see GW to John Augustine Washington, May 28, 1755, *GWP* 1: 290; "Diary of a Journey of Moravians from Bethlehem, Pa., to Bethabara, N.C., 1753," in Newton D. Mereness, ed., *Travels in the American Colonies* (New York, 1916), 334; and David Holmes Conrad, "Early History of Winchester," *Annual Papers of the Winchester Virginia Historical Society* 1 (1931): 169–81. For proposed conference, see Dinwiddie to Dobbs, January 17, 1755, *DP* 1: 469; Peters to Shirley, May 12, 1755, *PA* 1st ser., 2: 308; and Morris to Croghan, April 23, 1755, *MPCP* 6: 372. The four iron 12-pounders were never at Fort Cumberland or buried at Dunbar's Camp: see Dunbar to Shirley, August 21, 1755, *MPCP* 6: 593.

87. JCB, 12–13; Seaman's Journal, 370; BOB, xxvi–xxvii. The modern intersection of roads is at Clear Brook, Va.

88. Orme, 312 (press); HOB, 85–87 (Gage's route and provincials); St. Clair Instructions to John Hamilton, April 21, 1755, JSCL, 112, and Orme, 309 (Opequon bridge); *GWP* 1: 263 n. 3 and 268 (Winchester).

89. John W. Wayland, ed., *Hopewell Friends History, 1734–1934, Frederick County, Virginia*, 2 vols. (Westminster, Md., 2007), 24–25 (Ballenger), 31–32 (Littler); Hofstra, *The Planting of New Virginia: Settlement and Landscape in the Shenandoah Valley* (Baltimore, 2004), 1–4, 29–33; Hough, *Braddock's Road through the Virginia Colony*, 15–21; Harrison, "With Braddock's Army," 314–15.

90. Seaman's Journal, 371 (Cacapon or Leith Mountain); St. Clair Instructions to William Polson, April 21, 1755, JSCL, 111 (float); Journal of Captain Charles Lewis, cited in Andrew Wahll, *Braddock Road Chronicles* (Westminster, Md., 1999),477; GW to Orme, March 2, 1756, *GWP* 2: 321 (Enoch's).

91. Seaman's Journal, 372 (weather); Baker, *Braddock's Road*, 36–44; Hough, *Braddock's Road through the Virginia Colony*, 31–48.

92. Evelyn C. Adams, "The Coxes of Cox's Creek, Kentucky," *Filson Club Historical Quarterly* 22 (April 1948): 75–103; Friend Cox lived from 1720 to 1785.
93. Seaman's Journal, 372; Harrison, "With Braddock's Army," 315 (Cresap); BOB, xxvii and St. Clair Instructions to William Polson, April 21, 1755, JSCL, 111 (Potomac float); Journal of Captain Charles Lewis, December 2, 1755, cited in Wahll, *Braddock Road Chronicles*, 484; *GWD* 1: 14–15 (Cresap's); Kenneth P. Bailey, *Thomas Cresap: Maryland Frontiersman* (Boston, 1944), 101; Carson I. A. Ritchie, ed., *General Braddock's Expedition* (Woolwich, UK, 1962), University of Virginia Special Collections, 5–6 (race).
94. Seaman's Journal, 373 (the "Grenadiers' March" was used near Fort Cumberland and again during the Monongahela River crossing of July 9).
95. William A. Hunter, ed., "Thomas Barton and the Forbes Expedition," *PMHB* 95 (October 1971): 431–83, at 469–70; Charles Morse Stotz, *Outposts of the War for Empire: The French and English in Western Pennsylvania: Their Armies, Their Forts, Their People, 1749–1764* (Pittsburgh, 1985), 91–94; Harrison, "With Braddock's Army," 316.
96. Both Dinwiddie and Captain John Rutherford referred to the place as Fort Cumberland in letters written in February–March 1755, months before the general's arrival. The fort may have been named that winter by John St. Clair or James Innes: see Dinwiddie to Robinson, February 12, 1755, *DP* 1: 494; Rutherford to Morris, March 22, 1755, *PA* 1st ser., 2: 276–77. Dinwiddie also references a draft labeled Cumberland Fort, which may be the "Plan of Fort Cumberland on Will's Creek & Potomack River," dated February 12, 1755 (BL Cartographic Items, Maps K Top. 122.38, and in Stotz, *Outposts of the War for Empire*, 94). Braddock's orderly book also titled the very first entry at Wills Creek, on May 10, 1755, at the "Camp at Fort Cumberland" (BOB, xxx).
97. Braddock Warrant to James Innes, May 1, 1755, LO 579 (warrant as governor); Braddock Warrant, Feb. 28, 1755, LO 553 (storekeeper); *GWP* 1: 302, n. 8.
98. Orme, 312 (Allen); Seaman's Journal, 374–80; JCB, 15–16; HOB, 89 (field days on May 15 and 23).
99. Seaman's Journal, 374; *Expedition of Major General Braddock*, 18–21; Orme, 329, and HOB, 91–92 (orders), JCB, 15; *MPCP* 6: 395–97 (Peters). Peters stated that the general had issued orders forbidding Indian women from coming into the British camp, but no such orders appear in any of the orderly books. Peters also claimed that the Ohio Iroquois were "extremely dissatisfied at not being consulted with by the General," a claim that loses credibility given how frequently Braddock met with the Indians that month. Charles Lee to Sidney Lee, June 18, 1756, *CLP* 1: 5; Seaman's Journal, 378; Charles Davers to Gates, June 30, 1770, Horatio Gates Papers, NYHS (Boiling Water). Lee's adoption took place while the 44th was encamped in the Mohawk Valley in 1756.
100. George Croghan Account, Penn Papers Indian Affairs, Vol. 1 (1687–1753), 52, HSP (also *PA* 2nd ser., 6: 521–22); Croghan to Johnson, May 15, 1755, *SWJP* 1: 497; Orme, 311, and *MPCP* 6: 374–75 (messages).
101. JCB, 14; Seaman's Journal, 375; Bland, *Treatise of Military Discipline*.
102. "General Braddock's Speech to the Indians, May 10, 1755," CO 5/15, ff. 294–95, TNA. Thomas Gill's paraphrases match all of the points of that manuscript speech: it pictured all misunderstandings being buried under "that great mountain" (perhaps pointing to Wills Mountain conveniently before them); that the Indians' enemies were their enemies; that Braddock's army was joined by Shirley, Pepperell, and Johnson's forces; and most important, that the British were coming to "settle them happy in their country" (Seaman's Journal, 375). The speech was dated May 10 but delivered on May 12, 1755 (Orme, 309).
103. JCB, 15 ("Congrace" or congress with Indians); for the meeting on May 18, see Orme, 310, Seaman's Journal, 377–78, and Moreau, *Memorial*, 144–45; and WO 64/11, f. 349 (Bromley).
104. The speeches in Moreau, *Memorial*, 143–45, were "made, and pronounced to the Indians by Order, and under the Inspection of Colonel Johnson," and may have been the ones that Braddock received (along with wampum) from Johnson in mid-May (see *PA* 1st ser., 2: 321).

105. Seaman's Journal, 378; JCB, 15; Orme, 310; HOB 90.
106. In August 1755, a group of seven Native allies appeared at a council in Philadelphia and were rewarded for having fought at the Monongahela (*MPCP* 6: 524): Scaroyady, Cashuwayon (Kos Showweyha or Kanuksusy), Attschechokatha, Froson (perhaps Aroas?), Kahuktodon (Gahickdodon), Kashwughdaniunto (Kaghswaghtaniunt), and Dyioquario (Jonathan Cayenquerigo). Only six of these men, however, could have possibly been in the battle, as Scaroyady's son had been killed and Jerry had deserted from the original eight. Some men in the August 1755 council were likely other Iroquois who rejoined the army by July 10. Little is known of Attschechokatha, who may have been the eighth warrior with Braddock. Other possible candidates Dyioquario (Jonathan Cayenquerigo), Jagrea (Scaroyady's son-in-law) and Moses Contjochqua (the Song) do not appear to have fought at the Monongahela (Paul A.W. Wallace, *Conrad Weiser: Friend of Colonist and Mohawk* (Philadelphia, 1945), 367, 386–87, *MPCP* 6: 536, 551).
107. *MPCP* 6: 287; *Sharpe Corr.*, 6: 234; Barbara Sivertsen, *Turtles, Wolves, and Bears: A Mohawk Family History* (Bowie, Md., 1996), Table 11-4 (Scaroyady). Scaroyady had a tattoo of a bow and arrow on each cheek, according to a description in the *Gentleman's Magazine* (September 1756), 414.
108. On Kanuksusy/Canachquasy/Kos Showweyha, see *MPCP* 6: 589 (son of Aliquippa); *MPCP* 7: 6; *GWP* 1: 135, 140, n. 20; James H. Merrell, *Into the American Woods: Negotiators on the Pennsylvania Frontier* (New York, 1999), 236–37. Kanuksusy died of smallpox in 1756.
109. Seaman's Journal, 378 (quoting original journal in Ritchie, *General Braddock's Expedition*, 9); *MPCP* 6: 614; William A. Hunter, "Kaghswaghtaniunt," *DCB* 3: 319–20.
110. Speech of Silver Heels, September 21, 1769, enclosure in Charles Edmonstone to Thomas Gage, September 20, 1769, Gage Papers, AS 87, WLCL; Seaman's Journal, 378; Wallace, *Conrad Weiser*, 391 (at Monongahela).
111. *PA* 8th ser., 6: 4008 ("late Half King's Son"); *MPCP* 6: 552; 524; Wallace, *Conrad Weiser*, 378, 382, 391; Hunter, "Tanaghrisson," *DCB* 3: 613–14.
112. *SWJP* 1: 544, n.1 (Skowonidous); cf. *DRCHNY* 7: 178 (Showonidous); Seaman's Journal, 378 "Jerry Smith").
113. *PA* 8th ser., 6: 4008; GW to Montour, October 11, 1755, *DP* 2: 243.
114. Seaman's Journal, 380; George Croghan Account, HSP, 52; Orme; 311.
115. Seaman's Journal, 380; Orme, 311, 314. The original manuscript of the Seaman's Journal does not contain the phrase "these people are villains, and always side with the strongest," an addition that occurred following the Monongahela battle (see Ritchie, *General Braddock's Expedition*, 11–12); Beverly W. Bond, "Captivity of Charles Stuart, 1755—57," *Mississippi Valley Historical Review* 13 (June 1926): 58–81, at 63. Stuart's account claimed that two Shawnee leaders were present, but no other sources record the presence of Shawnees, many of whom were already at war with the English.
116. Moreau, *Memorial*, 145; Braddock to Morris, April 15, 1755, *PA* 1st ser., 2: 290. George Croghan also confirmed Braddock's reconciling approach to the Ohio Indians in a letter to William Johnson of May 15, 1755 (*SWJP* 1: 496).
117. Bond, "Captivity of Charles Stuart," 63; see John K. Rowland, "Treating American Indians as 'Slaves', 'Dogs', and Unwanted Allies: George Washington, Edward Braddock, and the Influence of Ethnocentrism and Diplomatic Pragmatism in Ohio Valley Military Relations, 1753–1755," in Edward Lengel, *A Companion to George Washington* (New York, 2012), 32–52.
118. John Craig Deposition, March 30, 1756, Penn Papers Indian Affairs, HSP, Vol. 2 (1754–1756), 78 (emphasis mine); see *Pennsylvania Gazette*, September 9, 1756 (Craig's captivity); *New York Mercury*, March 8, 1756 (Fleming); Duquesne to Marin, 13 juin 1753, ASQ-VV 5: 62, f. 5; Hitchen Holland to Dinwiddie, January 1, 1755, LO 539A; *Papiers Contrecoeur* 363; *PA* 1st ser., 3: 548–49 (French propaganda).
119. "Major William Sparke," 553; *ABF*, 132; Croghan Account, HSP, 52.
120. Johnson to Croghan, April 23, 1755, *SWJP* 1: 476; Johnson to Braddock, July 15, 1755, *SWJP* 9: 204–205; George Croghan Account, HSP, 52; Dinwiddie to Glen, September 25,

1755, *DP* 2: 212; see also *Maryland Gazette,* June 12, 1755 ("they were all kindly entertained by His Excellency"). On scalping, see HOB, 113 (bounty), and Breslaw, "A Dismal Tragedy," 130, n. 44 and 132.

121. Braddock to Morris, *PA* 1st ser., 2: 290 (Braddock's plans); Johnson to Braddock, May 17, 1755, *SWJP* 1: 513; Croghan to Morris, May 1, 1755, *MPCP* 6: 375 (Aughwick reluctance) and 379 (Peters). In 1755, Croghan clearly expected more warriors to rejoin the army, which casts doubt upon his later assertion that Braddock ordered all but eight to ten warriors away: see Edward Shippen to William Allen, July 4, 1755, *MPCP* 6: 460 and Shirley to Peters, May 21, 1755, *PA* 1st ser., 2: 321–22.

122. HOB, 89–90, 98; *PA* 1st ser., 2: 348; *MPCP* 6: 426; Brumwell, *Redcoats,* 122–23; Carol Deakin, "Support Personnel: Women with General Braddock's Forces," in Braden, *Alexandria: Empire to Commonwealth,* 85–94; Thomas L. Elder, "Women in Braddock's Army," *New York Evening Post,* 1926, Copy in HSP.

123. Braddock to Johnson, June 9, 1755, *SWJP* 9: 187; Johnson to Braddock, July 15, 1755, *SWJP* 9: 208 (Dinwiddie); *DRCHNY* 7: 19–24; Ian Steele, "Shawnee Origins of Their Seven Years' War," *Ethnohistory* 53 (Fall 2006): 657–87.

124. Shirley to Peters, May 21, 1755, *PA* 1st ser., 2: 321–22; Johnson to Braddock, July 15, 1755, *SWJP* 9: 205; Dinwiddie to Keppel, February 24, 1756, *DP* 2: 357; see also *GWP* 1: 206, n.3 (Innes); Croghan Account, HSP, 52.

125. Glen to Board of Trade, May 29, 1755, in *BRPO-SC* 27: 212; "Monecathootha to the Catawbas," "Six Nations to the Catawbas," (ca. 1754) and "Catawba King and Headmen to Governor Glen, January 21, 1755," in *DRIA* 28–29, 33–34; William Johnson also confirmed the six Mohawks' deaths, though his rendering of the details was not as accurate as Glen's (see *DRCHNY* 7: 23); Contrecoeur to Vaudreuil, August 14, 1755, *Papiers Contrecoeur,* 419 (Iroquois-Cherokee conflict in 1755).

126. Orme, 314; *GWP* 2: 159, 161, n. 9; *DP* 1: 268 and 2: 77; Account of James Beamer, June 18, 1761, and Manuscript on Saluda Conference [1755], June 18, 1761, James Glen Papers, 1738–1777, South Caroliniana Library; Thomas Hatley, *The Dividing Paths: Cherokees and South Carolinians through the Era of Revolution* (Oxford, 1995), 75–77.

127. Orme, 310; St. Clair to Braddock, June 10, 1755, JSCL, 138; *MANA,* 79; *MPCP* 6: 142, 181, 224–25.

128. Braddock's guides included Christopher Gist and apparently his two sons, Nathaniel and Thomas, John Fraser, John Walker, and Thomas Burney. See Kenneth Bailey, *Christopher Gist: Colonial Frontiersman, Explorer, and Indian Agent* (Hamden, Ct., 1976), 92 ("office of head Guide"); *BP* 2: 61 (St. Clair); *GWP* 2: 72 and 210, n.2; Hanna, *Wilderness Trail,* 2: 327, 332, 341; *Journals of House of Burgesses* 8: 364 (Burney); and John Fraser, "A List of Guides Employed in His Majesty's Service," undated, John Forbes Headquarters Papers, Box 7, Folder 505, UVA. "Guides," in Smith, *Universal Military Dictionary.*

129. GW to John Carlyle, June 7, 1755, Fort Cumberland, *GWP* 1: 306; Braddock to Napier, June 8, 1755, *MANA,* 85, 92; Edward Braddock to Newcastle, June 5, 1755, Add. Mss., 32855, f. 338–39; Montcalm to Paulmy, April 10, 1758, *DRCHNY* 10: 697 (live letters); St. Clair to Count Brown, September 3, 1755, JSCL, 174; Alberts, *Adventures of Stobo,* 130. See Duke of Cumberland to Loudoun, October 22, 1756, LO 2065 (distrust); *GWP* 1: 274 (reinforcement).

130. Braddock to Robinson, June 5, 1755, in Moreau, *Memorial,* 137–38.

131. Orme, 315; Dinwiddie to Braddock, May 12, 1755, *DP* 2: 40; McCardell, *Ill-Starred General,* 185, 192–93; 185; *GWP* 2: 44, 127, 128, n.5, 222.

132. Orme, 313–15; Seaman's Journal, 372, 375, 379–80; *MPCP* 6: 400, 406–407 (Daniel Cresap); Houston, "Wagon Affair," 276 and n. 93; Bailey, *Thomas Cresap,* 97–102; *Sharpe* 1: 143–45, 149–50, 200 (salt beef). See Roger Knight and Martin Wilcox, *Sustaining the Fleet, 1793–1815: War, the British Navy and the Contractor State* (Suffolk, 2010), 62–63 (casks).

133. Orme, 314; *MANA,* 88–91; Sarah Fatherly, "Tending the Army: Women and the British General Hospital in North America, 1754–1763," *Early American Studies* 10 (Fall 2012): 566–99.

134. Orme, 317–22 (councils), 327–28 (brigade organization); Seaman's Journal, 380; Orders to St. Clair, May 28, 1755, JSCL, 133; *PA*, 1st ser., 2: 331–32; *MPCP* 6: 410–11; and *GWP* 1: 299–300 (intelligence).

135. Orme, 312; Allan Macrae to GW, May 13, 1755, *GWP* 1: 270; Seaman's Journal, 381; *Pennsylvania Gazette*, May 29, 1755 (uniforms); *GWP* 1: 271, n.7 (Dobbs); Mapp, *Elusive West*, 261–64; John Mack Faragher, *Daniel Boone: The Life and Legend of an American Pioneer* (New York, 1992), 36, 69; John Maass, *The French and Indian War in North Carolina: Spreading the Flames of War* (Charleston, 2013). Returns of Braddock's Army, June 8, 1755, *MANA*, 86–91; Orme, 312 (not including numbers of sick in hospitals).

136. Dinwiddie to Braddock, June 3, 1755, *DP* 2: 48; *MPCP* 6: 397 (Peters's warning was also recorded in *The Expedition of Major General Braddock*, 24); St. Clair to Napier, June 13, 1755, *MANA*, 94–95; William Shirley, Jr. to Morris, May 23, 1755, *MPCP* 6: 404–406.

137. GW to John Augustine Washington, May 14, 1755, *GWP* 1: 272, 278; Thomas Gage to GW, November 23, 1755, *GWP* 2: 179–80 (esteem); Gage to Washington, July 26, 1756, *GWP* 3: 296–97 ("most affectionately"); Orme to GW, August 25, 1755, *GWP* 2: 9–10; Roger Morris to GW, *GWP* 2: 155–56; GW to Dinwiddie, March 10, 1757, *GWP* 4: 112–15, n. 2; Shirley on Orme: MPCP 6: 404–406. Washington befriended many of the leading officers in the campaign, including Shirley, Morris, Burton, Gage, and Dobson (*GWP* 1: 287, 347, 248, n. 7 and 272).

138. GW to John Augustine Washington, May 6, 1755, and GW to William Fairfax, June 7, 1755, *GWP* 1: 267, 299.

139. GW to William Fairfax, April 23, 1755, *GWP* 1: 258: *GWR*, 18–19; GW to John Augustine Washington, May 14, 1755, *GWP* 1: 277–78 (trifling); GW to Sarah Cary Fairfax, May 14, 1755, *GWP* 1: 280 (impatience).

140. Braddock to Robinson, April 19, 1755, Moreau, *Memorial*, 130; Braddock to Morris, May 24, 1755, *MPCP* 6: 400; Braddock to Napier, June 8, 1755 *MANA*, 85.

141. Conway Robinson Howard, ed., "Extracts from the Diary of Daniel Fisher, 1755," *PMHB* 17, no. 3 (1893): 263–78, at 272; *MPCP* 6: 475–76. GW to William Fairfax, June 7, 1755, GWP 1: 299; *MANA*, 84; Braddock to Morris, May 24, 1755, Gratz Manuscripts, HSP, Colonial Wars, Case 4, Box 6. Braddock's bitter letters: April 19, 1755, May 24, 1755, June 5, June 8 Braddock to Robinson, June 5, 1755, Moreau, *Memorial*, 136–39; *MPCP* 6: 400. For political effects, see Marshall, "View from London," 69–92, and Simmons and Thomas, *Proceedings and Debates* 1: 198–99, 208–11 (Braddock and Loudoun letters).

CHAPTER 4

1. Contrecoeur to Vaudreuil, June 21 and July 31, 1755, *Papiers Contrecoeur*, 364–66 (Kent, 222–23) (fortune, prayer); Duquesne to Contrecoeur, October 30, 1754, 266 (relief). Contrecoeur's devotion is especially evident in his vows for communion, [n.d.], ASQ-VV, Carton 3, no. 196, reel 2; and in Contrecoeur à son fils, ca. 1755, ASQ-VV, Carton 3, no. 226d, reel 2.

2. Duquesne to Vaudreuil, July 6, 1755, *DRCHNY* 10: 300.

3. Stotz, *Outposts*, 80–87; William A. Hunter, *Forts on the Pennsylvania Frontier, 1753–1758* (Harrisburg 1960), 97–136.

4. "Tableau des mouvements que Duquesne a fait faire principalement en 1755," ANOM COL C¹¹A 100, ff 17–23, at 17–18. In addition to the 21 officers and cadets and 237 men at Fort Duquesne, there were 15 men and 1 officer at Venango; 1 officer, 2 cadets, and 85 men at Riviere au Boeuf, and 1 officer, 2 cadets, and 100 men at Presque Isle.

5. Duquesne to Vaudreuil, July 6, 1755, in Stevens and Kent, *Wilderness Chronicles*, 91; Stotz, *Outposts*, 80–87; Laperière to Contrecoeur, April 20, 1755, *Papiers Contrecoeur*, 321 (cannons); Stevens and Kent, *Léry Journal*, February 24, 1755, 92, 239 (siege); Charles W. Dahlinger, "The Marquis Duquesne, Sieur de Menneville, Founder of the City of Pittsburgh," *WPHM* 15 (August 1932): 219–62, 238–39, n. 43 (flooding); "Memoir of Chevalier Le Mercier on the Artillery of Canada, Oct. 30, 1757," *DRCHNY* 10: 656; Pariseau, "Le Mercier," *DCB* 4: 458–60.

6. Contrecoeur to La Galissonière, July 31, 1755, *Papiers Contrecoeur*, 398–99 (Kent, 244) (accident); Pierre Pouchot, *Memoirs on the Late War in North America between France and England*, trans. Michael Cardy and ed. Brian Leigh Dunnigan (Youngstown N.Y., 1994), 107.

7. Benoist to Contrecoeur, June 30, 1755, *Papiers Contrecoeur*, 370–71 (Kent, 225).

8. Machault to Duquesne, February 17, 1755, *DRCHNY* 10: 275.

9. Duquesne to Contrecoeur, April 27, 1755, and February 15, 1755, *Papiers Contrecoeur*, 323 (Kent, 209) (trench), 275 (Kent, 201) (impossible); Kent, *French Invasion*, 43. See also Pouchot, *Memoirs*, 75; Lotbinière to Argenson, October 24, 1755, in Jean Marie Shea, ed. *Relations diverses sur la bataille du Malanguelee, gagné le 9 Juillet, 1755* (New York, 1860), 41–42; Dumas to Makarty, November 10, 1755, *DRCHNY* 10: 407 (Contrecoeur also "did not expect that he was to be attacked by such a considerable force": *DRCHNY* 10: 382).

10. G.F.G. Stanley, *New France: The Last Phase, 1744–1760* (Toronto, 1968), 95; Ronald D. Martin, "Confrontation at the Monongahela: Climax of the French Drive into the Upper Ohio Region." *PH* 37 (April 1970): 133–50.

11. Monongahela de Beaujeu, *The Hero of the Monongahela*, trans. G. E. Hawes (New York, 1913), 4–5; John Gilmary Shea, "Daniel Hyacinth Mary Liénard de Beaujeu," *PHMB* 8 (1884) 121–28; even Beaujeu's finest modern biographer, Malcolm MacLeod, in "Daniel-Marie Liénard de Beaujeu, 1711–1755: Empire Builder at Work and War," *Dalhousie Review* 53 (Summer 1973): 296–309, anachronistically refers to him as a "Yank-slayer" (304).

12. Contrecoeur to Beaujeu, June 7, 1755, and Duquesne to Contrecoeur, October 30, 1754, in *Papiers Contrecoeur*, 356, 266.

13. Joseph L. Peyser, trans. and ed., *Letters from New France: The Upper Country, 1686–1783* (Chicago, 1994), 103 (father); Malcolm MacLeod, "Liénard de Beaujeu, Daniel-Hyacinthe-Marie," David A. Armour, "Liénard de Beaujeu, Louis;" and David Daniel Ruddy, "Liénard De Beaujeu De Villemonde, Louis," *DCB* 3: 400–402; Acte des six nations iroquoises pour leur indépendance, 2 November 1748, Archives de la Province de Québec (microfilm reel 950 at PSA).

14. "Liste de M.ᵣˢ les officiers qui se sont trouvé dans l'affaire des Mines," 1747, ANOM COL C¹¹A 87, f. 283.

15. Liénard de Beaujeu, "Journal de la Campagne du Détachment de Canada à l'Acadie et aux Mines, en 1746–47," in *Le Canada Français* 2 (Quebec, 1889): 16–75, at 66 ("la joye") and 67 ("Nous entendions partout grand feu. Nous voyions de tout costé du monde en mouvement, sans pouvoir distinguer si c'étoit de nos gens, ou l'ennemy").

16. Claude De Bonnault, ed., "Pièces au sujet de M. Landriève," *BRH* 33 no. 8 (août 1927): 497–512, at 501; André Lachance, "Landriève des Bordes, Jean-Marie," *DCB* 4: 435–36.

17. "Tableau des mouvements que Duquesne a fait faire principalement en 1755," ANOM COL C¹¹A 100, ff 17–23, at 18–19; *Papiers Contrecoeur*, 87, n.1 (Carqueville), 343, n. 1 (Saint-Martin). It is likely that the young cadet Pierre-Philippe de Saint-Ours led this detachment, but his brother, François-Xavier, a lieutenant, might have led it. A cadet named Saint-Ours was at the Monongahela in 1755, and Pierre-Philippe was killed in 1757 near Fort Duquesne. See Yves Drolet, *Dictionnaire généalogique et héraldique de la noblesse canadienne française au XVIIe au XIXe siècle* (Montréal, 2010), 477, FrancoGène, http://www.francogene.com/dossiers/noblesse-quebecoise.pdf.

18. Franklin B. Hough, *A History of St. Lawrence and Franklin Counties, New York* (Albany, 1853), 182–83; Darren Bonaparte, transc., Eleazar Williams, *The Life of Colonel Louis Cook*, 1851, http://www.wampumchronicles.com/colonellouis.html, accessed March 12, 2010.

19. Monongahela de Beaujeu, ed., *Documents inedits sur le Colonel de Longueuil* (Montréal, 1891), 10–11 (May 15, 1755: "Il est ordonné au Sr. de Longueuil, enseigne en 2d des troupes de cette colonie de conduire les Hurons de Laurete à la Belle-Rivière, sous les ordres du Sr. de Courtemanche, lieutenant... "). See also ANOM COL E 290 (dossier Le Moyne de Longueuil), ff. 75–76.

20. "Tableau des mouvements," ANOM COL C¹¹A 100, ff 17–23: in Duquesne's recapitulation of the 1755 Detachment, only 617 French forces and 100 Indians went to the Belle Rivière posts, because the "Sieur de Villiers with a detachment of 200 men and 70 sauvages" had been ordered to remain at Niagara. By Duquesne's account, then, the total forces at the la Belle Rivière posts numbered 1,082 French marines and militia, and 200 *domiciliés*, once assembled.

21. Depending on the route over Lake Ontario, the journey from Montréal to Presque Isle is about 500 miles; the portage road to Rivière au Boeuf was 16 miles long; Rivière au Boeuf's circuitous course is a journey of 70 miles from Fort Le Boeuf to Venango; the distance from Venango to Pittsburgh along the Allegheny River is about 125 miles.

22. Pouchot, *Memoirs*, 323 (Montreal), 363 (river), 365, n. 1089, 399, n. 1245 and 459–60; *Léry Journal*, May 3, 1754, 3; Dale Standen, "Canoes and *Canots* in New France: Small Boats, Material History and Popular Imagination," *Material Culture Review* 68 (June 2008), 34–47.

23. Pouchot, *Memoirs*, 363, 366–67; *Léry Journal*, 4–6, 51 (canoe), 69 (Buisson); Adjutant Malartic to Count d'Argenson, October 6, 1755, *DRCHNY* 10: 349–50.

24. Pouchot, *Memoirs*, 127, 379, n. 1155; Stevens et al., *Travels in New France by J.C.B.*, 25. My rendering of the journey along the St. Lawrence is drawn from a variety of French travelers' accounts, including those by Pouchot, Céloron de Blainville, Joseph-Pierre Bonnecamps, Chaussegros de Léry, Pierre-François-Xavier de Charlevoix, and "Jolicoeur" Charles Bonin, among others.

25. ANOM COL C¹¹A 100, f. 22; Orders of May 17, 1754, in Beaujeu, *Documents inedits*, 9; *Léry Journal*, 7, 12; Pouchot, *Memoirs*, 421.

26. "Examination of Jean Silvestre and Wife," *SWJP* 1: 508–11, at 511; Hitchen Holland to James DeLancey, May 14, 1755, *MPCP* 6: 411; John Bradstreet to Colonial Governors, May 29, 1755, *SWJP* 1: 547–48.

27. Laperière to Contrecouer, June 11, 1755, *Papiers Contrecoeur*, 359–60: "Since May 18th, which was the date of M. de Beaujeu's arrival…" (Kent, 219); Pouchot, 415 (Niagara); Brian L. Dunnigan, "Portaging Niagara," *Inland Seas* 42 (Fall 1986): 177–83, 216–23.

28. A. Roy, ed., "Lettres de Daniel-Hyacinthe Liénard de Beaujeu, Commandant au Fort Niagara," *BRH* 37 (1931): 355–72; Robert L. Emerson and Callista L. O'Brien, "Agent of Empire: The Life and Letters of Daniel-Hyacinthe Liénard de Beaujeu," *Fortress Niagara* 2, no. 4 (June 2001): 3–11. I am grateful to Robert Emerson for bringing these letters to my attention in 2001.

29. Beaujeu to Galissonière, July 7, 1749, in Roy, *Lettres*, 358 ("cette garnison est composée d'anciens ivrognes de Montréal") and 355 ("il est très difficile d'en réprimer l'insolence").

30. Beaujeu to Galissonière, July 7, 1749, in Roy, *Lettres*, 359 ("l'arsenal de ce poste étant composé en partie de fusils à traite qui ne sont pas surs, que je crois qu'il conviendrait de les remplacer par des grenadiers, ou fusils de chasse"); Beaujeu to Galissonière, August 23, 1749, in Roy, *Lettres*, 364 (bedbugs).

31. Beaujeu to Galissonière, August 23, 1749, in Roy, *Lettres*, 364 ("un fort qui ne sera jamais solide, et toujours menacé de tomber dans le Lac").

32. Beaujeu to Galissonière, July 7, 1749, in Roy, *Lettres*, 358 ("j'ai travaillé inutilement").

33. Beaujeu to Galissonière, July 31, 1749, in Roy, *Lettres*, 361 ("Je suis surpris que vous me parliez de la sorte…").

34. Dunnigan, "Portaging Niagara," 177–83, 216–23; Frank Severance, *An Old Frontier of France: The Niagara Region and Adjacent Lakes under French Control*, 2 vols. (New York, 1917), 1: 378 and 2: 2–13; Pouchot, *Memoirs*, 62–63 (Seneca laborers).

35. Beaujeu to Contrecouer, June 1, 1755, Laperière to Beaujeu, June 11, 1755, and Laperière to Contrecouer, June 11, 1755, *Papiers Contrecoeur*, 353, 359–60; *Léry Journal*, 18 (repairs). Jean-Baptiste Phillipe Testard de Montigny accompanied a party of Kanesetake Iroquois: Laperière to Contrecoeur, June 1755, ASQ-VV Carton 2, no. 135, reel 1.

36. Laperière to Beaujeu, June 11, 1755, *Papiers Contrecoeur*, 358; Stotz, *Outposts*, 74–75, Hunter, *Forts*, 61–79.

37. Hunter, *Forts*, 74 (Bougainville); Benoist to Contrecoeur, June 30, 1755, *Papiers Contrecoeur*, 369–70 (Kent, 225); Étienne Taillemite, "Benoist, Antoine-Gabriel-François," *DCB* 4: 54–55.

38. Lévis à Mirepoix, 4 September 1757, in H. G. Casgrain, ed., *Collection de manuscrits du Maréchal de Lévis*, 12 vols. (Québec, 1889–1899), 2: 143.

39. Autumn L. Leonard, "The Presque Isle Portage and the Venango Trail," *Pennsylvania Archaeologist* 15, no. 1–4 (1945): 4–9, 59–64, 75–87, 119–27; Paul A. W. Wallace, *Indian Paths of Pennsylvania* (Harrisburg, 1965), 140, 170–73; Stotz, *Outposts*; History of Erie County, Pennsylvania, Vol. 1 (Chicago, 1884), 194.

40. Duquesne to Contrecoeur, August 14, 1754, *Papiers Contrecoeur*, 246 (Kent, 181).

41. St. Blin to Contrecoeur, July 7, 1755, *Papiers Contrecoeur*, 386: "The portage road is ruining my horses. Almost all the bridges are ruined and are miring the teams" (Kent, 233). See *Papiers Contrecoeur*, 413–17, for additional discussion, and ANOM COL E 168, ff. 493–94 (dossier Duverger de St. Blin).

42. *Léry Journal*, 43–45, contains his careful survey of the portage road in 1754 and records eleven different bridged areas (i.e., corduroy road, not actual bridges) along the route; *Wilderness Chronicles*, 172; Thomas Forbes Journal, in Darlington, *Christopher Gist's Journals*, 150 (travel time); *Travels in New France*, 55 (delays).

43. Laperière to Contrecouer, June 11, 1755, and Benoist to Beaujeu, June 30, 1755, *Papiers Contrecoeur*, 359, 369.

44. Kent, *French Invasion*, 68 (cadavers); Lake Erie's southern shore had been a "common resort of 'Lake Indians,'" a name applied to the Ottawas, Chippewas, and related Indians" who seasonally hunted there. Mississaugas also came to settle permanently in the area, as a French document from 1756 refers to the "domiciliated Mississagués of Presqu'isle" (see Vaudreuil to Machault, August 8, 1756, *DRCHNY* 10: 435; Hunter, *Forts*, 65, 81).

45. St. Blin to Contrecoeur, July 3, 1755, Benoist to Contrecoeur, July 6, 1755, *Papiers Contrecoeur*, 374–75, 381 (Kent, 229–31); Joseph L. Peyser, *On the Eve of the Conquest: The Chevalier de Raymond's Critique of New France in 1754* (East Lansing, 1997), 86 (charrette); wine and brandy consumed by Beaujeu's detachment, 1755, ASQ-VV, Carton 4, no. 379, reel 3; See also Duquesne to Vaudreuil, July 6, 1755, *Wilderness Chronicles*, 90, and Pouchot, *Memoirs*, 62 (portages).

46. Saint-Ours to Contrecoeur, July 7, 1755, *Papiers Contrecoeur* 384 (Kent, 232); Stotz, *Outposts*, 74–75; 79–97; Hunter, *Forts*, 83 (dockyard).

47. La Chauvignerie to Contrecoeur and Beaujeu, July 9, 1755, *Papiers Contrecoeur*, 388 (Kent, 235) (low waters); Stevens, *Travels in New France by J.C.B.*, 55 (trees); GW to John Augustine Washington, May 28, 1755 *GWP* 1: 289, 287 n. 5 (drought).

48. "Garrisons on the Belle Rivière, June 1755," *Wilderness Chronicles*, 65 (ANOM COL C¹¹A 100, f. 20); La Chauvignerie to Contrecoeur, June 9, 1755, *Papiers Contrecoeur*, 357; Vaudreuil to Machault, August 8, 1756, *DRCHNY* 10: 436 (dispositions); Hunter, *Forts*, 138–41 (Venango). See dossier of Desmarets de la Chauvignerie, ANOM COL E 242, ff. 249–51, and Serge Goudreau, "Michel Maray de La Chauvignerie," *Mémoires de la société généalogique canadienne-française* 48 (hiver 1997): 317–30.

49. La Chauvignerie to Contrecoeur and Beaujeu, July 9, 1755, *Papiers Contrecoeur*, 389 (Kent, 235) (Indians); Hunter, *Forts*, 151–54 (Delawares); Severance, *Old Frontier*, 2: 154–58 (La Chauvignerie); Malcolm MacLeod, "Chabert de Joncaire, Philippe-Thomas," *DCB*. I use John Fraser's own spelling of his name—not Frasier or Frazier—from a 1774 Bedford County court paper that he signed (in the collections of the Braddock's Battlefield History Center, Braddock, Pa). On Venango and Ticastoroga (Custaloga's Town or Cussewago), see *PA* 1st ser., 3: 296 and George P. Donehoo, *Indian Villages and Place Names in Pennsylvania* (Harrisburg, 1928), 52–53, 243–45.

50. Contrecoeur to De Léry, July 29, 1755, La Chauvignerie to Contrecoeur, July 29, 1755, and La Chauvignerie to Contrecoeur, August 27, 1755, *Papiers Contrecoeur*, 404, 401–2, 425–27; Vaudreuil to Minister, January 20, 1759, *Wilderness Chronicles*, 129 (quote); Stotz, *Outposts*, 76–79; Hunter, *Forts*, 136–67 (quote at 153). See Brian L. Fritz and William

Black, "Finding Fort Machault," *Pennsylvania Archaeologist* 82 (September 2012), 34–43, for recent excavations of the fort site in Franklin, Pa.

51. Contrecoeur to Beaujeu, June 7, 1755, and St. Blin to Contrecoeur, June 17, 1755, *Papiers Contrecoeur,* 356–57 (Kent, 217–18), 364 (Beaujeu's supplies); De Bonnault, "Pièces au sujet de M. Landrième," 501.

52. De Bonnault, "Pièces au sujet de M. Landrième," 502.

53. Benoist to Beaujeu and Contrecoeur, June 30, 1755; Benoist to Contrecoeur, July 6, 1755; St. Ours to Contrecoeur, July 7, 1755; and La Chauvignerie to Contrecoeur, July 18, 1755, *Papiers Contrecoeur,* 369–73, 381–84 (departure), 395 (party's ordeal).

54. Thomas Forbes Journal, *Gist's Journals,* 150–51; Andrew Gallup, *The Céloron Expedition to the Ohio Country 1749: The Reports of Pierre-Joseph Céloron and Father Bonnecamps* (Westminster, Md., 1997), 71; *Travels in New France by J.C.B.,* 93; Indian God Rock Petroglyphs Site, National Register of Historic Places Nomination, https://www.dot7.state.pa.us/ce_imagery/phmc_scans/H064449_01H.pdf. Observations of the Allegheny River are from personal canoeing trips.

An English captive at Fort Duquesne, named Staut, witnessed the arrival of large contingents of French and Indians beginning on July 2 and continuing for the next few days: see the *Pennsylvania Gazette,* August 7, 1755, p. 2 (article dated July 24 at Annapolis).

55. La Chauvignerie to Contrecoeur and Beaujeu, July 9, 1755, *Papiers Contrecoeur,* 388 (Kent, 235).

56. There has never been a concerted attempt to accurately define which Native peoples were present at Braddock's Defeat; a brief though partial attempt was Henry Rowe Schoolcraft's "Nationality of the Indians in Braddock's Defeat," in *History of the Indian Tribes of the United States: Their Present Condition and Prospects, and a Sketch of Their Ancient Status,* Volume 6 (Philadelphia, 1857), 215–18.

57. See the appendices in Dechêne, *Le Peuple, l'État et la Guerre,* 468–509, and Jay Cassel, "Troupes de la Marine in Canada, 1683–1760: Men and Materiel" (Ph.D. Diss., University of Toronto, 1987), 69–70 and Appendix D, 522–33.

58. Dechêne, *Le Peuple, l'État et la Guerre,* 194.

59. MacLeod, *The Canadian Iroquois,* chap. 3; ANOM COL C¹¹A 100, f. 28 (*Wilderness Chronicles,* 69) (Abenakis from St. Francis and Bécancour).

60. Contrecoeur to Vaudreuil, July 14, 1755, *MANA,* 130 ("les Sauvages du Détroit et de michilimakinak"); Roucher Account, in Kopperman, *Braddock,* 270 ("Utoweawas, Misillimakinaks, & Poutiawatamis at the Narrows"); *DRCHNY* 10: 401 and *Papiers Contrecoeur,* 224 (Miamis at war in 1754–1755); Capt. Thomas Morris's Journal, in Reuben G. Thwaites, *Early Western Journals, 1748–1765* (Cleveland, 1904), 1: 311 (Maumee Valley); Croghan, in Kopperman, *Braddock,* 184–85 (Wyandots); Contrecoeur to Vaudreuil, July 26, 1755, *Papiers Contrecoeur,* 400 "Hurons from the west"; Vaudreuil au ministre, 8 aout 1756, ANOM COL C¹¹A 101, f. 88 (*Wilderness Chronicles,* 94–96) also mentions Captain Dumas's diplomacy with Winnebagos and Chippewas in 1756; these nations could also have been at Fort Duquesne in 1755; John Joseph Matthews, *The Osages: Children of the Middle Waters* (Norman, 1961), 222–28; R. David Edmunds and Joseph L. Peyser, *The Fox Wars: The Mesquakie Challenge to New France* (Norman, 1993), 202 (Sac and Fox).

61. Vaudreuil au ministre, 8 aout 1756, ANOM COL C¹¹A 101, f. 88 (*Wilderness Chronicles,* 94–96) (Mississaugas, Ohio Iroquois, Shawnees); Contrecoeur to Vaudreuil, July 14, 1755, *MANA,* 130 ("ceux de la Balle Riviere"); Roucher notes Missassaugas, and "Shawanons & Iroquois of the five Nations, who are all near Fort Duquesne," in Kopperman, *Braddock,* 267; "Conferences between M. de Vaudreuil and the Indians, 1756," *DRCHNY* 10: 509 (Senecas); Vaudreuil to Machault, August 8, 1756 *DRCHNY* 10: 435–36 (Mississaugas and Ohio Iroquois); *Léry Journal,* July 20, 1754, 20 (Mississaugas at Fort Duquesne); Barsotti, *Scoouwa,* 20, 24, notes that some Delawares were warring against Pennsylvania and Braddock before July 1755; Croghan, in Kopperman, *Braddock,* 184 (Delawares and Shawnees).

62. Vaudreuil to Machault, August 8, 1756 *DRCHNY* 10: 435–36; *Léry Journal,* 40–41 (Missassaugas in 1754 campaign). French sources contradict what an Indian informant told James Kenny in 1763, that "not One of ye Delawares & only four Mingoes & three Shawanas" were present at Braddock's Defeat: John W. Jordan, ed., "Journal of James Kenny, 1761–1763," *PMHB* 37 (1913), 1–52, 152–201, at 183. In his 1850 interview with Lyman Draper, the Seneca Captain John Decker (Dah-gan-non-do) places Shawnees, Delawares, Wyandots, and Senecas at Braddock's Defeat: "Conversations with Capt. John Decker," 1850, Series S, Vol. 4, f. 94, Draper Manuscripts. Ackowanothio's speech in *PA* 1st ser., 3: 548–49 also remarks on Shawnee and Delaware participation against Braddock.

63. *Léry Journal,* February 24 and March 4, 1755, 92–94; Severance, *Old Frontier,* 2: 65; Duquesne to Contrecoeur, April 27, 1755, and Contrecoeur to Beaujeu, June 1, 1755, *Papiers Contrecoeur,* 322, 352.

64. Kevin Gélinas (Gladysz), *The French Trade Gun in North America, 1662–1759* (Woonsocket, R.I., 2011), chap. 3, quotes at 70 (Le Mercier); 78 (preference). Thomas Crocker's *Braddock's March,* contends (based only on research in English sources) that some Native warriors used rifles at the Monongahela and that rifles affected "the outcome of the battle" (309, n.6). I have seen no evidence in French sources that rifles were available in the Ohio Valley or used at the Monongahela, a judgment confirmed by historian Kevin Gélinas, the leading expert on eighteenth-century French firearms (e-mail communication, August 26, 2014). While it is in the realm of historical possibility that a handful of Native warriors may have acquired and used them, such speculation ignores a more obvious point: that Native warriors were incredibly accurate marksmen with smoothbore French trade guns.

65. Robert Scott Stephenson, "The Decorative Art of Securing Captives in the Eastern Woodlands," and Scott Meachum, "'Markes upon Their Clubhamers': Interpreting Pictography on Eastern War Clubs," in J.C.H. King and Christian F. Feest, eds., *Three Centuries of Woodlands Indian Art* (Altenstadt, Germany, 2007), 55–65, 66–74.

66. Dechêne, *Le Peuple, l'État et la Guerre,* 198–201; Cassel, "Troupes de la Marine," 46–50, 59; Andrew Gallup and Donald F. Shaffer, *La Marine: The French Colonial Soldier in Canada* (Westminster, Md., 1992).

67. Gélinas, *French Trade Gun,* chap. 2; René Chartrand, *Louis XV's Army (5): Colonial and Naval Troops* (London, 1997), 7–9; Gallup and Schaffer, *La Marine,* 53–133; and *Papiers Contrecoeur,* 273 (fuzils).

68. Cassel, "Troupes de la Marine," 70, 87–97, 118, 131, 135, Table 13 (173–76); Louis Franquet, *Voyages et mémoires sur le Canada* (Montréal, 1974), 118, 197–200; *Léry Journal,* 65 (Natives laughing). Cassel concludes that the Troupes du Canada were on the whole "not an impressive fighting force" (197), as does W. J. Eccles, in *France in America* (East Lansing, 1990), 103.

69. Cassel, "Troupes de la Marine," Appendix C, at 520; Dechêne, *Le Peuple, l'État et la Guerre,* 114–19, 201–208; Martin L. Nicolai, "A Different Kind of Courage: The French Military and the Canadian Irregular Soldier during the Seven Years' War," *Canadian Historical Review* 70 (March 1989): 53–75; W. J. Eccles's interpretations especially influenced the idea of the Canadian militia's effectiveness (e.g., *France in America,* 73). For French army officers' views of Canadians, see Julia L. Osman, "The Citizen Army of Old Regime France," (Ph.D. diss., University of North Carolina, 2010), chap. 2.

70. Contrecoeur à Vaudreuil, 14 juillet 1755, in *MANA,* 130 ("Ils…n'etoient malheureusement que des Enfant…les meilleurs avoient Resté a LaR[iviere] aux Boeuf a faire les portage des vivres"); "Detachement de la Belle-Rivière," and "Detachement de M. de Beaujeu," *Papiers Contrecoeur,* 329–45.

71. Pouchot, *Memoirs,* 314, and n. 155; Steven Delisle, *The Equipment of New France Militia, 1740–1760* (Bel Air, Md., 1998).

72. W. J. Eccles, "The Social, Economic, and Political Significance of the Military Establishment of New France," in *Essays on New France* (Toronto, 1987), 110–24.

73. Dechêne, *Le Peuple, l'État et la Guerre,* 201; Cassel, "Troupes de la Marine," 74–85, 105–13.

74. "Relation de l'affaire de la Belle-Rivière," in "Les 'mémoires' du Chevalier de la Pause," *Rapport de l'Archiviste de la Province de Québec* 13 (1932–1933): 307–16, at 308.

75. Duquesne to Contrecoeur, May 9, 1754, *Papiers Contrecoeur*, 123 (Kent, 136); *Léry Journal*, 41.

76. Duquesne to Contrecoeur, July 1, 1754, *Papiers Contrecoeur*, 209 (Kent, 163); see Lignery's narrative, dated 30 octobre 1755, in ANOM COL E 125 (Marchant des Ligneris), ff. 138–40; C. J. Russ, "Le Marchard de Lignery, François-Marie," *DCB* 3: 378–79; Edmunds and Peyser, *The Fox Wars*, 111; until Beaujeu's arrival, Lignery acted as Contrecoeur's second-in-command (Hunter, *Forts*, 115); Madame de Contrecoeur to her Husband, May 23, 1755, *Papiers Contrecoeur*, 348, and Lignery to Contrecoeur, July 30, 1755, ASQ-VV, Carton 1, no. 89, reel 1 (relationship between Lignery and Dumas).

77. Russel Bouchard, *Jean-Daniel Dumas, héros méconnu de la Nouvelle-France* (Montréal, 2008), 9–49.

78. ANOM COL E 153 (dossier Dumas), f. 413; Audet, *Jean-Daniel Dumas*, 20–21, 49–50; Dumas, quoted in Kent, *French Invasion*, 38–39; Étienne Taillemite, "Dumas, Jean-Daniel," *DCB* 4: 242–43; see also Duquesne to Contrecoeur, August 15, 1754, *Papiers Contrecoeur*, 247 for his praise of Dumas's abilities.

79. *DRCHNY* 10: 591 (Corbière); Gallup, *Céloron Expedition*, 27, 58; on Bailleul, see *Papiers Contrecoeur* 16 (Kent, 22); "Liste de M.ᴿ les officiers," ANOM COL CᴵᴵA 87, f. 283; Beaujeu, "Journal de la Campagne," 51, 65; *DRCHNY* 10: 262. See dossiers in ANOM COL E 14 (François de Bailleul), ff. 584–87; E 100 (Croisil de Courtemanche), ff. 399–408; and E 266 (Chevalier Le Borgne), ff. 233–35; and biographical sketches in *Papiers Contrecoeur* 87, n.1 (Carqueville); 44, n.3 (Courtemanche); 44 n. 2 and 205 n.2 (Le Borgne).

80. Paul Trap's exhaustive study of Langlade's career in the French and Indian War concludes that Langlade was probably not present at Braddock's Defeat. See Appendix A of Paul Trap, "Charles Langlade" (Unpublished Manuscript, Mackinac State Historic Parks, 1980). Michael McDonnell's forthcoming book on Langlade also confirms Trap's judgement (e-mail communication with author, April 3, 2014). See also Michael McDonnell, "Charles-Michel Mouet de Langlade: Warrior, Soldier, and Intercultural 'Window' on the Sixty Years' War for the Great Lakes," in David Curtis Skaggs and Larry L. Nelson, eds., *Sixty Years' War for the Great Lakes, 1754–1814* (East Lansing, 2001), 79–103.

81. See "List of Officers now on the Belle Rivière," *Léry Journal*, 32–33; C. F. Bouthillier, ed., "La bataille du 9 juillet 1755," *BRH* 14, no. 7 (1908): 222–23; Roucher, in Kopperman, *Braddock*, 267–68. One may posit that Langlade *may have been* present, based on the fact that Langlade was verifiably at Michilimackinac on May 25 and August 18, 1755, and records do not reveal his location between those dates (Trap, "Charles Langlade," Appendix A). But one cannot possibly justify through eighteenth-century French sources that Langlade had any shaping hand in the battle.

82. Augustin Grignon, "Seventy-two Years' Recollections of Wisconsin," *Wisconsin Historical Society Collections* 3 (1857): 195–295 (an account with dubious and unconvincing descriptions of the battle); Burgoyne to Germain, July 11, 1777, in John Burgoyne, *A State of the Expedition from Canada* (London: J. Almon, 1780), appendix 8, xxi, reported that the Canadian Indians and Ottawas among his army were "under the directions of a M. St. Luc, a Canadian gentleman of honour and parts, and one of the best partizans the French had last war, and of one Langlade, the very man who projected and executed with these very nations the defeat of General Braddock." The story was repeated in other British accounts and later adopted by Francis Parkman.

83. ANOM COL E 315bis (dossier Testard de Montigny), ff. 506–508, 531; David A. Armour, "Testard de Montigny, Jean-Baptiste-Philippe," *DCB* 4: 733–34; Laperière à Contrecoeur, Juin 1755, ASQ-VV, Reel 1, Carton 2, no. 135 ("Montigny avec les sauvages du lac"). Montigny departed Montréal in late May 1755 (*Papiers Contrecoeur*, 348).

84. *Léry Journal*, June 14, 1754, 17, 28 (Chauvignerie), 66 (Normanville); Laperière to Contrecoeur, June 1755, ASQ-VV Carton 2, no. 135, reel 1 (Courtemanche); Dumas, in Kopperman, *Braddock*, 254. In a 1757 "Special Return of the Indians" who were in the

1757 campaign against Fort William Henry, the "Officers attached to them" are listed in a separate column (*DRCHNY* 10: 607–8).

85. White, *The Middle Ground*, 142–43, 177.

86. *Léry Journal*, 74, 77, 87; MacLeod, *The Canadian Iroquois*, x (parallel war), and 41 (tensions).

87. *PA* 1st ser., 3: 548–49 (Ackowanothio); "Paroles de Contrecoeur aux Sauvages" [June 16, 1755], *Papiers Contrecoeur*, 363 (Kent, 221–22). See also Appendix E for another instance of the French warning Ohio Indians of the British threat.

88. Gregory Evans Dowd makes this same point for Pontiac's War, which was also true in 1755, in *War under Heaven: Pontiac, the Indian Nations, and the British Empire* (Baltimore, 2002), 34, 91.

89. MacLeod, *The Canadian Iroquois*, xv, 64, 126; Barsotti, *Scoouwa*, 28, 35; *Wilderness Chronicles*, 64–65 (garrison); Gallup, *The Céloron Expedition*, 45, and *Léry Journal*, 105 (multiethnic Ohio); *DRCHNY* 10: 232–33 (Ohio and hunting) and 509 (rampart); Vaudreuil to Minister, February 28, 1758, *DRCHNY* 10: 691 (height); *PA* 1st ser., 3: 548–49.

90. *Léry Journal*, 81–85 (quote at 85).

91. *Léry Journal*, February 24, 1755, 89.

92. *Léry Journal*, January 1, 1755, 79–80. See also Steele, "Shawnee Origins," 661–72.

93. Vaudreuil to Machault, July 24, 1755, *DRCHNY* 10: 307; see Hunter, *Forts*, 112–13, for a synopsis of French critiques of Fort Duquesne over the years.

94. Vaudreuil to Moras, July 12, 1757, and Vaudreuil to Machault, August 8, 1756, *DRCHNY* 10: 583, 426; the Illinois Country became crucial to the supply of Fort Duquesne after Braddock's Defeat: see Dumas to Makarty, November 10, 1755, *DRCHNY* 10: 407. See also *DRCHNY* 10: 583–84; Hunter, *Forts* 112; Deposition of John Charles Vian, January 30, 1758, in *DRIA-SC 1754–1767*, 443 ("Fort Chartres supplies Fort Duquesne with Flower"). The small French garrison of forty-four men at Fort Presque Isle temporarily abandoned the post in 1757 for lack of provisions: see Pouchot, *Memoirs*, 112.

95. Contrecoeur to Vaudreuil, June 2, 1755, *Papiers Contrecoeur*, 366 (Kent, 222).

CHAPTER 5

1. Instructions to Sir John St. Clair, May 28, 1755, JSCL; HOB, 94–95; Orme, 323; Seaman's Journal, 380–81; *MANA*, 86–89 (numbers in detachment).

2. Norman Baker estimates the total length of Braddock's march from Alexandria to the field of battle at 288.5 miles, including Dunbar's march through Maryland. There were twenty encampments during the 115-mile march from Fort Cumberland to the field of battle: Baker, *Braddock's Road*, 176, n. 393; Christopher Gist, *The Draught of Genl. Braddocks route towards Fort Du Quesne, 15th of Sept. 1755*, John Carter Brown Library Map Collection, 01541; in 1758, John Forbes estimated the exact mileage from Fort Cumberland to Fort Duquesne at 125 miles (*BP* 2: 265).

3. My descriptions of Braddock's Road and its surrounding terrain are based on fieldwork in hiking or driving the Braddock Road between 2003 and 2013, and in the past few years with my friend and colleague Norman Baker, the foremost scholar of the road. Any student must consult the John Kennedy Lacock Collection at the Lewis J. Ort Library at Frostburg State University, Maryland, an exquisite photographic resource and supplement to Lacock's famous article, "Braddock Road," *PMHB* 38, no.1 (1914): 1–38, and that of his companion, Henry Temple, in "Braddock's Road," *Ohio Archaeology Quarterly* 18 (1909): 432–42.

4. Cohen, "Major William Sparke," 550; Vice Admiral Samuel Graves, quoted in Spring, *With Zeal and with Bayonets Only*, 34 (see chapter 2 for British logistical constraints).

5. Charles Lee to Sidney Lee, June 18, 1756, *Lee Papers*, 3; Sir John St. Clair to Napier, June 13, 1755, Little Meadows, *MANA*, 94–95; *Expedition of Major General Braddock*, 16; St. Clair to Loudoun, January 12, 1756, LO 753. Such testimonies on American warfare were repeated twenty years later, during the War for American Independence. See Spring, *With Zeal and with Bayonets*, 47–48.

6. One of the key findings of Braddock Road scholar Bob Bantz is that the military road followed modern Fayette Street and proceeded toward the crest of Haystack Mountain, while a later colonial road was located along the lower flanks of the mountain. The two roads eventually intersected at Sandy Gap. See Baker, *Braddock's Road*, 51–54. There is no evidence that an Indian named Nemacolin blazed the trail west of Fort Cumberland for the Ohio Company, nor was the term "Nemacolin's path" used in the eighteenth century, to my knowledge. The source of the myth is John J. Jacob, *A Biographical Sketch of the Life of the Late Michael Cresap* (Cincinnati, 1866), 33. See also Lois Mulkearn's accurate discussion in *George Mercer Papers*, 510, 565–66.

7. Orme, 323; *GWP* 1: 293–94.

8. Peters to Morris, *PA* 1st ser., 2: 315; Orme, 325, 331; Seaman's Journal, 381.

9. Orme, 330; HOB 94–95.

10. My attribution of Gordon's authorship of *A Sketch of General Braddock's March* is based on a reference to such a "sketch" that Gordon mentions in a letter (in *MANA*,108), and also the close resemblances between the sketch of Braddock's Road and his earlier work on roads in Scotland: Harry Gordon, Maps of Scotland: Perthshire and Argyllshire, ca. 1749–1751, MR1/497, TNA.

11. St. Clair to Orme, April 13, 1755, and St. Clair to Napier, November 24, 1756, JSCL, 98, 312; BOB, liii (hatchet men); Orme, 318 (twelve-foot width). See Eric Sloane's classic *A Museum of Early American Tools* (Mineola, N.Y., 1964) on the road building tools described by St. Clair.

12. *Expedition of Major General Braddock*, 13–16: *Lee Papers* 1: 10.

13. Gordon Map; St. Clair to Orme, April 13, op cit.; BOB, xxxi; Orme, 323–24, 327; WO 116/5: Admission Books (1755–1764), Royal Hospital, Chelsea, f. 4, March 22, 1756 (Hilton was "disabled in the right shoulder" at Braddock's Defeat); RCB, 17–18 (halt, blasting); JSCL 134, 137; John St. Clair to Napier, June 13, 1755, *MANA*, 95 (arrival at Little Meadows on June 5, which corresponds to the date in Cholmley's batman's journal); HOB, 100–101 (Chapman's return); Seaman's Journal, 382 (weather).

14. HOB, 107; Brumwell, *Redcoats*, 137 (horses), 143 (labor), 147–48 (clothing); *MANA*, 235.

15. GW to George William Fairfax, June 7, 1755, GW to John Augustine Washington, June 28–July 2, 1755, *GWP* 1: 302–3, 323; *Carlisle Gazette* 3, no. 150 (June 18, 1788) (a Guinea slave with "many scars on his back" who claimed to be present at Braddock's Defeat and the conquests of Canada and Havana was recaptured in Pennsylvania in 1788).

16. "Inquiry into the Behaviour of the Troops at the Monongahela, Albany, Nov.r 21, 1755," WO 34/73, ff. 45–46.

17. Orme, 311; *Expedition of Major General Braddock*, 15, 26: Seaman's Journal, May 15, 1755, 377; Dunbar to Morris, September 12, 1755, Gratz Mss, HSP Case 4, Box 6; see also *GWP* 1: 305, n. 3; RCB, 20–21, 27; Cassel, "Troupes de la Marine," 350–64 (calories and salt provisions).

18. *Expedition of Major General Braddock*, 16; HOB, 107 (laurel); Dinwiddie to Dobbs, July 28, 1755, *DP* 2: 123; Robert Beverley, *The History and Present State of Virginia, In Four Parts* (London, 1705), Book II, 24; Brumwell, *Redcoats*, 149–50. Dobbs's encounter with this poisonous plant possibly saved his life, as he and his North Carolina contingent would remain with Dunbar's second division and not see action.

19. Seaman's Journal, 382; Orme, 322; Gordon Map; Harry Gordon Journal, *MANA* 104.

20. [Edward Braddock], "Instructions to James Innes, Esq:r Governor of Fort Cumberland," June 9, 1755, LO 583; JBO, 40; Orme, 322, 326; BOB, xlix, lv; Sharpe to Calvert, June 28, 1755, Sharpe Corr., 6: 234.

21. Orme, 331–32; GW Memorandum, May 30, 1755, *GWP* 1: 294, 298, n. 15.

22. Orme, 331–32.

23. JBO, 42; Orme, 333.

24. BOB, xxxv (Mr. Martin's); Gordon Map; HOB, 105; and Orme, 333.

25. Elizabeth Marshall Martin to Thomas Marshall, June 15, 1755, Breckinridge-Marshall Family Papers, 1755–1869, Filson Historical Society, Louisville, Ky. Though the letter

accurately dates Braddock's actual presence (June 15), there is reason to suspect its authenticity; the letter claims that Abram Martin participated in Braddock's expedition, for which there is no record. I include the letter here with the hope that other researchers may flesh out this mystery. See also "Locating Martin's Plantation," Western Maryland History Forum, http://wmdhistory.org/forum/index.php?topic=25.0;prev_next=prev#new, and "Martin's Plantation, "Maryland Historical Trust, Inventory of Historic Properties," http://www.msa.md.gov/megafile/msa/stagsere/se1/se5/000001/000001/000562/pdf/msa_se5_562.pdf (accessed November 14, 2012); "Marshall Family Genealogy," http://homepages.rootsweb.ancestry.com/~marshall/esmd1.htm, accessed November 14, 2012; and Sarah Susannah Adams, *As I Remember and Other Reminiscences* (New York, 1904), 38–42. Elizabeth Marshall (1726–1797) was the aunt of future Chief Justice John Marshall.

26. Orme, 334–35; BOB, xlviii (wagoners); "Anonymous Letter," *MANA*, 124 (never have done, [emphasis mine]); "Diary of a Journey of Moravians," in Mereness, *Travels in the American Colonies*, 335, 340, 349 (wagon travel); Baker, *Braddock's Road*, 59–66. See the 1908 US Geological Survey Map of the Frostburg (Md.) Quadrangle for the old course of Braddock's Road and the climb of 1,900 feet to 2,880 feet from George's Creek to Big Savage's crest.

27. Orme, 335, 342 ("let our carriages down a hill with tackles"); See "Diary of a Journey of Moravians," 338, 341, 345, 346, 349, for common techniques of eighteenth-century wagoners.

28. Stephen to Bouquet, August 8, 1758, *BP* 2: 341 (referring to the similar Shades of Death in Pennsylvania); William H. Love, ed., "A Quaker Pilgrimage: Being a Mission to the Indians from the Indian Committee of the Baltimore Yearly Meeting, to Fort Wayne, 1804," *Maryland Historical Magazine* 4 (1909): 1–23, at 5 (trees); Cresswell, 62 (dismal). See also Steve Colby, "The Shades of Death," *The Cumberland Road Project*, http://www.cumberlandroadproject.com/maryland/garrett/the-shades-of-death1.php, accessed March 5, 2012, and Baker, *Braddock's Road*, 67–71. Descriptions of old-growth forest are based on field work in extant old growth deciduous and coniferous stands in Cook Forest State Park, Pennsylvania.

29. Orme, 335 (corduroy); St. Clair to Napier, June 13, 1755, *MANA*, 95; RCB, 19; Gordon Map. For elevations, see USGS Topographic Map, Grantsville, Md. Quadrangle, 1914 (from 2,580 ft. in Wolf Swamp, where the corduroy bridges were located, to the saddle of the ridge, at 2,820 ft. is 240 ft.).

30. JBO, 42 (hills); *Expedition of Major General Braddock*, 26 (arms); Orme, 335–36 (marches, last water); Memorandum, May 30–June 11, 1755, *GWP* 1: 293 (deposit); Sharpe to Morris, July 15, 1755, *MPCP* 6: 477 and Gordon Map (abattis).

31. JBO, 42; Gordon Map (bad water); *MPCP* 6: 477 (illness).

32. Orme, 335–36; GW to John Augustine Washington, June 28–July 2, 1755, *GWP* 1: 320.

33. GW to John Augustine Washington, June 14 and June 28–July 2, 1755, GWP 1: 312, 320–22.

34. Shirley to Morris, June 11, 1755, *PA* 2: 357; St. Clair to Napier, July 22, 1755, and Dunbar to Napier, July 24, 1755, *MANA*, 102, 109; see discussion of this point in *GWP* 1: 325 n. 9: Orme's journal noted four formal councils of war: two at Fort Cumberland, one at Spendelow's Camp on June 11, and another at the Salt Lick Camp on July 3 (possibly another on the evening of July 8). Dunbar's letter may have been written with an eye toward defending his own reputation and castigating Braddock. But if Dunbar's account is true, it casts severe doubt on Washington's conviction that an actual council of war had been called to discuss the division of the army.

35. Braddock wrote to William Johnson from Fort Cumberland on June 9, 1755, that "I have receivd you[r] Letter by Mr Butler, informing me of the present situation of Indian Affairs," in *SWJP* 9: 187.

36. William Johnson to Edward Braddock, May 17, 1755, *SWJP* 1: 512–17 (n.b. that Johnson sent "this dispatch by Mr Butler whom I have appoitned a Lieut. over the Indians, these are Young Indian Warriors of the Mohawk Nation who go with him to pay their Duty to yr Excellency," and Johnson's endorsement, "Coppy of my letter to Generl. Braddock §

Lieu^t. J^n. Butler and Some Indians" (516). See also *SWJP* 1: 633. John Butler went on to have a distinguished and important career in the Seven Years' War and more famously, the American Revolution (see R. Arthur Bowler and Bruce G. Wilson, "Butler, John," *DCB* 4: 117–20).

37. "Examination of Jean Silvestre and Wife," *SWJP* 1: 508–11, at 511 (Johnson's endorsement shows that he had sent copies of Silvestre's examination to generals Shirley and Braddock); and Johnson to Braddock, May 17, 1755, *SWJP* 1: 517.

38. Shippen to Morris, June 17, 1755, and Burd to Peters, June 17, 1755, *MPCP* 6: 431 (quote on Butler's charge), 435–36; a letter from one of Dunbar's officers, dated June 22, 1755, confirms the general outline of Butler's charge and the influence of this recent intelligence on Braddock's decisions: "'Tis said this Morning the General has had Advice that 500 Regulars are in full March to the Fort, which is the Reason he is determined to be there before them" (Sharpe to Morris, July 15, 1755, *MPCP* 6: 477). On their way back to New York, Butler and his entourage made contact with James Burd, building the supply road, and met a Pennsylvania Indian trader, James Lowry, both of whom provided verification on the timing of Butler's visit to and from Fort Cumberland.

39. Bradstreet to Morris, May 29, 1755, *MPCP* 6: 412, says, "I have sent an Express with these Accounts this Day to the General across the Country, and have wrote to the several Governors from New York to Virginia also." Presumably Native couriers carried his express to Braddock well within two weeks' time. See also John Bradstreet to Colonial Governors, May 29, 1755, *SWJP* 1: 547–48.

40. Braddock to Morris, June 21, 1755 (*MPCP* 6: 446), written just two days after he had departed the Little Meadows, shows that Braddock had already received Bradstreet's overland couriers. Governor Sharpe had received Bradstreet's and Silvestre's information some time before June 4 and 8, respectively, and sent that information to Braddock (see *Sharpe*, Vol. 6: 213–16).

41. The term "flying column" appears to be of twentieth-century vintage, but it fits the spirit of Braddock's detachment. Smith's *Universal Military Dictionary* defined "Flying Camp" as "a strong body of horse and foot, commanded for the most part by a lieutenant-general, which is always in motion, both to cover its own garrisons, and to keep the enemy's army in a continual alarm."

42. JBO, 42 (Old Standers); *Duncan Cameron*, 10; HOB, 108–10. My estimate of 913 officers and men drawn from the 44th and 48th Regiments is based on the numbers in Halkett's Orderly Book (763) plus an estimate of 150 in the two grenadier companies. Total numbers of Irish regiments upon embarkation are drawn from "State and Condition of his Maj.s hired Transports on board which the Troops are Embarked for Virginia under the Care of Capt:n Hugh Palliser in Cork Harbour 10th Jan:y 1755," ADM 1/2292: Captains' Letters, 1755, Section 9, Hugh Palliser. Joseph Shippen, a civilian eyewitness who was at the Great Meadows when the army divided, also estimated the flying column's numbers at 1,200: Diary of Joseph Shippen, Jr., Misc. Microfilms # 1130, PSA.

43. Return of Ordnance by Thomas Ord and James Furnis, July 18, 1755, *MANA*, 96–97; Orme, 336. On the number of wagons in the flying column, principal reliance has been placed on the accounts of Orme, 336 ("about thirty"), and especially Gordon's accurate accounting of "three or four & thirty," matched almost perfectly in Mackellar's Map # 1 (thirty-six carriages drawn in the train, including artillery). The two additional wagons came as a result of Adam Stephen's party, along with George Washington rejoining the column in a covered wagon on July 8, bringing the total on July 9 to thirty-six carriages.

44. Orme, 336 (Indian presents).

45. *London Evening Post*, July 24–27, 1756, p.1; Dinwiddie to Braddock, June 16, 1755, *DP* 2: 65; see 1755 Army List, WO 65/2, pp. 62 and 66 (Floyer and Stone).

46. John Rutherford to Richard Peters, August 15, 1755, Richard Peters Papers, HSP, Volume 4, p. 41 (e.g., quoted in Anderson, *Crucible of War*, 96; Crocker, *Braddock's March*, 184; and Matthew Ward, *Breaking the Backcountry: The Seven Years' War in Virginia and Pennsylvania, 1754–1765* (Pittsburgh, 2003), 42).

47. Horatio Sharpe to William and John Sharpe, August 11, 1755 *Sharpe*, 1: 268; Sharpe to William Sharpe, September 15, 1755, *Sharpe*, 1: 284; Sir John St. Clair to Napier, July 22, 1755, JSCL, 123.

48. Gage to Albemarle, July 24, 1755, BL Add. Mss. 32857, f. 338.

49. Lily Lee Nixon, "Colonel James Burd in the Braddock Campaign," *WPHM* 17 (December 1934): 235–46.

50. [Thomas Pownall] "The New laied out Roads by Order of ye Assembly of Pennsylvania from Shippensburg to a Branch of Yohiogenni & from Alliquipis Gap to Wills Creek," [ca. 1755], LO 530. See also James P. Myers, Jr., "Mapping Pennsylvania's Western Frontier in 1756," *PMHB* 123 (January/April 1999): 3–30.

51. Peters to Burd, May 27, 1755, in Thomas Balch, ed., *Letters and papers Relating Chiefly to the Provincial History of Pennsylvania* (Philadelphia, 1855) 1: 39 (see 39–45 for western terminus); Orme, 316, 325; *MPCP* 6: 395–96 (forwardness), 425–26 (SC money), 430–31, 434–37; Houston, "Wagon Affair," 253, n. 28.

52. Contrecoeur to [Col. James Innes], March 22, 1755, *Papiers Contrecoeur* 305 ("hauteur des terres") and Duquesne to Contrecoeur, March 5, 1755 *Papiers Contrecoeur*, 281 [Kent, 203] (see also 308).

53. There were two "Normanville brothers" serving at la Belle Rivière in 1755 (Shea, *Relations diverses*, 10). Joseph Godefroy de Normanville (1727–1805) was likely the cadet whom Contrecoeur referred to as "Normanville the elder": a 1767 list of Canadian nobles residing in Québec shows a former lieutenant named Normanville, age forty, which corresponds to the year of his birth (1727). The younger brother may have been cadet Jean-Baptiste Godefroy de Normanville (b. 1736), who appears as a thirty-year-old ensign in the 1767 list. The French account of the battle in Appendix F, however, also mentions a "Vieux Pont Normanville," which may have been Jean-Baptiste Godefroy de Vieux Pont. See Douglas Brymner, *Report on Canadian Archives, 1888* (Ottawa, 1889), 44; Pierre-Georges Roy, *La famille Godefroy de Tonnancour* (Québec, 1904), 105–106, 109; and Appendix F.

54. Contrecoeur to Beaujeu, June 1 and 7, 1755, and Contrecoeur to Vaudreuil, June 21, 1755, *Papiers Contrecoeur*, 352 [Kent, 218], 356, 365. On the deserter from St. Clair's detachment, see St. Clair to Braddock, June 10, 1755, JSCL, 138.

55. Quaker missionaries later noted that images of the black soldier and Indian warrior were "cut upon the trees behind which they fell, as a memento of the circumstance" (Love, "Quaker Pilgrimage," 5); Gordon Map; Orme, 337–38.

56. Orme, 336–37.

57. JBO, 44; Contrecoeur to Vaudreuil, June 21, 1755, *Papiers Contrecoeur*, 366.

58. Four Abenakis departed on June 12; a party of twelve Senecas, Shawnees, and Cayugas left along with Louis-Amable Pertuis, a French interpreter among the Six Nations, on June 16. The following day, a party of fourteen reluctant Shawnees and Delawares went out, accompanied by two of the Baby traders who lived among the Shawnees (Louis, Jacques, or Antoine Baby). Contrecoeur significantly described the Shawnees and Delawares as having had "great difficulty in deciding to strike against the English." On June 20, Montisambert led a large force of around 150 Potawatomis and Ottawas who had come from Détroit, where he had ties to the French community there. On June 22, Ensign François de Bailleul departed with around 150 Wyandots and Ojibwas. On June 28, 120 Détroit-area Natives led by Lieutenant Jean-Baptiste-Marie Blaise Des Bergères de Rigauville departed. See Contrecoeur to Vaudreuil, June 21, 1755, *Papiers Contrecoeur*, 365–66; ANOM COL E 322, dossier Montizambert de Niverville, ff. 289–91; Dale Miquelon, "Baby, dit Dupéront (Dupéron, Duperron), Jacques," *DCB* 4: 38–39; Drolet, *Dictionnaire généalogique*, 42, 53. On Louis Pertuis, see Nancy L. Hagedorn, "'A Friend to Go between Them': Interpreters among the Iroquois, 1664–1775," (Ph.D. diss., History, College of William and Mary, 1995), 236.

59. Contrecoeur to Vaudreuil, June 21, 1755, *Papiers Contrecoeur*, 365–66 [Kent, 223].

60. Gordon Map; GW to John Augustine Washington, June 28–July 2, 1755, *GWP* 1: 322; Baker, *Braddock's Road*, 77–82.

61. GW to John Augustine Washington, June 28–July 2, 1755, *GWP* 1: 319 and 324, n.3. *GWR*, 19; Morris to GW, June 23, 1755, *GWP* 1: 315.

62. RCB, 22–23, Orme, 338; Gordon Map (Braddock's Run crossings); Baker, *Braddock's Road*, 83–94.

63. Orme, 340.

64. JBO, 44–45; Orme, 340–41; on stripped trees and pictographs, see Scott Meachum's pioneering work, "'Markes Upon Their Clubhamers'," 67–74.

65. JBO, 44–45; Batman, 23, HOB, 112.

66. JBO, 45; Orme, 342; McCardell, *Ill-Starred General*, 231.

67. JBO, 45; Orme, 343; Gordon Map, Baker, *Braddock's Road*, 99–101; Contrecoeur to Vaudreuil, June 21, 1755, *Papiers Contrecoeur*, 364–65.

68. Duquesne to Contrecoeur, April 27, 1755, *Papiers Contrecoeur*, 322 [Kent, 209]; Contrecoeur to Vaudreuil, July 14, 1755, in *MANA*, 129.

69. Orme, 344; RCB, 24; Gurney, *Northamptonshire Regiment*, 352, n. 19 (Dobson).

70. JBO, 46; RCB, 24; HOB, 114; Trimble, "Christopher Gist," 15–27.

71. William Johnston, "General Braddock's Campaign," *PMHB* 11 (1887): 93–97. 94; RCB, 24; Orme, 345; HOB, 114–15.

72. Orme, 345; JBO, 45; HOB, 115 (ammunition); Franklin B. Dexter, ed., *Diary of David McClure, Doctor of Divinity, 1748–1820* (New York, 1899), 108 (fort); Baker, *Braddock's Road*, 107–10.

73. Orme, 345; RCB, 24; Gordon Map; JBO, 46; GW to John Augustine Washington, June 28–July 2, 1755, *GWP* 1: 324; "Diary of a Journey of Moravians," 333, 340–41, 349, 354 (river crossings); Baker, *Braddock's Road*, 111–16.

74. GW to Orme, June 30, 1755, *GWP* 1: 329 (emphasis mine); GW to John Augustine Washington, June 28–July 2, 1755, *GWP* 1: 322–24. See also *MPCP* 6: 477.

75. Johnston, "General Braddock's Campaign," 93–94 (forage); GW to John Augustine Washington, June 28–July 2, 1755, *GWP* 1: 322–23; Dunbar to Napier, July 24, 1755, *MANA*, 109–11; Penn Papers Indian Affairs, Vol. 2 (1754–1756), 27, HSP; "Memorandum on Braddock's Road," *BP* 2: 654 (forage).

76. Three separate accounts mention the boy scalped alive: Harrison, "With Braddock's Army," 317; Seaman, 383; and *MPCP* 6: 457–58. On frontier attacks, see GW to John Augustine Washington, June 28–July 2, 1755, *GWP* 1: 319; Braddock to Morris, June 30, 1755, *MPCP* 6: 475–76; Dinwiddie to Shirley, June 3, 1755; Dinwiddie to the Several County Lieutenants, June 17, 1755, *DP* 2: 51, 67; *Maryland Gazette*, July 3, 1755; Ward, *Breaking the Backcountry*, 61, and Norman L. Baker, *French & Indian War in Frederick County, Virginia* (Winchester, 2000), 12, 16–17 (attack locations).

77. Barsotti, *Scoouwa*, 13–14, 18–20. The reliability and accuracy of James Smith's narrative can be confirmed by his account of his capture, compared to James Burd's letter to Governor Robert Morris of July 5, 1755. See also Patrick J. Spero, "Recreating James Smith at the Pennsylvania State Archives," *Pennsylvania History* 76 (2009): 474–83.

78. Roger Morris to GW, June 1755, and GW to Innes, July 2, 1755 *GWP* 1: 324, 328, n. 24, 330, 331; GW to Orme, June 30, 1755, *GWP* 1: 329; HOB, 119; JBO, 47.

79. JBO 46–47; Orme, 346; RCB 24; Wallace, *Indian Paths in Pennsylvania*, 27–30; Baker, *Braddock's Road*, 117–26; in addition to field work along the route, the author was privileged to attend a 2012 seminar on Braddock's Road in Westmoreland County, organized by the Mt. Pleasant Historical Society. On Captain Jacobs, see Preston, *The Texture of Contact*, 126, 174–75, and Donehoo, *Indian Villages and Place Names in Pennsylvania*, 73–74.

80. Gordon Map; JBO 47; Sir John St. Clair to Napier, July 22, 1755, *JSCL*, 123; Orme, 346–48. During the 1758 Forbes Expedition, British officers, including Washington, considered advancing from Loyalhanna, fortifying at the Salt Lick, then proceeding toward Fort Duquesne on Braddock's old road (see *BP* 2: 374, 380, and GW to Bouquet, August 2, 1758, *BP* 2: 302).

81. Orme, 347–48. If St. Clair was included in Orme's tally, the baronet had obviously been persuaded by these arguments and reversed himself.

82. *MPCP* 6: 589; Orme, 348–49; Gordon Map; JBO, 47; Baker, *Braddock's Road*, 127–36. See also Paul A.W. Wallace, "'Blunder Camp': A Note on the Braddock Road," *PMHB* (January 1963): 21–30.

83. HOB 115–16, 118; Orme, 346. Crocker, in *Braddock's March*, 193, and McCardell, *Ill-Starred General*, 232, both create a self-fulfilling prophecy about nervous Redcoats.

84. Gordon Map; Orme, 350; RCB, 25; Roucher; Roy, *La famille Godefroy de Tonnancour*, 110.

85. JBO, 47–48; Orme, 350; cf. RCB, 25–26; HOB, 119.

86. *MANA*, 129; Roucher, in Kopperman, *Braddock at the Monongahela*, 266; Beaujeu to Contrecoeur, June 1, 1755, and Contrecoeur to Minister, July 20, 1755, *Papiers Contrecoeur*, 354 (La Pérade) 397.

87. Orme, 349–50; RCB, 25–26; JBO, 47–48; Shea, *Relations diverses*, 10 (Simard); Roucher; A. A. Lambing, ed. and trans., *Register of Fort Duquesne, 1754–1756* (Pittsburgh, 1885), 58–59 (Simard); Baker, *Braddock's Road*, 137–38. After the battle, a rumor developed that Braddock had forbade his Indian allies from scalping. There is no evidence that such an order was given, and the scalping of Pierre Simard, along with Braddock's approval of scalp bounties, contradicts the rumor.

88. Gordon Map; Orme, 350–51; Baker, *Braddock's Road*, 141–46; Wallace, "Blunder Camp," 21–30.

89. [John Montresor], Copy of a Sketch of the Monongahela with the field of battle done by an Indian, ca. 1750s–1760s, Library of Congress, http://www.loc.gov/item/gm71002314/; Map of Fort Duquesne and Vicinity, ca. 1758, Dalhousie Muniments, 1748–1759, GD45/2/102, National Archives of Scotland (microfilm at PSA).

90. Gordon Map; Orme, 350–51; JBO, 48.

91. Gist Map, John Carter Brown Library (Camp 19 is named Blunder Camp, while Gordon's Map labels it the Turtle Creek camp). Orme, 351, JBO 48, and the Montresor Map all blame the guides; Wallace, "Blunder Camp," 27–30. Darlington, *Christopher Gist's Journals*, 33, 73–74, 86–87 (Gist's previous travels in the area). Fraser later told Washington that there was a route that "shunned" both the Monongahela and the Narrows—but did not specify where it was (GW to Bouquet, August 2, 1758, *BP* 2: 299).

92. On the Sewickley Old Town Path, see Wallace, *Indian Paths*, 251–52. Though Wallace does not cite it, James Burd's letter to Henry Bouquet, September 29, 1758, offers conclusive proof that the Sewickley Old Town Path led to the ridge route: "Captn Trent Reports that he has found a good road from the Breast work to Turtle Creek" (*BP* 2: 546); Bouquet's breastwork was a fortification on the Forbes Road to the north of Turtle Creek. Other corresponding evidence of the network of Indian trails, and how Indians and soldiers used them in Forbes's 1758 campaign can be found in Bouquet's Papers: *BP* 2: 325–29, 573, 578.

93. Thomas Mante, *History of the Late War in America and the Islands of the West Indies* (London, 1772), 27, states that Contrecoeur planned a defense that "might entitle himself and his garrison to the honours of war," for which there is no evidence in any French sources; Dumas, French C, and Roucher accounts, in Kopperman, *Braddock at the Monongahela*, 251, 255–56, 266–67 (French C's account states that the detachment was organized on July 8, while Roucher's account states that it was organized on July 7, with the intention of striking on July 8). *Pennsylvania Gazette*, October 28, 1756 (the soldier in Polson's Company "defected to the French about three Days before the Battle of Monongahela"). When Captain Dumas was in command of Fort Duquesne in 1756, he also believed that "to go out to meet the enemy and give him battle appeared inevitable" in case of enemy attack (*DRCHNY* 10: 410).

94. French B, in Kopperman, *Braddock at the Monongahela*, 256 (also *DRCHNY* 10: 337–38); Roucher, in Kopperman, *Braddock at the Monongahela*, 267 (Beaujeu sings war song on July 8). The French account in Appendix F also confirms that Beaujeu was at the July 8 conference.

95. "French B Account," in Kopperman, *Braddock at the Monongahela*, 256. An account entitled "Conference between M. Vaudreuil and the Five Nations, July 28, 1756, is one of

many examples of the French appealing to Indians by the metaphor of father—which may have been reflected in Beaujeu's appeal in July 1755 (*DRCHNY* 10: 447).

96. Barsotti, *Scoouwa*, 20–24.

97. Kopperman, *Braddock at the Monongahela*, 253; *MANA*, 130; Shea, *Relations diverses*, 10; Godefroy, Kopperman, *Braddock at the Monongahela*, 259; Roy, *La famille Godefroy de Tonnancour*, 104–10; Yves Drolet, Tables généalogiques de la *noblesse Québécoise* (Montréal, 2009), Table 89. "Transport, à Montréal, du permis de traite de Louis Godefroy de [Normanville], commandant aux Ouantanons, à François Augé et Pierre Bissonnet, marchands de Montréal, 4 juin 1738," Indiana History Mss., 1725–1973, Indiana University Archives Online http://webapp1.dlib. indiana.edu/findingaids/view?brand=general&docId=InU-Li-VAA1332&chunk .id=d1e654&startDoc=1.

98. French accounts reference a plan to ambush or dispute Braddock's crossing of the Monongahela; and an English captive at Fort Duquesne caught on to French intentions "to have disputed his Passage over the Monongahela, but coming too late for that Purpose, found him entered into the Valley where the Action happened" (*Pennsylvania Gazette*, August 7, 1755).

99. HOB, 119–20; *Expedition of Major General Braddock*, 27; Gordon Map (Defilé); Gordon Journal, *MANA*, 105; RCB, 26; JBO 48–49 confirms Gordon's account.

100. Memorandum, 8–9 July, *GWP* 1: 331; *GWR*, 19.

101. The Seaman's Journal specifically mentions that on July 8, Braddock "held a Council of War."

102. St. Clair to Henry Fox, July 22, 1755, JSCL; Sir John St. Clair to Robinson, Sept. 3, 1755, CO 5/46, ff. 32–33; Orme, 352; also St. Clair to Napier, July 22, 1755, *MANA*, 102.

103. Sargent, *History of an Expedition*, 215, has misled many scholars, but the ultimate source of the fable is John Entick, *The General History of the Late War: Containing It's Rise, Progress, and Event, in Europe, Asia, Africa, and America*, 5 vols. (London: Dilly, 1766) 1: 145.

104. Orme, 352; Seaman's Journal, 384; Sir John St. Clair to Robinson, Sept. 3, 1755, CO 5/46, ff. 32–33. Why the guides were called to describe what Braddock should have already known is puzzling. He had known enough about the narrows of the Long Run and Monongahela to try to avoid them altogether on July 7: had he and guides never previously discussed the possibility of fording the Monongahela?

105. St. Clair to Henry Fox, July 22, 1755, JSCL.

106. Contrecoeur the younger to his father, July 5, 1755, *Papiers Contrecoeur* 377 [Kent, 229]; *DRCHNY* 10: 307 (Vaudreuil); Dinwiddie to Halifax, June 6, 1755, *DP* 2: 55; Titus, *Old Dominion at War*, 69; Allan Macrae to GW, May 13, 1755, *GWP* 1: 270; James Wolfe to his father, June 29, 1755, in Beckles Willson, *The Life and Letters of James Wolfe* (London, 1909), 267.

107. *Maryland Gazette*, June 5, 1755; *South Carolina Gazette*, August 14, 1755; *ABF*, 135; John Gates Diary, 1755–1790, Pre-Revolutionary War Diaries, P-363, reel 4, f. 6. MHS.

CHAPTER 6

1. HOB, 120; RCB, 27; Orme, 352–53.

2. JBO, 49; RCB, 27; Dulany, "Military and Political Affairs," 17–18; Kopperman, *Braddock at the Monongahela*, 186–87 (Dunbar); David Jones, *A Journal of Two Visits Made to Some Nations of Indians on the West Side of the River Ohio in the Years 1772 and 1773* (Burlington, 1774), 18 (Mehmonawagehelak); Gordon's Journal, *MANA*, 106 (banks). Today, the railroad embankments running along the south side of the Mon near the old Duquesne Works convey a sense of those steep earthen banks that Braddock's men climbed.

3. Orme, 353–54; JBO, 49.

4. Orme, 354 (posted); JBO, 49 (embankment); RCB, 27–28.

5. Seaman's Journal, 384–85; Orme, 354 (pickets); *GWR*, 19; "Judge Yeates Visit to Braddock's Field," *Hazard's Register* 6 (August 1830): 104–5; Jared Sparks, ed. *Writings of George Washington* (Boston, 1833), 2: 469: "Washington was often heard to say during his lifetime, that the most beautiful spectacle he had ever beheld was the display of the British troops on this eventful morning."

6. Gordon Journal, *MANA*, 106; Seaman's Journal, 385; JBO, 49; Adam Stephen to John Hunter, Fort Cumberland, July 18, 1755, BL Egerton Mss., 3429, ff. 277–82; *Expedition of Major General Braddock*, 28.

7. "Mémoire des services de M. Landriève," in De Bonnault, "Pièces au sujet de M. Landriève," *BRH* 10 (1927): 626–40, at 626 ("il contribua en tout ce qui dépendoit de lui à sa défaite, en pourvoiant à tous les besoins du détachement de François et sauvages qui marcha contre ce general"); on French supplies of powder and ball, see Barsotti, *Scoouwa*, 24–25; Peyser, *Jacques Legardeur De Saint-Pierre*, 86–87, 93–95; Benoist to Contrecoeur, June 30, 1755, and St. Blin to Contrecoeur, July 7, 1755, *Papiers Contrecoeur*, 371, 385; e-mail correspondence with Dr. Keith Widder, August 25, 2011 (shots).

8. Beaujeu's tactical skill, confidence, and aggressiveness are clearly shown in the new French account (Appendix F) and deflates Captain Dumas's claim that he suggested the attack.

9. Lambing, *Register of Fort Duquesne*, 62–63; Roucher, in Kopperman, *Braddock at the Monongahela*, 267.

10. None of the accounts by eyewitnesses at Fort Duquesne mention Indian reluctance to *fight* on the morning of July 9. Beaujeu's speech happened on July 8, when there was an actual council at which he sang the war song. French B was a French Army regular in the Champlain Valley and not an eyewitness to events at Fort Duquesne: see the original and complete published versions of French B's account in Shea, *Relations diverses*, 26–29, and *DRCHNY* 10: 337–40.

11. For total strength and officers in the detachment, see appendices.

12. Historians and filmmakers have interpolated Beaujeu into a reference in a British account: the "Seaman's Journal" related that engineer Harry Gordon, who was indeed among the first to spot the French, saw "the Officer who was their leader, dressed like an Indian with a Gorget, on, waved his Hatt, by way of Signal to disperse to ye Right and left, forming a half moon" (387). Whether or not the officer Gordon spotted was Beaujeu cannot be proven. The story became entrenched in the literature through Parkman, *Montcalm and Wolfe*, 116–17, and John Gilmary Shea's 1884 article on Beaujeu that was, for many decades, the only biographical sketch in English. Shea wrote (without citation) that Beaujeu "came bounding on, rifle in hand, his hunting dress relieved only by the silver gorget which betokened his rank." Shea's story was picked up by later writers such as McCardell, *Ill-Starred General*, 244, and Crocker, *Braddock's March*, 202.

13. Godefroy, in Kopperman, *Braddock at the Monongahela*, 259 (Shea, *Relations diverses*, 10); Contrecoeur to minister, July 20, 1755, *Papiers Contrecoeur*, 397. Godefroy describes himself as an "officer in the garrison" of Fort Duquesne (Shea, *Relations diverses*, 9). There were four cadets named Godefroy who participated in the campaign and who could have written the relation: Joseph Godefroy de Normanville, Jean-Baptiste Godefroy de Normanville, Hyacinthe Godefroy de Linctot, and Daniel-Maurice Godefroy de Linctot. Whoever the author, his presence at Fort Duquesne gives greater credence to his account.

14. My colleague Peter MacLeod deserves all credit for the discovery of this map, published as an illustration in his superb book *The Canadian Iroquois in the Seven Years' War*. I only claim to have fully contextualized this important map to show how it changes our understanding of Braddock's Defeat. I am grateful to Peter and to archivist Isabelle Charron at the LAC for their help in locating this crucial map.

15. Appendix F (Le Courtois); Stevens, *Travels in New France*, 82 (three columns). Cf. French C, in Kopperman, *Braddock at the Monongahela*, 259 (Shea, *Relations diverses*, 10); French A, in Kopperman, *Braddock at the Monongahela*, 253–54 (Shea, *Relations diverses*, 27); and Roucher, Kopperman, *Braddock at the Monongahela*, 268.

16. St. Clair to Napier, July 22, 1755, *MANA*, 103; RCB 28. It should be noted that only Cholmley's batman mentions such a conversation between Gage and St. Clair. Morris to Robinson, CO 5/16, ff. 19–20, mentions a letter from Braddock that wrote of his plan to arrive at Fort Duquesne on July 10, 1755.

17. "Inquiry into the Behaviour of the Troops at the Monongahela, Albany, Nov.r 21, 1755," WO 34/73, ff. 45–46; Gage to Albemarle, July 24, 1755, BL Add. Mss. 32857, ff. 338–339

(scouts); Harry Gordon's journal also confirms Gage's report, referring to "the Guides which were all the scouts we had" (*MANA*, 106). Randy E. Gaborko, in "Intelligence and Security in Major General Edward Braddock's Campaign against Fort Duquesne, 1755" (M.S. thesis, National Defense Intelligence College, 2007), is the first to raise an intriguing question about the exact location of Braddock's Indian scouts, long presumed to be at the head of the entire army. I am grateful to Randy for sharing his work with me. Yet unless some new primary source is discovered, any attempt to state *definitively* where Braddock's Indian scouts were located remains speculative.

18. General John Forbes perceived the lack of timely intelligence as a major reason for Braddock's and Grant's defeats: see his undated memorandum (ca. 1758), "Explanation to the Plan of the line of Battle," Box 7, Folder 500, John Forbes Headquarters Papers, UVA. "Guides," in Smith, *Universal Military Dictionary.*

19. Pargellis's inaccurate descriptions of the battlefield's actual terrain and Braddock's route of advance along area trail networks have misled countless historians: Pargellis, "Braddock's Defeat," 259; Kopperman, *Braddock at the Monongahela,* 50, 115; Gipson, *The Great War for Empire,* 94. With an elevation of 1,200 feet, the ridge above Braddock was no "hillock" but as high and as steep as Quebec's Heights of Abraham above the St. Lawrence River.

20. USGS Topographic Map, Braddock Quadrangle, 1979; Raymond E. Murphy and Marion Murphy, *Pennsylvania: A Regional Geography* (Harrisburg, 1937), 37 (the Monongahela Valley is properly part of the unglaciated Appalachian Plateau, into which rivers have eroded deep cuts and channels that appear to be mountains).

21. On the trail leading from Fraser's and Turtle Creek to Shannopin's Town, see Gist's *Draught of Genl. Braddocks route,* JCBL, and "George Washington's Map, Accompanying His "Journal to the Ohio," 1754, LOC.

22. Map of Fort Duquesne, in "General Braddock's Military Plans, captured by the French before Fort Duquesne," 1755, HM 898, HL; Gist estimated the distance across the Allegheny at Shannopin's Town to be near a quarter-mile wide (76 poles or 19 chains) (Darlington, *Christopher Gist's Journals,* 34); the existence of a ford at Shannopin's Town also can be found on a ca. 1758 map of Fort Duquesne and its environs in the Dalhousie Muniments, 1748–1759, GD45/2/102. Seizing the ford at Shannopin's Town would not only have cut off the French line of retreat but enabled Braddock to continue his advance up the Allegheny River.

23. Mackellar's maps clearly indicate that those ravines did not run *parallel* to the British column. The French and Indians therefore did not fight from ravines along the length of the column, as some nineteenth-century accounts erroneously reported.

24. *MANA,* 107.

25. My estimates are based on the following sources: HOB, 120 ("The Grends: to March Compleat with Offrs & 70 Rank & File," which would yield a total of 73 by adding a captain and two lieutenants); Cohen, "Major William Sparke," 551, who was in the 48th, records the number in the grenadier company as 78 exactly; the Seaman's Journal, 388, also gives correspondingly accurate numbers on the grenadiers companies: "out of Dunbar's grenadiers, who were 79 complete that day, only 9 returned untouched, and out of 70 of Halket's, only 13." Those total numbers of 149–51 correspond to all other British accounts that place the strength of Gage's advance party at 300 (approximately 150 grenadiers and 150 from the battalion companies of the 44th and 48th): see accounts of Gage, Dunbar, St. Clair, and the anonymous British officer, who all report around 300 men in the advanced party. Orme also reports 300 men in the advanced party and 200 in the working party (see Robert Orme Letter, July 18, 1755, BL Add. Mss. 28231, ff. 359–60 and Orme to Keppel, July 18, 1755, in Charles Henry Lincoln, "The Keppel Manuscripts Descriptive of the Defeat of Major-General Edward Braddock," *American Antiquarian Society Transactions* 11 (1909): 171–76, at 175.

26. Robert Orme Letter, July 1755, BL Add. Mss. 28231, ff. 359–60 ("to proceed as Usual"); Cohen, "Major William Sparke," 552 (Gage on horseback).

27. Gage was following Braddock's standing orders that "a third of the effectives" be deployed as flankers to "prevent any surprise which the nature of the country made them very

liable to" (Orme, 318). My reconstruction of the advanced party's flankers is based principally upon Mackellar, CO 5/46, f. 135, TNA, and the Plate, "Plan of the distribution of the advanced party consisting of 400 Men," in Orme, following 353.

28. Kopperman errs in placing Gates's company with the main advanced party of Gage (Kopperman, *Braddock at the Monongahela*, 6–37). The accounts from members of the advanced party place their numbers around 300 (roughly 150 grenadiers and 150 from the battalion companies of the 44th and 48th). Since June 27, Gates's New York Independents had been under Sir John St. Clair's command, along with the Virginia companies of captains Polson, Waggoner, and La Péronie (HOB, 114). No alteration had been made to that organization of the working party between June 27 and July 9, and being assigned to rearguard duty was certainly in keeping with British officers' attitudes toward the Independent Companies. I also base this placement of Gates's company on Mackellar's map (letter h, "Rear Guard of the advanced Party," corresponding to Gates's company). Finally, St. Clair states clearly that there were four captains under his command in the working party (St. C to Commissioner Hughes, September 3, 1755, JSCL, 172) and identifies "Those Companys of Poulson's Wagoners and Peyroney's who were under my Command the 9ᵗʰ" (St. Clair to Dinwiddie, July 23, 1755, JSCL, 142–43).

29. JBO, 49; see Kopperman's very reasoned commentary on this "controversy" (112–13). Whether it would have made any substantive difference for the advanced and work parties to have been even more advanced ahead of the main body is impossible to know. I suspect that the results would have been largely the same, and that historians would then criticize Braddock for having his column too extended along the road.

30. St. Clair, *MANA*, 103, 94; Orme, 355; Kopperman, *Braddock at the Monongahela*, 187 (Dunbar); JBO, 50. See George H. Lamb, ed., *The Unwritten History of Braddock's Field* (Pittsburgh, 1917), 12, for a 1791 survey of Braddock's Field that included oaks and walnuts; *Gist's Journals*, 69–70, also describe largely deciduous trees in the region, and bullet-riddled oaks were the most common tree noted by later travelers. The daunting nature of this "rising ground" can only be appreciated by a drive through North Braddock, Pennsylvania, to the top of the ridge.

31. RCB, 28 (Indians); Gordon's Journal, *MANA*, 106; Seaman's Journal, 387 (Gordon spots a French officer); Croghan, Kopperman, *Braddock at the Monongahela*, 184; The "Anonymous Letter on Braddock's Campaign," July 25, 1755 ("British E") also notes the "french in Indian dress" and "the french mostly in Indian dress notwithstand[ing] several were seen in the french uniform" *MANA*, 113, 117. As British E is probably not an eyewitness account, the anonymous letter probably reflects information from actual participants, such as Gordon, Croghan, and the Royal Navy officer.

32. Gage to Albemarle, July 24, 1755, BL Add. Mss. 32857, ff. 338–339; Orme's plan of the advanced party, following 353; RCB, 28. Gage ordered the men to "form in Order of Battle," and the unknown British officer also confirms a line of battle, as he mentions wheeling to the right and left (JBO, 50).

33. Appendix F (Le Courtois); Dumas and Godefroy de Linctot, in Kopperman, *Braddock at the Monongahela*, 251, 259. Engineer Mackellar's unpublished map, entitled "Sketch of the Ground & Disposition of the Troops & Indians when the Engagement of the 9ᵗʰ July began" (1755), Cumberland Papers, Box 61/A3, shows "the Engagement began where the Daggers cross" (at a ravine indicated on the map). The Braddock Battlefield History Center has good claim to be located at the very site of the initial volleys of the battle. The steep brow of this ravine can still be perceived on Baldridge Avenue in North Braddock, looking west toward the intersection of Baldridge and 6th Street and the area beyond where the scouts first sighted the French columns, along the old mainline of the Pennsylvania Railroad. Pierre Pouchot's *Memoirs*, 82, states clearly that the battle erupted over this gully: "The horsemen who arrived at the top of the gully saw the French, who were advancing to proceed down it, and wheeled round on their advance guard who were only about a musket shot away from them."

34. Gordon's Journal, *MANA*, 106 (front rank kneeling).
35. The Le Courtois account puts to rest the contention that Gage blundered by not having his two 6-pounders with him. That account and others (Contrecoeur, Dumas, Godefroy de Linctot, French A and C) credited British artillery with coming into action quickly and provoking the initial retreat of French and Canadian forces (cf. Kopperman, *Braddock at the Monongahela*, 114). My estimate of rounds fired is derived from the total numbers of 6-pounder ammunition (250) listed in the "Return of Ordnance" in *MANA*, 97, compared to the varying numbers of captured ammunition listed in French sources (most say that only fifty-seven 6-pounder "boulets" or shots were retrieved, but one reports 200: see "Mémoires du Chevalier de La Pause," 310; *MANA*, 131; and Shea, *Relations diverses*, 14). If the French only found 57 remaining shots for the 6-pounders, it suggests that British gunners had expended 193 rounds (probably all 148 rounds of case shot and a good proportion of their 102 round shot).
36. Appendix F (Le Courtois); Shea, *Relations diverses*, 13, 36; ANOM COL E 266, f. 235 (Le Borgne), and E 315bis, f. 69 (Montmédy); Dumas, in Kopperman, *Braddock at the Monongahela*, 252, states that the officers suffered their wounds "at the outset" of the battle.
37. Audet, *Jean-Daniel Dumas*, 24–25; Godefroy de Linctot, in Kopperman, *Braddock at the Monongahela*, 259 (retreat); French Map of Battle of the Monongahela, LAC (my translation).
38. The accounts of Contrecoeur, Dumas, French C, Godefroy de Linctot, and Roucher all testify that Beaujeu was killed in the third volley, not the first, as some accounts incorrectly have it. The French Map, LAC, literally reads "Rallying of the French in order of the first" (i.e., back to their initial position).
39. Audet, *Jean-Daniel Dumas*, 25 ("Notre déroute se présenta à mes yeux sous le plus désagréable point de vu ; et pour n'être point chargé de la mauvaise manoeuvre d'autruy, je ne songeay plus qu'a me faire tuer"). Kopperman did not include this meaningful sentence expressing Dumas's sense of impending defeat and his death wish in his translation of the letter (Kopperman, *Braddock at the Monongahela*, 251).
40. French Map, LAC; Appendix F (Le Courtois).
41. Dumas, in Kopperman, *Braddock at the Monongahela*, 251–52; Contrecoeur to Minister, July 20, 1755, *Papiers Contrecoeur*, 397 (Kent, 239) (Lignery); Pouchot, *Memoirs*, 82; *Duncan Cameron*, 11 (overshooting). For the heroic image, see Audet, *Jean-Daniel Dumas*, 55–60. Dumas's most recent biographer, Russel Bouchard, in *Jean-Daniel Dumas, heros méconnu de la Nouvelle-France*, appears to reinforce the older image of Dumas, now an "unsung hero" in his view, but adds little on his role during the battle.
42. "Journal of Christian Frederick Post," in Reuben Gold Thwaites, *Early Western Journals: 1748–1765* (Cleveland, 1904), 1:177–291, at 231; Barsotti, *Scoouwa*, 162; Dr. Alexander Hamilton, quoted in Leroy V. Eid, "'A Kind of Running Fight': Indian Battlefield Tactics in the Late Eighteenth Century," *WPHM* 71 (April 1988): 147–71.
43. ANOM COL E 100, f. 401 (dossier Croisil de Courtemanche); Pouchot, *Memoirs*, 77; William Michael Gorman, ed., *A Concise Account of North America, 1765, Originally Published in 1765 by Major Robert Rogers* (Westminster, Md., 2007), 166. See also MacLeod, *Canadian Iroquois*, chap. 2, on these leadership dynamics and how they affected every campaign of the war.
44. Barsotti, *Scoouwa*, 170; Milo Milton Quaife, ed., *John Long's Voyages and Travels in the Years 1768–1788* (Chicago, 1922), 63 (warriors reading terrain).
45. JBO, 49 and Anonymous Letter, *MANA*, 115 (first fire from left); Gordon's Journal, *MANA*, 106 (emphasis mine); Brumwell, *Redcoats*, 204.
46. Roucher, in Kopperman, *Braddock at the Monongahela*, 268; Barsotti, *Scoouwa*, 22 (Smith's account of scalp cries).
47. Cf. the famed "Rebel Yell" during the American Civil War, or the Chinese Army's use of bugles and whistles in their mass attacks on American forces in the Korean War: Kie Young-Shim, "Racing from Mao's Bugles," *New York Times*, June 25, 2010, and S. L. A. Marshall, *The River and the Gauntlet: Defeat of the Eighth Army by the Chinese Communist*

Forces, November 1950, in the Battle of the Chongchon River, Korea (New York, 1962), 93–94, 123, 157.

48. The *Annual Register, or a view of the history, politicks, and literature, of the year 1759* (London, 1760), 34 (scream); Kopperman, *Braddock at the Monongahela*, 254; Brumwell, *Redcoats*, 201, 218. A Delaware Indian in 1758 related to a British emissary that "we take care to have the first shot at our enemies, and then they are half dead before they begin to fight" ("Journal of Christian Frederick Post," in Thwaites, *Early Western Journals*, 1: 231).

49. Matthew Leslie, in Kopperman, *Braddock at the Monongahela*, 204; I have had my doubts about the veracity of Leslie as a source, mainly as there was no Captain John Conyngham (whom Leslie mentions in his account) in the 44th or 48th regiments in 1755, and no such officer is listed among the wounded. But there was a Lieutenant John Conyngham in the 7th Royal Regiment of Fusiliers who purchased a captaincy in the 35th Foot (Otway's) in Ireland in the year 1755. Captain Conyngham may have been on some kind of detached or volunteer service. See WO 65/2, Army List, 1755, f. 37; *Gentleman's Magazine* 25 (June 1755): 284.

50. *Expedition of Major General Braddock*, 28; Gage to Albemarle, July 24, 1755, BL Add. Mss. 32857, ff. 338–339, and Gordon Journal, *MANA*, 106 (flanking parties); Pouchot, *Memoirs*, 82 (flank protection).

51. Appendix F (Le Courtois); Gage to Albemarle, July 24, 1755, BL Add. Mss. 32857, ff. 338–339; RCB, 28 (Cholmley); Anonymous Letter, *MANA*, 117; "Extract of a Letter from Cork, Nov. 18," *London Evening-Post*, November 27, 1755, p. 1 (Cholmley's death); and Nichols, "Braddock Expedition," 303, n. 68 (Tatton); Reid, *1745: A Military History*, 39 (Tatton at Prestonpans). The account of Cholmley's wounding is secondhand, derived from an unknown British officer in Philadelphia who claimed to have been at the Monongahela. The account correctly identifies Cholmley's regiment but seems to embellish his death with the detail that the two warriors rubbed Cholmley's brains on their joints, explaining that it invigorated them.

52. Gordon Journal, *MANA*, 106 (50–60 paces); Gage to Albemarle, July 24, 1755, BL Add. Mss. 32857, ff. 338–339 (vanguard running in and rising ground); *Duncan Cameron*, 11.

53. "Major William Sparke," 551; Seaman's Journal, 388; Horatio Gates, in Kopperman, *Braddock at the Monongahela*, 196 (Gates's figure of eighteen total officers indicates that Gage's advanced party had four to five companies, each company having three to four officers); Dunbar, in Kopperman, *Braddock at the Monongahela*, 187.

54. St. Clair to Napier, July 22, 1755, *MANA*, 103; St. Clair to Dinwiddie, July 23, 1755, JSCL, 142 (Polson); Kopperman, *Braddock at the Monongahela*, 170 (Italian); St. Clair to Robert Napier, July 30, 1757, John Forbes Headquarters Papers, Box 1, item 20; Horatio Sharpe to William and John Sharpe, August 11, 1755, *Sharpe* 1: 268, and St. Clair to Robinson, Sept. 3, 1755, CO 5/46, ff. 32–33 (wounds); *New-York Gazette*, No. 452, November 30–December 7, 1767 (St. Clair's wounds). Examination of Jacob House, July 17, 1755, Penn Papers-Indian Affairs, HSP, Vol. 2, p. 27 (sheet). St. Clair may have later informed Dr. Alexander Hamilton that he told Braddock in Italian that the battle was lost and that he should retreat (Breslaw, "A Dismal Tragedy," 135–36), but his letter to Napier clearly states just the reverse, that he encouraged Braddock to assault the rising ground and did not counsel a retreat.

55. GW to Robert Jackson, August 2, 1755, *GWP* 1: 350; Washington's letter to Dinwiddie, July 18, 1755, also testifies to how "very unexpectedly" the British sensed the attack, *GWP* 1: 339.

56. St. Clair to Napier, July 22, 1755, *MANA*, 103; Mackellar, Map 1 (troops around Braddock); Orme, 354 (Braddock rode ahead); Orme to Napier, July 18, 1755, *MANA*, 99 (taken post). I conjecture that Morris went forward, as neither Orme nor Washington wrote of going forward on reconnaissance in any of their accounts. Perhaps Morris received his wounds during this effort and failed to make a report.

57. Orme to Napier, July 18, 1755, *MANA*, 99; Orme, 354; and the Mackellar maps show how the train was drawn up in a tighter defensive formation, and that Braddock had ordered

all of the battalion companies forward, with the exception of the American rearguard, and the regular flanking parties (numbering approximately twenty-four on map 1). As Mackellar's maps show, and Kopperman has proven (299, n.34), criticisms of Halkett for supposedly moving the train forward into Burton's column are utterly groundless. Lawrence Henry Gipson is particularly guilty of creating a controversy out of thin air regarding the train's disposition (*Great War for Empire*, 95–96). It is clear from Mackellar's maps that the train had not moved an inch beyond the first hollow way.

58. ADP 5–0, The Operations Process (Washington, D.C.: Department of the Army, 2012), 3.

59. Orme, 355.

60. Breslaw, "A Dismal Tragedy," 137; Mackellar, Map 1, marks with the letter "o" a "Twelve Pounder Field piece in ye rear of ye Convoy" that has been moved to the right flank of the convoy in Map 2; Orme, 355 (Indians off). The French reported 192 howitzer shells recovered from the battlefield, out of the 200 that the British carried (cf. *MANA*, 97, "Mémoires du Chevalier de La Pause," 310, and Appendix F).

61. *MANA*, 121; Breslaw, "A Dismal Tragedy," 137 (the story); John Galt, *The Progress of Genius or Authentic Memoirs of the Early Life of Benjamin West, Esq.* (Boston, 1831), 51–57. Hamilton and his father-in-law, Daniel Dulany, both championed Halkett in their writings ("Dulany, "Military and Political Affairs," 14, and N. Darnell Davis, ed., "British Newspaper Accounts of Braddock's Defeat," *PMHB* 23 (1899): 310–328, at 327.

62. Stephen to Hunter, July 18, 1755, BL Egerton Mss., 3429, states that "Sr. Peter Halket fell in the beginning of the Day"; George Washington recalled that Halkett was "early killed," *GWR*, 20; and the anonymous British officer records that he was "killed at ye: beginning" (JBO, 20).

63. I am grateful to Martin West for impressing on me the very crucial point regarding annihilation.

64. "Major William Sparke," 553; "Journal of Christian Frederick Post," 1: 230–32, at 231 (Delaware); Adam Stephen perceived that the Indians "took particular Aim at our Men & Officers especially" (Stephen to John Hunter, July 18, 1755, BL Egerton Mss., 3429). See Leroy Eid, "A Kind of Running Fight: Indian Battlefield Tactics in the Late Eighteenth Century," *WPHM* 71 (April 1988): 147–71, and Eid, "'Their Rules of War': The Validity of James Smith's Summary of Indian Woodland War," *Kentucky Historical Society Register* 86, no. 1 (1988): 4–23.

65. SWJP 1: 544, n.1 (Skowonidous); Loudoun to Cumberland, August 20, 1756, Albany, *MANA*, 225 (Jerry); Seaman's Journal, 386 (in sight).

66. Pouchot, *Memoirs*, 139; "Journal of Christian Frederick Post," 1: 231; Gage to Albemarle, July 24, 1755, BL Add. Mss. 32857, ff. 338–339. See Spring, *With Zeal and with Bayonets Only*, chap. 7, for officer roles. An anonymous British officer known as "British E"—not an eyewitness to the battle—claimed that enemy shots made a "Whiszing noise" (*MANA*, 115). Some have assumed that the noise must be rifle rounds, but there is no evidence that rifles were used at the Monongahela, or that they had any consequential role. I concur with Kopperman's assessment that British E was not a participant in the battle (234–36).

67. Barsotti, *Scoouwa*, 24.

68. *MANA*, 106.

69. *MANA*, 106; Gates, in Kopperman, *Braddock at the Monongahela*, 196; Orme to Napier, July 18, 1755, *MANA*, 99 (confusion); Patrick Mackellar was in the rear of the work party and had a panoramic view of the advanced party and main body behind him: see Shirley to Robinson, Nov. 5, 1755, in Lincoln, *Shirley Correspondence* 2: 320–21.

70. Seaman's Journal, 385; *MANA*, 106, 115–16; Orme to Keppel, July 18, 1755, in Lincoln, "Keppel Manuscripts," 175.

71. "Anonymous Letter," *MANA*, 115–16; BOB, lvi (the two colors taken for the flying column); Officer of 1st Battalion of Light Infantry, quoted in Spring, *With Zeal and with Bayonets Only*, 323, n. 32; Gage to Albemarle, July 24, 1755, BL Add. Mss. 32857, ff. 338–339. For men crowding, see the accounts of Dunbar, the anonymous British officer, Gage, Gordon, and Washington.

72. Mackellar Map 2; *MANA*, 96, n.1 (Ord at Fontenoy); Keppel to Cleveland, October 30, 1755, ADM 1/2009, f. 18–19, and "An Account of the Detachm.t of Seamen," ADM 1/2009, f. 20. My estimate of 99 rounds fired by the 12-pounders was derived, as discussed earlier, from the 274 rounds listed in Ord's return, subtracted by the 175 rounds of 12-pounder ammunition that the French captured (*MANA*, 97; "Mémoires du Chevalier de La Pause," 310; Shea, *Relations diverses*, 14, and Le Courtois, Appendix F).

73. GW to Dinwiddie, July 18, 1755, *GWP* 1: 340; *Expedition of Major General Braddock*, 28; Orme, "Keppel Manuscripts," 175; Breslaw, "A Dismal Tragedy," 135. As both Spring and Brumwell observe, the lack of fire discipline among Braddock's men was not uncommon in the eighteenth century (Brumwell, *Redcoats*, 196, and Spring, *With Zeal and with Bayonets Only*, 173–77).

74. *GWR*, 19.

75. Otho Williams, quoted in Spring, *With Zeal and with Bayonets Only*, 232. My understanding of combat shock and panic has been informed by critical readings of S. L. A. Marshall, *Men against Fire* (New York, 1947); Richard Holmes, *Acts of War: The Behavior of Men in Battle* (New York, 1985), 224–30; Dave Grossman, *On Combat: The Psychology and Physiology of Deadly Conflict in War and in Peace* (Belleville, Ill., 2004), Sections 1–2; and battle histories that are analogous to Braddock's Defeat.

76. JBO, 50 (Mawhawking [i.e., tomahawking]); "Inquiry into the Behaviour of the Troops at the Monongahela," WO 34/73, ff. 45–46; Dunbar, in Kopperman, *Braddock at the Monongahela*, 188; RCB, 29–30.

77. For example, Kopperman, *Braddock at the Monongahela*, 77, 116 ("in the final analysis the day was lost, not because one or more officers blundered, but because the regulars panicked. It was they who threw away the great advantage held by the British").

78. Mante, *History of the Late War in North-America*, 28; Thomas Farrell was later a captain in the 62nd Regiment (Army List, 1767, WO 65/17).

79. St. Clair to Earl of Hyndford, September 3, 1755, JSCL, 169–70; St. Clair to Robinson, Sept. 3, 1755, CO 5/46, ff. 32–33. Horatio Gates also condemned the rush to judgment against the common soldiers (Gates, in Kopperman, *Braddock at the Monongahela*, 196).

80. General Court Martial of Private Martin Lucorney, New York Independent Company of Peter Wraxall, July 13, 1757, WO 71/65, f. 354. Stephen Brumwell first discovered Lucorney's important testimony.

81. "Anecdote of General Gates," *Independent Gazetteer* (Philadelphia), Issue 171, February 5, 1785; Hezekiah Niles, *Principles and Acts of the Revolution in America* (Baltimore, 1822), 276; Gates, in Kopperman, *Braddock at the Monongahela*, 196; John Rutherford to Wife, July 12, 1755, *SWJP* 1: 712; and JBO, 57 (officer casualties).

82. Roll of Non-Commissioned Officers and Soldiers of His Majestys Independent Company, April 8, 1757; Last Will and Testament of Horatio Gates, April 7, 1755; Pay Receipt of New York Independent Company, July 24, 1759; Francis Penford to Gates, January 12, 1773; Memorial 1763, Horatio Gates Papers, NYHS.

83. "Return of His Majesty's Independant Company of Foot Commanded by Captain Horatio Gates New York 29th: January 1756," Horatio Gates Papers, NYHS. This return lists the killed and wounded specifically from the Battle of the Monongahela, a source never before cited (e.g., Nelson, in *Horatio Gates*, 17, falsely claims that the company "suffered only light casualties"). Gates led a smaller detachment of fifty-seven officers and men of the New York Independent Company with Braddock's column on June 18. Lieutenant William Spering commanded the remaining forty-seven men of Gates's company left behind in Dunbar's column. See HOB 109, 114; *MANA*, 86–87; Rutherford to Wife, July 12, 1755, *SWJP* 1: 712.

84. JCB, 29 (the batman also concurs with Sparke that "Our Indiens behaved very well for the Small Quantity of them"); "Major William Sparke," 553; *GWR*, 19; JBO, 50.

85. H. R. McIlwaine, ed., *Journals of the House of Burgesses*, Vol. 8, *1752–1755, 1756–1758* (Richmond, 1909), April 17 and April 20, 1756, 8: 371–72 (John Stewart); April 28 and May 3, 1757, 8: 441, 449 (Thomas Longdon); November 12 and 19, 1756, 11: 24 (John

Harwood); cf. Roster of Virginia Regiment, 1754, Fort Necessity National Battlefield Park, http://www.nps.gov/fone/historyculture/roster.htm, accessed July 9, 2012.

86. C. Doyly to M. De Villelongue, Secretaire de Mons.ʳ D'Aubenton, Commissaire General de la Marine, Ordonnateur à Bourdeaux, June 26, 1764, WO 4/75A, f. 382, and Attestation of William Johnstone, John Adair, and Robert Stuart, June 26, 1764, WO 4/75A, f. 383.

87. Accounts on the Virginia officers are confused, as there was Captain Thomas Waggoner (not wounded) and his brother, Ensign Edmund Waggoner, who was in La Péronie's company. British C's account, for example, falsely states that Captain Waggoner was killed in action. Edmund was killed in action, while Thomas survived. The blending suggests a broad movement of Virginians that involved officers and men in a composite formation, as estimates on the numbers of Virginians in these attacks range from 80 to 170.

88. St. Clair to Dinwiddie, July 23, 1755, JSCL, 142–43 ("Captain Waggoner, Lieuᵗ Stewart, Lieuᵗ Woodard, and Lieuᵗ McNiel were the only surviving Officers"); Breslaw, "A Dismal Tragedy," 135–36; "British C," in Kopperman, *Braddock at the Monongahela*, 174 (also Davis, "British Newspaper Accounts," 321); Burd to Morris, July 25, 1755, *MPCP* 6: 501 (Burd's account accurately draws from conversations with John St. Clair and Thomas Dunbar and perhaps other British and Virginian officers while he was at Fort Cumberland).

89. *GWR*, 19; Martin West asserts that "When the 'Remarks' are compared with contemporary documents from 1753 through 1758, the general's memory of that period is generally accurate, if occasionally selective and incomplete" (*GWR*, 32, n.9).

90. There is much evidence to commend Washington's autobiographical remarks and his memory of the battle. As early as July 25, the story of Braddock's refusal to allow his men to fight from behind trees had surfaced. For other contemporary accounts that indicate requests to Braddock to fight as irregulars, see Burd to Morris, July 25, 1755, *MPCP* 6: 501; Thomas Birch to Lord Roydon, August 30, 1755, BL Add. Mss. 35398, ff. 280–82; William Hunter to Franklin, July 27, 1755, in Houston, "Wagon Affair," 283; *Gentleman's Magazine* 25, September 1, 1755, 426; Dinwiddie to Halifax, October 1, 1755, *DP*, 2: 221; *Public Advertiser*, October 3, 1755, in Davis, "British Newspaper Accounts," 319. All of these suggest that *something* transpired between Washington, Braddock, and other officers concerning battle tactics.

91. Breslaw, "A Dismal Tragedy," 136 (grenadiers); the anonymous British officer also mentioned that "Upon our right were a couple of immense large trees fallen on each other which the Indians were in possession of & anoyed us from very much; but an Officer & a party of men soon dislogded ym, & by a pretty brisk fire kept our right tollerably easy" (JBO, 50), but it is unclear whether the officer in view was a provincial or a regular. See Burd to Morris, July 25, 1755, *MPCP* 6: 501 for Braddock's refusal.

92. GW to Dinwiddie, July 18, 1755, *GWP* 1: 339 (quote).

93. Washington to Mary Ball Washington, July 18, 1755, *GWP* 1: 336; My estimates are based on "A Return of the Virginia Mary-Land & North Carolina Troops, Encamp'd at Will's Creek—June the 8ᵗʰ 1755," in *MANA*, 88–89; William Stark, "A Daily Return of the Nine American Companys, Fort Cumberland, Sepʳ 17th 1755," in George Washington Papers Online, LOC, 1741–1799: Series 4. General Correspondence. 1697–1799, http://memory.loc.gov/mss/mgw4/029/0200/0294.jpg, accessed June 22, 2012. These returns provide the *only* gauge available for the casualties in the Virginia companies. Because the latter return is two months after the battle, they undoubtedly reflect combat casualties and desertion after the battle. The actual casualty rates on July 9 may have been even higher, closer to Washington's estimate that there were "scarce 30 Men left alive" in three Virginia companies (presumably referring to La Péronie, Polson, and Waggoner): *GWP* 1: 339. La Péronie's Company shows a total strength of 59 on June 8, 1755, and of 27 on September 17, a loss of 32 killed, wounded, missing (54 percent); Waggoner's Company shows a total strength of 60 on June 8, 1755, and 23 on September 17, a loss of 37 (61 percent).

94. GW to John Augustine Washington, July 18, 1755, *GWP* 1: 343; GW to Dinwiddie, July 18, 1755, *GWP* 1: 340: "I luckily escap'd with't a wound tho I had four Bullets through my

Coat and two Horses shot from under me." Washington's memory in old age was still perfect on these near misses (see *GWR*, 20). Orme to Morris, July 18, 1755, *MPCP* 6: 488 (confirms two horses).

95. Orme to Keppel, in Lincoln, "Keppel Manuscripts," 175 (pickled); Orme to Franklin, July 27, 1755, in Houston, "Wagon Affair," 284 (leg wound); *South Carolina Gazette*, August 21, 1755 (Morris); GW to Mary Ball Washington, July 18, 1755, *GWP* 1: 336–37 (duty and early timing in battle); Breslaw, "A Dismal Tragedy," 137 (Shirley killed at same time as Halkett); Gordon Journal, *MANA* 107 (Orme and Morris in wagon).

96. GW to Mary Ball Washington, July 18, 1755, GW to Augustine Washington, August 2, 1755, and GW to Warner Lewis, August 14, 1755, *GWP* 1: 337, 352, 360.

97. GW to John Augustine Washington, July 18, 1755, Fort Cumberland, *GWP* 1: 343.

98. Loudoun to Cumberland, October 2, 1756, *MANA*, 235; JBO, 51 and Gordon, *MANA*, 107 (accounts of Burton's attack); Orme to Keppel, July 18, 1755, in Lincoln, "Keppel Manuscripts," 175 (Burton's wound); Orme, 356 (Burton's personal leadership); Spring, *With Zeal and with Bayonets Only*, 180, 256–59 (attacking in woods). Based on Gage's account, it seems that Burton's attack (and others like it) were drawn up in line of battle but devolved into "a line of march by files" (Gage, in Kopperman, *Braddock at the Monongahela*, 192–93).

99. These were the remarks of Colonel Henry Bouquet to William Smith, author of a *Historical Account of Bouquet's Expedition Against the Ohio Indians in 1764*, first published in Philadelphia in 1765 (reprint, Cincinnati, 1907), 89.

100. Gage, in Kopperman, *Braddock at the Monongahela*, 193; JBO, 52; *Journals of the House of Burgesses* 8: 330: A sum of £8 was given wagoner "W. Lewin," who was "wounded in his Arm, and is thereby rendered incapable of maintaining himself"; Faragher, *Daniel Boone*, 36–38; *Pennsylvania Gazette*, August 21, 1755 (the writer pointedly observed that it seemed "most remarkable" that all of the wagoners from Lancaster and York counties had safely returned from Braddock's army, with two exceptions (3). Another eyewitness, James Furnis, recorded that most of the drivers left at the beginning of the battle (Kopperman, *Braddock at the Monongahela*, 190). Mackellar's Map 2 shows that the drivers had led their teams forward into a more compact formation.

101. Philip Hughes, in Kopperman, *Braddock at the Monongahela*, 203. George Bolton, *Remarks on the Present Defective State of Firearms* (London: T. Egerton, 1795), 23–28, discusses what often happened in battle with flintlocks. Though it is a later source, his findings are borne out in the records of the 1750s and in my own experience firing dozens of live rounds.

102. Seaman's Journal, 386.

103. Orme to Morris, July 18, 1755, *MPCP* 6: 488 (wounds); JBO, 51 (bullet holes); GW to Dinwiddie, July 18, 1755, GWP 1: 340 (Braddock's wounds); Orme's letters in Lincoln, "Keppel Manuscripts," 175; Pargellis, *MANA*, 99; and Davis, "British Newspaper Accounts," 323. I am thankful to Martin West for the observation about whether Braddock wore his full regimental or his "undress" frock coat of scarlet. See Kopperman, *Braddock at the Monongahela*, and John S. Ritenour, *Old Tom Fossit: A True Narrative Concerning a Thrilling Epoch of Early Colonial Days* (Pittsburgh, 1926), for discussions of the various claims by Thomas Fausett and others that they killed Braddock during the battle (138–40). Those nineteenth-century myths are not only impossible to prove but lack any substantial evidence from eighteenth-century sources.

104. Historian Jonathan L. Bell discusses the "twisted history" of Braddock's sash over the centuries in his blog, *Boston 1775*, http://boston1775.blogspot.com/search/label/Edward %20Braddock, accessed June 10, 2013. Carol James, a weaver and artist, recently reproduced an eighteenth-century sash and tested it to prove that the strong silk sash could successfully support a man's weight, http://sashweaver.com/tag/sprang-sash/, accessed June 10, 2013.

105. *GWR*, 19–20; Croghan, Gage, and Stewart's accounts, in Kopperman, *Braddock at the Monongahela*, 185, 193, and 229; Seaman's Journal, 386. Stewart's account of helping and

saving Braddock is not "legendary" as Kopperman suggests (293, n. 35). An article in the *Public Advertiser*, August 18, 1775, p. 2, confirms the 1755 account.

106. "Inquiry into the Behaviour of the Troops at the Monongahela," WO 34/73, ff. 45–46; Orme, 356; Roucher, in Kopperman, *Braddock at the Monongahela*, 268; Le Courtois (Appendix F). Mackellar, Map 2, relates that Braddock was mortally wounded shortly after the 12-pounders had been captured by the French and Indians, and before the final retreat. The unknown British officer and Washington also placed Braddock's wounding around the time of Burton's charge and final retreat (JBO, 51 and *GWR*, 19–20).

107. Le Courtois (Appendix F); ANOM COL E 100, f. 401 (Courtemanche); Gordon's Journal, *MANA*, 107; "Inquiry into the Behaviour of the Troops at the Monongahela," WO 34/73, ff. 45–46.

108. "Major William Sparke," 552; GW to Dinwiddie, July 18, 1755, *GWP* 1: 339; JCB, 30.

109. JBO, 52. The accounts of William Dunbar, James Furnis, Thomas Gage, Harry Gordon, and Robert Orme also convey this sense of a collective turn or "right-about" in an instant.

110. JCB, 30.

111. *Expedition of Major General Braddock*, 27, 29, states that "the rear was brought up by Captain *Dumary's*, and another Independent Company," and that on July 9th, "Lieutenant *Grey* with a Party of *Dumary's* Company came by, who brought up the Rear." The strength of the South Carolina Independent Company detachment was "Lieut Gray [John Gray] with two Serjts & fifty Rank and file of the Detacht" (HOB, 119). Capt. Paul Demeré does not appear to have taken part in the battle, remaining with the rest of the South Carolina Independents in Dunbar's division. The return of Demeré's company on June 8, 1755, shows 10 officers and staff and 96 effective rank-and-file men (*MANA*, 86–87).

112. HOB, 119, mentions "Capt Stephens Lieut Brenns" as the officers of the detachment bringing cattle to Braddock's army. I have successfully identified this "Lieut Brenns" as Lieutenant William Bronaugh, who was in Adam Stephen's Virginia ranger company. I reconstructed the officer corps of the Virginia companies at Braddock's Defeat using *GWP* 1: 342 n. 10. Although that document only gives the officers assigned to Waggoner's, Polson's, and La Péronie's companies, I was able to reconstruct the officers in Stewart's and Stephen's companies by process of elimination. McIlwaine, *Journal of the House of Burgesses*, 8: 301 establishes the Virginia officers who were present at Braddock's Defeat (including Bronaugh), and Dinwiddie's letter to Stephen on August 11, 1755, *DP* 2: 149, indicates that Bronaugh was one of Stephen's lieutenants.

113. HOB, 119; the return of Adam Stephen's company on June 8, 1755, shows 10 officers and staff and 51 effective rank-and-file men (*MANA*, 88–89); Harry Ward, *Major General Adam Stephen and the Cause of American Liberty* (Charlottesville, 1989), chap. 2. The fact that Stephen brought his entire company is proven in *GWP* 1: 342, n. 10, which states that "Capt. Stephens came up a few days before with his Company to Escort a Convoy of Provisions."

114. Mackellar, Map 2; Anonymous British Officer, *MANA*, 117 (execution).

115. Gray died at Frederica, Georgia, in October 1762, a Captain of the Independent Company of South Carolina (*Papers of Henry Laurens* 1: 154); Howarth was still active as late as 1775 as commander of Fort Johnson in Charles Town; he was listed among loyalists subject to banishment and confiscation of property in 1782 but given citizenship in 1785 (*Southern History Association Publications* 2 (April 1898): 139, n.2, and *South Carolina Historical Magazine* 55 (1954): 198).

116. Based on July and September 1755 returns of Stephen's Company cited earlier, there were 63 officers and men in June 1755, and 39 officers and men in September 1755, an attrition rate of 38 percent.

117. *Expedition of Major General Braddock*, 28–29; Adam Stephen to John Hunter, July 18, 1755, BL Egerton Mss., 3429.

118. Stewart, in Kopperman, *Braddock at the Monongahela*, 229; Gordon's Journal, *MANA*, 107 (Braddock and cart); "Major William Sparke," 552; Croghan and Gage speak of Braddock's virtual abandonment by all but a few officers, and of the brief silence over the

battlefield (Kopperman, *Braddock at the Monongahela*,185 and 193). *The Expedition of Major General Braddock*, 29, also mentions this phenomenon.

119. I am remembering here Eugene Sledge's apt description of the "abyss" of war, in *With the Old Breed At Peleliu and Okinawa* (New York, 1981), xxi.

120. "A Return of the Drums Arms & Accoutrements of the Above Company New York 29th January 1756," Horatio Gates Papers, NYHS; (Francis Halkett), "Return of Cloathing, Arms, etc. Artificers & Recruits in His Majesty's 35th 42d, 44th, 48th, 50th & 51st Regiments," August 17, 1756, LO 1962 (10 sergeants' coats, 4 drummers' coats, and 76 regimental coats); "An Account of the Camp Equipage and Cloathing lost by the 44.ᵗʰ Reg.ᵗ at the Monongahela in July 1755," WO 1/1, f. 69, and "An Account of Cloathing and Pioneers Accoutrements Drums &c provided by His Majesty's 48.ᵗʰ Regiment," WO 1/1, f. 94.

121. Cohen, "Major William Sparke," 552; Gordon's Journal, *MANA*, 108; JCB, 31; JBO, 52; James Furnis, in Kopperman, *Braddock at the Monongahela*, 189. Pouchot's *Memoirs*, 82.

122. Gordon's Journal, *MANA*, 107 (Burton); "Major William Sparke," 551 (scattering into wood); *GWR*, 21 (Narrows); JBO, 52 ("utmost agonies"). Orme, 357, *GWR*, 19, and Mackellar, Map 2, indicate the high ground near the July 8 encampment as the most plausible site of Gage's rally. Gage, in "Inquiry into the Behaviour of the Troops," WO 34/73, ff. 45–46, states that "about a Hundred men" rallied there.

123. *GWR*, 20–21 (adamant); JBO, 52–53 (marks).

124. *Duncan Cameron*, 4–7 (battles), 13 (quotes). "Anonymous Letter on Braddock's Defeat" lends great plausibility to Duncan Cameron's experience. Some soldiers witnessed the plundering and scalping and lived to tell about it: "some [British soldiers] who were left in the field of Battle and Crawl'd off afterwards, saw the French take possession of our Guns and over sett some from the Carridges, likewise over turn the Waggons..." (*MANA*, 117).

125. *Duncan Cameron*, 11–12; Roucher account, in Kopperman, *Braddock at the Monongahela*, 272 (strip'd); "Etat de L'artillerie," *MANA*, 131; A "Money Tumbril" had been ordered for the expedition in 1754 from Woolwich Arsenal (WO 47/44, f. 226–27). See also Croghan's account, in Kopperman, *Braddock at the Monongahela*, 185, based on information given to Croghan by Wyandots who were present at the battle that wounded were killed on the field. *Travels in New France*, 83, also references that Indians "were the first to discover the military chest. They did not know the value of money, and scattered it right and left in the forest." *GWR*, 19 (pursuit).

126. *Duncan Cameron*, 11–12; Dumas, in Kopperman, *Braddock at the Monongahela*, 252; Pouchot, *Memoirs*, 83; Contrecoeur and Roucher, in Kopperman, *Braddock at the Monongahela*, 250, 270 (counterattack and rumor).

127. Dumas and Roucher, in Kopperman, *Braddock at the Monongahela*, 252 (Beaujeu's body), 269 (Carqueville and La Pérade); 271 (Beaujeu's burial); Shea, *Relations diverses*, 13; Lambing, *Register of Fort Duquesne*, 58–65. See Appendix D for French casualties. The most exact and detailed accounting, not included in Kopperman's book, appears in Shea, *Relations diverses*, 35–37, and also as "Etat des Morts Et blessés du detachmt. françois dans le combat du 9.ᵉ juillet 1755," *Papiers Contrecoeur*, 390–91. If the "gully" in view was the ravine running along current Sixth Street in North Braddock, Beaujeu's body was likely found in the vicinity of the current Braddock's Battlefield History Center. The cemetery of Fort Duquesne, where Beaujeu was buried, remains somewhere in the vicinity of Point State Park (see Lambing, *Register of Fort Duquesne*, 92, n. 23, on its location).

128. Barsotti, *Scoouwa*, 25–28; Roucher's account, in Kopperman, *Braddock at the Monongahela*, 271, confirms Smith's memory that the Indians "brought an infinite Number of Scalps." Contrecoeur to Vaudreuil, July 31, 1755, *Papiers Contrecoeur*, 404 (trampling).

129. Barsotti, *Scoouwa*, 26. Though written years afterward, there is no convincing reason to doubt Smith's *Narrative*, which is very accurate concerning the details of his capture, arrival at Fort Duquesne, and the day of the battle. In addition, both Charles Stuart's and

Mary Jemison's captivity narratives corroborate Smith's testimony of the post-battle torture of British soldiers: see Bond, "Captivity Narrative of Charles Stuart," 74, and James Seaver, ed., *A Narrative of the Life of Mrs. Mary Jemison* (Syracuse, 1990), 91. For the accuracy of Smith's other comments, see Eid, "'Their Rules of War,'" 4–23.

130. Roucher, in Kopperman, *Braddock at the Monongahela*, 270; "Etat de L'artillerie," in Pargellis, *MANA*, 131 ("20 hommes ou femme fait Prisonnier par les Sauvages"). I am especially grateful to Professor Steele for sharing findings from his authoritative and exhaustive work on European captives: e-mail correspondence with Ian K. Steele, February 21, 2011. See his *Setting All the Captives Free: Capture, Adjustment, and Recollection in Allegheny Country* (Montréal, 2013), 127–32, for a full discussion of captives at the Monongahela. Steele doubts Smith's narrative but admits that "at least two" captives were burned to death, based on a more problematic source, Seaver, *Mary Jemison's Narrative* (193).

131. *New-York Mercury*, January 2, 1758, p. 2; this may be the "Miss Hamilton" mentioned in a 1758 prisoner exchange, *DRCHNY* 10: 883. I am again grateful to Ian Steele for directing me to the *New-York Mercury* reference. Other key British sources are "Information of William Johnson, 1756," *MPCP* 7: 341 (states that three women survived Braddock's Defeat); *DRCHNY* 7: 282 (examination of a French officer, who stated that only three soldiers and five women were captured at the battle).

132. John Long, who escaped his captors in 1756, never heard of any "Wounded being saved," a judgment echoed by James Smith, who was a captive from 1755 to 1759: "I never could find that they saved a man alive at Braddock's defeat": *London Evening Post*, December 4, 1756, p. 1 (Long); *MPCP* 7: 289–90; Barsotti, *Scoouwa*, 29; and *Boston Post-Boy*, August 27, 1759 ("not one of the Wounded being ever heard of since, tho' there were many Hundreds").

133. Breslaw, "A Dismal Tragedy," 140 (John Hart); *Maryland Gazette*, July 31, 1755, contains an account by a colonial captive named Staut, who had been at Fort Duquesne on the day of the battle and shortly thereafter escaped to Fort Cumberland. Staut's account seems to be the ultimate source of the prevalent story in British sources of Indians killing wounded soldiers on their way back to Fort Duquesne (e.g., *Pennsylvania Gazette*, August 7, 1755). See also Croghan, in Kopperman, *Braddock at the Monongahela*, 185.

134. *Journal of the House of Burgesses, 1758–1761*, February 26, 1759, Vol. 9: 66–67 (Eger); Contrecoeur to Vaudreuil, August 3, 1755, *Papiers Contrecoeur*, 407 (Kent, 245).

135. "General Braddock's Military Plans, captured by the French before Fort Duquesne," 1755, HM 898, HL. The inscription translates as "Found in the military chest of General Braddock along with his campaign plans and instructions."

CHAPTER 7

1. The location of Dunbar's Camp is near the Jumonville Christian Camp and Retreat Center, east of the intersection of the Jumonville Road and Old Braddock Road and below Dunbar's Knob.

2. JBO, 53; Orme, 311, and Examination of Jacob House, July 17, 1755, Penn Papers Indian Affairs, Vol. 2 (1754–1756), ff. 27, HSP (also *MPCP* 6: 483) [sixteen Indian allies]; Raymond B. Abbott, "Braddock's War Supplies and Dunbar's Camp," *WPHM* 17 (March 1934): 49–52.

3. Examination of Matthew Laird, and "Information of the Road Cutters," July 20, 1755, Penn Papers Indian Affairs, Vol. 2 (1754–1756), HSP, 27–28.

4. *GWR*, 20; Orme, 356–57, and Gordon Journal, *MANA*, 108; JBO 53 and RCB, 31.

5. WO 71/65, f. 354 (Lucorney); "Gordon's Journal," *MANA*, 108 (fortifications). The Sergeant Anderson referred to by Lucorney was possibly sergeant "John Henderson" or sergeant "John Addison." See South Carolina Independent Company Muster Roll, August 25, 1756–October 24, 1756, LO 3057 (Anderson) and LO 3099 (Addison). Lucorney's "pair of colours" may have been actual regimental flags or a contemporary reference to an ensign's commission.

6. *Duncan Cameron*, 12; Orme, 357; RCB, 34; "Anonymous Letter," *MANA*, 124.

7. *Duncan Cameron*, 13; Johnston, "General Braddock's Campaign," 95; JBO, 53; Orme, 357.

8. HOB, 121; Sharpe to William and John Sharpe, August 11, 1755, *Sharpe* 1: 269 (destruction); on the decision, see St. Clair to Henry Fox, August 16, 1755, JSCL, 158; St. Clair to Robinson, September 3, 1755, CO 5/46, ff. 32–33, and Dunbar to Napier, July 24, 1755, *MANA*, 110; other British accounts such as the Seaman's Journal, James Furnis, and the anonymous British officer (*MANA*, 118–19) describe the order as Braddock's: RCB, 32 (burning supplies).

9. "Anonymous Letter," *MANA*, 118–19, 123 (the author cryptically mentions that "in the Generals name, was orders given" to destroy the camp, suggesting that another officer or aide issued the command); St. Clair to Robinson, September 3, 1755, CO 5/46, ff. 32–33 (ability to command). GW to Charles Lee, May 9, 1776, *CLP* 2: 12, compared the British evacuation of Boston in 1776 to Dunbar's hasty retreat, a comparison that he knew Charles Lee would well understand. No records show Lee's presence at the Monongahela.

10. "Anonymous Letter," *MANA*, 119; "Return of Ordnance by Thomas Ord," *MANA*, 97 (eight mortars "Distroy'd by order of Gen'l Braddock" at Dunbar's Camp, in addition to the three lost in battle on July 9); *MPCP* 6: 593 (guns at Winchester).

11. Dunbar to Napier, July 24, 1755, *MANA*, 110 (command); Seaman's Journal, 388; *ABF*, 134; *GWR*, 21. McCardell, *Ill-Starred General*, 260–61, and other historians use last words attributed to Braddock in a nineteenth-century account: "Is it possible" and "All is over." Franklin's version, even if secondhand, seems the more reliable of the two traditions.

12. RCB, 32 (maggots); *MANA*, 100; HOB, 121–26; Archer B. Hulbert, *Braddock's Road and Three Relative Papers* (Cleveland, 1903), 200; GW to James Innes, July 17, 1755, *GWP* 1: 334 and 334n–335n.

13. *Sharpe Corr.*, 1: 246; *MPCP* 6: 478–79, *DP*, 2: 98; *GWP* 1: 350.

14. Harrison, "With Braddock's Army," 317–18.

15. Dunbar to Morris, August 1, 1755, *MPCP* 6: 522; Willliam Plumsted to Overseers of the Poor, October 4, 1755, *PBF* 6: 214–15; "An Account of the Several Payments made by Thomas Calcraft Esq:r Receiver and Paymaster of His Majesty's Royal Bounty to the Widows of Officers who have been Killed or Died in the Service," WO 25/3021 and 3022, lists "Sarah Nartloo," who was mostly likely the spouse of Ensign William Nartlow, and Anne Handsard, who may have been the spouse of Lieutenant John Hansard. Petition of Rebecca Polson, in McIlwaine, *Journals of the House of Burgesses*, 8: 299.

16. Dinwiddie to James Abercromby, November 15, 1755, *DP* 2: 278; William Fairfax to GW, July 26, 1755, *GWP* 1: 345; Cholmley, *The Memoirs of Sir Hugh Cholmley*, 58; PROB 11/818/386, f. 2, TNA (Cholmley will). *East Riding Antiquarian Society Transactions* 10 (October 1902): 52 (Robert Cholmley's portrait was once at Howsham Hall in Yorkshire but its whereabouts are presently unknown).

17. HOB, 124; JBO, 54; see also Paul Kopperman, "The Medical Aspect of the Braddock and Forbes Expeditions," *PH* 71 (Summer 2004): 257–84.

18. Shirley to Fox, January 13, 1756, WO 1/4, f. 33, mentions nineteen soldiers of the 44th and 48th regiments who were recommended by their officers for Chelsea; all but one of these nineteen soldiers are listed in the Admission Books of the Royal Hospital in Chelsea, in WO 116/5, Admission Books (1755–1764), Royal Hospital, Chelsea, March 22, 1756, ff. 4–7 and f. 25, October 13, 1758. See also WO 120/4, Out-Pension Records, Regimental Registers, Royal Hospital, Chelsea, p. 575 (Higgins); Sir Thomas Robinson instructed Shirley that only those with "Certificates of their good Behaviour" at the Monongahela would be eligible for Chelsea pensions (Robinson to Shirley, August 28, 1755, Lincoln, *Shirley Correspondence*, 2: 242).

19. See Appendix. Both Mackellar and the Journal of the British Officer report a total of 96 officers, while Orme's tabulation and the Seaman's Journal report 85 officers. The difference is that the former included staff members. All of those lists of officer casualties

roughly agree: their numbers of killed or died of wounds range from 26 to 28; and 32 to 36 wounded in action.

20. *MANA*, 86–91 (June 8) and 125–27 (July 25); and John Gordon, "Weekly Return of the 48th Regiment with the Casualties since the 13th Instant July 30th 1755 at Fort Cumberland," LO 96. The July 25 return lumps all of the "Ammerican Foot" into one category, without distinguishing if the three Independent Companies were included in that section of the return, or whether it includes Captain Peter Hogg's detached company. The July 25 returns do not specifically account for desertion before that date.

21. CO 5/46, f. 135 (Mackellar's Map); "Return of the Troops," *Virginia Gazette*, September 5, 1755, p. 3; Orme to Franklin, July 27, 1755, quoted in Houston, "Wagon Affair," 284 (Orme's letter states 63 of 86 officers killed and wounded, and "714 men out of 1100 dead," which may reflect the July 25, 1755, returns already cited); JBO, 58. The statistics cited by civilian Alexander Hamilton (772 casualties) also nearly match Orme's statistics (Breslaw, "A Dismal Tragedy," 140). The Seaman's Journal, 388, citing army returns, lists a total of 896 casualties besides officers, and William Dunbar's narrative states that 823 were casualties out of 1,100 engaged (Kopperman, *Braddock at the Monongahela*, 188).

22. Orme to Dinwiddie, July 18, 1755, in Koontz, *Dinwiddie Correspondence*, 745; Duncan Cameron, 14 (cf. JCB, 34–35 on courts-martial); Stark, "A Daily Return of the Nine American Companys, Fort Cumberland, Sepr 17th 1755," in George Washington Papers Online, LOC, http://memory.loc.gov/mss/mgw4/029/0200/0294.jpg, accessed June 22, 2012; see also *GWP* 2: 203, n.10; *DP* 2: 196; and *Pennsylvania Gazette*, September 11, 1755, for the desertion problem. The total numbers of officers and men were 533 on June 8 (including the companies of Dagworthy, Dobbs, Stephen, Hogg, Mercer, Peyronnie, Polson, Waggoner, and Cocke). Those same companies numbered approximately 262 officers and men on the September 17, 1755, return, a loss of 271.

23. Dinwiddie to Sir Thomas Robinson, July 14, 1755; Dinwiddie to Fairfax, July 14, 1755; Dinwiddie to Charles Carter, July 18, 1755, *DP* 2: 99, 101–102; GW to Dinwiddie, July 18, 1755, *GWP* 1: 340.

24. Dinwiddie to GW, July 26, 1755, *GWP* 1: 344 (mistake); Dinwiddie to Fairfax, July 14, 1755, and Dinwinddie to Colonel David Stewart, July 16, 1755, *DP* 2: 98 (galling),100 (bad order).

25. Dinwiddie to William Byrd, July 22, 1755; Dinwiddie to Halifax, July 23, 1755; and Dinwiddie to Charles Carter, July 18, 1755, *DP* 2: 110 (banditti), 102, 114; Horatio Sharpe to John Sharpe, July 15, 1755, BL Add. Mss. 32858, ff. 110–13 (slaves). On Catholic fears, see Howard, "Diary of Daniel Fisher," 273–74 (cf. *MPCP* 6: 477); See *MPCP* 6: 503 and *PA* 1st ser., 2: 690; Sharpe to Baltimore, December 16, 1758, *Sharpe* 2: 315–17; and John Mack Faragher, *A Great and Noble Scheme* (New York, 2005), 324–25. *MPCP* 6: 503–4.

26. Dinwiddie to Dunbar, July 26, 1755, *DP* 2: 118, 173, 175 (offensive).

27. Dunbar to Morris, July 16, 1755, *MPCP* 6: 499; Orme to Shirley, July 18, 1755, in Lincoln, *Shirley Correspondence* 2: 209.

28. Dunbar to Dinwiddie, August 1, 1755, CO 5/16, f. 113 (council); Dinwiddie to Sharpe, August 25, 1755, *DP*, 2: 169 (immediate offensive); Sharpe to Dinwiddie, August 11, 1755, and September 2, 1755, Sharpe to W. Sharpe, May 2, 1756, *Sharpe* 1: 278, 266, 395–96 (abandonment); Houston, "Wagon Affair," 280 (Dunbar's friend); *MPCP* 6: 400 and *PA* 1st ser. 2: 325 (wintering at Philadelphia).

29. Sharpe to Dinwiddie, August 11, 1755, *Sharpe* 1: 266; Dunbar to Shirley, August 21, 1755, *MPCP* 6: 593–94.

30. RCB, 35–36.

31. Shirley to Peters, July 23, 1755; New York Council Proceedings, August 1, 1755; Shirley to Dunbar, August 6, 1755; Shirley to Robinson, August 11, 1755; and Shirley to Dunbar, August 12, 1755, in Lincoln, *Shirley Correspondence*, 2: 209–10, 214–16, 219, 231–34; Morris to Dunbar, August 19, 1755, *MPCP* 6: 563–69.

32. *MPCP* 6: 547–48; Dunbar to Shirley, August 21, 1755, *MPCP* 6: 593–94 (Pine Ford); RCB, 36 (timing of march); Dunbar to St. Clair, August 11, 1755, JSCL, 153; *MPCP* 6: 593–95; 604; *Pennsylvania Gazette*, October 2, 16, and 30, 1755 (journey to New York).

33. Keppel to Lawrence, July 26, 1755, "Keppel Manuscripts," 171; *London Gazette*, August 23–26, 1755, p. 1. Keppel transferred his broad pennent to *Sea Horse* before returning to London in August 1755.

34. Lady Jemima Montagu Meadows to Elizabeth Montagu, November 7, 1755, Elizabeth Montagu Papers, HL, MO 1537; Dulany, "Military and Political Affairs," 21; Phips to Robison, August 4, 1755, CO 5/16, ff. 143–44.

35. Thomas Birch to Lord Royston, August 30, 1755, and Royston to Birch, September 1, 1755, Add. Mss. 35398, ff. 280–84; Davis, "British Newspaper Accounts," 314–15; James Wolfe to his father, September 4, 1755, in Willson, *Life and Letters of James Wolfe*, 274.

36. George Marsden, *Jonathan Edwards: A Life* (New Haven, 2003), 414–17, 587, n.6.

37. William Vinal, *A Sermon on the Accursed Thing that hinders Success and Victory in War, Occasioned by the defeat of the Hon. Edward Braddock, Esq...* (Newport: James Franklin, 1755), 12; Charles Chauncy, *A Letter to a Friend; Giving a concise, but just, Account, according to the Advices hithereto received, of the OHIO-Defeat...* (Boston: Edes and Gill, 1755), 5; Thomas Kidd, *The Great Awakening: The Roots of Evangelical Christianity in Colonial America* (New Haven, 2007), 241; Samuel Davies, *Virginia's Danger and Remedy: Two Discourses Occasioned by the Severe Drought in Sundry Parts of the Country; and the Defeat of General Braddock* (Williamsburg, 1756).

38. Martha Brewster, *Poems on Divers Subjects* (New London: John Green, 1757); Samuel Niles, "A Summary Historical Narrative of the Wars in New-England with the French and Indians, in the Several Parts of the Country," *MHSC* 4th ser., Vol. 5: 309–589, at 467 (Braddock, Howe, and Wolfe as martyrs).

39. Lady Anson to Lord Royston (brother), August 23, 1755, Add. Mss. 35376, ff. 127–30; Lord Royston to Thomas Birch, September 1, 1755, Add. Mss. 35398, ff. 283–84; Halifax, quoted in Mercantini, *Who Shall Rule at Home?*, 139; Thomas Gage to Lord Gage, March 26, 1757, Add. Mss. 32870, f. 345; Newcastle to Holdernesse, July 11, 1755, Add. Mss. 32857, f. 53; Ayling, *The Elder Pitt*, 173

40. GWP 2: 15; PBF 6: 530; DP 2: 137 and LO 696 (names); *MANA*, 120.

41. Pargellis, "Braddock's Defeat"; Shirley to Robinson, November 5, 1755, *Shirley Correspondence*, 2: 319; Nichols, in "The Braddock Expedition," 428–32, offers the finest refutation of Pargellis's theory regarding Braddock's alleged failure to adhere to Bland. Pargellis held the British officers to a standard to which they did not hold themselves.

The suggestion that Gage should have occupied the ridge must be tempered by the fact that Native warriors overwhelmed James Grant's more seasoned and experienced forces who were posted on a commanding hilltop in 1758 and also drove Henry Bouquet's forces off a hilltop on the first day's action at Bushy Run in 1763.

42. St. Clair to Commissioner Hughes, September 3, 1755, JSCL, 172–73; James Oglethorpe, *The Naked Truth*, 3d ed. (London: A. Price, 1755), 30–31.

43. *Pennsylvania Gazette*, July 24, 1755, p. 2; Chauncy, *Letter to a Friend*, 9; Vinal, *Sermon on the Accursed Thing*, 19; John A. Schutz, ed., "A Private Report of General Braddock's Defeat," *PMHB* 79 (July 1955): 374–77, at 376 (Bolling's use of the phrase "die like Souldiers" suggests that he had read Washington's July 18 letter to Dinwiddie, describing the Virginia provincials' conduct).

44. GWP 1: 345; Orme, in "Keppel Manuscripts," 175; Gist to GW, October 15, 1755, GWP 2: 114–15, at 115; Samuel Davies, *Religion and Patriotism the Constituents of a Good Soldier* (London, 1756), 9.

45. Americanus to Loudoun, December 8, 1757, LO 4971; *Further objections to the establishment of a constitutional militia* (London: C. Henderson, 1757); Dulany, "Military and Political Affairs," 31.

46. See *DP* 2: 171, 175, 259; Thomas Birch and Lord Royston, August 30 and October 9, 1755, Add. Mss. 35398, ff. 280–82 and 293; William Livingston, *A Review of Military Operations in North America* (Dublin, 1757).

47. "British Newspaper Accounts," 316; Abbot, "Braddock in Alexandria," 212; Dulany, "Military and Political Affairs," 16; Dinwiddie to St. Clair, August 11, 1755, *DP* 2: 147.

48. Newcastle to Robison, October 5, 1755, Add. Mss. 32859, f. 386 (also Newcastle to Holdernesse, August 26, 1755, Add. Mss. 32858, ff. 289–91); James Abercromby to Dinwiddie, November 23, 1755, in Van Horne, *Letter Book of James Abercromby*, 170; Henry Fox to Colonel Dunbar, November 1755, WO 4/51, f. 38–39, and *GWP* 2: 115 n2 (Dunbar's later life).

49. Gordon Kershaw, "The Legend of Braddock's Gold Reconsidered," *Maryland Historical Magazine* 96 (Spring 2001): 87–110, rightly concludes that Braddock's main military chest was not captured.

50. Contrecoeur and Roucher accounts, in Kopperman, *Braddock at the Monongahela*, 256, 270–71. Referred to as "the elder," this officer was most likely Ensign Pierre-Hyacinthe Céloron de Blainville (b. 1732), and the son of the 1749 Expedition's leader: Roy, *La famille Céloron de Blainville*, 46.

51. Contrecoeur to Vaudreuil, July 29, 1755, *Papiers Contrecoeur*, 403–4 (feet, amount, 30 pirogues); 418 (shed of "quatre vingt piée") and 428; 404, 424 (detachments to battlefield); Hunter, *Forts on the Pennsylvania Frontier*, 111–12 (McKinney). On captured goods, see Shea, *Rélations diverses*, 14, 36–39, *MANA*, 131, and "Mémoires du Chevalier de La Pause," 310.

52. "Relation des divers mouvements qui se son passés entre les françois et les anglais à la bataille," Shea, *Relations diverses*, 35. Contrecoeur mentions these deserters in a letter to Vaudreuil of July 26, 1755, in *Papiers Contrecoeur*, 400.

53. Contrecoeur to Vaudreuil, July 26 and 29, 1755, *Papiers Contrecoeur*, 400, 403 (Du Buisson's mission and scouts beyond Fort Necessity). The eight mortars brought back (amenér) by Du Buisson were not included in some of the first inventories of cannon and materiel taken from the Monongahela battlefield (e.g., the list attached to Contrecoeur's letter in *MANA*, 131). But Pouchot, in his *Memoirs*, notes "12 cohorn mortars" taken, close to the total of 11 that the French seized (83).

54. Contrecoeur to Vaudreuil, August 14, 1755, *Papiers Contrecoeur*, 418 (party of 130). The first officer was Joachim-Louis Robutel de La Noue, an ensign who was not present at the Monongahela battle, but given an opportunity here to distinguish himself: see Cyprien Tanguay, *Dictionnaire généalogique des Familles Canadiennes depuis la fondation de la colonie jusqu'à nos jours* (Ottawa, 1871–1890) 7: 14, and "State of the Canadian Noblesse," in Douglas Brymner, ed., *Report on Canadian Archives 1888* (Ottawa, 1889), 46 (Robutel de la Noue is listed as a lieutenant who returned to Loches, France, by the 1760s); Drolet, "Tables généalogiques," Table 178.

55. *DRCHNY* 10: 425 (materials in 1756).

56. Contrecoeur to Vaudreuil, August 3 and 21, 1755, *Papiers Contrecoeur*, 407, 424; Lignery to Contrecoeur, July 30, 1755, ASQ-VV, Carton 1, no. 89, reel 1 (detachment); Duverger St. Blin to Contrecoeur, August 14, 1755; Contrecoeur to Vaudreuil, August 29, 1755, *Papiers Contrecoeur*, 417 (detachments); 427 (captured papers).

57. [Jacob-Nicolas Moreau], *Mémoire contenant le précis des faits, avec leurs pièces justificatives, pour servir de Réponse aux Observations envoyées par les Ministres d'Angleterre, dans les Cours de l'Europe* (Paris: L'Imprimerie Royale, 1756), 58. *DRCHNY* 10: 311–12, 380–81 (Vaudreuil's translation); David A. Bell, "Jumonville's Death: War Propaganda and National Identity in Eighteenth-Century France," in *The Age of Cultural Revolutions: Britain and France, 1750–1820*, ed. Colin Jones and Dror Wahrman (Berkeley, 2002), 33–61.

58. *DRCHNY* 10: 492 (Stobo), 379 (scarce), 390 (succors); "Answer of M. de Vaudreuil to the Five Nations," October 22, 1755, *DRCHNY* 10: 363.

59. Kerlérec to De Machault d'Arnouville, April 1, 1756, in Dunbar Rowland, A.G. Sanders, and Patricia Kay Galloway, eds., *Mississippi Provincial Archives*, Vol. 5, *French Dominion, 1749–1763* (Baton Rouge, 1984), 167–72; see also *DRCHNY* 10: 401 on Kerlérec.

60. Denys Baron, "D'une nouvelle terre," quoted in Fred Anderson, *The War that Made America: A Short History of the French and Indian War* (New York, 2005), 72–73 (my translation). The noël "Or nous dites, Marie" is attributed to Lucas Le Moigne (1520); Gabrielle Lapointe, "Daneau De Muy, Charlotte, *dite* de Sainte-Hélène," *DCB* 3: 161.

61. Letter of November 8, 1756, A. L. Leymarie, ed. "Lettres de Mère Marie-Andrée Duplessis de Sainte-Hélène, Supérieure des Hospitalières de l'Hôtel-Dieu de Québec," *Nova Francia* 4, no. 2 (mars–avril 1929): 110–23, at 113 ("cet homme raporte que les anglois virent sur le camp françois une dame vêtue de blanc qui étendoit les bras").

62. [Thomas Pichon], *Genuine Letters and Memoirs Relating to the Natural, Civil, and Commercial History of the Islands of Cape Breton and Saint John From the First Settlement There, to the Taking of Louisbourg by the English in 1758* (London: J. Nourse, 1760), 329; *DRCHNY* 10: 314–15, 528; Pouchot, *Memoirs*, 85.

63. Contrecoeur to Minister, July 20, 1755; La Chauvignerie to Contrecoeur, August 27, 1755; Benoist to Contrecoeur, August 21, 1755; Contrecoeur to Vaudreuil, August 21, 1755, and "Ordre de Vaudreuil à Contrecoeur de remettre son poste à Dumas, 8 août 1755," *Papiers Contrecoeur*, 398, 426–27(food), 423[Kent, 253], 418 (low water), 416; *DRCHNY* 10: 638 (Contrecoeur's fame); *Papiers Contrecoeur*, 403 (supply), 406 (request for relief).

64. Contrecoeur to Minister, November 28, 1755, ANOM COL C¹¹A 100, f. 250; Stevens and Kent, *Wilderness Chronicles*, 85–86, 96 (Illinois provisions). Vaudreuil to Contrecoeur, September 13, 1756, Viger-Verreau, ASQ-VV Carton 4, no. 361, reel 3 (exactness) and Machault to Contrecoeur, April 1, 1756 (prudence); *Papiers Contrecoeur*, 429; King's orders, May 26, 1759, Viger-Verreau, ASQ, Carton 4, no. 364, reel 3.

65. "Liste des officiers proposés par Vaudreuil de Cavagnial pour divers postes, 8 november 1756," ANOM COL C¹¹A, Vol. 101, ff. 158–62.

66. Marquis de Vaudreuil à Lotbinière, 27 janvier 1756, Canada Lotbinière Manuscripts, 1746–1790, NYHS; *DRCHNY* 10: 640 (veneration); Machault to Contrecoeur, April 1, 1756, *Papiers Contrecoeur*, 429; Aegidius Fauteux, *Les chevaliers de Saint-Louis en Canada* (Montréal: Les Éditions des Dix, 1940), 161–62, 174, 185–86, 191, 194.

67. Contrecoeur to Galissonière, July 20, 1755, *Papiers Contrecoeur*, 398 (victory); French newspapers and published French histories of the war (often drawn from English sources, tended to neglect the Monongahela battle; the *Alcide/Lys* incident and the capture of Braddock's headquarters papers garnered the lion's share of attention. See, for example, *Relation de la Victoire remportée par les François, sur un Corps de Troupes Angloises, commandé par le Général Braddock, près l'Ohio dans l'Amérique septentrionale* (1755), MHS; *Mercure de France* (août 1755), 254, and (octobre 1755), 226–27, LOC; and Étienne-Joseph Poullin de Lumina, *Histoire de la guerre contre les Anglois* (Geneve, 1759), 23–25.

68. Christian Ayne Crouch, *Nobility Lost: French and Canadian Martial Cultures, Indians and the End of New France* (Ithaca, 2014). For French Army officers' scorn for Canadian officers, see Montcalm à Lévis, 17 août 1756, in H. R. Casgrain, ed. *Collection des manuscrits de Maréchal de Lévis* (Québec, 1894), 6: 34.

69. Dieskau to Doreil, August 16, 1755, *DRCHNY* 10: 312 (treacheries); William Eyre to Napier, July 27, 1755, *MANA*, 128; Anderson, *Crucible of War*, chap. 10.

70. Count d'Argenson to M. de Montreüil, February 29, 1756; letter from M. Désandrouins, August 28, 1756, *DRCHNY* 10: 394 and 465; Osman, "Citizen Army of Old Regime France," 80–81.

71. Walpole, *Memoirs of the Reign of King George II*, 2: 46, 1846 edition; *London Chronicle*, November 14–16, 1758, p. 2; Stephen Hopkins to WJ, September 24, 1755, *SWJP* 2: 90 (see also Boleyn Whitney to Johnson, January 31, 1756, 2: 425); Thomas Birch to Lord Royston, November 1, 1755, Add. Mss. 35398, f. 304 (British chagrin); Fintan O'Toole, *White Savage: William Johnson and the Invention of America* (New York, 2005), 152–54.

72. Loudoun to Cumberland, October 2, 1756, *MANA*, 235; and "Memorial of Major Generals Abercrombie, and Webb," October 26, 1756, LO 5832.

73. *SWJP* 1: 544, n.1 (Skowonidous); Loudoun to Cumberland, August 20, 1756, *MANA*, 225; *SWJP* 1: 529 (Delaware lineage); *SWJP* 9: 499–500 (tutche); Gage to WJ, August 5,

1756, *SWJP* 13:89 (initial report); *SWJP* 2: 544 and 9: 825 (Tuscarora grievances); *SWJP* 1:533 and Duke of Cumberland to Loudoun, October 22, 1756, LO 2065 (collusion).

74. Daniel Disney Orderly Book, LOC, August 10–19, 1756; "Return of ye Detachment of ye 50th & 51st Regts and of ye Detachments from ye three Independent Companys," LO 1573 (Gates); *SWJP* 2: 554 (Silver Heels).

75. Disney Orderly Book, August 16–18, 1756; Stanley Pargellis, *Lord Loudoun in America* (New Haven, 1933), 163–65; Loudoun to Cumberland, October 2, 1756, *MANA*, 234.

76. Severance, *An Old Frontier of France*, 233–34; Dinwiddie to GW, July 26, 1755, *GWP* 1: 344; "Abstract of Despatches from Canada, July 1756," *DRCHNY* 10: 424–25 (ammunition from Dunbar's Camp); "Extract of a Council held at City Hall of the City of New York on Friday the 1st day of August 1755," LO 620; "Examination of Monsʳ. Belestre," *DHNY* 1: 498; "Abstract of Despatches from America, 1756," *DRCHNY* 10: 484 (Oswego); Pouchot, *Memoirs*, 104 (Oswego); Loudoun to Cumberland, August 29, 1756, *MANA*, 232 (Iroquois report).

77. Ian Steele, *Betrayals: Fort William Henry and the "Massacre,"* (New York, 1990), 104; Vaudreuil to Massiac, November 1, 1758, *DRHCNY* 10: 863 (ammunition).

78. SWJP 9: 518–19 (Aguiota); *Gentleman's Magazine*, October 1, 1757, 442–43.

79. Daniel Disney Orderly Book, LOC, August 18, 1756.

80. "Monthly Return of His Majesty's /35th/42d/44th/48th/ Regiments of Foot and Four Independent Companies, July 24, 1756," LO 6780; [Francis Halkett], "Return of Cloathing, Arms, etc. Artificers & Recruits in His Majesty's 35th 42d, 44th, 48th, 50th & 51st Regiments," August 17, 1756, LO 1962; and William Hervey, "Monthly Return of His Majesty's 44:th Regiment of Foot, Elisabeth Town 24:th Feb:y 1758," Box 2, f. 59, and "Monthly Return of His Majesty's 48th Regiment of Foot," February 24, 1758, Oversize Box, John Forbes Papers, UVA. The numbers given here are raw numbers, included those listed on the returns as present but sick or in hospitals. See Pargellis, *Lord Loudoun in America*, 104, and Brumwell, *Redcoats*, 75 (americanization).

81. Fred Anderson, *Crucible of War*, 286.

82. *MANA*, 132.

83. Pouchot, *Memoirs*, 83; MacLeod, *Canadian Iroquois*.

84. Pouchot, *Memoirs*, 80.

85. Council of War at Fort Oswego, September 18, 1755, LO 649; "Extract from the Journal of Major John Smith, 1756–1757," in Isabel Calder, *Colonial Captivities, Marches, and Journeys* (New York, 1967) 138; Captain Thomas Morris's Journal, in Thwaites, *Early Western Journals*, 1: 311. The British colors seen by the Virginia officer may have been derived from the wagon of Indian trade goods that Braddock carried.

86. William Leete Stone, ed. and trans., *Memoirs, and Letters and Journals, of Major General Riedesel During His Residence in America* (Albany, 1868), 1: 55.

87. Meachum, "'Markes Upon Their Clubhamers,'" 67–74.

88. Bonaparte, "Life of Colonel Louis Cook"; Charlotte Reeve Conover, ed., *Recollections of Sixty Years by John Johnston* (n.p., 1915), 11; Barsotti, *Scoouwa*, 25, 26, 28.

89. *DRCHNY* 10: 402, 625, 632; Pouchot, *Memoirs*, 120.

90. Christian Frederick Post, "Two Journals of Western Tours," at 230–31; Quaife, *John Long's Voyages and Travels*, 63 (Kanesetake); Thomas Butler to SWJ, March 14, 1757, LO 3046; Barsotti, *Scoouwa*, 24. Examples of other Native victories include Grant's defeat in 1758; the capturing of British military posts during Pontiac's War (including the defeat of James Dalyell's column at Bloody Run, and the Devil's Hole massacre in 1763); their near-victory over Bouquet at Bushy Run; and catastrophic routs inflicted on United States armies at Josiah Harmar's Defeat in 1790 and Arthur St. Clair's Defeat in 1791.

91. Account of Trader James Beamer, June 18, 1761, James Glen Papers, South Caroliniana Library; James Patterson Journal, 1758, *BP* 2: 327; *London Evening-Post*, December 4–7, 1756, p.1 (Long); *MPCP* 7: 289–90. See *GWP* 4: 213–15, 223, and *Sharpe* 2: 25 (Indian use of Monongahela fords).

92. Dinwiddie to St. Clair, August 11, 1755, *DP* 2: 147; GW to Dinwiddie, July 18, 1755, *GWP* 1: 340.

93. John Craig Deposition, March 30, 1756, Penn Papers Indian Affairs, Vol. 2 (1754–1756), 78; Preston, *Texture of Contact*, chap. 4; Kevin Kenny, *Peaceable Kingdom Lost: The Paxton Boys and the Destruction of William Penn's Holy Experiment* (Oxford, 2009); C. Vann Woodward, ed., *Mary Chesnut's Civil War* (New Haven, 1981), xxxv–xxxvi.

94. *GWR*, 21 Grenier, *First Way of War*, 89.

95. Responding to his experience at the Monongahela, Lieutenant Thomas Webb of the 48th Regiment wrote *A Military Treatise on the Appointments of the Army* (Philadelphia, 1759) [ECCO], which emphasized that war in America was unique and that two light infantry companies should be included in each regiment. He also presented tactical formations for "marching and drawing up a Regiment for Action in the Woods" (65). Webb later became a Methodist evangelical minister.

96. See Brumwell, *Redcoats*, 228–36; Ian McPherson McCulloch, "'Within Ourselves': The Development of British Light Infantry during the Seven Years' War," *Canadian Military History* 7 (Spring 1998): 41–55; Daniel J. Beattie, "The Adaptation of the British Army to Wilderness Warfare, 1755–1763," in Maarten Ultee, ed., *Adapting to Conditions: War and Society in the Eighteenth Century* (Alabama, 1986) and Russell, "Redcoats to the Wilderness."

97. Brumwell, *George Washington: Gentleman Warrior*, Lengel, *General George Washington*, and Hofstra, *George Washington and the Virginia Backcountry*.

98. *GWR*, 21; GW to Warner Lewis, August 14, 1755; *GWP* 1: 362; *GWP* 1: 357, n.1, and *GWP* 2: 1–3.

99. *DRCHNY* 10: 437 (grass); GW to Dinwiddie, May 3, 1756, *GWP* 3: 81–85; Adam Stephen to GW, September 25, 1755, and October 4, 1755, *GWP* 2: 61–63, 72–73; William Trent to James Burd, October 4, 1755, *MPCP* 6: 641 (Frasier); GW to Dinwiddie, and GW to Robinson, November 9, 1756, *GWP* 4: 4 (vigorous), 11–18; GW to Loudoun, January 10, 1757, *GWP* 4: 79–93 (offensive).

100. David L. Preston, "'Make Indians of Our White Men': British Soldiers and Indian Warriors from Braddock's to Forbes's Campaigns, 1755–1758," *PH* 74 (Summer 2007): 280–306; Norman L. Baker, *French and Indian War in Frederick County, Virginia* (Winchester, 2000).

101. GW to John Robinson, and GW to Dinwiddie, April 7, 1756, *GWP* 2: 334 and 337; "Speech to the Tuscarora Indians," August 1, 1756, *GWP* 3: 308–309.

102. Washington to Dinwiddie, March 10, 1757, *GWP* 4: 113.

103. Stephen to GW, August 20, 1757, *GWP* 4: 375; GW to Dinwiddie, January 13, 1756, and GW to Lewis, September 6, 1755, *GWP* 2: 278; *BP* 2: 183; for Washington's ideas on Indian dress, see Preston, "'Make Indians of Our White Men,'" 293.

104. James Baker to GW, June 10, 1757, GW to John Stanwix, June 15, 1757, *GWP* 4: 200, 215–17; *GWP* 3: 43, n. 7 (Baker); *DRCHNY* 10: 582 (French account); Pouchot, *Memoirs*, 115n; William Trent Manuscript, 1757, Native American History Collection, WLCL (Belêstre).

105. *SWJP* 9: 355, 362 (44th officers); Shirley to St. C, April 23, 1756, JSCL, 283; Preston, *The Texture of Contact*, 94–96.

106. *Scots Magazine*, November 1756, 559.

107. *SWJP* 2: 632–33, 636 (clothing); *SWJP* 9: 494 (scout); *Boston Weekly News-Letter*, October 7, 1756 (scalp); André Senécal, "New France in the Champlain Valley, 1609–1759," Map, n.p., 1998 (Levasseur's sawmill); *Pennsylvania Gazette*, November 2, 1758.

108. Bunford Samuel, ed., "The Ohio Expedition of 1754, by Adam Stephen," *PMHB* 18, no. 1 (1894): 43–50, at 46; Brumwell, *White Devil: A True Story of Savagery and Vengeance in Colonial America* (Cambridge, 2004), 147–49, 152–56; *London Evening Post*, February 16, 1760 (captaincy).

109. *Pennsylvania Gazette*, February 17, 1757, and November 2, 1758; Richard Mather to Thomas Mather, June 28, 1758, in Lothrop Withington, "Pennsylvania Gleanings in England" *PMHB* 31 (October 1907): 474–82, at 476; James Pottinger Memorial to Earl of Loudoun, July 21, 1757, LO 3975.

110. "Journal of Warren Johnson," in Dean Snow, Charles Gehring, and William Starna, *In Mohawk Country: Early Narratives about a Native People* (Syracuse, 1996), 255; Gage, "Queries of George Chalmers," 369.

111. Gage to Albemarle, July 24, 1755, and Petition of Thomas Gage to the King [July 1755], BL Add. Mss. 32857 ff. 338–40, and Newcastle to Holdernesse, August 26, 1755, Add. Mss. 32858, ff. 289–93.

112. "Lieutenant Colonel Thomas Gage's Proposal to His Excellency the Earl of Loudoun for raising a Reg.t of Light armed Foot," [1757] WO 34/46A, f. 1; Thomas Gage, "List of Officers proposed by Lt Col Gage for the Light armed Regiment," Dec. 19, 1757, LO 5044.

113. "Weekly Return of His Majesty's Forces Commanded by His Excel.y Major Gen:l Amherst," July 16, 1759, Gage Papers, AS 2, WLCL. On the 80th Foot, see John R. Cuneo, "Factors behind the Raising of the 80th Foot in America," *Military Collector & Historian* 11 (Winter 1959): 97–103; Eric I. Manders, Brian Leigh Dunnigan, and John R. Etling, "80th Regiment of Foot, 1757–1764," *Military Collector & Historian* 39 (Winter 1987): 172; and "Memorandum of Expences Rough Estimate of Cloathing of Light Armed Regt. of Foot," Dec. 23, 1757, LO 5075.

114. Loudoun to Cumberland, August 20, 1756, LO 1525A; Abercromby to Loudoun, December 18, 1757, LO 5038; Loudoun to Gage, January 2, 1758, LO 5319.

115. Duke of Cumberland to Loudoun, October 22, 1756, LO 2065; Abercromby to Loudoun, December 18, 1757, LO 5038; Lord Gage to Newcastle, August 23, 1758, Add. Mss. 32883, f. 64; Patrick Frazier, *The Mohicans of Stockbridge* (Lincoln, 1992), 129. Brumwell, *Redcoats*, 228–36.

116. Huck to Loudoun, May 29, 1758, LO 5837; Stephen Brumwell, "Band of Brothers," *History Today* 58, no. 6 (June 2008): 25–31.

117. "Return of the Names of the Officers of the Several Regiments, who were killed or wounded near Tienderoga, July 8, 1758," WO 1/1, f. 202 and "Return of Killed Missing & Wounded of His Majesty's Troops & Provincials in the Action near Tienderoge, July 8.th, 1758," WO 1/1, f. 225; Richard Middleton, "James Abercromby," *DCB* 4: 4–5.

118. *Grand Magazine of Magazines*, October 1, 1758, 253; Severance, *An Old Frontier of France*, 233–34; Pouchot, *Memoirs*, 153–54; *DRCHNY* 10: 821.

119. Douglas R. Cubbison, *The British Defeat of the French in Pennsylvania, 1758: A Military History of the Forbes Campaign against Fort Duquesne* (Jefferson, N.C., 2010), chap. 7; *BP* 2: 519.

120. GW to Francis Halkett, April 12, 1758, *GWP* 5: 125; *Pennsylvania Gazette*, December 14, 1758, in *BP* 2: 613–64; Shippen Orderly Book, quoted in Cubbison, *The British Defeat of the French*, 174–75; John Galt, *The Progress of Genius or Authentic Memoirs of the Early Life of Benjamin West, Esq.* (Boston, 1831), 51–57; for Benjamin West's sketch, see http://www .christies.com/lotfinder/lot/benjamin-west-pra-discovering-the-bones-of-4998425-details.aspx, accessed June 12, 2012.

121. *The Annual Register, 1759* (London, 1760), 34; Brian Leigh Dunnigan, *Siege—1759: The Campaign against Niagara* (Youngstown, N.Y., 1996), 92–98 (quote at 96), Appendix B; Pouchot, *Memoirs*, 232, n. 703; *CLP* 1: 19, 21.

122. Thomas Boone to Horatio Gates, August 19, 1759, Horatio Gates Papers, NYHS; Dunnigan, *Siege—1759*, 98; *Boston Evening-Post*, September 10, 1759, p. 4.

123. *CLP* 1: 26; Nichols, "Braddock Expedition," 358; WO 12/5637/1, 44th Regiment Muster Book, 1760 (the regiment numbered 608 officers and men); MacLeod, *Canadian Iroquois*, 186–87.

124. On the Cherokee War, see Daniel J. Tortora's forthcoming *Carolina in Crisis: Cherokees, Colonists, and Slaves in the American Southeast, 1756–1763* (Chapel Hill, 2015); Margaret Carrere McCue, "Lieutenant-Colonel James Grant's Expedition against the Cherokee Indians, 1761" (M.A. thesis, University of South Carolina, 1967); Scott Withrow, "Cherokee Field School: Marion in the 1761 Grant Expedition," *American Revolution* 1 (January 2009): 8–22.

125. Christopher French, "Journal of an Expedition to South Carolina," *Journal of Cherokee Studies* 2, no. 3 (Summer 1977): 275–301, at 288 (quotes), 295–96 (days/mileages); Appendix A, "Toll of the Grant Expedition," 336.

126. Quinton Kennedy to Loudoun, November 14, 1761, LO 6328.
127. Return of Troops, June 25, 1761, and Grant to Amherst, June 5, 1761, James Grant Papers, LOC (the return numbers the Indian Corps at 138). Kennedy himself places the numbers at 170 (LO 6318); Edith Mays, *The Amherst Papers, 1756–1763* (Bowie, Md., 1999), 162, 166–67, 202. Alexander Monypenny, "Diary of March 20–May 31, 1761," *Journal of Cherokee Studies* 2, no. 3 (Summer 1977): 320–31, at 326; and *South Carolina Gazette,* May 30 and June 20, 1761.
128. Christopher French Journal, 283–84; *South Carolina Gazette,* June 20, 1761; *Scots Magazine,* August 1761, 429 (also in *Maryland Gazette,* August 13, 1761). My description of the terrain is based on British accounts and a visit to the battlefield in 2013, located along Sam Corn Road near Otto, North Carolina.
129. Journal of the March & Operations of the Troops under the Command of Lt. Col: Grant of the 40.th Reg.t upon an Expedition from Fort Prince George against the Cherokees, June 7–July 9, 1761, ff. 8–21, at ff. 9–12 (quote at f. 11), reel 32, James Grant Papers, LOC; *Scots Magazine,* August 1761, 429 (quotes), 430 (Indian Corps' attack); Christopher French Journal, 283–84 (three hours).
130. James Grant, "Journal of the March," 35; Grant to Colonel Byrd, July 11, 1761, Grant Papers, LOC; Anne F. Rogers, "Archaeology at Cherokee Town Sites Visited by the Montgomery and Grant Expeditions," in Anne F. Rogers and Barbara R. Duncan, eds., *Culture, Crisis and Conflict: Cherokee British Relations, 1756–1765* (Cherokee, N.C., 2009), 34–44.
131. Christopher French Journal, 284; Mays, *Amherst Papers,* 243, 258; Grant to Bull, September 28, 1761, Grant Papers, f. 27.
132. Quinton Kennedy to Loudoun, October 23, 1761, and November 14, 1761, LO 6318 and 6328; *Public Advertiser,* February 17, 1762, 3 (Silver Heels); Robert Monckton to Lord Egremont, February 9, 1762, in *Gentleman's Magazine* 32 (March 1762): 126 (warmest); *Public Advertiser,* March 24, 1762, p. 3 (wounding); John Carden to SWJ, February 8, 1762, SWJP 3: 625–26 (Martinique); *South Carolina Gazette,* April 17, 1762 (rangers) and July 24, 1762 (death); Brumwell, *Redcoats,* 225 (halloo); Richard Shuckburgh to WJ, April 12, 1762, *SWJP* 3: 682 (slaves).
133. *Public Advertiser,* October 19, 1765, p. 4; Spring, *With Zeal and with Bayonets Only,* 251–52 (Townshend, Clinton); Brumwell, *Redcoats,* 47, 295. On the postwar British Army, see also John Shy, *Toward Lexington: The Role of the British Army in the Coming of the American Revolution* (Princeton, 1965).
134. Hulbert, *Braddock's Road and Three Relative Papers,* 209–12; see also "John Semple's Proposal for Potomac Navigation, 1769," *GWP* 8: 284–86. The role of military roads in opening of the west is a crucial part of the processes that François Furstenberg discusses in "The Significance of the Trans-Appalachian Frontier in Atlantic History," *American Historical Review* 113, no. 3 (June 2008): 647–677.
135. Stewart to GW, September 28, 1759, *GWP* 6: 359–60; Stotz, *Outposts of the War for Empire,* 127.
136. McIlwaine, *Journals of the House of Burgesses,* Vol. 9, *1758–1761* (Richmond, 1908), November 7 and 9, 1759, 9: 138, 143; *GWP* 1: 208, n. 12 (Finnie). On reopening Braddock's Road, see *BP* 2: 219, 222, 231, 270, 273, 277–78, 374, 446, 582, 615; *JHB* 1766–1769, 100 (March 27, 1767) and GW to John Blair, May 17, 1768, *GWP* 8: 87–88, n.1.
137. *Journal of Nicholas Cresswell,* 68; Capt. Harry Gordon to Gage, June 4 and 15, 1766, Gage Papers, AS 51, WLCL; "Extracts from the Journal of John Parrish, 1773," *PMHB* 16 (1892): 443–48, at 446; Joshua Elder to John Lukens, April 15, 1769, Misc. Mss., Box 8, WLCL; Preston, *Texture of Contact,* 246 and chap. 6. For postwar land grants, see GW to Botetourt, *GWP* 8: 272–75, 275n, and Lloyd DeWitt Bockstruck, *Virginia's Colonial Soldiers* (Baltimore, 1988); S. W. Durant, *History of Allegheny Co., Pennsylvania* (Philadelphia, 1878), 155 (Wright).
138. *BP* 2: 653; "Journal of John Parrish," 447; *Journal of Nicholas Cresswell,* 63; Frances R. Reese, ed., "Colonel Eyre's Journal of His Trip from New York to Pittsburgh, 1762,"

WPHM 27 (May–June 1944): 37–50, at 47–48; Will Lowdermilk, *History of Cumberland* (Washington, D.C., 1878), 256.

139. *Niles Weekly Register* 14, no. 11 (May 9, 1818): 179–80 (uncorroborated source that Washington may have searched for Braddock's grave); "Bones of Gen. Braddock," *New Hampshire Sentinel* 7, no. 325 (June 8, 1805): 4; Sargent, *History of an Expedition*, 261, n. 2, 277. Some of Braddock's bones were reportedly taken to both Charles Willson Peale's Philadelphia Museum as well as the Army Medical Museum in Washington, D.C., in the nineteenth century.

140. Thomas A. Chambers, *Memories of War: Visiting Battlegrounds and Bonefields in the Early American Republic* (Ithaca, 2012), chap. 1; Douglas MacGregor, "Braddock's Field: 'How Brilliant the Morning, How Melancholy the Evening,'" *Western Pennsylvania History* 88 (Winter 2005): 22–29.

141. See William Smith's 1757 sermon, in *The Works of William Smith, D. D.: Late Provost of the College and Academy of Philadelphia*, 2 vols. (Philadelphia, 1803), 2: 174–75.

142. Paul A. W. Wallace, *Thirty Thousand Miles with John Heckewelder* (Pittsburgh, 1958), 40; *Diary of David McClure*, 48; Charles I. Landis, "Jasper Yeates and His Times," *PMHB* 46 (1922): 199–231, at 212–14.

143. Bouquet to Cochrane, July 12, 1761, *BP* 5: 630; George Croghan to Thomas Gage, May 26, 1766, AS 51, Gage Papers, WLCL.

144. Gage to Burton, April 14, 1766, AS 50; and Gage to Johnson, May 5, 1766, AS 51, Gage Papers.

145. St. Clair had also become a friend of John Dickinson, author of the *Letters from a Farmer in Pennsylvania*. For St. Clair's final years, see Memorial of Sir John St. Clair, 1782, T1/577, TNA, ff. 299–30; *Boston News-Letter*, December 17, 1767, p. 2; Logan Papers, Box 40, HSP; Will of St. Clair, October 26, 1767, PROB 11/951/198, TNA. Other veterans of the Monongahela who faded from the scene include Robert Orme, whose military career never recovered following the death of his chief, and from his elopement with Audrey Townshend, the daughter of a prominent British aristocrat. Captain Roger Morris married into the wealthy Philipse family of New York following the war and remained loyal to Britain during the American Revolution. His Georgian estate in Manhattan was confiscated during the Revolution, and his former comrade George Washington briefly used the home as his headquarters in 1776 (the Morris-Jumel Mansion).

EPILOGUE

1. Council of War, July 9, 1775, in Philander D. Chase, ed., *The Papers of George Washington*, Revolutionary War Series (Charlottesville, 1985), 1: 79–82 (hereinafter cited as *GWP-R*).

2. Alden, *General Thomas Gage* and *General Charles Lee*; Paul David Nelson, "Lee, Gates, Stephen and Morgan: Revolutionary War Generals of the Lower Shenandoah Valley," *West Virginia History* 37 (April 1976): 185–200. For Gates's devotion to republicanism, see Horatio Gates to Charles Mellish, July 21, 1772, and April 11, 1774, Mellish Family Papers, Me C 29/2 and Me C 29/3/1, University of Nottingham Manuscripts and Special Collections.

3. "Letter of Harry Farrington Gardner, 1775," Colonial Society of Massachusetts Publications 26 (1927): 292–95, at 293; GW to John Sullivan, September 4, 1775, *GWP-R* 1: 414; GW to John Hancock, September 2, 1776, *GWP-R* 6: 200; John Hall, "Washington's Irregulars," in Lengel, *Companion to George Washington*, 320–43; Mark Kwasny, *Washington's Partisan War, 1775–1783* (Kent, 1996); and David Hackett Fischer, *Washington's Crossing* (Oxford, 2005).

4. Frederick County Committee of Safety, June 29, 1775, Theodorus Bailey Myers Collection, Daniel Morgan Papers, New York Public Library, No. 1081; Higginbotham, *Daniel Morgan*.

5. GW to John Hancock, August 4–5, 1775, and January 24, 1776, *GWP-R* 1: 223–39 and 3: 180–81; "List of Indians to have commissions," 1779, Schuyler Papers, Box 14, New York Public Library; Pickering to President of Congress, June 7, 1779, Papers of the Continental Congress, M247, roll 158, item 147, Vol. 3: 391. Joseph T. Glatthaar and James Kirby Martin, *Forgotten Allies: The Oneida Indians and the American Revolution* (New York, 2006).

6. Mark R. Anderson, *The Battle for the Fourteenth Colony: America's War of Liberation in Canada, 1774–1776* (Hanover, N.H., 2013); "Lettre du gouvenour Carleton au ministre Hillsborough, March 15, 1769," *BRH* 25: 123–24; "A General State of the Canadian Noblesse," 1767, in Douglas Brymner, *Report on Canadian Archives, 1888* (Ottawa, 1889), 44–48; *DCB* entries for Louis Liénard de Beaujeu, Gabriel Christie, Longueuil, Belestre, and Contrecoeur. Ironically, British officer Gabriel Christie of the 48th Regiment, who had remained with Dunbar's column in 1755, settled in Canada following the war and purchased the Lacolle seigneury or estate owned by the Liénard de Beaujeu family.

7. Adam Stephen to Charles Lee, July 13, 1776, *CLP* 2: 137. Howard C. Rice, ed., *Travels in North America in the Years 1780, 1781 and 1782 by the Marquis de Chastellux* (Chapel Hill, 1963), 1: 264–65.

8. GW to Robert Jackson, August 2, 1755, *GWP* 1: 350; GW to Samuel Washington, September 30, 1775, and GW to Adam Stephen, July 20, 1776, *GWP-R* 2: 74 and 5: 408–9 (spelling modernized); *GWR*, 55 (sash).

9. *ABF*, 134; John Adams to Nathan Webb, October 12, 1755, in *Papers of John Adams*, Ser. 2, ed. Robert J. Taylor et al. (Boston, 1977) 1: 4–7, at 4.

10. In addition to the contemporary references to America and Americans throughout this book, see J. M. Bumsted, "'Things in the Womb of Time': Ideas of American Independence, 1633 to 1763," *WMQ* 31 (October 1974): 533–64; Richard L. Merritt, *Symbols of American Community, 1735–1775* (New Haven, 1966), and Merritt, "The Colonists Discover America: Attention Patterns in the Colonial Press, 1735–1775," *WMQ* 21 (April 1964): 270–87. Merritt quantified how and when colonists began to write of themselves as Americans by counting symbols and words of American identity between the 1730s and 1770s. He found that Braddock's Defeat represented the "highest point" of such references during the French and Indian War (p. 273).

11. E.g., *Boston Evening-Post*, September 23, 1765, p. 1; *Boston Post-Boy*, December 26, 1763, p. 2; *Public Advertiser*, February 7, 1775, p. 2; *Pennsylvania Evening Post*, March 30, 1776, p. 1.

12. *Boston Evening-Post*, December 6, 1773, p. 4 (remains); Simmons and Thomas, *Proceedings and Debates*, 5: 347 (Grant); [Charles Lee], *Strictures on a Pamphlet, Entitled "Friendly Address to All Reasonable Americans, on the Subject of our Political Confusions."* (Philadelphia, 1774), *CLP* 1: 161–62; Arthur Lee, *An appeal to the justice and interests of the people of Great Britain, in the present disputes with America*, 3rd. ed. (London, 1775), 21.

13. Lord Germain to Lord Suffolk, June 16–17, 1775, Sackville-Germain Manuscripts, Vol. 3, WLCL; *Public Advertiser*, June 30, 1775, p. 3; Washington to Richard Henry Lee, April 4, 1776, *GWP-R* 4: 34–35; *Pennsylvania Evening Post*, March 30, 1776, 2, no. 186; *PBF* 22: 274–77

14. William Hunter to BF, July 27, 1755, in Houston, "Wagon Affair," 282–83.

APPENDIX G

1. Lt. Col. M.E.S. Laws, ed., "R.N. and R.A. in Virginia, 1755," *JSAHR* 57 (Winter 1979): 193–205.

2. "Extracts of a Journal of the Proceedings of the Detachment of Seamen," Royal Artillery Institution Library, Woolwich, UK; for a transcription, see Carson I.A. Ritchie, ed., *General Braddock's Expedition* (Woolwich, UK: n.p., 1962) in University of Virginia, Small Special Collections Library.

3. ADM 1/2009, f. 20.

4. ADM 1/2009, f. 20.

5. Cf. Sargent, *History of an Expedition*, 382 (hospital), and Ritchie, *General Braddock's Expedition*, 12.

6. Augustus Keppel to John Cleveland, Secretary to the Admiralty, October 30, 1755, ADM 1/2009, f. 18–19.

BIBLIOGRAPHY

MANUSCRIPT COLLECTIONS
Archives du Calvados, Caen, France
    Fonds Surlaville
Archives du Séminaire de Québec
    Fonds Viger-Verreau (microfilm at Pennsylvania State Archives)
Archives Nationales d'Outre Mer, Aix-en-Provence, France
    Archives des colonies
        Série C¹¹A: Canada et Colonies du Nord de l'Amérique
        Série D²C: Troupes des colonies. Canada et Ile Royale. Compagnies détachées,
        1737-1771
        Série E: Secrétariat d'État à la Marine—Personnel colonial ancien (XVIIe-
        XVIIIe)
British Library, London
    Burney Collection of Newspapers
    Hardwicke Papers
    Leeds Papers
    Newcastle Papers
David Library of the American Revolution, Washington Crossing, Pennsylvania
    Montresor Family Papers
Dorset History Centre, Dorchester, UK
    Ryder of Rempstone Archive
        Out Letter Book of Henry Fox, 1754-1755, D/RWR/X5
Historical Society of Pennsylvania, Philadelphia
    Braddock Expedition. Papers, 1754-1755
    Etting Collection
    Logan Papers
    Penn Papers, Indian Affairs
    Richard Peters Papers
Harvard University Archives, Cambridge, Massachusetts
    Franklin Thayer Nichols, "The Braddock Expedition, 1754-1755" (Ph.D. diss., 1946)
Huntington Library, San Marino, California
    Abercromby Papers
    Elizabeth Montagu Papers
    Huntington Manuscripts
    Journal of Captain Robert Cholmley's Batman
    Loudoun Papers
John Carter Brown Library, Brown University, Providence, Rhode Island
    Christopher Gist, *The Draught of Genl. Braddocks route towards Fort Du Quesne, 15th of Sept.
    1755*
Lewis J. Ort Library, Special Collections, Frostburg State University, Maryland
    John Kennedy Lacock Collection

Library and Archives Canada, Ottawa
    Archives Coloniales, Archives Nationales, microfilm
    National Map Collection
Library of Congress, Washington, D.C.
    Adam Stephen Papers, 1749–1849
    Daniel Disney Orderly Book, 1747–1757
    James Grant of Ballindalloch Papers, 1740–1819 (microfilm)
    John Montresor, Copy of a Sketch of the Monongahela with the Field of Battle
        Mercure de France (1755)
Library of Virginia, Richmond, Virginia
    Daniel Morgan Papers, 1763–1800
    Virginia Colonial Records Project
Massachusetts Historical Society, Boston
    Francis Parkman Papers
    Jonathan Belcher Letterbooks
    Pre-Revolutionary War Diaries
National Archives of Scotland, Edinburgh
    Dalhousie Muniments, 1748–1759 (microfilm at PSA)
National Archives (UK), Kew
    Admiralty Papers (ADM)
        ADM 1/480: Letters from Commanders in Chief, North America
        ADM 1/2009: Captain's Letters, 1754–1755
        ADM 1/2291–2292: Captains' Letters, 1754–1755
    Audit Office Papers (AO)
        AO 1/69/90
    Chatham Papers (PRO 30)
    Colonial Office Papers (CO 5)
        CO 5/15–17: Despatches, 1754–1755
        CO 5/46: Military and naval despatches, 1754–1755
    Maps and Plans (MR 1)
    Prerogative Court of Canterbury: Will Registers, 1384-1858 (PROB)
    State Papers (SP)
        SP 92/51–52: Sardinia, 1746–1747
    Treasury Warrants (T 1)
    War Office
        WO 1: In Letters
        WO 4: Out Letters
        WO 12: Muster Books and Pay Lists
        WO 24: Papers Concerning Establishments
        WO 25: War Office Registers
        WO 27: Inspection Returns
        WO 34: Amherst Papers
        WO 47/44: Board of Ordnance, Surveyor General Minutes, 1754
        WO 53/128: Ordnance Office Bill Books, Gibraltar, 1753
        WO 64: Manuscript Army Lists, 1736–1754
        WO 65: Army Lists, 1755–1763
        WO 71: Court Martial Records
        WO 116: Admission Books, Royal Hospital, Chelsea
        WO 120: Out Pension Records
        WO 284/3: Gibraltar Garrison, Orders, Vol. 3, 1748–1756
National Archives, Washington, D.C.
    Daniel Disney Orderly Book
    James Grant Papers
    Papers of the Continental Congress, 1774–1789

New-York Historical Society
    Canada Lotbinière Papers, 1746–1790
    Charlotte Browne Diary, 1754–1757
    Horatio Gates Papers, 1726–1828
New York Public Library
    Horatio Gates Papers, 1760–1804
    Emmet Collection
    Theodorus Bailey Myers Collection, 1542–1876
Pennsylvania State Archives (PSA), Harrisburg, Pennsylvania
    Archives du Séminaire de Québec, Fonds Viger-Verreau
    Dalhousie Muniments, 1748–1759
    Joseph Shippen Jr. Diary, 1755
Royal Archives, Windsor Castle
    The Papers of William Augustus, Duke of Cumberland
Royal Library, Windsor Castle
    Edward Braddock, *A Particular Description of the Peninsula of Gibraltar* (1753)
Royal Artillery Institution Library, Woolwich, UK
    Extracts of a Journal of the Proceedings of the Detachment of Seamen (microfilm
    at Library of Virginia)
Senator John Heinz History Center, Thomas and Katherine Detre Library and Archives,
    Pittsburgh, Pennsylvania
    Braddock's Campaign, Miscellaneous Materials
    Braddock's Field Print Collection
    Arthur S. Cunningham, "March to Destiny" (2001)
South Caroliniana Library, University of South Carolina, Columbia
    James Glen Papers, 1738–1777
South Carolina Department of Archives and History, Columbia
    Records in the British Public Record Office Relating to South Carolina, 1663–1782
    (microfilm)
Städtisches Museum Swäbisch-Gmünd im Prediger (Germany)
    Erhard Stiftung, Emanuel Leutze zu Julius Erhard, 22 February 1858
University of Nottingham (UK), Manuscripts and Special Collections
    Edward Braddock to Robert Monckton, April 14, 1755, Monckton-Arundell Family
    Papers, Ga M 3
    Horatio Gates, London, to Robert Monckton, April 3, 1762, Monckton-Arundell Family
    Papers, Ga M 87
    Horatio Gates to Charles Mellish, July 21, 1772, Mellish Family Papers Me C 29/2
    Horatio Gates to Charles Mellish, April 11, 1774, Mellish Family Papers Me C
    29/3/1
University of Pittsburgh, Archives Service Center
    Robert Stobo Papers, 1754, Darlington Collection
    William J. Gaughan Collection
        Sydney Dillon Maps (Series XII)
University of Virginia, Albert and Shirley Small Special Collections Library
    Sir John St. Clair Letterbook, 1755–1756
    Headquarters Papers of Brigadier General John Forbes
    Carson I. A. Ritchie, *General Braddock's Expedition* (1962)
Virginia Historical Society, Richmond, Virginia
    William Hill Sermon
    Notes from Benjamin Berry in relation to General Daniel Morgan
William Smith Morton Library, Union Theological Seminary, Richmond, Virginia
    William Hill Papers, 1769–1852
Wisconsin State Historical Society
    Lyman C. Draper Manuscript Collection

William L. Clements Library, University of Michigan, Ann Arbor
Thomas Gage Papers (American Series)
William Trent Manuscript, 1757, Native American History Collection

CONTEMPORARY NEWSPAPERS

Boston Gazette
Boston Post Boy
Boston Weekly News-Letter
Carlisle Gazette
Gentleman's Magazine
London Chronicle
London Daily Advertiser
London Evening-Post
London Gazette
London Magazine
Maryland Gazette
Middlesex Journal and Evening Advertiser
New-York Mercury
Pennsylvania Gazette
Public Advertiser
St. James Chronicle
Scots Magazine
South Carolina Gazette
Virginia Gazette
Whitehall Evening Post or London Intelligencer

SELECTED PRIMARY SOURCES

Abbot, W. W., ed. "General Edward Braddock in Alexandria: John Carlyle to George Carlyle, 15 August 1755." *VMHB* 97, no. 2 (1989): 205–14.

Abbot, W. W., Dorothy Twohig, and Philander Chase, eds. *The Papers of George Washington, Colonial Series.* 10 vols. Charlottesville: University Press of Virginia, 1983–94.

Abbot, W. W., Dorothy Twohig, Philander Chase, Edward G. Lengel, Theodore J. Crackel, and David R. Hoth, eds. *The Papers of George Washington, Revolutionary War Series.* 18 vols. Charlottesville: University Press of Virginia, 1985–.

Anderson, Fred, ed. *George Washington Remembers: Reflections on the French and Indian War.* Oxford: Rowman & Littlefield, 2004.

Barsotti, John J., ed. *Scoouwa: James Smith's Indian Captivity Narrative.* Columbus: Ohio Historical Society, 1996.

Beaujeu, Daniel-Hyacinthe-Marie Liénard de. "Journal de la Campagne du Détachment de Canada à l'Acadie et aux Mines, en 1746–47." *Le Canada Français* 2 (Quebec, 1889): 16–75.

Beaujeu, Monongahela de, ed. *Documents inedits sur le Colonel de Longueuil.* Montréal: Desaulniers & Leblanc, 1891.

Bond, Beverley W., ed. "The Captivity of Charles Stuart, 1755–57." *Mississippi Valley Historical Review* 13 (June 1926): 58–81.

Bouthillier, C. F., ed. "La bataille du 9 juillet 1755." *BRH* 14, no. 7 (1908): 222–23.

Breslaw, Elaine G. "A Dismal Tragedy: Drs. Alexander and John Hamilton Comment on Braddock's Defeat." *Maryland Historical Magazine* 75, no.2 (1980): 118–44.

Brock, Robert Alonzo, ed. *The Official Records of Robert Dinwiddie.* 2 vols. Richmond: Virginia Historical Society, 1883–84.

Browne, William Hand, ed. *Archives of Maryland.* Vol. 6. *Correspondence of Governor Horatio Sharpe, Vol. 1, 1753–1757.* Baltimore: Maryland Historical Society, 1888.

Brymner, Douglas, ed. *Report on Canadian Archives.* Ottawa: Maclean, Roger, 1886–89.

[Cameron, Duncan]. *The Life, Adventures, and Surprizing Deliverances of Duncan Cameron, A Private Soldier in the Regiment of Foot, late Sir Peter Halket's.* Philadelphia: James Chattin, 1756.

Casgrain, H. G., ed. *Collection de manuscrits du Maréchal de Lévis.* 12 vols. Québec: C. O. Beauchemin, 1889–99.

[Cresswell, Nicholas]. *The Journal of Nicholas Cresswell, 1774–1777.* New York: Dial Press, 1924.

Cohen, Sheldon S., ed. "Major William Sparke along the Monongahela: A New Historical Account of Braddock's Defeat." *PH* 62 (October 1995): 546–56.

Darlington, William M, ed. *Christopher Gist's Journals.* Pittsburgh: J. R. Weldin, 1893.

Davis, N. Darnell, ed. "British Newspaper Accounts of Braddock's Defeat." *PMHB* 23 (1899): 310–28.

De Bonnault, Claude, ed. "Pièces au sujet de M. Landrière." *BRH* 33, no. 8–10 (1927): 497–512, 558–76, 626–40.

[Dulany, Daniel]. "Military and Political Affairs in the Middle Colonies in 1755." *PMHB* 3 (1879): 11–31.

Expedition of Major-General Braddock to Virginia; with The Two Regiments of Hacket and Dunbar. London: H. Carpenter, 1755.

[Gage, Thomas]. "Queries of George Chalmers with the Answers of General Gage." *Massachusetts Historical Society Collections,* 4th ser., 4:367–72.

Gallup, Andrew, ed. *The Céloron Expedition to the Ohio Country 1749: The Reports of Pierre-Joseph Céloron and Father Bonnecamps.* Westminster, Md.: Heritage Books, 1997.

Grenier, Fernand, ed. *Papiers Contrecoeur et autres documents concernant le conflit anglo-français sur l'Ohio de 1745 à 1756.* Québec: Les presses universitaires Laval, 1952.

Hamilton, Charles. *Braddock's Defeat: The Journal of Captain Robert Cholmley's Batman, the Journal of a British Officer, Halkett's Orderly Book.* Norman: University of Oklahoma Press, 1959.

Hamilton, Edward P., ed. *Adventure in the Wilderness: The American Journals of Louis Antoine de Bougainville, 1756–1760.* Norman: University of Oklahoma Press, 1964.

Harrison, Fairfax, ed. "With Braddock's Army: Mrs. Browne's Diary in Virginia and Maryland." *VMHB* 32 (October 1924): 305–20.

Hazard, Samuel, ed. *Hazard's Register of Pennsylvania.* 16 vols. Philadelphia: W. F. Geddes, 1828–35.

Hazard, Samuel, ed. *Minutes of the Provincial Council of Pennsylvania.* 16 vols. Harrisburg: Theophilus Fenn, 1838–1853. Reprint, vols. 1–3, Philadelphia: Joseph Severns, 1852.

Houston, Alan, ed. "Benjamin Franklin and the 'Wagon Affair' of 1755." *William and Mary Quarterly* 66 (April 2009): 235–86.

Jackson, Donald, and Dorothy Twohig, eds. *The Diaries of George Washington.* 5 vols. Charlottesville: University Press of Virginia, 1978.

[Johnston, William]. "General Braddock's Campaign." *PMHB* 11 (1887): 93–97.

Kennedy, John Pendleton, ed. *Journals of the House of Burgesses of Virginia.* Vol. 10, 1761–65. Richmond: Virginia State Library, 1907.

Kent, Donald H., ed. "Contrecoeur's Copy of George Washington's Journal for 1754," *PH* 19 (January 1952): 1–32.

Koontz, Louis Knott, ed. *Robert Dinwiddie: Correspondence Illustrative of His Career in American Colonial Government and Westward Expansion.* Berkeley: University of California Press, 1951.

Labaree, Leonard W., et al., eds. *The Papers of Benjamin Franklin.* 40 vols. to date. New Haven: Yale University Press, 1959–2014.

Lambing, A. A., ed. and trans. *Register of Fort Duquesne, 1754–1756.* Pittsburgh: Myers, Shinkle, 1885.

[La Pause, Chevalier de]. "Les 'mémoires' du Chevalier de la Pause." *Rapport de l'Archiviste de la Province de Québec* 13 (1932–33): 307–16.

[Lee, Charles]. *The Charles Lee Papers.* 4 vols. New York: Collections of the New-York Historical Society, 1871–74.

Lewis, W. S., et al., eds. *Correspondence of Horace Walpole.* 48 vols. New Haven: Yale University Press, 1937–83.

Liebiger, Stuart, ed. "To Judge of Washington's Conduct: Illuminating George Washington's Appearance on the World Stage." *VMHB* 107 (Spring 1999): 37.

Lincoln, Charles Henry, ed. *Correspondence of William Shirley, Governor of Massachusetts and Military Commander in America, 1731–1760.* 2 vols. New York: Macmillan, 1912.

Lincoln, Charles Henry, ed. "The Keppel Manuscripts Descriptive of the Defeat of Major-General Edward Braddock." In *Transactions and Collections of the American Antiquarian Society* 11 (1909): 171–76.

Mante, Thomas. *History of the Late War in America and the Islands of the West Indies*. London: W. Strahan and T. Cadell, 1772.

McDowell, William L., ed. *Documents Relating to Indian Affairs, 1754–1765*. Columbia: South Carolina Archives Department, 1970.

McIlwaine, H. R., ed. *Journals of the House of Burgesses of Virginia*. Vol. 8, *1752–1755, 1756–1758*. Richmond: Virginia State Library, 1909.

McIlwaine, H. R., ed. *Journals of the House of Burgesses of Virginia*. Vol. 9, *1758–1761*. Richmond: Virginia State Library, 1908.

Mereness, Newton D., ed. *Travels in the American Colonies*. New York: Macmillan, 1916.

Molyneux, Thomas More. *Conjunct Expeditions: or Expeditions that Have Been Carried on Jointly by the Fleet and the Army*. London: R & J Dodsley, 1759.

Moreau, Jacob Nicholas. *A Memorial Containing a Summary View of the Facts, with their Authorities. In Answer to the Observations Sent by the English Ministry to the Courts of Europe*. New York: H. Gaine, 1757.

Mulkearn, Lois, ed. *George Mercer Papers Relating to the Ohio Company of Virginia*. Pittsburgh: University of Pittsburgh Press, 1954.

O'Callaghan, E. B. and Berthold Fernow, eds. *Documents Relative to the Colonial History of the State of New York*. 14 vols. Albany: Weed, Parsons, 1855.

O'Callaghan, E. B. and Berthold Fernow, eds. *Documentary History of the State of New-York*. 4 vols. Albany: Weed, Parsons, 1849–51.

Pargellis, Stanley, ed. *Military Affairs in North America, 1748–1765: Selected Documents from the Cumberland Papers in Windsor Castle*. New York: Archon Books, 1969.

Pease, Theodore Calvin, ed. *Collections of the Illinois State Historical Library*. Vol. 27: *Anglo-French Boundary Disputes in the West, 1749–1763*. Springfield: Illinois State Historical Library, 1940.

Pease, Theodore Calvin, ed. *Collections of the Illinois State Historical Library*. Vol. 29: *Illinois on the Eve of the Seven Years' War, 1747–1755*. Springfield: Illinois State Historical Library, 1940.

Pennsylvania Archives. 9 series, 138 vols. Philadelphia and Harrisburg, 1852–1949.

Peyser, Joseph L., trans. and ed. *Jacques Legardeur de Saint-Pierre. Officer, Gentleman, Entrepreneur*. East Lansing: Michigan State University Press, 1996.

Peyser, Joseph L., trans. and ed. *Letters from New France: The Upper Country, 1686–1783*. Chicago: University of Illinois Press, 1994.

Peyser, Joseph L., trans. and ed. *On the Eve of Conquest: The Chevalier de Raymond's Critique of New France in 1754*. East Lansing: Michigan State University Press, 1997.

Pouchot, Pierre. *Memoirs on the Late War in North America between France and England*. Edited and annotated by Brian Leigh Dunnigan. Translated by Michael Cardy. Youngstown N.Y.: Old Fort Niagara Association, 1994.

Quaife, Milo Milton, ed. *John Long's Voyages and Travels in the Years 1768–1788*. Chicago: R. R. Donnelly, 1922.

Quarters of the Army in Ireland. Dublin: George Faulkner, 1749 and 1752.

Quisenberry A. C., ed. "Virginia Troops in French and Indian Wars." *VMHB* 1, no. 3 (January 1894): 278–87.

Roy, A., ed. "Lettres de Daniel-Hyacinthe Liénard de Beaujeu, Commandant au Fort Niagara." *BRH* 37 (1931): 355–72.

Sargent, Winthrop. *The History of an Expedition against Fort Du Quesne in 1755*. Philadelphia, 1856. Reprint, Lewisburg, Pa.: Wennawoods, 1997.

Shea, Jean Marie, ed. *Relations diverses sur la bataille du Malanguelee, gagné le 9 Juillet, 1755*. New York: La Presse Cramoisy, 1860.

Simmons, R. C., and P. D. G. Thomas, eds. *Proceedings and Debates of the British Parliaments Respecting North America, 1754–1783*. Vol. 1: *1754–1764*. Millwood, N.Y.: Kraus International, 1982.

Smith, George. *An Universal Military Dictionary*. London, J. Millan, 1779.

Stevens, Sylvester K., and Donald H. Kent, eds. and trans. *Journal of Chaussegros de Léry*. Harrisburg: Pennsylvania Historical Commission, 1940.

Stevens, Sylvester K., and Donald H. Kent, eds. and trans. *Wilderness Chronicles of Northwestern Pennsylvania.* Harrisburg: Pennsylvania Historical Commission, 1941. Reprint: Lewisburg, Pa., 2002.

Stevens, Sylvester K., Donald H. Kent, and Louis M. Waddell, eds. *The Papers of Henry Bouquet.* 6 vols. Harrisburg: Pennsylvania Historical and Museum Commission,1951–94.

Stevens, Sylvester K., Donald H. Kent, and Emma Edith Woods, eds. *Travels in New France by J.C.B.* Harrisburg: Pennsylvania Historical Commission, 1941.

Sullivan, James, et al., eds. *The Papers of Sir William Johnson.* 14 vols. Albany: State University of New York, 1921–63.

Thwaites, Reuben Gold, ed. *Early Western Journals, 1748–1765.* Cleveland: Arthur H. Clark, 1904.

Van Horne, John C., and George Reese, eds. *The Letter Book of James Abercromby Colonial Agent, 1751–1773.* Richmond: Virginia State Library and Archives, 1991.

Wahll, Andrew, ed. *Braddock Road Chronicles, 1755.* Westminster, Md.: Heritage Books, 1999.

Walker, Lewis Burd, ed. *The Settlement of the Waggoners' Accounts Relating to Braddock's Expedition towards Fort Duquesne.* Pottsville, Pa.: Standard Publishing, 1899.

Washington, George. *The Journal of Major George Washington: An Account of His First Official Mission, Made as Emissary from the Governor of Virginia to the Commandant of French Forces on the Ohio, October 1753–January 1754.* Williamsburg: Colonial Williamsburg Foundation, 1959.

SELECTED SECONDARY SOURCES

Abbott, Raymond B. "Braddock's War Supplies and Dunbar's Camp." *WPHM* 17 (March 1934): 49–53.

Alberts, Robert C. *The Most Extraordinary Adventures of Major Robert Stobo.* Boston: Houghton Mifflin, 1965.

Alden, John R. *General Charles Lee: Traitor or Patriot?* Baton Rouge: Louisiana State University Press, 1951.

Alden, John R. *General Gage in America.* Baton Rouge: Louisiana State University Press, 1948.

Alden, John R. *Robert Dinwiddie: Servant of the Crown.* Williamsburg, Va.: Colonial Williamsburg Foundation, 1973.

Anderson, Fred. *Crucible of War: The Seven Years' War and the Fate of Empire in British North America, 1754–1766.* New York: Alfred A. Knopf, 2000.

Audet, Francis-Joseph. *Contrecoeur: Famille, Seigneurie, Paroisse, Village.* Montréal: G. Ducharme, 1940.

Audet, Francis-Joseph. *Jean-Daniel Dumas: Le Héros de la Monongahela.* Montréal: G. Ducharme, 1920.

Ayling, Stanley. *The Elder Pitt: Earl of Chatham.* New York: David McKay, 1976.

Bailey, De Witt. *Small Arms of the British Forces in America, 1664–1815.* Woonsocket, R.I.: Mowbray, 2009.

Bailey, Kenneth P. *Christopher Gist: Colonial Frontiersman, Explorer, and Indian Agent.* Hamden, Ct.: Archon Books, 1976.

Bailey, Kenneth P. *The Ohio Company of Virginia and the Westward Movement, 1748–1792.* Glendale, Calif.: Arthur H. Clark, 1939.

Bailey, Kenneth P. *Thomas Cresap: Maryland Frontiersman.* Boston: Christopher Publishing House, 1944.

Baker, Norman L. *Braddock's Road: Mapping the British Expedition from Alexandria to the Monongahela.* Charleston: History Press, 2013.

Baker, Norman L. *French and Indian War in Frederick County, Virginia.* Winchester, Va.: Winchester-Frederick County Historical Society, 2000.

Baugh, Daniel. *The Global Seven Years' War, 1754–1763.* London: Longman, 2011.

Beaujeu, Monongahela de. *Le héros de la Monongahéla : esquisse historique par Monongahéla de Beaujeu.* Montréal : Desaulniers, 1892.

Bell, David A. "Jumonville's Death: War Propaganda and National Identity in Eighteenth-Century France." In *The Age of Cultural Revolutions: Britain and France, 1750–1820,* ed. Colin Jones and Dror Wahrman. Berkeley: University of California Press, 2002, 33–61.

Bell, Whitfield J., and Leonard W. Labaree. "Franklin and the 'Wagon Affair,' 1755," *American Philosophical Society Proceedings* 101, no. 6 (December 1957): 551–58.

Berkebile, Donald H. "Conestoga Wagons in Braddock's Campaign, 1755." In *Contributions from the Museum of History and Technology, Paper 9, United States National Museum Bulletin 218.* Washington, D.C.: Smithsonian Institute, 1959, 142–53.

Bouchard, Russel. *Jean-Daniel Dumas, héros méconnu de la Nouvelle-France.* Montréal: Michel Brûlé, 2008.

Brown, George, et al., eds. *Dictionary of Canadian Biography.* 14 vols. to date. Toronto: University of Toronto Press, 1966–98.

Brumwell, Stephen. "Band of Brothers." *History Today* 58, no. 6 (June 2008): 25–31.

Brumwell, Stephen. *George Washington: Gentleman Warrior.* London: Quercus, 2012.

Brumwell, Stephen. *Paths of Glory: The Life and Death of General James Wolfe.* Montreal: McGill-Queen's University Press, 2006.

Brumwell, Stephen. *Redcoats: The British Soldier and War in the Americas, 1755–1763.* Cambridge: Cambridge University Press, 2002.

Brumwell, Stephen. *White Devil: A True Story of Savagery and Vengeance in Colonial America.* Cambridge: DaCapo Press, 2004.

Carter, Thomas. *Historical Record of the Forty-Fourth or the East Essex Regiment of Foot.* London: W. O. Mitchell, 1864.

Cassel, Jay. "Troupes de la Marine in Canada, 1683–1760: Men and Materiel." Ph.D. Diss., University of Toronto, 1987.

Charteris, Evan. *William Augustus Duke of Cumberland and the Seven Years' War.* London: Hutchinson, 1925.

Chartrand, René. *Canadian Military Heritage*, Vol. 1, *1000–1754.* Montréal: Art Global, 1993.

Chartrand, René. *Louis XV's Army (5): Colonial and Naval Troops.* London: Osprey, 1997.

Chartrand, René. *Monongahela 1754–55: Washington's Defeat, Braddock's Disaster.* Oxford: Osprey, 2004.

Chernow, Ron. *George Washington: A Life.* New York: Penguin Press, 2010.

Clayton, T. R. "The Duke of Newcastle, the Earl of Halifax, and the American Origins of the Seven Years' War." *Historical Journal* 24 (September 1981): 571–603.

Crocker, Thomas E. *Braddock's March.* Yardley, Pa.: Westholme, 2009.

Cubbison, Douglas R. *The British Defeat of the French in Pennsylvania, 1758: A Military History of the Forbes Campaign against Fort Duquesne.* Jefferson, N.C.: McFarland, 2010.

Dechêne, Louise. *Le Peuple, l'État et la Guerre sous le Régime français.* Montreal: Éditions Boreal, 2008.

Desbiens, Albert. "9 juillet 1755: la bataille du Malangueulé." In *Histoire du Canada: Une expérience tricentenaire.* Montréal: Éditions Sainte-Marie, 1967, 51–63.

Donehoo, George P. *A History of the Indian Villages and Place Names in Pennsylvania.* Harrisburg, 1928. Reprint, Baltimore: Gateway Press, 1995.

Drolet, Yves. *Dictionnaire généalogique et héraldique de la noblesse canadienne française du XVIIe au XIXe siècle.* Montréal: Dico, 2010.

Edmunds, R. David, and Joseph L. Peyser. *The Fox Wars: The Mesquakie Challenge to New France.* Norman: University of Oklahoma Press, 1993.

Eid, Leroy V. " 'A Kind of Running Fight': Indian Battlefield Tactics in the Late Eighteenth Century." *WPHM* 71 (April 1988): 147–71.

Fauteux, Aegidius. *Les chevaliers de Saint-Louis en Canada.* Montréal: Les Éditions des Dix, 1940.

Foote, William A. "The American Independent Companies of the British Army, 1664–1764." Ph.D. diss., UCLA, 1966.

Freeman, Douglas Southall. *George Washington: A Biography.* 7 vols. New York: Charles Scribner's Sons, 1948–57.

Frégault, Guy. *Canada: The War of the Conquest.* Trans. Margaret M. Cameron. Toronto: Oxford University Press, 1969.

Fuller, J. F. C. *The British Light Infantry in the Eighteenth Century.* London: Hutchinson, 1925.

Gale, R. R. *"A Soldier-Like Way: The Material Culture of the British Infantry, 1751–1768.* Elk River, Minn.: Track of the Wolf, 2007.

Gallup, Andrew, and Donald F. Shaffer. *La Marine: The French Colonial Soldier in Canada.* Westminster, Md.: Heritage Books, 1992.

Gipson, Lawrence Henry. *The Great War for Empire: The Years of Defeat, 1754–1757.* New York: Alfred A. Knopf, 1956.

Gladysz, Kevin. *The French Trade Gun in North America, 1662–1759.* Woonsocket, R.I.: Mowbray, 2011.

Goldstein, Erik, and Stuart Mowbray. *The Brown Bess: An Identification Guide and Illustrated Study of Britain's Most Famous Musket.* Woonsocket, R.I.: Mowbray, 2010.

Gurney, Russell. *History of the Northamptonshire Regiment, 1742–1934.* Aldershot: Gale & Polden, 1935.

Hanna, Charles A. *The Wilderness Trail; or, The Ventures and Adventures of the Pennsylvania Traders on the Allegheny Path.* 2 vols. New York: B. P. Putnam's Sons, 1911.

Hawes, G. E., trans. Monongahela de Beaujeu, *The Hero of the Monongahela.* New York: William Post, 1913.

Higginbotham, Don. *Daniel Morgan: Revolutionary Rifleman.* Chapel Hill: University of North Carolina Press, 1961.

Hildeburn, Charles R. "Sir John St. Clair, Baronet." *PMHB* 9 (1885): 1–14.

Hofstra, Warren R., ed. *George Washington and the Virginia Backcountry.* Madison, Wis.: Madison House, 1998.

Hough, Franklin B. *A History of St. Lawrence and Franklin Counties, New York from the Earliest Period to the Present Time.* Albany: Little, 1853.

Hough, Walter S. "Braddock's Road through the Virginia Colony." *Winchester Frederick County Historical Society Journal* 7 (1970): 1–79.

Houlding, J. A. *Fit for Service: The Training of the British Army, 1715–1795.* Oxford: Oxford University Press, 1981.

Hulbert, Archer B. *Braddock's Road and Three Relative Papers.* Historic Highways of America, Vol. 4. Cleveland: Arthur H. Clark, 1903.

Hunter, William A. *Forts on the Pennsylvania Frontier, 1753–1758.* Harrisburg: Pennsylvania Historical and Museum Commission, 1960.

James, Alfred Proctor, and Charles Morse Stotz. *Drums in the Forest.* Pittsburgh: Historical Society of Western Pennsylvania, 1958.

Jennings, Francis. *Empire of Fortune: Crowns, Colonies and Tribes in the Seven Years' War in America.* New York: W. W. Norton, 1988.

Kent, Donald H. *The French Invasion of Western Pennsylvania.* Harrisburg: Pennsylvania Historical and Museum Commission, 1954.

Kershaw, Gordon. "The Legend of Braddock's Gold Reconsidered." *Maryland Historical Magazine* 96 (Spring 2001): 87–110.

King, J. C. H., and Christian F. Feest, eds. *Three Centuries of Woodlands Indian Art.* Altenstadt, Germany: ZKF Publishers, 2007.

Koontz, Louis Knott. *Robert Dinwiddie: His Career in American Colonial Government and Westward Expansion.* Glendale, Calif.: Arthur H. Clark, 1941.

Kopperman, Paul E. *Braddock at the Monongahela.* Pittsburgh: University of Pittsburgh Press, 1977.

Kopperman, Paul E. "The Medical Aspect of the Braddock and Forbes Expeditions." *Pennsylvania History* 71 (Summer 2004): 257–84.

Lacock, John Kennedy. "Braddock Road." *PMHB* 38, no.1 (1914): 1–38.

Lamb, George H., ed. *The Unwritten History of Braddock's Field.* Pittsburgh: Nicholson, 1917.

Laws, M. E. S. "R.N. and R.A. in Virginia, 1755." *JSAHR* 57 (Winter 1979): 193–205.

Lengel, Edward G. *A Companion to George Washington.* New York: Wiley-Blackwell, 2012.

Lengel, Edward G. *General George Washington: A Military Life.* New York: Random House, 2005.

Leonard, Autumn L. "The Presque Isle Portage and the Venango Trail." *Pennsylvania Archaeologist* 15, no. 1–4 (1945): 4–9, 59–64, 75–87, 119–27.

Manders, Eric I. "Braddock's Troops, 1755: The 44th and 48th Regiments of Foot." *Military Collector and Historian* 14 (Spring 1962): 16–17.

MacGregor, Douglas. "Braddock's Field: 'How Brilliant the Morning, How Melancholy the Evening.' " *Western Pennsylvania History* 88, no. 4 (2005): 22–29.

MacGregor, Douglas. "The Shot Not Heard around the World: Trent's Fort and the Opening of the War for Empire." *PH* 74 (Summer 2007): 354–73.

Martin, Ronald D. "Confrontation at the Monongahela: Climax of the French Drive into the Upper Ohio Region." *PH* 37 (April 1970): 133–50.

McCardell, Lee. *Ill-Starred General: Braddock of the Coldstream Guards.* Pittsburgh: University of Pittsburgh Press, 1958.

McConnell, Michael N. *A Country Between: The Upper Ohio Valley and Its Peoples, 1724–1774.* Lincoln: University of Nebraska Press, 1992.

MacLeod, D. Peter. *The Canadian Iroquois and the Seven Years' War.* Toronto: Dundurn Press, 1996.

MacLeod, Malcom. "Daniel-Marie Lienard de Beaujeu, 1711–1755: Empire Builder at Work and War." *Dalhousie Review* 53 (Summer 1973): 296–309.

Mapp, Paul W. *The Elusive West and the Contest for Empires, 1713–1763.* Chapel Hill: University of North Carolina Press, 2010.

Messner, Robert T. *Reflections from Braddock's Battlefield.* Braddock, Pa.: Braddock's Field Historical Society, 2005.

Munson, James D. *Col.° John Carlyle, Gent.: A True and Just Account of the Man and His House.* Alexandria: Northern Virginia Regional Park Authority, 1986.

Neely, Sylvia. "Mason Locke Weems's 'Life of George Washington' and the Myth of Braddock's Defeat." *VMHB* 107 (Winter 1999): 45–72.

Nelson, Paul David. *Horatio Gates: A Biography.* Baton Rouge: Louisiana State University Press, 1976.

Netherton, Ross. "Braddock's Campaign and the Potomac Route to the West." *Winchester-Frederick County Historical Society Journal* 1 (December 1986): 1–22.

Nichols, Franklin T. "The Organization of Braddock's Army." *WMQ* 4 (April 1947): 125–36.

Pargellis, Stanley McCrory. "Braddock's Defeat." *AHR* 41 (Jan. 1936): 253–69.

Parkman, Francis. *Montcalm and Wolfe: The French and Indian War.* New York: Barnes and Noble Books, 2005.

Preston, David L. "'Make Indians of Our White Men': British Soldiers and Indian Warriors from Braddock's to Forbes's Campaigns, 1755–1758." *Pennsylvania History* 74 (Summer 2007): 280–306.

Preston, David L. *The Texture of Contact: European and Indian Settler Communities on the Frontiers of Iroquoia, 1667–1783.* Lincoln: University of Nebraska Press, 2009.

Reid, Stuart. *1745: A Military History of the Last Jacobite Rising.* New York: Sarpedon, 1966.

Russell, Peter E. "Redcoats in the Wilderness: British Officers and Irregular Warfare in Europe and America, 1740 to 1760." *WMQ* 35 (October 1978): 629–52.

Schumann, Matt, and Karl Schweizer. *The Seven Years' War: A Transatlantic History.* New York: Routledge, 2008.

Severance, Frank. *An Old Frontier of France: The Niagara Region and Adjacent Lakes under French Control.* 2 vols. New York: Dodd, Mead, 1917.

Shea, John Gilmary. "Daniel Hyacinth Mary Liénard de Beaujeu." *PHMB* 8 (1884) 121–28.

Silver, Peter. *Our Savage Neighbors: How Indian War Transformed Early America.* New York: W. W. Norton, 2008.

Spring, Matthew. *With Zeal and with Bayonets Only: The British Army on Campaign in North America, 1775–1783.* Norman: University of Oklahoma Press, 2008.

Steele, Ian. *Setting All the Captives Free: Capture, Adjustment, and Recollection in Allegheny Country.* Montréal: Queens-McGill, 2013.

Stotz, Charles Morse. *Outposts of the War for Empire: The French and English in Western Pennsylvania: Their Armies, Their Forts, Their People, 1749–1764.* Pittsburgh: University of Pittsburgh Press/ Historical Society of Western Pennsylvania, 1985.

Temple, Henry. "Braddock's Road." *Ohio Archaeology Quarterly* 18 (1909): 432–42.

Titus, James. *The Old Dominion at War: Society, Politics, and Warfare in Late Colonial Virginia.* Columbia: University of South Carolina Press, 1991.

Trap, Paul. "Charles Langlade." Unpublished manuscript, Mackinac State Historic Parks, 1980.

Van Creveld, Martin. *Supplying War: Logistics from Wallenstein to Patton.* London: Cambridge University Press, 1977.

Vineyard, Ron. "Virginia Freight Wagons, 1750–1850." Colonial Williamsburg Foundation Library Research Report Series #345. Williamsburg: Colonial Williamsburg Foundation, 1994.

Wallace, Paul A. W. "'Blunder Camp': A Note on the Braddock Road." *PMHB* 87 (January 1963): 21–30.

Wallace, Paul A. W. *Indian Paths of Pennsylvania.* Harrisburg: Pennsylvania Historical and Museum Commission, 1965.

Ward, Matthew C. *Breaking the Backcountry: The Seven Years' War in Virginia and Pennsylvania, 1754–1765.* Pittsburgh: University of Pittsburgh Press, 2003.

Webb, Stephen Saunders. *Marlborough's America.* New Haven: Yale University Press, 2013.

White, Richard. *The Middle Ground: Indians, Empires, and Republics in the Great Lakes Region, 1650–1815.* Cambridge: Cambridge University Press, 1991.

Yaple, Robert L. "Braddock's Defeat: The Theories and a Reconsideration." *JSAHR* 46 (Winter 1968): 194–201.

INDEX

Page numbers in bold indicate illustrations.